The Sociology
of Sports

The Sociology of Sports

An Introduction

Tim Delaney *and*
Tim Madigan

McFarland & Company, Inc., Publishers
Jefferson, North Carolina, and London

All photographs were provided by Tim Delaney unless otherwise noted.

Library of Congress Cataloguing-in-Publication Data

Delaney, Tim.
The sociology of sports : an introduction /
Tim Delaney and Tim Madigan.
p.   cm.
Includes bibliographical references and index.

ISBN 978-0-7864-4169-3
softcover : 50# alkaline paper ∞

1. Sports—Sociological aspects.   I. Madigan, Tim.   II. Title.
GV706.5.D463   2009   306.4'83—dc22   2008054525

British Library cataloguing data are available

Cover photograph: More than 33,000 orange-clad fans pack the Carrier
Dome at Syracuse University to watch a men's basketball game.

Manufactured in the United States of America

McFarland & Company, Inc., Publishers
Box 611, Jefferson, North Carolina 28640
www.mcfarlandpub.com

This text is dedicated to two
early founders of the sociology of sport
who had a great influence on Tim Delaney —
James H. Frey and the late Hal Charnofsky.

Contents

Preface 1

1. The Sociology of Sport 3
2. Social Theory and Sport 21
3. A Brief History of Sport 39
4. The Impact of Sport on Culture 59
5. Socialization and Sport 77
6. Youth Sports 96
7. High School and College Sports 116
8. Deviance in Sport 136
9. Violence in Sport 157
10. Gender and Sport 177
11. Race and Ethnicity in Sport 198
12. Economics and Sport 218
13. Politics and Sport 239
14. Religion and Sport 259
15. The Media in Sport 278
16. The Benefits of Sport Participation 298

Glossary 309
Bibliography 319
Index 331

Preface

Sport is a universal phenomenon. There is no known culture which has not engaged in some sort of sporting activity, and participating in and being a spectator of various sports is an important aspect of most people's lives. From early childhood, individuals start the process of taking part in organized games, and it is a rare person who has no interest at all in rooting for (or against) particular organized teams. Such activities are not only often physically challenging and mentally stimulating — they also provide a sense of belonging and personal meaning to people's lives.

The study of sport, therefore, is of value, both for its own sake and for what it can tell us about individuals and societies in the broadest way. *The Sociology of Sports: An Introduction* therefore gives both a micro and macro examination of sport as a human institution.

This book is designed to serve as a textbook for a wide variety of sport-related academic courses. It represents a fresh approach to the study of sport in society including a critical examination of sport but with an emphasis upon its positive features. The purpose of this book is to show the relevance of sociology to the study of sport: how it connects with every aspect of the field of sociology.

The Sociology of Sports provides a straightforward, student-friendly presentation of key sociological concepts and issues that pertain to the sociological study and analysis of sport in contemporary society. The primary focus is on American sports, but a cross-cultural examination is also provided throughout the book. This textbook highlights the many key components of sport sociology. Relevant discussion questions, which should stimulate student interest, along with a brief summary, are provided at the end of each chapter. A glossary of key terms is provided at the end of the book.

The Sociology of Sports is designed primarily to fit the sport sociology market. It will be most appropriate for upper division undergraduate courses but some professors may choose to use it for graduate courses. Unlike other textbooks, *The Sociology of Sports* provides a chapter about sports' impact on American culture (Chapter 4). It is a glaring oversight that other textbooks— many of which are edited anthologies with a bewildering array of authors— do not include such a chapter. There is also a chapter on the history of sports to help put the discussions within an historical framework. Fresh, up-to-date examples from the world of sport are used to illustrate the various sociological areas covered in the book.

Again, unlike other texts in this area, *The Sociology of Sports* is of manageable length. While covering all of the general categories of sport and sociology (such as socialization, economics, gender, race, ethnicity, religion, politics, the media, and the role of sport in society), the text is both concise and geared to the student's needs. Professors can teach from the text in the order they prefer, as each chapter has been written to stand on its own.

It is the authors' hope that students will find this text to be accessible and interesting, and

1

that it will provoke critical thinking on the many societal issues that arise through participating in and being concerned about sport as a social institution.

Tim Delaney would like to offer special thanks for the continued inspiration provided by Christina. Tim Madigan would like to offer special thanks to Tim Delaney for introducing him to the sociological study of sport.

CHAPTER 1

The Sociology of Sport

Sport is as much a part of American society and culture as are other social institutions such as family, religion, politics, economics and education. To ignore sport is to overlook a phenomenon that extends into a multitude of social arenas, including the arts, mass media, the economy, the community, and international diplomacy. In this book we will use the term "sport" to signify the totality of sporting activities, and "sports" to signify specific activities such as football, baseball, or cycling.

Sport reflects the mores, values, and general culture of a society. In American culture, as in most world cultures, winning and success are highly valued commodities. Sport can serve as an excellent exemplar of the cherished "win-at-all-costs" philosophy. This prevailing attitude often leads to elitism, sexism, racism, nationalism, extreme competitiveness, abuse of drugs (including steroids), gambling, and a number of other deviant behaviors. However, the true spirit of sport often reveals itself as well. The notions of cooperation and team work, fair play, hard work, dedication, personal excellence, obedience to rules, commitment and loyalty are also revered values of American society, and that is, perhaps, the primary reason that Americans love sports so much. There are far more positive stories in sport (despite the often negative media portrayal of sport) which help to reaffirm that our support of our favorite teams and athletes is not a wasted endeavor.

The institution of sport is very important, useful, and beneficial to American society. Sports adherents share the emotional roller coaster of the fortunes that their favorite teams experience. Both fans and participants find in sport a reaffirmation of central values and myths of the larger society that help give meaning and direction to their own lives. Athletic contests are important to the socialization of youth, to the integration of disparate groups and social classes, to physical and mental well-being, and to the enhancement of community pride.

The Sociological Perspective

Since this book is written from a sociological perspective it is important to clarify a number of fundamental sociological concepts and constructs relevant to the sociological study of sport. Let's begin with the sociological perspective. Among the core tenets of the sociological perspective are the following basic assumptions:

1. *Individuals are, by their nature, social beings.* There are two main reasons for this. First, newborn babies are completely dependent on others for their survival. Second, in order to survive as a species, humans have formed groups as a defense mechanism against the other animals and the environment.
2. *Individuals are, for the most part, socially determined.* As social beings, we are products of our social environments. Trial and error, reinforcement and modeling account for the primary methods of learning.

3. *Individuals create, sustain, and change the social forms within which they conduct their lives.*
Humans are both "puppets of their society" and "also puppeteers" (Eitzen and Sage, 1989: 5).
Our lives are not biologically predetermined; we are capable (within certain social limitations)
of making decisions to alter our life courses. "Through collective action individuals are capable of changing the structure of society and even the course of history" (Eitzen and Sage, 1989:
4–6).

Sociology is a broad field with many different theories, methodologies and areas of interest. Sociology is a member of the social sciences; it involves the study of groups, institutions,
organizations, cultures and societies. The social sciences, which also include anthropology, economics, history, psychology, and political science, concentrate their study on the various aspects
of human society. In contrast, the natural sciences, such as astronomy, biology, chemistry, geology, and physics, focus their studies on the physical features of nature and the manner in which
they interact and change. The social scientist is concerned with furthering knowledge for its
own sake.

Sociology is nearly always defined as a science that engages in rigorous research guided by
theory. The authors define sociology as the systematic study of groups, organizations, social institutions, societies, and the social interaction among people. The word "systematic" is used because
sociology is committed to applying both theoretical perspectives and research methods to the
examination of social behavior and also because sociologists generally study regularly occurring behaviors. By definition, sociology is a science. A science possesses such characteristics as
theory guided by empirical observations, measurement of variables, analysis, synthesis, and
replication/ public verification. Definitions of the term *science* usually include such criteria as
having knowledge and knowledge obtained and tested through the scientific method. The scientific method itself is defined as the pursuit of knowledge involving the stating of a problem,
the collection of facts through observation and experiment, and the testing of ideas to determine whether they are right or wrong. As we shall see throughout this book, sociology has a
strong commitment to research and to the testing (through statistical analysis) of its theories.

The roots of sociology are firmly entrenched within the scientific tradition. Auguste Comte
(1798–1857), one of the earliest sociologists, and the person who coined the term "sociology,"
was a strong proponent of positivism. Positivism is a way of understanding the world based on
science. Positivists believe that the social world can be studied in the same manner as the natural sciences and believe that "laws" exist that apply to the human species; they merely have to
be discovered by social scientists. Comte was an early positivist and his concept of positivism
is based on the idea that everything in society is observable and subject to patterns or laws.
These laws help to explain human behavior. The role of the sociologist is to reveal these patterns, or laws, of human behavior. "Comte believed positivism would create sound theories based
on sufficient factual evidence and historical comparisons to predict future events. The discovery of the basic laws of human behavior will allow for deliberate courses of action on the part
of both individuals and society" (Delaney, 2005: 25).

In an attempt to understand the laws of society, sociologists often utilize the *sociological
imagination*. The American sociologist C. Wright Mills coined the term the sociological imagination to show how our private lives are influenced by the social environment and the existing social forces. The sociologist gains insights into human behavior by utilizing the sociological
imagination. According to Mills (1959), "The sociological imagination enables its possessor
to understand the larger historical scene in terms of its meanings for the inner life and the
external career of a variety of individuals. It enables him to take into account how individuals, in the welter of their daily experience, often become falsely conscious of their social positions" (p. 5).

The sociological imagination stresses the importance of the historical social context in which an individual is found. Mills emphasized that it is important to understand the personal biography (life history) along with the current actions of an individual to truly understand the meaning of his or her behavior. To underscore the importance of this point, Mills made distinctions between personal troubles and public issues. This distinction is critical to fully understand the manner in which the sociological imagination operates. Personal troubles "occur with the character of the individual and within the range of her or his immediate relations with others. They have to do with the self and with those limited areas of social life of which the person is directly and personally aware" (1959: 8). An example of personal trouble would be an athlete who gets "cut" from the team because his or her performance was not good enough to make the team. Public issues "transcend these local environments of the individual and the range of her or his inner life. They have to do with the organization of many milieus into the institutions of a historical society as a whole and form the larger structure of social and historical life" (1959: 8). From this standpoint, "the sociologist acknowledges that social forces, often out of the control of the individual, affect the individual's life for both the good and the bad" (Delaney, 2005: 88). For example, let's say an athlete is good enough to make a team's roster but then the league folds due to financial shortcomings (e.g., the former XFL football league). Such an athlete was not "cut" from the team due to a personal shortcoming (personal troubles), but rather because of reasons beyond his control (public issues).

Another example of the application of the sociological imagination to the sports world is provided by Nixon and Frey's (1996) example of steroid use. They argue that when one individual out of hundreds of professional athletes uses steroids, that is an example of a personal trouble. However, when it becomes known that a relatively large number of athletes are using steroids, the problem becomes a public issue. (As we shall see in Chapter 8, steroid use in American society is as much a public issue as it is a personal trouble.)

The Sociology of Sport

The sociology of sport is a subdiscipline of sociology that focuses on the relationship between sport and society. Sport sociology is concerned with the behavior of individuals and groups within sport and the rules and processes that exist within the formal and informal design and makeup of sport. With a commitment toward objective analysis the sport sociologist places a great deal of emphasis on the *evidence.* It is the role of the sport sociologist to keep his or her own biases under control and to refrain from making value judgments while conducting research and presenting findings. In other words, as with any social scientist, sport sociologists are to remain objective and present facts. However, offering suggestions and courses of actions to correct the "wrongs" and injustices found within the institution of sport is within the reform tradition of sociology.

The objective sociological perspective represents a more viable alternative to biological and psychological attempts to explain sport. Sport psychology focuses on the mental processes and behavioral characteristics (e.g., motivation, perception, cognition, self-confidence, self-esteem and personality) of the individual almost to the point where it ignores the importance of social forces. As Eitzen and Sage (1989) explain, biological and psychological explanations of sport focus exclusively on the individual and not the social forces and processes that affect behavior. The sociological approach, in contrast, examines social conditions in the community or society (e.g., varying degrees of unemployment, leisure time, urban blight, restricted opportunities for minority groups, or distribution of power to a ruling class) that may affect individual decision-making and behavior.

As a discipline, sport sociology has been in existence for at least four decades. When people consider the early sport sociologists, most point to Kenyon and Loy's 1965 article "Toward a Sociology of Sport" and Harry Edwards' 1973 publication *Sociology of Sport*. In 1965, Kenyon and Loy had already declared that sport had "become a cultural phenomenon of great magnitude and complexity" and was "fast becoming a social institution" (p. 24). They also noted that "despite the magnitude of the public's commitment to sport, as a social phenomenon it has received little serious study" (p. 24). This pattern holds true today as sports play an even bigger role in society (than in 1965) and yet is still ignored (or considered somewhat frivolous) by some in academia. Kenyon and Loy (1965: 24) advocated the scientific-sociological approach to the study of sports: If sociology is the study of social order — the underlying regularity of human social behavior — including efforts to attain it and departures from it, then the sociology of sport becomes the study of the regularity, and departures from it, of human social behavior in a sports context. Sport sociology, as Kenyon and Loy see it, is a value-free social science. "It is not an effort to influence public opinion or behavior, not is it an attempt to find support for the 'social development' objective of physical education.... The sport sociologist is neither a spreader of gospel nor an evangelist for exercise. His function is not to shape attitudes and values but rather to describe and explain them" (p. 25).

There are many sport sociologists who disagree with Kenyon and Loy's assertion that the sport sociologist should remain neutral. In fact, they argue that it is the job of the sport sociologist to spearhead change where there are flaws in the system. Snyder and Spreitzer (1978) were among the early sport sociologists who advocated the need for an *applied* sociology of sport. "If the policy implications of sport sociology are not brought out in the research of social scientists, this burgeoning field will die on the vine of academic trivia" (p. 8). Many examples of applied sport sociology will be presented throughout this book.

Conflict theorists (see Chapter 2 for a review of Conflict Theory) have also questioned the commitment to the value-free approach. As Jack Scott stated in his introduction to *Rip Off the Big Game: The Exploitation of Sports by the Power Elite*, "Any serious social scientist must admit, however, that the value-free approach to social science has always had its critics both within and without the social-science movement.... It should go without saying that Marxist social scientists have never accepted the legitimacy of a value-neutral orientation" (Hoch, 1972: 3–4). Critics of the value-free approach to sport sociology claim that such an ideology is one of non-involvement and an attempt to free oneself from social responsibility. There remains a great debate among sport sociologists today as to whether the field should maintain a commitment to the roots of sociology as a value-free, scientific approach to the study of sport in society or whether it should be a critical field that concentrates on negative issues. This text will provide a scientific approach while pointing out many of the problems of sport.

Edwards' publication of *Sociology of Sport* (1973) represents a major turning point in the discipline. Edwards compiled an extensive amount of research material and established a leading textbook for the field. He also established the basic properties of sport sociology: "In its broadest sense, this field should be concerned with the descriptions and explanation of the interrelations between sport and other societal components. More specifically, these fragmentary writings have been concerned with the functions of athletics in relation to basic social institutions and processes. The unique feature of the sociological approach to sport, as distinct from that of psychology, has been a focus upon sport in its function as a component of social organization" (pp. 10–11).

Kenyon and Loy (1965) reference a work entitled *Soziologie des Sports* (published in Germany in 1921) as one of the first isolated works on sport sociology, but they do not elaborate on its contents. We believe that Thorstein Veblen's *The Theory of the Leisure Class* (1899) establishes Veblen as an early pioneer of sport sociology. Of particular importance are his descriptions and analyses of conspicuous consumption and conspicuous leisure, as they represent early theoretical explanations of the growing role of sport consumerism in the United States specifically and of Western societies in general. Veblen used the term conspicuous consumption to describe the *nouveau riche* (first generation wealthy people), who purchased luxury items as a means to convey to others their social position. In this regard, the nouveau riche were looking for approval from the upper socio-economic classes and envy from the lower socio-economic classes. Conspicuous leisure refers to living a lifestyle where the pursuit of leisure and the appearance of privilege are instrumental in one's behavior. In other words, it involves participating in nonproductive activities.

THE SOCIOLOGY OF SPORT DEFINED

The academic and scholarly interest in sport has grown tremendously over the years. And, although the interest in sport comes from a varied array of sources, "sport sociology has been defined to a great extent by the topics that have been investigated, both by those formally trained in the area, and by those who identify with the area in order to legitimate their own work" (McPherson, 1981: 10). As a subdiscipline of sociology, sport sociology has a focus on the processes and patterns found within the institution of sport and how these social forces impact human behavior. The authors define the sociology of sport as the systematic study of the processes, patterns, issues, values and behaviors found in the institution of sport.

As we shall see throughout this book, the social institution of sport has a relationship with all the other social institutions found within a society. Sport affects billions of people around the world either directly or indirectly.

Why Do We Study Sports?

Sport is one of the most significant and influential social institutions found in societies around the world. Sports are a major part of people's lives. Sport participation provides opportunities for intrinsic and extrinsic rewards and is an excellent way to help develop a physically fit body. The sports world also provides us with opportunities to gain insight on racism, sexism, labor struggles, structured inequality, and so forth.

SPORT IS SOCIOLOGICAL

Nearly every element of sport has sociological significance. The truth of this statement will be demonstrated throughout the text as entire chapters dealing with specific social institutions and their relation to sports are provided. In brief, sport participation provides personal health benefits for individuals. Sports play a significant role in the culture of a given society. Sports help to provide historical continuity (e.g., through record keeping and maintaining allegiances to a favorite team over a lifetime) and more important, sports have existed throughout recorded history. Sports help to provide continuity in life as sports allegiances formed in childhood generally persevere throughout adulthood. Sport often serves as a positive diversion from the negative aspects of life by providing people a temporary "escape" from the mundane, sometimes monotonous and painful elements in one's personal or social life. Interestingly, in 2005, ESPN ran a commercial featuring a female jogger in an urban environment followed by numerous people who have demands on her life (e.g., husband, son, daughter, boss, women's group, etc.) with the catch-phrase "Without Sports, How Would We Escape?" In short, sport is sociological because it is interconnected with all the other social institutions found in society.

SPORT IS PERVASIVE

The institution of sport has become increasingly important and dominant throughout a large portion of the world. To ignore sport is to ignore a significant aspect of any society and its culture. Add to this the realization that most people have a great deal of leisure time which, for many, involves sports— either as a participant, observer, or consumer. Although the pervasiveness of sport will be detailed throughout the text in a variety of fashions, for now, let's consider the following as samples of the pervasiveness of sport in society:

- Newspapers in most cities devote entire sections of their daily editions to the coverage of sport. *USA Today*, the newspaper with the highest circulation in the United States, allocates one-fourth of its print coverage to sports. In general, newsprint devoted to sport in North America usually surpasses the space given to the economy, politics, religion, the environment or any other single topic of interest.
- There are over 525 "sports talk" radio stations nationwide with 14 million weekly listeners (86 percent males, and the largest number from the 25–54 age group) (ESPN, 2007).
- Sports are so important to some people that they have named their children in honor of the 24-hour sports channel, ESPN. Variations of the names include ESPN, Espn and Espen (*The Post-Standard*, 6/30/04). In 2006, Leann and Rusty Real named their son ESPN Montana Real after the sports network and former football great Joe Montana.
- During "states of emergency" sports are cancelled because they seem unimportant. However, when sports resume, they are often viewed as a beacon of light, or a diversion.
- It is common for popular athletes to have food items, such as sandwiches, and drinks, named after them. For example, Reggie Jackson ("Reggie!" bars) and Ken Griffey Jr. have candy bars named for them and former Buffalo Bills quarterback Doug Flutie had corn flakes ("Flutie Flakes") named after him.
- Many sport contests are worldwide events (for example, the World Cup, the Olympic Games, the Tour de France, Wimbledon, and the Super Bowl). Children around the world are exposed to these sport events.
- In 2007, both the National Football League (NFL) and Major League Baseball (MLB) set paid attendance records. The NFL surpassed 22 million for the second time in two years (with 22,256,502 paying fans) and MLB drew 76,215,082 fans.
- On March 5, 2006, Syracuse University broke the NCAA on-campus attendance record (that they previously held) for a college basketball game when 33,633 attended the game in the Carrier Dome.
- The pervasiveness of sport is revealed through sport-related movies and videos. The 2004 Academy Award for best film went to a boxing movie, *Million Dollar Baby*. It was about a female boxer (played by Hilary Swank) and a trainer (played by Clint Eastwood). The film has grossed over $100 million and also garnered Academy Awards for best actress (Swank), best supporting actor (Morgan Freeman) and best director (Eastwood). A recent ESPN poll of the top 20 sports films of all time lists the following: *Bull Durham, Rocky, Raging Bull, Hoosiers, Slap Shot, The Natural, Field of Dreams, Caddyshack, The Hustler, The Longest Yard, North Dallas Forty, Jerry Maguire, Hoop Dreams, Breaking Away, White Men Can't Jump, The Bad News Bears* (the original version), *Chariots of Fire, Brian's Song, Eight Men Out*, and *When We Were Kings*. All of these are among the most popular films ever made.
- The pervasiveness of sport is revealed through Internet sites. In June 2008, the authors typed the word "sport" (on a Google search) and found that there were 1.25 billion sites.

Clearly, as these few examples indicate, there is a strong interest in sports in North America. There are just as many examples of the pervasiveness of sports around the world.

Sport as a Social Institution

As stated earlier in this chapter, sport is a social institution. Social institutions represent the means (e.g., a set of organized beliefs and rules) that each society develops to meet its fundamental needs. The original social institutions discussed in sociology were the family, religion, education, the economy, and the government or politics. Today, the mass media, sports, science and technology, medicine, and the military are also considered to be social institutions.

Functionalists argue that each social institution is designed to meet specific needs. The

More than 33,000 orange-clad fans pack the Carrier Dome on the campus of Syracuse University to watch a men's college basketball game.

family, for example, is responsible for, among other things, the replacement of members of society and teaching the next generation cultural expectations; the government is responsible for maintaining and preserving social order. Conflict theorists argue that social institutions exist to maintain the status quo and therefore disadvantage those without socioeconomic or political power. The interactionist perspective, with a micro focus, emphasizes that human behavior is influenced by the roles and statuses that we possess, the groups to which we belong, and the institutions within which we function. (See Chapter 2 for a more comprehensive review of theoretical perspectives on sports.)

Edwards (1973) describes sport as a "secular, quasi-religious institution" (p. 90). As a secular institution, sport takes on a functional, non-religious role in society by upholding and reaffirming basic values and norms found in that culture. It can serve as the functional equivalent of a religious ceremony that brings a community together under a coherent system of beliefs.

Sociologists are generally concerned with how a social system works; specifically, the norms, roles and structures that hold the system together. The institution of sport provides an excellent system for analysis by sociologists. It is characterized by regulation, formalization, ideological justification and the transmission of culture. Sport as a social institution possesses many general characteristics of all social institutions. The following is a brief review of four key characteristics of sport as a social institution:

1. *A Ranking System (stratification).* Within all institutions, groups and societies, a hierarchy (a ranking system) exists. This hierarchy is often based on something of value. In business, seniority and position are valued (e.g., a senior vice president has higher value than an entry-level clerk). In sport, a hierarchy exists based on such things as "skilled" positions, star performers, and, to a lesser degree, seniority.

2. *Roles and Statuses (the organizational/structural aspect).* One's role is determined by one's position in the hierarchy. Star players are expected to perform at peak levels at all times. Secondary players do not experience such demands. One's status reflects one's social position in the hierarchy (e.g., head coach, trainer, athlete, team manager, water boy).

3. *Social Control (the ability to provide rewards and levy punishments/sanctions).* Social control is a mechanism designed to maintain conforming behavior. Sport channels human actions so that they abide with predefined expectations. For example, a coach may have a team rule that if an athlete is late for a film session, team practice, or curfew, that athlete will not be allowed to start (or play) in the next game. Sport itself is filled with rules. There are rules that apply during the game and outside of the game. When rules are violated during the game, a referee will punish the violator with a foul or some other type of sanction. For example, the National Football League has a rule against "excessive" or preplanned celebrations. (Social control and deviance will be discussed in further detail in Chapter 8).

4. *Rules (norms and expectations of behavior).* The need for social control is the result of the large number of rules in sport. All organizations have formal (written) rules as well as informal rules (how things are *really* done). An example of a formal rule is the NCAA's ban on college athletes from gambling and taking illegal drugs. All groups have informal norms as well, such as making a teammate pay a "fine" for inappropriate behavior, or for making a bonehead play.

In sum, sport has the same characteristics as all other social institutions and is therefore accepted as a social institution in its own right.

What Is Sport?

We have discussed many aspects of sport, but what exactly *is* sport? Listing types of sport is relatively easy. Classifying sport as indoors or outdoors; professional or amateur; and so on; is only slightly more difficult. Nearly everyone believes that they know what a sport is; however, if one is asked to define "sport" that usually causes some difficulty. Formulating a definition that draws clear and clean parameters around what activities should be included and excluded is relatively difficult to do. For example, is the backyard leisure activity of badminton a sport? Years ago, the notion of badminton as a sport would have caused great laughter. Today, badminton is not only considered a sport by some people, it is an Olympic sport! Kickball is another youth activity that has been transformed into a sport. And yet, there are kickball associations throughout the United States. What about such activities as anvil shooting, elephant races, and cup stacking; are these activities sports? Let's find out!

In rural areas of the South anvil shoots have become an increasingly popular sporting activity. An anvil shoot involves participants blowing up the blacksmith's tool (anvil) as high as possible in the air. According to a spokesperson for the National Anvil Shooters Association, anvil shooting is "a guy thing" (Hoffman, 1996). "Anvil shooting involves placing one large blacksmith anvil upside down on the ground and filling its cavity with a fine grade of black powder. A second anvil weighing up to 150 pounds is then placed upright on top of the bottom one. The powder is ignited and the top anvil is thrust as high as 125 feet into the air. The earth literally shakes; and the deafening boom, it is said, can be heard from as far away as 15 miles" (Museum of Appalachia, 2005). According to the Museum of Appalachia, anvil shoots have a long history in the United States with "accounts that the shooting of the anvil was employed to celebrate the nation's independence, Christmas, and even Davy Crockett's election to the United States Congress." Anvil shoots are becoming increasingly common at events such as July 4th celebrations and are included with other activities such as rail splitting and crosscut sawing. "Odd as the sport sounds—and lethal as it could be among bumblers—it is growing in popularity among those fond of antique tools, rending noises and gravity-defying acts. The usual venues are old engine shows and blacksmith get-togethers along rural highways in the South" (Hoffman, 1996:A-18).

Another unusual example of sport is elephant racing. Elephant races occur at various locations throughout the world. A Google search for elephant racing will reveal a tourist site listing various elephant races, generally found in Asia. A well-publicized elephant race occurred in Germany in 2000. More than 40,000 spectators watched the event. The idea for the race came from the Indian-born mayor (Ravindra Gujjula) of the town of Altlandsberg, just east of Berlin. Elephant racing is a tradition in India, but only two states currently hold such events. Despite the large turnout in Berlin's Hoppegarten, elephant racing is very controversial. Elephants have protected status in India, since the pachyderm is revered by many Hindus because of its resemblance to the elephant-headed god Ganesh. BBC News (2000) reported that "members of the Animal Peace group objected to the race and were supported by French film star Brigitte Bardot, German rock singer Nina Hagen and India's Social Affairs Minister Maneka Gandhi" (p. 1). The event featured 14 circus elephants, half of them African and half Asian, and six races. Promoters of the race insist that the elephants enjoy racing. After crossing the finishing line, the elephants were rewarded with treats of fruits and vegetables (BBC News, 2000).

The child's game of cup stacking (sometimes known as "sport stacking") became very popular as a sporting activity during the 2000s. There are over 7,500 programs around the world promoting cup stacking. The World Sport Stacking Association (WSSA), formed in 2001 for the purpose of promoting and governing the sport stacking around the world, promotes the standardization and advancement of sport stacking worldwide. As the governing body for sport stacking rules and regulations, the WSSA provides a uniform framework for sport stacking events, and sanctions sport stacking competitions and records (WSSA, 2008). (The Guinness Book of World Records tracks records in cup stacking.)

Participants, mostly students ranging from elementary age to college, stack and unstack 12 plastic cups as fast as possible. Cup stacking is both an individual and team sport. Contestants place cups in multiple stacks and sequences (such as "three-six-three" or "one-ten-one") and compete against the clock or each other. Stacking cups has long been popular at summer camps, church youth groups, and special-education classes; but now, professionals are promoting and endorsing the virtues of cup stacking. "Therapists use it with stroke victims to help them regain strength and coordination. Athletic trainers, amateur and professional, encourage clients to stack" (Sefton, 2004:A-16). Exercise and sports scientists report findings that indicate cup stacking significantly improves eye-hand coordination and reaction time among participants. Proponents of cup stacking also point out size and strength are not variables to successful stacking; therefore, anyone can excel at this activity.

Will cup stacking some day gain professional sport status? Should cup stacking, anvil shoots and elephant races be considered as sports? Might they even become Olympic events? What do you think?

DEFINING SPORT

Labeling activities such as anvil shooting, elephant racing, and cup stacking as sports is contingent on one's definition of sport. The word "sport" has its origins rooted in the idea that it is an activity designed to divert people from the routines of everyday life. "Sport derives its root from 'disport,' meaning 'to divert oneself.' It carried the original implication of people diverting their attention from the rigors and pressures of daily life by participating in the mirth and whimsy of frolic—some physical activity" (Edwards, 1973: 55).

There is a lack of consensus among sport sociologists on how to define sport. John Phillips (1993) even suggests that "in one sense the word *sport* need not be analyzed. Anyone who speaks English knows what sport is and is not" (p. 30). As a sport sociologist, Phillips takes a unique stand as sociologists are known for establishing standardized and operational definitions of key concepts. Phillips reflects the mentality of most students and followers of sport that we all unconsciously *know* which activities our culture defines as a sport and we therefore take for granted what is and is not sport. Snyder and Spreitzer (1978: 11) state that it is important for social scientists to have "workable analytical handles" on the meaning of sport. We agree. Simply being able to list sport will not help the social scientist understand sport sociologically.

Among the earliest social scientists to define sport was Günther Luschen. Luschen (1967, 1970) defines sport as an institutionalized type of competitive physical activity located on a continuum between play and world. He felt that it was particularly important to emphasize the fact that sport is a physical activity which would therefore automatically eliminate such activities as playing cards as being considered a sport — an important point to make as there are some members of the contemporary media (especially ESPN) that would have us believe that playing poker is a sport. Edwards (1973) states, "One of the most salient features of sports is that they always involve physical exertion. This physical exertion is an imperative characteristic that cannot be overstressed. Without it there simply is no sport activity" (p. 55). In his own definition of sport, Edwards emphasizes the physical aspect, as well as the organizational, rule-making, and goal-directedness of sport. Edwards goes on to define sport as "involving activities having formally recorded histories and traditions, stressing physical exertion through competition within limits set in explicit and formal rules governing role and position relationships, and carried out by actors who represent or who are part of formally organized associations having the goal of achieving valued tangibles or intangibles through defeating opposing groups" (pp. 57–58).

Nixon and Frey (1996) adapted Edwards and Luschen's definition and define sport "as institutionalized physical competition occurring in a formally organized or corporate structure" (p. 3). Describing sport as institutionalized reflects the earlier discussion in this chapter of sport as a social institution possessing such key elements as norms, statuses, roles and social relationships. The second significant element of this definition of sport is physical competition. Physical competition mandates that physical activity and skills are involved in order to determine a winner or loser.

Curry and Jiobu (1984) believe that sports are physical actions but also nondeviant activities: "*Sport* is a physical activity that is fair, competitive, nondeviant, and that is guided by rules, organizations, and/or tradition" (p. 8). Once again, the idea that sport is a physical activity is a part of this definition of sport. The idea that sports are fair is an idealistic view of sport that we all like to believe is true, but realize is not. The most unusual aspect of the Curry and Jiobu definition of sport is the stipulation that sport is nondeviant activity. "In general, deviant activity does not fit our cultural ideas about what sport is or should be. Sport has moral overtones about it. It's supposed to represent the ideals and high goals of our society, something deviance does not do. We therefore find it advisable to keep deviance separate from sport" (p. 11). Idealism should no longer be confused as a primary element of sport. Deviance not only occurs in sport (as Curry and Jiobu do acknowledge) it is sometimes taught and engaged in freely by athletes, trainers, league officials, referees, and owners.

Jay Coakley (2006) defines sports as "institutionalized competitive activities that involve rigorous physical exertion or the use of relatively complex physical skills by participants motivated by internal and external rewards" (p. 21). Note once again the idea that sports are physical activities (in this case rigorous) is included in this definition. However, there is a very critical addition to this definition of sport: "*or* the use of relatively complex physical skills."

The importance of this amendment is that it allows many other forms of recreation to be included as sports. For example, Delaney has had many students comment to him in his sociology of sport classes, "How can golf be listed as a sport when there is little physical activity involved; especially if golfers use a golf cart?" As anyone who has ever played golf can attest, there most certainly is an element of skill involved; whether it is "complex" or not is debatable. Coakley also includes motivational factors in his definition of sport. Internal or intrinsic rewards are those which come from "inside" the person, a feeling of accomplishment for having achieved some sort of athletic goal (e.g., finishing a marathon regardless of "place" or climbing a mountain and reaching the highest peak). Extrinsic rewards refer to "outside" accolades that one may receive for successful sport participation (e.g., monetary rewards, trophies, cheering and adoring fans).

We define sport as institutionalized, structured, and sanctioned competitive activity beyond the realm of play that involves physical exertion and the use of relatively complex athletic skills. We maintain the consistent perspective that sport must imply physical activity and the ability to use skill to gain an advantage over an opponent and we want to make it clear that there is a distinction between play and sports. (This point will be elaborated on later in this chapter.) Thus, although neighborhood kids may play football in backyards across the United States, it is a far different game than when professional or highly skilled athletes play football as a sport.

UNIVERSAL AND REGIONAL SPORTS

We will discuss a wide variety of sports in a variety of settings throughout this book, but the authors feel it is necessary to briefly distinguish between universal and regional sports here. Remember that sport reflects culture. The great diversity of sport is a result of the diverse world we live in. Specific sports have appeal in particular regions of the world, while other sports, because of their popularity, enjoy a universal following. In the United States, football represents the American sport. Around the world, however, *futbol* is soccer, and is the most popular of the two. It would appear that Americans prefer the hard-hitting violence, strategic planning and offensive scoring of *their* football over the world's obsession with the low-scoring, defense-minded *futbol* (soccer).

Universal sports (e.g., running, swimming, throwing things, soccer) are those sports which appear throughout most of the world. Some sports, such as archery and wrestling, are indigenous to nearly all cultures in the ancient world (Craig, 2002). Running and throwing things, such as big rocks and disk-shaped items, are also universal sports. As mentioned above, the world's most popular sport is *futbol*, or what Americans call soccer. "Soccer is the world's dominant sport.... The Soccer World Cup draws an audience larger than the Olympics, but barely registers with American viewers. The antipathy that many Americans feel for the way soccer is played is matched only be the distaste of many Europeans for the American style of play.... Americans and Europeans have absorbed the structure and rules of their sports into their psyches, turning the arbitrary rules of nineteenth-century administrators into a way of life" (Szymanski and Zimbalist, 2005: 2).

Regional sports are those sports which are not played universally. They may be isolated to specific countries or regions (e.g., Afghanistan's *buzkashi*) or specific areas within a society (e.g., lacrosse has greater appeal in the Northeast than in the Southwest regions of the United States). In light of recent world events, Americans have learned a great deal about Afghanistan's culture, including sports. Under the rule of the Taliban, most Afghan sports were banned. Many national sports have returned to the forefront in Afghanistan since the U.S.-led forces removed the Taliban from power. These sports include cockfighting, kite fighting and buzkashi. Cockfighting is controversial throughout the world and yet it appears in many "back alleys" across the United States. (As of 2008, cockfighting was legal in Louisiana and New Mexico.)

Cockfighting is a centuries-old blood sport in which two or more specially bred birds, known as gamecocks, are placed in an enclosure to fight, for the main purposes of gambling and entertainment. A cockfight usually results in the death of one or both of the birds. A typical cockfight can last anywhere from a few minutes to more than a half hour. In Afghanistan roosters do not fight to the death, but the combatants are bloodied and sometimes blinded before a winner is declared.

Kite fighting is another Afghan sport. Under the rule of the Taliban, participants of kite fighting were imprisoned. "The competition is slow and beautiful, but it's also serious business. The idea is to cut the string on your opponent's kite while it is in the air before he can cut yours.... Kite fighters wager as much as 600,000 Afghans, or about $5 per match — a hefty sum in a country where most people live hand-to-mouth. The Taliban regime, which banned music, television and most other forms of entertainment, had a particular loathing for kite fighting. Gambling is forbidden in Islam" (Haven, 2002:A4). In 2006, Pakistan banned kite-fighting after 7 people were killed in a competition (Shahzad, 2006). The kites have glass-coated strings meant to cut an opponent's kite loose. Low-flying kites often cut participants and observers; in some cases they slit the throats of victims. (A best-selling novel, *The Kite Runner*, by Khaled Hosseini, describes in great detail this potentially bloody sport.)

The most popular sport in Afghanistan is the traditional game of buzkashi — jostling on horseback with other riders trying to grab a decapitated goat.

> Buzkashi is a contest between two teams of horsemen over the possession of a dead calf or goat carcass, with the object being for one talented and fearless rider to gain control of the slippery carcass and then separate from the pack of horsemen vying for the same prize. "Buzkashi" means goat, but a calf carcass is often used because it reportedly stays intact longer. The animal is beheaded, bled, and behooved [*sic*] before being used. It can be either gutted or not [Craig, 2002: 154–155].

In the movie *Rambo III* Sylvester Stallone's character, Rambo (in an ironic U.S. political misfortune), is in Afghanistan to help rebel forces against Russian "aggressors." Rambo plays the Afghan sport of buzkashi and quickly dominates, earning the praise of the Afghan rebels.

Buzkashi was spread by the Mongol hordes that swept out of China and across central Asia. Today, the sport is played mostly by Turkic people, including the Uzbek, Turkomen, Kazakh, and Kirghiz. Interestingly, the Navajo of North America played a game similar to buzkashi called "the chick pull," with a live rooster replacing a four-legged carcass (Craig, 2002).

Among the most entertaining and demanding regional sports in the United States is lacrosse (lax for short). As reported in *Sports Illustrated* (4/25/05), lacrosse was once a longtime niche sport played primarily in New York State, New England, and the Baltimore area; today, it is the fastest-growing sport in the U.S.— at every level. "The number of youth-league players in the U.S. aged 15 and under is estimated to be 186,000, more than twice it was in 2001. The explosion is similar at the high school level, where no other team sport has anything close to lacrosse's rate of growth" (*Sports Illustrated*, 4/25/05: 59–60). The proliferation of lacrosse is occurring among both men and women. There are multiple reasons for the appeal of lacrosse. It is a fast-paced game that combines elements of soccer (constant running), hockey (play behind the net), and football (wearing pads, violent, controlled collisions, one-on-one defenses, zone defenses, set plays). It is an imaginative and wide-open game where most of the participants are not huge, hulking athletes. Youth sport leagues and high schools like lacrosse because it is much cheaper to fund than sports such as football and hockey. As a Native American sport, it could be argued that lacrosse is the *true* American sport. (There will be more on lacrosse in Chapter 11.)

Have you ever heard someone say, "I used to be an athlete?" Such a statement generally implies that when that individual was younger he played a sport (most likely a traditional sport such as football, baseball, tennis, track and field, etc.), but now that he is older, he does not. In other words, many people agree with Nixon and Frey (1996) that athletics is a synonym for sport played in school or college settings. But what if an individual, who is in his or her 40s, works out for 75 minutes a day, including a three mile run — is he or she an athlete? Or, do you have to play an organized sport in order to be considered an athlete? A lot of people play golf but we would not refer to all of them as athletes. On the other hand, there are athletes who play golf. Where do we draw the line of distinction between someone who is "physically active" and "athlete"?

A physically active person is someone who puts forth physical energy while engaged in some sort of activity that involves exertion. This may include walking, gardening, hiking, sightseeing, and so on. A physically active person engages in such activity simply for the enjoyment or benefit it provides. Thus, one may walk on a regular basis for health purposes as opposed to training for some athletic event. An athlete, on the other hand, is in training for some specific event or participates in a sport. According to the Merriam-Webster Dictionary, an athlete is someone who trains to compete in athletics. Athletics is defined as exercises and games that requiring physical skill, strength and endurance. Note that sport is not specifically mentioned as part of the definition of athletics. Most sport sociologists believe that an athlete is someone who is involved in a sports activity. For Harry Edwards, the distinction is clear. "It is only in sports that the participant can accurately be termed an 'athlete'" (p. 55). Thus, Tiger Woods, a professional golfer, is an athlete, whereas the typical weekend golfer is not.

Phillips (1993) views a rock climber, because he or she is engaged in sport, as an athlete, but not someone who walks through Yosemite Valley (p. 30). They would, however, be considered physically active. Perhaps the importance of competition should be stressed as well — in sport, one competes against other athletes, against previous records, or "a time," or against one's own previous best.

Distinctions Between Leisure, Play, and Sport

As stipulated in our definition, sport goes beyond the realm of play. Consequently, it is important to make distinctions between a number of related terms including, leisure, play and sport.

Most economists and sociologists generally regard leisure as unobligated time that is free of work or maintenance responsibilities. The term leisure suggests fun, distraction, and pleasure. "Leisure came to use through the Latin word *licere* by way of the French, *leisir*, the Middle English *leisere* and finally to its present spelling, leisure. The root word, *licere*, meaning to be permitted, evolved into another word — license. The word leisure literally meant exemption or permission as applied to opportunity afforded that was free from legal occupation" (Arnold, 1980: 13).

Leisure provides time and opportunity for creative growth, self-actualization, and intrinsically motivated goals. Historically, most people had little time to pursue leisure; they were too busy trying to meet primary needs (food, clothing and shelter). Leisure was reserved for the upper class, the privileged members of society. All of this would change with the rise of industrialization and the resulting formation of a middle class. Industrialization afforded an opportunity for the masses to enjoy leisure. Among the most notable economists/sociologists to examine the relationship between industrialization and rise of leisure prospects was Veblen.

Veblen defined leisure as non-productive consumption of time. "Time is consumed non-productively (1) from a sense of the unworthiness of productive work, and (2) as an evidence of pecuniary ability to afford a life of idleness" (1934: 43). The primary concept of Veblen's theory of the leisure class is *conspicuous consumption*, "according to which the consumption of goods from the very early 'predatory' stage of history to the present, has served not so much to satisfy men's true needs or to provide what Veblen chooses to call the 'fullness of life' as to maintain social prestige — status" (Adorno, 1981: 75). Thus, Veblen noted that when people acquired an economic surplus they did not purchase necessity items; instead, in an attempt to build their self-esteem, they purchased products that conveyed to others their increased socio-economic position.

Veblen believed that individuals participated in "wasteful" behaviors as a means of attaining self-esteem. Sport participation (even as spectators) allows members of the lower economic classes to engage in some of the same activities as the wealthier members of society. Obviously, this can be very meaningful to people. As for the wealthy, Veblen theorized that merely possessing wealth and power is never enough. Instead, wealth or power must be put into evidence for esteem to be awarded. Veblen stated, "Not only does the evidence of wealth serve to impress one's importance on others and to keep their sense of importance alive and alert, but it is of scarcely less use in building up and preserving one's self-complacency. In all but the lowest stages of culture the normally constituted man is comforted and upheld in his self-respect by 'decent surrounding' and the exemption from 'menial offices'" (Mitchell, 1964: 230). Thus, Veblen understood why some people participated in leisure activities; however, he felt that leading a good productive life should be enough for one's positive self-image. Outside verification from others should be unnecessary. Clearly, Veblen's upbringing is reflected in his view of the leisure class. His parents worked hard so that their children had an opportunity to pursue advanced education. Their frugality afforded this opportunity. As a result, Veblen learned to appreciate and value hard work.

Many people disagree with Veblen's conclusion about leisure. Beginning with industrialization and continuing in contemporary society, individuals who work hard feel "entitled" to leisure time. They also feel a need to remove themselves, at least temporarily, from their work environments and enter preferred leisure domains. "The very development of capitalist society has thus produced forms of physical leisure pursuit ... for getting away from it all, for escapism and ecstasy" (Brohm, 1976: 88). Many sport sociologists believe that leisure is important to so many people because these activities often reflect one's social identity — they define who people really are, more so than other labels (e.g., occupation).

It should be noted that Americans have more leisure time today than in the past. According to the American Sociological Association (2008), 100 years ago, Americans averaged 57.7 working hours per week, earning $3.75 per hour, and life expectancy was 48.7. By 1980, the average work week was 39.7 hours per week at $11.53 per hour and life expectancy rose to 73.7. According to the United States Department of Labor, in 2008 the average work week was 33.7 hours per week at $18.01 per hour and life expectancy was 78.1 years— a very dramatic growth in such a short amount of time.

PLAY

Play is a universal concept. It is as old as culture itself. Play, in contrast to work, represents an absence of obligated time. Play is an activity that is performed voluntarily during leisure. "Play is an enjoyable experience deriving from behavior which is self-initiated in accordance with personal goals or expressive impulses; it tolerates all ranges of movement abilities;

its rules are spontaneous; it has a temporal sequence but no predetermined ending; it results in no tangible outcome, victory or reward" (Snyder and Spreitzer, 1978: 12). For example, two girls wander toward the swing set and begin to swing aimlessly. Next, they pick up a basketball and haphazardly take shots at the hoop. When they are bored they drop the ball and walk away. This type of behavior is the direct opposite of seriousness— it is play. "Play provides an opportunity to temporarily shelve reality and thus find one's inner self again" (Hellendoorn, van der Koolj, and Sutton-Smith, 1994: 25).

Guttmann (1988) describes two types of play: spontaneous play and organized play (games). Spontaneous play is voluntary, flexible, and uncertain with latitude for innovation. For example, at family picnic baseball games, youths may be allowed four or five strikes (instead of the customary three) and adults may be required to bat from their "opposite" side (left-handed for natural right-handed batters). Adaptations to rules are allowed, such as "do-overs"— repeating the play for some reason (e.g., the batter wasn't paying attention when a called "strike" pitch was made). In sports, there are no do-overs; you must comply with the rules and be ready to play. Recreation is a type of spontaneous play. As Nixon and Frey (1996) explain, it is a leisure activity designed to refresh the mind or body. Arnold (1980) explains the origins of recreation:

> In Latin, *recreatio* carried a connotation of restoration or recovery from something. Its root is in the word *re-creo* (to create again) to refresh, invigorate, or revive. Further references include such inferences as to amuse oneself after obligation: *laxandi levandique animi gratia*, having to do with which we are dealing has a metaphysical quality. If we are to accept the various synonyms given, we would need to substantiate activity as a means for attaining relaxation or rest. The assumption indicated would produce a dichotomy: rest from activity or a cessation of movement on the one hand and diverting activity on the other hand [pp. 9–10].

Thus, recreation has a strong component of leisure. It is meant to be a refreshing activity, and it is playful. It may, or may not, be productive.

As play becomes more serious, more organized, we have the beginnings of competitive contests and sports. According to Guttmann (1988), organized play, or games, involves both noncompetitive games (e.g., kicking a ball with friends) and competitive games (contests). Competitive games can be divided into two categories: intellectual contests (e.g., chess) and physical contests (sports). With organized play, games tend to have less freedom, they are bound by rules. There are designated time limits and boundaries (e.g., organized baseball has a set number of innings, bowling has 10 frames a game) and there is nearly always a clear winner (and loser) at the end of organized games. "Since games imply winners and losers, there may be a degree or emotion or ego investment involved, although such investment tends to be small compared to that found in sports and athletics" (Figler and Whitaker, 1991: 14). Incorporating the elements of games described above, Snyder and Spreitzer (1978) define games as "activities with an agreed-on organization of time, space, and terrain, with rules that define the objective and limit the pattern of human behavior; the outcome, which is to determine a winner and a loser, is achieved by totaling or accumulating objectively scored points or successes" (p. 12).

Contests may be between two individuals, between two teams, between an individual and a group, between an individual or team and inanimate nature (such as mountain climbing, white water rafting), between a person or group and animate nature (e.g., hunting, fishing, or bull fighting), or between an individual or team and an ideal standard (e.g., a home run–hitting contest). A number of "competitive eating" contests have sprung to life in the past decade. In fact, there is an international governing body, the International Federation of Competitive Eating (IFOCE), that oversees all competitive eating contests. The IFOCE requires that all competitive eaters must be at least 18 years old. Contests who throw up during competition are disqualified. The IFOCE sponsors over 100 contests a year internationally. The IFOCE, based in New York City, keeps official eating records and ranks its professional eaters (a top 50). In

2008, the number one ranked competitive eater was Joey Chestnut. Top-ranked "professional eaters" earn hundreds of thousands of dollars.

Among the most famous eating competitions is Nathan's annual July 4th hot dog eating contest held on New York City's Coney Island. The first hot dog eating contest at Nathan's was held on July 4, 1916 (Nerz, 2006). The hot dog eating contests pits numerous competitors against one another in a timed match to see who can eat the most hot dogs (with buns). Competitors at Nathan's annual hot dog eating contest compete for cash prices and the "mustard yellow belt." In 2008, Joey Chestnut reclaimed the top spot from his archrival Takeru Kobayashi. After first tying by eating 59 franks in 10 minutes, Chestnut won in a last-minute tiebreaker (a five dog "eat-off") by gobbling down another five dogs faster than Kobayashi. It was the first time the contest went into overtime. Because the Nathan's hot dog eating contest was reduced from twelve minutes to ten minutes, Chestnut set a new record.

Contests may also involve a struggle between animals (e.g., dog racing or horse racing) or between a real and an artificial animal (as in a greyhound race against a mechanical rabbit) (Calhoun, 1987). Games and contests are rule-bound, earnest and organized. As our definition of sport implies, the more institutionalized and structured competitive games and contests become, the more sport-like they turn out to be. This is not meant to imply that we consider competitive eating a sport, or competitive eaters as athletes. Furthermore, considering that numerous people around the world starve to death every day, the concept of competitive eating hardly seems sporting.

SPORT

Sports, by design, are highly structured, involve institutionally defined rules, give rise to a hierarchical authority pattern, and are often so over-regulated that they seem only nominally related to play. Although it is commonly said that athletes "play" sports, the rules and customs that control the behaviors of athletes often distances sport from the realm of play. "With the rise of sport we reach the ultimate in the organization and formalization of play. A game, says philosopher Paul Weiss, is an occurrence; a sport is a pattern" (Calhoun, 1987: 49). The participants of sports (athletes, owners, trainers, etc.) have an investment with sport. Their very livelihoods are dependent upon success in the sports world. Generally, the investment aspect of sport outweighs the recreational, playful aspect of the game itself. Thus, as Edwards (1973) notes decades ago, sport is often "anything but a diversion to its participants. In fact, for many participants it is sport that produces the primary stresses and strains in their lives" (p. 55).

As we will demonstrate throughout the text, for many people, sport is so important to them, it is like a religion. Sport is not a religion in the same sense as Catholicism, for example, is a religion, but in terms of the secular meaning and self-identification that sport allegiances provide. There are members of society who do not closely follow sports. They will have a hard time understanding how sport can provide such significant meaning to their lives. This same rationale is applied by those who do not adhere to a particular religion and have a hard time understanding another's devotion to a religion.

SUMMARY

Sociology involves the systematic study of society; especially the social institutions and people found within a given society. Sport continues to grow in importance in societies around the world. The scientific study of sport will help provide great insights regarding human behavior in their cultures.

Sport reflects the mores, values and general culture of a society. The systematic study of sport, therefore, can provide a mirror into such negative issues as elitism, racism, sexism, nationalism, competitiveness, the abuse of drugs, and other deviant behaviors. More importantly, though, it can help one understand the positive aspects of societies such as cooperation, hard work, dedication, loyalty, understanding rules, and ethical norms.

Sociology is a scientific endeavor which teaches us to look beyond "common sense" and utilize "the sociological imagination" in order to understand how our lives are influenced by social forces. Sociologists generally look at the big picture and study institutions that make up society and the corresponding cultures that are connected with them. The sociology of sport is a subdiscipline of sociology that focuses on the relationship between sport and society.

Sport sociology has existed as a discipline for at least four decades, although Thorstein Veblen was a pioneer in this field with his 1899 book *The Theory of the Leisure Class*. In his time, sports were primarily considered an activity of the wealthy class. Today, sports as recreation are played by the masses as well as by elites and represent a $160 billion industry.

While interest and participation in sport have increased, it is not easy to define what activities fall within it. There is a lack of consensus among sports sociologists on how to define sport, but such key elements as institutionalization, competition, external and internal rewards, and physical exertion seem to be constant. In addition, sports can be said to be whatever people label as sports.

Distinctions can be made between universal sports, which appear throughout the world, and regional sports. Regardless of such distinctions, sport reflects culture. It is connected to the universal concept of "play," voluntary activities performed during leisure time. As play becomes more organized and less spontaneous, societies experience the beginnings of competitive contests and organized play. Sports, then, are highly structured, rule-bound, hierarchical activities which play a major role in binding people together and giving meaning to their existences. The scientific study of sport, therefore, is a means to understand the processes, patterns, issues, values and behaviors found in the activities.

KEY TERMS

Athlete A person who trains to compete in athletics.

Athletics Exercises and games that require physical skill, strength and endurance.

Conspicuous Consumption A term coined by Thorstein Veblen; it refers to spending money, time and effort quite uselessly in the pleasurable business of inflating the ego.

Conspicuous Leisure A term coined by Thorstein Veblen; it refers to living a lifestyle where the pursuit of leisure and the appearance of privilege are used instrumental in one's behavior. In other words, it involves participating in nonproductive activities.

Contest An organized competition. It may be between two individuals, between two teams, between an individual and a group, between an individual or team and inanimate nature, between a person or group and animate nature, or between an individual or team and an ideal standard.

Culture The shared knowledge, beliefs, values, and rules about behavior that exist within a society.

Leisure Unobligated time that is free of work or maintenance responsibilities.

Leisure Class A term used by Thorstein Veblen to describe people who engaged in non-productive economic behavior.

Natural Sciences Disciplines such as astronomy, biology, chemistry, geology, and physics, which focus their studies on the physical features of nature and the manner in which they interact and change.

Organized Play Activities which are bound by rules, in which there are designated time limits and boundaries and nearly always a clear winner and loser.

Play An activity that is performed voluntarily during leisure.

Positivism A way of understanding the world based on science. Positivists believe that the social world can be studied in the same manner as the natural sciences and believe that "laws" exist that apply to the human species; they merely have to be discovered by social scientists.

Recreation A leisure activity designed to refresh the mind and/or body.

Scientific Method The pursuit of knowledge involving the stating of a problem, the collection of facts through observation and experiment, and the testing of ideas to determine whether they are right or wrong.

Social Institutions A set of organized beliefs and rules that establishes how a society will attempt to meet its basic social needs.

Social Sciences Disciplines such as sociology, anthropology, economics, history, psychology, and political science, which concentrate their study on the various aspects of human society.

Social Structure The organization of society — its social positions and the ongoing relationships among these social positions, the different resources allocated to these social positions, and the social groups that make up the society.

Society The largest collection of people in group form.

Sociological Imagination A term coined by C. Wright Mills. Sociological imagination stresses the importance of the historical social context in which an individual is found, and the ways in which our private lives are influenced by our social environment and existing social forces.

Sociology The systematic study of human society and social interaction. Note the difference from page 3, where sociology is defined as the systematic study of groups, organizations, social institutions, societies, and the social interaction among people.

Sociology of Sport The systematic study of the processes, patterns, issues, values and behaviors found in the institution of sport.

Spontaneous Play A type of play which is voluntary, flexible, and uncertain with latitude for innovation.

Sport An institutionalized, structured, and sanctioned competitive activity beyond the realm of play that involves physical exertion and the use of relatively complex athletic skills.

DISCUSSION QUESTIONS

- What do you think the term "win at all costs" means? Can you think of examples where this attitude has occurred in a recent sporting event?

- It is often said participating in a sport can build one's character. Think of examples that could demonstrate this. Do you agree or disagree with this claim?

- If an athlete is cut from the team not because of his or her shortcomings but due to financial problems of the team or league, would this be unjust?

- Is cockfighting an ethically acceptable sport? What are the arguments for and against it? How does this relate to the question of whether ethics is universal or relative?

- Why do so many popular films deal with issues of sport? Do you think this is a good or bad thing? Think of some recent examples of films that have sport as their central theme.

- What do you think of the statement "Winning isn't everything; it's the only thing"? Compare and contrast this with the statement "It isn't if you win or lose, it is how you play the game."

CHAPTER 2

Social Theory and Sport

Two friends are cheering for their beloved hometown baseball team. The starting pitcher for the home team has been dominant throughout eight innings. In the ninth inning the visitors begin to mount a rally and load the bases with two outs. The go-ahead runner is on second base. One of the friends begins to yell, at no one in particular, "Bring in a relief pitcher; this guy is done!" This fan believes that the starting pitcher has tired and therefore a "fresh" pitcher will have a better chance of getting the last batter out. In essence, this fan has expressed a theory, albeit a simple one, on baseball strategy.

The second friend has a different opinion. She believes that the manager should keep the starting pitcher in the game because he has a history of getting the next scheduled batter out. She cites research that the batter has just one hit in twelve previous at-bats, striking out seven times. This fan has expressed a different theory, one which is supported by data, rather than tradition (bringing in a relief pitcher when the starter appears fatigued).

Social theory involves expressing ideas about human behavior and the social world. As demonstrated in the story above, every one of us is capable of formulating a theory about social life. Sport sociologists use theory as a "guide" in their attempt to understand the institution of sport. Sport sociologists, like other sociologists grounded in the scientific tradition, incorporate research, the use of statistical data, and analysis to support their theories.

The Importance of Social Theory

Sociology attempts to provide insights and explanations as to why people behave the way that they do and why social institutions exist the way they do. Social theory, then, focuses on interactions, patterns and events found in the social environment and attempts to explain such observed phenomena. A theory on social reality reflects one's perspective on the nature of society. There are numerous perspectives and theories within the sociological tradition. A sociologist's preference for one theory over another often reflects his or her own values and possible biases. Preference for a particular theory or perspective is also impacted by current, in vogue, and fashionable trends found within sociology. "Theories about society are shaped by people's past experiences, current needs, and future hopes, and it is more likely that at given points in history one perspective may be more popular or more reflective of current events than others, rather than one being 'true' and the others 'false'" (Figler and Whitaker, 1991: 25).

What exactly is social theory? "The word *theory* is often misunderstood. It seems to imply speculation or uncertainty because it is viewed *merely* as a theory, not a statement of 'truth.' Theories are generally contrasted with 'facts.' It is usually believed that facts are established truths, whereas theories are speculations about what might be true" (Delaney, 2005: 1). However, to social scientists, the word "theory" does not imply mere speculation as theories may already be established as true. Theories provide explanations or accounts concerning social events or phenomena. As Gabriel Abend (2008) explains, a theory is "a general proposition, or logically-connected system of general propositions, which establishes a relationship between two or more variables" (p. 177). The authors define theory as a statement that proposes to explain or relate observed phenomena or a set of concepts through a logically-based system of general propositions. Theory involves a set of inter-related arguments that seek to describe and explain cause-effect relationships. Portraying ideas (theories) in the form of statements allows for empirical testing. Thus, any theory that can be tested for empirical verifiability is considered a "good" theory.

Although sociological theory has existed since the time Auguste Comte coined the term "sociology," most sociologists ignored sport as an academic study. George Herbert Mead represents one of the earliest sociologists to examine critical aspects of play and games—essential elements of sport.

GEORGE HERBERT MEAD AND PLAY

George H. Mead (1863–1931) was an American pragmatist, philosopher, social scientist and the primary founder of symbolic interactionism. Mead established a developmental theory (of self) centered primarily on the play of children. Mead (1934) described play as the stage which precedes organized games. Play is important in development because, as children grow, they learn to take on the role of others. "A child plays at being a mother, at being a teacher, at being a policeman; that is, it is taking different roles" (p. 150). According to Delaney (2004), "To learn the role of others, the child must come to understand the meanings of symbols and language. Much of this learning takes place through various forms of play" (p. 181). As the emphasis on the importance of learning would imply, Mead's theory is not biological, and therefore it has greater interest to contemporary sport sociologists than the other pioneering theories. Mead's developmental theory has four stages.

1. *The Imitation Stage.* During this preparatory stage, infants develop an emerging awareness of other people and physical objects found in the environment. Babies learn to grasp, hold and use simple objects like spoons, dolls, bottles, and blankets. As their physical skills continue to develop, they learn to play with objects by imitating the people around them. The infant may observe an older sibling playing and may try throwing a ball like the other, older children. A parent might pick up a ball and toss it, in an attempt to coax the child to do the same thing. Imitation implies learning, as infants find out that some behaviors are positively rewarded and other behaviors bring punishments. Interactions with significant others are especially important for the infant's development of self. Significant others are those specific individuals with whom a child interacts with on a regular basis, generally the child's immediate family members and friends.

2. *The Play Stage.* Mead was among the first theorists to emphasize the importance of symbols in the socialization process. In the play stage, the child has learned to use language and understands the meanings of some symbols. Language allows the child an opportunity to adopt the role or attitude of other persons—they can speak with the mannerisms of the other. They not only act out the roles of others, but their imaginations allow them to pretend to be that person (Pampel, 2000). Although lower animals also play, only humans "play at being someone else" (Aboulafia, 1986: 9). Through role-playing, the child learns to become both subject and object, a critical step in the development of self (Ritzer, 2000). It is important to note that children are also developing their own personalities at this stage. "In play, the child takes on and acts out roles which exist in his immediate, but larger, social world. By acting out such roles he organizes particular attitudes about them. Moreover, the child in the course of role playing becomes cognitively capable of 'standing outside himself' and formulating a reflected view of himself as a social object separate from but related to others" (Loy and Ingham, 1981: 197).

3. *The Game Stage.* At this stage, the child is capable of putting herself in the role of several others at the same time, and of understanding the relationship between those roles (e.g., teammates).

"If we contrast play with the situation in an organized game, we note the essential difference that the child who plays in a game must be ready to take the attitude of everyone else involved in that game, and that these different roles must have a definite relationship to each other" (Mead, 1934: 151). Mead, who taught at the University of Chicago, was a fan of the Chicago Cubs and enjoyed watching baseball. He used the game of baseball to illustrate his "game stage" theory. For example, when the ball is hit into play, the fielder must make the play, but must also know the role of his teammates and the complexities of the game — such as, where to throw the ball if there are already runners on base, and so forth.

Understanding the roles of others is not enough in the game stage; participants must also know and understand the rules of the game (Miller, 1973). As Mead explained, abiding by the rules involves the ability to exercise self-control and implies that the child has learned to function in the organized whole. Mead insisted that children take a great interest in rules. "They make rules on the spot in order to help themselves out of difficulties. Part of the enjoyment of the game is to get these rules. Now, the rules are the set of responses which a particular attitude calls out. You can demand a certain response in others if you take a certain attitude" (1934: 152). Thus, games teach children to take multiple roles but also teach them to abide by rules. "The game is viewed as a sort of passage in the life of a child from taking the role of others in play to the organized part that is essential to self-consciousness" (Delaney, 2004: 182).

4. *The Generalized Other*. This marks the final stage of development. The generalized other refers to the attitude of the community, a specific group, or society in general. It is the universalization of the role-taking process (Pfuetz, 1954). The generalized other is not a person; it is a person's conscious awareness of the society that she or he is a part of (Cockerham, 1995). Such associations occur with multiple, diverse others in the community (e.g., geographic community, church-group, sport-booster team, the greater society).

The development of self is dependent on interactions with others within the community. These interactions help to shape and determine the individual's personality. Whereas the play stage requires only pieces of selves, the game stage requires a coherent self (Ritzer, 2000). Mead's development of self theory is very sociological. It considers interactional patterns, past experiences, and the impact of "outside" social forces on the individual. The impact of social forces on sport participants and the creation and maintenance of the institution of sport is the central theme of contemporary theory.

In the following pages a number of contemporary sociological theories are applied to the study of sport. The first theory to be examined is functionalism.

Functionalism

Functionalism, or structural functionalism as some sociologists prefer to call it, was the one-time dominant theory of sociology (especially during the 1950s and early 1960s). Functionalism is a macrosociological theory that explores the characteristics of social patterns, structures, social systems, and institutions. Functionalism views society as an organized system of interrelated parts that seeks equilibrium or balance. These interrelated parts work in cooperation with one another so that the entire social system functions properly.

Functionalism has two basic postulates. The first is the concept of interdependent parts, where all of society's social institutions (e.g., sports, religion, politics, economics, and the media) are linked together. "Functionalism begins with the idea that any stable system (such as the human body) consists of a number of different, but interrelated, parts that operate together to create an overall order" (Levin, 1991: 76). With this reasoning, a change in one institution inevitably leads to changes in other institutions. For example, if the NCAA were to mandate that all athletes must maintain a 2.4 (4.0 grading system) GPA, member institutions would be forced to enact many changes. Because social systems wish to run smoothly, they constantly seek equilibrium, or stability. Functionalists recognize that certain behaviors cause a disruption in

the system — they are labeled dysfunctional acts. Robert Merton (1910–2003) was the first sociologist to articulate the potential dysfunctional features of certain aspects of the social system.
Merton stated that dysfunctional aspects are those which disturb the normally functioning social
system. Furthermore, Merton argued that aspects of the social system may be functional for
some, but not for others. For example, it is common for sporting events to be held during
national holidays. This is convenient for the fans who wish to watch the games, but not so convenient for the athletes who may have preferred to spend time with their families. Functionalists prefer the status quo over change (especially rapid change); and any change in the system
is generally introduced in such a manner that allows ample time for a smooth transition. Thus,
if the NCAA did mandate higher grade requirements among its athletes (currently, the NCAA
requires a 2.0 GPA), it would undoubtedly provide ample time for a smooth transition.

The second postulate of functionalism is centered on the idea that individual members of
the social system (e.g., society, sports league or team) generally endorse the same basic values
and beliefs. A common agreement on issues of right and wrong, basic values, and morality
allows for the system to function appropriately. If members of a social system lose faith in their
society (the system) they will seek change. Rapid social change within the system is something
the functionalist approach is not geared to handle.

Among the leading structural functionalists of the twentieth century was Talcott Parsons
(1902–1979), a major sociologist at Harvard University. Parsons's analysis of social systems and
social action remains as the cornerstone of the functionalist perspective. As with most social
thought, Parsons's ideas were a reflection of the era in which he lived. The post–World War II
era was highlighted by great prosperity among many Americans. The 1950s was a decade of relative social calm and stability. Parsons reasoned that social systems strive for stability in order
to function at peak levels, and "argued that the overall system and subsystems of which it is
composed work together to form a balanced, stable whole and that the system naturally tends
toward stability rather than toward disorder" (Levin, 1991: 77). Systems have parts, or subsystems. The social system also includes the interaction of a plurality of individual actors oriented
to a situation (e.g., a sports team). "Reduced to the simplest possible terms, then, a social system consists in a plurality of individual actors interacting with each other in a situation which
has at least a physical or environmental aspect" (Parsons, 1951: 5). Importantly, the social system is designed to continue to exist even when some individual members leave. For example,
as members of a college sports team graduate, transfer, or drop out, they are replaced by other
individuals. This cycle of individuals coming and going continues year after year and yet the
social system (the team, the league) manages to maintain itself (with varying degrees of success).

Although social systems are quite diverse (some are small, some large; some are complex,
others relatively simplistic) a number of general assumptions about social systems can be made:

1. Systems are orderly and made of the interdependence of parts.
2. The system and all the subsystems strive for equilibrium (normal activity, a self-maintaining
   order).
3. Systems are generally static or move in a progressively deliberate manner.
4. A disruption in the "normal flow" of one subsystem can cause a disturbance throughout the
   whole system.
5. Systems have boundaries, which may involve actual physical space, or time and distance
   [Delaney, 2005: 48–49].

By the 1970s, there were many criticisms of functionalism. One criticism is that functionalism is too conservative and fails to explain social change. Functionalism's focus on systems
equilibrium leads functionalists to ignore conflict. People do not agree on all the values and

beliefs of the dominant society and, as a result, functionalism is criticized for failing to acknowledge socioeconomic inequalities that lead to different perspectives of the social system. Because of its conservative nature and focus on the status quo, functionalism is also criticized for ignoring such social patterns as "discrimination, exploitation, and political dominations by elites or ruling classes who have a vested interest in maintaining their power and prestige" (Nixon and Frey, 1996: 10). Despite these criticisms, the staying power of functionalism as a dominant sociological theory cannot be denied. The relevancy of this perspective is demonstrated in the sports world as well.

FUNCTIONALISM APPLIED TO SPORT

The functionalist perspective has great relevance to sport. Sport, as a social institution, may be viewed as a social system with interrelated parts and a plurality of individual actors interacting with one another. As the authors shall demonstrate throughout the text, sport possesses both functional and dysfunctional aspects.

Sport provides many societal functions, some of them manifest (intended or planned) and others latent (unintended or unplanned). Merton (1949/1968) described manifest functions as those consequences that are expected, or intended; they are conscious motivations for social behavior. For example, the manifest function of two friends attending a baseball game is to watch the athletes perform or to cheer for a favorite team. Merton described latent functions as consequences that are neither recognized nor intended; they are by-products of the original intended behavior. Thus, the same two friends who attended the ballgame are also afforded an opportunity to reaffirm their friendship by spending time together. Parents and children may also bond over sports activities. Individuals bond with the community of the sports team they support. Eitzen (1989) adds:

> Most people view society and the role of sport in terms very similar to those used by functionalists. They look for the ways in which sport contributes to the communities in which they live. They see sport providing valuable lessons for their children and opportunities for themselves to release the tensions generated by a job or other life events. Sport gives them something to talk with strangers as well as friends and it provides occasions for outings and get togethers. Many people believe that sport can serve as a model of the goals we should strive for and the means we should use in trying to achieve those goals [p. 28].

During the 1970s many sport sociologists (for example, Allardt, 1970; Wohl, 1970; Luschen, 1970B; Gruneau, 1975; and Sage, 1979) embraced the functionalist perspective by describing sport "in functionalist terms as supportive of the social order" (Figler and Whitaker, 1991: 28). Stevenson and Nixon (1972) detailed five general functions by which sport helps the social system maintain equilibrium and operate smoothly and efficiently:

1. *Socioemotional Function.* Sport provides opportunities for conflict and tension management, camaraderie and community bonding, and ritualistic behaviors that people find comforting.
2. *Socialization.* All people learn society's expectations through the socialization process (See Chapter 5). Of primary concern to functionalists is the transmission of cultural values from one generation to the next.
3. *Social Integration.* A commonly cited function, sport, it is argued, provides opportunities for diverse groups and individuals to interact with one another.
4. *Political Functions.* The role of politics and sport is both functional and dysfunctional (See Chapter 13). The singing of the national anthem before sporting events is among the more obvious manifest functions of politics in action within the sports world.
5. *Social Mobility.* A recurring theme in contemporary society as well, it has long been argued that sport provides individuals with opportunities to improve their socio-economic status (SES). Sport does provide both direct (through professional sport participation) social mobility and indirect (through college scholarships with afford athletes an opportunity to earn a valuable education needed in the job market) social mobility.

Vogler and Schwartz (1993) argue that sport is so strongly endorsed by most people in American society that it has been given nearly "sacred status" and that the majority of people feel that sport is "compatible with American values" (p. 6); and thus is congruent with the functionalist perspective. As a result, sport is viewed as having a positive function in society. Among other things, sport transmits cultural values; is educational; provides a release for physical and psychological pressures; provides a feeling of group membership; provides a means of social mobility; and generates a sense of personal competition (Vogler and Schwartz, 1993: 6).

Functionalists, in the tradition of Parsons and his conception of functional imperatives (adaptation, goal attainment, integration, and latency; or AGIL), argue that there are four basic "system needs" in order for any society (club, organization, team, etc.) to run smoothly. This principle can be applied to the sports world as well.

1. *Adaptation*. Members of society must learn to adapt to changes in the social structure and culture in order to survive. The emphasis on being physically fit (a requirement for most sports) is an important element in survival. For example, being able to adapt to changes in coaching philosophies is often critical for athletes when a new coach/system is introduced to the team.
2. *Goal Attainment*. Individual societal members are expected to seek society's goals. The predominant goal in Western societies is to be successful. Sport teaches participants that working hard leads to victory, and, therefore, success. Sport is preoccupied with tracking the successes and failures of its participants. As former Green Bay Packer coach Vince Lombardi is reputed to have said, "Show me a good loser, and I'll show you a loser."
3. *Integration*. Sport brings people together. Sport provides people an opportunity to bond with a group and a community. It provides a sense of social identification as well as a source of personal identity.
4. *Latency (pattern maintenance and tension management)*. Sport provides many forms of pattern maintenance — primarily through participation where participants are taught to accept a well-defined authority structure (e.g., athletes know they must abide by their coaches' rules and the authority of referees, etc.). Sport also provides spectators and participants a socially approved outlet for their aggressive energy.

Despite the criticisms of functionalism, this theoretical perspective is still relevant to the sports world. However, it represents just one outlook on sport. Among the leading challenges to the functionalist approach is conflict theory.

Conflict Theory

Functional theory is centered on the idea that there is a general consensus in values and norms of society and that the social institutions found within a society are integrated into a functioning whole. In contrast, conflict theory examines the role of power and the inequality found methodically throughout society. Conflict theory is based primarily on the ideas of Karl Marx (1818–1883) and rose to prominence during the 1970s because of growing disillusionment with structural functionalism. As Turner (1975) explains, "The growing disenchantment with structural-functional theory has been marked by the rise of alternative theoretical perspectives over the last two decades. One of the most conspicuous of these alternatives has been 'conflict theory' which has presumably rediscovered for the discipline such phenomena as power, force, coercion, constraint, and change in social systems" (p. 443).

Marx did not "create" conflict theory; rather, it was his ideas on such subjects as human potential, the historical method, class conflict, economic inequalities, class consciousness, and communism that influenced future social thinkers. Marx noted that all of human history was highlighted primarily by a class struggle between those with power (the elites, or owners of the means of production) and those without power (the masses, or workers). The result is predictable: the people who possess power will want to keep it, while those without power will want to gain it. People may react to class differences in a number of ways including open hostility and revolt against the existing social system (and those who benefit from it) to simple acceptance of how things are in society. Marx referred to this latter response as false consciousness—the inability to clearly see where one's own best interests lie.

Marx viewed religion as an example of false consciousness and as a weapon of the power elite to keep the masses in their place. He recognized that the power elites encouraged the masses to embrace afterlife considerations because it diverted people from taking action against social inequalities on earth. (For example, *Psalms* 37: 11 states that "the meek shall inherit the earth.") Religious institutions, therefore, are useful to the power elites as means of keeping the powerless from questioning their status. Marx suggested that "religion is the opiate of the masses" (McLellan, 1987; Hadden, 1997). An opiate is a drug used to dull the senses; if one is not thinking clearly, one is likely to believe almost anything. Likewise, religions can help dull the pain of reality by encouraging a feeling that, no matter how oppressed or unfulfilled a person may be, there will be a joyous and exciting afterlife for those who endure such inequalities on earth. Using this Marxist perspective, Paul Hoch (1972) argued that sport has replaced religion as the opiate of the masses. "Five generations ago, Karl Marx called religion the opiate of the masses. Today that role has been taken over by sports" (Hoch, 1972: 19). At the time Hoch made this statement he suggested that perhaps the word "opiate" was a little strong, but he felt it was the best possible answer to the climate of the time. Hoch noted that people were more concerned with baseball and football scores than with the Vietnam War. Additionally, people appeared more concerned with whether Muhammad Ali would defeat Joe Frazier than the possibility of the Vietnam War extending into Laos. "To many, sports are such an escape from reality that the political economy is too mundane to be mentioned in the same breath" (Hoch, 1972: 11).

The idea that sport is the opiate of the masses is reinforced by the realization that sports are in an "age of the spectator" and the "age of the sport consumer." This is evident by rising attendance figures (see Chapter 1), the large number of hours fans spend watching televised sporting events, the growing popularity of sports fantasy leagues, sports gambling, the amount of space dedicated to sports in most newspapers, and the everyday casual conversations centered on sports among the populace. As Yiannakis and associates (1978) argued more than three decades ago, sport has taken on the quality of a secular religion because it provides the "followers" an escape from the mundane (as other opiates provide), and provides a sense of belonging. In addition, many sports fans say they follow their favorite teams "religiously" and pray for favorable outcomes. These are truly "devout" fans. (See Chapter 14 for a further discussion on the relationship between sport and religion.) Such terminology, sociologists argue, is not merely ironic but is in fact descriptive.

The conflict perspective seems relevant today as well as many Americans rely on sport to divert their attention away from the wars in Iraq and Afghanistan, the rising costs of oil-related products, global climate change, disarray in the mortgage industry, and so on. That sport serves a diversionary role in society also reflects the conflict perspective on power. This means the polity is afforded an opportunity to continue "business as is" because so many people have become "fed up" with the socio-economic reality of society and rather than concentrate their collective efforts to bring about change; they turn to sports for a diversion.

Conflict Theory Applied to Sports

Although Marx did not write much about sports, a Marxist perspective proves to be quite enlightening, as well as relevant. Marxist interpretations of the rise of modern sports are related to the organization of ownership over the means of production. Sport sociologists who utilize the Marxist point of view analyze the rise of modern sports from a materialistic perspective. Today, many elite sport teams and events are controlled by corporations, corporate sponsors, and those whom could be labeled as "power elites." Even the individualistic sports, such as tennis, golf and surfing, are controlled by corporate sponsors. Although most fans are aware of this corporate domination, few find it overly threatening. Marx would most likely identify this behavior as a form of false consciousness. Conflict theorists in general and Marxists in particular, are concerned about the role of power and domination found in sport. Marxists argue that the power elite promote sports as a means of keeping the masses preoccupied with more mundane things than matters of the state. Those who participate in sport are taught to accept authority (from coaches, administrators, and officials).

From this perspective, sports are not only viewed as an opiate of society, but the power elites of society may also be viewed as the ones "pushing" or "selling" the opiate to the masses. Furthermore, the power elites use sport to help socialize the masses into accepting rules. The power elites, it is argued, determine the rules and laws of the land, and individuals have little or no say in their formation and modification. Likewise, athletes have no chance of changing a rule while the game is being played; and, aside from sports with "instant replay," the decision of the referee/official is final. (Have you ever seen a home plate umpire change his mind after a called third strike is disputed by the batter? It doesn't happen!)

The idea that power elites control society is underscored by the conflict perspective's central tenet that power is differentiated unequally, resulting in oppressive and coercive relationships that are manifested in the social system of sport. According to Gruneau (1975) this includes the following:

1. Sport is wedded to material gain and must be seen in this light [not simply as recreation and entertainment].
2. Sport is intimately associated with differences in wealth and power.
3. Competitive sport reflects bourgeois (i.e., middle class, upwardly mobile) ideology; as a meritocratic, mobility-oriented institution, it fosters a false consciousness and false hopes for the lower class.
4. Sport, particularly the professional variety, alienates the athlete-workers from each other and, in fact, pits them against each other (e.g., many athletes vying for few positions), thus undermining social revolution.
5. "Competitive sport" cannot exist in a classless society because competitive sport is not, by its nature, egalitarian. [Its outcome draws a clear line of distinction between participants — rewarded winners and nonrewarded losers.]

Many of today's "holdouts" and "strikes" are all based on a demonstration of power. The owners, in an attempt to maintain their power position, attempt to weaken the power of player unions, and use holdouts as a sign of their power (e.g., the NHL's cancellation of the 2004–05 season). Players, on the other hand, will often go on strike in an attempt to demonstrate their power — they are, after all, the product that owners promote to the fans in an attempt to generate revenue. The owner-player relationship in a classic example of the Marxist analysis of a two-class society — although this two-class system has become distorted in the contemporary era because of the high salaries earned by athletes. The result is the masses (the fans) viewing the players as a part of the ruling, or elite, class. Conflict theorists also believe that

1. *Sport generates and intensifies alienation.* Standardized rules and a rigid structure destroy the spontaneous freedom characteristic of play.
2. *Sport is used by the state and the economically powerful as a tool for coercion and social control.* Sport, as an opiate, provides a temporary "high" (for both fans and participants); it diverts attention from political and economic realities; it masks the problems of everyday life; and it emphasizes success through hard work, leading to people to disparage "losers" — often failing to acknowledge the unequal opportunities to succeed.
3. *Sport promotes commercialism and materialism.* Sport is viewed as a product to be consumed;

athletes are commodities to be exploited; and advertising makes consumers believe that they must have certain products.

4. *Sport encourages nationalism, militarism, and sexism.* Many powerful countries use sport as a showplace for displaying their national symbols and military strength (e.g., Germany's Adolf Hitler attempted to use the 1936 Berlin Olympics to showcase his Aryan "superior" athletes, the East German government tried to legitimize its Communist regime through the medal winnings of its athletes, and most major U.S. sporting events include military "flyovers" just prior to the start of the game — especially in the NFL). Nationalism and militarism will be discussed in further detail in Chapter 13 and sexism in Chapter 10.

Among the criticisms of the conflict perspective is the realization that many people do not feel alienated or exploited by sport. They enjoy the recreational aspect of sporting events and find the release that sports provides as invigorating. Because of its concentration on power differentials, conflict theorists often ignore the many areas in which most people arrive at an uncoerced consensus about the important values of life. Conflict theorists fail to acknowledge the numerous elements of shared morality, values and beliefs held by citizens of a society. Furthermore, sports can be sites for positive experiences that individuals find rewarding and fulfilling. The fact that many people have found alternatives to corporate sports underscores the fact that sport still provides meaning — free from coercion — in many people's lives. The conflict perspective's focus on materialism, and economic issues, shields its discovery of the quasi-spiritual experience that many athletes and sport and leisure participants enjoy. Both conflict theory and functionalism are subject to criticism because of their macrosociological orientation. The major sociological theory that addresses micro concerns is symbolic interactionism.

Symbolic Interactionism

As essentially a social-psychological perspective, symbolic interactionism focuses on how people interact with one another through the use of symbols (e.g., language and gestures). Language is the primary method used to communicate symbolically. Language allows individuals to discuss and comprehend ideas and events that transcend the immediate environment.

Herbert Blumer (1900–1987) coined the term symbolic interactionism in 1937. According to Blumer (1969):

> Symbolic interactionism rests in the last analysis on three simple premises. The first premise is that human beings act toward things on the basis of the meanings that the things have for them. Such things would include everything that the human being may note in his world — physical objects, such as trees or chairs; other human beings, such as a mother or a store clerk; categories of human beings, such as friends or enemies; institutions, as a school or a government; guiding ideals, such as individual independence or honesty; activities of others, such as their commands or requests; and such situations as an individual encounters in his daily life. The second premise is that the meaning of such things is derived from, or arises out of, the social interaction that one has with one's fellows. The third premise is that these meanings are handled in, and modified through, an interpretative process used by the person in dealing with the things he encounters [p. 2].

Symbolic interactionists presume that human behavior involves choices and that choices are made based on *meanings*, or *definitions of the situation*. Because objects found in human environments carry no intrinsic meaning, humans are capable of constructing meanings for them. Sports are filled with symbolic meanings. Examples are found through its rituals, rhetoric, culture, emotion, "coach talk," and trophies. The Stanley Cup, awarded to the National Hockey League's champion, for example, is not aesthetically the greatest piece of art, but it has great meaning to NHL players and fans. During the NHL playoffs, fans often craft their own mock version of the Cup with such crude instruments as aluminum foil. Clearly, there is little,

While visiting his hometown of Oswego, New York, Erik Cole shows off the Stanley Cup that he won with the Carolina Hurricanes.

if any, monetary value to these makeshift trophies, but the meaning behind its design is not lost among the fans and participants.

Symbolic interactionism is a micro theory with a focus on individuals and group behavior. "Symbolic interactionism takes as a fundamental concern the relationship between individual conduct the relationship between individual conduct and forms of social organization. This perspective asks how selves emerge out of social structure and social situations.... The interactionist assumes that human beings are capable of making their own thoughts and activities objects of analysis, that is, they can routinely, and even habitually, manipulate symbols and orient their own actions towards other objects" (Denzin, 1969: 922–923). The interactionist perspective maintains a belief in the ability of individuals to alter their behaviors to meet the needs of the present and the immediate environment. Humans come to define their acts and the social environment during interaction. Additionally, human interaction involves both covert and overt elements, both of which are capable of being modified to meet the actor's expectations and needs. For example, players and fans alike are capable of adding extra meaning to a game that pits two bitter rivals competing against one another (even if each team has a losing record at the time of the game).

SYMBOLIC INTERACTIONISM APPLIED TO SPORTS

The symbolic interactionist perspective of sport is easily recognized by fans and participants, primarily because of its personal and up close analysis of sporting action. Sports fans like to hear "stories" about their favorite players and teams. The symbolic interactionist micro orientation provides this. Furthermore, sports fans understand the importance of symbolism in sports (e.g., the baseball catcher flashing signs to the pitcher and the symbolic importance of playing for a championship "ring").

There are a variety of symbolic interactionist approaches (those with a micro focus). The phenomenological approach to sport examines "sport through the senses and emotions of the player. A crunching tackle or a dive into water are intrinsically rewarding and satisfying experiences for the tackler and the diver. Some of these specific experiences are remembered for a lifetime, as though they had happened the day before" (Vogler and Schwartz, 1993: 8). In fact, most people who participated in sports can think back to a sporting event that has significant meaning to them. The old story of the fisherman who retells the story (defining the situation) of catching a prize fish, only to have the length of the fish grow over the years of storytelling, reflects the phenomenological approach.

Because of its micro orientation, symbolic interactionism has great cross-over appeal to psychological theories; especially those which examine personality traits and relaxation techniques. This should not surprise too many people as sport psychology, oddly, has enjoyed greater success than sport sociology. "The primary goals of sport psychology are to describe, to explain, and to predict the attitudes, feelings, and behaviors of sport participants— including athletes, coaches, and even crowd members" (Anshel, 1994: 16). However, as will be demonstrated throughout this text, most problems, issues and events encountered by sport participants are sociological in nature.

Psychological theories that examine personality traits of athletes have found that

> successful athletes differ markedly from their less successful counterparts in several ways. Despite flaws in personality research, studies have shown that successful participants tend to be self-confident, have a high need to achieve, maintain a relatively high self-image, at least in the sport environment, and score low on personality inventories in trait and state anxiety, tension, depression, mental fatigue, confusion, and anger. They often score relatively high in mental toughness, intelligence, sociability, creativity, stability, dominance, aggression, and extroversion. Still, personality scales should not be used to predict the level of an athlete's future success, the type of sport for which a person is best suited, or any other sport-related measure [Anshel, 1994: 51–52].

The simple reason why individual psychological personality theorizing alone cannot predict future success in sport is because of all the social factors (e.g., opportunities to play, grades in school, family support, coaching, school funding) involved between an athlete and the sports world (thus reaffirming the importance of the sociological analysis of sport).

Relaxation theory teaches athletes how to handle tense situations so that they do not "choke" when the pressure is on to perform. Relaxation, as defined by theorist Bud Winter (1981), "involves getting the tension out of muscles not directly involved in the task at hand. Relaxation also involves getting rid of mental tensions so that you can have peace of mind to think or not to think, as you choose" (p. 27). Winter is convinced that anyone can learn to relax physically and/or mentally at a high level of proficiency. An athlete learning how to relax so that he can perform basic tasks is perhaps the most legitimate area of psychological study in the field of sports. Relaxation theory teaches the need for repetition of behavior to the point where it becomes so routine that one can visualize in their minds before it happens (e.g., making a free-throw in basketball). However, at times, some athletes have trouble performing basic tasks; why is this the case? For example, many basketball fans marvel at Shaquille O'Neal's dismal free-throw shooting percentage (just over 50 percent for his career). Many "professionals" have worked with O'Neal, but to no avail. Despite being one of the most dominant "big men" in NBA history, O'Neal fails at the easiest task in basketball — an uncontested set shot from relatively close distance. O'Neal appears to be relaxed, and his gentle demeanor off-court would seem to imply that he is a mellow fellow and therefore casts doubt on the idea that he is not relaxed at the free-throw line.

Among the criticisms of symbolic interactionism is its overly individualistic approach and reliance on personal definitions of events—thus ignoring social process. Psychologists interested in the same topics as symbolic interactionists tend to criticize the perceived lack of scientific rigor utilized in their methodology. Because of its commitment to, and overemphasis on, everyday life and the social formation of self, symbolic interactionists tend to ignore social structure, especially structured forms of inequality.

One of the leading sociological perspectives to study structured forms of inequality is feminist theory.

Feminist Theory

Historically, and cross-culturally, women have fallen victim to discrimination and oppression in nearly all spheres of social life. This includes sports. Mary Wollstonecraft (1759–1797), author of *A Vindication of the Rights of Woman* (1792), was one of the first to argue that this state of affairs was unacceptable and immoral. Patricia Altenbernd Johnson writes,

> In a *Vindication of the Rights of Woman*, Wollstonecraft advocated an education for women based on the principle of independence rather than obedience. In addition, she advocated changes in social practices that would enable women to actualize this independence. She was optimistic about the political changes that were possible and about the speed at which changes could take place [Johnson, 2000: 81–82].

While Wollstonecraft (whose daughter, Mary Shelley, would write the bestselling novel *Frankenstein*) might have been optimistic that such social changes would occur quickly, such was not to be the case. Although a number of social thinkers (both men and women) promoted the idea of equality for both sexes, it was not until the early 1800s that any significant women's rights movement took place. In the United States, the origins of feminism can be traced to the abolitionist movement of the 1830s. Seneca Falls, New York, lays claim as the birth place of American feminism. A small group of women led by Elizabeth Cady Stanton spearheaded the first Women's Rights Convention, in Seneca Falls, in 1848. More than 300 people attended the convention that was held in the Wesleyan Methodist Chapel. The convention highlighted the many ways social institutions were designed to keep women subordinate to men. For example, "once a woman married, she forfeited her legal existence. She couldn't sign a contract, make a will, or sue in court of law. If she received property from her father or some other source, her husband could sell it and keep the money for himself" (Gurko, 1978: 8).

Feminism is as much a social movement to empower women worldwide as it is a theory. As a social movement, feminism is an ideology in support of the idea that a larger share of scarce resources (e.g., funding for women's athletics, equal pay for coaches) should be distributed to women. In short, feminists fight for the equality of women. As a social theory, feminism is a women-centered, broad-based theoretical perspective designed to reveal how sexual discrimination is a result of historic man-made conditions and not biological inferiority. "Through analysis of gender roles and gender appropriateness, feminist theory demonstrates how women have historically been subjected to a double standard in both their treatment and in the evaluation of their worth" (Delaney, 2005: 202). It is important to note that there are a variety of feminist theories (for example, liberal feminism, Marxist feminism, radical feminism, critical feminism, socialist feminism, and postmodern feminism) that advocate different approaches and solutions to end the male supremacy that dominates most cultures of the world. With this precaution in mind, feminism can be defined as "a recognition and critique of male supremacy combined with efforts to change it" (Hartmann, 1998: 41). Feminists argue that women should enjoy the same rights in society as men and that they should share equally in society's opportunities and resources.

FEMINIST THEORY APPLIED TO SPORTS

The women's rights movement reached new heights during the 1960s—a decade of unprecedented social change in the United States. The feminists of the 1960s ignored inequality found in the sports world. They were more concerned with socio-political issues designed to empower women in the workplace and in the home. This would change in the 1970s—a decade that would forever alter the role of women in sports. In 1972, the United States passed Title IX of the *Education Amendments to the Civil Rights Act of 1964* (see Chapter 10 for a further elaboration of Title IX). Title IX is perhaps the single most important event that ever occurred in regard to women's participation in sport. In brief, Title IX declared, "No person in the United States shall, on the basis of sex, be excluded from participation in, be denied the benefits of, or be subjected to discrimination under any educational program or activity receiving federal financial assistance." Initially, this piece of legislation was overlooked in the sports world. In 1971, there were nearly 3.7 million boys playing varsity high school sports, but just 295,000 girls (a 12.5: 1 ratio). A number of lawsuits followed and women's participation rates soared in the 1980s and 1990s (See Chapter 10 for current participation statistics).

In the 1970s, feminists realized that with sport, they had a social institution that provided a clear arena to document and measure sexual inequality. Feminists critiqued sport as "a fundamentally sexist institution that is male dominated and masculine in orientation" (Theberge, 1981: 342). As Messner and Sabo (1990) describe feminism of the 1970s and 1980s:

> Feminist analyses uncovered a hidden history of female athleticism, examined sex differences in patterns of athletic socialization, and demonstrated how the dominant institutional forms of sport have naturalized men's power and privilege over women. The marginalization and trivialization of female athletes, it was demonstrated, serve to reproduce the structural and ideological domination of women by men. In the decade that has followed, the feminist critique both of the institution of sport and of the androcentric biases in sport studies has had a profound impact. Feminism now makes a major contribution to defining terrain of scholarly discourse in sport studies [p. 2].

Feminists and equality minded theorists and professionals have so successfully increased the role of women in sport (both in terms of perception and participation) that many young female athletes today take for granted their opportunity to play sports and have seldom faced outright discrimination like their female predecessors had experienced. This is not to imply that full gender equality is found in sport today. As we shall see in Chapter 10, gender issues are still relevant in the sports world.

Among the criticisms of feminist theory is its primary focus on just half of the population—women. As the role of women in society (and sport) has changed so too has the role of men. The issues facing men must also be addressed, especially if feminists hope to change the once-dominant view held by men against women's increased participation in sports. Focusing a theory on just one issue—gender—leaves the feminist approach open to objections that it ignores other critical variables (e.g., social class, race, and willingness and desire of individuals to play sports). There are feminists, such as Sandra Harding, who have noted that gender, class, and race are interlocking variables and cannot be separated. In addition, Carol Gilligan, author of *In a Different Voice* (1993), raises the possibility that women, in general, may have a different concept of competitiveness than men do, rooted in their moral concerns. She writes: "Sensitivity to the needs of others and the assumption of responsibility for taking care lead women to attend to voices other than their own and to include in their judgment other points of view" (p. 16). Such an "ethics of care" could mean that men and women fundamentally differ over the importance of competitiveness and the need for a hierarchical structure in sports contests.

Thus, the wide variety of approaches to feminist thought demonstrates that feminists lack a clear and comprehensive agreed-upon theory to explain human behavior and gender differences in sport.

Functionalism, conflict, symbolic interactionism, and feminism represent four of the more "traditional" theories of sociology that may be applied to the sports world. We now address a pair of related theories that has been mostly applied to the sports world and not to other social institutions. The first concept is "basking in reflected glory" (BIRG) and the second is "cutting off reflective failure" (CORF).

BIRG and CORF Theories

In 1976, Cialdini and associates uncovered a phenomenon which they called "Basking in Reflected Glory" (BIRG). In their study of "big-time" college football programs, they noticed that students had an increased tendency to wear their schools' logo (e.g., on items of clothing) on Mondays following Saturday victories. Additionally, Cialdini and associates note that students are more likely to use "we" in discussing wins, but use "they" when describing losses. The BIRG theory is based on the premise that individuals purposely manipulate the visibility of their connections with winners and losers in order to make themselves look good to others. Individuals showcase positive associations and try to bury negative ones, thus encouraging observers to think more highly of them and to like them more.

Subsequent research (Snyder, Lassegard, and Ford, 1986; Wann and Branscombe, 1990) reveals that in additions to increasing their association with successful others (BIRGing), people also tend to increase the distance between themselves and unsuccessful others. This phenomenon is called "Cutting Off Reflective Failure" (CORF).

Wann and Branscombe (1990) theorize that the extent to which allegiance to a group or team that a person has will modify the effects of BIRGing and CORFing. They suspect that individuals high in identification would demonstrate a stronger tendency to BIRG in their team's success when compared to persons low in identification. The reverse was anticipated for CORFing; persons high in identification should CORF less than those low in identification. The results of their study support their hypotheses. Persons high in identification did show an increased tendency to BIRG following the team's victory, relative to persons moderate or low in allegiance. In addition, persons highly identified with the team appeared to maintain their association with the team even when faced with defeat, thereby showing a reduction in the tendency to CORF when compared to those lower in identification. Consequently, Wann and Branscombe show that the effects of BIRGing and CORFing are affected by one's identification level to the group or team.

The pervasive nature of group identification has shown that fans identify not only with sport teams but with the institutions represented by sport teams they support. In fact, fans who maintain high levels of identification with a sports team also show feelings of bonding with other fans of that same team (Wann and Branscombe, 1993). Throughout time people have derived much of their identity and self worth from groups to which they have membership (Baumeister, 1991).

In an attempt to replicate Wann and Branscombe's (1990) findings, Delaney (1999) conducted research on a sports booster group (the Southern California Browns Backers Association) in 1993. Delaney's research analyzed BIRG and CORF techniques based on respondent's identification and self esteem levels. Respondents were asked a number of questions that reflect BIRG (Questions 1, 2, 3, 4, 7, 8) and CORF (5, 6, 9) tendencies (See Table 2.1).

TABLE 2.1. BIRG AND CORF (IN PERCENT [N = 502])

BIRG and CORF Variables	Strongly Agree	Agree	Disagree	Strongly Disagree
Wear more apparel after a win	4	25	58	13
Read sports pages regardless of outcome	51	40	7	2
Read additional sports articles after a win	37	34	25	4
Buy more newspapers after a win	9	16	58	17
Do not read newspapers after a loss	1	2	54	42
Try to block out a Browns defeat ASAP	5	37	45	13
Try to relive Browns' highlights after a win	13	46	35	6
After win, watch as many highlights as possible	39	43	16	2
After a defeat, watch one, or no, highlights	8	34	47	11

Based on past research, Delaney (1999) hypothesized that highly identified fans will display increased tendencies to BIRG and decreased tendencies to CORF. In contrast, moderate fans are less likely to BIRG and more likely to CORF. In Table 2.2, BIRG and CORF tendencies are examined by high and moderate levels of identification. Nearly all variables reveal a statistical difference based on one's identification level (Question 1 did not). The results show that highly identified fans exhibit many signs of BIRGing but not of CORFing. Meanwhile, the moderately identified fans are less likely to BIRG, but also less likely to CORF. Thus, the tendency to BIRG is consistent with past research, but the tendencies to CORF are not consistent with past research. One explanation for this is, perhaps, the fact that the entire group under study may have been more highly identified fans than non-booster fans.

TABLE 2.2. BIRG AND CORF BY IDENTIFICATION LEVEL (IN PERCENT [N = 502])

BIRG/CORF Variables	Strongly Agree		Agree		Disagree		Strongly Disagree	
	High	Mod	High	Mod	High	Mod	High	Mod
APPVICT	3	4	27	24	58	58	12	13
RDSPRTPG	35	61	52	33	10	5	3	1
ADDSPRT	25	44	41	31	31	21	3	5
MORNSP	4	12	13	18	66	53	17	17
DEFPAP	0	2	3	1	59	52	38	45
BLOCK	2	8	34	38	52	41	12	14
RELIVE	4	18	37	52	49	27	10	3
HILIGHTS	20	51	56	36	21	13	3	0
DEFLIGHT	4	10	37	33	52	45	7	13

Variable Key (For Tables 2.2 and 2.3):
APPVICT — Wear more apparel after a win
RDSPRTPG — Read sport pages regardless of outcome
ADDSPORT — Read additional sport articles after a win
MORNSP — Buy more newspapers after a win
DEFPAP — Do not read newspapers after a loss
BLOCK — Try to block out a Browns' defeat ASAP
RELIVE — Try to relive Browns' highlights after a win
HILIGHTS — After a win, watch as many highlights as possible
DEFLIGHT — After a defeat, watch one, or no, highlights

In Table 2.3, the relationship between one's level of self esteem and BIRG/CORF techniques is examined. (Self esteem was measured by using Rosenberg's Self Esteem Scale.) As with the highly identified fan, it is hypothesized that those individuals with high self esteem will show increased tendencies to BIRG and decreased tendencies to CORF. This is because those who are high in self esteem can increase positive feelings of self through BIRGing and yet, they will not have to CORF because they possess a higher level of self-confidence than those with low self esteem. Thus, it is should follow that those with low self esteem are less likely to BIRG and more likely to CORF. Those with low self esteem are more likely to CORF because it provides a means of self-protection. An examination of the results revealed in Table 2.3 indicate that those with high self esteem have a slightly increased tendency to BIRG compared to those with low self esteem. The tendency to CORF is nearly identical for members of both high and low self levels of self esteem. Based on the results of this study, the argument that BIRGing and CORFing are techniques used in the maintenance of self esteem is tenuous, at best.

TABLE 2.3. BIRG AND CORF BY SELF-ESTEEM LEVEL (IN PERCENT [N = 502])

BIRG/CORF Variables	Strongly Agree			Agree			Disagree			Strongly Disagree		
	Low	Mod	High	Low	Mod	High	Low	Mod	High	Low	Mod	High
APPVICT	3	6	2	21	25	29	66	60	51	10	10	17
RDSPRTPG	43	54	56	49	37	37	7	7	7	1	2	0
ADDSPORT	28	38	42	44	34	28	25	25	25	4	3	5
MORNSP	8	8	42	13	18	16	69	60	49	10	14	24
DEFPAP	1	1	2	1	1	2	64	58	46	34	40	50
BLOCK	3	5	8	43	35	35	45	48	42	9	12	16
RELIVE	10	13	15	47	46	44	40	35	34	3	6	8
HILIGHTS	33	37	47	50	46	36	17	16	15	0	2	2
DEFLIGHT	8	7	8	34	36	33	53	48	43	5	9	16

The study of BIRG and CORF techniques explores some of the many ways in which individuals attempt to associate themselves with successful others while distancing themselves from those perceived negatively. It is believed that the BIRG and CORF phenomenon is not limited to the realm of sports. Future research should attempt to apply these same techniques within other social worlds such as family, religion, and national pride.

Summary

Social theory involves expressing ideas about human behavior and the social world through the formulation of theories about social life. A theory is a statement that proposes to explain or relate observed phenomena or a set of concepts. "Good" theories are those which can be tested empirically.

George Herbert Mead described play as the stage which precedes organized games. He also described a developmental theory of the self which is dependent upon interactions with others in the community.

Contemporary sports sociology theories can be applied to sport. Functionalism views society as an organized system of interrelated parts that seek equilibrium. Sports can play a vital role in maintaining such balance. However, critics of functionalism feel it is too conservative and fails to explain social change. Conflict theorists examine the role of power and inequalities found within society. For them, sports often exemplify such power inequities. Sports are the functional equivalents of religions, shielding people from harsh realities and inculcating a false sense of achievement. Sports also encourage commercialism, sexism, racism and nationalism, all conditions which further unequal class distinctions. However, conflict theorists do not acknowledge that sports is not necessarily exploitative and many people enjoy sports without feeling alienated.

Both functionalists and conflict theories are subject to criticism because of their macrosociological orientation. Symbolic internationalism takes a micro approach, by focusing on how people interact with each other using symbols. Humans construct the meanings they give. Sports are filled with symbolic meanings. For instance, trophies, which may not be aesthetically great works of art, have tremendous significance to those who win them. Symbolic internationalism has connections with psychological theories, which examine personality traits of athletes and fans. However, critics of symbolic internationalism say that it is overly individualistic and ignores social processes and structures.

Feminist theory is one of the leading sociological perspectives which focuses on the discrimination and oppression that women have undergone in all societies. As a social theory, feminism is designed to reveal how sexual discrimination is a result of man-made conditions rather than biological differences. While focusing on sexual equality as its aim, feminist theory has been criticized for ignoring other critical variables, such as class and race. In addition, the wide varieties of feminist thought demonstrate that such a theory lacks a clear and comprehensive theory to explain human behavior and gender differences in sport.

Two other sociological theories— BIRG and CORF —can be applied to the understanding of sports. BIRG stands for "Basking in Reflected Glory" and is based on the premise that individuals purposely manipulate the visibility of their connections with winners to make themselves look good to others. CORF stands for "Cutting Off Reflective Failure" and is based on the premise that individuals distance themselves from losers. These theories help to explain the allegiance which persons have to sports teams and individuals. However, statistical studies show that the relationship between one's level of self-esteem and BIRG/CORF connections with sports teams is tenuous.

Both macro theories such as functionalism and conflict theories and micro theories such as symbolic interactionism, feminism, BIRG and CORF may be applied to the sports and help one to understand the importance of sport to everyday life.

Key Terms

BIRG ("Basking in Reflected Glory") Individuals find meaning in their lives through their identification with successful people and teams.

Conflict Theories Theories which examine the role of power and the inequality found methodically throughout society.

CORF ("Cutting Off Reflective Failure") Individuals distance themselves from unsuccessful people and teams.

False Consciousness A term used by Marxists to signify the inability to clearly see where one's own best interests lie.

Functional Imperatives A term coined by Talcott Parsons, who argued that there are four basic "system needs" (adaptation, goal attainment, integration, and latency; or AGIL) necessary in order for any society (club, organization, team, etc.) to run smoothly.

Functional Theory The idea that there is a general consensus in values and norms of society and that the social institutions found within a society are integrated into a functioning whole.

Phenomenological Approach A type of symbolic interactionism which examines sport through the senses and emotions of the player.

"Significant Others" Those specific individuals with whom a child interacts with on a regular basis, generally the child's immediate family members and friends (a term used by George Herbert Mead).

Social Theory Focuses on interactions, patterns and events found in the social environment and attempts to explain such observed phenomena.

Symbolic Interactionism The view that that human behavior involves choices and that choices are made based on *meanings,* or *definitions of the situation.*

Theory A statement that proposes to explain or relate observed phenomena or a set of concepts through a logically-based system of general propositions. It involves a set of inter-related arguments that seek to describe and explain cause-effect relationships.

DISCUSSION QUESTIONS

• Does play "make a human complete?" Can one be a fulfilled individual without engaging in activities purely for fun?

• Do you agree or disagree with the statement that "Sports are the opiate of the people"? Why or why not?

• Do you think that men and women have different views on the nature of competition? Explain.

CHAPTER 3

A Brief History of Sport

Undoubtedly, all sports fans have heard stories about the legendary "Mighty Grog," the all-time qualfire leader. The qualfire record is the most treasured of all in the sport of *Kalrina*—which has its roots in the Quarryville League circa 150,000 B.C.E. The "Mighty Grog" solidified his immortal status, and eventual induction into the Quarryville Hall of Fame, during his final fire appearance. Grog needed to last four seconds in the "pit of fire" and emerge with the elusive *qual* to secure his team's victory. The crowd was at a frenzy pitch cheering their hometown hero. As Grog emerged with the elusive qual he grunted his superiority and turned his back on his unworthy opponents. The fans threw rocks into the air, batting them with their clubs, as they descended to earth as a sign of their approval. The beaten foes threw themselves headfirst into the fire to demonstrate their shame. Poems and stories would immortalize this great athlete and his accomplishments. Cave paintings gave vivid depictions of his victory. His legendary status has only grown over the centuries.

Well, as most students have quickly figured out, the above story is fantasy. The truth is, although no one knows for sure when humans first played sports, there is no evidence to indicate that sport existed in prehistoric times. Thus, our discussion of the history of sport begins with the "ancient" societies.

Ancient Sports (Circa 1400 B.C.E.–800 B.C.E.)

The word "history," when applied to humanity, refers to the period of time when humans first provided a formal written account of events and, thus, not the entire scope of our civilization. This realization helps to underscore the selection of the chapter's fictional account of a pre-historic sporting event. That is, prehistoric humans may have participated in some sort of sporting activity, but without documentation, how would we know?

Sports in Ancient Africa

The first variations of sports and games of the ancient world would reveal a pattern that held consistent until the time of the Romans; namely, that early sport reflected religious significance combined with activities associated with physical survival. For example, Africans participated in archery because it was valued as a warring skill and dance because it held religious value.

Sports in ancient Africa are divided into two uneven categories: Egypt and the rest of the continent. Egypt, because of its geographical location (at the crossroads of Africa, Asia, and Europe), has always been different from the rest of Africa. The ancient Egyptians were a highly advanced society that had a written language and left behind visual biographies in the form of wall paintings, thereby providing archaeologists with a wealth of information on their sporting activities. On the other hand, the rest of Africa remains mostly a mystery. We do know that archery and dance were popular throughout Africa, as were a wide variety of games that required dexterity and skill.

As for Egypt, a number of identifiable sports were played, including archery, stick fighting, wrestling, dance, running, swimming (especially in the Nile River), *mancala* (a counting strategy game), and *senet*, also called *senat* (one of the world's oldest recorded tabletop games) (Craig, 2002). Poliakoff (1987) also mentions boxing and pankration as sports played in ancient Egypt. "Pankration (or in Latin spelling, pancratium) is a Greek word that means 'complete strength' or 'complete victory'.... These terms reveal a lot about the sport: pankration allowed boxing, kicking, wrestling throws, strangleholds, and pressure locks. The bout ended when a competitor signaled unwillingness or inability to continue the fight" (Poliakoff, 1987: 54). The ancient sport of pankration is actually much like today's "ultimate fighting." (This helps to explain why some people consider ultimate fighting as an ancient, barbaric sport.)

Stick fighting is a particularly interesting sport in Egypt as it was a minor sport elsewhere in antiquity. The Egyptians held formal stick fighting contests and their artwork shows crowds of spectators watching the fighters. Some stick fights involved combatants wearing a shield on the left arm, keeping the right arm free to swing. As Mandell (1984) explains, "The sticks, which are about a meter long, were swung with the right hand, the left arm being shielded. Some stick fighters wore a light helmet to protect their faces and ears" (p. 21). It remains unclear, unfortunately, how a winner was determined, although most believe a record of "hits" were recorded and perhaps a knockout blow also determined a winner.

SPORTS IN ANCIENT ASIA

As in other parts of the world, sports in ancient Asia were tied to physical survival. Participation in Asian sport also possessed a philosophical quality. There is great diversity in the Asian continent, and as a result, sports varied from one society to the next. Ancient Chinese culture was relatively advanced and served as "the major civilization of the Far East" (Freeman, 1997: 62). Chinese culture is rich in sport and game participation. The Chinese played many board games including chess. Early versions of soccer (called *t'su chu*, a regimented game involving a foot striking a ball is traced back to 770 B.C.E.), polo and competitions in archery and wrestling were practiced by the Chinese people. Polo, or *pula*, is believed to have begun in Tibet and then spread throughout Asia; recognizable evidence exists in Persia dating from 525 B.C.E. (Bell, 1987). In addition, "A program of mild exercises, similar to gymnastics-oriented calisthenics, was developed and called *cong fu*. The objective was to prevent disease, which the Chinese believed could result from a lack of physical activity. Dancing was also popular. Although it was primarily ceremonial, there were both religious and popular forms. The popular forms were informal recreational dances" (Freeman, 1997: 63). Martial arts, of course, were also popular in China, and throughout Asia. "In Mongolia, the men have participated for centuries in what they consider the 'three manly sports' of archery, equestrian races, and wrestling" (Craig, 2002: 58).

Japanese ancient sports are similar to the Chinese and include board games, archery, and sumo wrestling. The Japanese had their own version of chess called *shio-ghi*, played chiefly by the intellectual classes (Falkener, 1961). Sports were not as predominant in Indian society. There were some recreational sports and games dances that were used for ceremonial purposes and religious observances.

The review of ancient sports in Africa and Asia represent a mere sampling of sports and games played in the ancient world. As Craig (2002) summarizes, there are some sports, such as archery and wrestling, that are indigenous to nearly all cultures of the ancient world. Throwing objects (e.g., spears), dancing, and running are also common sports activities shared by all ancient people.

Sport and Ancient Greek Culture (800 B.C.E.–100 B.C.E.)

According to Bell (1987), the only non–Western game to influence the Greeks was *pula*, or polo, which (as stated earlier) originated in Tibet and spread throughout Asia. The Greeks were concerned with the use of the horse in sport, more than the sport of polo itself. "The combination of the horse and chariot in Asia soon evolved into a chariot race that would fascinate both the Greeks and Romans.... The first horse race as an Olympic event came at the twenty-third games in 624 B.C.E. — one of the first visible signs of cultural cross-pollenization, the Greeks playing the Asian game, which would lead to the Hellenistic world: everyone playing the Greek games" (Bell, 1987: 92–93).

The Minoan civilization had participated in two primary sports games, boxing and bull vaulting (Bell, 1987). Of historical note, the boxers wore boxing gloves. (The significance of this will be explained later in the chapter.) Bull vaulting involved an individual standing in front of a charging bull, catching it by the horns, and leaping over the back of the animal. The fascination of the Minoans with bulls did not appeal to the Hellenic world. Boxing, on the other hand, held such great appeal that certain matches were described in Homeric poems when the sport was adopted by the early Greeks. Poems were written to honor heroes. The most heroic quality in the era of ancient Greece, just as it was in ancient times, was one's ability to demonstrate physical strength and survival techniques. "A general and persistent feature of Homer's poems is emphasis on physical prowess, whether this be manifested in armed combat, in organized athletic contests, in acrobatic dancing, in erotic adventures or in the sheer capacity for survival displayed by Odysseus on his way home to Ithaca from Troy" (McIntosh, 1993: 20).

The Egyptian sport of pankration found its way to Greek society as well. "The object was, as in boxing, to force the opponent to acknowledge defeat, and to this end almost any means was allowed" (Gardiner, 1930: 212). Serious injuries occurred often. The Spartans used pankration as a means of training warriors. Eventually, rules prohibiting biting and gouging were introduced to the sport. As with ultimate fighting, or street fighting, participants work with their strengths. Generally, taller athletes, with a longer reach, rely on hitting; while short, stocky athletes rely on wrestling.

The ancient Greeks loved their sports; this characteristic reflected the highly competitive character of the Greeks, "who were not only avid participants in athletic contests but also regularly held competitions in, for example, dancing, lyre playing and drinking.... In a society as competitive as that of the ancient Greeks, it is not surprising that sports, particularly competitive sports, were very popular" (Sansone, 1988: 76–77). Homer's poems describe how sporting events were social gathering events. However, it was also clear that the "contests also reveal a near obsession with winning. The stratagems employed to win offend our sense of 'fair play' as, for example, in the case of the goddess who blithely trips the superior runner, Aias" (Mandell, 1984: 39). Greek society valued physical excellence and cities glorified athletic victories of their citizens, rewarded victors materially and honored them in legend in the form of statues and poems/stories. Every Greek city had athletic facilities (similar to the stadiums found in most major world cities today).

Greek sport was such a serious endeavor that it took on cultural and religious significance. The Greek culture, heavily influenced by mythology, infused religious rituals and significance with athletics. Many city-states throughout Greece participated in religious games and festivals. As Freeman (1997) explained, these religious events and festivals "were generally celebrated by athletic contests, dances, and music. Some of the festivals were celebrated within a single city-state and by only one sex, as in the case of honoring local gods. Other festivals, however, were broader in appeal and sometimes were celebrated by all of the Greek people" (p. 69). Freeman also acknowledges that there is some debate over the origins of the religious games.

Some scholars trace religious games to the great Irish funeral festival, Aonach Tailteann, which may be older than the Olympics games. Thus, "the Irish claim that it was the inspiration for the Greek games" (Freeman, 1997: 69).

Clearly, the most significant of the Greek festivals was the Olympic Games. The Olympic Games are the oldest of the four panhellenic festivals. The other three panhellenic Games were the Pythian Games at Delphi, held in honor of Apollo; the Isthmian Games held in Corinth for Poseidon; and the Games at Nemea, which, like the Olympics, were held in honor of Zeus (Swaddling, 1980). Bell (1987) argues that the Olympics did not reflect any high ideals of the Hellenes, but rather served as a way to keep the Hellenistic world unified. As we shall learn, it is common for competition, sport or otherwise, to divide rather than unite people.

THE OLYMPICS

The Olympics were held in honor of Zeus, the most revered and powerful of all mythical Greek gods. The first recorded Olympic Games took place in 776 B.C.E. We know that many festivals were held before this first recorded Olympic Games and there is speculation that the games "may have been held originally to honor Herakles, an early traditional hero, with the worship of Zeus appearing in the sixth century. Women were banned, perhaps because Herakles was a warriors' hero, and because the presence of women was thought to diminish the warriors' power" (Freeman, 1997: 69). The Olympics were greatly modified over centuries but every four years, from 776 B.C.E. to 395 C.E., the games continued. People flocked to Olympia, originally a small village existing for the purpose of hosting the most prestigious of all Greek sport spectacles. "There is no modern parallel for Olympia; it would have to be a site combining a sports complex and a centre for religious devotion, something like a combination of Wembley Stadium and Westminster Abbey" (Swaddling, 1980: 7).

The timing of the Games was sacred to the Greeks. They took place every fours years, on the second or third full moon alternately after the summer solstice, in the months of August or September (Gardiner, 1930). Months before the Games began "Truce Bearers of Zeus" would set out from Olympia wearing crowns of olive and bearing heralds' staves to proclaim a month-long peace. This truce was always honored, as the Games took precedence over war. The city-states leaders did not want war to interrupt the training of the athletes or the eventual five-day competition. Originally, women were not allowed to compete or view the Games. (The women would eventually create their own games and dedicate them to the Goddess Hera, sister-wife of Zeus. These games were held at a time separate from the male Olympics). The athletes competed in the nude and were often beaten for violating rules (e.g., a false start in a race led to a whipping from a referee). The athletes prepared themselves (trained) for a month before the Games began. Only those of pure Greek birth were allowed to compete (Gardiner, 1930). Many of the athletes spent their time exclusively on training for the Games (like professional athletes); they had coaches, and received medical advice and assistance. As this special treatment implies, Olympic athletes were generally privileged males from well-to-do families.

There are some romantic revisionists who look at the ancient Olympics as something the modern Olympics should strive to be. Ironically, perhaps the modern Games are already like the ancient ones. Consider, the ancient Olympics were sexist (did not allow women), elitist (only those from wealthy families could participate), racist (Greeks only), politically corrupt and full of displays of poor sportsmanship (poor sports, cheaters, and enviousness of winners). Students may want to examine other ways that the ancient and modern Olympics mirror one another.

Regardless of any criticism of the original Olympics, they stand alone as a monumental testament to the value of sport in ancient Greece. They also represent an idealistic view of how sport could/should be organized.

Sport and Roman Culture (100 B.C.E.–500 C.E.)

The Olympics stand alone as the longest running sporting event in human history. The Games survived early Roman occupation, but eventually disappeared after it lost Roman financial support due to a Roman public that preferred bloody gladiator sports.

Before the infamous gladiator games dominated Roman culture, citizens participated in a number of games. The Romans, especially the wealthy, loved to play ball games. Playing ball afforded participants an opportunity to increase coordination and provided a measure of physical fitness. Although harpastum (interpreted in a variety of ways, including as an early form of rugby, "keepaway," or "monkey in the middle," was played by of a group of players) and trigon were never major spectator sports, there was a following for these athletes and games.

Roman children and adults participated in hoop bowling, loosely described as a game that entailed participants throwing a spear, or stick, or stone through a rolling hoop. The hoop was pushed to keep it rolling through the streets. The Roman hoops generally had jingling rings attached to forewarn oncoming traffic to clear a path (Craig, 2002).

Initially, the Romans had a different perspective on sport than the Greeks. They did not consider sport to be a philosophical activity but were more interested in military development and popular entertainment. The Romans, unlike the Greeks, had no interest in the balanced development of the individual. For the Romans, sport was merely a practical activity.

As a predatorial regime, the early Roman Empire placed a great deal of importance on military training. General physical education and training for boys was directed almost exclusively toward military goals. Military training involved pace training in marching, weapons proficiency, and weight training. Swordsmanship was a valued trait for Roman soldiers. It should be noted that professional athletes, along with coaches and trainers, were also expected to maintain a strict physical training program.

Over the centuries, the Roman Empire continued to grow. During the later centuries of the Empire, the Romans no longer felt the need to train. The Empire paid armies to fight for it, and other armies to defend Rome from potential invaders. Slaves did most of the day-to-day work previously performed by poorer citizens. Romans no longer had to work to survive; the state even provided free food. Political corruption abounded. Roman societal morals and ideals of patriotism and self-sacrifice continued to deteriorate. Roman citizens became increasingly bored and restless. They needed a diversion. What they got was entertainment spectacles; especially in the form of the brutal gladiator games.

GLADIATOR GAMES

Rome's citizens had become lazy; they had transformed themselves into a nation of spectators more content with watching other people play sports and athletics than performing such activities themselves. (It could be argued that the United States has become a nation of spectators, much like Ancient Rome.) Greek festivals and the pursuit of athletic excellence was not enough for the Romans. Instead, the Romans wanted a show, a spectacle, and the bigger the better. Winning was everything; and the more decisive the victory, the better. After a few centuries, the Romans had completely transformed the Greek ideal of athletics and sports. As Dunning (1999) indicates, the ancient Roman gladiator "sports" represent a regression into barbarism. The Romans ignored the decay of sport and sportsmanship. The level of cruelty and violence in Roman gladiator sport, the massacres and the bloodthirst of the crowds, were very different from the contests engaged in by the ancient Greeks.

The gladiators of the Roman spectacles entered the arena with the intent to kill each other; the spectators were fully aware of this. Romans developed a great appreciation for the "art" of killing. The gladiators were fed three meals a day, received relatively good medical care, and if they performed well enough, they could gain their freedom. They were not allowed to become citizens, however. Females were allowed to be gladiators and the practice was rather widespread, until women were forbidden to participate by the Emperor Septimius Severus in the early 3rd century C.E. The gladiator games pitted "undesirable" people (e.g., criminals, captured soldiers, slaves, and Christians) against heavily armed and trained gladiators. Generations later, gladiators would be matched against such animals as lions, crocodiles, bears, and elephants. Beyond human death, it was common for hundreds of wildlife deaths to occur during a gladiator spectacle. During a "half-time," or lunch break, executions would be performed against those convicted of capital offenses. Burning at the stake or crucifixion was a common method of execution. These also served to entertain the Roman spectators.

Sport in the Middle Ages (500 C.E.–1500 C.E.)

The secularization of sport that started during the Roman Empire continued during the Middle Ages. This was a transitional period between a time when a large, unified nation or civilization (the Roman Empire) had disappeared and a later time when nations regained strength and stability (the Renaissance). Greek festivals and Roman spectacles were replaced by a variety of tournaments, hunts, and folk games. Sport participation during this era tended to be class specific.

Participation in tournaments was restricted to the upper class, although all classes were allowed to be spectators of the knights who displayed their prowess. The tournaments actually have chariot racing as their roots. During the early Middle Ages, chariot racing was quite common in Eastern Europe and the events staged were similar to what the Greeks had done a thousand years earlier (e.g., two- or four-horse teams driven by professionals on a roughly 900 meter course, generally running 7 laps) (Mandell, 1984). The medieval tournaments conducted by knights served the dual purpose of providing entertainment but also served a military purpose: training for fighting. The tournaments lasted for centuries (11th–16th) until the invention of gunpowder would make such an activity inane. (King Henry II of France died from jousting injuries in 1599, ending the tournament games there.) Performed primarily in France, England, Germany, and southern Europe, tournaments featured armed horsemen in simulated battle. They were held with great pageantry at the invitation of royalty or the nobility and were meant to display the ideals of chivalry (e.g., a knight fighting for "a fair maiden's hand"). Jousting (two knights in full armor ride at high speed directly toward one another with the object to unhorse one's opponent with a long tilting spear) was the most famous activity of the knights during the tournaments, but tourneys featuring two opposing factions of knights were also held. Death was common. The dead knights often had their possessions stolen from them. Those knights who lived but lost in battle were potential victims of hostage demands (the kingdom of the losing knight might pay a ransom for the safe return of the knight).

Jousting became obsolete as gunpowder became increasingly prominent in warfare. Today, interestingly, jousting is popular at medieval reenactment faires and is the official sport of the state of Maryland. Instead of two combatants riding at each other in full gallop and wearing armor, a solitary rider, without armor, attempts to place his or her spear through a small ring that is suspended roughly in the same position that an ongoing rider would be. In subsequent rounds the ring keeps getting smaller.

Hunts and other activities that lead to the death of animals are viewed by some as barbaric, and yet, most of these same activities exist today. Cock-fighting and dog-fighting, for example, occur in many places of the world, including the contemporary United States. Hunting was not restricted to the poorer classes, as "leisured Europeans hunted with horses, dogs, hawks, and falcons" (Mandell, 1984: 112). Mandell also points out that there are almost no literary

The medieval sport of jousting is reenacted at a Renaissance Faire.

records of fishing. He assumes, therefore, that either fishing was viewed as a degrading trade, or if it was pursued strictly for leisurely purposes, it would have been done only by illiterate, lower-class persons.

. During the Dark Ages, archery remained as a popular activity (as it had been in ancient Egypt and Greece). Archery had been popular in war for thousands of years, but now, a bull's eye target was established for sporting purposes — although, as Bell (1987) points out, the target could just as easily be a barbarian or a rival lord. The invention of the crossbow, a later development, proved to be a status symbol among archers, and because it was an expensive instrument, tended to identify people of a higher social status.

Because the peasants were not allowed to be participants in the upper class tournaments, they played a number of folk games, some with ancient origins. Dance, for example, remained popular during the Middle Ages just as it had for thousands of years prior. All social classes participated in dance, although their venues were quite different. The peasants, for example would dance at local festivals, while the wealthy would enjoy facilities equipped with stages and other conveniences of the time. Boxing, with its roots in the ancient world, was still common during the Middle Ages. The game soule, a French game (called *la soule*) similar to rugby, served to unite members of all classes (e.g., farmers, clergymen, and noblemen) from one city or town who teamed together against another city or town. After the game, it was common for members of both teams to share a communal meal, thus encouraging a sense of equality and fellowship.

Sports such as field hockey have their roots in medieval Ireland. The Celtics played with a curved stick and a rough style of play that was so physical; it is believed by some sport historians that the origins of the term "fighting Irish" originated from field hockey (Bell, 1987). The Irish also played a game called "fives" (five fingers to the hand) that is the forerunner to handball. They players bounced a ball off a single wall, alternated turns, and kept score.

Bowling has its roots in the Middle Ages. It was so popular that in 1366 King Edward III of England outlawed bowling to keep his troops focused on archery. Bowling lanes were roofed over for the first time during the mid–15th century in Germany and it became an indoor game after that. The Dutch would bring bowling to North America. In Connecticut in the 1840s, a tenth pin was added; this became the standard in the 20th century.

The high price of bows led many peasants to ignore archery and pursue games, most of which were prohibited. Football (soccer) was a popular sport in England during the Middle Ages and although its true roots are hard to determine, the first certain reference dates to 1314 from an edict of Nicholas de Farndon (Magoun, 1966). From this edict it is clear that football was regularly played in London and was regarded as a dangerous nuisance. The first recorded football fatality occurred in 1321. There were no recorded rules of the game during this era (although there is evidence that the playing fields may have been marked out), and it is, therefore, not known whether the ball was only kicked, or whether carrying the ball was allowed. Medieval English football was certainly viewed as an undesirable alternative to archery, however. King Edward IV specifically forbade football and urged archery instead. In 1477, he made playing football a punishable offense which led to imprisonment. In 1477 the king proclaimed that no person shall participate in any unlawful games such as dice or football and that every strong and able-bodied person shall practice archery for the purpose of the national defense of England (Magoun, 1966). By the 1700s, football was very common in England and still quite a violent game.

During the Middle Ages, the English also played a game called *stoolball*, in which a batter hit a ball pitched toward an upside-down milk stool and ran around three other stools before coming home safely. This game would be transformed into a game called *rounders* in the 17th century. Rounders, a game much like stoolball but with a diamond shaped field, would be brought over to colonial America, where it would eventually evolve into *town ball* (the rules varied from town to town). This game would eventually evolve into baseball.

Clearly, a couple of patterns of sport were established during the Middle Ages. First, many sports played in this era were also played in ancient times. Second, many sports played during the Middle Ages would evolve into sports played today.

Sport in the Pre-industrial Age (1500 C.E.–1750 C.E.)

After the Protestant Reformation, Calvinism and Puritanism took hold as dominant cultural influences in both Europe and colonial America. The ideals proclaimed by these social forces were in stark contrast to that previously represented in sport. "Sports were seen as frivolous, profane, useless distractions from religious observance, hard work, family devotion, and expressions of good character that Puritans associated with good, virtuous, godly lives" (Nixon and Frey, 1996: 20). These restrictive measures were aimed primarily at the peasants. The Puritans detested the English tradition of playing sport on the Sabbath. James I had proclaimed in a royal decree, published as the *Book of Sports*, that his subjects had the legal right, after religious services, to engage in lawful recreation (e.g., dancing, archery, vaulting, etc.). When the Puritans briefly took power in England, "they ordered the state executioner to publicly burn the *Book of Sports*" (Curry and Jiobu, 1984: 27).

In colonial America, the Puritans forbade sports on Sundays. They also sought to discourage horse racing (Radar, 2004). The occasional farm festival was allowed, but such activities were restricted to post-barn raising celebrations, quilting bees and cornhusking contests (Eitzen and Sage, 1989). The New England Puritans "permitted fishing and hunting if those activities were pursued for food, to refresh the body, or to rid the colony of vermin. Towns even paid bounties to those killing foxes, wolves, and bears" (Radar, 2004: 7–8). The Puritan influence was not so strong in frontier America, though there was seldom time for recreational activities on the frontier.

As time moved on, the Puritan influence would diminish in colonial America. The wealthy would enjoy more opportunities for sports and leisure than most others. Horse racing and yacht racing (not as we know yachts today) was fairly common. Yacht racing, or sailing, a sport where one yacht chases another, first became popular among the upper classes in Holland and then England in the 17th century. The first yacht club, the Walter Club of Cork Harbor, was founded in Ireland in 1720. Competitive sailing continued to gain popularity in England and the United States through the modern era. The less wealthy people enjoyed many sports, but especially bowling. At times colonial gatherings would feature a variety of games and contests on large open fields. Hunting and other contests that led to the killing of animals (e.g., cockfighting) were common. Because these contests involved the spilling of blood, the contemporary term used to describe these contests is "blood sports" (Radar, 2004). It was also common to gamble on sports and contests in colonial America.

In Europe, sports had become popular at the universities, although the amount of time students were allowed to participate in such activities was limited. University officials limited the amount of time students played sports because they did not want it to interfere with academics. (This is something that colleges and universities struggle with today.) Taking the Athenian approach — the need to balance mind and body — the Renaissance era encouraged the idea of an all-around person (i.e., a Renaissance Man). The sports played in colleges during the Renaissance were similar to student intramural sports today. As with education, sport was generally limited to the elite. They enjoyed such activities as swimming, running, horseback riding, acrobatics, archery, swordsmanship, and wrestling (Freeman, 1997).

Archery remained important for military purposes and became mandatory for English soldiers. The elites also enjoyed the skill of archery. The Finsbury Archers of London, who held tournaments in the 17th and 18th centuries, had their origins with Henry VIII, who provided a grant for the association in 1537. The world's oldest continuous archery tournament, the Ancient Scorton Arrow Contest, was commissioned by England's Charles II in 1673. Charles II viewed archery as a sport as much as a military and hunting technique. Settlers in the United States would also take up archery. The native people were already experienced with the bow and arrow. The first archery club in the United States, the United Bowmen of Philadelphia, was organized in 1828.

Sport During the Early Industrial Era (1750–1900)

The rather archaic versions of sports activities that had developed throughout the previous centuries were evolving to modern versions during the Industrial era. Industrialization was the process of transforming an agricultural (farming) economy into an industrial one, through an increase in large factories, rapid population growth, and urbanization. Standardized, written rules are a sure sign of the impending modern version of sports. Heavy bureaucratization would be one of the last developments to finish this transition from loosely-organized games to highly structured sports leagues. "Old traditions, customs, and rituals, as well as the folk groups of family and friends, were being replaced with such radically different social inventions as standardization, centralization, division of labor, impersonal authority, and rational planning. Bureaucracy and formal organization were proving to be effective ways to organize the emerging social order. This included recreation-sport" (Leonard, 1988: 33).

In the 1860s, the Marquis of Queensbury endorsed a set of rules, including requiring boxers to wear padded gloves and three-minute rounds that would become the standard of modern boxing. The American John L. Sullivan, "the Boston Strongboy," won the last bare-knuckles heavyweight championship in 1889.

In Germany, Friedrich Ludwig Jahn (1778–1852), who is often considered the "Father of Gymnastics," and someone who was an ardent Prussian patriot (he was against the provincialism of Germany), introduced gymnastics in an outdoor setting. Jahn described this outdoor exercise activity area as *turnplatz*, or "exercise group," which was basically a playground with various apparatuses for exercises. Adolf Spiess (1810–1858), another German, would later develop a system of "free exercises"—no apparatuses were needed.

During the late 1700s and early 1800s, Americans participated mostly in the same games and sports as they had during the colonial era. Furthermore, the Puritan ethic still surrounded American sport. Playing sports on Sunday was still forbidden and made officially taboo by the blue laws. Blue laws were given this name because they were printed on blue paper in New Haven, Connecticut, in 1781. These statutes restricted sports and recreation but did not forbid utilitarian activities such as hunting and fishing (Leonard, 1988). The slow transformation of American sport was primarily attributed to the fact that the urbanization of American cities did not take place until the mid–1800s. Urbanization is the process by which a country's population changes from primarily rural to urban. It is caused by the migration of people from the countryside to the city in search of better jobs and living conditions.

So what social factors occurred during the mid–1850s that would lead to a new outlook on sports in the United States? For one, massive Irish and German immigration to American cities such as New York and Boson led to a huge urban development in the United States and also created ethnic diversity. Traditional values were challenged and crime sky-rocketed. Overcrowded, unsanitary conditions characterized America's growing cities. Numerous reform efforts were spearheaded to alleviate social problems that plagued the cities. Although urbanization was in full bloom in the United States at this time, social critics condemned city life and looked idealistically at rural society. Farmers, especially, were portrayed as healthy, honest, self-reliant people (Riess, 1995). Now, physical fitness programs were promoted by social reformers as instruments of positive social change. It was argued that sport participation would benefit society by instilling traditional American values upon immigrants, lower and middle class persons.

The increased importance placed on sport participation hit a snag each winter in the northern U.S. states. As a result, a number of sports clubs emerged toward the end of the 1800s. Sports such as basketball and volleyball were created as a result of these sports clubs. By the late 1800s a number of sports clubs, including religious based groups such as the Young Men's Christian Association (YMCA), an evangelical organization founded in London in 1844, emerged throughout the United States. James Naismith invented basketball as a class YMCA project in 1891 in Springfield, Massachusetts. He had his players shoot a ball into half-bushel peach baskets attached to the gym balcony 10 feet off the ground. In men's basketball, the number of players on a side dropped from nine to five in 1895, a year before Chicago and Iowa played the first college game. Women starting playing basketball in 1892. A few years after the YMCA opened, the Young Women's Christian Association (YWCA) was formed and encouraged women to participate in "feminine" sports such as swimming, golf and tennis (Riess, 1995). Volleyball, created by William G. Morgan while he served as physical director of the YMCA at Holyoke, Massachusetts, was designed for older men who found basketball too demanding (Rader, 2004).

During the early industrial era, a number of sports were popular in the United States. Most of these sports have their roots with the colonial period. However, as society became urbanized, many sports changed as well. Horse racing, for example, became both a sporting enterprise and a business. Race tracks built in cities helped to transform horse racing from strictly a rural sport to an urban sport. The entrepreneurs that founded race tracks may have loved horses and horse racing, but they also loved the economic benefits associated with owning such a business. Betting on horse races was also very common and led to both opportunities to make money and corruption (e.g., fixing races, bribery) (Curry and Jiobu, 1984). Horse racing was also quite popular in Canada at this time as well. By the 1850s, there were horse races in forty towns and villages throughout the Quebec province (Eitzen and Sage, 1989). Rowing developed as the first big-time college sport and regularly attracted huge crowds (Curry and Jiobu, 1984). Cricket, an English sport, was quite popular at this time and was organized under the guidance of the American Cricket Club (1855). In the 1850s, cricket was a very popular American sport. Bicycle riding, although not as physically demanding as running, was viewed as an excellent form of physical activity. Kirkpatrick Macmillan (1812–1878), a blacksmith, invented the first completely self-propelled (with foot pedals) bicycle. Macmillan never bothered to patent his invention, but others were quick to realize that a great deal of money could be made in the manufacturing and sale of bicycles. The earliest recorded bicycle race was held in Paris in the late 1860s. As the bikes became lighter and safer, racing became fashionable in Europe and the United States. In 1891, the first international bicycle race was held at Madison Square Garden in New York City. Cycling events were held at the 1896 Olympics. The first Tour de France, the world's premier bicycle race, was held in 1903.

In brief, there was no shortage of sporting activities during early industrialization. It would be fruitless to try and provide a discussion of all the variations of sports and recreation endeavors during this time. However, baseball deserves special attention.

BASEBALL

By the Civil War, a number of baseball clubs were competing against one another in the United States. Baseball was especially big in the Northeast, with New York City leading the way in the number of teams. By 1858, there were ninety-six baseball clubs in the New York metropolitan area. There exists a great controversy over the origins of baseball. As mentioned earlier in this chapter, baseball is similar to the English game of rounders, but the modern version played in the United States is not nearly the same sport. The popular belief is that Abner Doubleday (1819–1893) is the founder of modern baseball. In 1905, the A.G. Mills commission, headed by Al Spalding, wrongly credited Doubleday with inventing the game of baseball in Cooperstown, New York, in 1839. In actuality, Doubleday was a cadet at West Point when he was supposed to have founded baseball. The commission made its ruling based primarily on a single, unsubstantiated letter from an elderly man named Abner Graves, who claimed to be a friend of Doubleday and present at the time when he allegedly invented baseball. The discovery of an old baseball in an attic of a farmhouse in Fly Creek, a village three miles from Cooperstown, was said to have substantiated the story. The stitched cover had been torn open, revealing stuffing of cloth instead of wool and cotton yarn, which comprise the interior of the modern baseball. The ball became known as the "Doubleday Baseball" and is still on display at Major League Baseball's Hall of Fame in Cooperstown.

The rules established by Alexander Cartwright include nine contestants at a time for each team during the play of the game and the use of a diamond field with ninety feet in between the bases. Thus, it is generally accepted that Cartwright and not Doubleday established the modern game of baseball. However, Cooperstown's claim to be host to the first game of baseball is a different argument.

After three years of unorganized play, Cartwright established a permanent site for his baseball club at Elysian Fields in Hoboken, New Jersey (1845). This is one reason why Hoboken claims to be the birthplace of modern baseball (Hoboken disputes Cooperstown's claim to have hosted baseball in 1839). Furthermore, as Adelman (1997) states, a report in the *Herald* mentioned that the New York Club played a baseball game versus the Brooklyn Club at Elysian Field as early as 1843. Despite the controversy over the exact origins of baseball, Adelman (1997) declares that "historians universally accept the Knickerbockers as baseball's pioneer club even as many of them recognize the existence of earlier teams" (p. 59). A number of New York Knickerbocker Club members claimed to have played a "bat-and-ball" game as early as 1842, in the Murray Hill section of New York at Twenty-seventh Street and Fourth Avenue before the club team moved to Elysian Fields in Hoboken (Riess, 1989).

Adding to the baseball origin controversy, city officials and historians in Pittsfield, Massachusetts, claimed to have evidence proving that baseball originated in their hometown in the late 1700s. A 1791 bylaw was passed to protect windows in Pittsfield's new meeting house by banning anyone from playing baseball within 80 yards of the building. Baseball was so common that it was necessary to pass the law, officials claimed. A librarian found the original Pittsfield document in a library vault and its age was authenticated by researchers at the Williamstown Art Conservation Center (*The Post-Standard*, May 12, 2004).

Claiming to be the first professional baseball club and the site of the birthplace of baseball depends on how people define *professional* baseball. For example, if baseball was indeed played in Cooperstown in 1839 (and Pittsfield, for that matter), but not by professional baseball players, was that really a baseball game? Most sport historians say it may be impossible to ever pinpoint the exact time and place that baseball was invented. As is often the case, according to the conflict perspective, those in power (in this case, Major League Baseball) generally dictate the official answer — which is, as of now, baseball was founded in Cooperstown by Abner Doubleday.

The story of baseball is far more important than a debate over its origins. Baseball attracted huge crowds; in many cases, people were turned away from the small stadiums of the 1800s. "Even before the Civil War, a crowd of 5,000 was not unusual for a baseball game in Brooklyn, and after the war, crowds of 10,000 to 15,000 were attracted to the more popular games" (Szymanski and Zimbalist, 2005: 16). Baseball and Brooklyn would go hand-in-hand for another 100 years (until the beloved Dodgers were moved to Los Angeles, breaking the hearts of Brooklyn Dodgers fans). Baseball games were usually followed by elaborate postgame festivities where food and spirits abounded (somewhat like pregame tailgating at American football games). Baseball was quickly on its way to becoming the "national pastime." And for most people, this meant being socialized into the role of spectator and consumer of a sports culture.

The Formation of the Modern Olympics

Another critical development during the industrial era was the reintroduction of the Olympics. In brief, the Games were revived by a Frenchman, Baron de Coubertin (1863–1937) in 1896. Paris-born Coubertin was an aristocrat, a well-versed intellectual and talented sportsman who took part in boxing, fencing, horsebackriding, and rowing. His passion for education extended to sports education. After visiting organized sports organizations in England and the United States, Coubertin returned to France to persuade officials to introduce physical education in schools. Coubertin did not promote physical education simply for sports purposes but rather, as a means of keeping his countrymen in shape. He was convinced that the humiliating French defeat in the Franco-German War (1870–71) was tied to the fact that the Germans were physically superior. Furthermore, in the spirit of French democracy, Coubertin viewed sports as a way to bring the social classes together (Hill, 1992).

Coubertin was convinced that sports education was an important part of the personal development of young people. He believed that sports education presented opportunities to develop what he called "moral energy." To publicize his plans to revive the Olympic Games, Coubertin established the International Olympic Committee (IOC) during a meeting held at the University of Sorbonne in Paris on June 23, 1894. Among the ideals that Coubertin hoped the Olympics would inspire was the concept of amateurism. Coubertin embraced this ideal when it was suggested to him by Professor William Milligan Stone during his 1893 visit to Princeton University. Sloan promoted what he called "clean sport" (Mandell, 1984). The IOC decided that the first modern Olympics would be held in Athens, Greece, and that they would be held every four years at a site to be determined by the IOC. The Athens Games were a huge success. Unfortunately, the Paris Games of 1900 and 1904 were not so successful and were overshadowed by international fairs. The 1906 Paris Summer Olympics was a success and the momentum carried on. Coubertin served as IOC president for 29 years and died of a heart attack in Geneva on September 2, 1937.

Thanks to the efforts of Pierre de Coubertin, the modern Olympics are now played on a regular basis, with the Summer and Winter Games alternating every two years. As with the original Olympics, new sports are regularly added and old ones are dropped. For instance, in 1996 beach volleyball became an Olympic sport, whereas baseball and softball have been eliminated from the Olympics beginning in 2012. Also, as with the ancient Olympics, the modern Games are filled with political controversy (See Chapter 13).

Sport in the Twentieth Century

A number of general aspects characterize sports in the twentieth century. According to Riess (1995), sport is used "to engender pride in one's hometown (boosterism) and country (nationalism). According to conventional wisdom, people could more easily identify with their neighborhood, city, region, or nation when they cheered for athletes or teams who represented them in sporting competition" (p. 26). Having a major league sports franchise became a way to express boosterism, to show pride in one's hometown. Sport provided a tangible comparison between cities that symphonies, for example, could not. Nationalism grew throughout the twentieth century. Once again, sport provided a tangible measurement through which comparisons between nations would be possible. Americans were especially eager to show the British and other European powers that their athletes were able to successfully compete in sports. Reiss also points out that technological improvements, especially in communications, helped to fuel the interest and importance that sport commands in the twentieth century.

Allen Guttmann (1978) suggests that there are seven characteristics of modern sports:

1. *Secularism*. Secularism means nonreligious. The sports of the Greeks were quasi-religious ceremonies. Modern sports are more like Roman sport with an emphasis on show and spectacle.
2. *Equality*. Modern sports are, more or less, equality-driven. Women, minorities, and lower class persons all have, at least theoretically, an equal chance to achieve in the sporting world. Equality is assured because of the standardization of rules and passage of laws that ensure egalitarianism. Of course, participants who lack athletic ability are less likely to seeing playing time as the level of competition increases; thus, there is always some form of inequality in sport.
3. *Specialization*. In an attempt to keep an edge over competitors, many advanced athletes practice their primary sport almost exclusively. Furthermore, there is great specialty in sport. For example, in baseball, there are starting pitchers, middle-relievers, "set-up pitchers" and "closers." Baseball's designated hitter position (which did not exist in 1978 when Guttmann established these characteristics) is the ultimate example of over-specialization and a clear example of diluting the quality of baseball.
4. *Rationalization*. Rationalization, a product of the scientific, lucid outlook on social life that characterizes modern society, is exhibited in the development of standardized rules.
5. *Bureaucracy*. As German sociologist Max Weber (1864–1920) articulated, bureaucracies are

goal-oriented organizations designed to meet rational goals. As sports evolved, the bureaucracy that oversees it also continued to grow (mirror-effect). Guttmann used the IOC as an exemplar of an overly bureaucratic sports organization. The modern world is so overly-bureaucratic that it often seems impersonal. Realizing this, Weber viewed future society as an "Iron Cage" (inescapable from bureaucracy and rationalization) rather than paradise (Delaney, 2004).

6. *Quantification.* The rationalistic approach to social life involves documenting everything. Measurement and keeping performance records is a critical aspect of modern sport. The beauty of quantification (numbers and statistics) is that it provides something tangible for the athlete and participant. A bowler realizes the significance of a 300 game. A golfer wants to shoot below par. Major League Baseball hitters want to reach the 762 number (Barry Bonds' career record). Quantification is equated to precision. It provides a specific goal to strive for.

7. *Records.* Directly tied to quantification, the concept of keeping records is mirrored by society's idea of progress. As long as records are being broken, progress is being made. Thus the cliché, "Every record was made to be broken." Fans and athletes alike love the chase of famed records; it reflects our continuous desire to improve, to be "the best ever."

The characteristics of sport described in this section are meant to provide a highlight of the primary features of modern sport. In the proceeding chapters, the review of a number of specific topics (e.g., gender, race, politics, and economics) will focus on a number of specific characteristics (both positive and negative) that characterize sports today.

SPORTS PLAYED

Most of the same sports played since industrialization still exist today. In the following pages, we will provide a highlight of some of the more popular ones. Among the more popular sports *played* is billiards (or pool). The ancient activity of lawn game (dating back to ancient Persia) is most likely the forerunner of billiards. A similar table game developed in England and France in the 14th century, although it is unknown if this game evolved into billiards. Pocket billiards, or pool, originated in the 1800s. In the twentieth century billiards became hugely popular. Tables were found in pool halls and saloons. In the mid–1920s there were about 42,000 poolrooms, over 4,000 in New York City alone (Riess, 1989). Poolrooms also had a bad public image, as they were viewed as places where young males went to gamble and drink and otherwise engage in deviant behavior. In the early 1900s poolrooms outnumbered bowling alleys, but this would change by the end of the century, as bowling is the number one participatory sport in the United States.

Tennis and golf are two relatively popular participant sports; both have often been viewed as semi-elitist sports, played mostly by upper-class persons. Dwight Davis, for whom the "Davis Cup" in tennis is named, attempted to make tennis accessible for all — not just the country club crowd — early in the twentieth century. Davis was a world class tennis player and a World War I hero who served as President Coolidge's secretary of war and as President Hoover's governor general of the Philippines. Davis realized that most inner city children did not have adequate places to run and play. He promoted building playgroups where people from all social classes could enjoy recreational activities such as tennis. As park commissioner of St. Louis, Davis was responsible for a boom in parks development. By late spring 1913 there were tennis courts at four parks (including 32 new courts at Forest Park alone) in St. Louis. Many other cities followed suit and before long parks across the country had tennis court facilities. Today, tennis is played at most public high schools, but overall, it has remained primarily a sport for upper-class white persons.

Throughout most of the twentieth century, golf was played on private country club courses. These private clubs restricted play to a mostly upper-class, male, white clientele. Although the multiracial Tiger Woods is a household name, when he first joined the professional tour (PGA), he was confronted with the reality that some golf courses still did not allow blacks to play. Today, many public courses have extended the participation of golf to middle-class persons.

As mentioned earlier, baseball evolved from the English sport rounders. Throughout most of the twentieth century, baseball was known as the "national pastime" because it was the most popular sport in the United States. Youth played baseball, followed professional baseball, collected baseball cards, and dreamed of playing for their favorite Major League team. For many, baseball is a simple game to understand, but filled with chess-like strategic moves and displays of physical excellence. Baseball is both a rural and urban game. And many of today's Major League Baseball (MLB) players are from economically-depressed Central American countries.

Football is a game derived from English football (soccer) and rugby. Toward the end of the twentieth century, football replaced baseball as America's favorite sport. American football is controlled violence and it is poetry in motion. It is chaotic and it is planned precision. In many respects it is very primal and yet quite evolved in sophistication and technology. Football is the number one sport in high schools across the United States and the passion for this sport continues at the collegiate level and peaks at the professional — the National Football League (NFL).

The Post-modern Era: An Interest in "Extreme" Sports

Traditional sports remain hugely popular in American and Western societies. However, the increasingly prominent role of sport in society has led to a nontraditional backlash. Many people, especially the younger generation, have become frustrated with the overly specialized, overly competitive and highly selective character of most traditional sports. Many sports have become so rule-oriented that people have sought alternatives to "traditional" sports. Collectively, these "nontraditional" sports are known as "alternative sports." The most prevalent of these alternatives are known as "extreme sports." In this section, we will discuss the development of extreme sports and provide a brief review of some of the more prevalent extreme sports. As we shall see, ironically, or maybe predictably, many of these extreme sports are becoming as bureaucratized as the sports these participants shunned.

EXTREME SPORTS

The term extreme sports (sometimes called action sports) is a collective idiom used to describe a number of relatively newer sporting activities that involve risky, adrenaline-inducing action. Adrenaline junkies are susceptible to all kinds of dangerous activities not limited to sports. Many behaviors that attract such people are often dangerous and risky, defying common sense.

The longer any sport is in existence, the more likely it is to become standardized and commercialized; many extreme sports have been unable to escape this inevitability. For example, in 1995, ESPN created the "X Games." The X Games are a made-for-television phenomenon that features a number of extreme sports. The popularity of the X Games led ESPN to create annual Winter X Games and Summer X Games. Some of the events include aggressive in-line skating, bicycle stunt riding, snowboarding, sky surfing, street luge and skateboarding. Advertisers who covet the audience drawn to the X Games have been eager to join the extreme bandwagon. Sponsorships have guaranteed the success of the Games for both ESPN and the participants.

As with any discussion of traditional sports, it would not be practical to try and provide a complete analysis of all extreme sports. Consequently, our review will be brief and begins with post-modern variations of surfing. The thrill enjoyed by water surfers is shared by land-lovers who transformed traditional surfing into such sports as skateboarding, snowboarding, sky surfing and elevator surfing. Skateboarding represents one of the first activities to be classified as an "alternative" or "extreme" sport. Skateboarding has actually been in existence for decades dating back to its California origin during the 1950s. Skateboarding started as a dry land hobby for surfers while they weren't in the ocean. By the 1960s, skateboarding was so popular that a number of competitions with various styles (e.g., downhill slalom and freestyle) of competition were judged (Cave, 2006). Skateboarding is so popular today that it enjoys subcultural status and has been immortalized by skating movies and long-time television rebel Bart Simpson.

Snowboarding is another extension of surfing. Adopting a similar stance to the surfer and skateboarder, the snowboarder seeks gravity free moments of excitement and adrenaline rushes. Snowboarders first appeared at ski slopes in the early 1980s. They quickly earned the reputation as "bad boys" which only fueled the attraction of this sport to nontraditional sport enthusiasts. By 2000, the popularity of snowboarding led to its claim as the fastest growing sport in the United States with a total of 7.2 million participants (an increase of over 50 percent from the previous year) (Arnold, 2006). Sky surfing is an extreme sport that combines "getting air" with attempts to make "turns" on waves or slopes prior to parachuting to safety. Elevator surfing is one of the newest extreme sports. It involves daredevils riding, or "surfing," on the top of elevators. The inherent danger of elevator surfing includes being crushed between the elevator and the top of the elevator shaft or simply falling off the elevator top and falling to one's death. Elevator surfing typically takes place in skyscrapers and college campuses with tall buildings. Participants generally enter the building early or late in the day or whenever there are few people around. They pry the doors open and use emergency hatches to enter the elevator shafts.

Another example of an extreme sport is street luge. Street luge, as with most extreme sports, evolved from existing traditional sports; in this case from a combination of ice luge and skateboarding. Street luge races may be conducted legally (sanctioned events) or illegally (a hill in any neighborhood). Street lugers lie down on a skateboard-like apparatus that is equipped with four large urethane wheels and no brakes. The luges are generally made with aluminum frames. Steering is accomplished by leaning the body weight from side to side. Starting from the top of a hill (this could be in any neighborhood) lugers allow gravity to take them on their thrilling joy ride. One variation of illegal street luging involves the rider grabbing a hold of a moving vehicle for a "free ride."

One of the most dangerous extreme sports is BASE jumping. BASE jumping is defined as parachuting from stationary objects (e.g., buildings, bridges, steep mountains). BASE is an acronym for building, antenna (an uninhabited tower such as an aerial mast), span (bridge, arch, or dome) and earth (cliffs or other natural formation). Unlike skydiving, no aircraft is involved with BASE jumping. BASE jumping is a very dangerous sport and has a high fatality rate. There have been isolated examples of BASE jumping since the early 1900s (e.g., Frederick Law jumped from the Statue of Liberty in 1912), but these were usually done for publicity purposes. BASE jumping is somewhat like parachuting except BASE jumping is done from lower heights and at lower airspeed than a skydiver. Furthermore, an off heading landing is most likely to lead to fatal consequences for BASE jumpers, whereas skydivers have some time to maneuver. Most BASE jumpers already know how to skydive. It is advisable that BASE jumpers learn skydiving first so that they know how to safely fly and land a parachute (there is more room for error when learning how to sky dive than when learning how to BASE jump).

Unlike skydiving, the FAA has no jurisdiction over BASE jumping. However, to legally BASE jump, the jumper must secure necessary permissions to use the object that is being jumped and the area used for landing. Obviously, due to risk concerns, there is great reluctance among most owners of jumpable objects to allow BASE jumping. However, there is one bridge in the United States where it is legal to BASE jump — the Perine Bridge in Twin Falls, Idaho. The bridge is a perfect site for jumping. It sits 487 feet above the canyon and Snake River below.

There is a flat area to land. Tom Aiello, a BASE jumping trainer at Twin Falls, has taught many people. However, he makes all jumpers write a letter (just prior to their jump) to their family or loved ones explaining why they are jumping and promising not to sue Aiello, Twin Falls, or the state of Idaho, if they should get injured or die as a result of their jump (ESPN, 7/24/05). Two people have died from their jumps at Twin Falls.

As a matter of historic sports interest, the Perine Bridge is 2 miles west of the area where, in 1974, legendary daredevil and ultimate thrill seeker Evel Knievel attempted to jump the Snake River Canyon in his rocket-propelled motorcycle (he called it his "Skycycle"). Knievel made it over the quarter mile wide chasm but strong winds blew the malfunctioning parachute back into the canyon, and just a few feet away from the river in which he most likely would have drowned. Knievel would recover from his injuries and would attempt other extreme jumps before retiring. He died in November of 2007, shortly after a rock opera based on his life opened with excellent reviews in Los Angeles.

One of the more brutal extreme sports is ultimate fighting. Ultimate fighting has grown in popularity during the early 2000s. Ultimate fighting combines such traditional sports as karate, wrestling, boxing, kickboxing, and a variety of marital arts. Ultimate fighting generally involves participants beating up one another where the rules are flexible enough to allow for a number of fighting styles. This sport has become standardized already under the Ultimate Fighting Championship (UFC). The UFC is a series of international competitions televised internationally several times a year. Ultimate fighting is little more than sanctioned gang warfare or a bully who beats someone for the sheer enjoyment of harming another human being. Despite the brutality of this sport and its challenge to the premise of a civilizing movement in the premodern era, the popularity of ultimate fighting has not reached its peak.

It is important to reiterate the point that many sports classified as extreme have existed in the past. For example, many people climbed rocks, mountains and ice glaciers before these activities became labeled as extreme sports. Surfing is sometimes classified as an extreme sport, and yet it has a relatively long history in the United States. Running with the bulls in Pamplona, Spain, is certainly an extreme way to get one's kicks in life, and yet this event dates back to the 13th century. The annual running with bulls became popular in the late 1800s. Numerous people are gored each year and fatalities are common in this action activity.

Participation in extreme sports is steadily growing. However, participation rates for females in extreme sports remain distant to that of males. As with traditional sports, males generally control access to participation and the processes by which females could become accepted as fellow extreme athletes. Boys generally control the local parks and high school parking lots often used by extreme sport enthusiasts, thus depriving girls of the opportunity to develop their skills. Nonetheless, the popularity of extreme sports has increased so quickly that some of these sporting activities have become so standardized that they are included in such international sporting contests as the Olympics. Snowboarding, for example was included in the 2002 Winter Olympic Games.

Sport in the Future

In this chapter, a brief review of the history of sport was provided. It was not intended to be an exhaustive listing of sports and games played throughout history, as that would take volumes of published works. Rather, it was our intention to provide an accurate glimpse of sport throughout human history. As we have demonstrated, a number of specific sports and activities have existed for thousands of years. One other thing should be quite clear as well: sport has existed for so long, and is such a pervasive aspect of humanity, it will certainly remain as a major social institution for the foreseeable future.

Sport has always served a diversionary function in society, especially Western society (the primary focus of our historical review of sport). Games, and to a lesser extent sport, are also important in non–Western societies, although generally they are not as well developed and organized. For example, in Bolivia, indigenous women participate in a freestyle form of wrestling called *lucha libre*, based loosely on the World Wrestling Entertainment in the United States and Triple A in Mexico. The *cholitas* (women wrestlers) wear bowler hats, multilayered skirts and pumps while wrestling in packed and frenzied arenas. In Bolivian cities such as El Alto, lucha libre provides a much needed diversion for people who have little time or money for recreation (*Sports Illustrated*, 8/1/05). Members of the Sri Lanka swim team competing in the 2005 World Swimming Championships (held in Montreal) did not expect to win many medals, but they were happy to temporarily escape the problems of their homeland caused by the 2004 tsunami that killed over 30,000 in Sri Lanka alone. Many Sri Lankan swimmers lost their homes in the natural disaster. After it occurred, the Sri Lanka government mandated that all children learn to swim. Sadly, swimmers from other nations competing in the World Championships have had to escape their own problems. Angola, for instance, has been ravaged by disease and is still recovering from a civil war that lasted more than two decades. Eight members of the national team were killed in bombings during the conflict. Cameroon swimmers have a different type of challenge to overcome. The longest pools in their country are only 18 meters, and they are all located at resorts. Olympic-sized pools are 50 meters in length.

History has taught us that most people face hardships on a regular basis. Sport is used as a diversion from such misfortunes. Additionally, those who have leisure time at their disposal will also spend a great deal of time involved in sports and recreation. Future history books will reveal sports' continuing importance in society.

SUMMARY

It is difficult to trace when sport first began. This is connected with the continuing debate as to when humans first appeared on earth. The ancient Egyptians played a number of identifiable sports, including archery, wrestling, running, swimming, and tabletop games. Many sports and games in Ancient Asia had a philosophical quality, which helped to humanize their martial aspects. The ancient Greeks loved their sports, which characterized their highly competitive nature. This was reflected in the Olympic Games, which combined cultural and religious aspects and helped to produce unity throughout the Hellenistic world. The Roman Empire continued the traditions begun by the Greeks, but during this period sports became increasingly professional and secularized. Eventually, the Roman Empire became dominated by the infamous gladiator games, which led to a debasement of the culture.

In the Middle Ages, the secularization of sport that started during the Roman Empire continued with the rise of tournaments. These were held with great pageantry at the invitation of royalty and displayed the ideals of chivalry. Such tournaments were limited to the upper classes, but folk games were popular with the lower classes. The Pre-industrial age (incorporating the Renaissance, Reformation and Enlightenment) marked a major period of transition where religious and philosophical debates had an impact upon the sports being played. Calvinism and Puritanism, for instance, became dominant cultural influences in both Europe and America, and looked upon sports as frivolous, profane distractions from religious observances. Sports did become popular in universities, which had risen during the Middle Ages, although officials limited the time students played because they did not want it to interfere with academics.

In the mid 1700s the Industrial Revolution radically changed the Western world, through the introduction of machinery and mass production. With the rise of a middle class, there was an increase in the number of people with disposable income and the time to spend on leisure and sport pursuits. Urbanization also had an important influence on the rise of spectator sports. This transition marked a development of higher-level organization and standardized rules.

The modern Olympics were founded in 1896 by Baron de Coubertin as a way of bringing social classes together and encouraging international cooperation. As the twentieth century began, sports and leisure activities enjoyed a valued status in the Western world.

Today, sport is such a well-established social institution that it is as much a part of the character of a nation as are its politics, economics, and religion. Sport has been seen as a vital part of the civilizing process. However, due in part to increasing frustration with over-specialized, rule-oriented sports, the late twentieth and early twenty-first centuries have seen the rise of extreme and alternative sports.

KEY TERMS

BASE Jumping Parachuting from stationary objects (e.g., buildings, bridges, steep mountains). BASE is an acronym for building, antenna, span and earth.

Blue Laws So-called because they were once printed on blue paper, these are laws restricting activities or sales of goods on Sundays or holy days.

Boosterism Efforts to engender pride in one's hometown. Having a major league sports franchise can be a means to show pride in one's hometown.

Chivalry The qualities idealized by knighthood in the Middle Ages, such as bravery, courtesy, honor, and gallantry toward women.

Extreme Sports A collective idiom used to describe a number of relatively newer sporting activities that involve risky, adrenaline-inducing action. Features of extreme sports may include speed, height, danger, peril, stunts, and illegality.

Folk Games Popular and traditional games, primarily played in rural areas and passed along from one generation to another.

Industrialization The process of transforming an agricultural (farming) economy into an industrial one, through an increase in large factories, rapid population growth, and urbanization.

Jousting Competition between two knights in full armor who ride at high speed directly toward one another with the object to unhorse one's opponent with a long tilting spear.

Marquis of Queensbury Rules Set of rules agreed upon in the 1860s which became the standard of modern boxing, including requiring boxers to wear padded gloves and limiting rounds to three minutes.

Middle Ages A transitional period between a time when a large, unified nation or civilization (the Roman Empire) had disappeared and a later time when nations regained strength and stability (the Renaissance).

Pankration A Greek word that means "complete strength" or "complete victory."

Secularism The process of moving from a religious orientation toward one that is focused on the world.

Tournaments Public contests held in the Middle Ages between armed horsemen in simulation of real battle; these were restricted to the upper classes.

Urbanization The process by which a country's population changes from primarily rural to urban. It is caused by the migration of people from the countryside to the city in search of better jobs and living conditions.

DISCUSSION QUESTIONS

- What do you think were the earliest "sports?"
- What is "Pankration" and how does it relate to contemporary "ultimate fighting" events?
- Why was the ancient Olympics started by the Greeks? What is the idealized view of the ancient Olympics, and how does this differ from the reality of the Games?
- How did the Romans differ with the Greeks on the role of sport in society? How did gladiator fighting originate, and what were its effects on the Roman character?
- What do you think "chivalry" means, and how does it relate to the Middle Ages' development of sport?
- What objections did the Puritans have toward sport? Which sports did they approve of?
- In what ways did the Industrial Revolution impact upon the development of modern sport? Why have sports become more rule-oriented and bureaucratized? Is this a good or a bad thing, in your opinion?
- What are "extreme sports" and how are they a reaction to the civilization process?

CHAPTER 4

The Impact of Sport on Culture

Once upon a time, there was a legend of a man who could "walk on water." Imagine that, walking on water. How could that be possible? This man resided in the tropical paradise of Honolulu, Hawaii, but word of his accomplishments reached faraway lands. The legend grew so big that people in the United States wanted to see for themselves someone perform such an extraordinary feat. And so, this mysterious fellow left his tropical homeland for America so that he could showcase his talent. Tens of thousands of people descended upon the beautiful Redondo Beach, California, shoreline to witness this miracle. The curious wanted to know who was this "man who could walk on water." His name was George Freeth, and although he was descended from Hawaiian royalty, he was no god. Freeth was a surfer. Henry Huntington, a wealthy Californian entrepreneur, had witnessed Freeth surfing while he was on vacation in Hawaii in the early 1900s. Huntington convinced the part royal Hawaiian and part Irish beach boy to come to Redondo Beach in 1907 to promote Redondo Beach tourism. Freeth was advertised as the "Man who can walk on water."

George Freeth did much more than simply bring surfing to the United States; he helped to transform the Southern California culture. For many, surfing is not just a sport, it is a lifestyle with a quasi-religious feel to it. Beach communities throughout the United States have developed a highly identifiable subculture centered on surfing and the beach way of life. Surfing as a subculture will be discussed later in this chapter.

Defining Culture

No review of the sociology of sport is complete without a chapter on sports' impact on culture. The study of culture is one of the most important things sociologists do. The study of culture is critical to sociologists because of the impact of culture on individual human behavior and societal makeup. Culture is defined as the shared knowledge, values, language, norms, and behavioral patterns of a given society that are handed down from one generation to the next and form a way of life for its members. The prevailing culture of a society will dictate what is "proper" and "improper" behavior based on a number of variables, including the context and circumstances of a situation. For example, a child who throws a temper tantrum in a store is engaging in unruly behavior and is the cause of onlookers' scorn, but such behavior is discounted by the fact that the child is immature and has not learned to control his or her own behavior. An adult throwing a temper tantrum is not acceptable and deemed odd or peculiar.

Oddly, a number of professional athletes, managers and coaches feel that it is okay to throw a temper tantrum. Lou Piniella, for example, a long-time MLB manager (he was manager of the Chicago Cubs in 2008), is known for his emotional outbursts in dugouts and on the playing field. (Piniella has been known for kicking dirt on umpires, picking up bases and throwing them, making a number of strange gestures, and in short, "blowing a fuse!") Although

Piniella (apparently) finds this behavior acceptable, it is considered highly immature and child-like among viewers. If his antics were not so pathetic, they would be comical.

It is culture that influences members of society. A society refers to a group of people who interact with one another as members of a collectivity within a defined boundary. A society also consists of a number of highly structured systems of human organization and this organized system helps to form the social structure of society.

Sociologists generally identify two components of culture: material and nonmaterial. Material culture refers to the physical, substantial creations of a society (e.g., clothing, merchandise, football stadiums, sporting equipment, automobiles, art, and so on). In societies obsessed by conspicuous consumption, the material culture plays a prominent role. A preoccupation with conspicuous consumption and conspicuous leisure leads to a consumer culture. The possession of material goods are, in essence, "social communicators" of cultural values. In this manner, a season ticket holder of a particular sports team is "socially communicating" to others that he or she has the time and money to support the team on a full-time basis.

Nonmaterial culture includes the more abstract creations of society, such as beliefs, values, ideology, and norms. To illustrate how these two components of culture work, let's examine the merits of building a new stadium. Most fans, owners and players value a new stadium with all the modern amenities over an old and deteriorating stadium. However, Boston Red Sox and Chicago Cubs fans love the character of their respective old stadiums and value the sentimentality of the stadium over the idea of a new luxury one. The point is, no matter what type of stadium one prefers, culture has played a role in that fan's preference.

There are other aspects of culture that sociologists examine. We will limit our examination to a few key aspects of culture that are of particular interest to the sociology of sport; specifically, symbols, language, cultural diversity, and subcultures. (Social norms, the rules that govern behavior, will be examined in Chapter 8, when we discuss the role of deviance in sport.)

SYMBOLS

The use of symbols is another important aspect of culture. Symbols are items that represent something else by association, resemblance, or convention to a people in a society. We come in contact with a large number of symbols on a daily basis, including road signs, parking instructions, male and female bathroom signs, and so on. Members of a society generally share an understanding of the meaning behind symbolic representations.

Sport, as an institution of society, is also consumed with symbolic gestures. For example, in baseball, it is common for a catcher to flash signals to the pitcher. Elementary signals include the index finger as symbolic of a fastball, two fingers for a curveball, and three fingers for change-up pitch. If a catcher flashes a sign for a fastball "down the middle" (directly over home plate) but the pitcher "reads" the sign as a pitch-out (throwing outside and away from the batter) the ball is going to sail away from the catcher's reach. The third base coach is responsible for flashing signs to the batter. If a "run and hit" (the base runner takes off immediately for the next base and the batter is suppose to "protect" the runner by swinging at the pitch — no matter what) is called by the third-base coach but the batter fails to recognize the symbols the coach is flashing and does not swing at the pitch, the runner is "hung out to dry." Referees in sports use symbols. One of the most common referee symbols in football involves the ref raising both arms straight in the air signaling a touchdown. A soccer referee may pull out a yellow (warning) or red (suspension) card from his or her pocket and flash it toward a player indicating a violation has occurred. All soccer fans understand the significance of the red or yellow card symbol. Trophies and championship rings become the ultimate symbols of achievement in sport. There is a cliché in certain sports that athletes play for "the ring." "It's all about the ring." Of course, it's not really the ring itself the player wants. Anyone can order a "championship" ring (and some are available on eBay); it's the symbolic nature of the ring that is important to athletes.

LANGUAGE

Among the most important symbols used by a society is language. Language is a set of symbols that make up a body of words and provides systems for their common use by people who are of the same culture or society. The language developed by a society reveals the aspects of culture that are deemed most important. Language is used to describe events, to express feelings and beliefs, and to convey the importance of specific values and norms.

Just as language tells us a good deal about what is important and relevant to a culture, subcultural groups modify language to fit their needs. This is especially true in the world of sports, as all sports utilize language in a symbolic manner relevant to their domain. Tennis uses the term "love" instead of the number "zero." Thus, after an opening point has been won, the score is 15-Love. Soccer uses the word "nil" instead of "zero." Thus, after the first goal of a soccer match is made, the score becomes "one" to "nil." Baseball uses such expressions as: "Texas Leaguer" (a weak hit to the outfield), "can of corn" (a type of catch made in the field), "sacrifice bunt" (attempt to hit the ball in play to move a runner, rather than going for a "hit"), "grand slam" (a bases loaded homerun) and "infield fly rule" (a rule used with runners on base and less than two outs). Football uses such phrases as "blitz" (when the defense sends extra players to rush after the quarterback), "post pattern" (the receiver runs a pattern that ends near the goal post), and "going deep" (the receiver runs a long distance down the field).

Language is used to emphasize important aspects of the sport. It is also a method of introducing the basics of the sport to novice fans. As Extreme sports become increasingly commercialized, a language that reflects the events being played has developed correspondingly. The media (primarily ESPN) encourages the use of subcultural language to convey the uniqueness of extreme sports. During the 2007 X-Games held in Los Angeles, television announcers used such phrases as "no hander lander" (ending the trick ride without hands on handlebar), "back flip no handlebar" (doing a back flip without holding onto the handle bar), "360-tail flip" (a complete circle spin while shaking the back of the bike), and "double tail whip" (shaking the back of the bike twice while airborne). The E-games have adopted the format of such sports as figure skating to incorporate basic moves within the structure of language.

Sport language emerges from the obvious elements of sport (as described above), and terms and expressions developed over time by sport participants, fans, and clever announcers. One of the most colorful sports announcers of all time is the late voice of the Los Angles Lakers, Francis Dayle "Chick" Hearn (1916–2002). Hearn, who "was instrumental in introducing professional basketball to Southern California sports fans when the team moved from Minneapolis in 1960," coined unique phrases that became known as Chickisms (Stewart, 2002: D3). *Los Angeles Times* writer Larry Stewart compiled a list that included the following:

- *Slam dunk.* A shot that is thrust down hard into the basket
- *Airball.* A shot that badly misses the rim
- *Dribble drive.* A player is driving hard toward the basket
- *"No harm, no foul."* A player might have been fouled, but no damage was done, so no foul was called
- *Ticky-tack.* A foul not worth calling
- *Frozen rope.* A line-drive shot
- *"You can put this one in the refrigerator. The door's closed, the lights are out, the eggs are cooling, the butter's getting hard and the Jell-O is jiggling."* The game has been decided (Stewart, 2002: D3).

Although sport language is vibrant, curse words remain the most colorful and trouble-some. There are times when people find it necessary, no matter how inappropriate, to curse. Cursing is so common in English soccer that one British educator called for the games to be banned from television during daytime hours. English soccer officials have proposed a ban on cursing. Politicians have called for civility in English soccer. Martin Ward, deputy general sec-retary of the Secondary Heads Association, called the behavior of many English soccer players "very childish." England's Premier League players' union has even joined in for the call of proper language in soccer by printing posters urging its members to straighten up. Under a photo-graph of a player and referee arguing — but smiling — a caption reads: "Respect the Game. Respect the Ref" (*The Post-Standard*, 8/11/05).

DIVERSITY OF CULTURE

Every culture found around the world possesses aspects that are unique when compared to others. The diversity of culture is the result of each society's adaptation to its specific natu-ral environment (e.g., climate and geography) and a number of traditions, customs, routines, values and norms that develop over time a form a way of life for people. Some nations, such as Sweden, are referred to as homogeneous societies because they mostly consist of people who share a common culture, language, religion, ideology, customs, norms, and values. Conversely, some nations, such as the United States, are heterogeneous societies because they consist of people who do not universally share key social characteristics such as language, religion, race, ethnicity, politics, and economic backgrounds. Heterogeneous societies are likely to be charac-terized by conflict and tension, as behaviors that may have been acceptable in one's old culture are not acceptable in the host society. Each unique group tends to view their culture as the "best" and the others as inferior. Such an attitude is referred to as ethnocentric thinking. Ethnocen-trism is the belief that one's own culture is superior to all others and is the standard by which all other cultures should be judged.

Cultural differences are often reflected in sport. This may include styles of play, the level of deference shown to authority figures, the willingness to "win at all costs" philosophy versus ideals of sportsmanship, and so on. As Luschen (1981) explains, "Games of strategy are found in societies where obedience [is stressed], games of physical skill in those where achievement is stressed. Individual sports would mainly qualify as games of physical skill and again show achievement as their basic cultural value. Team sports as well are games of strategy. Their rela-tion to training of obedience would support exactly what we called earlier the value of collec-tivity" (p. 291). The prevailing cultural value of the United States, as with other nations of the West, is winning and achievement. These cultural values are reflected in America's most pop-ular sports.

Cultural diversity is an important topic for the business of sport as well. For example, in 2004, Nike learned that the success of a marketing campaign in one culture does not assure its acceptance by another culture. A series of ads in Singapore designed to resemble graffiti stirred negative emotions in the Asian nation known for its obsession with cleanliness and civic order. Small, page-size posters featuring NBA star LeBron James were pasted on 700 bus stops, shock-ing commuters throughout Singapore (*USA Today*, 11/26/04). Numerous complaints led to Nike pulling the ads that were viewed as offensive in a culture where public spaces are immaculate and stiff penalties for offensive behavior await violators.

SUBCULTURES

A subculture refers to a distinctive group within a greater culture that possesses its own cultural values, behavioral patterns, and other traits distinctive enough to distinguish it from the dominant group. Members of a subculture generally abide by the prevailing norms and values of the greater society, but distinguish themselves on a specific criterion that provides them with a sense of identity. There are many examples of subcultural groups, including "Trekkies" (fans of *Star Trek*), gang members, drug users, students, and surfers. Members of a subculture identify one another in a number of ways, including greeting styles, outlooks on life, priorities in life, mannerisms, clothing, and language. It is their language, or jargon, that really helps to differentiate subcultural members. Surfers for example get "stoked" about "duck-diving" and executing an "alley-oop. " They don't want to "wipeout" or look like a "barney" in front of a "nugget" (Quintanilla, 1998). Surfers understand this language, but others may not. Quintanilla (1998: D1) has complied a list of surfer terms. Below is a sampling:

- *Air.* When the surfer and board take off into the air and land on the wave again
- *Alley-oop.* When a surfer rotates 360 degrees backward above the wave
- *Barney.* A clueless surfer
- *Duck-dive.* While paddling out, the technique of submerging the surfboard under oncoming waves
- *Filthy.* Flawless waves
- *Lineup.* The area where surfers linger for waves
- *Nugget.* An attractive member of the opposite sex
- *Stoked.* Excited
- *Wipeout.* Crash

In the United States, surfing is mostly a subcultural sport restricted, obviously, to beach communities. Thus, logic dictates that surfing will enjoy greater subcultural participation in California and Florida as compared to Nebraska and Iowa.

An interesting aspect about subcultural language and its usage is that as the popularity of a subculture increases, it begins to become mainstreamed in the greater society. From the list above, most people understand the expression, "I was stoked about my grade in class" or, "Did you see that alley-oop pass to Kobe Bryant?"

Professional Sports and Their Relation to the Community

Community members generally have a strong emotional commitment toward their home professional sports team. They care a great deal about the outcome of a game, perhaps caring too much in some cases. Sports fans rejoice together in victory and console one another in defeat. They invest a great deal of leisure time following the fortunes and tribulations of their favorite teams. They believe in the old adage, "We'll get 'em next year." Year after year fans show up at the start of the season and support their team. They give freely of their time and energy because they have a feeling of loyalty and commitment to the team. But, what if there is no next year? What if the fans show up, but the team is no longer there? Does professional sport have the same level of commitment and loyalty to its fans as the fans have for the professional franchise? Often, sadly, they do not.

The owners of professional sports expect the fans and taxpayers of the community to support them (frequently) unconditionally. The owners are motivated by greed and when they feel that they are not making enough revenue they threaten to relocate the franchise, hold the community "hostage" for better stadium deals and revenue sharing agreements, or use any number of other tactics to maintain their profit margin. What can the average fan do about such power moves? In short, nothing. They are powerless. The undying loyalty to the team does not guarantee permanence of the franchise. The shared history between a franchise and its community does not promise a continued relationship. Fans want to know that their team will be there next year, and the year afterwards. The problem with supporting a professional sports team is the realization that they may not be there next year. A stadium public address announcer may excitedly yell, "And now, your...," but realize that it's "your" team only as long as the owner wants "your" money. The following season the owner may want some other community's money.

Even when a team has a long history of support from the community (e.g., the Brooklyn Dodgers and the Cleveland Browns), that alone does not guarantee the stability of the franchise in a community. Art Modell, owner of the Cleveland football team, broke the hearts of millions of Browns fans when he moved his franchise to Baltimore for the 1996 season. The city of Cleveland managed to secure the Browns' franchise name, colors and history, and was awarded a new franchise in 1999, but it certainly isn't the same thing. And die-hard Browns fans will never forgive Art Modell or the NFL for allowing the move in the first place. The Brooklyn Dodgers abandoned New York for California in 1958 because of civic inducement factors offered by the city of Los Angeles, even though Brooklyn fans were among the most loyal of all baseball fans.

Assuming the community wants the franchise to stay, there is still very little they can do to stop the owner from relocating a franchise. In the NFL, Cleveland accomplished the most — they saved everything (e.g., the "Browns" nickname, the records, and team colors) but the team. No community is safe from the realization that their beloved franchise may relocate. Fan groups, which come and go, and legislative attempts have failed to stop owners from moving their team from one community to another. The Professional Sports Community Protection Act of 1982, for example, has failed to stop franchise relocation (Johnson, 1983). A number of municipalities have attempted to gain ownership of franchises through the laws of eminent domain, which enable municipalities and states to acquire private property, so long as the owner is compensated for the value of the property. This strategy has been tried and failed on a number of occasions: A Massachusetts lawmaker introduced legislation to seize the Boston Red Sox during the 1994 baseball strike; the city of Oakland attempted to stop the Raiders' move to Los Angeles; and the city of Baltimore challenged when the Colts fled to Indianapolis (Katz, 1994; Euchiner, 1993).

In 2008, Seattle went to court to stop the NBA's Super Sonics franchise from leaving the city. Seattle used the same legal principle — specific performance — that Cleveland used in 1996 to ultimately secure a replacement NFL team. The "specific performance" clause used by Cleveland against Art Modell stemmed from exact language in Cleveland's lease requiring that the Browns must occupy the stadium until the lease expired, and that a lease buyout was not an option. In 2008, the Sonics still had two years remaining on their contract. As it turned out, Seattle and Sonics fans shared the same fate as Cleveland and its fans— the franchise moved to Oklahoma City but the city retained the nickname, colors and records of the team.

Other team owners seldom speak out against franchise relocation because they realize they may want to move their own team someday if a better deal comes along. There are two possible solutions to ending franchise relocations, however. The first involves empowering the league commissioner with the authority to refuse to schedule games for the team that relocates. This will never happen because the owners pay the commissioner's salary; and they certainly are not going to give the commissioner power to supersede their wants and desires.

The best solution to keeping franchises in the communities that support them is to allow the community itself to own the franchise; not an individual or corporate ownership, but community ownership. If the team is really a representation of the community, let the community own it. The Green Bay Packers (NFL) have enjoyed this type of relationship within their community for several decades. In a city of just 96,000 residents, the business of football is secondary to the game of football, thanks mainly to the structure of Green Bay Packers, Inc. The Packers have a management team to run the franchise. Fans know that the team will not be relocating, and stadium concerns become public concerns because the money going in is shared through the revenue generated by tenants. All fans should be as lucky as Packers fans. The time has come for communities and fans to own the sport franchises that they cheer. Unfortunately for communities, the owners do not want to give up this type of power and it is not likely that many communities will own franchises in the near future.

Followers of college sports do not have to worry about their team relocating — although occasionally, sport teams are dropped from the program. College sport fans enjoy a greater degree of loyalty in their sports. In professional sports today, there are far too many examples of the lack of loyalty. Often there is a lack of loyalty shown by owners and the community in which teams reside; there is a lack of loyalty shown by owners toward players; and there is a lack of loyalty among players and the franchise they were drafted by. And yet, the vast majority of professional sports fans remain loyal to their favorite teams despite the strikes, holdouts, lockouts, franchise relocation, and greedy demands perpetrated by owners.

Mike Lupica (1996) offers some suggestions to improve the relationship between the fans (and community) and owners of professional sports. First, give rebates to fans when a player displays unsportsmanlike conduct and then gets thrown out of the game. Second, team owners should sign a "prenuptial" agreement with the league and the community in which the team operates. The language should be simple. If an owner makes a mess of the team, sell it, don't move it. Third, offer cheap seats for every game. The fact is, professional sports events (and many "big-time" college sports for that matter) are too expensive for the average fan. There should be a cheap-seat section at every major arena, for every sport. And Lupica emphasizes the seats should be inexpensive, not bad seats. Additionally, Lupica believes that the fans should have a league commissioner, one that assumingly would assure the best interests of the fans.

Leisure Groups as Community

Social interaction plays an important role in an individual's life. Everyone wants to feel as though they are a part of a group or community. Individuals want to experience a sense of unity with their fellows. Group membership allows an individual to become a part of a whole. Group members are still individuals but at the same time the group provides them with a distinctive group identity as a result of their membership (Lee, 1993). Group membership provides opportunity for, and a sense of, community. A number of people form a sense of community through leisure group participation. Leisure activity may be viewed as one of the most telling indicators of who a person really is, more so than other labels such as occupation. Work is, after all, something that most people do in order to pay the bills and earn a living. We engage in sport participation or spectatorship because we want to (Rojek, 1985). Leisure-based communities provide individuals an opportunity to bond with others and fulfill the need to belong. In fact, there exists a vast network of leisure-oriented organizations that can collectively be called the "Leisure Establishment" (Frey, 1978).

The search for community is an extension of a lifetime of small-group participation. We are born into a family, form playgroups during childhood and later enter into cliques of primary association, and eventually many will form or establish a new family group of their own. Throughout adulthood individuals form work groups and leisure groups. Through these associations individuals develop a sense of self. One type of leisure-based group is a sports booster group. Sport booster groups help to provide people with a social identity, serve as a primary group and bring people together, forming a sense of community. Sport booster groups provide a network of social relations marked by mutuality and emotional bonds. Relationships in booster groups are close, often intimate, and usually face-to-face. Individuals are bound together by affective or emotional ties rather than by a perception of individual self-interest. Sport booster groups provide a community setting and members experience a sense of "we-ness." In this regard, sport booster groups may be viewed as a primary group. (See Chapter 5 for a further review of a primary group.)

Participation in sport booster groups (leisure groups) provide valuable bonding opportunities. Zillman, Bryant and Sapolsky (1979) propose that a taken-for-granted assumption is that watching a sports contest alone is less enjoyable than watching it in the company of friends (fellow boosters), or in the midst of a cheerful crowd (a viewing site where boosters can watch a game together). Expressed enjoyment or disappointment carries over to group members. Feelings are intensified through group empathy and enhanced through the expressions and emotions of others.

In research conducted on a sports booster group, Delaney (1999) examined the role of leisure group participation as community in his research on a sports booster group, the Southern California Browns Backers Association (SCBBA). A large number of the members were recent transplants to Southern California, mostly from Ohio. New to the area, they enjoyed the company of fellow Browns fans while watching Browns football at various viewing sites throughout Southern California. The formation of this new community centered on Browns football, but also provided individuals a chance to bond over a common interest. The viewing sites (bars and restaurants) provided valuable opportunities for bonding and development of camaraderie with one's fellows, which in turn allows for the development of a sense of community. Sixty-two percent of respondents indicated that the SCBBA provided them with a sense of community while 79 percent agreed that the SCBBA helped respondents feel more at home in Southern California (See Table 4.1). Seventy-three percent of the members agreed that they felt as though they were a real part of the group and 98 percent agreed that fellow members were friendly (See Table 4.1). With such strong feelings of friendship within the group, important bonding and camaraderie opportunities exist. Group members were also asked if being able to watch Browns games at the viewing sites had made the relocation to Southern California less stressful. Sixty-five percent agreed and 12 percent strongly agreed. Sixty-nine percent of the members agreed that SCBBA provided them with chances to meet other people who share many of their same interests (See Table 4.1). Thus, joining the leisure-based SCBBA lessens the impact of residential mobility. This is especially important because, as Fischer and Stueve (1977) note, since residential mobility involves disconnection from a place, it can have long-term negative consequences. Thus, if someone moves a great distance from friends and family, a quick way to develop a sense of community (and reconnect) may be through leisure groups. Sports booster groups help to provide a sense of community in a timely manner.

TABLE 4.1. LEISURE GROUP AS COMMUNITY (IN PERCENT [N=506])

Community Variables	Strongly Agree	Agree	Disagree	Strongly Disagree
Community	8	54	35	3
At Home	21	58	16	5
Real Part	13	60	26	1
Members Friendly	31	67	2	0
Relocate	12	53	29	6
Same Interests	19	59	25	6

(This is a revised and original table of data collected by Delaney.)

Variable Key for Table 4.1
Community — SCBBA provides a sense of community
At Home — SCBBA has helped me feel like I'm at home
Real Part — Feel as though I'm a real part of SCBBA

Members Friendly — Groups members that I have met are friendly
Relocate — SCBBA has helped me to make the geographic move less stressful
Same Interests — SCBBA provides chances to meet others who share my same interests

In short, sports booster groups provide people with a social identity, serve as a primary group and bring people together, forming a sense of community. Frey and Dickens (1990) believe that leisure groups often provide the most significant community bond that people may experience. Leisure-based communities have also helped to solidify the vital role of sport as a major social institution.

Sport Heroes

Who is a hero? A hero is usually someone who is admired for his or her achievement, courage, skill, dedication, or integrity. Heroes are recognized for feats of courage or notability of purpose, especially when one has sacrificed his or her own life for the betterment of others. But must one save another's life in order to qualify as a hero? Kirk Gibson is a hero to Dodgers fans. He did not save anyone's life to become a hero. Is someone a hero just because he can hit a dramatic homerun? Should athletes even be considered heroes? Shaquille O'Neal once said that the only hero is a sandwich. Charles Barkley feels that a child's parents should be heroes, not athletes. Perhaps the word "hero" is used too freely in our culture. Just doing the right thing should not qualify someone as a hero, and yet, that is often the case. What if someone's job *is* to save lives (e.g., firefighters and police officers) and they do indeed save a life of another, is this person a hero?

The ancient Greeks, who coined the word, had a precise meaning and limits for "hero." A hero was a person who was descended from a god or goddess on one side of the family, either by father or mother, and from a mortal on the other side. This definition is flawed, as the Greek gods never existed. But there are common themes in the various stories about heroes. Psychologist Otto Rank, in his influential 1909 book *The Myth of the Birth of the Hero,* argued that all cultures have heroic figures who share a similar story: they are fathered by supernatural beings and born to queens or goddesses but the birth is kept hidden; they are raised by either animals or people from a low status; they eventually discover their true origins and finally receive the proper honors due them after engaging in some significant courageous activity.

According to Webster's dictionary, a hero is a mythological or legendary figure endowed with great strength, courage, or ability, and favored by the gods. It also says a hero is a man admired for his achievements and noble qualities and considered in a literary or dramatic work. A heroine is a woman admired for her achievements and qualities, or the leading female character in a literary or dramatic work.

REPRESENTATIVES OF CULTURE

Heroes have existed in society since ancient times. The study of heroes in any given culture is very revealing, as the people proclaimed as heroes gain such a status because they reflect cultural ideals and values. As Leonard (1988) explains, "Cultural heroes or heroic archetypes typically manifest the major value orientations and symbols that a society holds in high regard.... Values provide directives and motivation for action; hence, it is predictable that cultural heroes, individuals who personify such values, become objects of admiration and emulation" (p. 72). Heroes, then, reflect the character traits most desired by members of a society. In this regard, heroes help to reaffirm and maintain the social structure of a society by perpetuating cultural values and norms. As Crepeau (1985) elaborates, "The hero shows us what we ought to be, and we make him a hero because we wish to be what he is. He calls us beyond ourselves, toward the ideal" (p. 76). A hero is someone that we admire. Consequently, heroes are chosen, whether they want to be or not. Conversely, someone cannot claim to be a hero. Such status needs to be conferred by others.

One difficult issue is the role which heroes play in a democratic society. Traditionally, heroes were either godlike figures or members of royalty who rise above the common crowd. How might heroes fit into a society which places emphasis on equality rather than superiority? In his book *The Hero in History,* philosopher Sidney Hook (1943) noted that: "A democratic society has its 'heroes' and 'great men,' too. It is no more exempt from sharp political crisis than other societies, and rarely lacks candidates for the heroic role. It selects them, however, on the basis of its own criteria. Where a democracy is wise, it will wholeheartedly co-operate with its leaders and at the same time be suspicious of the powers delegated to them — a difficult task but one which must be solved if democracy is not to become, as often in the past, a school for tyrants" (p. 14).

Contemporary American society views someone as a hero based on such criteria as achievement, courage and skill. Heroism also involves the ability to overcome extreme adversity, requires dedication and integrity, and involves a willingness to accept responsibility. With these qualities in mind, the authors define a hero as a person of distinguished courage or ability who is admired for brave deeds, noble qualities, achievement, dedication, integrity, or skill. Certainly, many athletes demonstrate these qualities. Sports heroes are admired and idolized figures in American society. The sports hero has become the central role model of young children and has gained enormous adoration from his or her fans. "Hero worship in sport is common and its manifestations are multitudinous.... The nature of the sport hero is the United States has changed throughout the present century and these changes mirror significant alterations in dominant cultural values" (Leonard, 1988: 72). In the first half of the twentieth century sports heroes such as Jack Dempsey, Babe Ruth, Knute Rockne, Joe Louis, Lou Gehrig, and Joe DiMaggio "were all portrayed as embodying various positive qualities of the American character" (Crepeau, 1985: 76). In the years following World War II, most sports heroes were clean-cut, modest, all–American boys like Johnny Unitas of the Baltimore Colts (Carroll, 1999). By the end of the century, flamboyant, brash, and often boastful athletes (e.g., Joe Namath, who played in the NFL from 1965 to 1977, or boxer Muhammad Ali, who became heavyweight champion in 1964 and referred to himself as "the Greatest") became heroes. Many of today's athletes are brash and boastful. They are also fueled by a desire to achieve and be flashy, if possible.

There is a great deal of evidence to support the claim that athletes are among society's leading heroes. Children play video games (e.g., *Madden 2009*) that include their favorite sports stars; sports enthusiasts seek autographs (sometimes to be sold at high prices on eBay); sports fans memorize statistics; read box scores, newspapers and sports features; attend publicity events; visit sport Halls of Fame (e.g., the NFL in Canton, Ohio, and MLB in Cooperstown, New York); fans collect trading cards; and many fans play "fantasy" sports. Fantasy sports are quite fascinating. Fans will draft and trade "players" like real sports owners, belong to a fantasy league where records are kept, and compete against others. It's just a matter of time before someone creates a "Fantasy Hall of Fame"— one that can be visited only in cyberspace!

FUNCTIONS OF HEROES

Sociologically speaking, heroes represent culture and value components. By understanding a country's heroes, one has an idea of what is culturally important in that society. Heroes become representatives or symbols of a given culture. Thus, heroes serve many functions in society.

First, sport heroes help to perform a pattern maintenance function in society. Key beliefs and values such as hard work, achievement and success are essential in society and sport. Sport

Baseball fans head into the National Baseball Hall of Fame and Museum in Cooperstown, N.Y.

heroes are shining examples of these cultural beliefs. They shape our lives with lessons of their fervor and follies, their tragedies and triumphs (Chua-Eoan, 1999). Second, heroes serve as agents of social control. Behaviors of heroes help to control, or at the very least, influence, other members of sport, as well as citizens of a society. Young athletes hear their coaches, parents and teammates say, "Why aren't you more like _____?" This particular person shows up for practice early, doesn't complain, accepts his or her role, and so on. In the film *Rudy*, high school and college teammates of Rudy constantly heard from their respective coaches about the heart and determination of Rudy, despite his overall lack of athletic talent. In this real-life-based story, Rudy served as an agent of social control because the coaches were able to use him as an example of how others should behave. Likewise, in the famous film version of the life of Notre Dame football coach Knute Rockne, Rockne inspires his team to victory by reminding them of their late teammate George Gip (played by future U.S. president Ronald Reagan), whose inspirational words were to "go in there with all they've got and win just one for the Gipper."

A third function of heroes is that they help to provide for social integration. It is often said that sports serve a valuable function to society by helping to bring disparate groups together. At ball games we will see spectators of all ages, races, ethnicities and social classes joined together while cheering for their shared favorite player or team. The social integration function is not limited to fans. In many ways sports was ahead of society in the integration of blacks into mainstream society. Athletes such as Jackie Robinson, Larry Dolby, Jack Johnson, and Jesse Owens helped to change the course of sport and society and helped to shape the future of sports. These athletes are known as "political-social-athletic leaders" (Dorison, 1997). The African American sport hero served as role models for black youth. Guidance from identifiable role models is imperative if the greater culture is to be assimilated.

Jack Johnson (1878–1946) is considered a sports hero because of his efforts to overcome white supremacy by defeating white boxers. Johnson inspired black youth to think that they too could attain success in a white dominated society. Johnson became the heavyweight champion of Negro boxing in the early 1900s. Jim Jeffries, the white champ at the time, refused to fight Johnson. After Jeffries retired, Johnson became heavyweight champion of the world when he defeated Tommy Burns in Australia in 1908. Johnson officially received the title in 1910 after he defeated Jeffries, who came out of retirement. Race rioting was sparked after the Johnson-Jeffries fight. Johnson was clearly a trailblazer in the attempt to integrate sport in the United States. He gave hope to all blacks that they might find an equal place in American society.

The Brooklyn Dodgers broke the color barrier in Major League Baseball by signing Jackie Robinson in 1947. But it was Harold "Pee Wee" Reese, Robinson's teammate, who showed the game and a nation how the integration process would be possible. Reese did this with a simple gesture of purposely putting his arm around Robinson's shoulders while he was enduring a high degree of harassment from Cincinnati Reds fans during a game at Crosley Field early in his career (Smith, 1999). Reese, the Dodgers' captain, endured the wrath of some bigots for his thoughtful embrace, but he became a hero to others by taking a stand against racial injustices. At Reese's funeral (August 18, 1999) Rachel Robinson, widow of Jackie, said that she was not sure whether the integration of baseball would have worked without Reese (Whitmire, 1999).

Serving as a source of identity is a fourth function of heroes. The once popular "Be like Mike" (Jordan) media campaign is an extreme example of heroes serving as a source of identity — the ad flat out said, *Be* like Mike. Athletes often serve as role models for youth. This is especially true among minority or discriminated persons. Former MLB player Roberto Clemente (1934–1972) instilled great hope to young Puerto Ricans. Clemente played for the Pittsburgh Pirates from 1955 to 1972. During the off season, Clemente would travel around his home island of Puerto Rico and conduct baseball clinics as a way of reaching out to youngsters. He spoke about the importance of sports, the importance of being a good citizen, and the importance of respecting parents (Feldman, 1993). The economically poor Puerto Ricans were able to identify with Clemente because he was one of them.

Some athletes become heroes at a regional level. They have a "cult-like" following in their own communities; they are what we would call heroes of community association. The New York Yankees have a cult following for Derek Jeter; Boston Red Sox fans with Manny Ramirez, and so on. NASCAR fans have a cult following for Dale Earnhardt, Jr. Fans that share an admiration for a particular sport hero form a sense of community based on this hero "worship. "

CATEGORIES OF HEROES

There are a number of categories of heroes. We will briefly review some of the more common types. Perhaps the most identifiable category of sports hero is the winner. This type of hero is determined by outcome assessment — did he or she win a championship or individual honor of achievement? If yes, this athlete is winner. The emphasis is on outcome and not the processes that were involved to achieve such a winning performance. Some athletes are not always the most graceful while performing, or they may appear not to be the most physically talented, and yet, they find a way to win. Generally, such heroes become winners because of good old-fashioned hard work and dedication. Eli Manning, Peyton Manning and Robert Horry are examples of this type of hero. Not all winners are necessarily heroes, however. Baseball legend Ty Cobb, for instance, was one of the greatest players in the history of the game, but it is usually noted that he was also violent, ungracious to other players and a bigot, and his own teammates often refused to associate with him.

Skilled performers are a second category of heroes. These athletes do possess exceptional skill. They give off an aura of invincibility and have usually psyched out the opposition by their mere presence. Michael Jordan, Kobe Bryant, Tiger Woods, Roger Federer, Mohammed Ali, and

Annika Sorenstam are examples of skilled performers. The skilled performers generally rise to the occasion of key events and big games. They are show persons for their sport and shine before an audience. As Dick Vitale, an ESPN men's college basketball analyst, is known to say about exceptional athletes, "He's a prime-time player." Most fans prefer the "skilled performer" over "winners" because they love the dramatic, theatrical play; the long touchdown pass versus the 9-minute drive, the winning home run in the bottom of the 9th inning, or a winning putt on the 18th green.

The hero of social acceptability, a third category, is admired because he or she upholds the values of society. Through their efforts on the playing field these athletes instill and uphold such beliefs as good sportsmanship and dedication. The hero of social acceptability often transcends the sport they participate in. Jesse Owens, at the 1936 Berlin Olympics, not only shattered Adolf Hitler's delusional concept of Aryan superiority, he helped to unite whites and blacks in the United States. All Americans cheered for Owens because of his athletic prowess and his virtues. Heroes of social acceptability demonstrate great character and become excellent role models. Athletes that overcome personal tragedies and hardships and still perform admirably are especially admired. It is easier to relate to an athlete who seems as "human" as we are; they have some of the same problems as non-athletes and still find a way to perform.

Lance Armstrong is an excellent example of this type of hero. Having successfully won his battle against life-threatening testicular cancer that had spread to his lungs, abdomen, and brain, Armstrong went on to win an unprecedented 7 straight Tour de France bicycle races. Since most of us know someone who has died from cancer it is refreshing to hear of stories like Armstrong's because it gives hope to us all. (However, allegations that he might have taken performance-enhancing drugs have, at least for some people, tarnished Armstrong's heroic image.) Soccer great Pelé is another example — he has been declared the "football ambassador to the world" by the FIFA, the international football association. Baseball great Cal Ripken, Jr. (discussed in Chapter 6) is also a socially acceptable exemplar.

The group servant, similar to a martyr, represents a fourth category of hero. The group servant is willing to put the needs of the team above individual needs, wants and desires. The group servant wants to do what is best for the team even if it means sacrificing individual statistics. This type of behavior is rare in professional team sports today, although there are occasions where athletes are willing to restructure their salaries in order to free up "cap space" (a professional sport's league "ceiling" limit on team salaries) to sign other players. Tim Duncan of the San Antonio Spurs (NBA) is an example of a group servant. He sacrificed his own numbers early in his career while David Robinson was still on the team, and continues to do so with new stars like Manu Ginobili, and through it all, he continues to win NBA championships. Pat Tillman (former NFL player with the Arizona Cardinals) is an example of a group servant, for he gave up his own career, and ultimately his life, to serve the U.S. Army team, and thus, all of the United States. This is one of many reasons why a large number of Americans consider Tillman a hero. Other examples include gymnast Kerri Strug and Daniel "Rudy" Ruettinger, whose dream to play in a Notre Dame football game was depicted in the beloved 1993 film *Rudy*.

Most people will not take great risks in their everyday lives; they do however, admire the risk takers. The risk taker category of hero is reserved for athletes who are inclined to place themselves in peril — and thus, become the object of fans' affection. Risk takers are found in most sports, especially in contact sports. For example, in football, a wide receiver who is willing to run a pattern across the middle of the field; in baseball, a catcher who will dive into the opponent's dugout for foul ball; and in basketball, a player who will drive the middle of the paint. Athletes who thrive on the action and danger of the game they play are risk takers. They give their all and they have no fear. Many extreme sport athletes are risk takers. Danny Way is a perfect example of a risk taker. Is there any wonder why he has become so popular? He fears no injury and he continues to raise the bar on the risky behavior. Evel Knievel, the famous daredevil, made a living on taking risks. Jackie Robinson took a huge risk (especially in terms of the abuse he would take from fans) when he signed with the Brooklyn Dodgers. Race car drivers and down-hill skiers are also examples of risk taking heroes.

A sixth category of hero is the reluctant hero. The reluctant hero would rather lead by example (on the playing field) than by trying to motivate teammates with an inspiring speech, pep talk, or some other indirect method of leadership. These athletes are usually unselfish and assuming. They may, in fact, be shy individuals. Marvin Harrison, Dwayne Wade, and Tim Duncan are examples of reluctant heroes. Tom Brady, quarterback of the New England Patriots, is a relatively quiet and unassuming person and yet he has led his team to three Super Bowl victories. Baseball great Lou Gehrig, the "iron man" and "the Pride of the Yankees," was also known for his quiet competence and dedication to the game.

The charismatic hero represents a seventh category. The charismatic hero is "viewed as exceptional, autonomous and unique, as endowed with super-human powers, and commanding a divine violence.... The triumphant moment of charisma is the moment of effervescence on the part of the community of followers. They hail, cheer, cry and try desperately to touch or be close to the heroes" (Giesen, 2005: 276–277). The charismatic sports hero possesses unique qualities that distinguish him or her from the rest of the group. This person need not be the most talented on the team, but is likely to be the team captain, or clubhouse leader. Thus, any team leader that is not necessarily the most talented would serve as an example. Derek Jeter and Shaquille O'Neal are specific examples of charismatic heroes.

Perhaps the most fascinating category of hero is the anti-hero. What makes the anti-hero such an enigma is the fact that he or she does not demonstrate the desired values or norms of society and yet still possesses a fan following. Traditionally, heroes have been noted for outstanding achievements, bravery, nobility of actions, moral and intellectual qualities, or some other contribution to society that has improved the quality of life for others. But hero identification is specific rather than diffused, and in most instances the hero is not a model of behavior in other spheres of social life. The anti-hero is the opposite of the group servant. The anti-hero thinks of him or herself first and the team second. The anti-hero is "someone who says that he does not need other people" (Crepeau, 1985: 77).

Terrell Owens, wide receiver for the Dallas Cowboys, has a long history of acting unprofessionally and fighting with teammates and ownership (he was kicked off the Philadelphia Eagles, leading to his trade to Dallas). And yet, Owens still has his fans. He is after all, an excellent receiver; but he is not a "team player" and does not care how his immature behavior affects others— he is the anti-hero. Former Chicago Bulls player Dennis Rodman was noted for his bizarre behavior, including multiple body-piercings, numerous tattoos, and unprofessional conduct. Yet this "bad boy" of basketball was a hero to many people because of his insubordination and colorful antics. There is a seemingly growing list of anti-heroes in contemporary sports, including Alex Rodriguez, Kobe Bryant, Barry Bonds, Bode Miller, Kyle Busch, Jason Giambi, Randy Moss, Pedro Martinez, and Allen Iverson. Past anti-heroes include Pete Rose, Billy Martin, John McEnroe, and Tonya Harding.

Heroes Survey Data

In 2005, Delaney and Madigan replicated earlier research conducted by Delaney (1999) on college students and whether they have heroes. Students were asked whether they had a sports hero when they were younger and if they had one currently. Respondents were also asked whether they presently have a hero of any kind, other than a family member or religious figure. In addition, students were asked whether or not they believe that there are as many heroes in this country today as in the past.

The data in Table 4.2 reveals that a higher percentage of males report having had a hero when they were young compared to females in each of the three sample years. In the 1999 and 2005 sample years a significant change occurred among females; specifically, they no longer report (as in 1994) that they had a sports hero in childhood.

TABLE 4.2. DID YOU HAVE A SPORTS HERO IN CHILDHOOD?
IN PERCENT. 1994 N=199 (82 MALES, 117 FEMALES); 1999 N= 201 (97 MALES, 104 FEMALES); 2005 N=239 (110 MALES, 129 FEMALES)

	1994		1999		2005	
	Yes	No	Yes	No	Yes	No
Males	79	21	64	36	69	31
Females	62	38	36	64	35	65

As people age, they are more likely not to view sport athletes as heroes. The data in Table 4.3 reveals that the percentage of respondents, both males and females, who report currently having a sports heroes drops considerably compared to childhood. In each of the sample years the pattern holds true that males still are more likely to report having a sports hero than are females.

Respondents were also asked to indicate who their sport hero was, if they had one. The list of all these different athletes is not provided here, but a startling and sociologically significant pattern, first noted in 1999, has continued in 2005 — 100 percent of all male respondents who indicated having a hero named a male hero. In contrast, only 50 percent of females in the 1994 study had a same-sex hero. In 1999, this figure rose only slightly to 53 percent. Consequently, not a single male reported having a female hero, while one-half of females had males for a sport hero. Delaney (1999) had anticipated that the number of women who report having a female sports hero would increase throughout the 2000s with the continued growth of girls and women's sports. The 2005 results were surprising, as only 40 percent of reporting females identified a female as there sports hero. Among the questions raised by this data are: do males really not see females as hero-material, or are they worried about a possible negative label from male cohorts if they identify with a female as a sports hero? Further, why do so many females report male athletes as heroes? Continued research in this area is warranted.

TABLE 4.3. DO YOU HAVE A SPORTS HERO CURRENTLY?
IN PERCENT. 1994 N= 199 (82 MALES, 117 FEMALES); 1999 N= 201 (97 MALES, 104 FEMALES); 2005 N=239 (110 MALES, 129 FEMALES)

	1994		1999		2005	
	Yes	No	Yes	No	Yes	No
Males	54	46	35	65	40	60
Females	38	62	14	85	24	76

The data in Table 4.4 indicates that a growing number of people report currently having a non-sports hero. The authors speculate that since the events of September 11, 2001, there is a groundswell of support for people who act admirably in the light of terrorist events.

TABLE 4.4. DO YOU CURRENTLY HAVE A HERO
(OTHER THAN A FAMILY MEMBER OR RELIGIOUS LEADER)?
IN PERCENT. 1999 N= 201; 2005 N= 239

	Yes	No
1999	24	76
2005	51	49

Respondents were asked whether they believe people have as many heroes in this country today as in the past. The data in Table 4.5 reveals a growing percentage of people believe we have as many heroes today, as compared to data for 1999. However, a vast majority of people still believe that there were more heroes in the past than today.

TABLE 4.5. DO WE HAVE AS MANY HEROES TODAY AS IN THE PAST?
IN PERCENT. 1999 N= 201; 2005 N=239

	Yes	No
1999	30	70
2005	41	59

It is ironic that Americans are quick to bestow the label "hero" so often, especially on athletes, and yet most Americans report that they themselves do not have heroes. Why is this the case? The answer can be found in the demise of the hero.

THE DEMISE OF THE SPORTS HERO

Heroes have existed for a long time. Flattering stories and generous embellishment of the facts over any given period of time eases the accession of mortal beings to hero status. Often, these tales of accomplishments were unchallenged, further enhancing heroes to legendary proportions. Heroic behaviors in one sphere of life were assumed to carry over to all other spheres as well. When a person displayed an admirable trait in one field, it was assumed (or ignored) that this person must demonstrate the same qualities consistently in all endeavors. Newspaper writers wrote heroic stories of such icons as Babe Ruth and Mickey Mantle, leaving their personal shortcomings out of print and away from the public's knowledge. Mickey Mantle, for example, admitted in 1985, years after his retirement, that most players can look back on their career and say that they gave it their best; he could not do that. He admitted that he never worked out or trained as he should have. He went boozing regularly. The general public was unaware of this. Mantle was a hero for many kids growing up in the 1960s. The truth was revealed in 2005, in a HBO 60-minute presentation on Mickey Mantle, titled *Mantle*. Bob Costas stated, "On the ball field there was something very dignified and heroic about the way he carried himself. But Mickey's life overall was not always a study of dignity" (Poliquin, 2005).

Today's heroes (in all fields) no longer receive star treatment. If a player is out "hitting the town" it will make the newspapers. No athlete is immune from media coverage and the sports hero (or any other type of hero) no longer holds the mythical status once enjoyed. We know about the private aspects of public persons, and consequently they do not stand apart from us anymore. Thus, the media have had a tremendous impact on the demise of the hero. On the one hand they help to create an image of a sports star as some type of larger-than-life character that we should admire because of their athletic ability; on the other hand, the media cannot wait to air dirty laundry capable of crushing the once positive image they created of an athlete for their audience's consumption. Sport stars are treated like any other celebrity, a life to be consumed. As a result, many athletes see themselves as celebrities that need to entertain the public. And while athletes want to be celebrities, celebrities want to be athletes. ESPN found a way to combine them both with their annual production of the ESPYs. This award ceremony combines celebrities—who hand out the awards—with athletes. It seems that each group wishes to be the other!

The study of a society's heroes is indeed quite revealing, as the attributes possessed by a hero reflect the values and norms of the greater culture. We often judge a society by the individuals it holds up as its own exemplars, so learning about those individuals granted heroic status by their own fellow citizens can be highly educating and a cause for further reflection.

SUMMARY

Sport has a tremendous impact on culture. Culture provides people with a "script" for what is acceptable behavior, and puts order into our lives. Sports usually have tangible elements such as uniforms, stadiums and equipment, as well as nonmaterial elements such as attachment to locations, values of fair play, and preferences for specific teams. In addition, symbols are used to represent meanings within a society.

Cultures can vary a great deal, and such differences are often reflected in sport. For instance, cultural values, such as fair play or competitiveness, can be reflected in a country's most popular sports, such as soccer or baseball. Subcultures are groups within a culture who share beliefs and behaviors which distinguish them from the larger society. They do so through the use of clothing, mannerisms, and language. Many sports are a type of subculture, such as surfing, which is specific to certain geographical areas.

A community is a group of people who organize together for a common purpose and form a network of social relationships. Traditionally, communities had the same physical location, but this has changed in recent times. There are many ways in which sport can unite a community—through both active participation and passive support. Such identification with a team can provide a healthy diversion from mundane reality and a sense of identification with the larger group. Sport can also divide communities, particularly when athletes and owners do not seem to have the interests of the community itself as their primary concern.

Sports fans generally have a strong emotional attachment toward their team. This can help them to feel as though they are a part of a group or community. One way to do this is through participation in a sport booster group. Such identification with a sport can reaffirm the fan's established values and beliefs and provide for identity enhancement. It can also allow individuals to express loyalty, commitment and emotional ties, which leads to group cohesiveness. Athletes also experience deep emotional highs and lows, especially when they are treated as heroes or ostracized by the general society.

Heroes were once thought to be semi-divine, and they still have a legendary status in societies. Such criteria as achievement, courage, dedication, integrity, and responsibility are admired by most societies, and athletes often demonstrate these qualities. There is a great deal of evidence to show that, whether they wish it or not, athletes are among societies' leading heroes. However, the media has had a tremendous impact on the demise of the hero in today's society, and the mythical status of sports heroes is no longer so evident.

KEY TERMS

Consumer Culture Using consumer goods to express cultural categories and principles, cultivate ideals, create and sustain lifestyles, construct notions of the self, and create (and survive) social change.

Culture The shared knowledge, values, language, norms, and behavioral patterns of a given society that are handed down from one generation to the next and form a way of life for its members.

Diversity of Culture The result of each society's adaptation to their specific natural environments (e.g., climate and geography) and a number of traditional customs, habits, values and norms that develop over time to form a way of life for people.

Ethnocentrism The tendency for members of a society to use their culture's norms and values as standards for judging other cultures.

Hero Someone who is admired for his or her achievement, courage, skill, dedication, or integrity.

Heterogeneous Societies Consist of people who are dissimilar in regard to social characteristics such as religion, race, ethnicity, politics, and economic backgrounds.

Homogeneous Societies Consist of people who share a common culture and are generally from similar social, religious, political and economic backgrounds.

Language A set of symbols that can be strung together in an infinite number of ways that expresses ideas and abstract thoughts and enables people to think and communicate with one another.

Material Culture The physical, tangible creations of a society, such as clothing, merchandise, football stadiums, sporting equipment, automobiles, and art.

Nonmaterial Culture The more abstract creations of society, such as beliefs, values, ideology, and norms.

Social Norms The rules that govern behavior.

Society A group of people who interact with one another as members of a collectivity within a defined boundary. A society also consists of a number of highly structured systems of human organization and this organized system helps to form the social structure of society.

Subculture A distinctive group within a greater culture that possesses its own cultural values, behavioral patterns, and other traits distinctive enough to distinguish it from the dominant group.

Symbols Items that represent something else by association, resemblance, or convention to a people in a society.

DISCUSSION QUESTIONS

• How do sports figures mirror the values of a given society?

• What are some of the differences between material and nonmaterial cultures? Think of some examples relating to a specific sports team — what would be the material and nonmaterial aspects of the team?

• What role do symbols play in helping people identify with a sports team?

• Come up with some examples of sports subcultures and list various types of argot and behaviors they use to separate themselves from the larger culture.

• List some recent examples where sport has helped to unify a community, and where it has divided a community.

• Why are franchises important to communities? Do you agree with Mike Lupica's suggestions for ways in which communities can protect a franchise from relocating?

• Do you think that athletes should be "heroes" in modern-day societies? What do you think are the characteristics of a hero?

• Why are so many "anti-heroes" in sports admired by the general public?

CHAPTER 5

Socialization and Sport

A father is telling a story to his young children about his favorite football player, and hero, Joe Montana. As he tells of the legendary passing skills of Montana the father becomes increasingly excited reminiscing about past glory. His enthusiasm is contagious. The children eagerly pry their father for more details, as if listening to a favorite bedtime story. The heroic tale told by the father will influence his children for some time. As they grow older, whenever these children hear the name "Joe Montana" they will think of him as a hero based primarily on the testimony of their father. Soon, these youth will search for their own "bigger than life" person to admire, just as their father did.

Many students reading this text have heard of Joe Montana and know him as a former great NFL quarterback. And yet, it is unlikely that most of you remember seeing him play. Still, despite never having seen Joe Montana, most young 49ers fans admire him as a hero. This is also true for football fans (and fans of all sports) across the country. Thus, young San Diego Chargers fans admire LaDainian Tomlinson, Indianapolis Colts fans admire Peyton Manning, and young Philadelphia Eagles fans idolize Donovan McNabb.

Admiring athletes as heroes represents an example of how the socialization process can influence people. Sociologists firmly believe that nearly all human behaviors are learned through the socialization process. It is through the socialization process that individuals learn cultural norms, values, beliefs and social expectations. As with all spheres of life, socialization plays an important role in the sports world. Sports are not just physical activities and games; they serve as focal points for the formation of social worlds. Social worlds consist of group members who share a subcultural perspective and are held together through interaction and communication. In order to fit into a social world, group members will adjust their behavior and mindsets to revolve around a particular set of activities. Social worlds are like reference groups, they provide us with a certain perspective on social matters (Shibutani, 1955). People are socialized into sport worlds by the agents of socialization.

The Socialization Process

Despite the focus on early childhood development, socialization is actually a life-long (from infancy to old age) process of learning. Socialization is defined as a continuing process of social development and learning that occurs as individuals interact with one another and learn about society's expectations of proper behavior so that they can participate and function within their societies. At the micro level, the socialization process also enables an individual an opportunity to acquire a personal identity wherein he or she learns the norms, values, behavioral expectations, and social skills appropriate to his or her social position. Thus, an athlete is expected to conform to certain expectations that correspond to her role, just as a coach is expected to conform to specific expectations attached to his role.

Every person we come in contact with, either directly (face-to-face) or indirectly (e.g., via a media portrayal), has influence over our behavior. However, socialization is most effective when enforced by significant others—family, peer groups, schools, the media, and so on. We learn *directly* from others who inform us about expectations of proper behavior and how to survive life's many obstacles, and we learn *indirectly* by observing others. It is through the socialization process that each of us (ideally) learns how to conform to society's norms and values.

At the macro level, socialization is critical for the survival and stability of society, as it is critical that members of a society are socialized to support and maintain the existing social structure. Furthermore, it is through the socialization process that members of a society learn about culture. Thus, just as children learn about culture from their parents (or other primary caregivers), these same children will some day grow up to become adults who must teach the next generation. In this manner, culture reproduces itself.

It should be noted that in some cultures, the socialization process may encourage people to make necessary changes in the social structure for the betterment of society or disadvantaged persons. For example, at one time African Americans were not allowed to play professional sports (see chapter 11). Eventually, enlightened individuals decided to challenge policies that discriminated against minorities. It was the socialization process that changed previously held norms of behavior.

Whether we are talking about accepting old customs, values and norms or new ones, the effectiveness of the socialization process is predicated by the need for individuals to internalize the messages being sent to them. Messages become internalized when people react automatically to certain stimuli. For example, when teaching the fundamentals of running the bases in baseball, young (or new) players are taught that they must "tag" before advancing from one base to the next when there is one "out" or no "outs." Players are also taught that when there are two outs they run as soon as the ball is hit into play. Before long, players do not need to be reminded of such fundamentals because they have internalized the norms of base running. This is why it is so frustrating to others when an experienced player forgets (or makes a mental error) how many outs there are and runs on an infield pop-up only to be tagged out.

Nature or Nurture?

How does the socialization process work? That is, are we born (the nature perspective) with the knowledge of a culture's norms and values? If this were true, there would be no need for a learning process, as a society's social expectations would be innate. Or, must we learn (the nurture perspective) about the demands and expectations of society? Clearly, sociologists lean heavily toward nurture. While it is true that biology dictates a number of physical attributes of an individual (e.g., skin color, hair color, eye color, ancestry) and plays a role as to whether or not an individual is mentally capable of learning, it does not dictate behavior. The nurture perspective states that socialization, experience, modeling, and motives— in short, the environment — determines human behavior. Sociologists argue that humans are free to make their own decisions and therefore our behavior is not predetermined by biology.

If a child sees their best way to get ahead in the world is via sports, for example, they will pursue sports as a possible career. Conversely, no one is born an athlete; one becomes an athlete. All athletes, even Michael Jordan (who was once cut from his high school basketball team), rely on individual effort, and not some natural biological or genetic predisposition to play ball. "The notion of a natural or 'born' athlete is misleading because it belies the fact that individuals must learn a host of social, psychological, and kinetic movements associated with a particular activity. Typically, an individual is referred to as a 'natural' if he or she possesses the 'tools' or motor skills (i.e., coordination, agility, speed, strength, power, and stamina) enabling one to perform sport feats with relative ease" (Leonard, 1988: 112). Clearly, possessing certain physical attributes (e.g., in basketball, having significant height and large hands to palm a ball) are important, but so too are socio-psychological skills such as desire, opportunity, coaching and encouragement, to mention just a few. Being tall is not much of an asset in basketball if the individual is not willing to run up and down the court to play ball. (The topic of genetics will be discussed in further detail in Chapter 11.)

PRIMARY AND SECONDARY GROUPS

What if someone tells you, "I am very disappointed in your behavior?" Does such a statement bother you more if expressed by someone close, like a parent, sibling, significant other, or best friend, or if it is expressed by a complete stranger? Most of us are more concerned about the sentiments and opinions of someone close rather than someone who hardly knows us. This is because the people closest to us are supposed to know us the best. The people closest to us are known as primary groups. Because primary groups have the greatest effect on us, socialization is most effective when taught by primary groups. A primary group may be defined as a relatively small group of people with whom members share a sense of "we-ness," intimacy, and mutual identification.

Charles Cooley (1909), an early symbolic interactionist, described primary groups as "those characterized by intimate face-to-face association and cooperation.... The result of intimate association, psychologically, is a certain fusion of individualities in a common whole, so that one's very self, for many purposes at least, is the common life and purpose of the group" (p. 23). It is the face-to-face association between group members and the high degree of intimacy (especially when compared to non-primary individuals) that leads to a sense of "we-ness." Every one of us uses various expressions with "we" in it. For example, "We went to the game last night;" "We won our game today;" or "We wished my brother a happy birthday." Think about how many times you have used the word "we" in a conversation as a means of identifying yourself with a group of significant others. Chances are it is far more common than you might suspect.

As of point of clarification, Cooley (1909) highlighted five fundamental properties of a primary group: face-to-face association, unspecified nature of associations, relative permanence, a small number of persons involved, and relative intimacy of participants. As social beings, humans are prone toward forming groups. For most of us, the first primary group in our lives is our family. As a child grows older, she will seek friends of her same age (peers) in an attempt to form a bond of friendship. Ideally, individuals will also learn to form a number of other relationships that involves forming a bond with their school, neighborhood, community, and eventually, with society as a whole.

Cooley also acknowledged that individuals often have interactions with others that are, more or less, impersonal. That is, we associate with a number of people on a fairly regular basis but our relationships are not very deep. For example, many of us shop at a favorite grocery store and see the same clerks time and time again. We say hello to each other, but other than that, we do not spend any time with each other. Most of us do not know our postal carrier on a personal basis, and yet, he or she comes to our homes six times a week. As a result, of the impersonal nature of secondary relationships we can define a secondary group as a collectivity whose members interact with one another in a relatively formal and impersonal manner.

AGENTS OF SOCIALIZATION

A sports team may be viewed as a primary group because it consists of a number of significant others. This is one reason why athletes generally value the opinions of teammates, coaches and other team-related personnel. Symbolic interactionist George Herbert Mead used the term significant others to refer to those who play a major role in shaping a person's sense of self. Significant others may also be viewed as agents of socialization. In brief, agents of socialization are sources of culture. They are the people, groups or institutions that teach us what we need to know in order to function properly in society. The most important agents of socialization for any individual are the ones that are most highly revered and trusted.

The agents of socialization include:

1. *Parents and families.* They provide the early preparation for life; primary socialization. The role of parents and the family will be explored in Chapter 6 with our discussion of youth sports.
2. *Schools (and day care).* Parental influence usually declines as the child progresses through school. This period marks the beginning of the secondary socialization process.
3. *Peer groups.* Friends of about the same age. The opinions, values and norms of peers are especially significant to school-age children.
4. *The mass media.* The media includes television, radio, magazines, motion pictures, video games, Internet, and the like. There is a great debate as to the role of media in society (see Chapter 15). In short, the influence of the media is very powerful for some, less so for others.
5. *Religion.* The importance of religion varies a great deal from one individual to another. Many athletes attribute their success to a divine source, while others attribute success to hard work, determination, and sometimes, luck. (See Chapter 14 for a review on the relationship between sports and religion.)
6. *Employment.* Many people's lives are dictated by their work environment; it either hampers or allows for opportunities for individuals to pursue sports and leisure activities.
7. *The government.* The type of socio-political structure found in a society will have a great deal of influence on individuals and the sports world. (See Chapter 13 for a further discussion.)

These are the primary examples of the agents of socialization. They impact individuals in varying degrees, but collectively, the agents of socialization are responsible for the transmission of culture from one generation to the next.

Development of Self

Although the socialization process continues throughout one's lifetime, early childhood is a critical time in the initial development of self. Consequently, primary group participation is very important for children. It is within the primary group that children develop a sense of self. "The self develops in a group context, and the group that Cooley called the primary group is the real seat of self-development" (Reynolds, 1993: 36). The development of self is the result of a number of interactions with others over a period of time in a variety of social and cultural contexts.

Throughout time people have derived much of their identity and sense of self from groups to which they have membership. Identity involves those aspects of one's life that are deemed as essential to the character and maintenance of self. A sense of self, which develops in a social group context, provides an individual with an identity. Thus, individual identities are socially constructed. Correspondingly, if such an identity is to sustain, it must be worked on and maintained in a group context (Berger, 1963). For example, someone may claim an identity as the team captain, but that identity can only be sustained in the context of a group (team) setting. As individuals come to see themselves by a particular identity they must meet the expectations of that role (e.g., the team captain must take on a leadership role and be an exemplar of expected behavior). Loy and Ingham (1981) elaborate: "As the individual takes a position (status) in a group, he learns to define himself in response to the expectations which the group has of a person occupying that status. That is, the person attempts to introject a group-defined identity into his own identity. The more congruent the projected self is with the group-defined self, the more social sustenance (reinforcement) one expects. Once having established one's claim to an identity, one works to preserve it, and if possible to enhance it" (p. 190).

While engaging others, individuals attempt to present themselves according to their identity constructs. "The 'self label' is an identity that one presents to others in an attempt to manage their impression of him or her" (Delaney, 2005: 122). Individuals are secure in their identities for as long as they interact within their primary group. As college freshmen learn, the identities held in high school do not necessarily remain attached in college. The "big man" on campus in high school, who once basked in all the glory that comes with that identity, finds himself a mere freshman in college where people are rarely impressed with high school achievements. Athletes that dominated in high school sports are often shocked by the decreased identity they possess in college. Whenever someone joins a new group they encounter new people who come to define them with a new identity. Modifications to self-identity are often necessary with new involvements. The individual must know how to adjust his or her role to meet the new group's requirements.

In team sports it is critical for everyone to play their role and accept the responsibilities that come with that role. The new person to the group will be accepted as long as they perform their role up to preconceived expectations.

Acceptance into the group is also dependent upon the actor's willingness to take on and internalize the communicated values and norms of the group. In turn, it is the responsibility of the group to socialize the neophyte within the idealized ideology. When the individual shares the perspective of a reference group, she has, in Mead's (1934) terms, taken on the attitudes of the generalized other (the community). At this stage of development the individual not only identifies with significant others (specific people) but also with the attitudes of the group or community as a whole. The generalized other is not a person; instead, it is a person's conscious awareness of the society that he or she is a part of. The ability to adopt the attitude of the reference group is what allows for diverse and unique persons to share a sense of community.

Thus, every team is composed of individuals who maintain their own sense of individuality while working cooperatively as a functioning whole. In a team context, any individual member has the power to disrupt the functioning operation of the whole by inappropriate conduct. Thus, the group influences the development of individual self and, individuals influence the group. For example, when a college football player wins the Heisman Memorial Trophy (considered the most prestigious award in American college football, awarded annually to the top NCAA football player of the year), the whole team benefits because of the prestige involved and the fact that football is a sport where individual achievement is accomplished only through teamwork.

Sports Identity

Participation in sport is generally recognized as a positive endeavor for at least two crucial reasons: sports provide valuable opportunities to develop physical skills, competency and proper conditioning, and sports are a powerful socializing agent that promotes the values and norms of the prevailing culture. Because of the cultural importance of sport in society, many people have their identities directly, or indirectly, tied to sports. Sport participants have a generic identity as an athlete. Within the athlete identity label are a number of subcategories based on such criteria as success (elite versus marginal); professional status (amateur or paid professional); team sport or individual sport; team leader (or captain) or backup player; and so on. Clearly, an elite athlete has a higher status than a marginal athlete. Non-athletes with a sports identity include sport consumers and sport producers.

An elite athlete is someone who has reached a top performance level of competition. Most elite athletes begin their sports involvement at an early age and generally enjoy success in their chosen sport. Elite athletes generally have a strong support system from significant others. As Kenyon and McPherson (1981) explain, "The elite athlete emerges from an environment which was highly supportive; that is, he was exposed from an early age to an abundant opportunity set (middle-class values and ample facilities, equipment, and leadership) and much encouragement, reward, and reinforcement from a variety of meaningful others" (p. 234). A team leader or team captain enjoys an elevated sense of self, as generally these labels are bestowed upon individuals because they have displayed character traits deemed most desirable in a team context. Team captains lead by example. They are especially significant to younger team members who look up to and admire team leaders. Possessing an identity such as an elite athlete or team leader comes with great responsibility and a conscious effort by such individuals to maintain such a status.

The effects of sports on self-identity and self-image are not fully understood. However, we know that boys learn at an early age that masculinity is related to achievement in sports and the more successful a boy is in sports, the more masculine he appears and the more likely he will be accepted by his peers. Furthermore, all boys are judged according to their ability, or lack of ability, in competitive sports. Because they equate a positive sense of self through becoming a successful athlete, boys learn to develop instrumental relationships—those based on pragmatic principles that assist individuals in their pursuit of goals (Messner 2002). Understandably, young males who are successful in sports benefit from such an identity. Boys who are not good at sports, or shun sports, will have to find another way to attain an identity. Some find identities through becoming waterboys, scouts or other related roles connected with sports while not actually involved in active participation. Considering how important sports are for boys, alternative identities seldom have the same level of status as that of an athlete.

Research on the effects of sports on girls is not as extensive as it is with boys. (The effects of sport participation on female sense of self will be examined in Chapter 10.) As more girls and women participate in sport, it would stand to reason that females will also benefit from a sports identity. For instance, a popular photo exhibit called "Game Face: What Does a Female Athlete Look Like?" opened in the Smithsonian Institution's Arts and Industry Building in 2001 to celebrate the increasing role of women in sport. It focused on the revision of beliefs about womanly and feminine behavior, and the positive ways in which women use athletics to enhance their sense of self.

The sport consumer (anyone who purchases sport-related products, including game tickets and sports merchandize) is an identity embraced by millions, and thus, far outnumbers the athlete as a sports identity. The pervasive nature of group identification has shown that sport consumers identify not only with teams but often with the institutions represented by the teams they support. In fact, fans who maintain high levels of identification with a sports team also show feelings of bonding with other fans of that same team (Wann and Branscombe, 1993). Research indicates that discriminating between groups can increase self-esteem (Lemyre and Smith, 1985; Oakes and Turner, 1980). As a result, sport consumers who have formed an identity by pledging an allegiance to one team (an in-group) view fans of another team (an out-group) as rivals. (Rival teams are also viewed as out-groups.) As described earlier, identity involves those aspects of one's life that are deemed necessary to the character and maintenance of self. For many sport consumers a fan identity to a particular team or favorite athlete is in fact deemed as a critical identifier of self.

Agents of Sport Socialization

Why is it that some people love sports and others ignore them completely? How is it possible within the same home environment that siblings do not share the same passionate level for sports, and why don't they always cheer for the same teams? Socialization, life experiences, opportunities and individual motives are among the explanations to these complicated questions.

American society provides ample opportunities for youth sport participation. Most schools have sports programs, a number of community centers provide safe venues for those interested in sport, and organized youth leagues such as Little League and Pop Warner Football abound throughout the United States. Children form informal playgroups in their neighborhoods and engage in sports. In short, if a child is motivated enough, there are plenty of sporting options available in every community.

Not every child is motivated to play sports. Some children played sports, had initial bad experiences and never returned to the sports world. Others never were interested in playing sports, and did so only under duress. As Turner (2006) explains, we need motives to occupy positions in life. We need to be energized to play certain roles in life. Some people simply never possessed a motive or desire to play sports when they were young. The motivation for sports participation is affected by a number of variables, including:

1. *Individual ability.* Possessing skill in a sport is a prime motivator to continue participation. Youth who lack skill in certain sports (or all sports) are less motivated to play when compared to those who demonstrate sporting skills.
2. *The availability of opportunities to play sports.* Sports programs and teams must be available for youth to try out. Unfortunately, many school districts face budget constraints that sometimes lead to the elimination of sport programs. Geography plays an important role as well. For example, youth in Los Angeles have far more opportunities to surf than youth in Montana do.
3. *Socioeconomic factors.* A number of sports (e.g., club hockey, polo, tennis, and golf) are too expensive to participate in and thus limit participation. On the other hand, other sports (e.g., soccer and basketball) are less expensive to play and therefore are accessible to youth of all socio-economic backgrounds.
4. *The influence of family and friends.* Youths who are encouraged to play sports and who are positively reinforced for their efforts by friends and family are more likely to start and continue their sport participation.
5. *The prestige and power of the socializing agents.* Possessing a sports identity is a great motivator for youth and provides them with an edge in the social world. Conversely, when sport participation loses its appeal, the prestige attached also decreases.

Individual motivation toward sport participation, or away from it, is greatly influenced by the agents of socialization. While the agents of socialization prepare individuals "for many roles in life that have little or nothing to do with sport, they also play a significant part in the individual's sport socialization" (Vogler and Schwartz, 1993: 15).

THE FAMILY AND SPORT

It should not come as a surprise that parents, as the primary agent of socialization, especially the father, and other immediate family members have the greatest impact on a child's socialization into sport. As Phillips (1993) states, "Children are more interested in sports when they receive encouragement from parents" (p. 86). Nearly all parents engage in ball playing with infants as a means of developing coordination, balance and basic motor skills. Rolling a ball to a baby and encouraging active participation in such an activity provides the child its first introduction into sport. It is also a non-threatening and fun way of developing a bond between a guardian and child. American boys are almost always encouraged to play catch or bat a baseball. Sports equipment (e.g., ball, glove) is a common gift for a newborn baby boy. Messner's (2002) research on male former athletes revealed that their earliest experiences in sports came in childhood from male family members, including uncles and older brothers, who served as "athletic role models as well as sources of competition for attention and status within the family" (p. 128). Messner (2002) also found that in some cases, attempts by younger aspiring athletes to meet the standards of older siblings was too much pressure and was difficult to contend with. Still, as adult males, these aspiring athletes looked back upon their childhood relationships with their athletic older male family members in a positive light.

Many parents also encourage their children's participation in board games and other fun activities as a way of providing entertainment but also as a way of introducing the child to the world of rules and clear-cut winners and losers. Children who learn to enjoy competition will become increasingly drawn to sports and other contests. Some children may be turned off by the physical activity or the competition and will begin to turn away from sports. Additionally, parents who encourage their children to engage in more passive activities such as reading and starting a coin or stamp collection are more likely to have children who shun sports.

The age and physical condition of the parents can affect a child's socialization into or away from sport. A father or mother who is physically fit and active will be more likely to encourage sport participation in the child. Conversely, if the parents are physically incapable of sport participation, their children may not be exposed to as many sport opportunities. The age of the parents in relation to the child can have an effect as well — many older parents are less able or willing to play sports with their children. A family's economic status and geographic residence are two additional factors that influence a child's socialization into sport. Families with limited disposable income will generally be limited to sports that they can afford to register their children into. Thus, the wealthy have opportunities to play the vast array of sports, including polo and golf, while the poor are more likely to play street basketball, soccer, or stickball.

The ethnicity of the family has also been cited as a variable in sport participation. Phillips (1993) examines the "ethnic influence" from the standpoint (and tradition of Harry Edwards) that certain ethnic and racial groups that are discriminated against are more likely to participate in sport. Blacks have valued sports excellence for decades and view it as a way of getting ahead and therefore have a higher percentage participating than whites (Edwards, 1973). This trend has continued into the early twenty-first century and explains, in part, why blacks dominate many American sports. Today, many other minority ethnic groups are beginning to use sport as a means of getting ahead and have begun to re-shape the elite strata of sport. (This topic will be discussed in further detail in Chapter 11.) Phillips (1993) notes that whites have a higher participation rate in sport than Asians and that this difference holds across all income and social class levels. Vogler and Schwartz (1993) examine the ethnic influence as a socializer in sport from a different perspective. Their focus is on ethnic neighborhoods that have a fondness for a specific sport (e.g., a Brazilian neighborhood would encourage soccer participation among its youth) that leads to a greater interest and participation in such sports. Furthermore, parents who are highly identified by their ethnicity and active in the community are more likely to encourage their children's participation in the ethnically preferred sport.

PEERS AND SPORT

A child's playmates will also have an influence on sport participation. In simplest terms, if a child's friends play ball, the child is more likely to play ball. As the level of importance in ball playing increases among peers, so too will the commitment level to participate in sport increase. As the child plays with others, talent levels are compared. A child that receives praise for his or her sports propensity is more likely to continue participation. Conversely, if a child's performance level is sub-par he or she may be subject to ridicule from peers. This will result in a negative self-concept and a negative outlook on sports, thus decreasing the likelihood of continued participation. Most children are somewhere in between the elite and inept extremes of athleticism. These children will continue to play sports for as long as it remains fun and relatively fulfilling. They will most likely remain fans, or consumers, of sports after their playing days have ended. The bond shared among peers who cheer for the same team or individual athlete is a very strong and important one.

Kenyon and McPherson (1981) summarize the peer-induced factors related to sport socialization:

1. The greater the peer involvement in sport, the greater the propensity for sport involvement.
2. The greater the positive sanctions from peers, the greater the propensity for sport involvement.
3. The greater the amount of sport-oriented face-to-face interaction with peers, the greater the propensity for sport involvement.
4. The higher sport is placed in the peer group's hierarchy of values, the greater the degree of sport role socialization (p. 235).

SCHOOL AND SPORT

Obviously, children need opportunities to participate in sports and to develop a passion for sport and physical play. Ideally, all schools would mandate physical education. Unfortunately, and as hard as it is to believe, some school districts have cut back on physical education (due to budget cuts) and do not require regular physical activity among their pupils. For most children, however, physical education is provided in school. Before long it becomes clear who has athletic ability and who does not. Physical education instructors, who often serve dual roles as coaches, will identify those kids with potential for school sports and encourage more advanced and specialized training. Since most junior high and middle schools have interscholastic teams and intramural leagues, children with sports ability are given a platform to showcase their skills. Success, to any degree, will most likely lead to a continuation in sport participation. Accolades from classmates, teachers and school personnel will enhance the ego of these young athletes and will, in turn, generally lead to a further commitment to sport. Schools with a winning tradition in sports will especially value athletic excellence, leading to both more pressure to succeed among elite athletes, but also providing an even bigger stage from which to shine when successful.

Socialization Into Sport

The agents of socialization pave the way for the socialization into sport. Socialization into sport is a process whereby an individual is encouraged by the agents of socialization to partake in sport either as a participant or as a spectator and consumer. Generally speaking, individuals are socialized "into" sport by significant others (agents of socialization) because of the perceived positive attributes of sport. As stated earlier, parents introduce games to children because they are rule-bound and encourage conforming behavior. A game that involves multiple players means that each participant must know the role of others. Behaviors must be adjusted to conform to group or team needs and game rules. Once a child learns how to play games, he or she is mature enough to be socialized into sport.

Socialization into sport is most effective when it begins in early childhood. This is especially true if a father shows an interest in sport and encourages his son or daughter to play sports. A highly identified fan and parent may try to "force" socialize a son or daughter into sport by dressing him or her in baby clothing of a favorite team, including pajamas, t-shirts or baby bibs; giving the child a stuffed animal that is either a replica of the mascot of a favorite team or one that is simply wearing clothing that supports a favorite team; watching the favorite team on television with the child in hopes that the excitement and passion will carry over; and so on. Clearly, children who are raised in a family where the parents, or older siblings, already demonstrate an interest in sport (either directly as participants, or indirectly as consumers) are more likely to embrace sports as well. Some parents want to live vicariously through their children's sport participation. These parents encourage their sons and daughters into sport either to recapture (indirectly) their loss athletic glory and the attention that sport participation garnered, or they hope to experience the glory that sport can provide and that they never enjoyed themselves when they were younger. The level of parental vicarious attachment and encouragement of sport participation increases as the level of competition (e.g., from intramurals to interscholastic sports) and corresponding prestige increases (Nixon and Frey, 1996).

It is interesting to note that regardless of the sex of the child, the father typically has the most influence over whether a child will be socialized into sport. Fathers are also more likely to "type" sport activities that are gender "appropriate." For example, fathers are more likely to tell their sons that sports such as football and baseball are more appropriate than ballet and dance to participate in. Because of socialization influences, boys are more concerned than girls about sports that are deemed "gender appropriate." A child's ordinal position in the family is also a factor in socialization into sport. First born children do not have the same opportunity to imitate siblings and lack older sibling role models to shape their behaviors.

Historically, boys, especially in American culture, have been encouraged to play sports. Girls have not. As we shall see in Chapter 10, women have had to overcome a great number of obstacles in their attempt to reach gender equity in the sports world. Socialization into sport is the first barrier that women had to shatter. Sports were believed to be a male's domain and most parents, fathers and mothers, socialized their children into this gendered view of sport. For instance, as J. C. Reeser (2005) notes: "Historically, female athletes have been subjected to a variety of discriminatory and prejudicial practices that have affected their access to sport. For example, women were not permitted to compete in the ancient Olympics, nor were they included when the modern Games were first organised in 1896" (p. 695).

With the rise of the women's rights movement in the 1960s and the passage of legislation in the 1970s, a number of sporting opportunities became available for girls and women. Initial inroads made by women seeking gender equity in sport were met by a variety of challenges. For example, in 1980, Iris Marion Young questioned whether women should participate in sport and utilized the sexist putdown in baseball, "You throw like a girl" as her central theme (Wedgwood, 2004). In a later version of her 1980 article, Young (1998) suggested that women underestimate their physical power and skills and approach tasks with timidity, doubt and hesitancy because they are afraid of getting hurt. Conversely, boys and men are not afraid of getting hurt. People get hurt playing sports; ergo, boys are more suited for sports. Twenty-five years later, few people in sport share this sentiment.

Nikki Wedgwood turned the phrase "throwing like a girl" around to "kicking like a boy" in her study of a schoolgirl Australian Rules football team. Wedgwood's (2004) research centered on why the girls played football; whether they played football as a means of consciously resisting male domination; whether they felt empowered by playing football; and how they handled gender role conflicts. Among Wedgwood's (2004) findings:

- Because some of the women on the team felt physically strong and confident before playing football, it is hard to conclude that they felt more empowered after playing football.
- However, for the women who had not previously felt strong and confident, football encouraged them to come out of their shells and "playfully experiment with their bodies" (p. 159).
- The exhilaration of physical play and assertiveness boosted their overall confidence.

Wedgwood concludes that these young women benefited by their socialization into a male-dominated sport and that their participation in football provided them "the opportunity to resist the traditional ideal of women as fragile, defenseless, weak sexual objects" (p. 159). Furthermore,

Wedgwood found that most of the women were not inspired by tenets of feminism to play football; rather, just like boys, the inspiration to play football was attributed to a love for the game. More than a decade prior to Wedgwood's study, Ryckman and Hamel (1992) concluded that adolescent girls participated in sport to maintain and prolong friendships more than any desire to develop and improve their athletic skills or nurture a love for the game.

The social characteristics of race, ethnicity and social class are also factors involved in the socialization into sport. Wealthy people are often socialized into sports that reflect their status and perceived dignity (e.g., fox hunts in England, rowing at Oxford and ivy league schools, polo "at the club," golf in private country clubs). People from lower socio-economic classes and those who are discriminated against are generally attracted to sports that provide accessibility and enjoyment, and also a chance for economic success.

Geographic location plays a role with the socialization into sport. Children raised in Syracuse, New York, are more likely to play lacrosse than children in Los Angeles. Conversely, children living in the beach cities outside of Los Angeles are more likely to surf than kids in Syracuse. This is despite the fact that someone from one geographic area may have a greater ability to play a sport popular in another area. Certain geographical areas are known for their sports: basketball in New York City; hockey throughout Canada; football in Texas, Florida and Alabama. Whether someone resides in a city, the suburbs, or a rural community can also affect the socialization into sport (e.g., what sports will be made available, funding, coaching, interest from the community to field a specific sports team).

Socialization Via Sport

Once an individual has entered the sports world, what keeps him or her interested? From the functionalist perspective, continued participation is related to individual ability, the influence of family and friends on the individual, the continued availability of resources, and whether one experienced success, or a positive experience, while playing sport. Developing a commitment to sport participation involves a number of factors, including:

1. A willingness to accept a sports role and the corresponding relationships and networks affiliated with it. This includes a willingness to abide by the rules.
2. The continued development of the web of personal relationships connected to sport participation.
3. Assessed potential for achieving success.
4. Degree of involvement in the sport. Those who play a lot have a vested interest in continuing their participation. Those who primarily sit on the bench are likely to lose interest.
5. Whether participation is voluntary or involuntary. Youths who are pushed into a sport (involuntary) by a parent, coach, or some other significant person are less likely to *want* to keep playing, compared to someone who participates voluntarily.
6. The prestige and power associated with playing the sport and how rewarding an individual finds sport participation will affect one's willingness to continue playing.
7. Gradually accepting the established personal reputation and identity as an athlete; in other words, seeing oneself as an athlete.

As athletes increasingly accept their role and position within the sports world, they acquire a number of character traits. Proponents of sport love to point out the positive attributes of participation, such as working hard, dedication, loyalty, teamwork (where applicable), and commitment. Detractors point to the undesirable attributes, such as athletes who cheat, take drugs, or employ a "win-at-all-costs" mentality instead of fair play and cooperation among all participants.

Socialization via sport involves the social processes and significant others that influence an individual's decision to remain in sport. This process can only occur through participation.

Individuals who decide to continue their athletic careers do so at many costs. They must give up free time to practice. They may need to diet and exercise. Strength and conditioning programs are often a part of an athlete's "off season" training. Some athletes, such as football players, often need to bulk up. Other athletes, such as wrestlers, must meet a weight limit before each match. Athletes learn that they must abide by their coaches' rules, team rules, school rules, and league rules. They must also accept any negative sanctions for non-conforming behavior.

Ideally, all participants learn good sportsmanship. Poor sportsmanship, according to John Rosemond, a family psychologist, is a show of self-centered disrespect for others. Children should develop positive sportsmanship by age 10. To instill good sportsmanship, Rosemond (2000) recommends that a child (at age 7) who begins to gloat or get upset during a game should be immediately removed and not allowed to continue unless he or she apologizes to everyone — the coaches, teammates, and the other team members. If the child refuses, then he or she should be removed from the game. Rosemond recognizes that the disciplined child will feel embarrassed and believes that's the point in properly socializing a child. "He must be required to experience a negative emotional consequence powerful enough to cause him to begin controlling his anti-social behavior on the field" (2000:C3). Most likely, readers will find Rosemond's approach a little extreme, but imagine if all of today's professional athletes had been required to meet such criteria in sportsmanship.

Athletes on teams often retreat to their own social worlds. It is here that they feel most comfortable. Peer pressure is a powerful form of "socialization via sport" technique. Not only is there pressure to follow the formal rules (e.g., meet curfew, no gambling) there is pressure to follow the informal rules of the team. Some of these rules are harmless forms of socialization. For example, baseball players may have a "donation" cup for every time a player makes an error. This mild form of sanction serves to bond teammates. Players begin to regret and fear making an error as much for the informal ridicule they will receive (along with the "donation" sanction) from teammates, as the fact that the error could cost the team the game.

An important element of the "socialization via sport" process is the fraternal bond. The fraternal bond is a process whereby members of a group foster and reinforce team camaraderie and a commitment to group goals. Curry (1991) describes the fraternal bond as a force, link, or affectionate tie that unites men. It provides bonding opportunities among teammates. The fraternal bond is a crucial element of fraternities, sports teams and other subcultural groups. The fraternal bond is not inherently negative or positive. Cooperation among team members who work hard to achieve a goal is one of many positive examples of the fraternal bond. However, the fraternal bond may also promote negative character traits. Curry (1991) suggests that "doing gender" in the locker room (e.g., communication among team members that involves putting down women, treating women as sexual conquests, mocking gays and bragging about sexual conquests) is a means of strengthening the fraternal bond. Kane and Disch (1993) claim that "an act of sexual assault such as gang rape becomes an important mechanism for male bonding in two interdependent ways: It creates in-group solidarity by clearly establishing dominance over an inferior outsider, and it temporarily erases pre-established hierarchies within the group by creating a 'level playing field' for all group members."

The contrasting viewpoints of the fraternal bond underscore the debate over whether sport participation actually promotes positive or negative character traits. Nixon and Frey (1996) conclude that any differences between the behaviors of athletes and non-athletes is most likely attributed to differences between individuals in the first place, rather than because sport changes individuals. Thus, people who display "good" character traits and who play sports will continue to develop positive attributes via sport socialization; while those people who display "negative" character traits will continue to develop negative attributes regardless of their sport participation. Delaney and Madigan believe there are exceptions to both categories of sport participants.

In other words, sport socialization can improve the character traits in individuals who previously had questionable ones; and people who generally display good character traits may also display negative traits, at least periodically, in sport.

Socialization Out of Sport

Eventually, sport participants are socialized out of sport. This can be voluntary (e.g., retirement, quit) or involuntary (e.g., being cut from the team, career ending injury). Socialization out of sport involves a desocialization process where an individual leaves sport and experiences a modification of sense of self. For professional athletes, exiting can be very difficult. (Think of all the tearful retirement speeches shown on television.) Drahota and Eitzen (1998) describe the role transition of athletes out of sport as a difficult one because: "They *lose* what has been the focus of their being for most of their lives, the primary source of their identities, the physical prowess, the adulation bordering on worship from others, the money and the perquisites of fame, the camaraderie with teammates, and the intense 'highs' of competition. All of these are lost to professional athletes who are in their twenties and thirties when they exit sport" (p. 263).

Big-time athletes have heard deafening crowds chant their names and have had adoring fans nearly worshipping them throughout their playing days. But when the career ends, so to does the cheering. Many professional athletes miss this type of attention after retirement. This is especially true if the person's primary identity was tied to sport participation. Many athletes stay close to sport by becoming coaches or sports media personnel. Tim Green, the former Atlanta Falcon who became a color analyst for *FOX Sports*, discusses what he calls the "The Second Death" phenomenon:

> They say that football players die two deaths. The first death comes when their career finally ends. My career has ended. No more cleats, no more banging helmets, no more cheers, no more headaches. Instead of the stress and worry of an impending football season, the notion of autumn is nothing more than brilliantly colored orange trees, just like in the postcards. I hear stories in the news about my former teammates losing weight in the heat, having last-minute battles over their contracts, getting injured.... As great as it is to stay close to this game, to talk about it, to be there watching, to get excited about doing television broadcasts, it really isn't quite the same, is it? [1996: 263–264].

EXITING SPORT VOLUNTARILY

There are a variety of ways for individuals to leave sport voluntarily. One simple reason for leaving is because participation has merely lost its appeal — it is no longer viewed as a rewarding endeavor. The sport participant may come to a realization that the personal time allocated (e.g., practice, training, game day) is taking away from the time needed to pursue other interests (e.g., dating, school work, family). In other words, at some point in time, usually during childhood, most people stop playing sports because it has lost its appeal. But how does sport lose its appeal? Most young children play sports because they are fun. However, as the level of competition increases and becomes more structured and the emphasis on skill and success becomes paramount, the lesser talent participants simply turn away. These young athletes desire that their sporting activities remain fun and do not like the intrusion of seriousness (e.g., emphasis on improving skills, utilizing techniques that attempt to maximize the chances of winning versus a commitment to playing everyone) creeping into their leisure activity.

From the participant's point of view a lost appeal in sport is one of the easiest ways to exit. However, the individual may find that significant others have objections to this decision. Friends, teammates and coaches may try to assert pressure on the individual to remain. Many parents become upset when their children quit sports because they had an emotional, communal and financial (e.g., purchased specific equipment that now will now go unused) attachment and involvement with their children's sport participation. Parents and family members that made a number of sacrifices so that their child could play sports may try to influence or coerce the young athlete back into sport. Parents who were living vicariously through their children's participation will especially be upset when their kids quit. However, it is also true that some athletes will quit or retire voluntarily to spend more time with their families. Professional athletes who retire voluntarily (especially those with seemingly more years of playing time ahead of them) often cite the desire to be with their families as their primary reason for leaving.

Many athletes are also pressured by friends, spouses and business associates who have a financial as well as emotional interest in their remaining in the game. This is often the case, for instance, with professional boxers, who have significant entourages and who find it difficult to voluntarily break away from the perks and privileges their status provides them in their community. Quite often, even after retiring, such athletes will find themselves returning to the sport they had voluntarily left, due to such financial, emotional and status pressures.

Another reason participants exit sport is because of burnout. Burnout occurs when individuals feel overwhelmed by their sport participation; to the point where they feel (or fear) that they have lost control over their lives and believe that their identity is too closely tied to sports. These young athletes come to believe that they may be missing out on other opportunities and identities apart from sports.

Retirement represents an exit strategy out of sport for the professional athlete. Voluntary retirement is different for professional athletes than it is for "other retirees who, typically, are elderly and leaving the occupational world altogether" (Drahota and Eitzen, 1998: 264). Although common sense alone should serve as a reminder to athletes that when they retire (even if it is after a long and successful career) they will have decades remaining in their lifespan, many are not prepared for life after sports. This is usually because of their single focus on their sport and the failure to plan ahead. Drahota and Eitzen (1998) believe that many athletes know but do not necessarily accept the fact that playing sports is a temporary role to be performed for a relatively short period of their lives. Often this failure to realize that a career will come to an end is tied to denial. Most athletes view retirement as the only acceptable way of exiting sport because it implies they left on their terms— ready, or not, for life after sports. And there does seem to be a special status for athletes who retire on their own accord, often at the top of their game or at least before inevitable decline in their skills sets in. Rocky Marciano, "The Brockton Blockbuster," retired as Heavyweight Champion in 1956, after holding the title for four years, and remains the only undefeated champion. He was noted for his courage, dignity and sense of grace, and managed his money and career well after leaving the ring, unlike many other athletes who find it difficult to adjust to life after sports.

EXITING SPORT INVOLUNTARILY

The two primary ways that sport participants exit sports involuntarily is through injury and being cut, or kicked off, the team. Injuries are a common occurrence, as the playing field can be a violent, risky and hazardous environment. "Not even the risky and labor-intensive settings of mining, oil drilling, and construction sites can compare with the routine injuries of team sports such as football, ice hockey, soccer and rugby" (Delaney, 2002: 1560). According to the Centers for Disease Control and Prevention, for instance, between 1997 and 1999 an average of 7 million Americans per year received medical attention for sports and recreation-related injuries. Youths aged 14 and under comprise about half of this annual total.

Ending a sports career due to injury is one of the cruelest things to happen to an athlete.

The years of hard work and training and fighting off competition (both from those trying to take your job and the competitors) comes to a brutal end when injuries cut short a career.

Being cut from or kicked off a team is the other major way of exiting a sport involuntarily. There are a variety of reasons that someone might be cut from a team: skills level is not high enough to successfully compete; diminished skills; increased competition; poor attitude; off-the-field problems; and so on. Lately, there has been an increase in the number of veteran professional players being cut because they carry too high of a salary. For example, in the National Football League (NFL) salary contracts are not guaranteed and as a result, if a player is earning a high salary and a younger player is available for less money, a number of franchises have decided to cut the veteran as a cost-saving mechanism. This veteran must now decide whether to take a playing offer for substantially less income (and "lose face" in the process), hope that some other team will sign him, or her, or retire. According to the National Football League Players Association (NFLPA), 400 players are socialized out of the game each year. The NFL is a 4-year turn-around business (meaning that the average player lasts four years in the NFL). Will Leitch notes: "The average NFL player's career lasts 3.5 years, according to the NFLPA, and the average annual salary is $1.25 million. That's good money, of course, but this fact complicates matters: NFL teams do not guarantee contracts, meaning that if a player is injured or does not perform up to expectations, he can be cut and the team is not required to pay his salary" (2005: 1).

There is another example of exiting sport involuntarily that occurs in rare cases—death. The causes of death include the athlete having a previous health ailment, injuries sustained while playing, or negligent medical treatment. In 2005, San Francisco 49er Thomas Herrion died from complications of heart disease. Herrion collapsed in the team's locker room following a preseason NFL game against the Denver Broncos. There are numerous sport activities that may lead to death. Among the most common are horse racing, sky-diving, hang-gliding, mountaineering, scuba diving, motorcycle racing, college football and boxing.

Athletes certainly are not the only ones being forced out of their occupation. This is something that many Americans can relate to, especially in light of economic uncertainty, corporate downsizing, jobs moving overseas, and so forth. No one wants to lose their job, especially if they are qualified and capable of doing the work.

Resocialization

Just as we are socialized into new roles, we are also socialized out of existing ones. Being socialized out of a role means being re-socialized into yet another new role. Socialization "out of" sport involves a re-socialization process, as one's sense of self changes when the athlete stops playing sports. This is true whether a participant exits voluntarily or involuntarily. Some athletes handle the transition quite well. They find jobs in the professional workforce or start their own companies. A number of former athletes will find jobs in the sports world (e.g., coaching, administration, the sports media). As we shall see in Chapter 13, some athletes even make a successful transition into the world of politics.

The NFLPA claims that upon retirement, 66 percent of NFL players report having emotional problems, 50 percent report personal problems, and 1 of 6 were divorced within 6 months. The NFLPA compares the experiences that professional jocks have after leaving sport to that of war veterans—the transition into civilian life is difficult, almost shocking (Leitch, 2005: 4). This difficulty in transition of roles is partly explained by the realization that the athlete can no longer perform his or her role successfully—he or she has been replaced. The truth of this reality can be painful both physically and psychologically. Resocialization out of sport will be especially difficult and stressful under these conditions:

1. The athlete's level of intensity of involvement in the sport was high.
2. Retirement from sport was involuntary.
3. Retirement will result in a loss of income and prestige (celebrity).
4. The athlete has not come up with a substitute career to fill the void that sport once filled.
5. The athlete's self-concept and sense of self were directly tied to sport participation.
6. The athlete does not seek counseling or assistance during the resocialization process (Figler and Whitaker, 1981).

The successful transition from sport athlete to non-athlete involves a process known as role exit. "Role exit is depicted as a process of disengagement, disidentification, and resocialization. Disengagement involves the actual means of withdrawing from the type of behavior associated with a role. Disidentification refers to the time when individuals stop associating their self-identity with the role being exited. The process of leaving a role means that one also is being socialized into a new role" (Drahota and Eitzen, 1998: 266). The key to resocialization for the athlete is to re-identify one's sense of self. Many athletes have a difficult time with this. Identifying with the "ex-athlete" role identity is something that takes years for many athletes. Tim Green, the former defensive lineman with the Atlanta Falcons and an athlete who has made a successful transition, believes that "it's hard for pro players to retire — regardless of how long or successful their careers were — after dedicating their lives to going pro" (Gifford, 2004:A-5). Green, who became a lawyer and best-selling author, ended his eight-year career in 1994. His book *The Dark Side of the Game: My Life in the NFL* chronicles some of the problems that players face after exiting sport. Green (1996) reports that many players have problems with alcohol, other drugs, and marital relationships, and engage in reckless behavior.

Research conducted by David Frith (2001) on cricket players reveals that they have the highest suicide rates of all ex-athletes. Since the early 1900s there have been 143 documented cricket player suicides worldwide. The largest percentage of cricket suicides occurs in South Africa. Frith reports that cricket athletes do not seek professional counseling for their emotional problems after exiting sports. Frith believes the high suicide rate is related to the pressure of the game. The most important matches take 6 to 8 hours a day for 5 days. As with other athletes that dedicate their lives to sport, the loss of night and day involvement in sport and the idea of being a "has been"— despite a relatively young age — is too much to handle for many athletes. Frith (2001) insists that it is not cricket that causes personal problems for its players; rather, it is the loss of cricket that is responsible. Frith's conclusion seems plausible. After all, golf matches often take 6 to 8 hours and last for four days, and Major League Baseball players play 162 games in less than six months. Consequently, the high suicide rate for cricket players cannot be attributed to being over-stressed due to the demands of the sport.

Successful transition into the "ex-athlete" mode is a difficult for many athletes. As Drahota and Eitzen (1998) found, some professional athletes never completely exit the role of professional athlete.

SUMMARY

Sports are not just physical activities and games; they serve as focal points for the formation of social worlds. In order to fit into a social world, group members will adjust their behavior and mindsets to revolve around a particular set of activities. People are socialized into sport worlds by the agents of socialization.

Socialization is how we "become" human. Without it children would not learn a language or how to behave in society. The so-called "nature versus nurture" debate continues in many academic circles, but for most sociologists human behavior is primarily determined through socialization. This takes place most effectively in primary groups—intimate associates who play a direct role in shaping one's sense of self. Significant others are those who play the most major role in such developments. Such agents of socialization not only foster a sense of self, they also help to sustain it over a lifetime.

Sport is instrumental in creating self-identity for many individuals, through their interactions with primary groups involved in sport activities, and through their identification with specific teams and players as well. In team sports, it is critical for all members to play their role and accept the responsibilities which come with it. The values and norms of the group are internalized and new members must learn these rules.

Many achieve identity in sport through participation as an athlete. Some reach elite status or become team leaders, while others are primarily followers or sport consumers. The latter form an identity through practicing allegiance to a team and often through rooting against the chief rivals of that team.

One question is, "Why do some people love sports whereas others do not?" For many, this is due to the motivations experienced in childhood. Initial bad experiences can cause a lifetime of aversion to sport, whereas positive experiences and availability of opportunities to play can instill a lifetime of enthusiasm. The influence of family and friends is also crucial in such developments. This is usually a positive experience, but at times parents might wish to live vicariously through their children to recapture past glories. This places an undue strain on the offspring to perform.

Children are more interested in sports when their parents and family are supportive. Such characteristics as the age, physical condition, economic status and ethnicity of the family serve as variables in sport participation. Peers also have a major influence—if a child's friends play ball, the child is more likely to do so. The role of schools is crucial as well, in mandating individual physical education and teamwork. This can help in showing which students have athletic abilities and which do not.

Maintaining interest in the sports world throughout one's life is another important consideration. There are many sacrifices involved, including financial costs and time commitments. An important aspect of socialization via sport is the fraternal bond, where camaraderie is constantly reinforced. Such a bond is neither inherently negative nor positive, but its effects remain a source of contention.

Socialization out of sport can be difficult, especially for former athletes who are no longer able to adequately perform. Some remain involved as coaches or sports media personnel. One major topic is whether such exiting is done voluntarily or involuntarily. In the latter case, injuries or being kicked off the team can curtail a career before its natural end. Being cut is a type of degradation ceremony. Re-socializing can become an issue, as one's sense of self must change in light of the new situations. Such a transition from sport athlete to non-athlete is known as "role exit." The transition can be a difficult one for those whose personal identities are interwoven with the sport they excelled in.

KEY TERMS

Agents of Socialization The people, groups or institutions that teach us what we need to know in order to function properly in society.

Development of Self The result of a number of interactions with others over a period of time in a variety of social and cultural contexts.

Elite Athlete Someone who has reached a level of competition at or near a national standard.

Fraternal Bond A process whereby members of a group foster and reinforce team camaraderie and a commitment to group goals.

Generalized Other A person's conscious awareness of the society that he or she is a part of; the community or communities one belongs to.

Identity Involves those aspects of one's life that are deemed as essential to the character and maintenance of self.

Instrumental Relationships Those relationships based on pragmatic principles that assist individuals in their pursuit of goals.

Primary Group An intimate association where members share a sense of "we-ness"—a sort of sympathy and mutual identification for which "we" is a natural expression. The primary group is relatively small, often informal, involves close personal relationships, and has an important role in shaping an individual's sense of self.

Role Exit A process of leaving a role through being socialized into a new role.

Secondary Group A collectivity whose members interact with one another formally and impersonally.

Significant Others Those who play a major role in shaping a person's self.

Social Worlds Group members who share a subcultural perspective and are held together through interaction and communication.

Socialization A process of social development and learning that occurs as individuals interact with one another and learn about society's expectations of acceptable behavior.

Socialization into Sport A process whereby an individual is encouraged by the agents of socialization to partake in sport either as a participant or as a spectator or consumer.

Socialization Out of Sport A desocialization process where an individual leaves sport and experiences a modification of sense of self. For professional athletes, exiting sport can be very difficult.

Socialization Process The ways in which individuals learn cultural norms, values, beliefs and expectations.

Socialization via Sport The social processes and significant others that influence an individual's decision to remain in sport.

DISCUSSION QUESTIONS

• Do you admire any athletes whom you never actually saw play? If so, how did you learn about their careers, and what is it you admire about them?

• How does the socialization process help a person learn what his or her athletic skills are? Give some examples, based upon the role which the following agents play: parents, peers, the school, the community, and the media.

• What does it mean to "internalize" social messages? How might this occur for individuals who from a very early age root for a specific team or athlete?

• Why is the notion of a "natural born athlete" misleading?

• In what ways does an elite athlete differ from a marginal athlete? Give some examples based upon your knowledge of current sports.

• What might be some reasons why children who grow up in the same household, under the same influences, can differ in their commitment to or participation in sports?

• Why do parents usually encourage children's participation in sporting events and games? What is your own opinion as to whether or not this is beneficial or harmful to the children involved?

• Do you think that schools should support physical activity and sports involvement? Why or why not?

- Why is it so difficult for athletes to retire from sports participation? Can you think of examples of athletes who should have retired earlier than they did?
- What is a "fraternal bond" and how does it relate to socialization via sport? What are some of the positive and some of the negative attributes of such bonds?

CHAPTER 6

Youth Sports

It is only natural for children to play. Participating in organized sport, however, is different. The highly structured design of formal sports is not attractive to all youth. Children should be allowed to make their own decisions as to whether they want to play organized sports. Encouraging children to participate is certainly acceptable; however, pressuring a child is not. Marv Marinovich, co-captain of the undefeated 1962 football national champion University of Southern California (USC) Trojans and former offensive lineman for the Oakland Raiders, was obsessed with the idea that his son, Todd, would become a quarterback for USC and then the Raiders. Marv trained his son with the assistance of over 20 specialists while Todd grew up. They were designing a quarterback, a "Robo-quarterback," as Todd was known. Todd's youth was totally regimented. He slept and woke at his father's direction and worked out in between. He was not allowed to eat any junk while he grew up; cake at his friends' birthday parties was also banned. Marv Marinovich would make Todd run several miles home after a poor performance (Weiner, 1999). Todd Marinovich did become the quarterback for both USC and the Raiders. But his professional career was short-lived and his off-the-field problems include two drug-related arrests and an arrest for sexual assault (Weiner, 1999; *USA Today*, 6/7/99; *USA Today*, 4/27/00). As a youth, Todd Marinovich was physically prepared to play football. Clearly, all this training did not prepare him for life as an adult.

Has Marv Marinovich learned his lesson, that you cannot force someone to be an athlete? Well, the answer is "no." Marv has another son, Mikhail (Todd's half-brother), who is the one now being prepared for life as a professional athlete. Mikhail was once described as the "greatest 6-year-old athlete" his American Youth Soccer Organization team coach had ever seen (*Los Angeles Times*, 7/4/94). Should six-year-olds be described in terms of "greatest athlete" ever, at that age? Is this too much pressure for a child to handle? These are among the concerns of youth sport participation that will be discussed in this chapter. (After starring in football at Jserra High School in California, Mikhail signed with Syracuse University to further his football career. Unfortunately, before taking a snap for the Orange, Marinovich was arrested and charged with misdemeanor criminal mischief following an alleged break-in of a sports equipment room at Manley Field House.)

Should Children Play Sports?

Should children play sports? And if so, when and what sports should children be allowed to participate in? Are organized sports worth all the time, money and effort put into them? These are questions that confront parents, and to a lesser extent, society in general. In most countries, organized youth sports are a luxury. They cost money and time that many people cannot afford. This is true even in the United States and Canada. The authors believe that it is important to indicate that youth sports benefit the vast majority of participants, including youths and parents. Furthermore, most parents have the best intentions when they encourage their children to play sports and certainly do not go to the extremes of Marv Marinovich.

BENEFITS OF YOUTH SPORT PARTICIPATION

It has long been argued that sport participation helps to develop motor skills and physical fitness in youths. Play and sport are healthy behaviors that should be encouraged. Beyond the physical benefits, most people who support the idea of youths playing sport cite the character development aspect. In the United States, the "sport builds character" concept can be traced back to the post–Civil War era. It should be noted, however, that this character development concept was applied primarily to boys. As Rader (2004) explains, a number of social leaders were concerned that modern life had become too soft and effeminate:

> Frontiers and battlefields no longer existed to test manly courage and perseverance. Henry W. Williams observed that the 'struggle for existence, though becoming harder and harder, is less and less a physical struggle, more and more a battle of minds.' Apart from sports, men no longer had arenas for testing their manliness. Theodore Roosevelt worried lest prolonged periods of peace would encourage 'effeminate tendencies in young men.' Only aggressive sports, Roosevelt argued, could create the 'brawn, the spirit, the self confidence, and quickness of men' that was essential for the existence of a strong nation [p. 105]. [For the Williams quote reference see Williams, 1895; see Dubbert, 1979 for the Roosevelt quotes.]

The post–Civil War period marks a point in history where the traditional expression of manliness took on new meanings. Rapid industrial and technological advancements were making life increasingly "easy" (less dependent on physical brawn as a means for survival) for those in Western societies, especially the United States. Sports, especially aggressive ones, were viewed as a way for males to express their manliness.

Although this bit of historical information provides a framework for when advocates first touted sport as a means of building character, it does not inform us as to what character is, and whether sport can provide it. "Character" has a different meaning for people. Generally, it is assumed that "good" character is displayed when someone abides by the rules and acts according to social expectations. "Aristotle said that character is the composite of good moral qualities, whereby one shows firmness of belief, resolution, and practice about such moral values as honesty, justice, and respect. He also said that character is right conduct in relation to other persons and to self. Our humanness, he continues, resides in our ability and capacity to reason, and virtue results when we use our reasoning ability to control and moderate our self" (Stoll and Beller, 2000: 18). Others would argue that reasoning alone is not enough to determine good character; instead, one must have a strong value system as well. As Stoll and Beller (2000) explain, "To say, 'Cheating is wrong,' is inadequate. One must know why it is wrong and put into action what one values, knows, and reasons is right. It is easy to say that one does not cheat but another thing not to cheat when surrounded by others who are cheating" (p. 19).

There are a number of personal qualities associated with "character." "They include responsibility, persistence, courage, self-discipline, honesty, integrity, the willingness to work hard, compassion for others, generosity, independence, and tolerance" (Griffin, 1998: 27). The authors define character as individual personality and behavioral traits, both good and bad, which define who a person is. Those who abide by societal rules are said to have good character; whereas those who flaunt society's rules or become overly self-absorbed do not.

Griffin (1998) states that "good character" comprises four traits:

1. *Responsibility.* Someone who can be depended upon to get the task or job done. This person works hard and is self-disciplined and persistent. Furthermore, a responsible person does not blame others for his or her own shortcomings or failures.

2. *Integrity*. A person with integrity "lives according to personal values" and possess deep conviction for his or her conduct in the social world.
3. *Decency*. "This person is directed by a firm sense of what is just and fair.... They respect the rights and dignity of others."
4. *Independence*. A free thinker who "is not the tool of someone else" [p. 56].

Childhood and adolescence is a critical time in character formation and social development. "Social development comprises such things as friendship, social ranking, status, power, rejection and acceptance, inclusion and exclusion, dominance and submission, leadership, connection to the group, cooperativeness, aggression and passivity and withdrawal, and conflict" (Griffin, 1998: 27). The ability to get along cooperatively with others and a willingness to accept society's rules are signs of good character and proper social development. Sports provide a good mechanism to develop character, and it does so under the watchful public eye. Because of this, youth receive immediate feedback regarding their behavior. At the same time, they become increasingly aware of their sense of self and role in the community.

Stoll and Beller believe that sports can build positive character traits in participants if the athletic programs themselves are designed to contribute positively to the ethical and moral development of athletes. "While teaching the will to win does not have to be eliminated, coaches, athletic administrators, and others in sport leadership positions must re-evaluate their philosophy regarding the importance of winning as it relates to character development, particularly when the participants are children and young adults. Without this fundamental shift in philosophy, sport will never fulfill its potential as a tool to educate and build positive character traits in our nation's youth" (2000: 27).

Schreiber (1990) argues that sport *does* build character. "Perhaps more important, sports *reveals* character — in kids and adults. Just watch a group of kids play basketball, and see if you can't immediately discern who looks to pass, who looks to shoot, who hollers at teammates when they make a mistake, who berates herself for the slightest error, who's the leader, who's eager to take the ball during crunch time, and so on.... Sports is an uncanny truth-detector" (9). Schreiber makes a good point about sport revealing character. It is quite enlightening watching children play, as many of their character traits are revealed. However, it is important to note that some people transform themselves when playing sport in order to perform at a maximum level. Thus, a youth who plays football very aggressively is not necessarily an aggressive person off the field. In short, it is difficult to make general statements regarding sport participation and the building of character.

Griffin (1998) concludes, "No matter how one wants to define character, athletes very likely have no more of it than members of any other group" (p. 67). Some athletes display very positive character traits; in some cases these values were learned in conjunction with sport participation and in other cases these values were learned by other agents of socialization. Unfortunately, all athletes do not display positive character traits. Throughout the remainder of this book a great number of negative character traits displayed by athletes will be detailed (see, for example, Chapter 8, Deviance; and Chapter 9, Violence).

WHEN SHOULD YOUTHS BEGIN SPORT PARTICIPATION?

Infants, from birth until about eighteen months, are just beginning to learn to interact with their environment. A physically active infant is an important foundation for a healthy life. Infants learn to play through interaction with caregivers (e.g., family members) and by self-exploration. There are very few "skills" that can be encouraged at this age. However, playful slapping, smacking, and pounding a ball can be encouraged by placing a ball in the baby's crib. When the infant can sit up, rolling a ball is a good way to develop motor skills. Infants can kick a ball before they can walk, so parents should encourage this activity as well. Parents who take their young children on walks and bike rides provide another way to encourage early active participation. When toddlers begin to walk, it is important to encourage the activity, so that the child will feel proud of his or her accomplishment. From around eighteen months to 2 and a half years of age, children develop a well-organized autonomous achievement orientation that evolves from increasing mastery of competence motivation. Around age two or three, children learn to throw items; if not a ball, then a doll, or food. At this age, the child throws only with his or her arms and does not use any body motion. Catching a ball is more difficult than throwing one. Playing catch with toddlers is another excellent motor skill development activity.

In short, it is never too early for physical play, as infants can be encouraged to roll a ball or kick one. When a toddler has learned to walk, running is the next type of development, and this activity should be encouraged. Caroline Silby (2000) argues that at young ages, it is very important for

A young child playing with a toy football appears to make the "Heisman pose" (courtesy Shannan Delaney).

children to discover the numerous ways their body can move. Relying a great deal on imitation and trial and error, youngsters will develop most of their complex motor skills by age six or seven. At this age of maturation, children are beginning to develop self-perceptions of physical, social, and cognitive competency. As a result it is very important for adult care-givers to emphasize a positive social environment (Silby, 2000).

The early school years of a child mark an important stage in development, and thus, athletic competencies. Around age seven, most children experience a growth spurt; including the size of the brain, which increases to 90 percent of its total weight (compared to 25 percent at birth). Along with body growth comes an increase in ability to handle more challenging physical activities. Children tend to cling to rules and organization at this age.

Early elementary age children have learned the basic skills necessary to play any sport of their choosing. "It is crucial for youngsters to practice their newfound skills in order to gain proficiency in sports" (Small and Spear, 2002: 14). At this age it is advisable for youths not to specialize in one sport, as they are still developing and may enjoy or excel at another sport. From ages 10 to 13, children generally undergo their adolescent growth spurt as they reach puberty. During this growth spurt, many children are often physically awkward. As these children become comfortable with their new physiques, they may find that they have new athletic grace and ability (Schreiber, 1990).

Sports become increasingly competitive with each succeeding year. Selection for team sports comes to the forefront. "By age eleven, more than half of children have quit organized sports. Kids cite several common reasons for quitting: sports cease to be fun; sports become too competitive; she does not receive enough playing time" (Small and Spear, 2002: 17). Kids who drop out of organized sports have the option to participate in informal sports such as hiking, skateboarding, skating, snowboarding, bicycle riding, and walking.

In short, by age 7 or 8, children have developed a capacity for reason and an understanding for rules and are therefore ready for organized physical activities. At the very least, children at this age are capable of participating in physical education classes in school. Organized sports before the age of 7 should be matched with that child's needs and abilities. As for contact sports, Martens and Seefeldt (1979) believe that youth at age 6 are ready for noncontact sports (e.g., swimming, tennis, track and field); 8-year-olds are ready for contact sports (e.g., basketball, soccer, wrestling); and 10-year-olds are ready for collision sports (e.g., ice hockey, tackle football).

Origin and Development of Organized Youth Sports

One of the outcomes of industrialization and urbanization of the United States and Canada midway through the nineteenth century was the emergence of leisure time for many children, especially urban youth. The large number of children roaming the streets convinced social policy makers and citizens alike to find a way to organize children's lives through a combination of sport and education. The linking of sport with formal education began in the United States around the time of the Civil War. This idea was influenced by European sports programs of early nineteenth century.

Toward the end of the nineteenth century, advocates of youth sports were proclaiming the moral value of participation. Combining sport and morality with education was accomplished through an ideology known as "Muscular Christianity." Muscular Christianity, then, refers to the religious philosophy of teaching morals and values through sport. The idealism of Muscular Christianity had a great impact on the development of sport in English and American society. Muscular Christianity triggered the development of sports in American schools; especially for boys. Sport activities were organized for boys in schools, on playgrounds, and in church groups. Team sports were supposed to teach boys how to cooperate and work productively together with others. It was believed that boys would become strong, assertive, competitive men.

Ideas of Muscular Christianity and boys acting manly influenced the establishment of the Young Men's Christian Association (YMCA). "Founded by laymen in England in 1851 and subsequently transplanted to the United States before the Civil War, the original purpose of the YMCA had been to offer spiritual guidance and practical assistance to the young men who were flooding into the nineteenth-century cities" (Radar, 2004: 106). After the Civil War, the YMCA broadened its sports programs but maintained a commitment to developing a spiritual "physical culture."

The development of organized youth sports was not limited to the schools or a religious realm. A "play movement" developed outside the schools and gained momentum toward the end of the nineteenth century. Massive immigration during the nineteenth century had led to overcrowded cities and youth with no place to play. "In an effort to provide suitable play space for children in this environment, sand piles were first erected in Boston in 1885. In 1888, New York passed the first state legislation that led to an organized play area for children. By 1899, the Massachusetts Emergency and Hygiene Association sponsored 21 playgrounds" (Lumpkin, 1994: 213). Jane Addams' Hull House in Chicago also had a playground. As the twentieth century began, a large number of political and community leaders worked to ensure that children had a place to play, either at parks, playgrounds, or indoor facilities.

With the development of sports in and out of school it became necessary to train people to teach physical education courses and to coach sports. By the end of the nineteenth century many colleges offered degrees in physical education. It became a recognized subject by the National Education Association in 1891. As the twentieth century progressed, schools across the nation provided competitive sports for youth. Slowly the number of sporting opportunities for girls would increase. Summer sport programs ensured that children had an opportunity to remain active in sports year-round. During the 1950s, general fitness programs were established in schools. And although the popularity of sport has continued to grow in the United States since the 1950s, American school children have tested poorly on fitness (Lumpkin, 1994). The 1950s also marked the beginning of the "Baby Boomer" generation. For the first time in history, a large number of children had a great deal of leisure time on their hands, with families that had the means to provide for their children's athletic pursuits. Sports were funded by a combination of public, private and commercial sponsors. Parents were active. Some fathers would serve as coaches, managers and league administrators and mothers became chauffeurs and short-order cooks so that their kids could be on time for practices and games and still have time to eat. During the late 1970s, girls' participation in sport began to grow in earnest.

In the following pages we will take a closer look at youth sports in the twentieth and twenty-first centuries in our analysis of formal and informal youth sports.

Formal Youth Sports

It should be fairly well established by this point that sport plays an integral role in American culture and is a major social institution in society. Furthermore, because of the free time afforded children (because they are not expected to work full-time) and a general concern that idleness leads to delinquency, it comes as little surprise that formal sports are strongly encouraged.

The main objective of organized youth sports was to provide opportunities for all youths to participate in sport in a wholesome character-building environment as they made the transition form childhood to adulthood (Berryman, 1988). The concept of character development has always been associated with youth sport. As described earlier in this chapter, sport is promoted as a setting where youth can develop good character traits such as positive attitudes about competition, sportsmanship, authority, and discipline. Martens and Seefeldt (1979: 11) identify a number of objectives for youth sport programs:

1. To develop motoric competencies.
2. To develop physical fitness.
3. To teach children how to cooperate.
4. To develop a sense of achievement, leading to a positive self concept.
5. To develop interest in, and a desire to, continue participation in sports in later years.
6. To develop healthy, strong identities.
7. To help develop independence through interdependent activities.
8. To promote and convey the values of society.
9. To contribute to moral development.
10. To have fun.
11. To develop social competencies.
12. To help bring the family together.
13. To provide opportunities for physical-affective learning, including learning to understand and express emotion, imagination, and appreciation for what the body can do.
14. To develop speed, strength, endurance, coordination, flexibility, and agility.
15. To develop leadership skills.
16. To develop self-reliance and emotional stability by learning to make decisions and accept responsibilities.
17. To teach sportsmanship.
18. To develop initiative.
19. To teach children how to compete.
20. To help children learn about their capabilities through comparisons with others.

Formal youth sport leagues were formed to help keep the idealized view of sport as a character-building activity for youths. Children would develop positive character traits and their idle time would be minimized. There are a number of organized youth leagues in the United States (as well as Canada and other Western nations). In the following pages we will examine a few examples of organized youth leagues beginning with, perhaps the most famous of them all, Little League Baseball.

FORMAL YOUTH BASEBALL

Little League Baseball was founded in 1939 in Williamsport, Pennsylvania, by Carl E. Stotz and Bert and George Bebble. There are many divisions (decided by age) in Little League Baseball. The most popular division is the Major League Division (for boys and girls between the ages 9 and 12). It is this division that receives the most media attention during its annual World Series. (A 2006 rule change now allows 13-year-olds to play in the World Series as long as they turned 13 after May 1.) The Major League Division utilizes a 60 foot diamond and the pitching distance is 46 feet. The Junior League Division is a program for boys and girls ages 13–14, using a conventional 90-foot diamond with a pitching distance of 60 feet 6 inches. The Senior League Division is for boys and girls ages 14–16, using a conventional field (*Little League Baseball*, 2008).

More than three million youths world-wide play Little League ball, making it the world's largest organized youth sports program. Little League baseball teaches sportsmanship and promotes the ideals of character building. One of the characteristics that makes Little League Baseball (Major Division) so special is its annual World Series. Little League baseball teams from all 50 U.S. states, more than 70 countries, and six continents (understandably, Antarctica is the lone continent which does not have Little League Baseball) compete against one another for the opportunity to play in the Little League World Series (LLWS), held in Williamsport every August. The top 16 qualifying teams from around the world are invited to the 6 week tournament. A local league has the option to choose a "Tournament Team" (or "All Stars") of 11 and 12-year-olds from within its division and enter the International Tournament leading to the series. All expenses for the teams advancing to the LLWS (travel, meals, housing) are paid by Little League Baseball. The LLWS is broadcast live in the United States and in many other countries around the world, adding to the overall formal, organized nature of the game. Furthermore, Little League Baseball has its own Hall of Fame Museum located in Williamsport.

Another organized baseball league is the Babe Ruth League. The Babe Ruth baseball and softball program uses regulation competitive baseball and softball rules and teaches skills, mental and physical development, a respect for the rules of the game, and basic ideals of sportsmanship and fair play (*Babe Ruth League*, 2008). The first Babe Ruth League was formed over 50 years ago by a group of men, dedicated to the youth of America, who met in a suburb of Trenton, New Jersey. This group eventually agreed to name Marius D. Bonacci as the founder of the program. They initially named their league the "Little Bigger League." It was renamed in 1954, when Claire Ruth, Babe Ruth's widow, learned of the merits of the organization and agreed to lend Babe's name to the league. Since its humble 10-team league start, the Babe Ruth League now has over 886,000 players on more than 45,000 teams in more than 7,300 leagues (*Babe Ruth League*, 2008). The 13–15 age division is the most popular and the one that most boys join after Little League. There is a Babe Ruth division for 16- to 18-year-olds that has been increasingly growing in size over the years. A softball division (with different age groupings) is designed for girls. The Babe Ruth League also has an annual World Series.

In 1999, the Babe Ruth League announced the renaming of one of its youth baseball division from the Bambino Division to the Cal Ripken Baseball Division. This division is for kids

12 and under. This league promotes providing every youngster the opportunity to play baseball and have fun while learning to play the game "The Ripken Way" (*Babe Ruth League*, 2008). Cal Ripken, Jr., the former Baltimore Orioles great and a graduate of the Babe Ruth program, is often cited as one who played the game "right." Ripken is also an example of a hero of "social acceptability" because he upholds the values of society, especially those of sportsmanship and hard work.

Little League and Babe Ruth League baseball are highly organized youth sport programs. They are adult-centered, meaning adults run the operation and children follow the standardized rules. Many people support these organized youth sport programs for those very reasons. Others, however, complain that a formal and rational organization deprives young people of playlike experiences. Nixon and Frey (1996) use the term little leaguism to describe youth sports that have become bureaucratic, standardized, efficiency-driven, rationalized, calculated, and predictable.

FORMAL YOUTH FOOTBALL

The most recognized formal and organized youth football program is Pop Warner Football. The history of Pop Warner Football can be traced to Philadelphia in the late 1920s and a group of factory owners who were tired of having youth throw rocks through their factory's windows. They attributed this delinquent behavior to the idleness of children with nothing better to do (Powell, 2003). As a result, they formed an athletic program for kids. They also assumed that football would be best sport to keep idle kids occupied and out of trouble. The league was called the Junior Football Conference and operated for the first time in 1929.

Today, over 360,000 boys and girls, ages 5–16, mostly in the United States (there are teams in Japan and Mexico), play in eight different age categories of Pop Warner Football (*Pop Warner*, 2005). In some areas of the country Pop Warner Football is taken very seriously. For example, as Powell (2003) describes, there were more than 6,500 fans in attendance for a Miami Pop Warner championship game at the 65 pound division. In the poorer neighborhoods of Miami, like so many other areas, sports, in this case football, is viewed by some community members as the best way to escape their impoverished environment. Powell describes one Pop Warner playoff game in Miami that was marred by gun fire in the nearby neighborhood. Just as colleges and professional teams compete for athletes, rival youth football leagues in Miami vie for youth talent. "But Pop Warner is the only league that offers the possibility of playing for a national championship at Disney World. For that reason, Pop Warner is far and away Miami's dominant youth football league, home to the best players and the toughest competition" (2003: 5).

TENNIS

Tennis is a sport that historically has been linked to the wealthy socio-economic classes. At private clubs, the girls wore white skirts and boys wore hip-hugging white shorts and swung wooden rackets while adults often drank cocktails courtside (McKibben, 2006). Many public schools offered tennis in the 1950s and 1960s and baby boomers began to embrace the sport as way to stay fit. The interest in tennis reached its peak in the 1970s when an estimated 36 million boys and girls played tennis (McKibben, 2006). Court time was coveted. Private clubs and public tennis courts were rapidly built to meet the growing demand. "During the sport's peak in the mid–1970s, developers couldn't build private clubs fast enough to satisfy the public's urge to whack a fuzzy yellow ball. The building boom continued through the 1980s, even as the number of recreational tennis players fell by more than half and cheap-to-build suburban public courts flooded the landscape" (McKibben, 2006: A21). Today, many of the private clubs have closed their doors. "The demise of the private tennis club has touched nearly every region of the country, from San Francisco to Kansas City to New York, where four Manhattan facilities recently closed. Hardest hit is Southern California, where private clubs, once only for the rich, proliferated after World War II to serve a growing upper-middle class. Half of Orange County's 22 tennis-only private clubs have been bulldozed and replaced by shopping malls, condos and homes in the last 15 years" (McKibben, 2006: A21).

Many youth today prefer to play soccer. But that does not mean that tennis is dead, as nearly 25 million Americans still play the game (McKibben, 2006).

FORMAL YOUTH SOCCER

Soccer has gained popularity in the United States over the past two decades. Many youth soccer leagues have developed across the nation. Soccer is often a preferred sport because it is an inexpensive sport to fund (all that is really needed is a ball and an empty field with a goal at each end) and smaller children can compete more evenly than in contact sports such as football, rugby, and basketball. Soccer is appealing because it is a simple game to comprehend and youth can easily pick up the few critical rules. Today's youth also prefer soccer over baseball because they get to run around in soccer, whereas in baseball there is a great deal of standing around doing nothing—especially for outfielders. The recent success of the men's and primarily the women's U.S. National Soccer teams has led to many American youth idolizing soccer stars.

Among the more popular formal youth soccer associations are the American Youth Soccer Organization (AYSO), which helps to support and manage youth soccer leagues, and the U.S. Youth Soccer, association which assists those who wish to organize youth soccer leagues. Approximately 13 million Americans under the age of eighteen play soccer (U.S. Embassy, 2008). The popularity of youth soccer created the "soccer mom" phenomena. A soccer mom is someone who drives her children to soccer games and watches them compete. Since the parents were probably never soccer players, the children get to play a sport for which parents are not "armchair quarterbacks"—constantly suggesting better playing techniques based on their own overstated knowledge of the game.

SPECIAL OLYMPICS

Sports are typically viewed as physical activities performed by individuals who possess the necessary physical attributes to play. Physically-challenged youth have historically been shunned from the sporting world. But what if someone who is wheelchair-bound really wants to play basketball? Shouldn't they be allowed the opportunity? They will not be able to "run" up and down the court, but they can wheel themselves up and down the court.

To that end, the Special Olympics was created. In 1968, Chicago played host to the First International Special Olympics Games. The Special Olympics provides year-round sports training and athletic competition to people with disabilities in more than 180 countries. There are more programs than ever before for persons with disabilities. The Special Olympics now involves more than 2.5 million athletes who train and compete in countries around the world (The Special Olympics, 2008). The Special Olympics has helped to create a global community of inclusion, helping to change stigmatizing attitudes while fostering acceptance and understanding. At the start of the twenty-first century, there exists a general acceptance of the idea that youth and adults with disabilities should no longer be automatically excluded, as they once were, from a wide range of activities (Fink, 2000).

CHARACTERISTICS OF FORMAL YOUTH SPORTS

As our brief review reveals, there are a number of general characteristics of formal youth sport. Obviously, formal sport involves the realization that such activities of youth are organized in a highly structured manner. Listed below are the primary attributes of formal sports:

- Activity is adult-controlled
- Activity may be repetitious and boring, especially practices
- The best athletes play the most, and the less-talented youths may not play at all
- Players run set plays, often utilizing a playbook; spontaneity is generally discouraged — especially if "creative" plays initiated by the youth are unsuccessful
- Great emphasis is on specialization and playing a specific position
- Rule enforcement is via referees; the youth do not work out their own differences
- Coaches assess the quality of play of each participant
- Activity is played for a set period of time (a certain number of minutes or innings)
- The impact on family life can be quite high as schedules may need to be adjusted to fit the sporting requirements of the youth.

Some scholars believe that formal youth sports, because of their highly structured design, create more harm than good for participants. As a result, there are a number of criticisms of formal youth sport.

CRITICISMS OF FORMAL YOUTH SPORT

Despite the many benefits of formal sport programs, there are a number of detractors of organized sports and criticisms of formal youth programs. A number of sport sociologists argue that formal youth sports have taken away the playful character of sport (Nixon and Frey, 1996; Devereaux, 1976; Horn, 1977). As the focus shifts from play-centered to performance-centered, a corresponding overemphasis on winning occurs. A "win at all costs" approach is not appropriate for youth sport. The overemphasis on winning is often encouraged by over-zealous coaches. In his research of Pop Warner football, Powell (2003) found that coaches at the elite 95-pound division conduct drills and practices like a "boot camp. " These practices consisted of sprints, rope-netting skip drills and agility tests. After an hour of conditioning drills, the team breaks down into groups to run drills and plays. Powell (2003) quotes one coach barking commands to one of his young players, "Get mean! Wipe that smile off your face. Get ready to hurt somebody. Get mean! Come on, get mean!" (p. 3).

In addition, the play aspect is compromised in formal youth sports because of the regimentation of organized sport programs. As sports become increasingly regulated, the spontaneity of the game is greatly compromised. Many youth turn to informal sport because it is less structured and offers greater freedom and creativity.

Another criticism of formal sports is that league officials and coaches often forget, or fail to understand, the physical (motor skills), cognitive, emotional and developmental stage of their youth athletes (Chalip and Green, 1998; Nixon and Frey, 1996; Hellison, 1995; Hutslar, 1985; and Martens, 1988). The case described by Powell (2003) regarding "boot camp" practices may be applied here as well. In her book *Little Girls in Pretty Boxes* (2000), sports columnist Joan Ryan describes the often harrowing experiences which young female gymnasts and figure skaters undergo in their training. Many of them end up suffering from eating disorders such as bulimia and anorexia. She writes:

> Coaches push because they are paid to produce great gymnasts. They are relentless about weight because physically round gymnasts and skaters don't win. Coaches are intolerant of injuries because in the race against puberty, time off is death. Their job is not to turn out happy, well-adjusted young women; it is to turn out champions. If they scream, belittle or ignore, if they prod an injured girl to forget her pain, if they push her to drop out of school, they are only doing what the parents have paid them to do. So, sorting out the blame when a girl falls apart is a messy proposition; everyone claims he was just doing his job [Ryan, 2000: 11].

Furthermore, many youth find organized, formal sport as not only too restrictive, but filled with anxiety and angst. They are turned off by adults who bark orders and league officials who impose standardized rules. This is one reason my so many youth have turned to informal sports.

Informal Youth Sports

Informal sports are those which are player-controlled, free from governing bodies and adult supervision and allow the participant an opportunity to have fun in a self-expressing format. Informal sports include skating boarding, bicycle riding, jogging, and so on. They also include most of the extreme sports described in Chapter 3. (As noted in Chapter 3, some of these extreme sports have become formalized in some settings.) According to 2001 statistics complied by the American Sports Data (SGMA International "Superstudy"), many of the most popular sports for youngsters are informal sports (Connors, 2002):

Activity	Participants (in millions)
1. Basketball	11.287
2. Soccer	7.692
3. Inline Skating	7.482
4. Baseball	4.719
5. Scooter riding	4.469
6. Freshwater fishing	3.712
7. Running/jogging	3.340
8. Calisthenics	3.327
9. Stretching	3.169
10. Skateboarding	3.144

Sports such as inline skating and skateboarding continue to gain in popularity due in part to increased media exposure. Furthermore, for many youth, skateboarder Tony Hawk is their favorite athlete and sports hero.

Informal youth sport participation usually involves family members such as siblings and cousins, along with friends and neighborhood peers. These youths get together, without the help or interference of adults, and ascertain for themselves what sporting activities to engage in. There must be a general agreement on what to play, and how to play it, in order for team play to occur. Whether kids are playing stickball on city streets (where they must determine what serves as "bases") or football in an open field (where boundaries may be determined by corn fields or hedgerows) they must work out for themselves how the game will proceed. When cooperation fails, kids go off to do their own thing.

There are a number of characteristics that distinguish informal sports from formal ones. The significant characteristics of informal sports include:

• Activity that is player-controlled
• Activity that involves action, especially that which leads to scoring opportunities
• Activity that maximizes personal involvement in the sport
• Spontaneity of play; that is, the plays do not come from a pre-written "playbook"
• No referees, the youth work out disputes for themselves
• A close score and relatively even teams, which lead to a competitive sporting activity
• Activity can end at any time; even if its just because the kids are bored of playing or they are called to dinner
• Opportunities to reaffirm friendships through participation in the sporting activity
• Seldom impacts the total family life; family schedules are not adjusted so that youths can participate in informal play.

These are just generalizations of informal play. Nowhere should it be implied that informal play is problem-free. For example, disputes between participants may be settled by the bigger kids imposing their will on the smaller ones. As we all know, kids can be very cruel to one another. Because of the lack of adult supervision, the informal setting allows unrestricted opportunities for the dominant kids to pick on others.

HEALTH FITNESS

Perhaps the most important aspect of youth sport participation involves the idea that youths actually engage in some type of sporting or physical play activity. There currently exists an obesity epidemic among American youth. Many children are playing video games sitting on a comfortable couch indoors. If the cliché "The youth are our future" is true, and certainly it is, adults of today need to make sure that the future generation is physically fit to run the world. Health fitness is, therefore, a critical element of the future of humanity. Health fitness can only be achieved through regular exercise and a proper diet.

There are three components to health fitness: heart-lung endurance (cardiovascular fitness), strength and flexibility (musculoskeletal fitness), and a good ratio of body fat to muscle (nutritional fitness). "All three components are essential for children's short- and long-term good health. Kids who exercise regularly have bigger hearts, more muscle mass, less fatty tissue, stronger bones, and more flexible joints. Being fit in childhood helps people fight off a host of diseases in later life, including heart disease, back pain, and osteoporosis. Fit children are far less likely to be injured in sports than youngsters who aren't in shape" (Micheli and Jenkins, 1990: 26). Individuals who play sports or engage in healthy physical activities when they are young are also more likely to continue their healthy habits in adulthood.

According to a recent study on sports participation and health-related behaviors among youth in the United States:

> Female sports participants were significantly less likely than female nonparticipants to report not eating fruits and vegetables on the previous day and were more likely to report 3 or more 20-minute sessions of vigorous physical activity during the previous week. In addition, female sports participants were less likely than female nonparticipants to report cigarette smoking, using marijuana or cocaine, having sexual intercourse during the past 3 months, and contemplating or attempting suicide.... Male sports participants were less likely than male nonparticipants to not report eating fruits and vegetables on the previous day and were more likely to report 3 or more 20-minute sessions of vigorous physical activity during the previous week. In addition, male sports participants were significantly less likely than male nonparticipants to report cigarette smoking; using marijuana, cocaine or other illegal drugs; sniffing glue, contemplating suicide; carrying a weapon, and trying to lose weight [Pate, Stewart, Levine and Dowda, 2002: 906].

The study does note, however, that sports participants were equally as likely as nonparticipants to report eating fatty foods, engaging in one or more binge drinking episodes in the past month, being involved in a physical fight, and using laxatives to lose or control weight. Clearly, societal pressures to consume fast foods, drink to excess, solve problems through violent means and adhere to narrow models of beauty remain problems for everyone, athletes and nonathletes alike. But regular participation in sports program does seem to correlate to an overall healthier lifestyle.

Disturbing Trends in Youth Sports Today

There are some disturbing trends in youth sports today and these include a sports culture run amok, stressed out youth sport participants, steroid use and a great deal of violence perpetrated mostly by overzealous parents. Increasingly, the youth sport environment is often one where coaches scream, sideline parents act out angrily, and children just do not have as much fun as they deserve. As Bigelow (2000) states, "We have a youth sports system that is wildly out of control or, at a minimum, one with badly misplaced priorities" (p. 7).

STRESS

Youth sports are supposed to provide pleasurable experiences for children. The sports environment should be a place where youth have fun, reaffirm friendships, burn off excess energy and receive positive reinforcement from their parents and family members. Unfortunately, many youth experience a great deal of stress during their sports participation. "At all competitive levels, athletes are subjected to both physical and psychological resources of the competitor, athletic stress is said to exist. While stress is endemic to the athletic setting, it is well recognized that extreme levels of stress can have adverse consequences on performance, enjoyment of the activity, and the physical and psychological welfare of the athlete" (Smith, 1986: 107). Stressful situations are the result of demands that test or exceed the resources of an individual (Smith, 1986). As a result, we define athletic stress as forces that cause bodily or mental strain. Bodily strain is caused by excessive physical demands on the body, such as fatigue as a result of a strenuous workout. Mental strain can be caused by internal pressure that the youth places on self-performance.

An increasing number of young athletes are experiencing stress. The source of this stress is not sport participation itself; rather, it is often caused by parents of these athletes. Instead offering encouragement and supportive praise, many parents yell at their children during their youth games. The authors have attended numerous youth sports events over the years and have heard a number of parents yelling at their children by calling them "bums" and "useless" when they make a bad play. The children who are screamed at not only feel bad about themselves, they are embarrassed by their parent's behavior, and experience a great deal of stress. The consequences of experiencing such stress may be both immediate and delayed. Youths who no longer value sport participation because of stress will most likely quit and find some other activity free from parental involvement. For other youths, years of stress caused by fanatical parental interference may boil over in early adulthood when the young athlete becomes free from direct parental supervision. The case of Todd Marinovich, described at the beginning of this chapter, serves as an exemplar of behavior of youth who have experienced harmful stress. When Marinovich was old enough to go to college and live on his own, he finally allowed himself the opportunity to express his newfound freedom. Some of these youthful transgressions had harmful results. Todd's brother, Mikhail, appears to be following in his footsteps.

Marv Marinovich's extreme efforts to push his son Todd into college and professional sports were fulfilled, but at a great cost. Although few parents go to the limits of pushing their children into sports as Marv Marinovich, there are many parents who do push their children toward the unrealistic goals of college sport scholarships and professional sports contracts. These slightly-delusional parents hear and read about all the money professional athletes make and believe that their children can also do it. The odds, of course, are strongly against any youth making to the professional level. Fewer than 2 percent of high school athletes will receive a college athletic scholarship and only one in 13,000 high school athletes will ever receive a paycheck from a professional sports team (Relin, 2005). When youth are made to feel that their self-worth depends on how they play the game, they are likely to experience stress (Martens and Seefeldt, 1979).

Most parents find it very important that their children win at the sports they play. Winning is a high priority to parents. However, when children are asked why they play sports, they overwhelmingly indicate that winning is a low priority (until around high school age). "Children play sports for other reasons, the most common being, in order of importance, to have fun, to develop skills, to get exercise, and to socialize.... But when adults are queried about their priorities relating to involvement in youth sports, winning places much higher on the list" (Bigelow, 2000: 10). Clearly, youth and adults have different ideas about the important aspects of youth sports. As a result, "Across the country, millions of children are being chewed up and spit out by a sports culture run amok. With pro scouts haunting the nation's playgrounds in search of the next LeBron [James] or Freddy [Adu], parents and coaches are conspiring to run youth-sports leagues like incubators for future professional athletes" (Relin, 2005: 4).

ANABOLIC STEROID USE

Steroid use is generating great discussion and concern in the sports world. (See Chapter 8 for a full definition and explanation of how anabolic steroids work.) It is important to note that the nonmedical use of steroids is illegal and banned by sports organizations. Although much of the discussion on steroid use centers on professional athletes, many "prepubescent athletes are experimenting with performance-enhancing drugs" (Relin, 2005: 4). Furthermore, the use of anabolic steroids is not limited to athletes, bodybuilders or males. "Studies show that nearly 5% of 12- to 18-year-old boys and up to 2% of girls have tried steroids. And in a 2004 survey, 19% of eighth-graders, 29% of 10th-graders and 42% of 12th-graders said that steroids were 'fairly easy' or 'very easy' to obtain" (O'Shea, 2005: 8). Parents should look for a number of warning signs that their child may be using steroids: mood swings (which are, unfortunately, common with many teens), obsession with body image, excessive acne that appears suddenly (generally on the face and back), and rapid gains in muscle size and strength (O'Shea, 2005).

VIOLENCE

The increasing number of violent incidents found in the youth sport culture over the past few decades is enough to frighten sensible people. (See Chapter 9 for an in-depth look at violence in sport). The United States is the most violent society of the Western world and this is reflected in youth sport. A great deal of violence in youth sports is caused by out-of-control adults. "The behavior of adults has been at the center of the debate about reforming kids' sports ever since 2002, when Thomas Junta of Reading, Mass., was convicted of beating Michael Costin to death during an argument at their sons' youth hockey practice" (Relin, 2005: 7). The types of violence found in youth sport includes parents fighting parents, parents attacking youth participants, parents attacking referees, coaches attacking referees, youths attacking referees, and referees attacking coaches.

Consider these stories as examples of the escalating levels of violence in youth sport:

- A 2000 soccer match involving teams of boys ages 8–9 ended in a fistfight among parents and coaches in South Brunswick, N.J. Police were summoned to separate the combatants (*USA Today*, 9/11/00).
- A youth football (14- and 15-year-olds) game in Port Orange, Florida, ended in a brawl involving more than 100 parents, coaches and teenagers in 2000. One player was punched and a number of adults were arrested for assault, including one for assaulting a police officer (*Buffalo News*, 9/25/00).
- In a 1993 youth football (13- to 15-year-olds) game in Oakland Park, Florida, a youth quit in during the game and left the field. A teammate's mother yelled at him to return to the game. The youth attacked the woman and punched her in the face and began fighting with her relatives. The attacking youth's mom pulled out a gun and threatened those who tried to intervene (*Los Angeles Times*, 9/9/93).
- The 2005 Little League baseball season in New Bedford, Massachusetts, was suspended after a series of violent incidents, including two mothers who got into a fistfight in the stands. One woman's son jumped the playing field fence and helped his mother attack the other woman (*ABC News*, 8/13/05).
- A father, who also served as an assistant coach, ran out on a football field and attacked two 9-year-old players from the opposing team whom he accused of blocking his son too hard (Ernst, 1999).
- Former New York Islander defenseman Gerry Hart was accused of assaulting a 14-year-old Syracuse boy during post-game handshakes at a youth hockey tournament (Albanese, 1997A).
- A brawl erupted during postgame handshakes in a youth hockey league game in Potsdam, New York, that even involved the Zamboni driver (*The Post-Standard*, 2/26/97).
- A youth hockey association in New York State barred a parent from home games for one year because he punched a referee (Albanese, 1997B).

- In 2000, a 15-year-old boy was banned for life from playing competitive soccer anywhere in the world after hitting a referee twice in the face at the end of a South Ceredigion Junior Football League match in west Wales (*The Post-Standard*, 8/19/00).
- A Massachusetts father, who was angry about the rough play in a youth hockey game, beat a hockey coach to death. "In North Carolina, a mother attending her child's soccer game was charged with assault for slapping a 14-year-old referee. A 36-year-old coach in Florida attacked an umpire and broke his jaw during a baseball game, while a police officer who was thrown out of his son's baseball game for unruly conduct later retaliated by pulling the ump over at a traffic-stop for allegedly making an illegal left turn" (Fridman, 2004: 1).
- Referees are not always the victims of violence. In Fayetteville, Georgia, a youth basketball referee, who was apparently angry that his calls were being criticized, slashed an assistant coach with a knife after a game involving 7- and 8-year-old players as their stunned parents watched (Stacy, 2001).

The above are just a few examples of out-of-control and violent behavior occurring in youth sports. Each of them depict unacceptable forms of behavior. We have saved this story for last because it is perhaps the most difficult one to accept in a civil society. T-ball is a game designed to indoctrinate young children (starting around age 5) into the game of baseball. In June, 2005, a North Union Township, Pennsylvania, T-ball coach (Mark R. Downs) allegedly paid one of his players $25 to hurt an 8-year-old mentally disabled teammate so he wouldn't have to put the boy in the game as the league rules mandate (all players on the team must play). The disabled child was hit in the head and in the groin with a baseball by his teammate just before the game started. Downs was arrested on a number of criminal charges. In 2006, Downs was sentenced to consecutive six to 36-month sentences for corruption of minors and criminal solicitation to commit simple assault. Clearly, there is no reason to emphasize winning in T-ball. This ultra-competitive coach who had a burning desire to win at T-ball should never have been in coaching.

Emphasizing Sportsmanship

Many communities have taken action to implement, and in some cases, force, sportsmanship ideals onto parents. In 2000, Florida's Jupiter Tequesta Athletic Association, which sponsors basketball, soccer, football, softball and baseball for 6,000 boys and girls in the community, required parents to take a mandatory lesson in sportsmanship. After completing the sportsmanship lesson, parents had to sign a code of behavior agreement. If they failed to abide by the rules, they risked the expulsion of themselves and their children from youth sports (Meadows, 2000). Although most parents think this is a good idea, others protest, claiming they have the right to yell and scream and say whatever they want while watching their children play sports. Clearly, these people are lacking in good sportsmanship character. Today, the Jupiter-Tequesta Athletic Association allows parents to take an online course on how to behave at their children's athletic events (Relin, 2005).

A girls' soccer youth league in Northern Ohio instituted a "Silent Sunday" where cheering, clapping, griping and chattering is forbidden (Mihoces, 1999). Most of girls who play soccer in this suburban Cleveland league agreed with the idea. But many parents expressed that they have a right to cheer for their daughters if they want to.

Educators, student athletes and others in the state of Maine have launched a "counterrevolution" called Sports Done Right with a goal of transforming the way Maine, and the rest of the nation, conduct youth sport programs. Their first step is de-emphasize competition so that kids stay in sports for the fun of it, instead of dropping out because of stress and turmoil sometimes associated with competition. "The program has identified core principles that it insists must be present in a healthy sports environment for kids, including good sportsmanship, discouragement of early specialization and the assurance that teams below the varsity level make it their mission to develop the skills of every child on every team, to promote a lifelong involvement with sports" (Relin, 2005: 7).

At the youth sport level it is important for parents to realize that winning is *not* everything; in fact, it is of small consolation. Fun should be the top priority and emphasized as such. No child should be belittled, in private or public, and all children should be encouraged regardless of their skill level. Parents should cheer all players, even the opponents— these are children, remember?! Parents need to stop trying to live their lives vicariously through their children's sport participation. Furthermore, parents should talk with each other, and never yell or assault someone. Participation in multiple sports should be emphasized over specializing in one sport. Parents need to let the coaches coach and not worry so much about playing time. In addition, parents should compliment coaches and referees for doing their jobs the best they can.

Parents also need to be realistic about the skill levels of their children and their potential to play sports at the college or professional level, although, with the economic reality of players' salaries, it is easy to understand why so many parents (especially those from lower socioeconomic families) encourage their children to pursue a career in sports. It is true that winning is an American value and virtue. However, there are other American virtues that should be emphasized, especially at the youth level, including teamwork, loyalty, commitment, and sportsmanship. If parents would take heed of these issues the youth sports environment would be a much happier and safer place for children. Furthermore, parents would serve as positive role models for their children and sportsmanship ideals would be passed from one generation to the next.

Evaluating Youth Sports

It would seem that youth sport participation has both positive and negative consequences. The majority of youth have a positive experience with sports, but clearly, many others do not. One of the sources of stress for parents of youth athletes and a source of pain and discomfort for youth athletes is sport injuries.

Sport Injuries

Most parents, coaches and league officials do their best to assure that injuries in youth sport are minimized. As a result, most children who play sports will not be seriously injured. Nonetheless, sports injuries are fairly common for young athletes. More than half of all youth sport injuries occur at practice rather than during competition (National Center for Sport Safety, 2006). The two most common types of sports injury for youth athletes are sprains (in injury to a ligament such as tearing or stretching) and strains (an injury to a tendon or muscle). Growth plate injuries (the growth plate is at the end of the long bones in developing children before it is replaced by solid bone) are also common for youngsters. Immature bones (growth plate), insufficient rest after an injury, and poor training or conditioning contribute to a large number of sport injuries for youngsters (National Center for Sport Safety, 2006).

It is common to divide injuries into two major categories: acute and chronic. Acute injuries occur quickly as a result of a traumatic event followed immediately by a pattern of signs and symptoms such as pain, swelling, and loss of function (Pfeiffer and Mangus, 2002). Cuts, bruises, sprains and fractures are a common type of acute injury. Chronic injuries are those which linger and develop over an extended period of time and are not tied to a single traumatic event. A chronic injury could be the result of knee damage or arthritis. In extreme cases, an athlete may suffer from a catastrophic injury, which involves damage to the brain or spinal cord and is potentially life threatening or permanent (Pfeiffer and Mangus, 2002). Tackles in football that result in a broken neck or spinal cord are an example of a catastrophic injury. As more children play organized youth sports, the number of injuries is expected to increase. Limiting children to one sport in hopes of minimizing sports injuries is a fallacy, as specialization in year-round sport at an early age is often cited by doctors as a source of injury (Relin, 2005).

According to the National Center for Sports Safety (2008) more than 3.5 million children ages 14 and under receive medical treatment for sport injuries each year. The Center also reported that in 2001, the number of sport-related injuries for youth ages 5–14 were basketball — 680,307; football — 413,620; baseball — 170,902; soccer — 163,003; gymnastics — 99,722; hockey — 63,945; and volleyball — 55,860. Injuries are also common for youth who do not play organized sport. More than a half million youth are injured each year from bike riding (The Center for Disease Control, 2002). More than 300,000 youth are injured each year playing roller sports and on playgrounds. Sustaining an injury is, indeed, very common for young athletes.

Injuries in sports cannot be eliminated completely, just as injuries off the field cannot be eliminated. Injuries are more likely to occur when youth overtrain. It is important to recognize the physical signs of overtraining. The American Council on Exercise warns that if exercise leaves someone more exhausted than energized, then overtraining may the culprit.

In short, it is important to provide as safe an environment as possible for youth while they participate in sport.

EVALUATING EFFECTIVENESS

Evaluating the effectiveness of youth sport programs has a lot to do with one's own personal experiences and their perception as to the role of sport in youth development. John Underwood (1989), for one, has a very negative outlook on organized youth sports. "I am against little league sport. Not *some* little league sport. *All* little league sport. In principle, in fact, in perpetuity. I will go to my grave believing little league sport is bad for the youth of America, because I don't see the swamp being cleared in my lifetime. Just the opposite. The swamp gets bigger every day" (Underwood, 1989: 120). Underwood is against organized youth sport for many of the same reasons we documented previously. He views little league sports as an ultimate form of exploitation, where adult domination of organized youth sport deprives children the chance to grow naturally in sport and where parental misbehavior causes harm to young people's development. Anyone who concentrates on the negatives in sport will find enough examples of it to support their belief.

Underwood (1989) expresses an idealistic view of a sport grounded in an era of the past when it was safe for children to leave the house and play all day on their own. The world has changed drastically over the past few decades. Organized youths sports are designed, today, to provide a safe environment for youth to play with adult supervision; and thus, protection from potential predators. Underwood (1989) is certainly accurate about one critical issue, namely, "The most important thing about playing sports is to *play*. To take part, with all the good that implies. It is okay to try to win, and there is an undeniable joy in winning. But it is enough to take part" (p. 132).

The vast majority of children and parents involved in organized youth sports have positive experiences. Chalip and Green (1998) promote the virtue and value of modified youth sport programs. "Research shows that modified programs can broaden the base of youth sport participation, enhance children's affective experience of sport, and evaluate the level of skill they attain" (326). Parents of children who play modified youth sports generally like the idea that adult imposition in the organization of the sport is minimized and the aspects of having fun while developing skills is emphasized. Chalip and Green warn, however, that modified youth programs will have difficulty maintaining their distinctiveness from traditional organized youth sport programs if they are implemented within established sport club structures.

Youth with Attention Deficit Hyperactivity Disorder (ADHD) (officially identified in 1994) may benefit from sport participation. ADHD is identified by three characteristics: inattentiveness, impulsiveness, and hyperactivity. Some children with ADHD may be able to sit still and contain their behavior but find it difficult to pay attention. Others may be able to pay attention for a while, but quickly lose focus and become impulsive. Children with ADHD can play organized sports. As Small and Spear (2002) explain:

> There is no reason why your child with ADHD cannot fully participate in some kind of sport. But a hyperactive child usually does not do well with a team-based sport unless that child has lots of adult supervision. This does not mean that they can never play a team sport.... The key to keeping your child with ADHD physically active is to find a sport that has more individualistic attention. Activities such as martial arts and dance instruction are less competitive, yet allow a child to participate in a group environment.... A good coach for an ADHD child must be patient, able to explain things clearly, and able to direct your child. One-on-one activities would also be great choices for ADHD kids. You might try rollerblading, walking, biking, or skateboarding. These are sports you can do with your child to help keep him in focus [p. 71].

A 2000 study of more than 14,000 teenagers found that those who participated in team sports were less likely to use drugs, smoke, have sex, carry weapons or have unhealthy eating habits (Tanner, 2000). The researchers attributed their findings in part to team rules that forbid unhealthy (e.g., smoking) behavior. Sport participation contributes to healthy behaviors by encouraging a well-balanced diet and physical conditioning. Furthermore, the greater the length of time youth participate in sport, the less time they have for deviant activities.

SUMMARY

Children and play go hand-in-hand. Play should be encouraged, as it develops a child's imagination, intelligence, perceptual-motor development, and it is a healthy activity. Sport represents an evolutionary growth of play. Sport may be formalized or performed informally. Organized formal youth sports are viewed by some as a means of social mobility. They believe that if the child hones his or her skills while young, that he or she may some day find fame and fortune at the professional level.

There are those who believe youth sports have become corrupted by the increasing level of organization and structure. Changes in the family structure (e.g., divorce and children splitting time with parents) have made organized youth sport programs attractive for those parents who simply do not have the time to keep an eye on their children or to provide them with sport instruction and coaching.

An important factor in whether children should participate in sports is their own desires to do so. There are a wide variety of sport options, both formal and informal, that should be made available to youths so that they can try them out and decide for themselves which, if any, they enjoy playing.

There is a good deal of debate over whether sports "builds character," particularly whether abiding by societal rules is a sign of good character.

Organized youth sports have arisen throughout the Western world since the middle of the nineteenth century, and have been linked with physical education. Such formal youth sports, including Little League Baseball, Pop Warner Football, and Youth Soccer Leagues, have become an integral part of American culture. Despite their many benefits, there are a number of criticisms, which focus on the overemphasis upon winning at any cost. Informal sports, which are more player-controlled and less regimented, have arisen partly in response to such criticisms.

Health fitness is a major component of youth sport. Perhaps the most important aspect is the idea that youths engaging in such activities will be more physically fit. Related to this, however, are the health risks involved, including physical injuries and mental stress. The use of performance-enhancement drugs and the danger of violence both off and on the playing field is as real for youths as it is for adult athletes. Still, recent studies have shown that sports participation among U.S. youths is associated with numerous positive health behaviors.

Key Terms

Acute Injuries Sports injuries which occur quickly as a result of a traumatic event and are followed immediately by a pattern of signs and symptoms such as pain, swelling, and loss of function.

Athletic Stress Forces that cause bodily or mental strain.

Attention Deficit Hyperactivity Disorder (ADHD) A behavior disorder identified by three characteristics: inattentiveness, impulsiveness, and hyperactivity.

Babe Ruth Baseball/Softball Program Using regulation competitive baseball and softball rules, this program teaches skills, mental and physical development, a respect for the rules of the game, and basic ideals of sportsmanship and fair play.

Bodily Strain Physical impairment caused by excessive demands on the body.

Cal Ripken Baseball Division Part of the Babe Ruth Baseball/Softball Program, this division is for kids 12 and under.

Catastrophic Injury A sports injury which involves damage to the brain or spinal cord, or both, and is potentially life threatening or permanent.

Character Individual personality and behavioral traits, both good and bad, which define who a person is.

Character Development Gaining qualities that will make a person better able to deal with life's problems; many believe sports enhance character development.

Chronic Injuries Sports injuries which linger and develop over an extended period of time and are not tied to a single traumatic event.

Informal Sports Those which are player-controlled, free from governing bodies and adult supervision, and allow the participant an opportunity to have fun in a self-expressing format.

Little League Baseball A program for youth, geared to provide a safe and healthy environment where they can learn the fundamentals of baseball while becoming good and decent citizens.

Little Leaguism A term used to describe youth sports that have become bureaucratic, standardized, efficiency-driven, rationalized, calculated, and predictable.

Mental Strain Distress caused by internal pressure that the youth places on self-performance.

Muscular Christianity A term used to describe the religious philosophy of teaching morals and values through sport.

Pop Warner Football The most recognized formal and organized youth football program.

Soccer Mom Someone who drives her children to soccer games and watches them compete.

T-ball A game designed to indoctrinate young children (starting around age 5) into the game of baseball.

Discussion Questions

• In 2005, a baseball team of 11- and 12-year-olds was kicked out of a league in Canal Winchester, Ohio, because they were too good. The Columbus Stars were removed from their league because they were humiliating their opponents by such scores as 18–0, 13–0, 24–0, and 12–2. The other teams began complaining and cancelled their games against the Stars. Do you think the league did the right thing? What type of messages do you think the coaches of the other teams sent to their players by asking the league to cancel their games against the Stars? Explain.

• What are some of the reasons why parents encourage their children to participate in sports? What do you think are positive reasons and what are negative reasons?

• How does participation in youth sports correspond to a child's mental and physical development? What are some steps that can be taken to make sure that these progress in an acceptable way?

• What are some of the key differences between formal and informal youth sports? Why is informal youth sport becoming more popular in the Twenty-First Century?

• Do you think that sports "builds character"? What does this phrase mean to you, and how can it be applied to youth sports in particular?

CHAPTER 7

High School and College Sports

"John Doe Scores Six Touchdowns in Final High School Football Game," reads the local newspaper article. Doe has the perfect combination of speed and power, two important tools for a running back. Doe has set state records in career touchdowns scored and rushing yardage. College recruiters are drooling over the hope that Doe might play for them. Community members from Doe's high school assume he will star in football at the college ranks. Unfortunately, Doe does not possess the perfect combination of athletic and academic skills. He has struggled every year to remain academically eligible for high school sports and, recently, Doe has learned that he has failed the SAT. His low high school grade point average does not qualify him for colleges offering football programs. Doe had spent far more time preparing himself for college as a football player than college as a student. What will he do now? Academic eligibility is just one of many concerns related to sports in the educational setting.

Interscholastic Athletics and Academics

Nearly all secondary schools offer interscholastic athletics. In the United States, and most other nations of the West, colleges and universities also routinely field sports teams. Sports and education would seem to go hand in hand. As discussed in chapter 6, proponents of sports in schools often cite the long-held belief that sport teaches positive character traits and values (such as teamwork, dedication, loyalty and success due to hard work) that will transcend from the playing field onto the game of life. The schools themselves benefit from the increased commitment of alumni and local supporters. Others, however, argue that the priority placed on sport programs often distract the school (administrators, students and parents) from prioritizing educational goals (e.g., intellectual development through a rigorous curriculum). In addition, they claim that the costs involved in promoting and recruiting are not offset by ticket sales and contributions, and that teams are detrimental to the ultimate bottom line.

THE CONSEQUENCES OF INTERSCHOLASTIC SPORT PARTICIPATION

High school and college athletes receive fame and accolades from peers, community members, and sometimes the media. Males have long enjoyed the benefits of being an athlete in high school and college and more recently females have also begun to experience this. This is because high school sports accomplishments generally receive more attention than academic ones. The primary reason for this is the fact that interschool sports competitions provide a means of unifying the entire school. For example, individuals from diverse racial and social class groups are afforded a bonding opportunity through sports. Teachers that support school sports are generally more respected by students than those who do not support sports. The school benefits indirectly by sports because of the social control apparatus that accompanies participation. Athletes must abide by a number of rules in order to remain eligible. These rules apply to both on the

116

field behavior (team rules, league rules, and so forth) and off the field behavior (grades and personal behavior). Research has shown that, in general, athletic participation does *not* lead to poorer academic performance or lower academic aspirations (Nixon and Frey, 1996). High school sports often provide local communities with a rallying point of local pride. In addition, individuals who play sports feel an increased attachment to the school, school values, and community.

There are, however, a number of potential problems associated with interscholastic and intercollegiate sport. Sport specialization has led many athletes to concentrate on just one sport, year-round, instead of enjoying participating in multiple sports. Proponents of sport specialization, however, argue that when athletes concentrate on one sport, they increase their chance of becoming dominant in that sport. Sports are often fields of elitism. The elite interscholastic and intercollegiate sports (football and basketball) generally dominate the athletic budgets of schools. Elite athletes often have such inflated egos that they begin to think they are better and more important than other students. Cheating in its multiple forms (e.g., violating rules of sportsmanship, taking performance-enhancing drugs) undermines the idealism of sport as an institution of character building. The excessive pressures to win often "cheat" participants from the fun of playing sports. Many athletes become disenchanted by the over-emphasis on rules and the pressures to win. They end up feeling like they are doing work rather than engaging in play. The authoritarian coach may also ruin the sport experience of participants. (The role of the coach will be discussed later in this chapter.)

High School Sports

Youth sport participation is mostly about having fun. When athletes reach high school the pretense of having fun is overtly replaced by an emphasis on winning. The best athletes receive the most playing time while others are relegated to the bench. The responsibilities of the high school athlete are far more intense than those of the nonathlete, as far as school-related activities are concerned. The high school athlete must manage educational, athletic, and social responsibilities that are very time consuming and too demanding for many young people. High school athletes not only have to study and do classroom assignments, they must also attend athletic practices. Research has also shown that negative life stresses affect student athletes much more than non-student athletes (Petrie and Anderson, 1996). Thus, high school athletes may face stress from off the field, like their nonathlete peers, but also on the field stress— something nonathletes cannot encounter. Finding the proper balance between educational, athletic and social time requirements potentially presents challenges too difficult for young people. On the other hand, athletes that are successful at accomplishing this balance as teenagers should have an advantage in adulthood. The careers they will be entering, especially in the fast-paced twenty-first century, will probably involve multi-tasking, and the need to balance many competing responsibilities will come to the forefront.

ACADEMIC REQUIREMENTS

Most students today would be surprised to learn that during the 1970s and early 1980s many high school jurisdictions did not have a minimal academic requirement for athletic eligibility. It was argued that academic requirements were unfair to disadvantaged youth. Some people even believed that sport participation was a right rather than privilege. Predictably, the lack of a minimal academic requirements led to many athletes concentrating on sports and ignoring academics.

Today, it is common for all high schools to maintain minimal academic requirements for sports participation. However, such requirements still vary from state to state, and often from city to city. In December 2005 National Collegiate Athletic Association (NCAA) President Myles Brand organized a national working group of academic and athletic experts to review the standards currently being enforced, in light of concerns expressed by NCAA member institutions over the legitimacy of high school academic credentials being presented by some incoming student-athletes. It is the student-athlete's responsibility to maintain his or her grades to the minimal requirement in order to play sports. However, the athlete is generally given a support system in the form of school guidance counselors and coaches who may intervene when a problem arises between a student and teacher. In the state of New York, the New York State Public High School Athletic Association oversees the rules and regulations when it comes to academic eligibility. Each county is allowed to set other guidelines but they all must meet the state's minimal requirement. In Erie County for example, the requirements for athletic eligibility include:

- Student participants in extracurricular athletics must complete a minimum of 4½ credits, including physical education, by the end of each academic school year (August).
- At each ten week marking period students must be passing four subjects as well as physical education to remain academically eligible.
- In mid report card periods, any student who has an average below 65 percent in two or more subjects has one week to raise his or her grades. If after that week the student is still below 65 percent in more than one course, he or she will be ineligible until the close of the marking period.
- Students who are academically ineligible will still be considered a member of the team or activity. They will participate in routine meetings and team practices during the period of ineligibility.
- Ineligible students will be required to receive academic intervention services (Erie County Interscholastic Conference, 2001).

While stereotypes of "dumb jocks" might lead one to think otherwise, student athletes generally perform better than their nonathlete counterparts (this is true at both the high school and college levels). In many cases, sport participation may actually enhance academic achievement (Phillips, 1993). There are many possible explanations for this, including the following:

- The athlete pays closer attention to school work in order to maintain eligibility.
- The students who play sports, because of eligibility concerns, are already better students in the classroom.
- Teachers are more lenient in grading athletes' school work.
- There is a spillover effect — hard work on the playing field results in hard work in the classroom.
- Tutors provide special assistance to athletes in order to keep them eligible.
- The lure of college sport participation keeps some athletes interested in performing well academically.

Athletic eligibility for student-athletes is a subject of great scrutiny. Administrative offices must constantly monitor the academic progress of high school athletes.

INTERSCHOLASTIC PARTICIPATION AND ADMINISTRATION

According to the National Federation of State High School Associations, there are nearly 7 million high school athletes (CNN, 2003). There are nearly 4 million boys who play high school sports and over 2.8 million girls. The number of total athletes in high school has steadily increased for the past 14 years, although the total is still less than in the 1970s when high school sport participation reached its height because of the baby boom era. Football remains far and away the most popular sport for high school boys (over 1 million participants), followed by basketball (540,874), outdoor track and field (498,027), baseball (453,792), soccer (345,156), and other. Basketball is the most popular sport for girls (457,165), followed by outdoor track and field (415,602), volleyball (396,682), softball (357,912), soccer (301,156) and other. Texas (771,633 participants), California (652,333) and New York (336,987) are the three states with the most high school athletes.

It should be noted that there are alternatives to interscholastic sports for high school aged students. We are not referring to the rare case of the high school athlete who turns professional in sport (e.g., golfer Michelle Wie turned professional at age 15 and promptly signed endorsement deals with Nike and Sony which will pay her as much as $10 million a year), but rather sports leagues that exist outside of the high schools. Elite soccer players play on club sport teams, cheerleader club teams train just to compete rather than cheer for a team, baseball players play in leagues such as the American Legion, and hockey has junior hockey leagues. For example, Junior "A" Hockey represents the pinnacle of the skill development program of USA Hockey and the Canadian Amateur Hockey Association. The program is open to high school students and graduates seeking a greater challenge than that available at their high school or club team. The purpose of such leagues is to prepare the athlete for a career at the collegiate or professional level (O'Toole, 2005).

With such large participation numbers comes the need for administrative control and oversight. Many of today's administrators were trained in academic administration and not in athletic administration. As a result, most schools have athletic administrators who oversee the sports program and such issues as academic eligibility and handles grievances (challenges to ineligibility). These athletic administration positions developed slowly and gradually. As secondary schools have grown in size (especially through the consolidation of school districts) and interscholastic programs expanded (particularly because of the addition of girls' programs), the need for sport administrators became increasingly evident. At many of the larger high schools, the athletic department has an athletic director (similar to the college ranks).

Athletic directors inevitably exert great influence in the forming of policies and practices at their respective schools and athletic conferences. Furthermore, a number of high school associations sponsor athletic directors conferences and meetings that further strengthen their role and power. Athletic directors typically oversee standards of eligibility for interscholastic athletic competitions, contest regulations and preparation for out-of-town games; meet with tournament management; establish and define high school athletic policies; oversee athletic awards policies and banquets; administer the purchase, issuing and general care of equipment; direct athletic budgets; oversee safety essentials, programs and travel; manage the general layout and maintenance of athletic facilities; oversee intramural activities and the development of junior high school programs; and administer legal aspects of interscholastic activities.

Clearly, there is a great deal of work involved in interscholastic sports that goes unnoticed by most fans and participants of high school sports. Another important aspect is dealing with the media: sending out press releases and notices of games, interacting with sports reporters from newspapers and television, and monitoring the stories that appear about the teams. In many U.S. cities high school sporting events are covered as aggressively as college and even national sporting events.

ATHLETIC TRAINING

Among those providing overt benefits to sport participants are the athletic trainers. The National Athletic Trainers Association (NATA) is the governing body of athletic training. The association sponsors certification through the NATA Board of Certification (NATABOC). "Historically the practice of athletic training was confined to the collegiate sports setting with an emphasis on caring for injuries in tackle football. It was not until the 1970s that this situation changed significantly, as the services of athletic trainers began to be recognized as extremely valuable in the high school sport setting" (Pfeiffer and Mangus, 2002: 23). Despite the obvious

High school football played under the lights on a Friday night.

need for, and the benefits of, athletic trainers, less than half of all high schools in the United States have access to a NATABOC-certified athletic trainer (Pfeiffer and Mangus, 2002). Most school administrations argue that they cannot afford athletic trainers. NATA hopes to increase the number of athletic trainers at high schools, even if it means training a teacher already at the school to serve in this capacity. The less-affordable, but NATA preferred option, is for all schools to hire a full-time athletic trainer. This person would be free from teaching responsibilities and would work full time implementing a comprehensive sports medicine program.

ECONOMICS

When school boards face budget constraints, sports and the arts are usually the first victims of cuts. Understandably, academics must always be the first priority at all schools (and at every level); but it is always disappointing when extra-curricular activities are eliminated. (This economic reality helps to explain, in part, why there are so few athletic trainers.) All across the United States and Canada school budgets are subject to cuts. When school budget cuts result in the elimination of the funding for sports teams, many sports booster groups spring into action in an attempt to save school sports.

Curtis, McTeer and White (2003) examined the role of high school sport participation and earnings as an adult. They found that "those who participated in organized sport as a youth tended to have higher annual earned incomes as adults than those who did not participate in this way" (Curtis, et al., 2003: 60). The researchers also found that this relationship was more prevalent for males than for females. They indicate that participation in other school activities may also present economic benefits (capital) in later life, and state, "Of course, each type of early school activity may involve social capital and cultural capital" (p. 73). Students interested in a career in journalism, for instance, can benefit by working on the school newspaper and yearbook, and students who volunteer on the library staff gain vital skills that can be useful in information-based careers. Still, sports participation is usually the best-known and most influential extracurricular activity found on most high school campuses.

NEGATIVE EFFECTS OF HIGH SCHOOL SPORTS

A number of negative effects surround high school sports. The disproportionate attention given to athletics over academics (among some students, teachers, administrators, parents, communities and schools) compromises the primary goal of schools— education. The most important aspect of education must involve the pursuit of knowledge. High school sports provide a great diversion from the daily grind of homework and attending classes, but they should remain as a diversion and not a focal point. Due to the importance placed on athletics at most high schools, athletes enjoy a superior sense of self. Critics claim that such an inflated ego or status leads to elite deference. Elite deference refers to the special privileges that are afforded athletes (Lipsyte, 1985).

The over-emphasis placed on winning has led to many of the same problems witnessed in youth sports (See Chapter 6). Fans have been known to attack other fans, referees and game officials at high school sporting events. For example, several fans rushed the field in Massillon, Ohio, and were arrested for trying to attack officials who called back a Massillon Washington touchdown that would have given the Tigers the lead in the closing seconds. Washington lost the game. When the game ended fans attempted to reach the game officials but were tackled by police officers (*The Cleveland Plain Dealer*, 2000).

College Sports

For many sports fans, college sports are more important and entertaining than professional sports. College football, for example, commands huge legions of followers, and the sheer number of teams alone guarantees a wider audience for college football than for professional football. The focus and attention given to collegiate sport in the United States is unparalleled compared to the rest of the world. Nearly every college and university in the United States has a sports program and fields multiple teams. Many of these teams play in organized leagues and just as many teams engage in intramural sports. Furthermore, many college sports (e.g., football and basketball) have a longer history than professional sports. As Richard Goldstein (1993) notes, "As far back as the 1820s, the meadows at Cambridge and New Haven were scenes of semi-organized mayhem for college men. On the first Monday of the school term at Harvard and Yale, the sophomores would battle the freshmen in games that ostensibly involved kicking a round canvas ball, but seemed mostly directed at kicking the opponent" (p. 3).

THE STUDENT-ATHLETE

Just as the high school athlete must find the proper balance between time constraints tied to athletics and academics, so too must the college athlete. The demands on a college student-athlete are far more intense than on high school athletes. Furthermore, the amount of time spent in the classroom compared to the athletic arena is dramatically different from high school. A full time college student (defined as taking a minimum 12 hour course load per semester) spends far less time in the classroom than does a high school student. The typical full-time college student takes 15 credit hours and, therefore, attends class about 13 hours per week. A high school student generally attends school for close to 35 hours per week. Theoretically, the college student has far more free time than a high school student — but it is assumed that the college student is studying significantly longer than a high school student. The college-athlete does not enjoy the free time of non-full-time-working college students. College athletes (in-season) will typically follow a six-day-a-week practice schedule that includes team workouts, film sessions, conditioning, and weightlifting. Thus, the student-athlete faces all the challenges experienced by non-athletes (e.g., social adjustment, career exploration, and school work) along with unique challenges that include scheduling classes that do not conflict with athletic commitments, visiting the athletic trainer for injury treatment, traveling for road games, learning an athletic play book, studying game films, and training. Different sports will emphasize certain aspects of training over others (e.g., football players will be encouraged to lift weights more than synchronized swimmers). It should be noted that the NCAA limits the amount of time an athlete may practice. Practice is defined as:

> Any meeting, activity or instruction involving sports-related information and having an athletics purpose, held for one or more student-athletes at the direction of, or supervised by, any member or members of an institution's coaching staff. Practice is considered to have occurred if one or more coaches and one or more student-athletes engage in any of the following activities: (1) Field, floor or on-court activity; (2) Setting up offensive or defensive alignment; (3) Chalk talk; (4) Lecture on or discussion of strategy related to the sport; (5) Activities using equipment related to the sport; or (6) Discussions or review of game films, motion pictures or videotapes related to the sport, except for the observation of an officiating clinic related to playing rules that is conducted by video conference and does not require student-athletes to miss any class time to observe the clinic [NCAA Manual, 2004–05: 125].

The loophole that most colleges use to avoid an NCAA infraction on extra practice time for athletes is to make sure that no coach is present. Weight-lifting is a good example of non-reported practice time. Many student-athletes experience a time crunch because of travel. In some cases, college athletes will be on the road for days at a time. Often, when student-athletes return to campus they have to immediately go back to class and, in some instances, take scheduled exams.

During the off-season, student athletes are still expected to work out and maintain their conditioning program. Some may participate in informal practice sessions with teammates. Student athletes, as representatives of their school and sports team, are often expected to donate their personal time for charity events and the promotion of their school and their sport. In addition to athletic and academic demands are the many personal responsibilities (grocery shopping, house-cleaning, dating, and family, for example) that every other college student has. Clearly, student-athletes are very busy.

SCHOLARSHIPS, RECRUITMENT, ELIGIBILITY AND ACADEMIC REQUIREMENTS

High school athletes hope to earn athletic scholarships to attend college. This is not an unusual situation, as many colleges offer nonacademic financial support to numerous students who do not play sports. Athletic scholarships (some are full and some are partial) provide financial assistance, usually in the form of "room and board" (paying for admissions, textbooks and school supplies) as well as per diem (meal allowance). If a graduating high school does not receive a scholarship to a Division I school, he or she may either try out for the team as a walk-on (a nonscholarship athlete that tries out for a sport), or play for a Division I-AA (Division I-AA in football has been relabeled the NCAA Football Championship Division), Division II, or Division III school. Division III schools may provide an athlete an opportunity to play, but they do not offer scholarships.

Some high school athletes are recruited; that is, colleges seek them out, rather than the athlete seeking out a college. "Recruitment of college athletes is hardly new.... In the period from 1895 to 1905 ... there was widespread recruitment of schoolboy athletes" (Bowen and Levin, 2003: 43). What has changed the most about recruiting over the past 100 years is the aggressive nature of recruiters today, some of whom do not even provide "lip service" to educational values (Bowen and Levin, 2003). A related trend in sports such as ice hockey is the recruiting of athletes who have had extensive experience playing on club teams or even national teams, often honing their athletic skills after graduation from secondary school. "The result is a roster that contains a number of somewhat older, more experienced players" (Bowen and Levin, 2003: 49).

Today, promising athletes will receive letters of invitation from college officials in the athletic department to visit their campus and may be invited or encouraged to attend sport camps on campus or those run by college coaches that are off campus. The recruitment process can be stressful to both the athlete and the sports programs (especially the coach). "Coaches are under enormous pressure to recruit the most outstanding high school athletes each year, since this has become the key determinant of competitive success in major college sports. The intensely competitive nature of the recruiting process is aggravated by the perception, real or imagined, that many coaches and institutions use negative or illegal recruiting tactics" (Duderstadt, 2003: 192). Illegal recruiting tactics may include rival recruiters spreading misinformation, lies or innuendos to prized athletes in such ways as suggesting the other school is about to be placed on probation, they are going to raise admissions requirements, or that the head coach is about to quit or be fired. For example, colleges and universities that recruit the same high school football players as Penn State have been known to "warn" recruits that Joe Paterno (Penn State's football coach) is likely to retire in the immediate future because of his old age. (In 2008, Paterno was 82 years old and still going strong.) Other illegal recruiting tactics involve sport boosters who provide cash, merchandise, cars and jobs to athletes or their family members if the athlete promises to play for a particular school. The NCAA has many rules (e.g., the number of phone calls and unofficial and official visits to a recruit) regarding recruitment, and violations are punishable by such means as a reduction in the number of scholarships an athletic department many offer.

The stress that a coach at a high profile school experiences due to recruiting (especially in basketball) is highlighted by the fact that one or two great players can make a program. The fact that such a high profile player may only stay at a school for one or two years before being lured away to the professional ranks adds to the pressure of recruiting from the coaches' perspective. A few years ago, for example, Carmelo Anthony was a highly desired high school basketball player. He chose Syracuse University and immediately helped Coach Jim Boeheim win his first NCAA national championship (in 2003). Anthony, despite pleas from legions of Syracuse Orange fans, left the university after his freshman year. He now earns millions of dollars in the NBA. Boeheim won his championship but was forced to find the next great recruit after just one year.

The athlete being recruited also experiences stress. This young athlete must make the "right" decision. Among the athlete's concerns are playing time, the team's chances of winning, the amount of television exposure, the coaches' ability to "teach," the social life of the college, the academic environment, and the support system designed to help the serious academic-minded athlete. When the athlete decides what college to attend, he or she signs a "letter of intent." The letter of intent, which is treated as a legal contract, states that the athlete promises to attend a particular school for four years. If the athlete changes his or her mind and wants to transfer to a different Division I school, he or she may forfeit a year's eligibility and must sit out a year. An athlete who wishes to turn professional may do so but risks losing any remaining college eligibility.

Once the recruit has signed a letter of intent, he or she must still meet academic admissions requirements. These requirements vary a great deal depending on the academic standards of particular colleges and universities. Many recruited athletes do not academically qualify for college. "All too frequently, the competitive pressure on coaches leads them to recruit athletes who are clearly unprepared for college work or who have little interest in a college education. While few universities engaged in big-time sports have truly competitive admissions processes, most do have certain minimum standards that must be met for admission. In all too many cases, recruited athletes fail to meet even these minimum standards" (Duderstadt, 2003: 193). Ideally, all colleges would emphasize academics over athletics. In that manner, all those who attend college would make academics their top priority and the term student-athlete would then be appropriate. Lisa Saxon (1999) insists that the term "student-athlete" should be used more judiciously. "Reserve it for athletes who are serious students, for those who had the SAT scores and high-school grade-point averages to qualify under general university admissions standards. Call the others athlete-students. Then encourage them to earn the title student-athlete. And a degree" (Saxon, 1999: 85).

ATHLETIC SCHOLARSHIPS

Athletic scholarships provide student-athletes an opportunity to attend college while they pursue the sports interests. "Awarding athletic scholarships as inducements for playing sports violates long-standing amateur principles. Still, for the most part, the scholarships that existed before 1967 did not constitute employment contracts" (Sack and Staurowsky, 1998: 79–80). Today, a number of expectations (e.g., follow team rules, maintain adherence to codes of conduct) are attached to athletic scholarships; although the NCAA is quick to point out that scholarships are not employment contracts. Full athletic scholarships include free tuition, room and board. Athletic scholarships are very controversial. Some argue against giving scholarships to people who would not otherwise qualify for college, while others argue that the athletes should receive more money. As for the former argument, it should be noted that "athletes who are recruited for reasons *other* than their cognitive abilities receive about $600 million in full or partial athletic scholarships. Many schools award more merit-based scholarship money to athletes than to all other scholarship students combined. Not only that, but many of these athletic scholarships are given to athletes who have little chance of making it academically or even to those who do not care about receiving a college education" (Eitzen, 1999: 107).

One of the most unfortunate aspects of granting a college scholarship to an athlete to play sport is that he or she pays more attention to athletics than academics. "Every year hundreds of college athletes buy into the dream of a professional sports career. Convinced they will be among the fortunate few to land a lucrative contract, they devote much of their energy and concentration to the practice field, barely sliding by academically in dubious majors like 'human potential'.... The vast majority of hopefuls suddenly face the fact that their dreams will never be anything more than that" (Easterbrook, 1999: 79). Even successful college athletes may not be drafted and some of those who are drafted may not make the team or may be injured before they play a single professional game.

Despite the fact that most college sports programs lose money, there are a number of advocates who promote the idea that college athletes should receive a cash allowance in addition to free tuition, room and board. These advocates may fail to point out where this money will come from, especially if the program is losing money. The NCAA and the vast majority of colleges and universities are against this idea for economic and amateur-status reasons. It should be pointed out, however, that the NCAA places limits on how much money a student athlete can earn and how many hours a student-athlete can work. A workable compromise to the idea that student athletes should be paid a salary or stipend involves the NCAA loosening some of these "off-the-field" money earning opportunities an athlete would be allowed to pursue. However, many problems may arise then, including "phantom" jobs provided by boosters, and money-making opportunities offered to recruits to attend a college that provides "employment" opportunities.

ADMINISTRATION

The primary administrative head of college athletics is the athletic director. Typically, the athletic director (AD) is the most powerful and central figure in regard to all aspects of athletics; the president is clearly second in power (Sperber, 1990). The AD has full control over all aspects of college athletics, including the department's employees (staff, coaches, and student-athletes). The athletic department at nearly every college and university is an entity devoted entirely to varsity sports, and athletic directors enjoy freedoms that most other college and university department heads do not. Furthermore, "Athletic directors have the salaries and perks of CEOs in corporate America, but very few of them have the training to deal with business problems" (Sperber, 1990: 21). One might wonder, "Isn't there a better way to run an athletic department?"

Vanderbilt University believes it has found an alternative to the traditional way of running college athletics. Vanderbilt, a university with high academic standards and a member of the football powerful Southeastern Conference (SEC), has merged its athletic department and its student recreational activities department. Vanderbilt still competes in the SEC but the reorganization eliminates the traditional athletic department completely and places athletics under the supervision of the university administration. Vanderbilt University Chancellor Gordon Gee believes that the merger will create a culture where students, faculty, athletes and others involved with the university will come together and work collectively toward the core mission of the university (*Sports Illustrated*, 2003). The new department is called the Office of Student Athletics, Recreation and Wellness, which will coordinate both intercollegiate athletics and student recreation activities, and is led by Vice Chancellor David Williams II (as of 2008). Intercollegiate sports at Vanderbilt have seemed to benefit financially from this merger, as athletics programs are now funded by the university's multi-billion dollar endowment — one of the largest in the world (*Vandy Sports*, 2005). Vanderbilt is *adding* six varsity sports as a result of the direct access to the university's endowment. Chancellor Gee's goal is to reform college sports and emphasize the "athlete" in student-athlete.

SCHOOL SPIRIT AND ECONOMICS

In high school, sports serve as an important aspect of the social life of students, parents and the local community. Few programs are actually profitable; as described earlier, their value is found outside the economic realm. Some school districts operate at such deficits that they cannot afford to run athletic programs. In many cases high school sport boosters help raise money to save programs. At the collegiate level, most Division II and Division III programs lose money. At Division II and III schools, sports are played by athletes who have a true love of the game, and seldom does any athletic program actually make money. Some wonder if the money used to fund sports at Division II and III (and even I) schools is justified.

At the Division I level, sporting events often serve as the focal point of the school's social life. The sports programs provide school spirit and identity and are designed to make money. Most elite Division I schools have at least one program (football or basketball) that generates enough money to fund all the sport programs at that school. Filling football stadiums and basketball arenas with paying customers is a traditional method promoted by big-time colleges in generating revenue (Sperber, 1990). As Sperber (2000) explains, "In the 1970s and 1980s, big-time athletic departments became franchises in College Sports Inc., a huge commercial entertainment enterprise with operating methods and objectives frequently opposed to the educational missions of the host universities. Feeding the growth was the increased revenue from the television networks for the rights to broadcast college sports events, notably the NCAA's men's basketball tournament" (p. 33).

There is a debate over the effects of a "winning" college sports program and a rise in enrollment. Until recently there wasn't any conclusive research conducted to show such a relationship. However, based on recent research, there now appears to be a positive correlation between a winning program and enrollment. This correlation has been dubbed the "Flutie Effect'—named after Doug Flutie, former Heisman Trophy winner at Boston College (Potter, 2008). College applications jumped about 30 percent in the two years after Flutie's exploits on the football field in the mid–1980s. As a rule, applications increase 8 percent at schools that win an NCAA football or men's basketball championship. Research was conducted at 330 NCAA Division I schools from 1983 through 2002.

The National Collegiate Athletic Association

All sports and games have rules. "Regulation of college sports began with debates over the still-being-formulated rules of the game themselves, before moving on to ask who should be allowed to play and under what conditions" (Shulman and Bowen, 2001: 12). Once the rules of the game were established (allowing for modifications over the years), there grew a concern about the enforcement of the rules. This concern was fueled by the reality that, if left unsupervised, many people involved in sports (as with all other social institutions) would violate the rules of the game in order to gain an unfair advantage during competition. Corruption and blatant cheating in sport forced the creation of a supervising body. In college sports, the most dominant ruling body is the National Collegiate Athletic Association (NCAA).

The Purpose and Development of the NCAA

The NCAA actually has a number of purposes. Page one of the 2004–05 NCAA Manual clearly states those purposes:

(a) To initiate, stimulate and improve intercollegiate athletics programs for student-athletes and to promote and develop educational leadership, physical fitness, athletics excellence and athletics participation as a recreational pursuit;

(b) To uphold the principle of institutional control of, and responsibility for, all intercollegiate sports in conformity with the constitution and bylaws of this Association;

(c) To encourage its members to adopt eligibility rules to comply with satisfactory standards of scholarship, sportsmanship and amateurism;

(d) To formulate, copyright and publish rules of play governing intercollegiate athletics;

(e) To preserve intercollegiate athletics records;

(f) To supervise the conduct of, and to establish eligibility standards for, regional and national athletics events under the auspices of this Association;

(g) To cooperate with other amateur athletics organizations in promoting and conducting national and international athletics events;

(h) To legislate, through bylaws or by resolutions of a Convention, upon any subject of general concern to the members related to the administration of intercollegiate athletics; and

(i) To study in general all phases of competitive intercollegiate athletics and establish standards whereby the college and universities of the United States can maintain their athletics programs on a high level.

The NCAA is an administrative body designed to enforce the rules of college athletics. It is also an organization of all the colleges and universities that voluntarily belong to it. Thus, the NCAA could not exist without the mutual agreement of member institutions. "The NCAA has been described as the fox watching the henhouse of college sports, but the Association's consolidation of power cannot be attributed only to its own ambitions; schools had demonstrated repeatedly that they were unable to protect themselves from themselves and, at the same time, that they had no desire to disband their programs. In response, the NCAA has organized and managed the flow of big money" (Shulman and Bowen, 2001: 16). Over the years, the NCAA has tweaked the rules and guidelines of intercollegiate sport in response to growing problem areas (e.g., steroid use, gambling, etc.).

Their ultimate purpose is to assure the smooth running of college sports while maintaining new ideals of sportsmanship and concepts of fair play. Other people have different evaluations of the NCAA. Economists, for example, "generally view the NCAA as a cartel. They hold this view because the NCAA has historically devised rules to restrict output (the number of games played and televised) and to restrict competition for inputs (student-athletes)" (Fleisher, Goff and Tollison, 1992: 5). This narrow economic analysis of the NCAA ignores the fact that member institutions agree to the rules and procedures of the NCAA. "The NCAA is a relatively ineffective cartel primarily because of the market structure in which it operates. The most destructive feature of this market structure, from the NCAA's standpoint, is the heterogeneity of member interests" (Koch and Leonard, 1981: 253). Although is questionable whether the NCAA would even want to act like a cartel (thereby viewing members' interest as a "destructive feature"), it is true that member colleges have a great deal of influence on the NCAA.

Furthermore, college conferences also exude a great deal of influence and power and it is doubtful that the NCAA would want to challenge a big-time conference (e.g., SEC, Big East, Pac-10, Big 10, Big 12) on a matter deemed critical by a conference. College conferences serve as collective units for instilling standards in college sports. Their power was established during the early 1900s while the NCAA was still in its early stages of development. "A league of eight to ten institutions was more important in college sports for shaping academic eligibility requirements and recruiting limits than was membership in a national association" (Thelin, 1994: 53). During the 1920s and 1930s college conferences adopted restrictions on athletic scholarships, standardized schedules to limit the numbers of games and practices, and set player eligibility standards, recruitment practices and so on. Thus, the NCAA has never operated as a true cartel in the sports world.

In short, the NCAA supervises the organization of college sports, the conduct of athletes, coaches and others involved with college sports, and the academic qualification to which athletes must adhere. It attempts to act in the best interests of college athletics.

Coaching

Coaches, as the old cliché goes, *coach*. They coach others in the rules of the game and methods of training, and ideally, help to develop the skills of athletes. One might assume, then, that coaches are highly trained people. This is often far from the case. In fact, the sole criteria for many youth sport coaches is being a parent of one of the players, liking children or having an interest in a sport. As each level of sport competition increases, so too does the level of training that coaches go through. Clark (2000) argues that the United States lags far behind other nations in the formal preparation of coaches.

> Many other nations have well-developed programs for educating coaches. Statements describing what is important for coaches to know at each level of play are common. Many countries require formal training, examinations, certificates, and even licenses to coach. Running counter to this increase in the professionalization of coaches internationally, American sports at all levels remain dominated by truly amateur coaches.... In many other countries, coaches are required to undergo

extensive preparation to progress through, or even enter, the profession. For example, Canada has a mandatory, national five-level program that has been in place long enough to undergo evaluation and change [Clark, 2000: 55–56].

The primary role of a coach is to teach athletes. "Coaching is teaching in its most perfect and rewarding form. No matter what the sport, coaches are basically giving information, waiting for a response, and then giving feedback on that response" (Dorfman, 2003: xi). Coaches are perceived by athletes as leaders, teachers, and mentors, and therefore they must think before speaking, be clear communicators, speak with clarity, be consistent yet flexible, and learn to establish a connection to all team members.

The idea of the coach as a teacher has roots in the time when athletics was formally incorporated into higher education as "coaches were usually faculty members who were given coaching assignments" (Gerdy, 1997: 91). The role of the coach as an educator changed dramatically at the collegiate level when sports became a commercial enterprise and institutions began to employ full-time professional coaches. "This fundamental change in the coaching profile has not stopped those in the athletic community from continuing to insist that coaches are, before all else, educators. The playing field or court, they insist, is a coach's classroom, and the lessons taught there in discipline, teamwork, and sportsmanship are just as important as the lessons being taught in the lecture hall or chemistry lab. The realities of major college athletics, however, suggest otherwise. Coaches are neither hired nor evaluated based upon their commitment to higher education" (Gerdy, 1997: 91). Today, many coaches are evaluated based on the graduation rates of their players. Furthermore, the NCAA is considering implementing rules that tie the number of scholarships a college sports program can offer to graduation rates.

At big-time colleges and high schools, the coach is often the most recognized personality on campus and perhaps in the community. For example, in Syracuse, New York, a city lacking many visible celebrities, men's basketball coach Jim Boeheim is a first-tier celebrity. The media plays a major role in the development of the coach as a celebrity. "Many coaches have become full-fledged entrepreneurs with their own television and radio shows, summer camps, shoe contracts, and endorsements" (Gerdy, 1997: 92).

Coaches who lead winning teams are often celebrities at their schools and in their communities, and are often better known (and better compensated) than college presidents. The pressure to be a winner may, unfortunately, lead to unethical practices. Eitzen (1989) states, "Many coaches cheat. They may hold practices in violation of the rules. They may 'doctor' the playing field or playing equipment to give their team an unfair advantage. At the college level, many coaches have violated the rules by giving athletes illegal payments, altering the transcripts of athletes, hiring surrogate test takers for their marginal student-athletes, and enrolling them in 'phantom courses.' What values are being transmitted to athletes by these kinds of coaches?" (Eitzen, 1989: 134). The desire to be "number one" can cause coaches to believe in the axiom that winning justifies the means. (See Chapter 8 for a review of a wide variety of deviant forms of sport behaviors.)

The pressure that college coaches feel to win has also led to a greater emphasis on recruiting star high school athletes than on teaching and serving as an educator. "The coaches of most major college sports programs have become full-time recruiters, always on the lookout for new talent. Their networks of coaches, friends, and alumni reach back into elementary and middle-school programs to begin tracking young athletes with potential. They monitor the development of these youngsters both through school programs and summer sports camps. By the time they approach the end of their high school careers, the best athletes are well known to and sought after by most of the major colleges" (Duderstadt, 2003: 192). Thus, with the great importance placed on recruiting, the college coach is seldom viewed as an "educator." In fact, at most colleges and universities, there exists academic support systems designed to keep student athletes academically eligible for sports. "The increased emphasis on the development of quality academic support programs has been taken as a sign by some coaches that the responsibility for the academic and personal development of student-athletes rests solely with the academic support staff" (Gerdy, 1997: 95).

AUTHORITY, POWER, AND CONTROL

When dealing with athletes, the role of the coach, at any level, is to provide leadership, direction, order, structure and discipline. Coaches, then, are in a position of authority. A person of authority is in a position of power because he or she can influence the thoughts and behaviors of others. Some coaches attempt to gain complete control over the actions of athletes while others take a more democratic approach to coaching. Coaches who have the ability to handle authority well generally know how to manage people. When coaches attempt to assert their power position, they place their credibility on the line. "A leader who knows how to manage athletes can direct their mental and behavioral efforts toward a common goal — a goal established by the leader. This becomes the organizational/team credo" (Dorfman, 2003: 4). The credo becomes the first expression of a coach's power position. It is important for coaches to establish their authority on day one. The coach will explain to his or her athletes what is expected from each of them as individuals and teammates. A coach can get the message across without being a raving maniac. Dorfman (2003) cites Bill Walton's (a basketball star at UCLA and in the NBA) reflection of Coach John Wooden's handling of a difficult or resistant player. According to Walton, Wooden would tell that player, "I admire and respect your position. We'll miss you here at UCLA. We've enjoyed your time. Thanks for coming" (Dorfman, 2003: 5). In this manner, Wooden was polite to his defiant players but made it clear that it was still his way or the highway.

There is a distinction between power and authority. Coaches who crave absolute power are like dictators. Coaches who want to establish authority are really concerned with gaining control. "Coaches don't want power; at least, the ones who care about the players they coach aren't power-hungry. What coaches want is *control*—control over the many variables that affect their on-the-job performance" (Warren, 1997: xvii). This idea is easy to grasp, as each of us would like to have some level of control — at least in our own lives. Of course, we all realize, sooner or later, that there are few variables in life that we can control. The manner in which we deal with adversity is what sets us apart from one another. This is especially true with coaches. Inevitably things will not go as planned. The players will look toward the coach to see how he or she is handling adversity and will generally feed off the coach's cues.

All coaches have their own coaching styles and philosophies. The primary goal of all coaches, however, is to be successful. The ability to recruit gifted athletes and improve the skills of athletes will lead to coaching success. Ultimately, successful coaches have gained control of their team and individual athletes by getting them to accept the credo of hard work, dedication and sacrifice. Some coaches, such as Bob Knight and the late Woody Hayes, remain controversial figures, as their determination to win often seemed to cross an ethical line — treating one's own players in a belittling fashion, skirting the rules of the game, using strong intimidation factors against opposing teams, and encouraging raucous behavior among fans. Opponents of such controversial coaches claim that they demean the very game they are advocates for, whereas proponents extol their winning records and ability to motivate players in ways unorthodox but clearly successful. If nothing else, coaches are powerful role models, and the ways in which they enforce rules and train their players can have long-lasting consequences. John Kerr (2005), summarizing several recent studies on the role coaches play in instilling values among their players, states:

As the authority figure, the coach then tends to transfer his values in terms of moral climate and attitude towards winning to the young athletes. If the team environment is one which encourages inappropriate action in pursuit of winning, then young athletes will tend to conform to the view that inappropriate behaviours are acceptable. They also report their intention to engage in inappropriate acts, and engage in them with greater frequency, when they perceive a team environment which permits or encourages unsanctioned acts of aggression and violence. In a nutshell, the results of these studies point to coaches as a (or even the) major influence on their young athletes in the use (or not) of unsanctioned aggression and violence in sport [p. 83].

Full time coaches, such as those found in the college and professional ranks, generally work long days (e.g., reviewing game films, preparing their athletes for competition, recruiting); especially during their respective seasons. Elite college and professional coaches are compensated quite handsomely for their time and dedication. Coaches at elite colleges and universities are often the highest paid employees on their campus. Jim Boeheim, Hall of Fame men's basketball coach at Syracuse, for example, earned over $1,125,850 during the 2006–07 fiscal year. His salary was highest of all university personnel (Webb, 2008). Boeheim, as with most coaches at elite programs, also earns financial compensation from camps, shoe contracts, and other endorsements. Connecticut's men's basketball coach Jim Calhoun earns between $1.5 and $2 million a season. Duke Coach Mike Krzyzewski earns in excess of $1.5 million, Florida's Billy Donovan earns an average of $1.7 million per season and LSU's Nick Saban, head football coach, is reportedly the highest paid college coach at $3 million per season. Professional sport coaches and managers are now receiving multi-year contracts in excess of $7 million per year. Larry Brown, for example, was hired in 2005 to coach the New York Knicks. His five-year contract was $50 million. In short, it is not just the owners and athletes benefiting from the economic riches of Western sport. A potential large financial contract and a powerful authority position make coaching a highly desirable profession. This is in spite of the stress and pressure associated with coaching.

Hazing

Among the more persistent problems associated with sports is hazing. "Hazing is an all-encompassing term that covers silly, potentially risky, or degrading tasks required for acceptance by a group of full-fledged members" (Nuwer, 2004: xiv). Crow and Rosner (2004) incorporate the aspects of humiliation and shaming in their legal interpretation of hazing. They define hazing as "any activity expected of someone joining a group that humiliates, degrades, abuses, or endangers, regardless of the person's willingness to participate" (p. 200). Hazing is fairly common in sports, fraternities and sororities, the military and street gangs. Incidents of hazing date back to 387 B.C.E. with Plato's account of the savagery of young boys' hazing behavior. Hazing was common during the age of the rise of European universities (1400s). Nuwer (2004) states, "Martin Luther endured hazing at Erfurt as a student. Later, in 1539, at Wittenberg, he advocated hazing as a means of strengthening a boy to face and endure life's challenges" (p. xxv). At American universities hazing was a method first utilized by upperclassmen against freshmen to "keep them in line." According to Ronald Smith (1988), hazing in American sport can be traced back to Harvard University in the late 1700s.

The sophomore-freshman hazing in sport became institutionalized in the early fall "rush." Annually, on the first Monday of the fall term in the late 1700s, Harvard sophomores would challenge individuals of the freshman class to wrestling matches. If the sophomore should by some chance be defeated by being thrown down, then the juniors would challenge. If the juniors lost, then the seniors would take on the freshmen. "It was a kind of initiatory process for newcomers," a member of the Harvard class of 1805 stated. The tradition of rushes or class battles, though not necessarily wrestling, was found on most nineteenth-century college campuses [Smith, 1988: 19].

Since the early 1800s, and until recently, hazing has endured as a relatively acceptable form of freshmen indoctrination into the subcultural world of sports by upperclassmen. In this regard, defenders of hazing practices view hazing as a "rite of passage" which all recruits must endure before becoming accepted as a member of the team.

Why Does Hazing Occur?

In most cases hazing is a tool utilized by upperclassmen, or higher ranking personnel, as a means of conveying to freshmen, or newcomers, the privileged status of being a higher ranking individual. Groups such as fraternities, sport teams and street gangs tend to reward with power and status individuals who are perceived as making the group better. Hazers are looked upon as providing a group service by teaching newcomers precedence while toughening them up (Nuwer, 1999). New recruits must show the experienced members of the group that they are "worthy" of admission. The tradition of hazing has long been upheld as an important ritual by groups and organizations that value extreme loyalty to the "team." The willingness among new recruits to endure a hazing ritual demonstrates the power and status of the group or team.

Hazing generally operates under the cloak of secrecy. Perpetrators and participants of hazing seldom admit to their involvement. The secret nature of hazing serves as a bonding experience among the participants. Those who perpetrate hazing have already experienced the victimization of hazing and easily justify victimizing newcomers. Newcomers who successfully survive their hazing experience look forward to the day when they become hazers. It becomes advantageous for all involved in hazing not to say anything to officials who may view such behavior negatively. Thus, a perpetual cycle of reinforcement guarantees the continuation of hazing. The adage "What was good enough for me is good enough for them" applies with hazing.

Proponents of hazing argue that such ritualistic behaviors stimulate team loyalty, bonding and solidarity — we're all in this together. The ever-growing legions of people (e.g., school administrators, faculty, and concerned parents) who are against hazing argue there is no place for degrading or humiliating activities in team-building (Meagher, 2005). Unfortunately, humiliating newcomers is a big part of hazing. In fraternities and male sports teams, newcomers are often humiliated in a sadomasochistic manner. Nuwer (1999) argues that sadomasochistic sexual assaults or threats of such assaults in fraternal hazing may be performed by older members to demonstrate their male dominance over newcomer males. (This is also the case in prison, where dominant males will rape weaker males. Such acts are not viewed as homosexual but rather as a sign of power and dominance.) Male dominance sometimes manifests itself in a sexual manner against women (e.g., gang rapes) (Nuwer, 1999). Former National Hockey League player Moe Mantha was banned for one year as general manager and 25 games as coach of the Windsor Spitfires for his role in a 2005 hazing incident where players were made to strip on the team bus.

Milder versions of male dominance over rookies are common in professional sports. In Major League Baseball, for example, rookies endure annual initiation rites. Rookies are generally made to dress like women (or in some degrading costume) in a public place, such as the airport for the last road trip of the regular season. Although this is meant to be "fun," many high school and college officials believe that the professional ranks are sending a negative message to young athletes for tolerating any type of humiliating hazing behavior. Beyond humiliation, there are times when people are physically injured and sometimes killed during hazing activities.

Presently, high schools, colleges and universities have taking a hard stand against hazing in sports and in fraternities and sororities. They have taken such a stand because of the increasing number of reports of injuries that continue to occur during secretive hazing ceremonies. "Hazing in sports has received a significant amount of media attention in the last several years, especially on high school and college campuses nationwide. More student-athletes are being prosecuted under state anti-hazing laws and more institutions are being held responsible for their care. This liability may soon be extended to professional athletes and sports organizations due to the frequent hazing of rookie players" (Crow and Rosner, 2004: 200). As of 2008, there was no uniformity among state statutes regarding anti-hazing policy and legislation.

HIGH SCHOOL HAZING

Anyone who has played high school sports has likely been hazed. "The Alfred University/NCAA survey released in 1999 revealed that nearly half of all collegian athletes say they were first hazed in high school or even middle school. Thus, hazing — a ritual that gives hazers a sense of power, entitlement, and occasionally sadistic pleasure — must also be addressed by educators who work with teens and preteens" (Nuwer, 2004: xv). Hazing has a long history with high school sports but many administrators want to see an end to such behavior, often which is very violent. "High school hazing of freshmen and rookies can be particularly vicious when directed toward nonconformists struggling to find an identity. In fact, hazing is part of a larger culture of violence and destruction" (Nuwer, 2004: xvi). High school hazers may not view themselves as bullies, but in essence, that is what they are. High school administrators are increasingly coming to view hazers as bullies and want to stop hazing altogether in their schools.

Anti-hazing proponents are often discouraged when they learn of stories that involve professional athletes who continue hazing traditions. Stoneham (Massachusetts) High School principal Tom Ryan was upset with the wide-ranging media coverage of the New England Patriots' (NFL) annual hazing tradition of veterans giving rookies atrocious haircuts and hosing them down (Borges, 2005). Hazing has been illegal in Massachusetts high schools and colleges since the late 1980s (Massachusetts General Law 269, Sections 17–19). Massachusetts defines hazing as "any conduct or method of initiation into any student organization, whether on public or private property, which willfully or recklessly endangers the physical or mental health of any student or other person" (Borges, 2005:C12). The hazing law was established in Massachusetts after a number of incidents with football and hockey teams and with college fraternities where newcomers were subjected to degrading acts of initiation. The Massachusetts anti-hazing law also mandates that high school and college administrators are to inform all students about the law.

The current anti-hazing trend in high school will most likely continue and those who continue this ritualistic behavior risk possible sanctions (e.g., suspension from school and possible criminal offenses).

COLLEGE AND UNIVERSITY HAZING

The Alfred University/NCAA survey of 1999 came about after an incident at Alfred University. "In 1998, Edward Coll Jr., president of Alfred University, an NCAA Division III school, forfeited one of the school's football games after five players were arrested for hazing freshmen players, including minors, by restraining them with rope and requesting them to drink alcohol" (Crow and Rosner, 2004: 201). The findings of this survey revealed that a great deal of hazing still occurs in collegian sport. Interestingly, what sport participants view as hazing and what administrators view as hazing differs a great deal. For example, 80 percent of respondents reported being subjected to one or more of the listed (from the survey) hazing behaviors, yet only 12 percent characterized or labeled those activities as hazing (Crow and Rosner, 2004).

Examples of hazing, especially sadomasochistic hazing, abounds in collegian sports. The University of Vermont's hockey scandal is among the most infamous. The heinous hazing acts and the subsequent attempted cover-up of the incident led the president of the university to cancel the remainder of the 1999–2000 hockey season. Among the hazing activities that freshmen were forced to endure were a pie-eating contest (the pie consisted of seafood quiche with ketchup and barbeque sauce), naked push-ups with their genitals dipped into warm beer beneath them, and parading around naked performing the "elephant walk" (players held each other's genitals) (Crow and Rosner, 2004). The state of Vermont enacted anti-hazing legislation as a result of the incident.

Females are also involved in extreme forms of hazing. A former University of Oklahoma female soccer player charged her former coach with "physical and mental abuse" in a federal lawsuit against the coach, her two assistants, and the university's board of regents because of a hazing incident that occurred in 1997. "The victim, then a freshman, was forced to perform simulated oral sex with a banana while blindfolded and wearing an adult diaper. The humiliated victim, out of fear of losing her scholarship, did not report the incident for a year" (Crow and Rosner, 2004: 202–203). The victim came forward after some of her teammates showed the university's athletic director photos of the incident. The coach resigned immediately. The original federal lawsuit was eventually dismissed.

Hazing is an outdated ritual that often causes mental and physical harm to those who are forced to bear the hazing ritual. A number of athletes are deterred from joining high school and college sports because of threat of hazing. Those involved in hazing risk being suspended and held criminally responsible for such behaviors. Hazing shames and humiliates athletes at least as much as it builds team camaraderie as proponents claim. For the good of high school and college sports, hazing should not be tolerated any longer.

SUMMARY

Most young athletes have positive experiences with high school and college sport participation. Nearly all secondary schools offer some sort of interscholastic athletics. In addition, most colleges and universities have sports teams, and encourage both intra and intermural competition. Proponents of sports in school argue that it teaches positive character traits and values. Opponents claim that it distracts from the educational experience, and encourages negative behaviors such as violence and cheating.

While most student-athletes participate in interscholastic sports, there are many alternatives unconnected with school systems. However, the fact that there is such large participation in organized school sports means that the need for administrative control and oversight continues to grow. Athletic directors exert great influence in the forming of policies and practices at their respective schools and athletic conferences.

Athletic trainers, whose job it is to help athletes prevent and recover from injuries, play an important role in youth sports. But due to budget constraints, many schools do not have such trainers, and coaches—who are often unprepared or unsuited for such roles—are looked upon to fulfill this position.

Sport participation can allow a student to bond with others, as well as stand out above the rest. School sporting events can provide an opportunity for school spirit activities, which can rally the entire academic community.

The National Collegiate Athletic Association attempts to regulate and watch over collegiate sports. Important functions of the NCAA include monitoring the following: how student-athletes are recruited, whether they are eligible to attend college, the manner in which athletic scholarships are administered, and the number of hours athletes can participate in sports, practice and working at on-campus jobs.

The proliferation of college games on television, the movement toward larger stadiums, and the occurrence of recruiting infractions have placed new demands upon the NCAA to regulate college sports. The amateur ideal—athletes playing for pure love of the game—is now in constant conflict with student-athletes who expect compensation for their abilities.

Coaches are central to the high school and college sports world. As each level of sport competition increases, so does the level of training that coaches go through. At one time, many coaches were also teachers, but this has changed dramatically at the collegiate level when sports became a commercial enterprise.

A major problem in high school and college sports is the prevalence of hazing. The growing number of injuries, as well as negative media attention, has made this ritual no longer an acceptable practice.

KEY TERMS

Academic Admissions Requirements Certain minimum standards that must be met for admission to a college or university.

Athletic Director A person who has full control over all aspects of college athletics, including the department's employees (staff, coaches, and student-athletes).

Athletic Scholarships Either full or partial, these provide financial assistance, usually in the form of room and board (paying for admissions, textbooks and school supplies) as well as per diem (meal allowance).

Athletic Trainers Professionals who specialize in proper health care for athletes and in prevention, evaluation, management and rehabilitation of injuries.

Authoritarian Coach An overbearing coach obsessed with winning who may ruin the sport experience of participants.

Authority A person in a position of power who influence the thoughts and behaviors of others.

Cheating In school sports it can take multiple forms (e.g., violating rules of sportsmanship, taking performance-enhancing drugs), all of which undermine the idealism of sport as an institution of character building.

Coaches Individuals who guide athletes on the rules of the game, methods of training, and ideally, help to develop the athletes' skills.

College Conferences Collective units which serve for instilling standards in college sports.

Elite Athletes Those considered the best in their sport; they are often shown special favor by coaches and schools.

Elite Deference Refers to the special privileges that are afforded athletes.

Hazing An all-encompassing term that covers silly, potentially risky, or degrading tasks required for acceptance by a group of full-fledged members.

Illegal Recruiting Tactics These may include rival recruiters spreading misinformation, lies or innuendoes to prized athletes in such ways as suggesting the other school is about to be placed on probation, they are going to raise admissions requirements, or that the head coach is about to quit or be fired.

Letter of Intent Treated as a legal contract, this states that the athlete promises to attend a particular school for four years.

National Collegiate Athletic Association The NCAA supervises the organization of college sports, the conduct of athletes, coaches and others involved with college sports, and the academic qualification to which athletes must adhere. It attempts to act in the best interests of college athletics.

Practice Any meeting, activity or instruction involving sports-related information and having an athletics purpose, held for one or more student-athletes at the direction of, or supervised by, any member or members of an institution's coaching staff.

Recruitment Where colleges seek out an athlete, rather than the athlete seeking out a college.
Sport Specialization Concentrating on just one sport, year-around, instead of enjoying participating in multiple sports.
Walk-on A nonscholarship athlete who tries out for a sport.

DISCUSSION QUESTIONS

- Should academic achievement be considered an important part of a student-athlete's role? Suppose he or she is outstanding in a given sport but unable to perform well academically. Why would this be an issue?

- What are some of the pluses and minuses of participating in interscholastic sporting events?

- Who are "athletic trainers" and what arguments can be given to show why they play an important role in school sports?

- What is the NCAA and how did it come into existence? What are its chief functions today?

- What are some possible recruitment violations of student-athletes, and how can these be avoided?

- Should student-athletes be paid for their services? Give your reasons pro or con.

- Are you aware of any hazing incidents? Why is hazing a concern in youth sports, and what can be done to prevent it?

CHAPTER 8

Deviance in Sport

All sports are guided by numerous rules and regulations. Some of these rules seem rather silly and relatively meaningless. Golf, for example, has a few trivial rules that are strictly enforced. One such rule was cleverly articulated in a *Seinfeld* episode ("The Big Salad") where Kramer describes his golf outing to Jerry and Elaine. Kramer was playing with his friend, Steve Gendason, who on the fifteenth hole picked up his ball and cleaned it. Elaine wondered what the big deal was. Kramer responded, "Umph, sorry! But the rules clearly state that you cannot clean the ball unless it's on the green. The rules are very clear about that." Jerry concurred; the rules are very clear about that. Consequently, Kramer penalized Gendason a stroke. Gendason became extremely angry with Kramer and almost came to blows with him. Elaine still did not understand the seriousness of the rule. Kramer, once again explains to her, "A rule is a rule. And let's face it. Without rules there's chaos."

The *Seinfeld* episode illustrates the prevailing theme of deviance — if you break the rules you are subject to sanctions or punishments. As we have already learned from the earlier chapters, the social institution of sport is not immune from deviant or criminal behavior. Among the types of deviance in sport to be discussed in this chapter are on-the-field forms; off-the-field acts; performance-enhancing drug use among athletes; and illegal and pathological gambling.

Deviance

Ideally, sport promotes many of society's desirable character traits, including fair play, sportsmanship, obedience to authority, hard work and dedication toward a desired goal, and a commitment to excellence. Unfortunately, this is not always the case. We begin our discussion with a definition of deviance.

Although most people tend to believe that they understand what the word "deviance" means, the sociological study of deviant behavior reveals that a number of circumstances influence how some behaviors come to be defined as deviant while others are defined as acceptable. Bear in mind that no behavior is inherently deviant; it must be labeled as deviant in order to *be* deviant. Most definitions include the basic idea that deviance entails any behavior that violates cultural norms and that such violations may lead to punishment. For the purposes of this text, the authors define deviance as any act or behavior that is likely to be defined, by some members of society, or specific subcultural groups, as an unacceptable violation of a social norm and elicits negative reactions from others. By definition, people who commit such deeds are deviants. For example, it is widely understood among athletes that what happens in the locker room stays in locker room. In other words, do not air "dirty laundry" to the public.

Explaining Social Deviance

There are a number of theoretical explanations of social deviance. Sociological theories are grounded by the belief that deviance is caused by environmental factors (e.g., family, community, and other social factors). They incorporate a diverse, multi-causal framework in their explanation of deviant behavior. In an attempt to support their theories about deviance and crime, sociologists utilize empirical data. Our discussion begins with functional and anomie/strain theory.

FUNCTIONALIST AND ANOMIE/STRAIN THEORY

Anomie theory, sometimes called strain theory, was articulated by Robert Merton, who borrowed Emile Durkheim's term *anomie*. Many of Durkheim's ideas were used in the formation of functionalist theory. Intrigued by Durkheim's focus on morality and his notion of anomie, Robert Merton examined the role of strain on individuals. Whereas Durkheim believed that anomie was the result of rapid social change, Merton believed that anomie, or strain, was a condition that existed permanently in certain societies, such as the United States. Merton introduced the concept of "dysfunction" to describe American society. Dysfunctions have a negative effect on society. Merton viewed the U.S. as a dysfunctional society because it places an overemphasis on the cultural goal of economic success. Merton stated that American society provided many appropriate, legitimate, or institutionalized means for attaining the success goal for a majority of the people of society. However, Merton argued that not everyone is equally endowed with desire or opportunity to reach the success goal. Merton believed that when certain members of society become frustrated and feel a strain because they cannot attain the cultural desired goals legitimately, they turn to illegitimate means. Thus, Merton believed that deviance was a result of the social strain that anomie created.

Merton's anomie theory (first published as "Social Structure and Anomie" in 1938) is based on the premise that society encourages all persons to attain culturally desirable goals, but the opportunity to reach these goals are not equal for all members of society. Furthermore, when people have difficulty reaching their desired goals they will feel strain. Some people become so frustrated that they resort to illegitimate (deviant) means of getting ahead. Thus, a MLB player who has a goal of hitting 50 home runs in one season but fails to do so may decide to take performance-enhancing drugs in order to reach that success goal.

SUBCULTURE/CULTURAL DEVIANCE THEORY

By the 1950s and early 1960s, sociologists were studying deviant behavior in the context of the new sociological term "subculture." A subculture refers to a group of people who possess distinctive cultural values, ethnicity, or some other trait that distinguishes it from other groups in the greater society. There are many subcultural groups within any society, including athletes.

Subcultures are formed with group members identify common goals, values, and traits that unite them. In this regard, the subculture becomes a reference group for individual members. One trait that may unite members of subculture is common activity, such as playing sports. As we learned in Chapter 4, athletes share a common lingo, or language, that has symbolic meaning to them. Reinforcing particular mannerisms and language are examples of reference points that unite subculture members. In many cases, the subculture's values and norms supersede that of the greater society. Consequently, members engage in behaviors that are acceptable within the subculture, but may be considered deviant by the greater society. For example, skateboarders— in need of paved areas to skate — might choose to skate in front of government building (e.g., City Hall) because of its ramps, rails (stairway rails), and adjacent parking lots.

To the skaters, this is a logical place to skate. Chances are, however, local ordinances will forbid skateboarding outside City Hall, and thus, these skaters will be labeled as "deviants" by the greater society (especially the police and city hall workers). In short, subcultural theorists believe that deviants who violate certain rules adhere more closely to the norms of their subculture group than that of the larger society.

SOCIAL LEARNING AND DIFFERENTIAL THEORY

As the name social learning theory implies, individuals *learn* how to become deviant within a social context. An individual learns behavior through interaction with others, whether directly (being taught) or indirectly (through observation, imitation, and modeling). Through interaction with others, individuals learn of the norms, beliefs, attitudes and values treasured by the interactants. That is to say, people learn by observing the behavior of others. A young aspiring ball player will closely watch the behavior of other ballplayers, especially professional athletes. The young athlete will model his or her behavior to that of the observed by mimicking (e.g., chewing on sunflower seeds, wearing a ball cap backwards in the dugout, using a fist bump instead of a "high five" for a greeting). Most people model their behavior after influential others. Generally, this is acceptable. However, if the model engages in deviant acts, the observer is likely to see this behavior as acceptable and engage in the same type of activity.

Edwin Sutherland, a leading social learning theorist, argued that it takes more than an occasional observation of deviant behavior on the part of the observer before it becomes an acquired behavior. Sutherland argued, in his differential association theory, that it takes continued association and reinforcement in order for a behavior to be indoctrinated. Thus, the more an individual associates with deviants (and criminals) the more likely he or she will learn and accept these behaviors, values, attitudes and beliefs (Sutherland and Cressey, 1978). Based on this theoretical explanation of deviance, if athletes associate with deviant significant others rather than conforming significant others, they are more likely to become deviants. Further, if athletes are taught various methods of cheating by significant others, they are more likely to accept these behaviors.

LABELING THEORY

At one time, labeling theory was the most prominent symbolic interactionist approach to the study and explanation of deviant behavior (the lack of consistent empirical verification has led to its decline in popularity). Labeling theory examines the effects of a "label" being placed on a person and his or her subsequent behavior. For example, what effect does the negative label of "bully" being assigned to a person have on the subsequent behavior of that person? That is, will he try to live up to such a label and start and continue to beat up on others, or will he go out of his way to help and protect others to prove that he is not a "bully?"

Labeling theorists believe that no one wants to acquire a label that they themselves consider to be an inaccurate assessment of their character (e.g., that he or she "chokes" at critical points of a game or competition). Everyone attempts to *negotiate* their *role-identity*. However, the allocation of labels is often determined by "outside" others, such as media personnel, fans, and bloggers. As a result, we cannot control the labels that others bestow upon us. Labeling theory also states that when an individual continually receives negative feedback from significant others and then begins to accept the negative label, a self-fulfilling prophecy has been created. The self-fulfilling prophecy occurs when people take to heart the labels bestowed upon them, come to see themselves in regard to those labels, and then act correspondingly to those labels. In short, they come to see themselves as others have labeled them. Thus, labeling is an important factor in the creation of a deviant identity. For instance, athletes who are constantly referred to as "losers" might internalize such a label, lose self-confidence and thereby perform unsuccessfully.

CONFLICT THEORY

Conflict theorists highlight the imbalance of power found in society, especially in light of economic and social inequalities found in all societies. Conflict theorists argue that those who control the means of production are in a social position to dictate to others what is "right" and "wrong" behavior. Class distinctions play an important role in complex societies. In sport, coaches, athletic directors, and owners possess power and make the rules that players must follow. These power elites are in a position of control and can impose their will and ideas of what constitutes deviance.

In 2005, NBA Commissioner David Stern instituted a mandatory dress code for all players. Stern required players to wear business casual attire whenever they are engaged in team or league business. Business attire is defined as: long or short-sleeved dress shirt (collared or turtleneck), and/or a sweater; dress slacks, khaki pants, or dress pants; appropriate shoes and socks, including dress shoes, dress boots, or other presentable shoes, but not including sneakers, sandals, flip-flops, or work boots (*NBA.com*, 2005). The NBA players are mostly members of the subcultural hip-hop generation and they prefer to wear gold chains and maintain their individual dress styles. Visible chains, pendants or medallions are not allowed over their clothes. Some players claim the dress code is racist (See Chapter 11 for a further discussion of racism in sport). Especially in light of the fact that athletes often set fashion trends, requiring them to wear clothing they consider unfashionable or "square" presents a dilemma between the need for conformity and the desire for self-expression.

On the Field Deviance

The most likely culprits for on-the-field deviance are the athletes themselves. Normative forms of deviance are abundant and especially manifest themselves in the form of denial of wrongdoing or the failure to admit to deviant behavior. For example, soccer players may occasionally be guilty of a "hand ball"—the illegal touching of the ball—but they will not report such violations to the referee; nor would their competitors expect them to do so. Perhaps the most famous case of a hand ball occurred in the 1986 World Cup quarterfinal game between Argentina and England. In this game, Argentine star Diego Maradona credited God for his goal against England. (The goal is known as the "Hand of God" goal in soccer lore.) Maradona appeared to punch the ball into the goal but officials allowed it despite the complaints by the English team. In 2005, Maradona admitted that he struck the ball with his hand (Bechtel, 2005).

In the spirit of respect for the game, baseball players are expected not to attempt to "steal" signs between the opposing pitcher and catcher. A batter might look behind his shoulder to see what signs a catcher flashes to the pitcher and runners on base (especially second base) may try to steal signs and relay them to his teammate who is at bat. On other rare occasions, one team accuses another of using cameras in the outfield and then relaying the information to a coach in the dugout who must then relay signs to the batter.

An example of deviant cheating is point shaving. Point shaving involves a player(s) "throwing" a game or performance (e.g., taking a "dive" in boxing; dropping a touchdown pass; deliberately missing free-throws in basketball) for money (usually from gamblers) or other goods ands services. Various point shaving scandals have surfaced over the years and it would be impossible to know how many times an individual or group of teammates have agreed to comprise the integrity of the game. Bookmakers in Nevada and the NCAA monitor unusual fluctuations in point spreads that might suggest a fix. Occasionally select games are "taken off the board" (no one is allowed to bet on the game) in Nevada because officials may believe a fix is in. One of sports history's most memorable point shaving scandals occurred in 1950 and involved college basketball players from Bradley, Kentucky, Long Island University and City College New York (CCNY). That year, CCNY won both the men's National Invitation Tournament (NIT) and the National Collegiate Athletic Association tournament (NCAA), becoming the only team to win both tournaments in the same year. As it turned out, 30 players from the four teams were implicated to have taken money from gamblers to "shave" points from the total score (Goldstein, 2005). In 1951, City College player Norman Mager was arrested and pleaded guilty to a misdemeanor offense. He later received a suspended sentence. Although CCNY won the championships, it was alleged that Mager made sure his team did win by a margin higher than the established betting lines (Goldstein, 2005). Many fans today still fear that some games are "fixed."

These are just a few examples of on-the-field deviance committed by players. Coaches, team doctors, and trainers are also capable of on-the-field deviance. Team doctors and trainers may act unethically by the means that they administer drugs to players. We will examine their role with deviance later in this chapter.

Coaches, Scouts and Deviance

Coaches may engage in a number of deviant behaviors, starting with lying on their resumes (e.g., George O'Leary lost his dream job at Notre Dame when it was revealed that he lied on his resume; he is currently serving as head coach at the University of Central Florida); belittling their players in practice and sometimes in public; running practice in an intimidating manner (like a "drill sergeant"); teaching players how to get away with certain deviant behaviors; deliberate attempts to intimidate officials and influence calls; encouraging players to take pain medication in order to play in pain; and violent outbursts. Violent outbursts range from Bobby Knight's infamous chair throwing incident during a basketball game, to baseball managers throwing temper tantrums, coaches ripping the ball away from an official, to Miami of Ohio defensive coordinator Jon Wauford being arrested for allegedly shoving a fan who was celebrating Marshall's last-second win over Miami in a 2002 game.

In individualist sports such as track and field, a coach may be tempted to encourage an athlete to take illegal drugs in an attempt to improve performance. Trevor Graham, a hugely successful sprint coach in track and field, has helped many athletes reach their goal of earning a gold medal in the Olympics. His athletes also have received drug suspensions (Patrick, 2005). Graham, among other things, portrays himself as a whistle-blower. It was Graham who provided "the U.S. Anti-Doping Agency a syringe containing the designer steroid THG in June 2003, which helped unravel the BALCO case, the biggest performance-enhancing drug scandal in U.S. sports history" (Patrick, 2005: 6C).

In 2007, Bill Belichick, the head coach of the New England Patriots (NFL), was labeled a "cheater" as a result of his unauthorized videotaping of opposing teams' coaches in order to pick up their play signals—a tactic that would provide the Patriots with an unfair advantage. NFL Commissioner Roger Goodell punished Belichick and the Patriots with $750,000 in fines and the forfeiture of a first-round draft pick. According to the NFL's office, Belichick had been conducting unauthorized videotaping for the past decade, thus casting doubts on the legitimacy of their Super Bowl (as well as other) victories during that span. The controversy surrounding the cheating scandal led to the term "Spygate." A Google search (in 2008) of the term "Spygate" revealed more than one-half million references to this act of deviance.

In 2008, we learned that scouts are also capable of committing deviance. The Baltimore Orioles fired veteran scout Alan Marr because he was allegedly linked to a sports betting probe.

According to an SI.com report, more scouts have also been implicated (*The Post-Standard*, 7/12/08: C-5). An investigative unit of MLB was working with the FBI as part of an inquiry into illegal gambling. During this investigation it was revealed that scouts have been skimming money from signing bonuses given to Latin-American players.

Referee and Officials' Deviance

Referees and officials are only human. They sometimes make mistakes. Honest mistakes are forgivable. Dishonest mistakes and improper behavior are examples of deviance. Officials have been known to make mistakes on the number of downs in a football game leading, to a team having a fifth down. Sometimes they put extra time on the clock that gives one team another chance to win; perhaps, undeservingly so. Other times, officials misinterpret rules, giving one team an unfair advantage. And in one odd case (2007), veteran NBA referee Joey Crawford challenged San Antonio Spurs star player Tim Duncan to fight! The NBA suspended Crawford indefinitely. In 2008, umpire Brian Runge was suspended for one game for bumping into New York Mets manager Jerry Manuel before ejecting him from a game.

Crawford's and Runge's embarrassing behavior paled in comparison to the shameful behavior of Tim Donaghy, who so soiled the reputation of the NBA that its very integrity is in jeopardy. In 2007, the FBI began its investigation into the allegations that veteran NBA referee Donaghy influenced the outcome of professional basketball games on which he or associates of his had gambled on the outcome during (at least) the 2004–05 and 2005–06 seasons. The disgraced Donaghy resigned from the NBA and NBA Commissioner Stern attempted to ease the concern of fans and related parties by saying the actions of Donaghy were an isolated incident. During the 2007–08 NBA championships finals, Donaghy stated in court that NBA officials tampered with games to assure certain teams advanced through the playoffs. Kobe Bryant (Los Angeles Lakers) was asked about Donaghy's possible tampering with NBA games during the 2008 finals. According to *Sports Illustrated*, 6/23/08, Bryant's answer was elusive and he apologized for his nonanswer by saying, "I'm sorry to be Belichicky"— a reference to Bill Belichick's vague responses to the media when he was asked about Spygate (p. 28).

In light of the Donaghy case, fans of all sports renewed their paranoia that "the game was fixed" any time their favorite team appeared to fall victim of a perceived bad call from a referee or umpire).

Sports Entertainment, Media and Deviance

Sports are entertainment. They also come equipped with other forms of entertainment including cheerleaders, mascots, stadium sound effects and pyrotechnics, and intermission entertainment such as marching bands. Nearly all spectators enjoy the musical performances of marching bands during halftime of football games. At the high school and college levels they are nearly institutionalized within the sport structure. Marching bands provide entertainment for spectators; they nearly always exude good sportsmanship and fair play. There was, however, one occasion where the halftime marching bands of Prairie View A&M and Southern University did not demonstrate proper behavior. Instead, they brawled. This unfortunate event took place on September 19, 1998. The musicians used their instruments as weapons, assailing one another. Each band was subsequently suspended from its next two football games (Patrick, 1998).

The media may be responsible for a great deal of deviance. (We will explore the role of the media in sport in Chapter 15.) Lately, they have come under great scrutiny by the FCC for possible breaches of decency. The FCC has decided to hold the media responsible for the acts of entertainers, for example, halftime performers at the Super Bowl. Janet Jackson's "wardrobe malfunction" during the 2004 Super Bowl halftime show became the lightning rod for federal regulators of what constitutes acceptable or deviant behavior. Ultimately, CBS paid a record $550,000 fine for indecency because Jackson's breast was temporarily exposed to the estimated 90 million television viewership.

SPECTATOR DEVIANCE

Much of spectator deviance is violent and occurs off the field (this topic will be discussed in further detail in Chapter 9). Some forms of spectator deviance are normalized. For example, many fans still try to sit in seats better than their own and then act surprised when they confronted by the proper seat-holders. Some spectators sneak alcohol and other forbidden products into sporting events. They may attempt to use cameras at events where they are forbidden. Some spectators neglect to stand during the playing of the national anthem, including some males who ignore the etiquette of removing their hats.

Other forms of spectator deviance are not normative and involve a direct confrontation between spectators and athletes. For example, in 1993 a crazed Steffi Graf fan stabbed her primary rival, Monica Seles, during a break in a tennis match in Germany. Houston Astros right fielder Bill Spiers was attacked on the field in the bottom of the sixth inning during a game at Milwaukee in 1999. Kansas City Royals first base coach Tom Gamboa was attacked during a 2002 game in Chicago by a father and son who ran onto the field. William Ligue, Jr., was sentenced to 30 months of probation for two counts of aggravated battery in the September 2002 attack on Gamboa. In April 2004, Ligue violated his parole when he was charged with breaking into a car in suburban Harvey and led police on a brief chase. If Ligue had been incarcerated for his unprovoked attack on Gamboa he would not have been free to commit his other crimes.

Spectators have increasingly been interfering with baseball players attempting to make plays near the stands. In many sports, spectators throw objects at players. It seems that many spectators interpret the price of admission as an opportunity to act in any manner they see fit. This is not true, of course. There are many possible explanations for the general lack of civility displayed by some spectators. Many are upset with players who act arrogant and are far-removed (especially financially) from the typical fan. Some spectators believe they need to "protect" their home turf and team's honor and direct their deviance toward opposing fans and players. Spectators must realize that the rules of fair play and sportsmanship also apply to them.

Off the Field or Court Deviance

Athletes, referees, and even marching bands may be involved with a wide variety of off-the-field deviant behaviors, including recreational drug use, athletes who have other students take tests for them, "sympathetic" teachers and professors who pass undeserving athletes, spousal abuse, deviant sex scandals and criminal behavior. Of particular importance are the topics of taking performance-enhancing drugs and gambling, which will be discussed later in this chapter. We will review sex scandals and athletes and crime.

DEVIANT SEX SCANDALS

Deviant sex scandals come in a variety of forms. Some are far more serious than others. For example, in 2003, a parent took members of the Massapequa High School (NY) varsity baseball team on a late-night visit to a Florida strip club. Coaches were dismissed and players disciplined for violating the school and athletic department's code of conduct (Eltman, 2003). Taking under-aged youths to a strip club reinforces the objectification of women that many teenage boys have already developed. If high school athletes are allowed to get away with deviant

As predicated by a long tradition, fans of the SUNY Oswego men's hockey team throw bagels onto the ice following the first goal against arch-rival SUNY Plattsburgh. Officially, administrators are against this tradition.

sexual behavior, they will expect to get away with other deviant behaviors in college. In turn, professional athletes often possess an even higher elevated sense of entitlement. In fact, some professional athletes have "groupies" in every city where they play, which reinforces their sense of entitlement with women.

Deviant sex parties, where women are objectified, occur throughout sports. For example, during the 2005 NFL season, some members of the Minnesota Vikings were "accused of participating in a floating orgy so debauched, Caligula would have blushed" (Rushin, 2005: 19). On October 6, 17 Vikings and their guests arrived in coach limousines to the shore of Lake Minnetonka where they then boarded two yachts. The outing was part of the team's annual rookie party (Silver and Dohrmann, 2005). Among the alleged activities reported to police were possible acts of prostitution, drugs and live sex acts (Rushin, 2005). Minnesota Governor Tim Pawlenty told the Minneapolis *Star Tribune* that he doesn't expect the Vikings to be role models but he does expect them to abide by the basic laws of the state (Rushin, 2005). In December 2005, four Vikings players were charged with misdemeanors alleging lewd or indecent conduct. Among the allegations were players receiving lap dances from naked women (Chanen and Shaffer, 2005). Young athletes learn about this behavior of professional athletes and the cycle of objectification of women continues on to the next generation of athletes.

Cheerleaders are also capable of deviant behavior. On November 6, 2005, two Carolina Panthers cheerleaders (Top Cats) were arrested after a nightclub incident. The two cheerleaders

(Angela Keathley and Victoria Renee Thomas) were having sex with each other in a bathroom stall at the Banana Joe's nightclub in Tampa, Florida. Other patrons became angry waiting to use the restroom and complained to the two women when they finally exited the stall. Keathley got into an argument with one of the other patrons and then punched her in the face, according to police reports (Poltilove, 2005). In January 2006, Keathley pleaded guilty to disorderly conduct and obstructing a police officer. Thomas denies the sex allegations. The incident occurred 11 hours before the kickoff of the Panthers' NFL game against the Tampa Bay Buccaneers. The two cheerleaders were in Tampa on their own, as the Top Cats perform only at home games. This incident is further evidence that anyone involved in sport is capable of committing acts of deviance.

There are times where the athlete is the victim. There are some "groupies" who hope to land a young successful athlete before he turns professional (or while he is a professional athlete) in an attempt to live the "good life." In 1999, a football player at Arizona State University was confronted with a rather bizarre form of marriage "entrapment." J. R. Redmond was suspended by the NCAA for one game for violating its "extra-benefits" rules. He used a cell phone from a part-time athletic department employee who later pointed out to Redmond that he had just violated NCAA rules. She promised to keep the infraction quiet if Redmond agreed to marry her. Redmond married her but then filed for divorce when she claimed half his future earnings in the NFL (*USA Today,* 11/2/99).

These are just a few examples of sexual deviance in sport. Perhaps more alarming is criminal activity committed by athletes and others in the sport profession.

ATHLETES AND CRIME

Deviant behavior that violates a law constitutes a crime. As humans, some athletes make poor decisions and commit criminal acts. The sports media report criminal activity committed by athletes as if they are publishing a "police blotter."

People in the sports industry have been involved in criminal activities for as long as there have been sports. However, in recent decades the number of athletes, sports agents, coaches and owners involved in criminal activity has seemingly skyrocketed. One merely has to listen to a *SportsCenter* broadcast or read a daily newspaper's sport section to find examples of crime in sports. The crimes range from misdemeanor offenses to felonies and include racketeering, fraud, extortion, murder, murder-for-hire, disorderly conduct, drug sale and distribution, spousal abuse, threatening people with weapons, running prostitution rings and so on. Some sport commentators argue that athletes committing crimes was as common in the past as it is presently, but that there were control mechanisms designed to protect the special privilege of athletes in the past that do not exist today. Thus, there only *appear* to be more crimes committed by athletes today than in the past.

It would be pointless to try to provide a list of criminal activities that involves sport participants. We will, instead, briefly review a few of the more recent sensational cases involving athletes and crime:

• Two University of Connecticut men's basketball players were disciplined by the University for their role in trying to sell stolen laptops in the summer of 2005. Guard A.J. Price was suspended from basketball for the entire 2005–06 season, while teammate Marcus Williams was allowed to return to the team in December. Both players had to complete several hours of community service.
• Former NFL defensive lineman Bob Buczkowski was charged with conspiracy, possession and delivery of a controlled substance and operating a prostitution and cocaine ring in Monroeville, Pa. Buczkowski and his girlfriend, Amy Schifano, made nearly $1 million through drug sales and prostitution between February 2003 and June 2005. In June of 2007 Buczkowski pled guilty and was sentenced to ninety days of house arrest and three years of probation.

- A high school athlete, awaiting an October 17, 2005, trial on six counts of aggravated robbery with a deadly weapon, each of which carries a sentence of five years to life, was allowed to continue playing football at his Lancaster (Texas) high school. Along with his helmet and shoulder pads, Brandon Jackson had to wear a court-ordered electronic ankle monitor. As Rick Reilly sarcastically wrote in his weekly *Sports Illustrated* column (August, 29, 2005), "Luckily, in this country, where shame is on permanent holiday, there are bleachers full of football coaches willing to give youngsters facing six-count felony charges another chance" (p. 72).
- Maurice Clarett, former running back at Ohio State (who unsuccessfully challenged the NFL's draft policy — he declared himself eligible for the draft after his freshmen year) was accused of robbing two people at gunpoint in an alley behind a downtown Columbus bar in January 2006. While on trial, he led the police on a chase after making an illegal U-turn and had to be forcibly subdued with mace after a taser gun did not work, as he was wearing body armor. Several guns, including a loaded AK-57 type weapon, were found in his SUV. On September 8, 2006, he pled guilty and was sentenced to seven and a half years in prison.
- In 2006, Thomas "Hitman" Hearns, a former champion boxer, was arrested on misdemeanor assault and battery charges for allegedly hitting his 13-year-old son.
- Former MLB All-Star Jeff Reardon was arrested for allegedly holding up a jewelry store in December 2005. He was found not guilty by reason of insanity, due to the anti-depressants and mood stabilizers he had been taking due to being distraught over his son Shane's death from a drug overdose in February of 2004.
- Former Virginia Tech quarterback Marcus Vick (brother of NFL's Michael Vick), who was booted from the Hokies' football team for his behavior on and off the field, was charged with pulling a gun on three teenagers during an altercation in a restaurant parking lot in January 2006. In a separate incident, Vick was charged with speeding and driving without a valid driver's license. In March 2006, Vick pleaded guilty to disorderly conduct as part of plea bargain for both offenses (brandishing a firearm at the teenagers and illegal operation of a motor vehicle). Among Vick's other off-the-field deviant behaviors are reckless driving and marijuana possession in 2004. His on-the-field deviant behavior included stomping on Louisville All-American defensive end Elvis Dumervil's left calf in the 2006 Gator Bowl as Dumervil lay on the ground after a play was blown dead.
- Michael Vick, meanwhile, was sent to prison for his role in encouraging and promoting dog-fighting activities at his home in southeastern Virginia. In July of 2007 Vick and three accomplices were charged with operating an unlawful dog-fighting ring for over six years. Vick pled guilty; while on bail he tested positive during a random drug test for marijuana. In December of 2007 he was sentenced to 23 months in Leavenworth, a federal penitentiary.

Unfortunately, this is merely a brief look at the deviant off-the-field transgressions of some athletes.

Drug Use and Blood-doping in Sport

In 2001, the NCAA released the results from its survey of drug use among athletes. Over 21,000 athletes from all three athletic divisions responded. Just 1.6 percent of Division I athletes indicated that they had used anabolic steroids in 2000. Less than 4 percent of respondents claimed to have used amphetamines and ephedrine. NCAA athletes participated in far greater recreational drug use, with 79 percent indicating that they had at least one alcoholic drink in the past year and 43 percent saying they had more than six beers in one sitting (labeled as binge drinking). Division III athletes are more likely to smoke marijuana (32 percent) than to smoke cigarettes (26 percent) or chew tobacco (19 percent). Fifty-eight percent of responding athletes admitted to using some kind of nutritional supplements other than vitamins; creatine was the top choice (26 percent of athletes) (*NCAA News*, 2001). Creatine is a simple nitrogenous compound that is found in most meat. Proponents of creatine argue that one's energy supply, which is depleted during strenuous exercise, can be improved by taking the substance (Kammerer,

2001). Creatine phosphate is a dietary supplement that is believed to help build muscle and provide brief bursts of energy (Kuhn, et al., 2000). Creatine does increase body weight, but it may not build muscle in all users. There is no evidence that creatine improves endurance (Kuhn, et al., 2000).

Blood-doping involves introducing an additional substance into an athlete's body in the hopes of improving performance. Unlike medical or recreational drugs, the substance introduced is the athlete's own blood. Blood doping is cheating and is a violation of fair play. Blood doping was rampant during the Olympics of the 1970s. Many athletes were suspected and ultimately shown to be guilty of this practice (Houlihan, 1999). Although blood-doping was not officially considered cheating by the IOC before 1986, it was considered cheating and dishonorable within the athletic community (Voy, 1991). The development of rEPO (recombinant erythropoietin), a synthetic drug, has provided blood dopers with an alternative in drug form (Houlihan, 1991).

Blood-doping is a process that involves taking two or more pints of an athlete's own blood (or that of a donor) about eight to twelve weeks before competition. Over this 8–12 week period, the athlete's body will gradually return to a normal level of red blood cells. However, the athlete must increase his or her intake of food, vitamins, and iron (Voy, 1991). The red blood cells from the transfused blood are (usually) separated from the plasma and freeze-preserved, carefully stored, and reinfused (injected) into the athlete about 24 hours before competition. This results in a significant increase in the number of red blood cells in the body and the overall oxygen-carrying capacity of the blood supply. Houlihan (1999) explains that the purpose of blood doping "is to increase the capacity of the blood to transport oxygen to the muscles and it is based on the principle that the amount of oxygen available to the muscles is determined by the quantity of red blood cells in the body. Therefore, if the number of red blood cells can be increased, so too can the volume of oxygen transported to the muscles during competition" (p. 41). The increased level of oxygen also increases endurance and therefore benefits athletes who participate in endurance-related sports such as the 5000 and 10,000 meters swimming events.

The sudden increase in the units of blood or red blood cells can cause dangerously high blood pressure and put the doper's heart at risk. In some rare cases, total heart failure is possible. The increased amount of blood may also cause clotting, which may also lead to serious and fatal health problems (Voy, 1991). Blood doping also involves the athlete being dependent upon a lot of persons handling the transfused blood. With all the potential risks associated with blood transfusions (e.g., AIDS infection), blood doping is a dangerous way to cheat in an attempt to gain an edge over the competition. By 2004, the World Anti-Doping Agency had turned its attention to a far more sophisticated form of doping — gene alteration. There are researchers developing plans to genetically alter an athlete's body for peak performance. Although it has not been accomplished as of this writing, the Anti-Doping Agency is aware of the research being done in this area and is prepared to stop genetically-altered athletes from competing in international sporting events (Ruibal, 2004).

And yet, many athletes are willing to risk almost anything, including their health and life, in an attempt to gain an advantage over the competition. Taking performance-enhancing drugs is among the most dangerous options.

Performance-Enhancing Drugs

As with most advanced societies, it is a part of American culture to strive and be the best. Competition is very evident in sport. At any level, but especially the professional, success is always measured in terms of winning. Winning is the ultimate goal. Society rewards winners with celebrity, status, admiration and, of course, wealth. Success in sport, as with any social institution, is achieved when someone gains an "edge" over the competition. In the pursuit of success, however, some people are tempted to gain an unfair advantage, or edge, through illegal or unethical manners. Athletes, because they want to achieve peak levels of performance, sometimes turn to techniques other than training in order to achieve the success goal. Performance-enhancing drugs, such as anabolic steroids, have an aura of success.

THE AURA OF SUCCESS THAT ENCOMPASSES ANABOLIC STEROIDS

Anabolic steroids are drugs that resemble androgenic hormones such as testosterone. "The effects of anabolic steroids mimic those of testosterone. Naturally synthesized hormones, such as testosterone, are types of lipids. They have a four-ring carbon skeleton and are synthesized in the adrenal cortex, ovaries or testes. Production of testosterone takes place in the male testes and the female ovaries; it is present in the male at significantly higher levels than in females, two of the main effects being androgenic and anabolic" (Lenehan, 2003: 2). An excessive amount of testosterone provides an athlete with an advantage over the competition. When this testosterone is introduced to the body in an unnatural manner, it becomes a form of cheating. Floyd Landis, winner of the 2006 Tour de France, was stripped of his championship when an international sports court upheld doping charges against the cyclist. It was determined that Landis had taken an illicit dose of testosterone to win the bicycle race that has been routinely subject to doping scandals. Landis, however, was the first tour winner to be stripped of his title for a doping violation.

Testosterone's main effects are androgenic, which controls the secondary sexual characteristics in the male (e.g., deep voice and hair in the "growth areas") and anabolic, which controls the growth and development of many body tissues, the most obvious being muscles (Lenehan, 2003). Any anabolic steroid that builds up muscle tissue will also cause secondary sexual changes, and therefore, as Lenehan (2003) suggests, steroids should really be referred to as anabolic-androgenic steroids. Despite this reality, most people use the term "anabolic steroid."

Anabolic steroids are synthetic versions of naturally occurring hormones. Athletes consume steroids in hopes of gaining weight, strength, power, endurance and aggressiveness. The anabolic effects help to accelerate the growth of muscle, bone and red blood cells. When combined with a strenuous conditioning program, steroids do in fact aid the athlete in reaching the goal of added strength, quickness, and bulk muscle.

Here is a theoretical model of how steroids work: the steroid hormone enters the cell and binds to a receptor molecule; the bound hormone enters the nucleus and activates specific genes to produce proteins; and these proteins, in turn, bring about the cellular changes triggered by the hormone.

The introduction of anabolic steroids into the body can have numerous unintended consequences, such as upsetting one's nitrogen balance, which can lead to a state of "catabolism" (the negative nitrogen balance leads to muscle consumption). Protein is an essential element for building muscle tissue. Muscle growth will occur under two conditions: (1) With heavy training and weight-lifting, the testosterone binding capacity increases—aiding the athlete in reaching the goal of added strength, quickness, and bulk muscle and (2) the body must retain more nitrogen (from protein) than it loses through the ongoing process of nitrogen excretion. In short, taking anabolic steroids represents an unnatural approach to muscle gain. Furthermore, steroids actually accomplish what they advertise. The "typical" steroid user is a white male, 18 to 45 years old (but most likely is between 25 and 30) who may have a part-time, minimum wage job and a minor criminal record (Yesalis, 1998). The obsession of young males with muscle gain and physical appearance has been referred to as "reverse anorexia"—when one believes he is not muscular (enough), when a rational person sees him as very muscular (Yesalis, 1998).

It is against federal law to possess and distribute steroids in the United States unless it is under direct medical supervision and for rehabilitative purposes.

HUMAN GROWTH HORMONE (HGH)

HGH is a synthetic human growth hormone that is being increasingly used as a therapy technique for nonathletes. Parents of short children have increasingly turned to HGH for their children in an attempt to stimulate growth. If parents believe HGH will assist growth development in children, it is just a matter of time before HGH is applied for other purposes. As Hoberman (2001) suggests, "Inevitably, some parents will want HGH to boost the athletic potential of their children" (p. 115). In June 2005, Tim Montgomery, the world's fastest man, told a federal grand jury that he used HGH and a steroid-like "magic potion" provided by the alleged ringleader of the BALCO (Bay Area Laboratory Cooperative) steroids scandal. The *San Francisco Chronicle* reported that Montgomery admitted to a grand jury that Victor Conte gave him weekly doses of growth hormone and a steroid-like drug known as "the clear" (because it is undetectable in drug tests) over an eight-month span ending in the summer of 2001. Athletes who take performance-enhancing drugs must also find a way to cheat the drug testing system implemented by governing agencies. Minnesota Vikings player Onterrio Smith, who has a history of violating the NFL's substance-abuse policy, was briefly detained by police at the Minneapolis–St. Paul International Airport on April 21, 2005, after a search of his travel bag revealed suspicious vials of white powder. Smith explained to officers that it was dried urine used in conjunction with a device called "The Original Whizzinator." The dried urine is used for making a "clean" urine (*The Post-Standard*, 5/12/05). The Whizzinator is a device sold on a web site by a company called Puck Technologies in Signal Hill, California. It is worn like a jock strap with a prosthetic penis attached to it (Hamilton, 2005). The device comes in different sizes and "skin" colors. It is believed that the Whizzinator is used extensively in baseball as well.

NEGATIVE ASPECTS OF TAKING PERFORMANCE-ENHANCING DRUGS

- So what's the problem with athletes taking performance enhancing drugs? Among the negative aspects that surround steroid use are:
- It gives the athlete who takes a performance-enhancing drug, such as steroids, an unfair advantage over those who remain "clean."
- It is a form of cheating; it is illegal.
- It violates ethical codes of proper behavior.
- It does not measure true athletic ability.
- It encourages further types of deviant behavior, by showing that people who cheat can still become successful.
- It is, perhaps, a reflection of a moral crisis in society (e.g., people refusing to play by the rules, they will cheat on drug tests as well).

Many people believe that records established by athletes who take steroids are tainted. The old cliché of "Say it ain't so, Joe" (a reference to "Shoeless" Joe Jackson, who was among the prominent members of the Chicago White Sox who were accused of throwing the 1919 World Series) applies to the steroid controversy today. Fans, especially young ones, want to know the truth — are today's athletes relying on steroids to accomplish their athletic feats? For example, is Barry Bonds' homerun record tainted because he allegedly took steroids? The jury, so to speak, is still out on Bonds, but the courts have reached a decision about the accomplishments of Marion Jones. Jones, who won three gold and two bronze medals in the 2000 Sydney Olympics and became one of the most marketable female athletes in the world, was sentenced to six months in prison in January 2008 (and 400 hours of community service upon her release from prison) as a result of her steroid and check fraud case. The check fraud scheme was Jones' major crime, but Federal Judge Kenneth Karas chastised Jones during sentencing (he imposed the maximum sentence) by claiming that the wide use of steroids "affects the integrity of athletic competition" (*The Citizen*, 3/8/08).

However, a fundamental question remains—can steroids actually affect a player's ability to hit a homerun? There has been no evidence to suggest that steroid use increases the hand-eye coordination so critical in one's ability to hit a ball. However, logic would dictate that a steroid-enhanced athlete, because he or she is stronger, will be able to hit the ball farther because of increased strength and power. In sports like football and rugby, where brute strength is often critical, it is easy to see how steroids can affect play. In track, where victories are often measured in tenths of seconds, any little advantage is enormous.

It should also be pointed out that athletes, whether they intend to or not, serve as role models for youth. When youngsters are told, directly (by coaches, parents, athletes) or indirectly (messages received from the media) that winning is the most important thing about sports, or life, the temptation to cheat becomes normalized. The number of American youths taking steroids is rapidly increasing. According to the Senate Caucus on International Narcotics Control, there are 350,000 American high school boys and 175,000 American high school girls using steroids each year (Orr, 2005). Research collected by the World Anti-Doping Agency reveals that "nearly 5% of 12 to 18-year-old boys and up to 2% of girls have tried steroids. And in a 2004 survey, 19% of eighth-graders, 29% of 10th graders and 42% of 12th graders said that steroids were 'fairly easy' or 'very easy' to obtain" (O'Shea, 2005: 9). The level of steroid use among young athletes exceeds the use of any drugs other than alcohol, nicotine, or marijuana (Kuhn, 2000). The risks to adolescents taking steroids are much greater than for the fully-grown adult.

Athletes and youth are not the only people illegally using steroids. This is evidenced by the large numbers of steroid users in training facilities across the United States. These muscle builders are motivated primarily by vanity and insecurity (Courson, 2005). Women want to be slim and have great body tone while men want big muscles with a strong upper body. An increasing number of female body builders are emphasizing their muscles and upper body strength as well. Looking good, or being big, represents the primary motive for anabolic steroid use among gym-based weight lifters. According to the Senate Caucus on International Narcotics Control, over 5 million Americans use steroids illegally each year (Orr, 2005).

The sports spectacle of professional wrestling is filled with steroid-induced entertainers. The costs of pumping up are often revealed after several years of use and abuse. A *USA Today* report in 2004 revealed that 65 wrestlers had died since 1997. The highest percentage of these fatalities were tied to heart attacks. Evidence has revealed that excessive steroid use can lead to an enlarged heart that may cause heart attacks (Swartz, 2004). Wrestler Chris Benoit, in June of 2007, killed his wife and child as well as himself in a case widely attributed to "'roid rage."

Anabolic steroids such as testosterone, progesterone, estradiol, zeranol and other growth hormones do promote muscle growth and strength. However, prolonged use has been implicated in breast, prostate and testicular cancer, heart disease, sexual and reproductive disorders, immunodeficiencies and liver damage, as well as abnormal growth and premature sexual development in young girls. And yet, those who avoid steroids may be ingesting their ingredients without consciously being aware of it. For example, all American consumers of beef and most milk drinkers are exposed to these hazards. Growth hormones are administered to most U.S. and Canadian beef cattle. Consequently, the European Union has banned imports of U.S. and Canadian beef since 1989, sparking a spiteful trade war. And yet, the American government finds it perfectly acceptable that its citizens are exposed to these growth hormones while forbidding athletes from voluntarily taking anabolic steroids. Some suggest that drug testing is against the Fourth Amendment. Supporters of the Congress's actions counterclaim that if organized sports will not regulate itself, the government must step in, much as it did in the 1920s during the rampant cheating in baseball.

The authors believe that athletes will continue to take performance-enhancing drugs in the future (for as long as the "winning is everything" doctrine remains dominant) despite the negative message they send youngsters, the unethical nature of taking steroids, the possible negative consequences of poor health (including possible death), suspension and expulsion from the sport, and possible jail time. Furthermore, we believe that the next wave of performance-enhancing techniques is just beginning to emerge.

What does the future hold for those who want to cheat in sport? The answer is "genomics." Genomics involves the use of genetic engineering to enhance athletic performance. Although gene therapy has been used mostly to treat disease (with only a handful of successes to date) the ability to enhance athletic skill is just a few steps away (Nesmith, 2007). As of now, there is no government intervention regarding genomics. Without regulation, genomics may trigger the beginning of "genetically supercharged" athletes (Nesmith, 2007).

Gambling in Sport

Gambling comes in a variety of forms, including bets between friends and family, lotteries, bingo, 50–50 raffles, and casino and sport gambling. The rising popularity of gambling makes it difficult for authorities to regulate and control legal gambling, let alone the multi-billion dollar illegal gambling industry. Nearly all of us have participated in some form of gambling, whether it involves purchasing a lottery ticket, playing church bingo, placing a bet at the track (or at an off-track location), casino gambling, playing cards for money, or making bets with friends, coworkers, or family members. Gambling among friends and co-workers is often called recreational gambling. A good example of recreational gambling involves a group of friends playing poker for minimum stakes or placing a small wager on a game.

Gambling has become a national issue as the result of the proliferation of all the various types of gambling, especially with the advent of casinos which have spread from Nevada and Atlantic City, New Jersey, to the riverboats and Indian reservations across the United States and Canada. Churches have long held bingo nights as an acceptable form of entertainment and fundraising. The Indian Gaming Regulatory Act of 1988 triggered the spread of casinos on Indian reservations. Billion dollar casinos have existed in Las Vegas for years. Most state governments argue that legalized gambling, especially lotteries, will help to generate increased revenues. As of 2008, only two states had no legalized gambling whatsoever — that includes no lotteries, horse-racing, dog-racing, jai-alai or casinos — Utah and Hawaii. Just two decades before, only two states had legal gambling.

Gambling is among the fastest growing industries in the United States. Many states have allowed the installation of a new generation of high-tech slot machines at race tracks and off-track betting (OTB) parlors creating "racinos" — slots at raceways. Indian casinos continue to pop up throughout the United States and Canada. Many Indian tribes believe that legalized gambling on their reservations will help to eliminate the extreme poverty that many of their people face. Approximately 400 Indian casinos were operated by 220 or so tribes in 28 U.S. states in 2008 and they pulled in $18.5 billion. (In 2008, there were 562 federally recognized Indian tribes in the United States.) Indian casino income is increasing by 10 percent or more every year (Werner, 2005). According to the National Indian Gaming Association, Indian gaming represented 23 percent of the total 2003 market share in the gambling industry. Because Indian tribes represent sovereign nations, they do not have to pay state or local taxes and are exempt from most zoning and other laws. Commercial gambling accounts for the largest percentage (39.4) of the total $72.8 billion gambled legally in 2003. Lotteries account for 27.4 percent of the total (Werner, 2005). New Yorkers alone spent more than $2 billion on lottery tickets in 2002.

The introduction of Mega Millions and Super Lottos (where states combine revenues and payouts) has dramatically increased the appeal of lotteries. Some single-winner payouts have exceeded $300 million. Forty states and the District of Columbia have lotteries; 43 have pari-mutuel wagering (dog and horse racing) and 35 states allow electronic gaming devices such as video poker and slot machines (Kuehn, 2005). Furthermore, as of 2008, 28 states allowed full-scale commercial casinos and there were more than 40 riverboat and dockside casinos with more on the way.

Critics of expanded legalized gambling worry that the United States is on its way to becoming "one large chapter of Gamblers Anonymous" (*The Post-Standard*, 5/26/04: A-12). Furthermore, most gambling is conducted *illegally* in an illicit market (estimated at $380 billion). In this regard, bets are made with bookies—people who take illegal bets. Illegality is just one of many potential problems associated with gambling.

Problems Associated with Gambling

Most people gamble low stakes and can absorb the defeat if their bet loses. Unfortunately, there are people who have a gambling problem. Some may even become compulsive or pathological gamblers. With the increase availability of gambling outlets, the number of problem and pathological gamblers will surely increase. Lesieur (1998) explains that a "problem gambler" is someone who has less serious problems than a pathological gambler. Whereas not all problem gamblers are pathological gamblers, all pathological gamblers are problem gamblers. Normally, the term "compulsive gambler" is used by the general public while the term "pathological gambler" is used by treatment professionals. "Pathological gambling" is classified as an "impulse control disorder" rather than a compulsion (Shafer, 2003). Research has shown that the prevalence of problem and pathological gambling has grown in states where the availability of gambling has increased and that pathological gambling is more common among males, youths, and minority populations (Volberg, 1994, 1996). Western New York, for example, has all the trappings of a bettor's paradise — professional sports teams, casinos, numerous OTB parlors, easy access to the state lottery — and it has a documented increase in the number of problem and pathological gamblers (Auer, 2003). In the Buffalo area, it is casino gambling that attracts the greatest number of pathological gamblers.

Pathological gamblers face several social and economic costs. Many may declare bankruptcy, and for others their gambling-related debts are often extreme. The pathological gambler's financial burden is extended to the family. The mortgage, the rent, gas, electric and other bills may be paid late or not at all. The pathological gambler's employment can also be hampered, either by missing work or arriving late, leaving early or sneaking out to place a bet. Between 69 and 76 percent of pathological gamblers report having missed time from work due to gambling (Ladouceur, Boisuert, Pepin, Loranger and Sylvain, 1994). Pathological gambling may lead to a number of illegal activities such as embezzling at work, forging checks, bouncing checks to cover gambling debts, lying on tax returns, committing fraud, and initiating a host of other illegal activities. Furthermore, the stress from gambling may lead to depression and anxiety, and impulsivity (Shafer, 2003). In extreme cases the pathological gambler may commit suicide when debts reach an extreme level. There is some hope for pathological gamblers— "Gamblers Anonymous," for instance, is an organization specifically designed to help them break their gambling habits. Patterned after the Alcoholics Anonymous program, Gamblers Anonymous is designed to help identify pathological gamblers and then to help them combat their deviant obsession.

Many other social problems are associated with gambling. The large number of youth participating in gambling is alarming. According to a 1999 Harvard Medical School study, about 35 million young teens are addicted to gambling (Auer, 2003). In the same year (1999), the National Gambling Impact Study Commission said in its final report that an estimated 7.9 million children and adolescents had problem or pathological gambling addictions (Kuehn, 2005). Although these two statistics are miles apart from each other, it should be clear that gambling is a problem for a large number of youth. Stinchfield and Winters (1998) reviewed many studies on youth gambling and came up with a number of conclusions, including: most youths have gambled at sometime; boys are more involved in gambling than girls; minority youth gamble more than white youth; prevalence rates of pathological gambling are higher among youths than adults; and youth gambling is directly related to parental gambling. The ease in availability of gambling on the Internet is one of the main culprits in this potentially epidemic gambling problem. Many youth have unrestricted access to the Internet, which provides ample opportunities for gambling. E-gambling (gambling on the Internet) reached an estimated $8.3 billion in 2004. In comparison, E-gambling in 2000 was estimated at $2.2 billion, demonstrating its rapid growth (Weir, 2003).

A great deal of E-gambling is done by setting up bank accounts in foreign banks and gambling with that money. As a result, the U.S. government becomes increasingly concerned because of lost tax revenue. "Although all types of gambling are controversial in some circles, Internet gambling may be more so because, though illegal in many states, operators can circumvent the law and state regulators by going 'off-shore.' Some experts also contend that Internet games encourage compulsive, addictive behavior that wreaks havoc on family finances" (Kuehn, 2005: 15). Most people pay off an offshore gambling debt (e-gambling) with a credit card. However, in 2006, President George W. Bush signed into law a bill that makes it illegal for banks and credit-card companies to settle payments for online gambling sites.

The E-gambling world and concern over youth gambling is highlighted by a 2005 promotion run by a Costa-Rican based website (absolutepoker.com) that held a virtual "Texas Hold 'Em" (poker) tournament with a controversial jackpot: a college scholarship. The site administrators hope to hold competitions at the beginning of each college semester. Critics, and there are many of them, have dubbed this promotion as offering "vice scholarships" (similar to scholarships offered by alcohol and tobacco companies) (Sefton, 2005). According to Keith Whyte, executive director of the National Council on Problem Gambling, college tuitions awarded due to winning a gambling event should set off the same level of concern as a student being required to smoke a carton of cigarettes a day for a year for a scholarship (Sefton, 2005).

Among the many fallacies upheld by those who promote gambling is the idea that economic windfalls are so abundant that everyone benefits. However, most casino jobs are low-wage, high turnover positions. Crime, once synonymous with gambling, is still a feature of gambling. Con games and rigged card games and gambling devices (e.g., slot machines) also exist. Gambling winners may be victimized by robbery from street criminals. On many Indian reservations that host casinos, there is actually an increase in social problems (e.g., alcohol abuse, crime, neglect and abuse of children and spouses, and missed work days). Indian casino gambling has not led to an improvement in the quality of life for most members of participating gaming tribes. An even bigger economic concern is the fact that gambling does not produce any tangible products for society. It merely provides a means for people to spend money gambling instead of buying other products. After all, most people have a limited amount of "disposable income" and if they lose it gambling, they cannot support other legitimate businesses.

GAMBLING IN SPORTS

At major casinos, especially those found in Nevada and Atlantic City, gambling is not limited to card games, roulette wheels, slots, and dice; there are also sport books, where gamblers can legally place bets on a wide variety of sporting events. In 1992, Congress made almost all sports gambling illegal, believing that the substantial sums wagered on sporting events are potential threats to the integrity of the competition. Sport books in Nevada and Atlantic City were "grandfathered" (meaning they were exempted from the legislation) (Will, 2000). Sport gamblers can bet on individual ball games or a combination of games (parleys), car races, tennis matches, and so on. During the Super Bowl there are so many gambling options that people can even bet on the coin toss (heads or tails).

The method that one uses to place a sports bet depends on whether the gambler is betting legally or illegally. Legal sport gambling options include off track betting outlets and the wide variety of casinos that exist throughout the United States. If a gambler bets illegally, as most sports gamblers do, the wagering behaviors are altered radically, as the gambler must find a bookie in order to place a bet. As Best and Luckenbill (1994) explain, whenever a good or service is forbidden but the demand for it continues, an illicit market will emerge. Placing a bet with a bookie is risky, primarily because of the criminal nature of such betting and the fact that the gambler has to trust the bookie to pay off a winning bet. Losing a bet to a bookie and being unable to pay off the debt is also risky and may result in physical harm.

Many people like to gamble on sports. In the U.S. people especially enjoy betting on professional football. A significant amount of the NFL's popularity is connected to gambling. Football is practically designed for gamblers, as the once-a-week format of football heightens the significance of each game to players (and fans). Gamblers watch the point spreads, track injury reports (which the NFL is requited to provide to the media), and keep an eye on the weather to see if it may interfere with playing condition (e.g., heavy rainfall may lead to more turnovers). The media (television, radio, and newspaper) promote gambling by discussing betting lines and point spreads and hosting gambling shows designed to give the gambler an "edge." It comes as no surprise to sports fans that gambling is a big part of sports; surely league officials are also aware of this reality.

Obviously, gambling involves risk-taking behavior on the part of the gamblers. The risks involve the understandable — you may lose your bet — to the not so apparent. Earlier in this chapter, we described a form of deviant behavior that involves an athlete taking a "dive." Gamblers have no idea when athletes may be on the take or willing to compromise their behavior. For example, it was recently revealed that former professional tennis player Andrea Jaeger (who is now a nun) purposely lost the 1983 Wimbledon women's final. Jaeger admits to feeling guilty for interrupting her Wimbledon finals opponent Martina Navratilova's prematch ritual the night before the match. To make amends, Jaeger (who was then ranked 3rd in the world) claims that she missed several shots on purpose and often hit the ball right at Martina (*Sports Illustrated*, July 14–21, 2008). This story underscores the many risks involved with gambling.

Pete Rose, former MLB great, presents us with an example of direct gambling involvement on the part of sport participants. While managing the Cincinnati Reds, Rose was accused of betting on a large number of games. Former Baseball Commissioner Peter Ueberroth and his successor, A. Bartlett Giamatti, initiated a formal investigation, which was run by attorney John Dowd. In 1989 the Dowd Report claimed that in 1987 Rose had bet on no fewer than 52 Reds games, at a minimum of $10,000 a game. To bet on a single game would have been enough to cause his expulsion from baseball. While vigorously denying this, Rose voluntarily accepted a permanent place on baseball's ineligible list (Delaney, 2007). In his 2004 autobiography, melodramatically entitled *My Prison Without Bars,* he finally admitted that he did indeed bet on

Reds games, but stated he had never bet against the Reds (which would have made him liable for criminal prosecution). Rose is the all-time MLB leader in hits but was placed on the "ineligible list" for Hall of Fame induction due to his alleged gambling on sports— something he has continued to deny. The commissioner's office feels that it has ample evidence of Rose's gambling involvement and has (basically) been waiting for Rose to admit his guilt and apologize publicly. This impasse has been going on since 1986, Rose's final season as a player. The rules for entry into MLB's Hall of Fame state that a player must have been retired for at least five years but no more than 20 to be eligible for election.

Many professional athletes and ex-athletes admit to gambling on sports because it makes the game more exciting for them. In 2006, Charles Barkley admitted that he has lost nearly $10 million in gambling, mostly at blackjack. Barkley explained that he does not have a gambling problem because "I can afford to gamble" (Hoffer, 2006: 18). In 2008, Barkley was in trouble with a Las Vegas casino for walking away from a $400,000 gambling debt (he was extended four $100,000 markers). Clark County District Attorney David Roger said that Barkley would face charges if he did not make good on the debt (*Sports Illustrated*, 5/26/08). Professional golfer John Daly claims to have lost between $40 million and $60 million in gambling — although most people in sport question whether he has even earned that much money. Daly also claims to have won $25 million gambling (Hoffer, 2006). Michael Jordan once made a very public announcement on *60 Minutes* that he has a gambling problem. Is it any wonder that sports governing bodies are concerned about athletes and gambling?

Gambling is also a problem in collegiate sports. Most alarming to the NCAA is the number of athletes who gamble. In 2005, the NCAA released the results of their study on gambling which showed that 35 percent of male athletes and 10 percent of female athletes had gambled on college sports during the previous year (Tuley, 2005). The NCAA requires that all athletes (at every level) sign a form that they will not gamble on sports. In its Bylaws of Ethical Conduct, the NCAA manual (2005) details its rules regarding gambling activities (Article 10.3). Staff members of a member conference, staff members of the athletics department of a member institution and student-athletes shall not knowingly:

  (a) Provide information to individuals involved in organized gambling activities concerning intercollegiate athletics competition;
  (b) Solicit a bet on any intercollegiate team;
  (c) Accept a bet on any team representing the institution;
  (d) Solicit or accept a bet on any intercollegiate competition for any item (e.g., cash, shirt, dinner) that has tangible value; or
  (e) Participate in any gambling activity that involves intercollegiate athletics or professional athletics, through a bookmaker, a parlay card or any other method employed by organized gambling [pp. 47–48].

Athletes in violation of this bylaw are subject to sanctions, which include losing all remaining regular-season and postseason eligibility in all sports, and may be ineligible for any further intercollegiate competition.

There are many lessons to be learned about sports gambling. Among the primary lessons are, as with all forms of gambling, the "house" always has the edge — just look at the billion dollar hotel casinos in Las Vegas for visible evidence. Athletes who gamble risk suspension and termination from future sports involvement, and those who gamble risk a strong negative stigma.

As we have learned in this chapter, the institution of sport is not immune to unethical, illegal, or deviant forms of behavior. Most people involved with sport recognize this and either live with it, or are trying to change it for the better. It is important to note, however, that for all the focus upon deviancy in sport, sportsmanship is not dead. It remains very much an ideal by which athletes, coaches, referees, owners and fans are judged by society as a whole.

SUMMARY

All sports are guided by numerous rules and regulations. How these are enforced, and whether they are good or bad, remain topics of debate, but if rules and regulations are broken, there will be sanctions and punishments.

There are a number of sociological and psychological explanations for deviant behavior. Sociological theories are grounded by the belief that deviance is caused by environmental factors. These include the functionalist and anomie/strain theory, subculture/cultural deviance theory, social learning and differential association theory, labeling theory, and conflict theory.

Types of deviant behavior associated with sport include on-the-field infractions, off-the-field acts committed by athletes, owners, referees and fans, the use of performance-enhancing drugs, and illegal gambling. Illegal drug usage is one of the most serious types of deviant sport behavior. Restorative and recreational drugs have been used to make players feel better and to enhance their performances. While knowing that they are breaking the rules, many athletes are willing to risk almost anything, including their health and life, to gain an advantage over the competition.

The use of performance enhancing drugs raises a host of ethical issues. In addition, the United States government has taken an active interventionist role in recent years due to the growing demand that something be done to end the perceived rampant use of steroids among players.

There are many forms of gambling in sports, both legal and illegal. Pathological gambling causes tremendous suffering. There are many social problems associated with all forms of gambling. In addition, one can make a distinction between "real" sports fans, which root for and identify with a team, and gamblers, who are only concerned with winning money.

KEY TERMS

Anomie Theory Developed by Robert Merton, the premise that society encourages all persons to attain culturally desirable goals, but the opportunity to reach these goals is not equal for all members of society.

Blood-doping Introducing a surplus of an athlete's own blood into his or her body in the hopes of improving performance.

Bookies People who take illegal bets.

Commitment Involves an emotional attachment to the object of loyalty.

Conflict Theory Highlights the imbalance of power found in society, especially in light of economic and social inequalities found in all societies

Deviance Any act or behavior that is likely to be defined, by some members of society, or specific subcultural groups, as an unacceptable violation of a social norm and elicits negative reactions from others.

Deviants Those who stray from the norm by committing acts of deviance.

Differential Association Theory The view that it takes continued association and reinforcement in order for a behavior to be indoctrinated.

E-gambling Gambling on the Internet.

External Social Control (Sometimes called direct social control) Regulation of behavior comes from "outside" social control agents, such as coaches, trainers, administrators and referees and umpires.

Genomics The use of genetic engineering to enhance athletic performance.

Labeling Theory The theory which examines the effects of a "label" being placed on a person and his or her subsequent behavior.

Recreational Gambling Gambling among friends and co-workers.

Self-fulfilling Prophecy Occurs when people take to heart the labels bestowed upon them, come to see themselves in regard to those labels, and then act correspondingly to those labels.

Social Learning Theories An individual learns behavior through interaction with others; whether directly (being taught) or indirectly (through observation).

Sport Books Legally placed bets on a wide variety of sporting events, allowed in some casinos.

Subculture A group of people who possess distinctive cultural values, ethnicity, or some other trait that distinguishes it from other groups in the greater society.

DISCUSSION QUESTIONS

- Why is it difficult to define "deviancy"?

- What is the difference between "normative" cheating and "deviant" cheating? Can you think of some examples of each?

- How can coaches encourage deviancy among players?

- Do you agree or disagree that Pete Rose should never be inducted into the Baseball Hall of Fame? Why did his alleged betting on baseball have an effect upon the judgment of whether he merits being in the Hall of Fame?

- What are some of the ethical issues raised by using performance enhancing drugs?

- Is there a moral distinction between legal and illegal gambling on sport?

- Why might being "specially privileged" create problems for athletes that can lead to deviant behavior?

CHAPTER 9

Violence in Sport

Intimidation, aggression and violence are aspects of sports, just as they are a part of society in general. Hence, no one should be surprised that violence exists in sport. As with most of human history, we live in violent times. Governments have longed used violence as a means of reaching a desired end; in fact, people have widely used violence as a way to "solve" disputes. Violence in sport occurs at all levels: youth, high school, college and professional. Certain sports, such as football, rugby and hockey, are designed for assertive, physical contact between competitors. Auto racing contains an element of violence in the very fact that at any time during a race a crash may occur that leads to the destruction of an automobile and serious injury and potential death to drivers. Participants, spectators, and fans of such sports seem to enjoy the element of risk involved. For example, it has often been said that die-hard hockey fans love to watch the fights between players as much as they enjoy the actual hockey skills displayed by the players. Player fights are an example of violence in sport. Despite attempts by hockey leagues such as the NHL to place a focus (e.g., by imposing penalties against overly-violent plays) on the wonderful skills necessary to play hockey, the fans still like to see fights. Athletes that play in violent sports view such risks as "part of the game."

What Is Violence?

The fields and courts that athletes play on are often environments filled with hazards and violence. "Not even the risky and labor-intensive settings of mining, oil drilling, and construction sites can compare with the routine injuries of team sports such as football, ice hockey, soccer, and rugby" (Delaney, 2002: 1560). Competitors in all spheres of social life attempt to gain an edge over the competition. As we learned in Chapter 8, there are times when some people will use deviant means (e.g., taking performance-enhancing drugs) to gain an edge. In this chapter, we shall discover that many people associated with sport utilize violence as well.

DEFINING INTIMIDATION, AGGRESSION, AND VIOLENCE

A common method of trying to gain an advantage over a competitor is through acts of intimidation. Intimidation involves words, gestures and actions that sometimes may threaten violence or aggression in an attempt to pressure and put fear in the opponent. A tennis player may use loud grunting sounds while playing and flash intimidating grimaces toward an opponent. In a pre-fight promo, former heavy-weight champion Mike Tyson once threatened to punch his opponent's nose to the back of his skull. An athlete attempts to intimidate his or her opponents in an attempt to demonstrate power and dominance. Intimidation is often a vital tactic in battle and competition. However, intimidation is only successful if the intimidator is capable of backing up such words, gestures and actions or if the opponent is weaker and easily intimidated. Acts of intimidation can also backfire. Intimidation in sport is of lesser consequence than aggression and violence. Consequently, it is important to make distinctions between aggression and violence.

The authors define aggression in sport as verbal and physical behavior grounded in the intent to successfully accomplish a task even if it means to dominate, control, or harm, physically or psychologically, an opponent. Aggression is often linked with violence. Aggression is an important feature of performance success in many sports. Coaches teach and encourage aggressive behavior and teammates reinforce it; after all, it is better to be aggressive than passive in contact sports. In several sports (e.g., football, wrestling, hockey) aggressive behavior is *required*. And yet, even in contact sports where aggressive behavior is expected, there are boundaries of acceptability, and athletes who exceed these boundaries face penalties by game officials for exhibiting behaviors that can be labeled hostile or physically abusive. For example, in football, a defensive end that is rushing the quarterback is expected to be aggressive in his pursuit of the quarterback. However, he may not hit the quarterback above the shoulders or after the ball has been thrown. A passive approach to rushing the quarterback will generally not produce a positive outcome for the defensive team. Thus, the defensive end who is attempting to tackle the quarterback needs to be aggressive to be successful; he does not have to harm the opponent, he just has to tackle him.

There are two forms of sport aggression: instrumental aggression and reactive aggression. Instrumental aggression refers to behavior that is non-emotional and task oriented and driven by the quest for achieving some nonaggressive goal (Delaney, 2002). Instrumental aggression involves the physical form (e.g., direct contact and body blows) and the nonphysical form. A nonphysical form of instrumental aggression between players usually takes the form of "psyching out" the opponent. Verbal taunts, "talking trash," or jokes about one's sexuality and family members are just the tip of the iceberg of nonverbal jawing between aggressive players. The second type of aggression in sport is reactive. Reactive aggression possesses an underlying emotional component in behavior with the primary goal of inflicting bodily injury or physical harm to an opponent (Delaney, 2002). An example of reactive aggression is baseball's "brush-back" pitch. A brush-back pitch involves the pitcher throwing the ball at or near the opposing batter in an attempt to send a message. Sometimes the pitcher will deliberately hit the batter in an attempt to intimidate the opponent and opposing team. Brush-back pitches are a relatively common way that a pitcher attempts to "take control" of the home plate area. They are most likely to occur after a pitcher has given up a homerun and he feels that he has been shown up; when the batter takes too long to "get in the box" (ready to bat); when the batter tries to intimidate the pitcher (e.g., glares at him, "digs into the box"); and especially after the pitcher's teammate had been hit by a pitch in the preceding inning. Brush-back pitches definitely increase the adrenaline in players and create a more aggressive feel to the game. Not surprisingly, reactive aggression often leads to violence.

Delaney and Madigan make a case that violence involves great physical force used to injure or harm or which has the potential to cause harm or destruction. As stated earlier in this chapter, aggression has its place in sport. However, there are unacceptable forms of aggressive behaviors in sport and they become labeled as violence. There is a great deal of violence in many contemporary sports. Violence in sport involves intentional aggressive behavior that crosses the line of acceptability. Thus, sport violence can be defined as intentional aggressive physical behavior that causes harm, occurs outside the rules of the game, is unrelated to ideals of sportsmanship, or which destroys the property of another sportsperson.

Contextually, violence in sport is evaluated differently from the general violence found in society. Simon (1985) argues that violence generally involves the use of force, but reminds us that every use of force is not violent. The tennis player, for example, uses force in serving, but few people would characterize a serve in tennis as an act of violence. It is possible, however, that a serve in tennis could be used in an aggressive, intimidating, and ultimately violent manner when the player serves *at* the opponent rather than at a place on a court where the opponent cannot return the serve.

Some sports, especially American football, have elements similar to the military and war. The language of football is filled with military references, for example, throwing a "bomb"; "blitzing" the quarterback; linemen working in the "trenches"; the quarterback as a "field general"; entering "enemy territory"; and so on. Rank is important in the military and in sports. The military designates personnel by titles (ranks) and expected duties. In the U.S. Army, for example, the private is subordinate to a sergeant, who reports to a platoon sergeant, and all of these people must submit to the authority of officers that range from lieutenants to generals. On the battlefield, a squad is composed of privates who are directly under the supervision of a squad leader, who is under the supervision of a platoon leader, usually a lieutenant. The chain of command goes all the way to the generals, and ultimately the commander-in-chief (the president).

In football, a team (squad) performing on the playing field (battlefield) is under the command of the quarterback (on offense) or the middle linebacker (usually) on defense. The offensive and defensive leaders receive their "orders" from their respective coordinators (assistant coaches), who are under the command of the head coach. The coach must report to a general manager, team owner, and ultimately, the league's commissioner. Furthermore, athletes and military personnel are subject to external and internal sanctions for committing deviant acts, and rewards for following orders and executing directives successfully. It should be noted, however, that among the glaring differences between sport and the military is the realization that literally killing the opponent is not an objective of sport. Also, in sport, many efforts are made to assure fair play and balance in available "weapons" (e.g., protective equipment, a ban on performance-enhancing drugs), whereas in the military, gaining an unfair advantage over the opponent is a goal consciously sought.

Many coaches, fans and even teammates expect athletes to perform at peak levels and to win by any costs, including inflicting injury onto an opponent. Players themselves often describe the game as a "battle" and have stated that they "are at war" with the other team. Immediately following the September 11, 2001, attacks on the World Trade Center and Pentagon and the subsequent start of the war on terrorism, many players consciously attempted to stop using war-analogous terms when describing their sporting exploits. However, by the mid–2000s, it became common once again for athletes to use the "going to battle" mantra.

Player Violence

Most athletes display the positive character traits promoted by proponents of sport. That is, they are disciplined, hard-working, and rule-abiding; they show respect for authority and maintain a positive work ethic. However, as we learned in Chapter 8, some athletes and other members of the sporting world engage in deviant behaviors. One specific type of deviant behavior that deserves its own special attention is the area of violence.

Many sports are inherently aggressive. There are times when athletes become overly aggressive and enter the realm of violence. There are numerous examples of sport violence in contemporary society. The authors will provide a brief review of some of the sports experiencing violence and provide examples of athletes acting violently in their respective sports.

FOOTBALL

By its very design and purpose, football is a violent sport. Controlled collisions highlighted by near hand-to-hand combat among linemen, hard hitting blocks that knock opponents down,

Defensive players gang tackle a running back in a display of acceptable sport violence (courtesy Cardinal Sports Imaging).

and gang-style tackles are among the violent elements of football. Players are taught to be aggressive; they readily accept this expectation. Fans love the aggressiveness and violence of football and scream encouragement for their brave "gladiators" to destroy the opponent. The aura of football is *controlled* aggression and violence. In Tim Green's (1996) words, "The difference between an NFL player and the average guy on the street is not that the player is more likely to break someone's nose. The NFL player has simply learned how to tap into the dark side of the human psyche. We all have it, that dark side. Most football players can turn that on and off like a blender. You need to be bad on the playing field, vicious and mean, that's part of the game. That is the game" (p. 65).

To mentally prepare themselves for "battle," football players psych themselves up so that they can raise their level of adrenaline in order to play at peak levels. There are occasions when football players become so excited they get involved in pregame fisticuffs. Ten players were fined for their roles in a fight between the Philadelphia Eagles and the Atlanta Falcons before a *Monday Night Football* game in September 2005. As a result of the fight, Falcons cornerback Kevin Mathis and Eagles linebacker Jeremiah Trotter were ejected from the game before the opening kickoff. During warm-ups, Trotter shoved Mathis, who responded by punching Trotter. Numerous teammates jumped into the fracas. The day after the infamous Detroit Pistons–Indiana Pacers brawl, football players from arch-rival universities, Clemson and South Carolina, were involved in an ugly all-out brawl before their game on November 20, 2004. Six players from each team were suspended and both schools gave up bowl bids as punishment. In 2005, South Carolina's new football coach, Steve Spurrier, recommended banning the pre-game handshake. Instead, players from both sides formed a line on their respective sides of the field and walked toward each other to shake hands as a team at midfield.

There are times when teammates fight each other. In the sports world, such incidents are supposed to stay "in house" so that they can be handled by the head coach. However, some incidents are so brutal that the outside world learns of the details. For example, in 2006, Mitchell Cozad, a backup punter on the Northern Colorado football team, brutally attacked starting punter Rafael Mendoza in an attempt to gain the starting position on the team. Cozad laid in waiting and then stabbed Mendoza in the knee of his kicking leg outside his apartment. The incident drew comparisons to the Tonya Harding–Nancy Kerrigan incident in which Harding's hitman clubbed Kerrigan in the knee in order to knock her out of competition. (Harding considered Kerrigan her chief rival in making the Olympic U.S. Figure Skating team.) In 2007,

Cozad was found guilty of second-degree assault (but acquitted of attempted first-degree murder) and sentenced to seven years in prison.

Players are not the only ones involved in violence in football. There have been occasions where coaches have gotten into fights with players, shoved referees, kicked dirt on umpires, and made obscene gestures to fans (*Sports Illustrated.com*, 2005). In 2005, Nebraska football coach Bill Callahan was accused of making a throat-slashing gesture toward a referee. In 2004, the NCAA Football Rules Committee made the throat-slashing gesture punishable by a 15-yard penalty for unsportsmanlike conduct. Owners can also be involved in acts of violence. In 2005, New Orleans Saints owner Tom Benson lunged at a television news crew cameraman. WWL-TV, a CBS affiliate in New Orleans, was videotaping Benson leaving the Saints game played in Baton Rouge. (Due to the 2005 Hurricane Katrina, the Saints could not play their home games in New Orleans during the entire 2005 NFL season.)

BOXING

Boxing is a carryover sport from ancient times. No sport has more inherent physical risk involved within its rules of acceptability than boxing. Every boxer who puts on a pair of gloves and enters the ring risks substantial harm, including possible death, to both the opponent and himself or herself. (It should be noted that many sports, including horse racing and sky-diving, have a far higher fatality rate than boxing.) The primary goal of contemporary boxing is pretty much the same as in the past — knock out the opponent. Many people in contemporary society believe that boxing should outlawed because of its primitive brutality. Despite the corruption involved in boxing, the sport is nowhere near disappearing from the sports world. Adding to the chagrin of the distracters of boxing is the growing number of women boxers (the 2004 Academy Award Winner for Best Film, *Million Dollar Baby*, dealt with this phenomenon).

The violence that surrounds boxing is not limited to the ring and the two designated fighters. There are occasional brawls during the pre-fight weigh-ins (boxers must get their weight measured) that may include the boxers themselves or their team representatives (e.g., managers, trainers, body guards). Post-fight brawls may involve the boxers and their representatives and even fans; in some rare cases, a fan may enter the ring (e.g., the "Fan Man" who entered the ring during a fight via a flight suit powered by a motorized fan). However, the greatest level of violence still occurs inside the ropes. Some fighters are beaten to death, others sustain serious injuries, and some are knocked unconscious. A rather bizarre form of violence occurred during a heavy-weight fight between Evander Holyfield and Mike Tyson in 1997. Tyson took a bite out of Holyfield's ear during the match. Such an act of violence is deemed unacceptable even in a sport where participants are allowed to literally beat each other.

HOCKEY

Hockey is an aggressive sport known for its rough play and tough athletes. It is not uncommon for a single professional hockey player to receive hundreds of stitches and incur numerous broken bones over the course of his career. The stereotype is that almost every player will have lost his teeth by the end of his career, either from getting hit with a puck or a stick or from fighting with other players. Sports commentators often remark after a hockey player has been injured and quickly returns to action, "What did you expect, he's a hockey player?!" The implication is that hockey players are so tough that they always play through pain and injury. The sport of hockey is conducive to fighting and overly aggressive play by its very design. For example, the slippery surface that hockey is played on may lead to inadvertent contact that opponents may take exception to. The enclosed rink with sideboards to slam into also encourages violent physical contact. Hockey players are "armed" with "clubs" (hockey sticks) and skate with blades; both are dangerous items used for violence under other conditions.

Hockey players, as with athletes in most sports (especially American football), are getting larger and faster and are in better shape than ever before. When these elements are added to a culture that encourages physical, aggressive play, acts of violence are almost certain to follow. In fact, a certain number of violent collisions are expected and demanded by coaches and teammates. Fans especially love to watch hockey fights. Certain players, known as "goons," are famous for their aggressive behavior. Hockey proponents warn that if fighting in hockey were eliminated (through regulations) the core hockey audience would stop being fans of the sport.

In a sport that requires even its weakest players to be aggressive, fighting is considered part of the game. During hockey fights players may gouge at an opponent's eyes, rub their gloves across the face of an opponent, and engage in any other number of violent acts. Beyond these infractions, there are other times when excessive fighting occurs. Most hockey teams employ "goons" for certain occasions. The primary job of a goon is to fight. Coaches send goons on the ice for a number of reasons, including when they want to "send a message" to their opponents, when the opponent has a big lead, or when a star player was hit too hard (the goon is there to defend the star players). Goons are highly paid enforcers, respected by teammates and adored by fans. Is there any wonder violence is so common in hockey?

Among the more extreme examples of violence in the National Hockey League (NHL) involves Chris Simon's (New York Islanders) attack on Ryan Hollweg (N.Y. Rangers) during a March 2007 game. Hollweg had driven Simon hard into the boards and did not receive a penalty. Simon collected himself and skated after Hollweg and delivered a vicious two-handed stick swing to his face. Hollweg laid motionless on the ice for some time. Simon was suspended for 25 games by the NHL. In December 2007, Simon was suspended for 30 games for a brutal attack on Pittsburgh Penguins player Jarkko Ruutu. Simon's acts of goon behavior followed other high profile cases involving Marty McSorley and Todd Bertuzzi. McSorley (then with the Boston Bruins) attacked Donald Brashear (Vancouver Canucks) on the ice during a game in February 2000. He slashed the side of Brashear's head with his stick. Brashear fell backwards and slammed his head on the ice, suffering a concussion and loss of memory of the incident. McSorley was suspended for the remainder of the season (23 games). The 17-year NHL enforcer never played another NHL game. Todd Bertuzzi (Vancouver Canucks) ambushed Steve Moore (Colorado Avalanche) during a hockey game on March 8, 2004. Bertuzzi dragged Moore down from behind as Moore was skating toward the other end of the rink. Moore hit the ice hard as Bertuzzi landed a sucker-punch on the defenseless player. Bertuzzi was suspended for the rest of the 2003–2004 season. He remained suspended throughout the 310-day lockout and was prohibited from playing in the 2004 World Cup of Hockey. After a four-month investigation, Bertuzzi was charged with assault in June 2005. He was reinstated by the NHL on August 8, 2005.

Violence in hockey is sometimes accidental. For example, a Syracuse youth ice hockey coach died after falling and hitting his head on the ice while teaching a group of 4- to 6-year-olds, including his own 5-year-old son (*USA Today*, 3/26/02).

BASKETBALL

Basketball, once labeled as a "non-contact" sport, has changed dramatically since its creation. Diving for loose balls used to be one of the most aggressive moves in basketball. However, basketball is no longer a non-contact sport and both instrumental and reactive physical aggression are a part of men's and women's basketball (Figler and Whitaker, 1995). Contemporary basketball has adopted a "street mentality" where talking smack and violently slamming and dunking the ball into the rim, especially if it is over an opponent standing under the rim (referred to as being "posterized"—because it makes for a great photo when one player shows dominance over another) has become commonplace. Basketball players have also adopted, either as part of their subculture or as the result of direct coaching, a "no lay-up" rule. The "no lay-up rule" means that the defender is never to give up an easy lay-up to an opponent; instead, the defender should make a hard (violent) foul against the opponent as a "warning" not to try such a fundamental move again.

Periodically, players engage in physical violence with spectators. For example, in 1995, Vernon Maxwell, then with the Houston Rockets, once charged up a dozen rows into the crowd at Memorial Coliseum in Portland, Oregon, and punched a spectator in the jaw. In the United States, the most disturbing incidence of violence in basketball (to date) occurred on November 19, 2004, when members of the Indiana Pacers, Detroit Pistons and fans at The Palace in Auburn Hills, Michigan, were involved in one of the worst brawls in U.S. sports history. The incident started when Indiana's Ron Artest fouled Detroit's Ben Wallace with 45.9 seconds left in a game that the Pacers had already essentially won (they were leading by 15 points). Upset with the foul, Wallace responded with a two-handed shove to Artest's chin, which, in turn, started a chain reaction where several players from both teams began pushing each other. Artest, wanting no part of the bigger Wallace, backed away and lay down on top of the scorer's table.

Just as the players had calmed down and were separated, a fan hit Artest with a cup filled with an icy beverage. The volatile Artest bolted into the stands in a rage and went after a fan he believed threw the cup. Artest's teammate, Stephen Jackson, followed Artest into the stands, swinging at fans. Artest and teammate Jermaine O'Neal later slugged fans on the court. As the Pacers finally left the court, they were belted by debris from Pistons fans (Lage, 2005). Nine players from both teams were suspended for a combined 143 games and Artest was suspended for the season (Sheridan, 2004). The 73-game suspension, plus playoff games, cost Artest almost $5 million. Jackson received the second longest suspension, 30 games, because he went into the stands and fought with fans, while O'Neal received the third longest suspension—25 games—because he fought with fans on the court. On May 1, 2006, John Green, the man accused of throwing the cup that sparked the brawl, was sentenced to 30 days in jail on an assault and battery charge and was placed on two years' probation after he was found guilty of assault and battery for punching Artest.

In January 2006, another NBA player, New York Knicks forward Antonio Davis, charged into the stands when he observed his wife and a fan seated behind her in a verbal argument. The NBA, which flat out forbids players from entering the stands, suspended Davis for just five days because league officials accepted Davis' argument that he believed his wife was in trouble.

Basketball has become so aggressive and violent that some teams have designated "goons" (physical enforcers) similar to hockey. These athletes generally enter the game when the coach wants to send a message—usually directed at the other team. One such incident occurred in March 2004 when Temple University basketball coach John Chaney proclaimed before his team's game with St. Joseph that he would get one of his players to "send a message" to their crosstown rivals. Chaney was upset because he believed that St. Joseph used illegal screens (a form of violent play) in a game between the two rivals weeks earlier. In the rematch game, Chaney proceeded to play little-used 250-pound forward Nehemiah Ingram, whom Chaney described as a "goon," to deliver his message (Zirin, 2005). Ingram committed five fouls (the maximum limit allowed) in four minutes of play. One of his fouls included throwing St. Joe player John Bryant to the floor. Bryant's arm was broken as a result of the foul. There was a public outcry from the media and sports fans against Chaney's use of a goon to send a message. This incident was a clear violation of sportsmanship and such violent displays of behavior should not be tolerated in basketball, or any other sport.

SOCCER

Soccer is known more for its violence off the field than it is for player violence on the field. Christopher Merrill (1993) writes:

Soccer may be a brutally simple sport, but for much of its history it was simply brutal. From the beginning, it seems, humans have loved to kick things—balls, doors, skulls; in the records of every civilization there is evidence of kicking games like soccer. Chinese court games, Japanese *kemari*, Pueblo kickball, the ball games of the ancient Egyptians, the *calcio storico* still played in Italy, village football—"the mob game for ruffians" the English invented or imported from the Continent, codified into the modern game of soccer in 1863, then exported around the world—in almost every culture humans have relaxed from the tedium of daily life by kicking something round over plains and fields, through streets and cities, in courts and stadiums [p. 15].

Soccer has moments of physical and violent collisions among players, and often there are heated exchanges between players (Vogler and Schwartz, 1993). In North America, the biggest soccer rivalry is clearly between the United States and Mexico. Although the Mexicans lead the all-time series against the Americans, 28-11-10, the United States has won six of the last eight matches. The Americans accuse the Mexicans of dirty play and unsportsmanlike conduct. For example, in 1997, Mexico's Ramon Ramirez karate-kicked Alexi Lalas in the groin. Lalas described the incident as "a full-frontal assault on my manhood" (Wahl, 2005: 56). During the 2004 Olympic qualifying tournament in Guadalajara, the Mexican crowd chanted "Osama, Osama." During the 2002 World Cup game between the two soccer rivals, Landon Donovan claimed that Mexican forward Luis Hernandez said to him, "I will find your mother and kill her" (Wahl, 2005: 56). And in the 2006 World Cup final game, French star Zinedine Zidane was expelled from the game for headbutting Italy defender Marco Materazzi. Zindane claimed that Materazzi had made a derogatory remark about his mother, which the Italian player vigorously denied. Whatever the reason, Zindane was the only player ever to be sent off the field during an overtime World Cup finale, and many feel this may have caused France to lose the game.

BASEBALL

Generally, baseball is not a very violent sport. There are potential violent collisions in the form of hard slides that may involve a defender being spiked or a catcher being "taken out" of the play. The "brushback" and "beanball" pitches could also be viewed as an act of violence, especially if the pitch was aimed at the head of the batter, or with harmful intent. According to Margolis (1999), only one Major League Baseball player—Ray Chapman of the Cleveland Indians—has died as a result of being hit in the head with a ball during a baseball game. This death occurred in the 1920s, long before MLB required the use of batting helmets. If an umpire feels that a pitcher deliberately threw *at* a batter, both teams will be warned and the pitcher may be thrown out. If a warning has already been issued, the offending pitcher will be thrown out of the game. Perhaps the most extreme form of violence in baseball occurs when a batter charges the mound, typically after being thrown at. Benches empty and players from the clubhouse trot onto the field just in case there is a real fight. Usually, such events involve verbal taunts and harmless pushing. On other occasions, punches may be thrown and people can be injured.

The New York Yankees and Boston Red Sox were involved in a bench-clearing brawl during Game 3 of the 2003 American League Championship Series. Yankees coach Don Zimmer ran toward Boston pitcher Pedro Martinez, who subsequently threw Zimmer to the ground. Zimmer was 72 years old at the time and Martinez was 32 years old. In June 2005, Texas Rangers pitcher Kenny Rogers was involved in and subsequently suspended for violently confronting two different cameramen a total of three times during an emotional melt-down prior to a Texas

Rangers game. Rogers had just missed his prior scheduled start because he broke a pinkie finger during an emotional outburst in the dugout. He sustained the injury during a violent display of behavior while throwing his temper tantrum.

On April 26, 2006, International League player and top Tampa Bay Devil Rays prospect Delmon Young threw his bat at the home plate umpire. This violent event occurred after Young was called out on strikes and while he was walking back toward his dugout. Young received the (believed) longest suspension — 50 games — in the International League's 123-year history. Young apologized for letting his emotions get the best of him. He did not appeal the suspension and considered the punishment appropriate for his misconduct.

Auto Racing

Auto racing is a highly competitive and aggressive sport that involves both human and machine. Drivers must make split decisions while driving race cars at high rates of speed. Any miscalculation may result in harm, injury or even death to the driver or other drivers. This risk factor also extends to pit crew members and fans in the stands. Some drivers are more aggressive than others and may nudge a competitor's car in an attempt to pass. Race car drivers have long memories and may retaliate against a competitor for a past transgression.

The September 2005 NASCAR race in New Hampshire provides a number of examples of road rage in auto racing. Kasey Kahne was fined $25,000 and penalized 25 points in the drivers' standings for intentionally hitting Kyle Busch's car in retaliation for an earlier accident. Busch had bumped Kahne hard into the wall and when he restarted his wrecked car he drove it out of harm's way along the bottom of the track. When Busch came by Kahne on the next lap, Kahne deliberately shot up the track and hit Busch's car in the left front. During the same race, Robby Gordon was fined $35,000 and docked 50 points in the drivers' standings for intentionally trying to hit Michael Waltrip's car with his helmet. The two drivers had collided shortly before the helmet throwing incident and Gordon blamed Waltrip for deliberately causing the accident. A year earlier at the same race, Gordon intentionally wrecked Greg Biffle in retaliation to an earlier event. Auto racing is dangerous enough without having drivers deliberately trying to knock each other out of competition.

In short, all sports have examples of violence and violence is more common in some sports than others. We will now examine a variety of violent behaviors committed by spectators around the sporting world. We will then offer a number of explanations as to why spectators act out violently at sporting events.

Spectator Violence

There are far more spectators than there are athletes. As a result, it should come as no surprise that spectator violence is far more common than player violence. Among the variations of spectator violence are verbal assaults, disrupting play, throwing objects (at opposing fans, athletes, coaches and referees), physical assaults (e.g., fighting, stabbings), and vandalism.

Verbal assaults refer to the use of obscenities, vulgarities, and threatening words directed by sports spectators at the targets of their scorn (e.g., other spectators, players, coaches, and game officials) (Wann, et al., 2001). As nearly anyone who has attended a sporting event in the United States can attest, numerous spectators use curse words, often with complete disregard for those seated nearby. It is very common at football and hockey games for fans to shout threatening words.

Disrupting play generally takes place in the form of a spectator(s) running onto the field or court. These deviants want to become "a part of the game" and usually mean no harm. They may want to shake hands with a player or kiss a player or even attempt to steal the ball. In fact, there is a subgroup of spectators, both male and female, who get attention by running onto the playing field nude. Most of these interferences are in good fun, and accepted as such. Yet ever since a fan ran onto the court and stabbed tennis player Monica Seles, there is an increasing level of fear that some fan disrupting play may actually cause physical harm and commit acts of violence aimed at players, coaches, or referees.

Fans do not have to enter the field of play to cause possible physical harm to sport participants; they can simply throw objects. Any object can become a possible missile of harm, including batteries, coins, plastic beer bottles empty or full of some sort of liquid (e.g., beer or urine), electronic devices, belts and other clothing items, food items, snowballs, and so on. The throwing of objects may also be directed toward opposing fans. Particularly vocal visiting football fans can expect to have objects thrown at them by the home fans at most professional football games.

Physical assaults may occur either in the stands or outside a stadium. The most common type of physical assault involves fighting among spectators. People who fight at sporting events typically have been drinking alcohol. Generally, the fans that fight each other are cheering for opposite teams. There are other occasions when a fight may ensue for reasons that are unrelated to the sporting event (e.g., a chance meeting of rival gang members, alcohol-induced confrontations). Fights outside the stadium may, once again, be related to the sports event just attended or some other non-sports-related reason. Beyond fighting, stabbings and gunfire would be considered examples of physical assault. There have been incidents of spectators shooting other fans outside a stadium and of stabbings both inside and outside a sporting arena. For example, in September 2003, a Los Angeles Dodgers fan was shot and killed in a Dodger Stadium parking lot during a dispute following a game between the Dodgers and Giants. The murderer was a Giants fan and the victim a Dodgers fan.

The very threat of violence in the stands may affect the scheduling of sporting events. Venues may be moved to neutral sites, night games may be moved up to day games, and in some rare instances, spectators may actually be banned from the game. For example, on October 21, 2005, two rival high school football teams from New York State, Mount Vernon and New Rochelle, played on a Friday morning in an otherwise empty stadium. Students were in school and not allowed to attend the game. No spectators were allowed to watch. The reason? The Mount Vernon superintendent feared violence as a result of an off-the-field incident wherein a Mount Vernon resident was killed in New Rochelle weeks earlier (7Online.com, 2005).

As with fighting, vandalism — the willful or malicious destruction or defacing of public or private property — may occur in the stands (e.g., ripping apart seats in the stands or toilets and sinks in the bathroom) or outside the arena (e.g., damaging vehicles, breaking neighboring store windows). Sports-related vandalism is usually caused by disgruntled fans, although a disturbing trend of victorious fans destroying property after winning a big game or championship developed in the 1990s.

There are a wide variety of examples of sports-related violence in both the United States and other parts of the world. In the following pages we will examine a few of these incidents of violence and describe a number of situational factors that lead to spectator violence.

Spectator Violence in the United States

The trend of sports celebrations turning violent and destructive takes place at both the college and professional levels (they occur at high school celebrations far less frequently). Rowdy sport celebrations are most likely to occur after a big game, like a national championship, or a league championship. A victory celebration in Detroit after the Pistons won the 1990 NBA championship degenerated into a riot that left 7 dead. Three people died in rioting in Chicago following the Bulls' 1993 NBA championship. In 2002, sport celebrations turned ugly at College Park, Maryland, and Minneapolis. University of Maryland fans celebrated the school's first national championship in basketball by destroying property. Riot police were called in to restore order. University of Minnesota fans were celebrating their school's national championship in men's ice hockey (O'Toole, 2002). Beyond the physical mayhem, a number of acts of vandalism occurred. In the College Park incident, six police cars were damaged and fire-fighters fought at least 16 separate fires. In Minnesota, street lights were damaged, furniture was torched, and rocks and bottles were thrown at police. While Maryland fans were causing havoc near their campus, fans of the losing team — Indiana — also took to rioting. Upset by their team's loss, fans torched couches, toppled street signs and threw objects at police.

Fans are allowed to cheer for their team and root against the opposing team. They are not allowed onto the field or court. As described earlier in this chapter, during the November 19, 2004, NBA game between the Pistons and Pacers, players went into the stands and fought fans, and fans came onto the court and fought players. Although this was one of the worst cases of fan-player violence in recent history, it is not the sole example of fans coming onto the court to fight. During a February 24, 1947, NBA game between the Syracuse Nationals and the Moline Blackhawks, the hometown Nationals fans became increasingly upset with the officiating and the perceived "bad calls" by the officials that went against Syracuse. After a particularly hard foul against a Syracuse player, home-grown John "Chick" Meehan, by Blackhawks player William "Pop" Gates, a Hall of Famer and one of the first African Americans to play in the NBA, hundreds of Syracuse fans stormed the court to get at Gates. One fan pulled a knife and tried unsuccessfully to get at Gates. Fistfights broke out across the court (Kirst, 2004). The NBA and *The Post-Standard* of Syracuse referred to the incident as a "race riot." The NBA responded by returning to an all-white sport the following year (Kirst, 2004). The similarity between the two incidents (Syracuse and Detroit) is the fact that officials lost control of the game and players and fans reacted by responding inappropriately.

One of the most extreme forms of violence is terrorism (war would be the most extreme example of violence). Attending sporting events in the 2000s — especially after 9/11/2001 — has been characterized by perceived threats of terrorism. In 2005, the NFL mandated that all fans are to be "checked" before they enter the stadium. (A Tampa Bay fan complained to the ACLU that such searches are unreasonable and violate First Amendment rights. The NFL lost the suit and in November 2005 was forced to abandon its security measures at Tampa Bay.) The security personnel search for explosive devices, especially those worn by suicide bombers. These check-points are far less obtrusive than airport checks and generally last just a few seconds. The NFL is concerned that football games might make an attractive venue for terrorists. Most sports leagues share this concern, as the large numbers of people crammed into a small area with relatively few exits are favorite targets of terrorists. The most infamous such attack occurred during the 1972 Olympics, when 11 Israeli athletes were brutally murdered by Palestinian terrorists while the world watched in horror.

Fans enter the playing fields and courts for reasons other than attempting violence. Even so, they risk disrupting play. "Rushing" the field or court after the game concludes has been relatively common in collegiate sports but has come under increasing disfavor. As a rule, fans simply want to bask in the glory of their team's victory, especially if it was an unexpected victory or a monumental one. Although players and officials are seldom injured, the risk factor is very high. Consequently, most schools are trying numerous measures to stop fans from storming the court.

With most sports, when fans storm the court or field, they have no real direction; that is, there is no central place to converge. Football is different. When fans storm the field at the conclusion of a football game most of them head directly toward the goalposts. Their purpose is to knock down the goalposts and parade around the stadium with them. The goalposts are similar to a hunter's trophy — proof of victory. Tearing down goalposts has a long tradition in football. It is considered good clean fun. Most spectators and fans of the victorious team look upon fans tearing down the goalposts with joy and happiness. Tearing down goalposts reached it peak in 2002 with 17 reported cases. However, tearing down goalposts can have dire and even deadly consequences. For example, on homecoming weekend at the University of Minnesota-Morris, October 22, 2005, the goalpost became a symbol of tragedy. Spectators stormed the field to knock down the goalposts. As is the typical fashion, fans stand on the crossbar and jump up and down until the parts of the goalposts snap off. These "parts" are made of strong metal. At Morris, as the dislodged goalpost tumbled down, it hit a student and caused his immediate death due to severe head trauma. In 2003, a spectator at Toledo became a quadriplegic after being hit by a goalpost being carried out of the stadium. At Ball State, in 2001, a fan became paralyzed as he was hit by a falling goalpost. As a result of these and other tragedies, college administrators are trying to find ways to stop it. Collapsible goalposts are used at some stadiums. The posts are made of aluminum. If the goalposts are already down it more or less defeats the purpose of storming the field. Some schools have goalposts on hydraulics so that they can collapse the goalposts quickly. Other schools grease the goalposts so that spectators cannot climb them. None of these measures would be necessary if officials could find a way to keep fans off the field.

Some spectators find it acceptable to throw objects at others during the game. Generally, these are isolated behaviors. There are times, however, when the "mob mentality" takes over and throwing objects becomes a collective endeavor. Mob mentality will be discussed later in this chapter as a possible explanation of collective violent behavior. In brief, a mob mentality develops when a group reacts nearly simultaneously to a stimulus. In sports, a bad call or act of violence on the field serves as the most common stimulus to collective behavior. A clear example of a mob mentality in action occurred during a December 16, 2001, NFL game between the Jacksonville Jaguars and Cleveland Browns. In this game, at Cleveland, fans reacted violently when game officials violated NFL rules. The Browns had the ball at the Jaguars' 9-yard line and appeared to be on their way to a last minute victory. The victory would keep the Browns' playoff hopes alive and therefore the game took on added importance. The Browns had already run a play when officials stated that they were reviewing a previous play. The rules state, once a play has been run, previous plays are not subject to review. The officials over-ruled a call that was made two plays earlier and awarded Jacksonville the ball. The Cleveland Browns bench erupted in anger. The ball was spotted in front of the end zone with the famous "Dawg Pound" (home to arguably the most loyal and ferocious fans in the NFL), which instantaneously responded by throwing beer bottles and other debris onto the field in an attempt to hit the game officials. Similar to the "wave" in sports, fans around the stadium immediately followed suit and threw objects onto the field. They were also aiming at the Jaguars but managed to hit the hometown Browns players as well. Many players and officials feared for their lives as the field became a sea of rubbish. The officials called an end to the game and cleared the field of players. Fans were ordered to leave the stadium. A phone call from the NFL commissioner told the game officials that all games must be completed, which led to the game being resumed 30 minutes later in a nearly empty stadium. One of the authors (Tim Delaney) was at the game and witnessed this wild scene.

Throwing objects onto the field certainly did not begin with Cleveland Browns fans in 2001, nor did it end there. The day following Thanksgiving 2005 the entire student section of Colorado was removed from their seats as numerous students threw objects onto the field during the Colorado-Nebraska football game. Security rushed to the area to maintain order after the referee halted play in the game.

There are times when spectators get hit by flying objects that originate from the playing field. Foul balls and homeruns are common in baseball and sometimes come at spectators like missiles. Many spectators have been injured as a result of being hit by a baseball. Hockey is another dangerous sport for spectators, as the puck periodically becomes deflected into the stands. People who get hit by errant hockey pucks risk great pain and potential death. In 2002, a 13-year-old girl was hit by a puck as a spectator at a NHL game in Columbus, Ohio. She was struck in the head. "Two days later she was dead, and the first such fatality and one of the few at an American sports event, other than auto racing, directly related to action on the field" (*Buffalo News*, 3/20/02: C6).

SOCCER HOOLIGANS

Perhaps the most infamous of all violent spectators are soccer hooligans. Hooliganism itself refers to violent and malicious behavior. When applied to sport, soccer hooliganism occurs when fans of soccer teams go on violent sprees of destruction that may involve verbal and physical violence, vandalism, physical altercations (often involving the use of weapons), rioting, burning objects, and causing general chaos. Soccer hooligans display behavior similar to street gangs. Their violence may occur before, during, or after soccer matches. Although many nations are home to hooligans, England's soccer hooligans are the most notorious. The English hooligans are so well-known that hooliganism has been referred to as the "English Disease." Other nations dread the arrival of England's teams because of the infamous acts of hooliganism that often accompanies them (Snyder, 2001).

There are two general categories of soccer hooliganism: spontaneous and deliberate. "Spontaneous hooliganism" is unplanned and a relatively low-level form of disorder caused by fans at, or around, soccer matches. Spontaneous hooliganism occurs at the arena between rival fans who are seated (or standing) next to each other or during chance meetings (e.g., at bars or train stations). "Deliberate hooliganism" refers to planned, organized violence caused by gangs of hooligans who have attached themselves to futbol clubs and fight "firms" from other clubs at soccer matches or in areas far removed from the pitch.

As mentioned above, soccer hooligans have similarities with street gangs, including core members who interact at a high frequency rate, possession of a group name, identity by specific types of clothing and color, claims of a specific territory, and participation in violent and criminal behavior. As with gang members, soccer hooligans justify their behavior, usually by insisting that they are simply protecting their neighborhoods or teams from outside rivals. In this regard, soccer hooligans, like street gangs, find it their duty to fight rival groups. As a result, there are a large number of incidents (too many to list here) of hooligan violence.

The seriousness of soccer hooliganism cannot be overstated. Firms (gangs) of soccer hooligans not only target other firms willing to fight, they also victimize innocent soccer fans who simply wish to cheer their team on to victory, free from violence. This helps to explain why *Sports Illustrated* (9/11/06) demonized an English toy company for creating a line of soccer-fan action figures called "Little Hooliganz" in its weekly "Sign of the Apocalypse" feature.

SITUATIONAL FACTORS THAT LEAD TO SPECTATOR VIOLENCE

Spectators that participate in violence range from the soccer hooligan who uses sport as an excuse to fight to a normally mild-mannered fan who finds him- or herself caught up in some sort of collective behavior. Consequently, there are a number of situational factors that lead to spectator violence:

1. *Hypermasculinity.* Hypermasculinity refers to a belief among young males that honor and respect are the result of one's ability to physically dominate another. Hypermasculinity is especially important to lower socio-economic class males. This idea is similar to Miller's (1958)

explanation of gang behavior and his use of focal concerns (trouble, toughness, smartness, excitement, fate and autonomy). These focal concerns become the basic feature of lower-class values and a way of life (Delaney, 2006). Hypermasculine males tend to be attracted to sports that encourage physical play. When males who value trouble, toughness and other masculine traits come into contact with one another, the possible for violence exists.

2. *A Strong Sense of Identity.* Many spectators have such a strong connection to the sports team that their very identity is shaped by the team. Soccer hooligans, for example, view the soccer team as an extension of the community in which they are based and consequently an important source of identification and pride (Semyonov and Farbstein, 1989). A strong sense of identification to the team coupled with hypermasculinity become two powerful situational factors that lead to soccer hooliganism. The soccer hooligan views the arena as a "battlefield" wherein turf must be protected. The soccer hooligan also views fans of an opposing team as the "enemy." Not only do the majority of soccer hooligans come from the lower social classes, most spectators who act violently tend to be young males (16–25 years old) from lower socio-economic group. It should also be noted that spectator violence is more likely to occur in team sports than it is with individual sports because it is easier for fans to identify with a group, which represents community, than with an individual.

3. *Alcohol Consumption.* Most spectators that engage in sports violence have consumed excessive amounts of alcohol. This is especially true with fan disturbances at college and professional sporting events (especially during football games).

4. *Frustration.* Fans realize that despite their passion and dedication, they have no direct effect on the outcome of the game. Thus, their role as spectator has a built-in component of stress and frustration. Some people react violently when frustrated; the hypermasculine male is the most likely candidate. Logic would seem to dictate that fans of the losing team would be the most frustrated and therefore most likely to engage in violent behavior. However, as we have already shown, many sports riots occur when fans celebrate a championship.

5. *A Dense Crowd.* A packed stadium creates a certain anxiety among spectators. It is also a source of frustration because spectators feel as though their personal space has been violated. Standing room crowds, which are extremely rare in the United States but common in other parts of the world, also contribute to violence because people on their feet are more active than those who sit throughout the game.

6. *A Large Crowd.* A large crowd increases the probability of violent spectators. A large crowd also creates a sense of anonymity by individuals (Mann, 1979). Members of large crowds feel a sense of power because they realize they greatly outnumber the security forces. A large crowd may also lead to a "mob mentality."

7. *Mob Mentality.* Individuals tend to lose their inhibitions and sense of "right" versus "wrong" when they become a part of a large crowd. They take on a group, or mob, mentality. As Gustave Le Bon (1952) explained in his "contagion theory," a "collective mind" forms within a large group and individuals abandon rational reasoning and become submerged into the groups' acts and mood (Vogler and Schwartz, 1993). Individuals experience a heightened sense of suggestibility when they are a part of a "mob." At many sporting events, alcohol fuels a mob mentality. A good example of the mob mentality in sports is the storming of the football field by spectators in an attempt to tear down the goalposts. As some fans jump on the crossbars, others join in. They revel at being a part of a group and simply follow the cues of others. Destroying property is a behavior that most of these people would never engage in if not for the "mob mentality."

8. *Important Games.* As a general rule, the more important the game, the more passionate fans become. Important events include playoff games, championship games and games against long-time rivals. If these rival teams are also from neighboring schools or cities, the importance of the game increases.

9. *In-game Player Violence.* Spectators respond to stimuli on the field. If an athlete(s) on the field reacts in an aggressive manner such behavior is likely to stimulate the fans of the athlete(s). For example, Smith (1974) found that nearly 75 percent of the incidents of hockey spectator violence in the stands were preceded by player aggression on the ice.

These are among the typical situational factors that influence the likelihood of spectator violence. Spectator violence in sport is an all too familiar occurrence. Civil societies frown upon spectator sports violence and attempt to control it via the civilizing process.

Sport Violence and the Law

Sport participants realize there is always a chance of injury when playing sports. This concept is based on the English common law notion of *volenti fit injuria*, or voluntary assumption of risk. Assumption of risk assumes that both management and labor understand the medical hazards inherent within sport (as with many other employment occupations). Injury, or harm, may occur as a result of actions that are within the realm of acceptable assumption of risk, or outside the realm of acceptability. In his 1859 publication *On Liberty*, British philosopher John Stuart Mill distinguished between *self-regarding* acts and *other-regarding* acts. Self-regarding acts refer to behaviors that may cause harm only to the individual performing them; and therefore, fall within the realm of acceptable violence. Other-regarding acts, however, are those which may cause harm to others; and therefore, fall outside the dominion of acceptable forms of violence. Mill (1859) argued that individuals should have the right to engage in risky behaviors (without interference) if they want because it is no one else's business what one does with one's own life. On the other hand, individual behaviors that cause harm to others are not acceptable and are subject to interference (e.g., government legislation or oversight by some regulatory agency). Robert Simon (1985) refers to Mill's concept as "The Harm Principle." In brief, The Harm Principle states that the only justification for interference with personal behavior is to prevent harm to others (Simon, 1985).

Athletes often risk personal harm. For example, a wide receiver who runs a pattern across the middle of the field and stretches himself to reach for a ball while surrounded by defenders realizes that he is vulnerable and will be hit hard. The wide receiver understands that his actions run a risk for harm (a self-regarding act) but runs such a pattern anyway. However, the wide receiver does not agree to be hit early, late, or illegally (other-regarding acts) by defenders. Although athletes have historically understood the risks involved in playing sports, an increasing number take exception to other-regarding acts. For example, in the past, it was uncommon for batters to charge the mound after a pitcher sent a "warning" pitch near the batter. Today, it has become commonplace for batters to charge the mound. These batters, as with many other athletes, are less tolerant of others whose behaviors may cause them harm. As Delaney (2002) explains, "While the concern with violence in sport is nothing new, what is new is the degree of legal intolerance to forms of player violence and player resistance to blind acceptance of risk of bodily harm. Legal forms of resistance by professional athletes are evidenced by the many cases in sports law and the growth of civil and criminal litigation" (p. 1561).

Over the years, efforts have been made to differentiate between acceptable forms of sport violence and those which are not. The most frequently used typology of on-the-field violence among athletes originated with Michael D. Smith (1983, 1996). His typology involves four categories: brutal body contact, borderline violence, quasi-criminal violence, and criminal violence.

1. *Brutal Body Contact.* This category of sports violence includes physical acts that conform to the official rules of the game and are accepted as part of the action and, therefore, are legal under the law. Examples include delivering extreme punches to an opponent in boxing, hard tackles in football, certain variations of elbowing an opponent in basketball, checking in hockey, and stick whacks in lacrosse. As Smith (1996) explains, "It is taken for granted that when one participates in these activities one automatically accepts the inevitability of contact, also the probability of minor bodily injury, and the possibility of serious injury. In legal terms players are

said to 'consent' to receive such blows (*volenti non fit injuria*— to one who consents to injury no injury is done)" (pp. 162–163). With "brutal body contact" athletes are suspending the usual moral standards of acceptability found in civil society. A pedestrian on a sidewalk does not consent to a blind-sided tackle from another pedestrian. A football player does give such consent. Thus, athletes on the playing field are working with a type of sports morality or ethics that is acceptable during game time, but a different type of ethical and moral behavior when they interact in the everyday world. In essence, morality and ethics are modified in the sports. But, as we will see, such modifications do have their limits.

2. *Borderline Violence.* This category of sports violence involves behaviors that violate the official rules of the sport and the law of the land but are widely accepted by all concerned as conforming to the norm of sport ethics when used as part of competitive strategy (Smith, 1983; Delaney, 2002). Examples include the "brush back" pitch in baseball, fist fights in hockey, late hits in football, high tackles in soccer, bumping cars in auto racing and talking smack in basketball. During the course of the game, such acts may be subject to sanctions (penalties). As Smith (1996) explains, "Borderline violence is essentially the province of referees, umpires, and other immediate game officials, higher league officials and law enforcement authorities seldom becoming involved. Sanctions never exceed suspension from the game being played, and perhaps a fine" (p. 165). These behaviors are often "expected," encouraged and positively reinforced within the sports world. "Borderline violence is tolerated and justified on a number of grounds, most of which boil down to some version of the 'part of the game' argument" (Smith, 1996: 165). However, public pressure is mounting to put a halt to the growing level of borderline violence in sports.

3. *Quasi-criminal Violence.* Involves assaultive physical acts that violate the formal rules of a given sport, the law of the land, and the informal norms of player conduct (Smith, 1996). Examples of quasi-criminal violence include swinging a bat at a player in baseball, kicking a player in the head in rugby or soccer, and sucker punches in any sport. Quasi-criminal violent acts usually result, or could have resulted, in serious injury, which brings it to the attention of top league officials (Smith, 1996). Athletes usually condemn this form of violence and fines or suspensions are often imposed. Quasi-criminal behaviors may generate outrage from the public but they are generally viewed as a sport problem to be handled internally and not involving courts of law (Nixon and Frey, 1996). Smith (1996), however, states that some episodes of quasi-criminal violence in professional sports have resulted in litigation.

4. *Criminal Violence.* This category consists of behaviors that are obviously outside the boundaries of official rules of the sport, the law of the land and players' informal norms, and are handled by the law. Athletes that commit criminal violence are subject to arrest and criminal prosecution. Deliberate or premeditated attempts to injure or seriously disable another athlete are examples of criminal violence. There are a growing number of sports-related acts of violence that come under the jurisdiction of the courts. Some of the more extreme cases criminal sports violence comes from the violent sport of hockey.

Sports and Leisure in Prison

If convicted of a violent offense, an individual may find him- or herself in prison. There has been little research conducted on sports and leisure in prison. A prison is a correctional facility for convicted felons. Roughly 1.4 million of the United States' 2.2 million inmates are in either state or federal prisons. Historically, prisons were viewed as institutions that emphasized harsh punishment and personal deprivation over inmate rehabilitation. Consequently, play, leisure and sport programs were discouraged. "In recent years, participation in recreational activities has been encouraged as a means of alleviating the monotony of prison life and as a safety valve to release built-up emotions and tensions. The National Advisory Commission on Criminal Justice Standards and Goals (1973) established standard policies and practices for recreation programs that included recommending that every institution employ a full-time director of recreation; that every offender be evaluated for interest in leisure services; that recreation programs provide some interaction opportunities with the outside community; and that a wide range of recreational activities be made available to inmates" (Frey and Delaney, 1996). What led to this change in philosophy? Proponents argue that sports and leisure programs in prison raise inmate morale, reduce boredom, and provide a "proper" avenue for blowing off or releasing pent-up frustrations.

SPORTS AND RECREATION IN PRISON

There are many potential functions of sports and recreations programs in prisons. Besides the possibility of providing a diversion, or escape, from the monotony of prison life, sports and recreation serve as a valuable treatment for individual rehabilitation (Brayshaw, 1974); provide inmates with the opportunity to experience the pleasures associated with non-prison life (Speckman, 1981; Williams, 1981); and increase inmate morale by providing healthy activity that stimulates positive attitudes among inmates (Telander, 1988). Corrections officials believe that sports can reduce medical expenses by improving the health of inmates (Dobie, 2004). Recreation programs may also reduce recidivism because inmates have enhanced their self-esteem by participation in a lifestyle that is acceptable in the outside world (Brayshaw, 1978; 1981). Most supporters of sport and recreation in prison argue that these activities serve as a safety valve or a way of "blowing off steam" or displacing aggressive energy in a legitimate manner (Mahon and Bullock, 1991; Bartollas, 1985; Leonard, 1988). Thus, an inmate who vents his aggressive tendencies by exerting considerable energy lifting weights or hitting a baseball is less likely to assault a fellow inmate or correctional officer. Frey and Delaney (1996) state:

> Recreation and leisure programs relate to the safety of the institution by serving as a barometer of prison climate. Guards get a 'feel' for the overall prison mood by observing how prisoners group together during leisure time. For example, if the groupings form along clearly racial lines then the possibility for conflict increases. If leisure groupings are racially integrated the climate may be less hostile. When there is extensive congenial interaction among various prisoners during leisure time, the guards know overall tension is low. The observation of recreation patterns gives prison administrators and guards the opportunity to detect potential conflict in the prison population. Tension management, skill enhancement, time management, and mood assessment are functions assigned to the place of sport and leisure in a prison setting. These activities augment prison control measures by providing a mechanism to promote the safety of prisoners and guards within the setting [p. 82].

Prison officials view sports and recreation time as something that has to be "earned." In that way, proper behavior is encouraged, as inmates who want recreation time learn to behave and follow the rules. Conversely, prison officials may take away recreational privileges for improper behavior. This is often an important function of sports and leisure opportunities in prison.

SPORTING ACTIVITIES IN PRISON

Recreational activities in prison include calisthenics, jogging, walking, playing cards, crafts, watching television and movies, taking music lessons, and talking with other inmates. The most common sports include weightlifting, basketball, softball, volleyball, flag football, handball, and soccer. Some prisons run rather serious sports programs. For example, the Angola Prison (Louisiana), known as "The Farm," runs a prison rodeo every Sunday in October. Most of the spectators of the rodeo are from the "outside" and come to cheer the high quality of rodeo skills displayed by the inmates. The inmates participate in the rodeo because it makes them feel good about themselves. Their self-esteem is enhanced when the regular citizens cheer their sporting skills. At the prison in McNeil Island (Washington), inmates play basketball in a league consisting of teams from the "outside." Obviously, McNeil plays all "home" games. Opposing teams are willing to go to McNeil to play hoops against the inmate team. McNeil has a unique home-court advantage and rarely loses. The inmate team members are very grateful that teams from the outside are willing to play them. Other inmates are allowed to be spectators as rewards for displaying proper behavior. There has never been any significant violence while the inmate and civilian teams have played one another at McNeil. Many other prisons have flag football teams and weight-lifting competitions.

In their study on the Nevada prison inmate population, Frey and Delaney (1996) divided sporting activities in prison into two categories: passive and active leisure pursuits. Passive activities, such as visiting other inmates, reading books, and watching television were among the most popular activities in prison. Active pursuits, such as weightlifting and jogging, involved less than half of all the inmates. Considering most inmates did not participate in a significant amount of active sporting endeavors, and those who did were on a very small scale, Frey and Delaney (1996) question the cathartic effect of recreation on the reduction of aggression. "It is not possible for significant tension release to take place if most inmates are either not participating in recreation or, if they do participate, do so in passive activities. These results suggest that building friendships and social relationships are the most important outcomes of leisure participation, not tension release. Thus, leisure time can contribute to building solidarity or a sense of community among prisoners" (Frey and Delaney, 1996: 84).

Today, many taxpayers question funding recreational programs in prison. Some critics target weight-lifting specifically as a sporting activity that should be eliminated from prisons. There are a couple reasons for this concern over weight-lifting. First, inmates who grow bigger and stronger become a greater threat to follow inmates, guards, and prison officials, and then citizens on the outside when or if the inmate is released. Second, there have been incidents where barbells have been used as weapons during prison riots. Arguments that sports and recreation programs cost taxpayers too much money is not supported by evidence, as budgets are modest (they vary from state to state). For example in New York State, the cost for recreational programs averages about $10 per inmate per year. Many state prisons run their sports programs entirely on profits generated from inmate commissaries (Dobie, 2004).

The authors suggest that there is a need for additional research into the role of recreation and sport programs in prison. This is a highly neglected area of study in sport sociology.

Summary

There seems to be an increasing level of sports rage in society today. The civilizing process seems to be making strides and losing ground at the same time. Since violence seems to be a part of society in general, it is not surprising that it exists in sports as well.

Some sports, such as football, rugby and hockey, are designed for assertive, physical contact between competitors. Violence is often seen as "part of the game." Intimidation is often used to gain a competitive edge. Aggressive behavior can be encouraged by coaches and teammates, and is sometimes *required*. It can be either nonphysical (such as using verbal taunts) or physical (such as deliberately throwing a ball at an opposing batter).

There are differing definitions of "violence." Not all acts involving deliberate force are necessarily violent in intent. In addition, violence in sport is evaluated differently than violence in the general public. There are several different theories given to explain the prevalence of violence in society. Some have a biological basis, attributing violence to innate drives or instincts, whereas others use a social learning approach.

Most sport participants and observers are nonaggressive; however, violent subcultures exist among players and fans. Violence has been a part of most sports since their inception.

One reason for the continuing problem of violence in sport is the fact that many sports are inherently aggressive by design. Football, for instance, involves controlled collisions, hard hitting blocks and gang-style tackles. Boxing, although it has been "civilized" through the imposition of the Marquis of Queensbury rules, still involves two people trying to knock one another unconscious. Hockey, while a game of intricate skill, is noted for its rough play and tough athletes (sometimes known as "goons"). Basketball, once labeled a "non-contact" sport, has changed dramatically, through the adoption of "street mentality" plays. Soccer is known more for its violence off the field than for player violence on the field.

Of special concern is spectator violence, including verbal assaults, disrupting play, throwing objects, and physical assaults on opposing players and fans. Such violence can occur both when fans' home team loses and when the home team wins; rowdy sport celebrations are more likely to occur after a big game, like a national championship. In the 2000s, fear of terrorism has added a new element to extreme forms of violence. Also, the ever-present danger of mob mentality can make attending sporting events a fearful experience.

There are a number of situational factors that lead to spectator violence, including hypermasculinity, a strong personal connection with a sports team, alcohol consumption, frustration, a packed or large crowd, and the importance of the game. Spectators also respond to stimuli on the field and can emulate violent athletes.

The law plays an important role in regulating violence in sport. Athletes often risk personal harm; over the years, efforts have been made to differentiate among acceptable forms of sports violence and those which are not.

One other area of concern is that of sports and leisure in prison settings. There are many potential functions of sports and recreation programs in prisons, including the possibility of individual rehabilitation.

KEY TERMS

Aggression Behavior which leads to personal injury, or the intent to harm others.

Aggression in Sport Verbal and physical behavior grounded in the intent to successfully accomplish a task even if it means to dominate, control, or harm, physically or psychologically, an opponent.

Disrupting Play Generally takes place in the form of a spectator(s) running onto the field or court.

Harm Principle Philosopher John Stuart Mill's view that the only justification for interference with personal behavior is to prevent harm to others.

Hypermasculinity The belief that ideal manhood lies in the exercise of force to dominate others.

Instrumental Aggression Behavior that is non-emotional and task oriented and driven by the quest for achieving some nonaggressive goal.

Intimidation Behavior that involves words, gestures and actions that sometimes may threaten violence or aggression in an attempt to pressure and put fear in the opponent.

Mob Mentality Collective thinking and action that develops when a group reacts nearly simultaneously to a stimulus.

Other-regarding Acts Behaviors which may cause harm to others and, therefore, fall outside the dominion of acceptable forms of violence.

Reactive Aggression Where one's primary goal is inflicting bodily injury or physical harm to an opponent.

Self-regarding Acts Behaviors that may cause harm only to the individual performing them and, therefore, fall within the realm of acceptable violence.

Sport Violence Intentional aggressive physical behavior that causes harm, occurs outside the rules of the game, is unrelated to ideals of sportsmanship, or which destroys the property of another sportsperson.

Terrorism The unlawful use of — or threatened use of — force or violence against individuals or property to coerce or intimidate governments or societies, often to achieve political, religious, or ideological objectives.

Vandalism The willful or malicious destruction or defacing of public or private property.

Verbal Assaults The use of obscenities, vulgarities, and threatening words directed by sports spectators at the targets of their scorn.

Violence Entails great physical force used intentionally by one person(s) to cause another person(s) harm or aggressive behavior which destroys the property of another.

DISCUSSION QUESTIONS

- What are the differences between "intimidation," "aggression" and "violence" in sports? Give examples based upon your own knowledge or experience.
- What are examples of actions that might seem to be violent but actually are not? Can you think of some that relate specifically to sporting events?
- How might nonphysical forms of instrumental aggression be used by athletes to gain a competitive edge? Do you think this is acceptable behavior?
- Why might violence in sport be evaluated differently from general violence found in society?
- Do you think that boxing is an acceptable sporting event? Why or why not?
- Have you ever experienced spectator violence at a game? What might be the causes for this deviant behavior?
- Should fans be allowed to tear down goalposts after a major victory? Why or why not?
- Do you feel that civility in sport is still of major importance? Give examples to show why or why not.

CHAPTER 10

Gender and Sport

Traditionally, boys and girls have been raised differently. Boys are generally taught and encouraged to play rough games like football and hockey and to play with such toys as trucks, airplanes, toy robots and toy soldiers. If they injure themselves by falling off a tree branch, for example, boys are told such things as "Big boys don't cry" and "Suck it up, and go back out there and climb that tree again." Messages such as these teach boys, subtly, to become emotionally distant and to face physical challenges head on. Conversely, girls have been encouraged to play with dolls, play "dress up," and have "tea parties" with their stuffed animal "friends." Girls, then, are being encouraged, subtly, to learn housekeeping skills and nurturing techniques. If boys and girls are raised differently and sent different messages by significant others, they tend to accept these gender differences as purely natural.

Gender stereotypes are learned in early childhood. The comic strip *Baby Blues* illustrates some gender stereotypes related to play. In one strip, the little boy named Hammie is playing with his army guy toy. His big sister Zoe, who is in the second grade, teases Hammie for playing with a doll. Hammie is offended by her remark and states, "Action Guy isn't a doll! He's a realistic action figure." Hammie's comment reflects the belief of most little boys, that girls play with dolls and boys play with "action figures." Like most boys, Hammie is offended by the mere suggestion that he is participating in a (perceived) feminine activity. He also points out that "Action Guy" is for boys because he wears steel-toed combat boots. Revealing aggressive male tendencies, Hammie then proceeds to hit Zoe's doll with his action figure. In the subsequent cartoon strip, Zoe is still teasing her little brother and asks, "Do your friends know you play with dolls?" Zoe is challenging Hammie's "manliness." Hammie, who is once again put on the defensive, describes all the reasons why "Action Guy" is not a doll. "He's a super-tough, solid, high-impact plastic action figure with realistic military accessories! Look at the box!" Hammie states. Zoe takes a look at the box and reads "From the makers of Barbie." Upon hearing this, Hammie is outraged. This comic strip reflects the fact that boys and girls become consciously aware of gender roles and their corresponding expectations at an early age.

As we shall see in this chapter, traditional views of gender have all but disappeared. Whereas girls and women were once discouraged from playing sports or flat-out denied opportunities, today female participation in sport is a given.

Patriarchy's Influence on Female Sport Participation

As stated above, women were once denied significant access to sport. Much of this had to do with the patriarchal (male dominated) design of most nations around the world throughout history. In a patriarchy, the female sex was viewed as inferior to the male sex. The term sex refers to one's biological classification. As we are aware, males and females differ biologically in regards to their internal and external reproductive organs and genitalia, types and levels of hormones and chromosomal structure (females have an XX and males an XY design). As social scientists, sociologists are more interested in gender classifications than they are with sexual classification schemes. Gender refers to socially determined expectations placed on individuals because of their sexual category. Traditionally, males have been expected to act masculine, while females were expected to act feminine. Because sport was viewed as a masculine endeavor, females were not encouraged to play sport as they are today.

However, as Morgan, Meier and Schneider (2001) explain, there is no sport that requires the possession of male genitalia in order to perform. Thus, if females are physiologically capable, why haven't they participated in sport in significant numbers before the 1970s? The answer must lie with culture, and in this case, a patriarchal culture. Needing some sort of justification to keep females out of sport, patriarchies created a number of myths associated with female sport participation.

MYTHS ASSOCIATED WITH FEMALE PARTICIPATION IN SPORT

Myths associated with female sport participation reflect both medical ignorance and negative stereotypes of women. As Patricia Vertinsky (1994) points out, during the late nineteenth century, "medical practitioners, many of whom were men, utilized pseudo-scientific theories about the effects of the reproductive life cycle upon women's physical capabilities in order to rationalize the life choices of middle-class women and define limits for their activities" (p. 39). Other researchers agree with Vertinsky's analysis. For example, Stanley (1996) argued that in the 1870s, the medical profession described the uterus as "a perilous possession" and the most dominant organ in the female body (p. 29). Dr. Edward Clark of the Harvard Medical School wrote an immensely popular book, *Sex in Education; Or a Fair Chance for the Girls* (1873), where he claimed that educating girls after the onset of puberty was a fundamental mistake because nature "had reserved that time for the process of ovulation and the development and perfection of the reproductive system. Education interfered with this critical process because the body never did two things well at the same time" (Stanley, 1996: 30). Education was considered unimportant for women because it might spoil women for family duties, thus "rendering them manly, indelicate, and unsexed" (Sack and Staurowsky, 1998: 52).

Combining primitive medical knowledge with negative stereotypes would lead to the creation of myths. One of the oldest myths of women and sports centers on the idea that they are too weak physically to play sport. Although modern medicine will confirm that the average male is physically stronger and faster than the average female, that does not mean women are too weak to play sport. (According to the National Center for Health Statistics— part of the Centers for Disease Control and Prevention — in 2002 the average American male was 5 foot 9½ inches tall and weighed 191 pounds, while the average American female was 5 foot 4 inches tall and weighed 164 pounds [Meckler, 2004].) The physical differences between men and women led to a myth that women are frail.

There are other physiologically-based myths regarding female participation in sport. "Some critics believe that sport participation defeminizes women (meaning that it makes some women less attractive, either physically or mentally, in some men's eyes), or that women (or sometimes their not-yet-conceived children) might suffer some physiological damage" (Morgan, et al., 2001: 208). Any assertion that women are harmed as a result of strenuous physical exertion while men are not is inaccurate. Further, if men are allowed to engage in "risky" behavior, then women should be allowed the same bodily and mental risks (Morgan, et al., 2001). The concept of a "macho female athlete" is a derogatory term used by those who argue female athletes become too masculine through sport participation (Sabo, 1996). Another myth related to the physiology of women is tied to the supposed delicacy of the female body. This myth is centered on the idea that women are easily injured; in particular, the breasts and reproductive organs are especially vulnerable. Female fragility is a big concern in patriarchal societies that view women primarily as care-givers to children.

Myths designed to keep women from playing sports are not limited to the physicality of the female body. They also extend to the psychological realm as well. "The 'myth of psychic damage' contends that women do not have the necessary psychological assets for athletic competition and, in contrast to men, women do not reap psychological benefit from sport. These notions are partly rooted in psychological theory.... Within the framework of psychoanalytic theory, for example, nonconformity to traditional roles and stereotypes was considered pathological. Hence, women's interest and involvement in business, engineering, athletics, or other 'masculine' activities were clinically suspect" (Sabo, 1996: 334–335).

Women can, however, benefit from sport participation. Just as males supposedly learn how to become better leaders and team players, females who play sports often grow up to become leaders. Research conducted in 2001 on 401 senior women business executives by Oppenheimer-Funds and its parent company, MassMutual Financial Group, revealed that 82 percent of the executives played organized sports after grammar school, including school teams, intramurals or recreational leagues (Johnson, 2002). Eighty-six percent of the women executives said that sports helped them to be more disciplined; 81 percent said sports helped them function better as part of a team; 69 percent said sports helped them develop leadership skills that contributed to their professional success; 68 percent said sports helped them deal with failure; and 59 percent said sports gave them a competitive edge over others (Johnson, 2002).

Patriarchal myths in sports designed to discourage female participation have nearly disappeared. There are still some lingering effects of these myths but most people in Western societies accept the idea that women should be allowed to play sports and realize that females do not face physiological or psychological damage for doing so.

The Early History of Women's Participation in Sport

As our discussion on the patriarchal nature of most societies and the negative myths associated with women's participation in sport implies, it is not surprising to realize that, until recent years, women have played a minor role in the history of sport. Women had little time to participate in sports and leisure when they were expected to keep busy child rearing and home making. The masculine ideals of sport led to social mores than discouraged women from participating in sport, as women were expected to engage in feminine pursuits.

Pre-Civil War

Discrimination against women participating in sports can be traced back to the ancient Olympics when women were forbidden from participating. Anshel (1994) states that women could be sentenced to death for simply watching men compete. However, as we pointed out in Chapter 3, women of ancient Greece established their own games in honor of Hera, the wife of Zeus. Spartan women were actually encouraged to keep healthy (through physical activity) in order to be good "breeders" (Leonard, 1988). During America's colonial period, wealthy women participated in a number of leisure activities, including horseback riding and foot racing. They were also spectators to men's sports. Women played cricket during the 1700s.

Prior to the Civil War, women as well as men participated in sports and leisure activities that were popular in their respective countries and social classes. Upper class women's sport participation was limited but generally included horseback riding and dancing. Middle- and lower-class women led lives that were more physical by necessity. Their recreational activities included dancing, horseback riding, skating, foot racing, and early versions of bowling and baseball (Howell, 1982; Figler and Whitaker, 1995). Men, on the other hand, were allowed much greater latitude in their physical pursuits. As a rule, men participated in more physical and aggressive sports than women and their everyday life events often presented physical challenges.

THE VICTORIAN ERA

During the Victorian Era (mid- to late-nineteenth century), upper-class women were treated as frail beings ruled by their hormones. It is important to note that hard physical labor was performed by lower-class and slave women on a daily basis during this era; a fact that seemed to escape the "educated" doctors of the wealthy class. Wealthy women were exposed to calisthenics in schools and private clubs, but most of the Victorian women participated in passive sports such as croquet, bowling, tennis, golf and archery. However, participation in these sports were for social purposes rather than competitive ones (Leonard, 1988). Well into the 1870s, aristocratic women considered it vulgar to strengthen the body. But this would slowly change with the advent of women's colleges.

By the 1870s a number of women's colleges had opened their doors. Calisthenics became increasingly popular. The Wellesley College catalog of 1876, for example, "proclaimed that good health was absolutely essential to good scholarship" (Stanley, 1996: 49). A number of colleges created remedial programs to prepare young women who could not successfully perform calisthenics. "Many students who previously had been excused from gymnasium work (mostly because of spinal curvatures or weak arches) received corrective therapy" (Stanley, 1996: 49). Women's colleges of the late 1800s were helping to reverse the popular cultural belief that sport participation was harmful to women. Many physical educators believed that sports would stimulate an interest in all forms of physical exercise for women. Gymnastics classes would determine those women (and men) that were capable of more strenuous forms of exercise that sports required.

The patriarchal society imposed ideals of proper dress for men and women. Full-length dresses and unrevealing clothes were the standard for women. Such clothing was not conducive to sporting activities. However, in the late 1800s a sports breakthrough for women occurred. As Leonard (1988) explains, "Although the pale and fragile woman remained a cultural ideal until the 1930s, the rosy-cheeked girl on her bicycle was providing evidence that exercise made a woman healthier for housework and childbearing. Amelia Bloomer's bloomers allowed women to move, but modesty in appearance was still an important consideration in sports participation" (p. 265). Middle-class women took to the bicycling rage of the 1890s as a means of testing the limits of female physical expression. Women dared to wear more comfortable and shorter dresses so that they could more easily ride a bicycle. Elizabeth Cady Stanton argued that bike riding "was the means, she said, by which health would be restored to an ever increasing number of nervous, overwrought women" (Vertinsky, 1994: 79). Physicians may have embraced the idea of women riding bicycles for the mild exercise benefits it produces, but many during the Victorian era feared that the freedom the "wheel" brought to women would lure them away from the home (and housework) to remote spots alone with men where they might succumb to seduction (Rader, 2004). Many members of society who embraced patriarchal notions also worried that women might ride bicycles to stimulate sexual organs (apparently through the vibration). Oddly, this same "logic" (genital stimulation as a result of vibrations) was not applied to horseback riding (as it is today). Feminists often view women cyclists as a symbol of emancipation from Victorian inhibitions, but the most enduring legacy of cycling appears to be tied to women who enjoyed riding because of the freer forms of clothing (Rader, 2004).

The sport of tennis evolved during this era thanks in part to the less restrictive clothes worn by both men and women. Stanley (1996) states, "Gentlemen began to abandon their formal attire in search of the freedom of movement required by the new game. Some women could be found playing the faster-paced game and wearing less restrictive clothing. Women playing tennis strictly for its own sake were apparently novel. In fact, in 1893 when socialite Ava Willing Astor played a vigorous tennis match (wearing bloomers) it created quite a stir. So arresting was the sight that *Vogue* devoted special coverage to the spectacle" (p. 76). Lawn tennis became increasingly popular with the women and men of the elite classes. Tournaments were designed so that only those of the "assured social position" were permitted to participate (Stanley, 1996). By the turn of the twentieth century, "Sports had become a necessary activity for anyone wishing to gain entry to polite and refined society" (Stanley, 1996: 77). Thus, anyone who was "someone" played sports. The masses, for the most part, were relegated to pursuits that assured basic survival.

THE EARLY 1900S

During the beginning of the twentieth century, more women became involved in various athletic activities. A group of wealthy sportswomen founded the Chicago Women's Athletic Club in 1903. Soon after that, other lavish women's athletic clubs opened in New York and other major cities around the country (Cahn, 2003). Women's participation rates in sports received a positive boost in the early 1900s when they were allowed to participate in the 1912 Olympic Games in Stockholm, Sweden. (It should be noted that Olympic founder Pierre de Coubertin and the American Olympic Committee were against women participating). Their participation in these Olympic Games was limited to swimming and diving. However, it was becoming evident that the cultural mores and gender expectations regarding women's sport participation were beginning to change in the early 1900s. For example, in 1923, a Women's Division of the National Amateur Athletic Federation was formed to stress "sports opportunities for all girls, protection from exploitation, enjoyment of sports, female leadership [and] medical examinations" (Simon, 1991: 123). The idea of this sports "creed" was to encourage girls and women to play sports while at the same time reassuring these female athletes that they were not unfeminine just because they played sports.

Another milestone in women's sports during the early 1900s occurred in England when Gertrude Ederle swam the English Channel. "When Gertrude Ederle swam the English Channel in 1926, two hours faster than any of the men who had preceded her, people began to think that women might not be so weak" (Heywood, 1998: 213). The athletic achievements of Babe Didriksen were likewise widely reported during the 1920s, but Heywood and Dworkin point out (2003) that "Babe was muscular and androgynous in the 1920s, but became increasingly 'feminine'— in the sense of growing her hair and wearing dresses— in the '30s and '40s in response to constant media criticism of her 'masculinity,' criticism that was a mask for fears about her sexuality" (p. xviii).

During the 1930s and 1940s several women's sports organizations were in place. They generally adopted position statements supporting educational-based sports programs for all girls and women. Track and field became popular sports for girls and women during the 1930s, '40s, and '50s. Beginning in 1924, the AAU (Amateur Athletic Union) sponsored annual national track and field events for women. The 1924 Olympics scheduled track and field events for women. Stanley (1996) recounted many stories by sports writers who covered the women's track and field events in a less than flattering manner (e.g., women could not handle the undue stress that competition placed upon their nerves); thus revealing that old cultural norms were prevalent among males in the sports world. Interestingly, the Great Depression drove most white women away from track and field (Rader, 2004). The economic turmoil caused by the Great Depression led to most sports and recreation programs for women being canceled or scaled down due to budget cuts. Black women filled the void. Nearly all segregated southern black high schools offered varsity competition in basketball and track and field to their students (Rader, 2004).

The Cold War between the United States and the Soviet Union that began in the late 1940s helped to stimulate renewed attention to women track athletes. The U.S. men had competed relatively evenly with the Soviet men, but the Soviet women easily beat the U.S. women in the 1952 Olympics. Attracting white women to a sport that was now dominated by black women was viewed both as essential in the quest to compete with the Soviets and difficult due to the massive recruitment efforts that would be necessary to attract larger numbers of women to the sport. Campaigns actively touted that women could be track athletes and feminine at the same time.

Enthusiasts for women's track enjoyed some mild successes at the 1960 Rome Olympics when Wilma Rudolph won praise for both her track performances (a triple gold medal winner) and her femininity (Rader, 2004). The astute reader may notice that this approach to female sports — that the athlete be both accomplished on the field while also being feminine — has continued to the present era.

Post World War II

During the 1960s, many American women (e.g., Wilma Rudolph, Wyomia Tyus in track, Donna de Varona in swimming, and Peggy Fleming in figure skating) achieved Olympic fame and commercial success. Tennis stars Billie Jean King and Margaret Court were gaining much public acclaim, as well as relative wealth, for their sports achievements. However, these women were the exception to the rule, as there were few opportunities for women at all levels of sports (high school, college and professional). The women's movement of the 1960s that fought so hard for the equality of women in many spheres of social life all but ignored the sports world. But the women's movement did advocate a sexual revolution and launched an all-out attack on the traditional mores and norms that placed restraints on physical freedom and the enjoyment of bodily pleasures (Rader, 2004). In the 1970s, the women's movement would find a "playing field" — sports — to test gender equality judicially. "With women's rapid postwar movement into the labor force and revived feminist movement, what had been an easily ignorable undercurrent of female athleticism from the 1930s through the 1960s suddenly swelled into a torrent of female sport participation — and demands for equity" (Messner, 2001: 274). In short, women were becoming organized and were fighting the system via the system.

A large number of collegian women's sports organizations that existed prior to the 1970s became unified in 1971 under the direction of the Association for Intercollegiate Athletics for Women (AIAW). "The AIAW hoped to bring about more intense and higher level competition while avoiding the abuses threatening men's college athletics. The AIAW placed strong restrictions on recruiting and took other steps to avoid cheating on transcripts and recruiting, exploitation of students and too much emphasis on commercialism. The AIAW's hope [was] for a separate but equal and purer existence than the governing body of male college athletics" (Beezley and Hobbs, 1989: 339). Among other things, the AIAW attempted to provide women with an opportunity to strive for excellence in sport; create new programs for women; and create local, state, regional, and national competitions. It emphasized educational achievement as well as academic and worked to secure the rights of female athletes who leave school to still be qualified for an Olympic bid (Morrison, 1993). The AIAW stressed the importance of being a student first and athlete second. They instilled a set of rules and regulations to assure that female athletes maintained their grades for eligibility. The AIAW also fought for the rights of female athletes. With the passage of Title IX in 1972, it promoted the idea that women's intercollegiate sports were to be viewed as the same as men's intercollegiate sports. In this regard, the AIAW represents one of the early major social institutions fighting for gender equity in sport and education. After spearheading a new ideal of women athletics that encouraged millions of young woman to participate in sports, the AIAW dissolved in 1982. The direction and supervision of women's athletics then came under the jurisdiction of the NCAA. "The AIAW left a heritage and a legacy of women leaders who examined, created, controlled, and supported a critical decade of intercollegiate athletics. That decade was a period of great accomplishment for women and for women's athletics" (Morrison, 1993: 65).

The number of women in sports grew slowly throughout the 1970s. Women met a general resistance from the masses who still thought that sports were for boys and men; from male athletes who wanted to dominate a domain they considered their own; and the NCAA, which fought the inevitable growth of women's participation in sport. Women won this battle, of course, as they participate in sports at greater rates today than ever before in history.

The most momentous single event to affect women's participation in sport occurred with the passage of Title IX of the Educational Amendments Act of 1972. (This topic will be discussed in detail later in this chapter.) Women did not experience immediate benefits from Title IX; they would come later. There would be other factors that contributed to the growth of female participation in sports beyond Title IX.

Factors That Led to Increased Women's Participation in Sport

Every social movement needs trailblazers. In the fight for gender equity in sports Maria Pepe of Hoboken, New Jersey, serves as a significant figure. In the summer of 1972, Pepe, then 12 years old, shattered the gender barrier in Little League Baseball. Pepe, who had a deep passion and desire to play baseball coupled with a mean fastball, tried out for the local Little League Baseball team. She made the team and played in three games. The governing body of Little League ruled her ineligible — because girls were not allowed to play — and threatened to strip the Hoboken Young Democrats team's status as a member of the Little League Association because it had allowed a girl on the team. After her coach informed Pepe of the news, with a heavy heart she turned in her uniform. Her plight made national attention. The National Organization for Women (NOW) worked with Pepe's family in an attempt to get her reinstated. Two years later, the New Jersey Superior Court ruled that girls must be allowed to play Little League Baseball. For Pepe, it was too late, as she no longer made the age requirement. However, since then, more than 5 million girls have played Little League (Read, 2005). Today, no one would even consider not allowing a girl to try out. Pepe's brief participation in Little League was enough to make ESPN's Top 10 list of the "Greatest U.S. Women's Sports Moments," coming in at number 5.

Billie Jean King was a major trailblazer in the fight for gender equity in sport. King was a brilliant tennis player who fought to end sexism in sport; especially the gender inequalities in pay (until the 1970s, women generally received about 10 percent of the amount of prize money available to men). King was able to convince other leading female tennis players to start their own women's circuit and formed the Women's Tennis Association. The feminist movement joined forces with King and helped to secure financial backing from the Philip Morris Tobacco Company, which promoted its Virginia Slims brand of cigarettes by sponsoring the WTA Tour (Rader, 2004). A television contract further increased the prize money for women. Today's female athletes owe a great deal of gratitude to Billie Jean King's vision of financial gender equity.

King was a feminist and an ostentatious tennis player who drew a great deal of attention on and off court during the changing cultural era of the 1970s. King made quite a stir when she told reporters that she did not want to have children and instead wanted to pursue her tennis professional career full time. Her attitude challenged the dying patriarchal order of American society. A far more flamboyant Bobby Riggs (a former triple-crown winner at Wimbledon in 1939) represented the voice of the "old school" patriarchal regime. In 1973, Riggs, who was 55 years old, challenged King, who was 29 years old and at the peak of her career, to a tennis match. Riggs (a famous braggart known as "the Mouth that Roared") was confident that because he was a man, not even a player as great as King could beat him. King refused to play Riggs, citing that she had nothing to gain by it.

Margaret Court, another leading women's tennis player, however, agreed to play Riggs on Mother's Day 1973. Riggs won in straight sets. King changed her mind and decided to play Riggs in a tennis match to be broadcast on live television from the Houston Astrodome in September 1973. Millions of viewers, including both of these authors, remember viewing this spectacle when it first aired. Riggs entered the arena in typical chauvinist flair accompanied by scantily dressed women and teased and taunted King before the match. It was King, however, who had the last laugh, as she easily defeated the outmatched Riggs. This "Battle of the Sexes" (as it was billed) was mostly show, but it generated huge interest and debate among Americans, Canadians, and sports enthusiasts around the globe. A great number of women began to believe that girls and women should have the same rights as males to play sports. They were also ready to challenge any male who stood in their way.

Jay (2004) explains that the "Battle of the Sexes" showed that tennis could attract a mass audience. Furthermore, it "brought tennis out of the country club and into the mainstream. Combined with a new crop of dominant American players, the much-publicized match helped to make tennis one of the most watched sports of the 1970s and early 1980s" (p. 171). Many stars emerged during this era, including Chris Evert and Martina Navratilova on the women's circuit and Arthur Ashe, Jimmy Connors, and Bjorn Borg on the men's circuit.

Throughout the 1970s a number of new opportunities presented themselves as many girls and women's sports programs were created in high schools and colleges. The desire of many girls to play sports coupled with an increasingly powerful feminist movement was responsible for a great deal of the growth in women's participation in sports. The numbers of girls participating in high school sports, funding, visibility, acceptance and popularity increased dramatically in the 1980s (35 percent of high school athletes were female) compared to the 1970s (7 percent) (Leonard, 1988). The average number of sports programs offered per college for women grew from 5.61 in 1978 to 7.31 in 1988 (*Chronicle of Higher Education*, 1988). The 1984 Los Angeles Olympics witnessed twice as many female athletes—about 2500—than any other previous Games (Leonard, 1988). However, this number still represented just 23 percent of the total Olympic athletes in 1984 (Figler and Whitaker, 1995).

Women's participation in sports would continue to grow throughout the 1990s; by this time there was a general consensus in Western societies that females should have equal opportunity to pursue sporting activities. The growth in sport participation was fueled by a health and fitness movement that encouraged women to work out. The development of physical strength and sports competence was now encouraged, rather than discouraged, for women.

The emergence of Venus and Serena Williams in the mid–1990s represents another marker of social change (Jay, 2004). Fans, sportswriters and critics commented on their every move. The Williams sisters served as a "commentary on race relations and gender norms, and the symbolism of being powerful black women in a nearly all white game" (Jay, 2004: 238). Today, the sisters are world renowned tennis superstars who possess a combination of speed, strength, and charisma, along with a fashion sense designed to be marketed. As L. Jon Wertheim notes in his book *Venus Envy*: "In the year 2000, Venus wouldn't just surpass her little sister; she would establish herself as the dominant player in women's tennis. In addition to claiming the U.S. Open and Wimbledon titles, she would run off a thirty-five-match winning streak and win gold medals in both singles and doubles at the 2000 Summer Olympics. To top off what had already been a pretty good year, she signed a $40 million endorsement deal with Reebok that made her the richest female athlete in history" (Wertheim, 2002: 3). And while the Williams sisters were helping to break down the racial barrier in a sport dominated by whites, Tiger Woods was becoming golf's first black superstar (Jay, 2004). (We will discuss racial issues in sport in Chapter 11).

Women have come a long way since their humble sport participation beginnings. Girls are competing with boys in many high school sports, including wrestling. In fact, in 2006, Michaela Hutchison emulated her two brothers, both of whom won state wrestling titles, when she won the 103-pound Alaska state title. She went into the tournament ranked number one in the state. Her accomplishment on the wrestling mat earns her the distinction as the first girl in U.S. history to win a state championship competing against boys (*Sports Illustrated*, 2/13/06). Today, many girls take it for granted that their decision to play sports will not be met with resistance and that opportunities exist for them to participate in a variety of sports. The increased media coverage of female sports further reinforces the legitimacy of sport participation as a reasonable course of action for females.

Obstacles to Continued Growth in Women's Sports

There are a number of obstacles interfering with the continued growth of women's sports participation. Schools at all levels (elementary, high school and college) are experiencing budget cutbacks that affect both men's and women's sports. The reality of limited finances in recent years has hampered the development and continuation of many sports programs. Beyond the general financial concerns, there are a number of specific obstacles that concern those striving for continued gender equity in sports.

LACK OF WOMEN IN POWER POSITIONS

Since the early 1970s, women's sports programs have increasingly been run as men's programs, resulting in women losing control over what they previously held. For example, as the total number of females participating in sports increased dramatically since the 1970s, the number of women coaches and administrators has decreased proportionately. In 1972, the year Title IX became law, over 90 percent of women's teams and programs were coached by women (Van Keuren, 1992). During the 2000s, the percentage was cut in half.

Most observers agree that women must be provided more opportunities in the power positions of women's sports in order to increase gender equity. Bailey (2000) makes a number of suggestions to help in that process:

1. *Aggressive Identification, Recruiting, and Retention Efforts.* Through such methods as an expansion of graduate assistantships, internships, and administrative fellowships and scholarship opportunities.
2. *Creating a More Supportive Work Environment.* Including such things as a flexible work schedule, liberal family leave policies and comparable salaries for men and women in coaching and administrative positions.
3. *Increased Professional Development Opportunities.* Developmental workshops and programs and encouraging women to take advantage of such opportunities when they are made available.
4. *More Access to Decision-Making Processes.* Especially in leadership positions with the NCAA and other appropriate ruling bodies of sports leagues.

Unfortunately, most of these suggestions as well as others are directly tied to financial support, and as we mentioned earlier, many athletic budgets are facing shortfalls, not excesses.

MALE RESISTANCE

As the conflict perspective articulates, those in power will attempt to keep it — it is in their best interest to do so— while those without power will attempt to change the status quo. It should come as no surprise that there are many men and some women who are still resistant to the trend of an increasing number of women in sports (including athletes, coaches and administrators, as well as people in peripheral positions in the sports world). There is resistance to government policies and legislation that have led to the funding of female sports at the cost of men's programs (to be discussed in further detail with our review of Title IX). This resistance is centered on the fact that sport, before the 1970s, was primarily a male preserve, and many males want to keep it that way.

AESTHETIC FITNESS

Women have come a long way since the early 1970s in regard to sport participation. Women have proven that they can compete in sports. But one myth lingers— that sport masculinizes females. As a result, most female athletes want to be viewed as both athletic and attractive (feminine). They want to be taken seriously as athletes, and yet because of increased public exposure, a number of marketing opportunities are now available for female athletes. One of the most basic marketing ploys involves sex appeal. After all, advertisers tell us that "sex sells." If women really want to achieve financial riches, they have to promote themselves outside of sport. And, if the adage that "sex sells" is correct, these women will have to possess aesthetic fitness— looking attractive and feminine. This reality helps to explain why tennis stars Anna Kournikova and Maria Sharapova have been among the highest paid female athletes of the 2000s. The (then) 19-year-old Sharapova, for example, earned more than $30 million in endorsements in 2007.

Many female athletes diet excessively in an effort to attain aesthetic beauty and fitness as well as for more "practical" athletic purposes. Long distance runners, for example, have relied on strict dieting to lose weight and be as thin as possible for running (Clark, Nelson, and Evans, 1988). However, a number of female athletes are dieting excessively in a variety of sports and are risking a number of health problems as a result of over training, inadequate diet and striving for thinness. Among the problems that can occur to a female athlete (at any level of competition) are disordered eating, body image issues, anorexia, bulimia, amenorrhea (no menstrual periods), osteoporosis, depression, attempts of suicide, career ending injuries and even death. This high price of success represents the darker side of sports' demands and athletes' desires, especially in women.

All athletes need energy. Our food intake provides the calories we need for conversion to energy. The average daily caloric intake for girls between the ages of twelve and fifteen is 2,200 (Berg, 1997). Otis and Goldengay (2000) state that the resting metabolic rate for young women is between 1,200 and 1,800 calories, depending on a number of factors. Athletes burn hundreds of additional calories during each practice. For example, on average, 450 calories are burned per one hour of aerobic activity, and jogging at 5.5 mph burns 660 calories per one hour (Ravage, 2001). As we can see, athletes need to eat more food than non-athletes in order to maintain a healthy body weight. Burning off more calories than one consumes can lead to such things as amenorrhea, osteoporosis, and long term health problems.

A number of athletes, especially females, may suffer from anorexia and bulimia. Anorexia may be defined as "an eating disorder characterized by a purposeful weight loss far beyond the normal range. Fear of being fat is almost always an overriding factor" (Kinoy, Holman, and Lemberg, 1999: 2). People with this disease have a distorted body image. When they look in the mirror, no matter how thin they are, they see themselves as fat. This can lead to even greater

A surfer stretches before heading out to tackle waves at the North Shore in Oahu, Hawaii.

problems, as the individual may be in denial that there is a problem and therefore not seek the medical attention they need. Anorexics may ingest diet pills, laxatives or water pills, causing some very serious medical problems and addiction later on. Anorexics suffer from feelings of inadequacy, self-doubt and low self-esteem. Coaches who belittle athletes repeatedly, making them feel fat, ugly and worthless, are one contributor to female athletes becoming anorexic (Ryan, 2000). Anorexics often feel the need to please everyone else before they try to please themselves. Athletes often feel that they must perform to please others. Gymnasts and figure skaters, for example, feel the need to please coaches, judges, parents and peers. Anorexics crave control in a seemingly chaotic world. Food intake is one thing they can control. Anorexics may feel constant anxiety and hyperactivity; that is, until their bodies begin to lose fuel (energy) and breakdown. The break down experienced by anorexics may be both physical and psychological. Providing a healthy, positive environment for athletes (as well as non-athletes) is the best source of prevention and treatment for the anorexic. Coaches need to identify warning signs in their athletes (e.g., when the athlete is acting sluggish when they have not been pushed). Coaches should document significant changes in athletes, especially weight loss and mood changes (Hornak and Hornak, 1997). Coaches, of course, are not the sole people responsible for keeping an eye on young athletes. Parents, family members, and friends need to provide assistance in identifying unhealthy behaviors in athletes as well.

Bulimia is another eating disorder that may affect female athletes. "Bulimia nervosa, from the Greek word for Ox hunger, is a complicated disorder characterized by repetitive cycles of dieting, then overeating — binging — followed by behaviors that get rid of, or purge, the food eaten" (Otis and Goldengay, 2000: 87). Bulimic behavior triggers an individual's body into a state of semi-starvation that in turn releases hormones that stimulate the person to eat uncontrollably. This disease feels like a "roller coaster" to its victims, filled with emotions of guilt and frustration followed by pleasure and happiness, only to be repeated over and over. The bulimic eats a huge amount of food in one sitting (binges) and then throws up the food (purges) so as not to put on weight. Not all bulimics are thin; they may even be slightly overweight. This is a secretive disorder that is often difficult to detect. As with anorexia, support from the family, friends, and coaches is extremely important.

Female athletes may also suffer from amenorrhea, the complete loss of menstruation. It can be termed as three or fewer menstrual cycles in a year or no cycle for six consecutive months (Wilson, 1995). A combination of poor diet and excessive exercise may set up a female athlete for amenorrhea. If a female is not menstruating, there is no release of estrogen and progesterone (necessary for bone cell maintenance), resulting in weaker bones and fragility, which in turn triggers the early onset of osteoporosis. Osteoporosis does not affect just older women. It can affect younger women who do not take care of themselves at an early age. The body needs a number of nutrients to keep the bones strong. Without these nutrients, bones can literally shatter. One of the most avoided nutrients is fat. Fat is an essential part of a healthy diet and yet many dieters steer free of it. Fats are needed for absorption of vitamins and for digestion. The U.S. Department of Agriculture recommends that no more than 30 percent of the total caloric intake should be from fats. When people try to restrict fats they also deprive themselves of very important nutrients. Calcium in the diet is extremely important for female athletes. Calcium strengthens bones, and therefore has a correlation between intake and stress fractures. The less calcium a person takes in, the more likely stress fractures will occur. Important sources of calcium are dairy products such as yogurt, milk, and cheese. It is important that coaches and parents make sure that young athletes eat properly by consuming foods that are filled with nutrients and that are from all food groups.

The shift toward aesthetically pleasing female athletes may compromise a great deal of the growth that women have attained and continue to seek in being treated equally with men as athletes. In an attempt to reach "ideal" weight, many female athletes engage in unhealthy eating behaviors and suffer from such health problems as anorexia, bulimia and amenorrhea. Younger girls need positive role models to admire. Athletes who suffer from eating disorders do not make good role models, and this in turn may stunt the continuing growth of female participation in sport.

Sexism

Sexism is another obstacle confronting women in their attempt to reach equity in sport. Sexism is defined as behavior that discriminates against a member(s) of one sex due to preferential treatment aimed to assist a member(s) of the other sex. Sexism leads to inequality. Historically, women have been victims of sexism far more often than men, but both men and women may be victimized by sexism. There are two primary forms of sexism, ideological and institutional. Ideological sexism is the belief that one sex is inferior to another and stresses gender-appropriateness based on gender roles. Ideological sexism in sport has long prevailed and is exemplified by men who consider women too weak to play sports. An example of ideological sexism is provided by the remarks of Formula One head Bernie Ecclestone, who told reporters before the 2005 U.S. Grand Prix that "women should be all dressed in white like all the other domestic appliances" (*Sports Illustrated*, 2005: 20). The 74-year-old Englishman's comments were directed toward race car driver Danica Patrick. A year earlier Ecclestone told a female writer that not only were women like appliances, but also "they shouldn't be allowed out. You don't take the washing machine out of the house, do you?" (*Sports Illustrated*, 2005: 20). Institutional sexism, on the other hand, refers to systematic practices and patterns within social institutions that lead to inequality between men and women. The lack of women in power positions in sport could be seen as a form of institutional sexism. Equal opportunity in sport for women and men will occur only when discrimination and sexism is removed from that social institution and society in general.

SEXUAL HARASSMENT

Sexual harassment is a byproduct of sexist attitudes. Sexual harassment is a violation of U.S. law. Sexual harassment is defined as the making of unwanted and offensive sexual advances, sexually offensive remarks or acts, unsolicited verbal comments, gestures, or physical contact of a sexual nature, especially by a superior or a person in a supervisory position. As a once all-male domain, the world of sport is often an environment wherein sexual harassment may be found. In some instances, sexual harassment occurs between coaches and athletes. The coach has an advantageous position of power over the athlete. At times, the coach may use his or her position to force an athlete to have sex in return for favors such as increased playing time, or a starting position (at the expense of another athlete). Sexual relationships between coaches and athletes are generally discouraged and in many cases may be explicitly forbidden in athletic handbooks. Sexual harassment may also occur when a woman plays sports on a men's team.

QUEST FOR EQUALITY IN THE MALE PRESERVE

Many males view sports opportunities as a "rite of passage." Since the 1970s, many males in the sports world have become increasingly fearful of the growing number of women in sports and the shrinking financial budgets for male sports as a result of this shift in the sporting landscape. Messner (2001) states, "Increasing female athleticism represents a genuine quest by women for equality, control of their own bodies, and self-definition, and as such represents a challenge to the ideological basis of male domination" (p. 267).

In order for gender equity in sport to become a reality, two key things must occur. First, men will have to change their perception of sport as a male domain and their ideas that masculinity in males is tied to excelling in sports. Second, more females will have to hold positions of power (e.g., coaching and administration). There is a conscious effort in the sports world to address the latter, but there is little chance of changing the former any time in the near future. Most (certainly not all) men *do* tie their identities and ideas of masculinity to the ideal character traits of most sports, competition, domination, toughness, and aggression. Most males have been taught since they were little boys to be tough. ("Big boys don't cry.") As males grow older this message is hammered over and over, be tough, play with pain, suck it up, don't let the opponent intimidate you, fight back. These same messages are common in sports, especially America's most popular sport — football. Whether males are biologically wired to be aggressive because of thousands of years of evolutionary growth and the need to be the "hunter," or whether males learn that toughness is a valuable and desired trait, aggressiveness, working hard and toughness remain valued attributes among males.

Interestingly, crying does seem to have its role in sport. Male athletes are "allowed" to cry under certain emotional conditions, such as during a retirement speech, or an induction speech into the Hall of Fame. Women, who are generally encouraged to be more open with their emotions, are expected to abide by the no crying adage of sports. The classic line "There's no crying in baseball" from the movie *A League of Their Own,* spouted by Tom Hanks' character to a professional women's baseball team, reflects this anti-crying creed in sports, even by women. In Chapter 9 we mentioned the attack on figure skater Nancy Kerrigan. Although she had actually been physically attacked, the media and public mocked her "selfish" crying, "Why? Why, me?"

as she sat on the floor immediately following the assault. The "rules" of proper behavior in sport are often as clouded as the rules of general society sometimes tend to be.

Changing the male's perception of what it means to be masculine in sport, or outside of sport, represents a much more difficult challenge than legislating equity via increasing the number of women in power positions and the number of female sports programs in schools. The number of women in sports has increased greatly in Western societies since the 1990s (Wedgwood, 2004). Women have entered the domain of many traditional male sports; for example, there are women who play rugby, football and hockey or participate in boxing and snowboarding. As more women enter the sports world, the male preserve is altered. To date, there are several women's professional sports leagues including full contact football, soccer, basketball, rugby, hockey, and track and field. This is in addition to the sports that women have long participated in, such as tennis, figure skating, and gymnastics. Female athletes are no strangers to pain and injury resulting from playing such sports. They have learned to suck it up, play in pain, and be aggressive and tough such as males have learned. This demonstrates, yet again, that regardless of any possible genetic predispositions a person may have as a result of their sex, this can be modified through the socialization and trial and error process. The authors join many other scholars who argue that the sports world serves as a site of empowerment for females.

HOMOSEXUALITY AND HOMOPHOBIA

Homosexuality in sport is an area that has received much attention in recent years. Most homosexual athletes want to keep their sexual lives private; this is especially true for gay men (Anshel, 1994). Coming "out of the closet" is a taboo for male athletes due to the threat of loss business sponsorships, the desire of sports clubs to retain their masculine image, and the likelihood that teammates will no longer accept them as peers. Although there is a growing acceptance of gay men in most Western societies, male athletes work in an environment that is still dominated by machismo. Billy Bean, a former Major League Baseball player who announced he was gay after his playing days ended, claims that male sports are society's last bastion for denial. According to a *Denver Post* report, Bean was one of only three male team-sport athletes to acknowledge at the time that he is gay (*Honolulu Star-Bulletin*, 1/8/06). The other two male athletes to "come out" are Glenn Burke (MLB) and Esera Tuaolo (NFL). Male athletes live in a testosterone world, and it is unlikely that a player who acknowledges being gay will be accepted by his teammates, as Mike Anderson (running back for the Denver Broncos) indicated in an interview (*Honolulu Star-Bulletin*, 1/8/06). Gay athletes may be unwilling to "come out" not only because of the fear of being rejected by teammates and fans, but also the potential loss in endorsement deals. In 2007, former NBA player John Amaechi came out and publicly announced that he was gay. His admission occurred three years after his playing career ended. The general public was not overly concerned. But NBA player Tim Hardaway said "I hate gay people" when asked about Amaechi during a radio interview (Murphy, 2007). Hardaway was blasted by the media and the Gay and Lesbian Alliance Against Defamation. NBA commissioner David Stern suspended Hardaway from playing in the 2007 All-Star Weekend festivities. Hardaway later apologized.

Sports marketers indicate that coming out would have a negative impact in endorsement deals (Wertheim, 2005). However, as people become more accepting of gay athletes, it becomes increasingly likely that more athletes will "come out." A 2005 *Sports Illustrated* poll reveals that nearly 80 percent of respondents agreed that Americans are more accepting of gays in sports today than they were twenty years ago (Wertheim, 2005). Twenty years from now we will most likely find that gay athletes is not a controversial topic.

Issues of sexuality are found in female athletics as well. In the 1800s, women were considered too frail to play sports. After women proved they could play sports, there were concerns that female athletes would become too masculine or engage in lesbianism. During the mid–1900s leaders of women's sports became aware of criticisms that female athletes were labeled as lesbians and "failed heterosexuals" (Cahn, 1994). This was based on assumed associations between mannishness and lesbians and between masculinity and sport. Based on these assumptions, critics of women's sport now claimed that women athletes were "mannish lesbians who were unattractive to men" (Griffin, 1998: 35). During the 1970s, the feminist movement had become quite strong. Lesbians no longer felt the need to hide their sexual preference. "The emerging gay and lesbian rights movement changed coming out from a personal declaration to a political statement and sparked the proliferation of a more visible and proud lesbian and gay subculture" (Griffin, 1998: 41).

During the Regan era (1980s) the U.S. became more conservative and lesbian athletes especially felt more compelled to keep their sexuality secret. In 1981, Billie Jean King held a press conference to reveal that a former lesbian lover was suing her for palimony. Most women on the professional tour knew King was a lesbian but kept it a secret, fearing loss of sponsorships. This reality affirms the perspective of that era that female athletes were accepted by society as long as they were heterosexual and that it was financially ruinous for lesbian professional athletes to publicly identify themselves (Griffin, 1998). Martina Navratilova, another dominant female tennis player, was "outed" in an article in the *New York Post*. The public was not too surprised by this. The Women's Tennis Association, fearing loss of sponsorships, warned other players they would not tolerate another player coming out (Zwerman, 1995). A general acceptance of lesbian athletes in sports like tennis and golf existed throughout the 1990s. This period of liberalism has been replaced by a focus on aesthetic beauty and athleticism in the 2000s. A new generation of professional tennis players and golfers has embraced femininity and has reaped the financial awards for doing so.

This is not to suggest that there are no lesbians in sports today. It is a commonly held belief that many women in basketball, professional and collegiate, are lesbians. And although society in general seems accepting of lesbians, there are still many individuals in power positions that are not. On December 11, 2005, ESPN's *Outside the Lines* aired a special on Penn State's women's basketball and coach Maureen "Rene" Portland. A long-time coach at Penn State (26 years as of 2005), she earned two "National Coach of Year" awards and had more than 650 victories, including seven conference titles. Portland had a strict "no lesbians" policy and throughout her career approached her players that she suspected of being gay. She forced them to admit to being gay and then threatened to "out" them (to the media and their family members) if they complained about her anti-gay attitudes. Portland kicked lesbians off the team. Throughout this *Outside the Lines* broadcast former Penn State players discussed their shock and dismay of Portland's outward hostility toward lesbians. One player recounted how Portland took players to a WNBA game in Seattle and later complained to her players about the audience members— many of whom consisted of lesbian couples and groups of lesbian women. After a lawsuit by one former player and an internal university review of Portland's practices, she resigned in 2007.

In 2005, Sheryl Swoopes of the Houston Comets (WNBA) announced that she was a lesbian. She was once married to a man and has an 8-year-old son. Swoopes claims not to have been gay while she was married but instead became a lesbian in recent years. Swoopes, the only player to be named league MVP three times, said that she never had feelings for a woman before she met Alisa Scott, a former Comets assistant coach. Swoopes hopes that she can remain a role model to young aspiring female athletes (Rieken, 2005). Interesting enough, in 1993 Swoopes' mother, Louise, had caused a national controversy by claiming that Sheryl, then trying out with the University of Texas Lady Longhorns, had been subjected to sexual advances by two members of the team. "To her credit," writes Perry Deane Young (1995), "Jody Conradt, the coach of the Lady Longhorns, refused to be intimidated by the accusations. Conradt said she knew nothing of the incidents Swoopes's mother described, but she said it was no problem for her or the team if there were active lesbian members. The winningest coach in women's basketball ... Conradt said the university had a policy not to discriminate against anyone because of sexual orientation. 'The best team I ever had had diversity,' Conradt said. 'When our society learns to embrace diversity, we'll be a lot better society'"(p. 37).

Gays and lesbians in sport will continue to be a topic of interest for years to follow. It is important to note that it is against the law to discriminate against athletes (or nonathletes) because they are gay.

Title IX

As we mentioned earlier in this chapter, the most significant single event to occur for women in sport was the passage of Title IX of the Education Amendments of 1972 (20 U.S.C., Sect. 1681). Congress enacted Title IX on June 23. Title IX legislation was the first comprehensive federal statue created to prohibit sex discrimination in education programs that receive federal financial assistance. This includes public elementary, secondary and post-secondary schools and public and private universities. Since nearly every educational institution is a recipient of some type of federal funding, nearly all educational institutions are required to comply with Title IX. Title IX is enforced by the Office for Civil Rights (OCR) of the U.S. Department of Education. This legislation requires educational institutions to maintain policies, practices and programs that do not discriminate against anyone based on sex. Under this law, males and females are to receive equal funding and treatment in all areas of education including athletics. The OCR has the authority to develop policy on the regulations it enforces.

Before Title IX, athletic budgets were overwhelmingly slanted toward male sports. Title IX was designed to eliminate such widespread examples of discrimination in educational settings. The implementation of Title IX meant that men would have to share the better facilities (gymnasium, weight rooms, swimming pool, etc.), the better practice times (women were usually given late night or early morning practice times), and most importantly, financial resources. "The impact of Title IX has been clear and dramatic. In 1972 only one girl in twenty-seven played a sport sponsored by her high school, and colleges spent a total of $100,000 on athletic scholarships for women. By 1996, one girl in three played a sport sponsored by her high school, and colleges spent a total of $180 million on athletic scholarships for women. The participation of women in college sports increased fourfold between 1970 and 1999, from 31,000 to 110,000" (Porto, 2003: 13–14).

Title IX and Compliance

Any school in violation of Title IX can be penalized for non-compliance; such penalties usually result in the loss of federal funds. Although most schools are not in compliance with Title IX, no institution has lost money for violating Title IX. Many schools have, however, paid substantial damages and attorney fees because of lawsuits brought to court. There are three basic aspects of Title IX that apply to athletics: participation and accommodation (offering sports programs), athletic financial assistance (scholarships), and "other" athletic program areas.

1. *Participation and accommodation.* Title IX is sometimes viewed as a quota system; but this is not accurate. To comply with Title IX institutions must show one of three things: proportionate (to the enrollment of the institution) athletic opportunities for male and females athletes; or demonstrate a history and continuing practice of expanding opportunities for the underrepresented sex; or the provision of sports of interest to the under-representative sex.

2. *Athletic Financial Assistance.* The total amount of athletic aid (scholarships) must be proportionate between female and male athletes. This is calculated by simple mathematics. If 53 percent of the participants are men and 47 percent are women, then 53 percent of the scholarship dollars must be awarded to men and 47 percent to women. Title IX does not impose scholarship limits by sport — the NCAA determines this.

3. *Other Athletic Program Areas.* Title IX mandates equal treatment in a number of other athletic program areas, including coaching, game and practice times, medical and training facilities, publicity, travel per diem, equipment and supplies (especially in regard to equal quality of equipment), locker rooms, recruitment of student athletes, tutoring opportunities, laundry service, and practice and competitive facilities.

Title IX does not require that men's programs be cut to accommodate women's programs. It is each school's choice whether to cut men's programs in an effort to comply with Title IX or to add women's programs. Due to the decreasing amount of money available to an increasing number of schools, cutting men's sports programs is often viewed as the best fiscal decision. It is also important to note that the law protects men as well as women; consequently, men may charge an institution with violating Title IX.

REACTIONS TO TITLE IX

The implications of Title IX were clear to all those involved in sports. Many males felt threatened by the passage of Title IX. As Francis (2001) explains, "Despite the phase-in, Title IX was met with resistance from coaches of men's teams, from university athletics directors, and from the National Collegiate Athletic Association.... The NCAA lobbied Congress to exempt athletics from Title IX, and, when this effort failed, brought suit challenging the regulations issues by the Department of Health, Education, and Welfare (HEW) to implement Title IX" (p. 252). The NCAA merely postponed the inevitable enforcement of Title IX. University athletic directors worried that equal funding for women's sports teams would financially cripple the men's programs, especially the revenue producing football and basketball programs, but started the phase-in of women's sports by the end of the decade. By the late 1970s, the typical pattern was for a university to offer roughly equal numbers of men's and women's teams in nonrevenue sports, men's and women's basketball teams, and a football team.

In 1982, the AIAW was swallowed by the NCAA. The NCAA started offering national championship games in women's sports— a symbolic victory of equality. National championship games had previously been reserved for men's sports. Since 1988 and the clarification on the program-specific interpretation of Title IX, numerous lawsuits have been brought against university athletics programs, by both male and female athletes. Most of these lawsuits were initiated by athletes who sought to block their schools from dropping specific sport programs. "Female members of varsity teams objected to cutbacks that eliminated the teams in equal numbers for both sexes. Male members protested cutbacks that were imposed unilaterally on men's teams. In several cases, women members of club teams sought to compel their university to upgrade their teams to varsity status, a step that the university was unwilling to take for financial reasons" (Francis, 2001: 253).

During the Bill Clinton presidential administration, Title IX took on a new momentum as the Office of Civil Rights laid down a new set of compliance guidelines (Rader, 2004). Among the new rules was a stricter interpretation of proportionality — that the total number of varsity male and female athletes be in proportion to the general student body. Since women outnumber men in college (overall), women would now be required to receive a greater number of total scholarships than men. Colleges with football programs were in real potential trouble, as the football team was once allowed to offer 85 scholarships. This number would have to be reduced, but even then, other men's programs were in jeopardy if football continued. When football is taken out of the equation, women receive more athletic scholarships than men. Critics argued that women may not have the same interest level in participating in sport and therefore questioned the legitimacy of proportionality as the criteria for athletic funding. Defenders of proportionality argue that if given a chance, women may wish to participate in sports as much as men presently do.

During the 1980s and 1990s at least 170 men's college wrestling programs were eliminated (Rader, 2004). A large number of men's swimming and diving, tennis and gymnastics teams have also been eliminated during this period. Men's programs continue to be eliminated in the 2000s. Roughly 400 men's college sports teams were dropped in the first 30 years since Title IX was passed (Brady, 2002).

TITLE IX IS UNFAIR TO MEN'S SPORTS

Large numbers of men's college sports programs have been cut in the past three decades. Title IX compliance is usually cited as the reason for all these cuts to men's programs. Critics of Title IX believe this is unfair to men. In 2005, for example, the Supreme Court rejected the National Wrestling Coaches Association's (NWCA) claim that Title IX was a form of discrimination against male athletes because of the large number of cuts in wrestling programs across the United States. The High Court argued that the NWCA failed to show that the law was directly responsible for the reduction in men's sports. The unfair treatment of athletes is not limited to the college ranks. Indeed, the Department of Education's Office for Civil Rights reports that only 25 percent of complaints involve colleges (Brady, 2002).

Proportionality requirements are deemed as unfair to male athletes by critics of Title IX. Elizabeth Arens (1999) believes that "more men than women are interested in taking part in college sports and that universities fail to take this into account when applying Title IX" (p. 127). Arens argues that *interest* in sport is more important than enrollment numbers of males and females. Arens argues that men's sports teams have been victims of misguided egalitarianism. "Thanks to pressure from the Clinton administration and the federal courts, schools are destroying men's athletics programs across the country. They are capping the sizes of teams, terminating long-standing programs, and driving thousands of male students off the playing fields. And they are doing so without regard to the level of interest in sports demonstrated by female students or to the resources of the schools they attend" (Arens, 1999: 128). The Commission on Opportunity in Athletics recommends that schools use surveys to determine the level of interest men and women on campus have in varsity athletics. Those findings would then be used to determine compliance (Fletcher and Sandoval, 2003).

Critics of Title IX argue that this legislation is unfair to male athletes and therefore it should be drastically altered. As Welch Suggs (2005) points out:

> The essence of the debate over Title IX comes down to the fact that Americans have not decided what "fair" means when it comes to opening up opportunities to people previously excluded. Conservatives hold that fairness has nothing to do with numbers of people involved in a certain activity, and that if colleges (or any other organization) try to fix the proportion of female participants to match the proportion of the overall female population, they are imposing a quota system.... The larger point, though, is Title IX does not require schools and colleges to make everything fair for everybody. Instead, it requires schools and colleges not to discriminate on the basis of sex. Because they schools and colleges have chosen to offer sports opportunities, and to do so in a way that male and female students are separated, then they need to find a way to prove that they are offering equitable opportunities. And nobody has come up with a better means of allowing colleges to define "equitable" for themselves than the three-part test [pp. 190–191].

TITLE IX IS FAIR AND NECESSARY

Proponents of Title IX argue that the legislation is still necessary and not unfair to men. They remind critics that proportionality is just one way for a school to prove it is complying with Title IX (Labinger, 1999). Athletic financial assistance (scholarships) and "Other" athletic program areas are the other two ways for schools to comply with Title IX. Furthermore, proponents of Title IX point out that individual schools could add women's programs instead of dropping men's programs; thus, revealing that the problem of decreasing numbers of men's sports programs is not the result of Title IX but instead each school.

In addition, proponents of Title IX point out that while the legislation is working, it has not accomplished its goal — equity. Labinger (1999) explains, "While women athletes on college campuses haven't yet achieved equity with their male counterparts, they've come a long way since Title IX's enactment. Title IX is working. It shouldn't be weakened because some universities would rather make excuses than give women their fair share" (p. 139). Porto (2003) concurs and adds that relatively few colleges are actually in compliance with Title IX, thus showing the need to continue it. Currently, approximately 42 percent of student athletes in college are female. In high school, the compliance gap is much smaller. According to the National Federal of High Schools (2003–04), girls comprise 42 percent of all athletes and while comprising 47 percent of the high school population (*Women's Sports Foundation*, 2005).

As for the claims that girls and women are not as interested in sports as males, proponents of Title IX point out that there has been an 847 percent increase in girls' participation in high school varsity sports since the passage of Title IX (Harrison and Lynch, 2005). It has been a relatively short period of time since girls and women were encouraged to play sports. It seems very plausible that their interest in sport will continue to grow throughout the 2000s.

Clearly, the debate over Title IX will continue for years to come.

SUMMARY

Young boys and girls are traditionally raised differently, and this can have an effect upon whether or not they play sports. Gender stereotypes are learned in early childhood. Role expectations in sports often begin at this stage. The perceived differences between the two sexes can help one understand the historically low participation of women in sports. Changes in cultural attitudes toward women have led to dramatic increases in the number of girls and women playing sports today.

The patriarchal design of most nations throughout history has supported a system of gender stratification that left most women in subservient roles. While the average male has always been physically stronger and faster than the average female, this perceived "weakness" has been used to further reinforce patriarchal societies. Sports, which require and emphasize physical strength and size, came to be viewed as more "natural" for males than for females.

The fact that men are bigger, on average, than women has no bearing on whether or not females can play sports. Anatomy is not athletic destiny. Cultural attitudes about the inappropriateness of women playing sports prevailed up until the twentieth century. Myths designed to keep women from playing sports were not limited to the physicality of the female body, but also extended into the psychological realm. These myths still linger in Western societies.

The single most momentous event to affect women's participation in sport occurred with the passage of Title IX of the Educational Amendments Act of 1972. Both the Civil Rights Movement of the 1950s and 1960s and the Feminist Movement of the early 1970s played a large role in encouraging equal opportunity for all, and an end to discriminatory practices throughout the United States.

There are still a number of obstacles interfering with the continued growth of women's sports participation, including budgetary cutbacks, lack of women in power positions, and male resistance. While women have come a long way since the early 1970s, one myth lingers — that sports masculinizes females. As a result, most female athletes want to be viewed as both athletic and feminine. "Aesthetic fitness" — highlighting of femininity and beauty — is another pressure many female athletes face. As a result, a number of them suffer from eating disorders and other physical ailments brought about by trying to attain unrealistic physical ideals.

Sexism, both ideological and institutional, presents a challenge to female equality in sports, as does sexual harassment. In some instances, sexual harassment occurs between coaches and athletes. In order for gender equality in sport to become a reality, two key things must occur. First, men will have to change their perception of sport as a male domain, and second, more females will have to hold positions of power (including coaching and administrative roles).

Homophobia is another issue which complicates the topic of women in sport. It is a commonly held belief that many women in sport, particularly basketball, are lesbians, and while society in general seems more accepting of this, there are still many individuals in power positions who are not.

Another controversy in the area of women and sports is whether cheerleading constitutes a proper sport. The cheerleader is a nationally recognized symbol of sportsmanship. While originally a male role, most cheerleaders today are female. There is much debate over whether they are positive role models or rather perpetuate sexist stereotypes. There is a growing acceptance for cheerleading as a sport.

Overall, women have made tremendous strides toward gender equity in sports over the past few decades, and interest in women's sports continues to grow.

KEY TERMS

Amenorrhea The complete loss of menstruation. It can be termed as three or fewer menstrual cycles in a year or no cycle for six consecutive months.

Anorexia An eating disorder characterized by a purposeful weight loss far beyond the normal range.

Bulimia An eating disorder characterized by repetitive cycles of dieting, then overeating — binging — followed by behaviors that get rid of, or purge, the food eaten.

Cheerleader A person who leads, calls for, and directs organized cheering at sporting events from the sidelines of the field or court.

Competitive Cheer Squads Groups which compete against other cheer squads in front of judges rather than cheering for a sports team.

Gender This refers to socially determined expectations placed on individuals because of their sexual category. Males are expected to act masculine, while females are expected to act feminine.

Gender Roles A social by-product of cultural expectations. Gender role expectations extend to all realms of the social life, including mannerisms, behaviors, attitudes, styles of dress, and activities, including sports, that are deemed appropriate for men and women.

Homophobia Fear and dislike of homosexuals, often leading to persecution and discrimination against them.

Ideological Sexism The belief that one sex is inferior to another; it stresses gender-appropriateness based on gender roles.

Institutional Sexism Systematic practices and patterns within social institutions that lead to inequality between men and women.

Osteoporosis A condition of decreased bone mass that can lead to bone fractures.

Patriarchy A male-dominated society or ideology.

Proportionality In Title IX, the total number of varsity male and female athletes must be equal to the general student body.

Sex This refers to one's biological classification. Males and females differ biologically in regards to their internal and external reproductive organs and genitalia, types and levels of hormones and chromosomal structure (females have an XX and males an XY design).

Sexism Behavior that discriminates against a member(s) of one sex due to preferential treatment aimed to assist a member(s) of the other sex.

Sexual Harassment Deliberate or repeated unsolicited verbal comments, gestures, or physical contact of a sexual nature that are unwelcome by the recipient and create an intimidating or hostile work environment.

DISCUSSION QUESTIONS

• Should little boys and girls play with different toys? Do you think that boys playing with toy soldiers and girls playing with dolls perpetuates stereotypes and has a harmful effect upon them? Why or why not?

• What is the difference between "sex" and "gender"? Why might this be significant in the discussion of women in sports?

• What is "gender stratification" and how does it relate to a patriarchal political system?

• What are some of the myths associated with female participation in sports? How did these myths arise, and how might one argue against them?

• What are some of the reasons the issue of female equity in sports became a major issue in the 1970s? How did Title IX try to address this issue, and what are the pros and cons that have arisen in trying to implement this policy in the past 40 years?

• Do you agree or disagree with the claim that women tend to "burn out" faster than men in high pressure jobs such as coaching and administrative positions?

• What is "aesthetic fitness" and why is it an issue in female sports?

• Do you think that cheerleading is a legitimate sport? Why or why not?

CHAPTER 11

Race and Ethnicity in Sport

Throughout its history, the image of a winning NFL quarterback (QB) was that of a man who bravely stood in the "pocket" while he "read" opposing defensive schemes before passing a winning touchdown. It was reasoned that it took a certain measure of intelligence in order to accomplish such a feat. It was assumed that such a person would have to be white. As a result, NFL owners only drafted white players as quarterbacks. Head coaches supported this reasoning because they believed that the QB position was a "thinking" position and therefore necessitated that someone white serve as the field general. So ingrained was this ideology that blacks were seldom allowed to be quarterbacks in college. What was the point? They would not be allowed to play QB in the NFL, so why should they play this position in college? Because of their physical skills they would be better off in "reaction" positions (e.g., defensive back and wide receiver).

Eventually, a number of black players broke the color barrier and were allowed to be quarterbacks. However, prejudices still existed, as these black quarterbacks generally possessed great running skills and they were expected to win with their legs more than with their ability to read defenses. This led to a new stereotype of black quarterbacks as *just* a running QB. In other words, the black QB achieved because of physical skills and not mental (intelligence) skills.

Slowly, a number of black quarterbacks started getting drafted by the NFL, and yet, they were expected to change their positions (e.g., become a defensive back or wide receiver) and give up their leadership role as quarterback. By the 2000s, a limited number of African American quarterbacks were found in the NFL (e.g., Donovan McNabb and Michael Vick). And yet, they were expected (by coaches and team owners) to run the ball as well as throw it. Why? It was assumed that black quarterbacks were not quite up to the thinking level of their male counterparts who could stay in the pocket, read defenses, and win games (e.g., Tom Brady and Peyton Manning).

Racism in Sport

The idea that the quarterback position in football is a "thinking" position while playing defensive back is a "reaction" position serves as an example of a traditional, race-based belief that has contributed to stereotyping and discrimination in sport. Such beliefs are based on social construction (cultural determinations) rather than biological realities. Social constructionism has also led to the creation of the terms "race" and "ethnicity." From a social constructionist approach, and the one adopted by sociologists, race is defined as a group of people who share some socially recognized physical characteristic (such as skin color, facial features, or hereditary traits) that distinguishes them from other groups of people. Thus a racial group is biologically determined through cultural constructs and interpretations. The most common biological feature used to determine races of people is skin color — despite the reality that this is a very imprecise way of determining races. An ethnic group refers to a category of people who are recognized as a distinct based on such social or cultural factors such as nationality, religion, language, geographic residence, a common set of values, and so on.

When a person, such as a quarterback, is negatively evaluated solely on the basis of his race, he is the victim of racism. Racism refers to unequal treatment of a person or group of people based on race. Racism leads to prejudice and discrimination. Although the terms "prejudice" and "discrimination" are related, there are distinct differences. Prejudice involves negative beliefs about a person without having knowledge of that person; whereas discrimination refers to actual behavior that leads to unequal treatment. If we revisit the QB position in football, if a coach believes that an athlete is not smart enough to be a QB because he is black, the coach is guilty of prejudicial thinking. However, if the coach gives the athlete a chance to try out for the QB position he is not guilty of discrimination. On the other hand, if a coach has a policy wherein black athletes are not allowed to try out for quarterback, he is guilty of discrimination.

RACISM IN SPORTS IN THE PAST

The roots of racism and discrimination in sports may be as old as sports themselves. Social class discrimination was common during the American colonial era and England's amateur rule was adopted "in order to block, or at least to limit, lower-class participation in modern sports; but social class has not been as high a barrier here as it was in Europe. In the United States, prejudices about race and gender have done more than class biases to hinder full development of modern sports" (Guttmann, 1988: 119).

Following the end of the American Civil War in 1865, slavery was officially abolished by the 13th Amendment. Social institutions, businesses and industry had to examine their inclusionary role in accepting blacks into mainstream society. Most of these institutions failed miserably. Sport, as a social institution, generally reflects the prevalent sentiment of any era. For example, in horse racing, it had been common practice that blacks were jockeys for their masters' horses in colonial and antebellum times (Guttmann, 1988). Immediately following the Civil War most jockeys were still black. A black jockey, Oliver Lewis, rode the winning horse (Aristides) in the first Kentucky Derby in 1875. Further, all but one of the fifteen jockeys in the first Kentucky Derby was black. Isaac Murphy, a black jockey, won the derby in 1884, 1889 and 1891, and was considered one of the best jockeys of his era. However, spectators and fans of horse racing attributed a first-place finish to the speed of the horse rather than any skill on the part of the jockey, thus making it easier for white Americans to accept black jockeys (Guttmann, 1988). This form of racism would end when white jockeys began to dominate the sport, as jockeys were now viewed as skillful athletes. The black jockey, in fact, became a symbol of racism.

According to Shropshire (1996), the lawn jockey is a symbol of racism. Lawn jockeys are small statues, approximately three feet high, of black jockeys featured with oversized lips and flared nostrils, usually dressed in bright red coats and holding a ring or lantern. Lawn jockeys first appeared on the lawns of suburban U.S. homes decades ago. There are many legends about the origin of the lawn jockey. One version has George Washington's eight-year-old slave "Jocko" as the inspiration of the original lawn jockey. "According to the anecdote, the slave froze while holding the reins of George Washington's horse after the crossing of the Delaware River in 1776" (Shropshire, 1996: 20). Shropshire states, "Other legends point to a slave frozen as he held the horse of his master while the master and friends drank inside a tavern. A less common explanation is that the statues are a salute to the formerly dominant African American jockey in horse racing" (pp. 20–21). The racist connotations of the lawn jockey have led to their near complete disappearance, although some people have painted the figure white — assumingly to conceal the racist image (1996).

Baseball became one of the first American sports to take a strong exclusionary position on the role of blacks. In 1867, the National Association of Base-Ball Players (NABBP) ruled that blacks would not be allowed to play in their league. As the first established baseball league, their policy forbidding members from a specific race from participating in sport would set the tone as an accepted practice for future American sports leagues. The NABBP's discriminatory policy "reflected the racism and segregation that were becoming facts of life in the North after the Civil War" (Bowman and Zoss, 1989: 136). The NABBP would disband years later, but it set the standard for future baseball leagues.

In 1876, baseball's National League was established. The National League became the premier league in all of baseball. (In 1901, the American League became baseball's second major league, establishing the structure that continues today.) As early as 1879, the National League and other lower-level leagues agreed to respect each other's player contracts and avoid raiding the rosters of other teams. However, this pact did not forbid the lower leagues from signing black players. During the 1880s, it is estimated that at least 55 blacks participated in organized baseball (Bowman and Zoss, 1989). Just like blacks who first broke the color barrier in Major League Baseball decades later, these black players were subjected to a great deal of prejudice and discrimination. Spectators heckled any black player. White pitchers often intentionally threw at the heads of black players, white players tried to spike black players while sliding into base, and verbal taunts by white players against black players were common (Bowman and Zoss, 1989). In 1887, organized baseball established the "National Agreement" which, in effect, eliminated blacks from the elite leagues. Thus, baseball was guilty of institutional racism, as the Jim Crow mentality had crept into "America's pastime."

Negro baseball would arise in response to baseball's color line and the establishment of separation ("separate but equal") in society. "As in the rest of American life, a period of experimentation with interracial activities, initiated after the Civil War, had been replaced by a period of increasingly rigid racial segregation. It was apparent to prospective black ballplayers that if they wanted to play baseball they would have to form all-black teams that played in all-black leagues" (White, 1996: 128). The Negro leagues were not one solitary league in which all black baseball players played; rather, it is a collective term used to describe the various teams and leagues that existed from the early 1900s until the 1950s. Eventually, exhibitions between Negro League teams and Major League Baseball teams were played. These exhibitions drew huge crowds from both white and black America. "Triumphs over big-leaguers were savored, recalled, elaborated upon. If black players could not play in the major leagues, they could show that they belonged there" (Peterson, 1984: 5).

Although the Negro Leagues were never as popular as Major League Baseball, they provided many players an opportunity to play ball in a racist society. Jackie Robinson's integration into Major League Baseball would lead to the demise of the Negro Leagues, but it would also signal an end to segregation in baseball.

Perhaps the most well-known racist of the 20th century is Adolf Hitler, who proclaimed his German people (the Aryan race) as the superior people of the world. Hitler had hoped to use the 1936 Berlin Olympics as a showcase for the superiority of fascism. James Cleveland "Jesse" Owens, a black American, would shatter Hitler's delusionary vision. Owens faced prejudice daily. As a track and field star at Ohio State, Owens and his black friends were forced to live in off-campus housing (away from white athletes) and were not allowed in university restaurants. Despite being a victim of racism, Owens flourished on the track. During one meet in 1935, Owens broke three world records— in the 220-yard dash, the 220-yard low hurdles, and the long jump — he also tied the world record in the 100-yard dash (Entine, 2000). His selection to the American Olympic team was an obvious choice. But would he be accepted by Americans? After all, he was a victim of racism on his home campus. Because of nationalistic pride, most Americans adored Owens.

Owens was treated as hero by the vast majority of Americans. The myth of Hitler refusing to shake Owens's hand further added to his hero status (Guttmann, 1988). The sudden emergence of a black sports hero presented a dilemma for the churchgoing black community of his era. Black church leaders had "long made a point of downplaying athletic success, instead stressing schooling as a way to accelerate assimilation into white society and shake the image of black inferiority. That strategy had not opened many doors. Now sports offered a more promising path to acceptance" (Entine, 2000: 173–174). Many black social leaders began to view sport as one of the best means of blacks becoming accepted, or assimilated, into mainstream society.

Like Owens, the boxing great Joe Louis provided a blow to racist ideology. In 1935, Louis beat Italian Primo "Italian Ox" Carnera in New York City. "That sixth-round knockout was particularly sweet for the black community with Mussolini's troops poised to conquer Ethiopia, an independent nation and another source of pride for many American blacks.... The white press conferred status on the young heavyweight for the fight was portrayed as a battle between Italian fascism and American democracy" (Entine, 2000: 188). Although hailed by Americans as an American hero, Louis was also a victim of racism in the United States. "Despite his great talent, Louis at first had found it almost impossible to break through the race wall that had been reinforced in the years since Jack Johnson had been driven out of the sport" (Entine, 2000: 189).

Basketball was another sport in which blacks were segregated from whites. Basketball slowly grew in popularity in the United States during the first three decades of the twentieth century. "By the 1930s, basketball had replaced track and baseball as the second most popular sport on college campuses, but professional basketball struggled for places to play.... Black youth often played basketball at community centers because few black high schools and relatively few colleges could afford gymnasiums, and black youth who attended integrated schools were often not allowed to participate in school activities" (Caponi-Tabery, 2002: 41). For the most part, blacks and whites played basketball separately. When integration in education became a reality in the 1950s, not everyone eagerly accepted it. For example, on January 2, 1957, Iona College was scheduled to play Mississippi in a men's college basketball game at the All-American City Invitational in Owensboro, Kentucky. When Mississippi Governor J.P. Coleman learned that Iona had a black player on the team, he refused to allow Mississippi to play against them. The game is listed in the Iona record book as a 2–0 victory, the official score for a forfeit. There is no sign of the game in the Ole Miss record book (Fitzgerald, 2001). Stanley Hill, Iona's black player, was shocked when he heard the governor state, "We're not going to play any blacks—against any blacks or with any blacks" (Fitzgerald, 2001: B11). Hill was pleased when all the Mississippi players went to his hotel room to apologize (Fitzgerald, 2001).

Whites and blacks played the game of basketball differently. White players' approach was to dribble, fake and move past the man guarding you for a lay-up or, if your path was impeded, for a "set shot." Blacks, however, incorporated jumping with their moves (Caponi-Tabery, 2002). Thus, blacks introduced the jump shot to mainstream basketball. At one time, the racist term "Negro basketball" was applied to this style of basketball; it has since been replaced by such phrases as "street ball" and "hotdogging" (Caponi-Tabery, 2002). The "slam dunk" was also introduced into basketball by black players. It was considered such an unnatural part of the game that in 1967 the NCAA instituted the "Alcindor Rule" banning the slam dunk. Kareem Abdul-Jabbar (then Lew Alcindor), a center for UCLA, was so dominant that the NCAA forbade the use of the slam dunk because it gave players like Jabbar an unfair advantage and was considered hotdogging (Caponi-Tabery, 2002).

RACISM IN SPORTS IN THE PRESENT

In 1954, the Supreme Court (*Brown v. Board of Education of Topeka*) invalidated the *Plessy v. Ferguson* 1896 court decision that had created the "separate but equal" American policy. The significance of the *Brown* case cannot be overstated, for among blacks, as well as other minorities, it provided the spark of hope that had begun to build in the 1940s. The 1954 decision, among many things, guaranteed blacks the opportunity to attend public schools, including colleges. Coupled with the G.I Bill of Rights, it enabled large numbers of blacks to attend college in the 1950s. These same opportunities would open the doors for college athletic participation among blacks.

The transition from segregation to integration of some college sports teams between the late 1960s and the mid–1970s may best be shown by the University of Alabama. In 1968, Alabama had no blacks on athletic scholarships. By 1975, its basketball team had an all black starting lineup (Nixon, 1984). In 1966, the University of Texas at El Paso (UTEP), known then as Texas Western, with five black starters, shocked heavily favored (and all-white) Kentucky in the NCAA men's college basketball final, winning 72–65 (Menez, 2006). (In 2006, the film *Glory Road* was released and although the filmmakers took some dramatic license, the film is based on this historic meeting between Texas Western and Kentucky.) College coaches across the United States began to seek talented black athletes, assuming this was their ticket to success. As Lapchick (1991) states, UTEP's triumph over Kentucky is often hailed as a sign of a breakthrough against racism, but none of the five starters on the basketball team graduated from the university. According to Lapchick, if UTEP had a true commitment to ending racism, they would have worked with these athletes to ensure their graduation from college. Low graduation rates remain a concern of many college sport observers.

Even the casual observer has noticed that blacks dominate many American sports today (especially team sports with high earning potential). However, black domination in sport was then, and remains today, mostly limited to the role of participant. There are still few minority owners, general managers, managers, head coaches, and trainers. The primary reason minority members are underrepresented in power positions in sports is because of racism. "The most visible nonplaying personnel in sports are those who reside in the front office. These parties include chief executive officers, team presidents, general managers, and the head coach, who straddles the line between the field or court and the administrative offices. The front office also includes such professionals as team doctors, lawyers, and accountants" (Shropshire, 1996: 76). Little has changed in the years since Shropshire's observation.

In 2005, the white corporate structure of the NBA decided to implement a dress code that the black player-dominated league viewed as racist. The league announced that during team and league business, players must dress in "business casual" attire, which includes a ban on sleeveless shirts, shorts, sunglasses while indoors, and headphones. Players are also expected not to wear gaudy, shiny chains (bling). Further, while on the bench, players not in uniform are expected to wear sport jackets, dress shoes and socks. Although few players complained about the dress requirement while on the bench, most black players viewed the new policy as an example of racism. The players have embraced the hip-hop culture associated with professional, street-style basketball that dominates the current NBA. Jason Richardson of the Golden State Warriors, for example, argues that it is racist to ban players from wearing chains outside their clothing, adding that just because someone wears a suit, that does not exempt them from being a crook. Richardson stated, "A guy could come in with baggy jeans, a do-rag and have a Ph.D. and a person who comes in with a suit could be a three-time felon" (*AOL Sports News*, 2005A:1). Allen Iverson argued that the league should pay for players' clothing if management wants the workers to dress in certain attire. The NBA believes that the players can afford their own dress clothing.

In recent years, there have been some positive changes in the power structure of organized sports. For instance, in 2005 Arizona millionaire Arturo Moreno bought the Anaheim Angels and thus became the first Mexican-American to own a U.S. major league team. The National

Football League has made it a public policy to encourage all team owners to interview members of minority groups whenever there is an opening for head coach, partly in response to a 2002 report released by famed attorney Johnnie Cochran, Jr., entitled "Black Coaches in the National Football League: Superior Performances, Inferior Opportunities." And Robert Johnson, billionaire founder of the Black Entertainment Network, became the NBA's first black majority owner in 2005 when he was chosen as owner of the new Charlotte franchise, the Bobcats. Yet these triumphs are still a very small percentage in the overall control of major league sports franchises.

This brief review of racism in sport reveals that sport has often reflected racist beliefs held in society. However, sport has also often led the way in desegregation. In the following pages we will review a few of the most significant racial break-throughs in American sports.

The Role of Genetics

The idea that blacks are innately superior athletes and that whites are innately more intelligent reflect racial ideologies that lead to prejudice and discrimination in the sports world. Beliefs of racial superiority based on genetics can have deadly results. Hitler's idea of the superior Aryan nation led to a justification of an "inferior" Jewish "race" that needed to be exterminated. The American colonies justified slavery on the ideological belief that black people were not equal to whites which helped to "justify" the ownership of one race by another race. In 1971, Martin Kane wrote an article, "An Assessment of Black Is Best," for *Sports Illustrated* and suggested that blacks dominate sports because American slave owners weeded out the weak blacks on plantations and made sure that strong black men and black women mated (thinking this would lead to stronger and better working slaves). Jimmy "the Greek" Snyder, a former sports analyst for CBS, suggested in 1988 that blacks made good ball carriers in football because they were bred to have big, strong thighs when they lived as slaves. Kane and Snyder conveniently ignored the millions of blacks with skinny thighs and were ignorant of the historical fact that the control of white slave masters over the sexual behavior of black slaves was never extensive enough to shape the genetic traits of even a small portion of the U.S. African American population.

Biological notions of racial predispositions are troublesome at the very least and deadly in more extreme cases. There are many flaws to the theory of genetic predisposition to sports. Primarily, there is no "pure" gene pool that guarantees an individual is genetically programmed to be an athlete, or a teacher or biologist for that matter. Further, the idea that blacks are naturally more gifted athletes is discounted by the fact that most blacks — like most whites — are not athletes and do not participate in sports. Focusing on physical attributes while ignoring work habits and intellectual characteristics is also problematic. It takes training, practice, dedication and positive reinforcement, among other social traits, for an individual to become a great athlete. Still, there are those who believe in such outdated concepts as "natural" athletes and "born athletes."

In chapter 10 we described how naïve the medical profession was in regard to women's frailty in during the Victorian era. As recently as the mid–1950s the medical profession considered the 4-minute mile a physical impossibility. Doctors feared that the athlete's heart or lungs might explode due to the stress of such a feat. In 1954, Roger Bannister accomplished the impossible when he ran a 3:59.4 mile. Bannister attributed his triumph to medical training, careful observation and logical deduction (Entine, 2000). Bannister was a medical student who trained himself to become a world-class runner. He had finished fourth in the 1,500 meters at the 1952 Olympics. Bannister later became a medical doctor. Bannister never claimed to be the best runner of his era. He attributed his accomplishments to hard work and training. Why is it then that some people cling to ideas of natural born athletes? Is there an "athletic gene" that gives some individuals an edge over others based on biology? Since blacks are dominating most major commercial sports in North America, do they possess this athletic gene? Most sociologists quickly discount any such claims.

As we stated in Chapter 4, geography has a great deal to do with sporting opportunities. Nigerians tend to make excellent long distance runners. Do they have a "running gene"? Or do Nigerians excel in distance running because the nation is very poor and rural and offers few other sporting opportunities? Do skiers from Switzerland excel because they have a "skiing gene" which brings them "natural" ability? Or do Swiss skiers excel because they reside in the Alps where skiing is a big part of their culture? Canadians are hockey players. Is there a "hockey gene"; or simply plenty of opportunities for Canadians to skate on frozen rivers and lakes? World-class sprinters are typically black. Many of the best sprinters in the world are African Americans. Do they have superior running genes over white athletes? In 2004, American Jeremy Wariner won the 400 meters in the Greek Olympics. Nothing surprising about an American winning a sprint, but this American was white. He was the first white American man to win a sprint medial since Mike Larabee's 400 gold in 1964, but does that mean that other white athletes are not capable of winning sprints?

Earlier we described the exploits of Marv Marinovich, who attempted to "breed" the genetically perfect athlete. He irrationally believed that two genetically elite athletes who mate would have a son or daughter who would be an even more superior athlete than either individual parent. Since he was an elite athlete, Marinovich reasoned that he needed a genetically "superior" female athlete to mate with. Marv should have learned his lesson with his first son, Todd, who was an elite athlete, but possessed a personality that was not congruent with achieving mechanical athletic success. Todd's dreams, as it turned out, were not the same as his father's. Clearly, hopes and dreams of parents for their children are not passed on through genetics; they may however, be learned through observation. Marv mated with a different elite female athlete to produce another son, Mikhail. The results were again not what he had hoped for.

The authors do not discount that some individual athletes have physical advantages over others. Clearly someone with big hands will find it easier to grip and palm a basketball. Being tall also helps in basketball. Lance Armstrong's heart is 20 percent larger than the normal person's heart, giving him a great advantage in endurance sports such as bicycling. Armstrong does not have this advantage because he is a white person — he is a biological fluke. Andy Roddick has unusually flexible ribs and spine, enabling him to arch his back and rotate his arm much more efficiently than the average professional tennis player, which helps to explain why he can hit a 155 mph serve. Once again, all white people do not share this "advantage." Achieving athletic success involves many elements, but genes are not among them. Opportunity, desire, reinforcement, and trial and error provide the basis for learning, not genes. Working hard, practice, and sometimes luck (e.g., remaining injury free) are elements that help athletes win in sporting contests. Athletes are not born, they are made. Skin color is not a precursor to athletic superiority or intelligence.

Sport and Upward Mobility

In Chapter 12, we will explore the role of social class and economics in sports. For now, it is important to point out that society is divided into strata, or layers of stratification. Economics is the primary way that most people identify stratification in society. In short, some people are poor, some are wealthy, and the majority are somewhere in between. It is the goal of all wealthy people to maintain or increase their wealth (e.g., no matter how much money an athlete makes, he or she will want more). Poor people, of course, want to escape poverty and enjoy the same benefits and privileges as others. The middle class, who are better off than poor people, but not as well off as the wealthy, want to increase their socio-economic status (SES). Everyone wants to climb upward in society. They will pursue the avenues of least resistance or paths that provide the greatest opportunity to get ahead in life. People with education and "connections" generally choose professional careers where they can use their intellect in jobs that will reward them financially. People who perceive limited legitimate opportunities to advance in life may choose illegitimate means (e.g., criminal activities) or they may choose a profession that offers great financial rewards but requires great physical effort (e.g., sports). From this standpoint, people who are the most disadvantaged in society will pursue sport as an avenue of success. Revenue-generating sports, then, are the most appealing sports to people who come from lower SES backgrounds.

Do Sports Provide Opportunities for Upward Mobility?

Is upward mobility via sport a myth or fact? Some people believe that sports are a powerful resource for minority athletes that provide an effective vehicle for upward social mobility. Others argue that the purported mobility benefits gleaned from athletic participation is entirely illusory (Melnick and Sabo, 1994). In short, sport can provide upward mobility for athletes, but those numbers are limited as there are only so many money-making positions available in professional sports. Nonetheless, sport can provide upward mobility in other ways as well. Thus, sport can provide direct and indirect upward mobility. Direct upward mobility is accomplished when an athlete signs a lucrative professional contract (and endorsement contracts). Indirect upward mobility occurs when an athlete earns a college degree and finds gainful employment because of his or her educational credentials. Taking advantage of the educational opportunity presented because of sports is the athlete's best hope of getting ahead

Major Racial Break-throughs in American Sports

Historically, whites have dominated every aspect of sports (in the U.S., Canada, and Europe), including participation, ownership, and coaching. Following World War II, blacks began to break the color barrier. Kenny Washington and Woody Strode (Los Angeles Rams) became the first blacks to play in the National Football League (NFL) in 1945 and Marion Motley of the Cleveland Browns became the first black in the All-American Football conference. Jackie Robinson broke baseball's color barrier in 1947 when he played for the Brooklyn Dodgers of MLB. In 1949, the American Bowling Congress (ABC) allowed blacks to join their association. Three black players, Chuck Cooper, Earl Lloyd and Nat "Sweetwater" Clifton, broke the NBA's color barrier in 1950 (Vogler and Schwartz, 1993). Willie O'Ree (Boston Bruins) became the first black player in the NHL in 1957. Since the 1970s, blacks have come to dominate the major team sports (as participants) of the United States. The inclusion of other racial and ethnic groups (e.g., Hispanic/Latino, Asian, and Native American) has come at a slower rate.

In the following pages, a few select major racial breakthroughs will be discussed.

White Ethnic Group Breakthroughs

There are times when racist attitudes are directed at white people, even in a society dominated by a white majority. In early American history, the Anglo-Saxon cultural ideal was designed to discriminate against all those who were not English or German. Every ethnic group that migrated to the U.S. fell victim to this form of prejudice and discrimination. Realizing that assimilation was the key to socio-economic success in the United States, some immigrants changed their last names in an attempt to fit in to the greater society and realize the "American Dream." The Irish and Italians were among the major ethnic groups to benefit as a result of their American sport participation.

In Ireland, the political and socio-economic status of the Irish Catholic was similar to that of blacks in the United States. The Irish experienced poverty, degradation, and oppression at the hands of the English. The hatred that the Irish had toward the English would carry over as part of their "cultural baggage" in the New World. In the United States, the Irish were still discriminated against — because of the Anglo-Saxon cultural dominance. In many cities, prominent signs announced "No Irish Need Apply" on many business windows and doors. The Irish were certainly not Anglo— they were Gaelic or Celtic — and they felt insulted when referred to as Anglo. The largest number of Irish came to the United States during the 1840s because of the Irish potato famine.

The Irish were a poor people, and the Irish immigrants who moved to the United States and settled (originally) primarily in New York City lived in filthy ghettos of New York's Five Points district. Charles Dickens visited the Five Points after a famous 1857 riot and declared the area much worse than the slums of London, which he made famous in *Oliver Twist*. In total, it is estimated that nearly 1.7 million Irish immigrants settled in the U.S. between the years 1841 and 1860 (Wilcox, 1994). In fact, by the late 1850s, the Irish comprised one-fourth the total population and one-third of the registered voters in New York City. Today, Irish-Americans are second only to German Americans in the number of U.S. residents who claim ancestry (Marger, 2006).

Some of the Irish success in assimilation can be attributed to sports, especially boxing. "More has been written on Irish success in the American prize ring than about any other ethnic group in sport" (Wilcox, 1994: 57). Boxing has long found appeal among the oppressed minorities. Boxing represents a rapid escape from poverty, prejudice and discrimination. Historically, the racial or ethnic group that dominates boxing is an oppressed group in that society. The Irish dominated boxing throughout the second half of the 19th century. Among the more prominent Irish-American boxers prior to the Civil War were Sam O'Rourke, Cornelius Horrigan, John C. "Benecia Boy" Heenan, James "Yankee" Sullivan, and John Morrissey. Sullivan demonstrated the "Irish way"— embrace American culture quickly and assimilation will follow all the more promptly. The "Irish way" was embraced by other European immigrant groups who had the racial advantage of being white in a white-dominated society. In the post–Civil War era, other Irish boxers also dominated. Among the more prominent fighters were Paddy Ryan, Jake Kilrain, John L. Sullivan, and "Gentleman Jim" Corbett. "World Champion from 1882 to 1892, Sullivan has been credited with anywhere between 75 and 200 victories in the ring. 'John L.' became the first modern sporting superstar" (Wilcox, 1994: 58).

The Irish also participated in other sports throughout the mid– to late–1800s. Among these sports were pedestrianism (later named track and field), a sport that offered poor Irish immigrants an opportunity to win prize money. In 1878, for example, American-Irishman Daniel O'Leary won the Astley Belt and $3,750 in prize and gate receipts before 30,000 spectators in London. Later in 1878, O'Leary beat fellow Irish-American John Hughes in New York City for prize money. O'Leary later established his own games, the O'Leary Belt Race for the Championship of America, with the first race taking place in Madison Square Garden in 1879 (Wilcox, 1994).

Rowing was a third sport that afforded poor Irishmen a chance to earn fame and fortunate. The Irish formed many rowing clubs in such cities as Buffalo, New York, and Boston, Massachusetts. Challenges between various sporting clubs regularly drew more than 30,000 spectators. Side bets among spectators were as common in rowing as they were in pedestrianism. Cricket clubs were also common and the Irish were among the best in the United States. The Irish also dominated early American baseball. "The Irish realized perhaps greater immediate success in baseball than any other immigrant group. By the turn of the century seemingly all the prominent clubs were captained by Irish Americans including Kelly (Brooklyn), Delehanty (Philadelphia),

Collins (Boston), Donovan (St. Louis), Doyle (Chicago), Gleason (Detroit), McGraw (Baltimore), and Duffy (Milwaukee)" (Wilcox, 1994: 61).

As the Irish became assimilated into society, they moved out of the ghettos and were replaced by the next large group of poor immigrants. Before 1890, most European immigrants who came to the U.S. were from northern and western European nations such as England, Germany, France and Ireland. By the mid–1880s, most immigrants were now coming from southern and eastern Europe; especially Italy, Austria-Hungary, and Russia. Because this wave of immigration was so distinct from previous, these immigrants became known as the "new immigrants" (Marger, 2006). Once again, questions of character and culture led to negative labels being attached to these new immigrants. The largest of these ethnic groups to immigrate to the U.S. were the Italians. The largest number of Italians came to the U.S. after the "Panic of 1873" (socio-economic unrest in Italy). Italian Americans were victims of Depression-induced violence in the U.S. during the 1880s and 1890s. Most Italian Americans lived in ethnic communities in the large Northeast cities—"Little Italy." These ethnic communities were consistent with previous (and present) ghetto living: over-crowding, environmental hazards, desperation and depression, crime and a sense of hopelessness.

Italian immigrants were against the idea of sports and recreation in schools. They were concerned especially about the Progressive Muscular Christianity movement which argued that it was healthy and advantageous to play sports. "Italian fathers, however, believed that play was a waste of time; children should get a job and contribute to the welfare of the family.... Among other reasons, they felt that play could cause injury, hence loss of income and burden to the family" (Bazzano, 1994: 109). As this quote reveals, many Italians came to the United States without any sporting traditions and reasoned that hard work alone would provide the path to self-sufficiency. However, many immigrants, facing prejudice and discrimination, decided to give sports a try.

At the turn of the 20th century, bicycle racing had become a popular sport. Bicycle racing "had supplanted pedestrian long distance running because its greater speed could create more excitement for the spectators. It was a well-organized sport. The Amateur League of American Wheelmen came to life in 1880. There were races for amateurs and professionals, and for a brief period — the late nineteenth and early twentieth centuries— it was the biggest sport craze" (Bazzano, 1994: 107). Bicycle riding was popular with Italian immigrants. In fact, one of the oldest Italian sports clubs, the Unione Sportiva Italiana, had a large number of bicycle racing devotees (Bazzano, 1994). The races drew large enthusiastic crowds and made heroes out of victors. For poor immigrants the draw to such a status was understandable.

Italians American immigrants also participated in Greco-Roman wrestling and bocce. Bocce ball was, perhaps, the most popular sport among Italian immigrants. "It was very popular because it required mild exertion and was appropriate for people whose work was physically demanding. As late as 1967, there was an active bocce league in Tontitown and in Chicago where five clubs enjoyed active participation in the sport and maintained fine facilities" (Bazzano, 1994). Following the lead of the Irish, many Italians took to boxing in an attempt to get ahead and get out of the ghetto. Some early Italian boxers fought under Irish names to avoid discrimination (Bazzano, 1994). Italians also played baseball. Indeed, one of the most beloved figures of Italian-Americans is Joe DiMaggio, the son of Italian immigrants. DiMaggio excelled for the New York Yankees from 1936 to 1951. His career statistics were compromised, as he served a tour of duty with the U.S. Army (1943–44) during World War II. Italian soccer clubs were also popular during the early 1900s. "In 1929 the Italian Soccer Club was organized in Chicago. This team, according to the organizers, was the first step in uniting the Italian soccer players into a club of their own. Previously, many Italian players had been playing for teams of other ethnic groups" (Bazzano, 1994: 112). Like the Irish, the Italians would become fully assimilated into mainstream society and sport pursuits, as a group, would become a secondary concern.

JACKIE ROBINSON BREAKS BASEBALL'S COLOR BARRIER

Throughout this chapter we have discussed many examples of black athletes (e.g., Jesse Owens and Joe Louis) who faced prejudice and discrimination and managed to overcome racism and went on to become sports stars. Perhaps the single most significant breakthrough in sports was Jackie Robinson's breaking Major League Baseball's color barrier.

Although we have shown that some blacks played Major League Baseball (MLB), the league had discriminated against blacks throughout most of its history. This changed in 1947 when Jackie Robinson played for the Brooklyn Dodgers. So significant is this event that MLB officially retired Robinson's jersey number "42" from all MLB teams on April 15, 1997 — the 50th anniversary of Robinson's breaking the color barrier in modern baseball.

In order to break the color barrier, a talented black player was going to need the help and cooperation of a powerful white executive. Branch Rickey, baseball executive of the Brooklyn Dodgers, served this role. There were numerous reasons why Rickey wanted to integrate baseball. For one, Rickey "had long felt that the ban on black players was morally wrong, but it was not until the war began to revolutionize the role of blacks in America that he felt that the integration of the majors would be accepted by the players and the fans" (Oakley, 1994: 25). Rickey also realized the practical benefits of integrating baseball. A truly talented black player could help the Dodgers win more games and Rickey reasoned that African American fans would come to Dodgers games to cheer on one of their own (Oakley, 1994). "He knew that black Americans, who had a share of the post–World War II economic boom, were a largely untapped market for organized baseball and the integrating of the game was the best way to get more blacks through the turnstiles" (Moffi and Kronstadt, 1994: 8). Rickey was able to conceal his true intent to integrate baseball by claiming he was scouting the Negro leagues to field an all-black team that would play at Ebbets Field while the Dodgers were on the road. At the end of the summer of 1945, Rickey found his man: a shortstop for the Kansas City Monarchs.

On October 23, 1945, Rickey made history by signing Robinson to a contract to play for the Montreal Royals, the Dodgers' minor league affiliate, for the 1946 season. He played the entire year at Montreal in 1946. During the spring of 1947, the Dodgers announced that they had purchased the contract of Robinson from Montreal and called him up to the parent Dodgers club in Brooklyn. As Rickey had foreshadowed, Robinson's integration into MLB was difficult. Robinson was the victim of numerous racist taunts by both players and fans. Robinson was a great player and quickly won over his Dodgers teammates who, for the most part, eagerly defended him from others. Pee Wee Reese, the Dodgers team captain, once put his arm around Robinson in an early game during the 1947 season to demonstrate to all that Robinson was accepted as player and teammate. Robinson was only human and he admits in his *Autobiography* that there times when the abuse tested his patience. The Philadelphia Phillies, led by manager Ben Chapman, were by far the most insulting and venomous. Robinson states that Chapman's and the Phillies' constant abuse was so awful that he almost went over the Phillies dugout to grab "one of those white sons of bitches and smash his teeth in with my despised black fist" (Robinson, 1995: 60). But then Robinson remembered all that Rickey had warned him about and he regained his composure. The entire Dodgers team and organization were often the recipients of abuse because of Robinson's participation in baseball.

As any casual fan of sport knows, Robinson went on to have a very successful career. His integration into baseball and his ability to control himself despite constant racial taunts opened the door for other black athletes in baseball and other American professional sports as well. Robinson represented an entire race of people during a time when prejudicial attitudes and discriminatory actions were widespread throughout a segregated American society. Although Robinson's integration into baseball may seem insignificant to those outside sport, his ability to perform at peak levels under extreme forms of duress served as an inspiration to an entire race of people and those who admire personal accomplishments against great odds, and those who simply believe in equality. April 15 has been named "Jackie Robinson Day" by MLB, and Robinson will always be remembered as a great player and pioneer of racial equity. Today, blacks dominate many team sports in the United States. Jackie Robinson represents one of the true pioneers toward this reality.

It is important to note that African Americans do not dominate participation in baseball. A recent study revealed that only 8.4 percent of the 2006 Major League Baseball players were black, the fewest since the mid–1980s (Michael, 2007). There are a few reasons for this. One, many young African Americans are no longer interested in playing baseball (they would rather play basketball or football). Second, there is a concerted effort by MLB to sign established Asian professional baseball players. And third, there are large numbers Hispanics and especially Latinos who are playing baseball.

Hispanic/Latino Breakthroughs in American Sports

The Hispanic/Latino experience in American sports is quite different from that of whites and blacks. African Americans had long been the largest minority group, and as a result far more attention has been placed on the black experience in sports. Hispanics now make up the largest minority group in the U.S. and their numbers are rapidly growing. Consequently, far more attention will have to be given to the role of Hispanics in sports in the coming years.

A number of Latinos had played in the Negro leagues, so Robinson's breaking MLB's color barrier served as a sign to Hispanic/Latino players as well as black athletes that opportunities existed in the United States professional sports leagues.

> When Jackie Robinson broke the color barrier in 1947 it sent "shock waves throughout the Caribbean baseball." Black and mulatto ballplayers from the Dominican Republic, Cuba, Puerto Rico, Venezuela, and Mexico could now consider major-league careers. During 1947, only Cuban-born catcher Fermin Guerra and Mexican pitcher Jesse Flores, both with the Philadelphia Athletics, were in the major leagues. Between 1950 and 1955, however, forty-two Latinos played in the majors. Historian Sam Regalado points out that given the fact that only fifty-four Latinos made the big leagues in more than fifty years prior to 1950, this was a considerable increase [Lomax, 2004: 75–76].

Latino players did not begin to enter the professional leagues in American sports in any significant numbers until the 1950s. Unlike blacks, many Latino players faced discrimination because of language barriers. The inability of Latino and Hispanics to speak English infuriated many Americans. Many Latinos, such as Roberto Clemente, were unprepared for America's obsession with racial categorization. Puerto Rico, Clemente's home country, does not use racial categories when dealing with others. Clemente stated, "I don't believe in color; I believe in people" (Lomax, 2004: 77). Latinos considered the Jim Crow practices of American society irrational. The resulting segregatory practices naturally upset Latinos. Because of hotel segregation, especially during barnstorming exhibitions in the southern states, there were times when the white players received police escorts through town so that their chartered buses could make it to the airport and ball fields on time. Blacks and Latinos had to take separate buses and fend through traffic on their own — sometimes missing flights to the next city (Lomax, 2004). A number of professional teams that played Latino ballplayers hired assistants to help Latinos deal with American culture. Still, black and Latino players did not feel that they should have to adapt to racist policies; rather, racist policies should be changed.

Roberto Clemente

One of most significant early Hispanic athletes to play American sports was Roberto Clemente. Clemente was an awesome player who excelled both defensively as an outfielder and offensively with a career batting average of .317. He was the eleventh player to reach the career 3,000 hit club. Clemente played in an era before cable television and during a "dead" period in baseball (low scoring, which translates to lower interest on the part of fans). Those who saw Clemente play will remember his uncanny ability to flag down fly balls in the outfield and his ability to stretch a single into a double with his speed and reckless abandon on the base paths.

Clemente always played with class and dignity and was proud of his Puerto Rican heritage. His off-seasons were spent providing endless public service and making personal appearances across his native island. Clemente felt a closeness with all Latinos. "Thus when a devastating earthquake shattered the countryside of neighboring Nicaragua on December 23, 1972, it was predictably Roberto Clemente who sprang into immediate action, hoping to exploit his status as a national sports hero as a focal point for marshaling the necessary relief effort" (Bjarkman, 1996: 79). Clemente decided to board a DC-7 plane in San Juan that was loaded with supplies for Nicaragua, even though the plane had a history of mechanical problems. The plane finally took off for Nicaragua, but it never made it. Moments after it departed, the crew attempted to circle back and make an emergency landing. The plane plunged into the sea, killing Clemente and the three crew members. Clemente, a 12-time All Star for the Pittsburgh Pirates, died at age 38.

Because of his humanitarian aid and his brilliant baseball ability, Roberto Clemente remains as a cultural hero to many youth today. On December 31, 2005, Clemente's son re-enacted his father's last trip by flying to Nicaragua to distribute humanitarian aid. It marked the 33rd anniversary of Clemente's untimely death.

Nancy Lopez

Nancy Lopez represents an early modern Latino athlete to achieve greatness in her sport. Lopez is a member of the Ladies Professional Golf Association (LPGA) tour. She first started playing golf at age 8 and by age 12 she won the New Mexico Women's Invitational (Chavira, 1977). Lopez joined the LPGA in 1978. "Lopez won nine tournaments, including an unprecedented five in a row, was named Rookie of the Year, Rolex Player of the Year (also won in 1979, 1985, and 1988), Vare Trophy Winner (also won in 1979 and 1985), Golfer of the Year, and Female Athlete of the Year (Jamieson, 1998: 343).

Lopez's arrival to the LPGA was very important, as the circuit was experiencing popularity problems at the time. Her Latina status seemed to be especially important for professional golf. "Similar to the rhetoric about Tiger Woods, Lopez's presence supposedly marked an opening up of golf to the masses, especially to 'young people' and other unlikely golf fans.... Both Lopez's and Woods' stories stand out as symbols of persistent, yet shifting inequalities in the lives of all women and men, but especially women and men of color" (Jamieson, 1998: 344). Lopez's triumphs on the playing field were hailed as a victory for Latina inclusion in a formerly all-white reserve. Lopez made the move to "mainstream" without "rage" or "controversy" and "may be read as discontent with radical and separatist tactics used by both the Chicano movement of the 1960s and of the 1970s (Jamieson, 1998: 351). Thus, any controversy was limited to those from her own racial group that felt, perhaps, she was not a "radical" spokesperson for political causes. Woods and Michael Jordan faced the same "controversy."

Decades later, Lopez's dramatic debut to golf, has not, in fact, led to a great influx of Hispanic/Latino participation or spectator interest. Still, the achievements of Lopez stand above nearly all other female golfers and she remains a giant in women's golf. She continues to be a prominent spokesperson for the game and has developed a brand of sporting equipment specifically for women golfers. In 2000 she was recognized as one of the LPGA's top 50 players and teachers.

There is another racial group that has faced racism, prejudice and discrimination in sport: Native Americans. Native Americans have not participated in sports in great numbers; yet, Indian imagery is commonly used in all levels of sports (from the pee wee leagues to the professional). Much of the Indian imagery used in sport has racist connotations and utilizes negative stereotypes of Native Americans.

The Use of Native American Nicknames, Logos, and Mascots

Sports teams routinely use nicknames, logos and mascots as a means of conveying a team identity. These nicknames, logos, and mascots possess symbolic meaning, usually meant to intimidate opponents because of their fierceness. For example, the NFL's Chicago franchise has "Bears" as a nickname and clearly, a bear is an intimidating figure. Although there are no wild bears running the streets of Chicago, it is one example of sports teams choosing symbolic representations that have a direct connection to the community they call home. In some cases, the relationship between the team and the community is obvious: Major League Baseball's Colorado "Rockies" (located in the Rocky Mountains); the Minnesota Twins (for the Minnesota "twin" cities of Minneapolis and St. Paul); Milwaukee "Brewers" (Milwaukee is known for its beer breweries); and the NBA's Philadelphia "76ers" (as in the spirit of 1776). Other times the relationship is not so obvious, generally when franchise relocation is involved; for example, the Utah "Jazz" made sense when the franchise was still in New Orleans, the Los Angeles "Lakers" when they were still in the "Land of 10,000 Lakes" (Minnesota), and the Los Angeles Dodgers when Brooklyn fans actually had to dodge the cable trolleys in order to enter Ebbets Field. (The Dodgers were once known as the "Trolley Dodgers.")

A large number of sports teams use Native American imagery for their nicknames, logos, and mascots. Those who support such team names, like the "Braves," believe that they are honorable symbols that reflect the greater community in a positive manner. They believe that ritualistic behaviors like the "tomahawk chop" and the "war cry" are merely ways of cheering for the team. The manner in which fans defend their right to hold on to and embrace their cherished symbols of the team reflects a type of totemism. Totemism, as described by Emile Durkheim, is a primitive form of "a religious system in which certain things, particularly animals and plants, come to be regarded as *sacred* emblems (totems) of the clan. With totemism, an image or representation is placed on a totem pole. The images at the highest points of the totem were the most sacred. In addition to the physical aspects of totemism is the moral character. There are occasions when the members of the tribe come together at the totem and share a number of emotions, sentiments, and rituals" (Delaney, 2004: 100). Ordinary items are transformed into sacred totems through special rituals and ceremonies (e.g., the wafer and wine at a Catholic mass which is ritualistically transformed into the body and blood of Christ). Team logos and mascots take on this totem quality for devout fans. It seems odd that people in the 21st century embrace totems, or symbols, with the same level of enthusiasm as primitive, pagan worshippers. However, sports often bring out the primitive inner being of people — including a passionate devotion to a belief or symbol.

In light of the fact that Native Americans were victims of genocide — the intentional attempt to exterminate a race of people by a more dominant population — a number of Native American groups, scholars, and sports fans consider the practice of using Indian imagery as a form of racism. Though there exist some other types of human mascots, Native American mascots are in a different category. Human mascots such as Hilltoppers, Oilers, Patriots, and 49ers are generally emblematic of the geographic area where their teams reside. Other human mascots (e.g., Crusaders, Friars, Knights, and Saints) have religious significance. Native American nicknames may be generic (e.g., Indians and Redmen), tribal (e.g., Florida State Seminoles, Utah

Utes, Central Michigan Chippewas and Eastern Michigan Hurons), or they may focus on an attribute (e.g., Braves, Warriors and Savages). In most cases, Indian nicknames do not represent a specific regional tribe, but rather, that the team has the fearsome characteristic of "Indian savages." The idea of Indians as "savages" corresponds to the threat that Indians posed to the early settlers. Furthermore, in many cases, it served as justification for taking their land.

In addition, this attribution of Native Americans as mascots is similar to those teams that use nicknames such as Tigers or Bears. For example, there are no wild lions running loose in Detroit; instead the usage of the nickname and mascot "Lions" by Detroit's NFL franchise is to imply that the team embodies the power of a wild and ferocious animal. Native Americans, however, are human beings, not wild animals. Using imagery of Native people as though they are fearsome, savage beasts is racist.

In response to Native American claims that Indian imagery is a form of racism, many high schools, colleges and universities have eliminated their use of Indian nicknames, logos and mascots. Syracuse University, for example, dropped its "Indian" logo and mascot in 1978. Syracuse University was one of the first institutions to employ Indian imagery. "Throughout the late nineteenth and twentieth centuries, Syracuse's Indian mascot was rooted in notions of 'noble savagery,' the 'vanishing Indian,' and eventually the Indian as wild creature" (Fisher, 2001: 25). By the 1970s, there were protests from local Native American groups to end Syracuse University's usage of Indian portrayals. Additionally, university officials decided to eliminate the Indian imagery because of "reason, truth, and fairness had prevailed over emotion, fiction, and prejudice" (Fisher, 2001: 38). St. Johns University changed its name from "Redmen" to "Red Storm" in response to cultural sensitivity. These are just two examples of schools that have voluntarily disassociated themselves from Indian imagery. Other schools and professional sports franchises have been reluctant to change.

A number of specific teams have been targeted by Native American groups in the hope that they will abandon their usage of Indian nicknames, logos and mascots. Among these teams are the Cleveland Indians, Atlanta Braves, Washington Redskins, and Florida State University.

The Cleveland Indians (MLB) have come under attack primarily because of their logo—a caricature of an "Indian" head smiling with huge glaring buckteeth and a single red feather, named "Chief Wahoo." This logo is highly objectionable to Native Americans and many American Indian organizations have asked repeatedly for it to be replaced. Slightly less objectionable to Native American groups is the generic nickname "Indians." The Cleveland Indians organization claims that the nickname was chosen by Cleveland fans in a newspaper poll as an honor to Louis Francis Sockalexis, the first Native American to play Major League Baseball. The "Indian" identity has been absorbed into the collective consciousness of Cleveland Indians fans, and fans of baseball in general, forming a shared tradition and common rallying point (Staurowsky, 1998). However, Staurowsky conducted an extensive content analysis of Cleveland newspapers from September 1914 through March 1915, the period of time when the fan voting supposedly took place, and concluded that the eventual selection of the "Indians" name by newspaper readers was improbable and difficult to prove. Further, Staurowsky claims that the assertion that a fan recommended "Indians" to honor Sockalexis, although not impossible, has no evidentiary foundation in the articles chronicling fan or writer preferences. This revelation that the Cleveland story lacks credibility has been reported before in the mainstream press by the *Cleveland Plain Dealer* (Aran and Sangiacomo, 1993) and by other sources.

The controversy facing the Atlanta Braves centers on such practices (of fans) as the use of the "tomahawk chop," the "warwhoop," wearing "Indian" face paint, etc. The primary disdain directed toward the Atlanta Braves franchise by Native American groups is the generic use of the term "Braves" and the stereotypical usage of Indian imagery and the mockery of Native American history, culture and religion.

The most offensive nickname in North American professional sports, by far, is the Washington Redskins. The Washington Redskins organization argues that the term "redskin" is a neutral term and that it uses "Redskins" as its nickname to honor American Indians. Native Americans strongly disagree. In fact, nearly all dictionaries provide the same description for "redskin" as it does for "nigger"— that is an "offensive term," or "offensive slang." People should be as uncomfortable saying the word "redskin" as they are saying the word "nigger." In other words, the term "redskin" should be viewed as "the 'R' word" just most people use the expression "the 'N' word" to refer to the offensive slang word for African Americans. Furthermore, it is more than ironic that the Redskins franchise is located in the U.S. national capital city. Washington, D.C., has long been the symbol of broken promises and treaties over the years to Native Americans.

It is the Florida State University Seminoles that seems the least offensive of all Indian nicknames, at least for most Native Americans. And this is because the Seminoles refer to a specific tribe indigenous to the Tallahassee, Florida, region (home of the university). Supporters of the Florida State University's usage of the nickname "Seminoles" believe that they are honoring a regional, specific group of brave warriors who refused to compromise and be forced to move westward. The student mascot is a male dressed as "Chief Osceola," who wears moccasins, a tasseled leather "Indian" outfit, face paint and a large bandanna, hoisting a large feathered lance. One of FSU's most visible traditions (created in 1978) involves the home-football game performance of "Chief Osceola," atop a horse named Renegade, charging onto the football field with a burning spear and then dramatically thrusting it into the logo centered on the playing field. The FSU fans cheer in a wild frenzy.

LEGAL ACTION

The NCAA is an organization that has the power to do something about schools that use nicknames, logos and mascots that are deemed inappropriate. The NCAA cannot forbid schools from using the nicknames they choose, but it does have the authority to dictate which schools are eligible to participate in NCAA tournament events. The NCAA can also encourage member schools not to schedule teams with offensive nicknames.

In 2005, the NCAA took aim at schools that use "hostile" and "abusive" nicknames, logos and mascots. "The NCAA identified 18 offending schools. Six play I-A football: Florida State University (the Seminoles), Illinois (Fighting Illini), Utah (Utes), Central Michigan (Chippewas), Arkansas State (Indians) and Louisiana-Monroe (Indians). Effective Feb. 1, those schools' teams will be barred from wearing uniforms with Indian references or imagery in NCAA championships or they must cover up the offending areas. Schools already selected as hosts of NCAA championships similarly 'must take reasonable steps to cover up those references' at the site, and the association won't award the 18 schools any future championships" (Wieberg, 2005: 9C). Each of the "offending" schools was allowed to explain to the NCAA why they use Indian imagery and were given an opportunity to prove that such imagery was not offensive to Native Americans. Among the first schools to respond was Florida State University. FSU president T.K. Wetherell stated, "That the NCAA would now label our close bond with the Seminole [tribe] as culturally 'hostile and abusive' is both outrageous and insulting" (*Sports Illustrated*, 8/15/05: 22). By the end of 2005, the NCAA had changed its position on both Florida State University and the University of Utah, as both schools were able to show documented proof that the respective tribes supported their imagery.

Other universities have not been as successful as FSU and Utah. Some universities are facing legal action for their Indian imagery usage. For example, the University of Illinois was sued in 2005 by the Illinois Native American Bar Association (NABA) to stop the university from using "Chief Illiniwek" as its mascot. "Chief Illiniwek" is a student dressed in authentic Illini buckskin and a headdress. The "Chief" has performed at home football and basketball games as far back as 1926. Illiniwek has not performed at an NCAA tournament game since 1989 (*Sports Illustrated*, 4/11/05). King and Springwood (2001) see Illinois' use of "Chief Illiniwek" at sporting events as a classic example of "playing Indian." The NABA lawsuit does not seek monetary damages; it simply seeks to persuade Illinois to retire the mascot (*Sports Illustrated*, 4/11/05).

The issue of sports teams using Indian imagery in its teams' nicknames, logos and mascots will not disappear until offending usages of such imagery no longer exist in sports. There are those who believe Native Americans are being honored by teams who use Indian imagery. In the military there is an expression, "No honor is given, if no honor is received." In other words, one cannot claim they honored another if the other does not view it as an honor. Other people try to ignore the Native American nickname, mascot and logo issue by saying, "It's just political correctness." That is not true. A case of political correctness applies to the renaming of Crayola's color "Indian Red" because some people equated it to the skin color of Native Americans — it was actually named for a brownish-red pigment found near India. (It is now called chestnut.) Native Americans are people. They are not mascots. Eliminating offensive Indian imagery is a matter of *correctness*.

Native American Participation in Sports

Once known as the "vanishing Americans," the American Indian population has increased at every census since 1940. In 1940, the Native American population was 345,000. In 2000, the Native American population was 2.5 million (Marger, 2006). The small population of Native Americans only partially explains their near complete omission from most American sports. Further, nearly half of Native Americans live on reservations. Transition from life on the reservation to American society is often very difficult. Furthermore, Native Americans' sense of tribal tradition plays an important role in keeping American Indians on the reservation. The Native Americans have a word for those who try to leave the reservation, "apple." An apple is someone who is "red" on the outside but "white" on the inside. This is similar to the use of the term "Oreo" when applied to black people who try to leave an older neighborhood for the suburbs. The pull of the reservation is intense.

Native Americans in Sports Today

One of the fastest growing sports in North America is lacrosse, which is an indigenous game created by Native Americans long before the European conquest of the Americas. Baker (1988) writes: "The earliest Indian inhabitants of North America played lacrosse the year round. The Winnebago tribe in Wisconsin, for example, not only competed in a spring festival game but also after the winter hunt. Indians everywhere played darts, dice, and guessing games on long winter evenings, but more hardy young warriors spent entire afternoons playing lacrosse on frozen rivers or lakes. Indians in the Canadian Northwest traditionally took to icy lacrosse fields after the winter hunts as well as during the summer" (p. 159).

Many of the best lacrosse players continue to be Native Americans. In New York State, four tribes (Oneida, Onondaga, Seneca and Tuscarora) have formed a box lacrosse league (the North American Minor Lacrosse Association) for Native American youth. (This league was a feature of ESPN2's *Timeless* series hosted by Philadelphia Eagles linebacker Dhani Jones and first aired in March 2006). Oneida Coach Ron Patterson explains the importance of lacrosse for Native Americans: "It goes back to the original request of the creator, and we continue to play his game for his amusement" (Potrikus, 2006: B-3). According to Oneida history, lacrosse is a symbolic rite sacred to the Thunders, the seven honored elders who move across the sky from west to

College women play the Native American sport of lacrosse (courtesy Cardinal Sports Imaging).

east, cleansing the earth with winds and rain (Potrikus, 2006). Native Americans used lacrosse to prepare for war, to develop strong men, as medicinal rites, to solve conflicts, and to amuse the "Creator." Lacrosse remains hugely popular with many Native tribes today. Native athletes from across the United States and Canada compete in the North American Indigenous Games. The Games were started in 1990 and are traditionally held every three years, although financial difficulties postponed the 2005 Games to 2006 (Moses, 2006). More than 10,000 Native athletes competed in the July 2006 Games held in Denver.

Hockey is also a sport which many Native Americans have grown up with and consider one of their own. There are some Native American hockey players in the National League — usually relegated to the "thug" role, unfortunately. Still, the number of Native Americans playing in major league sport remains small. Notah Ryan Begay III, for instance, was the only Indian (Navajo) on the PGA tour as of 2008.

The issue of race provides yet another example of sport mirroring society. As the demographics of the U.S. population continues to change, so to do the demographics within the sports world. Just as there are more Hispanic/Latinos in the United States, there are an increasing number in American sports. A number of athletes (e.g., Derek Jeter, Hines Ward, and Tiger Woods) are from "mixed" races, which reflects the growing amalgamation trend found in the United States. Sports are, indeed, a microcosm of society.

SUMMARY

The idea that blacks are innately superior athletes and that whites are innately more intelligent reflects racial ideologies that lead to prejudice and discrimination in the sports world.

Beliefs about racial superiority can have deadly consequences. Geography can have a great deal to do with sporting opportunities, as can unique physical characteristics such as big hands or larger hearts. Opportunity, desire, reinforcement, and trial and error provide the basis for achieving athletic success, not genes.

For many people, sports provide a means for upward mobility. However, racism — both individual and institutional — can be a barrier to this. In the past, social class itself was an impediment, as most sports were limited to "amateurs." After the American Civil War, when slavery was officially ended, the participation of African Americans in most major sports became an issue. They were effectively shut out of participating in baseball, football, horse racing, basketball and other activities.

Jesse Owens was one of the first African American athletes to bridge the color gap, when his victories in the 1936 Berlin Olympics were cheered by most Americans. The 1954 *Brown v. Board of Education of Topeka* ruling by the United States Supreme Court ushered in an era of increasing interaction among black and white athletes on the local and national level. Today, blacks dominate many American sports, but only as participants, not as owners, general managers, coaches or trainers.

Ethnic groups such as the Irish and Italian overcame initial discrimination through excelling in sports such as boxing, track and field, baseball and bicycle racing. For the most part, they are today fully assimilated into mainstream society. Jackie Robinson provided perhaps the single most significant breakthrough in sports when he became a player for the Brooklyn Dodgers in 1947, thereby breaking the color barrier.

Today other racial groups, including Hispanic/Latino, Asian, and Native American, face similar hurdles in participating in sports. They, too, have experienced discrimination and racist policies.

One of the major controversies in sports today is the use of Native American imagery for nicknames, logos and mascots. Those who support such team names as "Braves" or "Chiefs" believe they are honorable symbols that reflect the greater community in a positive manner. But opponents say that such terms are racist and demeaning, and should be changed.

The issue of race provides yet another example of sport mirroring society.

KEY TERMS

Direct Upward Mobility A rise in socio-economic status that is accomplished when an athlete signs a lucrative professional contract.

Discrimination Behavior that treats people unequally on the basis of an ascribed status, such as race or gender.

Ethnic Group A category of people who are recognized as a distinct group based on social or cultural factors.

Genocide The intentional attempt to exterminate a race of people by a more dominant population.

Indirect Upward Mobility A rise in socio-economic status that occurs when an athlete earns a college degree and finds gainful employment because of his or her educational credentials.

Negro Baseball A collective term used to describe the various teams and leagues that existed from the early 1900s until the 1950s.

Prejudice Negative beliefs and overgeneralizations concerning a group of people which involves a judgment against someone based on a rigid and fixed mental image of some group of people that is applied to all individuals of that group.

Race A group of people who share some socially recognized physical characteristic (such as skin color or facial features) that distinguishes them from other groups of people and are recognized by themselves and others as a distinct group.

Racism Any attitude, belief, behavior, or social arrangement that has the intent, or the ultimate effect, of favoring one group over another.

Totemism As described by Emile Durkheim, a primitive form of a religious system in which certain things, particularly animals and plants, come to be regarded as *sacred* emblems.

DISCUSSION QUESTIONS

- Why are black quarterbacks expected to run with the ball rather than be "pocket" quarterbacks?

- What are some of the difficulties in defining the word "race"? What is the difference between a race and an "ethnic group?"

- What is the difference between discrimination and prejudice? Can you think of some examples where this might pertain to the sports world?

- Why is it wrong to say that certain groups are "naturally" athletic? What are some problems with this claim and what are some alternative explanations for why people might excel in certain sporting activities?

- Why are there so few minority owners, managers and coaches in sporting teams today? What do you think could be done to try to change this?

- What do you think about the controversy over using Indian imagery for athletic team names and mascots?

CHAPTER 12

Economics and Sport

Both of the authors teach college students. We meet new students every semester. Nearly all students indicate that their primary reason for attending college is to "find a good job." Most students expect to receive a high salary right after graduation. (These expectations are usually crushed by reality!) For the most part, however, students looking for a productive career realize that they will be working for most of the rest of their lives. Inevitably, sociology professors (as professors in most disciplines) will hear such questions as, "What type of jobs can I find with a sociology degree?" and "How much money will I earn?" Although students may be disillusioned with the answers, they never expected to hear of an option that involved a profession where they could earn so much money that they could retire after 5 or 10 years. High paying jobs like that don't even exist. Or do they? Yes, in fact they do. Usually these positions are found in the field of entertainment (e.g., movie and television stars, popular singers, and elite athletes).

Sports are a part of the entertainment business. Elite members of the sports industry will earn huge sums of money. The average salary in Major League Baseball was $2.82 million in 2007 (New York Yankee players averaged $7.47 million). The highest paid MLB player in 2007 was N.Y. Yankee star Alex Rodriguez (A-Rod) at $27.7 million. When asked about his high salary, A-Rod stated, "I love being the highest-paid player in the game. It's pretty cool" (Blum, 2007). Pretty cool, indeed! Even the most mediocre players are guaranteed outrageous minimum salaries. For example, in the NFL, the annual minimum salary ranged from $235,000 for players with no experience to $770,000 for players with ten years' experience (in 2007). Imagine if sociologists belonged to a union strong enough to secure a minimum wage of a quarter million dollars for first year employees!

Oddly, many professional athletes believe that they *should* be paid enough money during their brief sports career so that they do not have to work after retirement — usually sometime in their 30s. Who enters any profession thinking that they can work for 5 to 10 years, earn millions of dollars, and live in comfort without needing to work again for the rest of their lives? Obviously, there are many of us who would love to be in that position.

Such is the design of economics in sport in contemporary society. The sport industry is a field where even marginal professional athletes can expect to earn millions of dollars annually. Today's athletes are lucky to be a part of such an odd profession. In contrast, as recently as 1981 many Major League Baseball players took jobs during the baseball strike because their salaries were far more in line with the median salary of all U.S. workers. In this chapter, we will examine the role of economics in sports and how, at times, loyalty to the "Almighty Dollar" has become far more important than loyalty to a community that supports a professional sports franchise.

Social Stratification and Socio-economic Status

Sports can provide upward mobility (directly and indirectly) for many athletes. Those most attracted to sports as a means of upward mobility are from the lower socio-economic classes, which are disproportionately composed of minority members. Socio-economic classes are a component of the stratification system that exists in all groups, organizations and societies. While geologists may concern themselves with such things as the layers of the Earth's subsurface, sociologists are concerned about the "layers" found in the social world. Social stratification is a ranking system of members of a social system into levels having different or unequal evaluations; it reveals patterns of social inequality. Most societies have three major dimensions of stratification: social prestige, political, and economic.

Most people want power and prestige, and many believe that money will provide both. As a result, the economic dimension of stratification systems is what holds most people's attention and focus. The economic dimension involves two key variables: income and wealth. Income refers to the amount of money that a person, or family, receives over a period of time; generally a calendar year (e.g., reported income on a tax return). The second element of economics is wealth. Wealth refers to the total value of everything that a person or family owns, minus any debts owed. It is similar in meaning to the term net worth. Economic success is often equated with prestige, as people with money generally garner more respect in western societies than the poor. Sociologists use the term socio-economic status (SES) to measure economic-prestige status. Socio-economic status is a composite term that includes a person's income, wealth, occupational prestige, and educational attainment.

The United States has an open stratification system. That is, people have the ability to climb, or fall from, the socio-economic ladder. The U.S. class system provides (at least theoretically) the highest degree of mobility in society. Both ascribed and achieved statuses have significant effects on people's income, wealth, and social position. Ascribed status states that those born in wealthy families generally enjoy a higher status than those born in poorer families. In addition, wealthy persons will have opportunities presented to them that the poor will not (e.g., access to better schools, private tutoring, and job "connections"). However, achieved status also plays a role in the class system because those people who attain high levels of education or make successful personal and economic decisions can influence their status as adults. It was revealed in Chapter 11 that members from multiple groups that faced discrimination used sports to get ahead in society. Sports provide an environment where objective reviews can be used to compare one person's performance to another person's (e.g., a 100 meter race). Athletes that excel in high school give themselves a chance to play sports in college. Those who do well in college athletically have a chance to earn big money professionally. College athletes who earn their degrees have a chance for socio-economic success in the employment sector.

Sport as an Extension of Consumerism

Sports are an enigma. On the one hand, they *are* games. Games are usually associated with play and play with frivolous, nonserious activity. Organized sporting activities—sports—are far different from children's games. Sports are so pervasive in society that they comprise a multibillion dollar industry. Much of the business of sport involves providing a "product" that is marketable. As a result, much of sport is designed for entertainment appeal—"Give the fans something to cheer about!" It is important to provide an entertaining product because people have so many options as how to spend their leisure time and money. This adage helps to explain why fans will pack a stadium to watch a winning, entertaining team, but will stay away from games involving losing, boring teams (an "inferior" product). The sports industry must compete with all the other consumer-driven businesses. And there are many options available, sports or otherwise.

In an attempt to reach an ever-expanding market, the sports industry has paid increasing attention to its entertainment appeal and methods of marketing its product to consumers.

SPORTS ENTERTAINMENT

Everyone enjoys being entertained. Life sometimes provides follies for our amusement and friends and family members tell stories to amuse us. In addition, an entire industry exists to manufacture entertainment in print, audio and visual format. Entertainment is the number one industry in Los Angeles and hires more people than any other single category of employment there. Hollywood is responsible for a large percentage of television programs and films consumed throughout the world. Studios across the country produce music for our audio entertainment. The list goes on. Sports also provide us with entertainment. For decades, sports and the media have development a symbiotic relationship where both may profit. (The media will be discussed in greater detail in Chapter 15.)

People watch sports for a variety of reasons. Some fans are only happy when their team wins; other sports fans are happy with a well-played game where all participants seemingly gave a maximum effort. Although there is little that sports personnel (e.g., marketing and media executives) can do about making all sports fans happy — especially those who are only happy with a favorable outcome — they can help to provide an entertaining event. Because of the great number of potential sport consumers, the sports industry attempts to lure fans beyond the established, die-hard fans. The key is to provide a product that people will want to consume. Major events, such as the Super Bowl, are so over-hyped that consumption has reached near staggering results. It is the most watched single sporting event of the year, every year, in the United States. In essence, it has become the number one "unofficial" holiday in the United States. The authors have been proposing for years that the Monday following the Super Bowl should be an official holiday (like many of the other three-day weekends). It only seems logical, especially when considering more people call in sick on this day than on any other day of the year. And this is in addition to people who go to work but are less than productive because they partied hardy during a Sunday Super Bowl party. (This seems especially true in the Eastern and Central time zones, where the game ends quite late.)

Today, sporting events are products designed for consumption. This includes ballgames, races of all sorts (e.g. auto and animal), or some other sports event (e.g., gymnastics, surfing, tennis matches). Auto racing is a commercial sport largely designed and created by automobile manufacturers to promote, advertise, and sell their products. The race cars themselves are like moving advertisement billboards. Many corporations promote their products at sporting events because of the exposure to a large audience. "The springboard for all sports promotions is the competition. Sporting events predictably gather audiences in person and over the airwaves. Broadcasters know that over 130 million people will watch the Super Bowl, thirty billion (yes, billion) total viewers will watch the fifty-two World Cup matches.... With so much interest focused on competition, shrewd sponsors pay to identify and interrupt the action to promote their products and services" (Schaaf, 1995: 23). The success of commercialized sport is, in part, dependent upon successful sports marketing.

SPORTS MARKETING

Marketing is an important function within the total operating system of any business and corporation. "The basic reason for the marketing function is to enable the organization to achieve its objectives in an effective manner. Marketing provides a foundation upon which objectives are set. The particular objectives of the organization will have an impact on the appropriate marketing strategy or strategies" (Stauble, 1994: 14–15). Marketers must find a way to influence consumers to purchase products they promote. Because people have numerous choices in the products they consume, marketing can be the difference in financial success or failure.

The right marketing campaign provides financial benefits for all involved. But major campaign advertisements are costly. The use of corporate sponsorships is an effective way to handle costs. Corporate sponsorships have proven to be an effective method of promotion in the sports world.

> The proven ability of sports to influence consumer behavior off the field of play drives the chameleon forces of 'sponsorship,' the powerful turnkey that identifies sports entertainment properties with products and services around the world. Sponsors choose from hundreds of events and sponsorship packages to identify with their existing markets and expand into others. The widespread popularity of athletic competition helps companies successfully sell breakfast cereal, soda pop, checking accounts, automobiles, shoes, underwear, and virtually any product manufactured [Schaaf, 1995: 22].

The sports world is a haven for corporate sponsors, as many events are viewed by millions of people. The network that broadcasts the sports event gets to display its corporate logo on the television screen. Stadiums are filled with commercial sponsorships that are strategically located to appear on normal television broadcasting. Most stadiums have corporate names attached to them (e.g., Petco Field, the Staples Center). Bowl games and NCAA conference tournaments have corporate sponsorship names. Many corporations even sponsor halftime shows and segments within broadcasts.

Sport Sponsorships

Sponsorships are so prevalent in sports today that they have contributed dramatically to the over-commercialization found in sport. Many corporations are involved with sport sponsorships. Sports are an attraction to corporations because of their popularity and large viewing audiences. Corporate leaders also recognize that their sponsorship of a particular team or athlete may establish, maintain, and enhance their identity.

CORPORATE SPONSORSHIPS

When corporations purchase sponsorships, they attain certain rights. As Schaaf (1995) explains, "Companies purchase various *sponsorship rights*, e.g., radio/television broadcast rights, stadium billboard placements, product logo on the event tickets, etc., to turn sporting events into important promotional campaigns for their products and services. Simply put, *sponsorship is the promotional mechanism by which sports entertainment penetrates consumer markets to create identifiable publicity and profits for corporate buyers/participants*" (p. 110). Corporations like to use sports events as a way to promote their products. "Companies have been giving away tote bags, caps, T-shirts, posters, mugs, key chains, and food items at sporting events for years. By spending money to be associated with the audience at a sporting event, companies buy the enthusiasm of the fans of that particular event, the access to the crowds, and all of the associated media efficiency benefits such as broadcast announcements, printed mentions in newspapers, printed mentions on schedules.... The stadium event is the oldest form of sponsorship, but that does not mean that it has not developed with the times" (Schaaf, 1995: 115).

Ideally, a symbiotic relationship is established between the sponsor and the sport organization (or individual athlete). As a case in point, in 1999, the European subsidiary of the Japanese electronics company SEGA Enterprises arranged for a shirt sponsorship with Arsenal FC of the English Premier League (Rosson, 2001). The deal benefited both SEGA and Arsenal. Arsenal

The outfield wall of a minor league baseball stadium is covered with commercial advertisements.

had just ended its 18-year shirt relationship with JVC and needed to find a new shirt sponsor. SEGA was about to launch its new video gaming console in European markets and needed to come up with a high-impact marketing plan to reach as large an audience as possible (Rosson, 2001). In Europe, especially England, soccer reigns as the king of all sports. Arsenal's elite status in the Premier League guaranteed large exposure for SEGA. The impact of corporate sponsorships is so prevalent in European soccer that players' jerseys contain a corporate sponsorship name instead of the team's logo.

Phil Schaaf, in his book *Sports, Inc.* (2005), points out several potential benefits for sponsors who wish to identify their product with an athlete or sports program:

- Reaching an event's audience at the event and through the available media.
- Building brand identity with on-site visibility and naming rights.
- Potential customers sample the product or service.
- Employee rewards and incentive programs may be created involving the property.
- Creating programs within the event.
- Leveraging special mailing or customer lists.
- Selling the product at the event via concession access privileges (167–169).

He adds the phenomenon of "lightning in a bottle"—when something beneficial or interesting happens that can be associated with the product. "Jerry Rice wore the CNS nasal strip (an antisnoring device) on *Monday Night Football*. The announcers talked about it all game. The next day, the stock of the company went up 11 percent" (Schaaf, 2005: 168).

There are many factors involved in a product's promotional success. Consequently, it is sometimes difficult to ascertain whether or not specific marketing sponsorship campaigns are successful. With sports-related event sponsorships increasing at a tremendous rate, marketers have had difficulties assessing the value of such advertising strategies (Miyazaki and Morgan, 2001). In their assessment of the market value of corporate sponsorship of the Olympic Games, Miyazaki and Morgan (2001) employed an event study analysis, a technique common to the finance discipline, and found that this type of sponsoring is of value to participating firms.

Corporate sponsors want to receive their money's worth of advertising. Often, additional sporting contests (e.g., NCAA conference championship games) are implemented to generate additional interest in the sports event, and in turn, the corporate advertisers. NASCAR has created a point series championship at the end of its racing season in an effort to generate both further fan interest and corporate dollars. The sponsors of the leading cars receive great additional exposure (e.g., the races themselves and media promotions). The increased popularity of auto racing, especially NASCAR in the United States, has caught the attention of the television networks. In December, 2005, NASCAR agreed to an eight-year, $4.48 billion television deal. Beginning in 2007, NASCAR will air on four different networks. The 36 racing events will air on Fox, ABC/ESPN, TNT, and the Speed Channel (Fryer, 2005).

When a corporation attaches its name to an event, it may potentially reap the benefits of success, but it also risks having certain deficiencies exposed. Michelin, a tire manufacturer, was embarrassed after 14 Formula One (F-1) cars refused to use their tires at the only F-1 event held in the United States in June 2005. As a corporate sponsor of F-1, race teams were required to use Michelin tires. After two Michelin tires failed in practice sessions—one causing a wreck that prevented Toyota's Ralf Schumacher from competing—Michelin said its tires were unsafe for the Indianapolis speedway (host of the F-1 event). Michelin wanted a curve installed going into turn 13, which would slow the cars and spare the tires. Fourteen drivers boycotted the U.S. Grand Prix event. Fielding only six cars, the event when on as planned. Many fans at the Grand Prix wanted their money back and world-wide media ripped into the event (Wade, 2005). The F-1 series, which is hugely popular around the world, had hoped to increase its presence in the United States—where stock car racing reigns as the fans' favorite. Joie Chitwood, CEO and president of the Indianapolis Motor Speedway, called the fiasco a dark day for the sport and believed that F-1's hope of making it in the U.S. had experienced a major setback (Wade, 2005).

It should be noted that smaller businesses often sponsor teams (e.g., high school, college, minor league sports teams) from within their community. The costs are significantly lower, but of course, the audience shrinks correspondingly.

PLAYER ENDORSEMENTS

Athletes have been endorsing products for corporations dating back to when Red Rock Cola hired Babe Ruth to endorse its soft drink brand in the 1930s. Companies spend more than one billion dollars a year on athlete endorsements. Corporations are buying into the commonly held belief that consumers are likely to purchase products endorsed by athletes. Many elite athletes may earn more income from their endorsement contracts than from their salaries to play sports. All elite athletes are not created equal. It helps to be an elite athlete in the "right" sports. The popular sports (e.g., football, baseball, soccer, and basketball) provide great visibility for its elite athletes and as a result, endorsement contracts are more likely to be extended to them. The obvious reason for this is that marketers need spokespersons that have popular appeal and name and face recognition. This list below is a mere sampling of athletes and their endorsement deals:

- *David Beckham (soccer), sponsor: Adidas.* Estimated value: $160 million (lifetime)
- *George Foreman (boxing), sponsor: Salton, Inc. (including such products as the "Lean Mean Grilling Machine).* Estimated value: $137.5 million (lifetime)
- *Tiger Woods (golf), sponsor: Nike.* Estimated value: $100 million (5 years)
- *LeBron James (basketball), sponsor: Nike.* Estimated value: $90 million (7 years)
- *Allen Iverson (basketball), sponsor: Reebok.* Estimated value: $5 million a year (lifetime)
- *Venus Williams (tennis), sponsor: Reebok.* Estimated value: $40 million (5 years)
- *Kobe Bryant (basketball), sponsor: Nike.* Estimated value: $40 million (5 years).

Olympic athletes are given a huge stage on which to shine. Usually, success brings endorsement opportunities. Mary Lou Retton, for example, is still popular with marketers more than 20 years after her gold medal 1984 Olympic performance. Retton was a star in gymnastics—traditionally, one of the most popular Olympic sports. Her bright smile, warm personality, and perfect "10" score all but guaranteed her endorsement success. She has earned millions in endorsements. But what if Retton was a gold medal winner in speedskating—would she have received as much attention? Not likely. American Bonnie Blair, a 1988 Olympic (Calgary) gold medal winner in speedskating, earned an estimated $100,000 in endorsements prior to the Albertville (France) 1992 Olympics. Blair did not receive endorsement offers anywhere near that of Mary Lou Retton; she was in the "wrong sport." "Although Blair's success is phenomenal, it's a far cry from how much she would have made if she were a figure skater—the big bucks are still in traditionally feminine sports. Athletes in figure skating, tennis, and golf are most likely to boost their incomes with contracts to sell things other than sporting goods" (Levin, 1996: 368).

Marketers want high profile athletes to pitch their products. Sponsors reason that athletes without mass appeal are not as effective in promoting products. "Although the sport in which an athlete competes largely determines her financial future, individual factors enhance an athlete's 'marketability.' Performance is 50 percent of the equation.... The other 50 percent is a combination of looks, personality, and brains that make a person 'a good promotion'" (Levin, 1996: 369). This idea reinforces the adage that "sex sells" via marketing opportunities.

Michele Wie provides us with an example of the "sex sells" mantra without the need to actually succeed, in her case on the golf course. In 2006, Wie received seven-figure appearance fees to play men's events in Korea, Japan, and Europe. As it turned out, she never made the cut in any men's events. Furthermore, she stumbled through eight LPGA events by missing three cuts, withdrawing twice, finishing last twice after making the cut, and finishing second from last (Sirak, 2008). In short, Wie is among the most over-rated golfers in history and yet, thanks to corporate sponsors Nike, Sony, and Omega, she earned over $12.5 million in 2006 (Sirak, 2008). (She earned less than $10,000 on the course.)

Endorsement contracts are not a "free ride" where athletes accept money from marketers and do nothing in return. There are expectations attached to endorsement deals. Athletes with endorsement deals are often at the beck and call of a sponsor. They must make themselves available for promotions, photo shoots, potential publicity stunts, and still perform athletically at peak performance levels. It is also important that athletes exercise a little common sense when they have endorsement deals to promote specific products. But logic and endorsement deals do not always go hand-in-hand. Consider the following samplings of "stinging endorsements" as complied by *Sports Illustrated* (11/14/05):

- *Ken Griffey, Jr., is the spokesperson for the "Ken Griffey Jr. Milk Chocolate Bars."* The problem: Griffey is allergic to chocolate.
- *Arnold Palmer promotes "The Callaway ERC II Driver."* The problem: Palmer was the honorary membership chairman of the USGA, which had declared the golf club illegal because the club face didn't conform to the rules of golf.

- *John Daly promotes "Trimspa."* The problem: The overweight Daly wears a Trimspa patch on the front of his shirts, but he also wears the logo of another company that pays him for an endorsement — Dunkin' Donuts.
- *DeAngelo Hall promotes "Reebok."* The problem: The Falcons cornerback wore Nike shoes. When Hall appeared on a Monday night football game wearing the Nike swoosh logo, Reebok dropped his endorsement deal two days later.

Most college basketball teams have endorsement deals for sneakers so that they can provide them to their players. The endorsement deal may be worked out with the coach, the athletic director, or the school. Either way, the players are generally obligated — or at the least, expected — to wear the shoes endorsed by the team. An interesting case involving shoe endorsement contracts occurred at Arkansas State when Jerry Nichols, a 6'6" senior, refused to wear team-supplied Adidas footwear. Nichols, who suffered a number of injuries in the past, said they occurred while wearing Adidas. He wore a different brand, taping over the logo of the Adidas competitor, but the athletic administration told Nichols that he had to wear Adidas or he would not be allowed to play. Nichols still refused. Adidas stepped in and told Arkansas State that Nichols would not be obligated to wear its brand. Adidas also encouraged Nichols to try out other styles of their sneakers before completely ruling out its shoes. Arkansas State went along with Adidas's decision (Alexander, 2005).

Corporate sponsorships and endorsements clearly have had a significant impact on the economics of sports.

The Globalization of Commercial Sport

The U.S. and its capitalistic system have created some of the most powerful business operations in the global market. Numerous American products such as Pepsi and Coca-Cola and fast-food restaurants such as Pizza Hut and McDonalds, for example, are found worldwide and are enjoyed by billions of culturally diverse people. Companies such as Nike "demonstrated how in the post–1970s world of new transnational corporations, money was free to move anywhere it could find quick profit" (LaFeber, 1999: 151). The Nike swoosh symbol is recognized internationally. The endorsement of worldwide celebrity Michael Jordan greatly assisted in the name recognition of Nike — thus justifying any amount of money Nike pays Jordan in endorsement compensation.

In order to survive, capitalism is dependent on further and further growth. When one marketplace becomes saturated, a new one must be developed. Societies of the West, especially the United States, dominate the global economic marketplace. Large corporations have expanded their markets throughout the world and have spread their cultural influence into previously diverse cultures. The continued expansion of industrialization, urbanization, and capitalism has triggered many trends of social change that are collectively referred to as modernization. Among the primary characteristics of modernization are: growth in technology (especially a reliance on the application of scientific knowledge); advances in agriculture (e.g., commercial production of corporate-run farms); the use of machinery (human and animal power being replaced by machines); and changing ecological arrangements (e.g., continued population shift from rural areas to urban ones) (Smelser, 1966; Delaney, 2005). Modernization fueled the development of commerce between nations. "Multinationals are not a new phenomenon, as commerce among nations is at least as old as the Phoenicians, whose trading ships sailed from what is now Lebanon to foreign lands more than 3,000 years ago. From then on, trading routes crisscrossed the globe, as silk, gold, spices, and tools were bartered or sold" (Delaney, 2005: 333). Modernization and multinational trading accelerated the globalization process.

GLOBALIZATION AS EVOLUTION

Modernization and the development of nation states transformed the concept of community to encompass the greater society, and eventually the world community. In *The Elementary Forms of Religious Life* (1912/1965), noted sociologist Emile Durkheim stated, "There is no people and no state which is not a part of another society, more or less unlimited, which embraces all the peoples and all the States with which the first comes in contact either directly or indirectly; there is no national life which is not dominated by a collective life of an international nature. In proportion as we advance in history, these international groups acquire a greater importance and extent" (p. 474). As this quote reveals, Durkheim recognized nearly 100 years ago the growing phenomenon of globalization. The world today is more closely tied into an interlinking economy than ever before in human history. The process of linking nations of the world together is called globalization. Globalization can be defined as "a social process in which the constraints of geography on social and cultural arrangements recede and in which people become increasingly aware that they are receding" (Waters, 1995: 3). The increasing interconnectedness of the nations of the world has led to an evolutionary transformation of heterogeneous cultures into a homogeneous culture that transcends all topographical boundaries placed on maps. On every continent, more and more people are embracing the American consumer lifestyle of convenience and seeming abundance.

Together, modernization and globalization affect all spheres of social life; including the sports world. For example, many sports are played on the international level and have an international audience. World Cup soccer and the Olympics are prime examples of sports in an international market. (Both the World Cup and the Olympics will be discussed in greater detail in Chapter 13.) Worldwide communications has allowed for the transmission of sports coverage in one nation to extend globally. European interest in American football coupled with American capitalism led to the development of NFL affiliates in Europe. And sponsorship of sporting events is a big part of the contemporary scene.

THE DIFFUSION OF SPORTS

Cultural diffusion refers to the spread of cultural aspects of one society to another. As described in chapter 3, most American sports were influenced by previously existing sports from different nations, especially European societies. Baseball, for example, was influenced by the English game of rounders. Today, baseball is played in England. Football was influenced by the European game of rugby and now American football is played in Europe. In addition, there are many sports (e.g., soccer and baseball), beyond the Olympic sports, played by people around the world, further demonstrating the diffusion of sports. Rees (1998), for example, found that there was great similarity between the sports played by adolescents from Berlin and New York City. The global expansion of professional sports mirrors the expansion pattern of development of multinational corporations that are motivated primarily by the pursuit of greater profits. American marketers in particular have invested huge sums of money in an attempt to introduce sports to new markets. Their ultimate goal is to sell commercial products. For example, American beer companies sponsor NFL Europe football games in an attempt to sell more beer in European markets. (NFL Europe was founded in 1990 as the World League of American Football, partially backed by the National Football League.) Thus, many franchises may lose money, but marketers can still profit if their sales increase beyond the costs to sponsor sports leagues in foreign countries. Marketers enjoy profits from the global expansion of professional sports in many other ways, including the sale of broadcast rights to television companies in a number of different nations and the sale of licensed products such as apparel with team logos to people worldwide (Nixon and Frey, 1996). The diffusion of sports around the world reflects the economic imperative of capitalism —find new markets when the old ones become saturated.

Major League Baseball, a corporate entity, envisions expanding its market by actively supporting the World Baseball Classic — a global baseball tournament that debuted in 2006. (In 2009, the second WBC will be held in Japan.) MLB Commissioner Bud Selig described the World Cup style event —16 countries played over 18 days in the U.S., Japan and Puerto Rico— as "the most important international baseball event ever staged" (Chen, 2006: 16). The winner of this event can more accurately claim to be world champs than the winner of MLB's "World Series," which only involves teams from the United States and Toronto, Canada. However, American baseball fans have shown little interest in the World Baseball Classic and generally view it as exhibition caliber baseball. MLB is not concerned with American viewers of the WBC, as it has already saturated the U.S. market with commercial products. As Chen (2006) explains, "The truth is, organizers don't much care if the WBC plays in Peoria as long as it bowls 'em over in Beijing. The target audience isn't American fans but those in untapped markets in Asia, Europe and Central America, where Major League Baseball would love to sell TV rights and licensed paraphernalia" (p. 17). MLB Commissioner Selig hopes to tap into a potential 1 billion plus viewers in Africa, Europe and Asia where potential consumers of American baseball are likely to purchase jerseys, ball caps, and a variety of other products. Under Bud Selig's global market vision, MLB earned more than $6 billion in 2008. Selig attributes the value of MLB to increased attendance in the U.S. and the concerted effort to expose its product to other parts of the world.

It is important to note that the successful introduction and spread of any product is still dependent upon an interest in that product. Thus, if Asian viewers are not interested in WBC, or if Europeans did not like the American game of football, the respective events would fail and all the marketers would lose out. The sport of cricket has not caught on in the United States, nor is it likely to any time soon. Americans don't like it or even understand it. On the other hand, ESPN once created a cult-like following of Australian Rules Football with its broadcast of the sport in the 1980s. Curiously, ESPN stopped broadcasting Australian football and has not resumed broadcasting it, nor has any other major network broadcast this sport with great potential American appeal.

Another example of cultural diffusion in sport is the migration of athletes from one nation to another. A number of Americans migrate to foreign countries in order to play sports. Conversely, foreign athletes are coming to the U.S. to play college sports and such professional sports as baseball and basketball. Furthermore, athletes are moving from one point of the globe to another. This is especially true with soccer. For example, while Iraqis celebrated their national team's first-ever Asian Cup championship (in 2007) with a victory over Saudi Arabia, the Iraqi government mostly ignored this event. Why? The Iraqi government does not support national soccer. In fact, very few of the national players live in Iraq and the team has not played a game in the nation in seventeen years. Their practices are generally held in Jordan (Greenwell, 2007). For millions of Iraqi soccer fans, the accomplishment of the national soccer team was hardly compromised by the fact most of the players are far removed from Iraqi society.

The Role of the Owners

Due to the high value of major sports franchises, owners of professional sport teams are very wealthy people. For example, Daniel Snyder is the owner of the NFL's Washington Redskins, and the Redskins franchise had the highest market value in 2006 at $1.26 billion (Forbes, 2006). In some cases, franchises are owned by corporations and in very rare instances, they may be publicly owned (e.g. the Green Bay Packers) with a management team that runs daily operations.

Professional sports leagues do not encourage "fair" competition; instead, they act as cartels and attempt to dominate all aspects of their respective businesses (sport).

SPORT CARTELS

The sports world is basically a self-regulating monopoly that acts as a socialist cartel. Professional sport leagues have often been characterized as sport cartels by economists. "A cartel is a collective of firms who, by agreement, act as a single supplier to a market" (Downward and Dawson, 2000: 31). From a sociological perspective, cartels are bureaucratic, large-scale social organizations. Many sports leagues take on the primary characteristics of cartels. The authors define a sports cartel is an economic body formed by a small number of teams within the same league that make decisions on matters of common interest (e.g., rules, revenue-sharing, expansion, scheduling, and promotion) and exchange money as resources. Buying and selling players and establishing minimum league salaries are examples of collective financial decision making made by league officials. "In a cartel mutual behavior is by agreement only and these agreements need to be enforced. If they are not, or better opportunities for members of the cartel appear elsewhere, then they can break down. Paramount to the success of a cartel thus is the ability to reconcile potential conflicts of interest within the group" (Downward and Dawson, 2000: 36). Sports leagues that act as a cartel provides numerous advantages for owners.

Cartel business activity is essentially illegal in the United States—as established by the Sherman Antitrust Law. Enacted in 1890, and named after Senator John Sherman of Ohio, it authorized federal action against any combination of trusts which engaged in a conspiracy to restrain trade or stifle competition. Companies, for example, that engaged in business across many states were thought to be in violation of the Sherman antitrust legislation. Sports leagues often extend business across many states. They also control player salaries, another feature of a cartel. The Sherman Act, however, was vaguely worded and has been difficult to enforce.

Over the years, the courts have allowed a variety of exceptions to the cartel behavior of many American corporations and businesses, especially in sports (Daymont, 1981). Among the more significant court decisions was the 1922 Supreme Court decision that essentially ruled Major League Baseball free from antitrust legislation (Metzenbaum, 1996). Supreme Court Justice Oliver Wendell Holmes "reasoned that the antitrust laws did not apply because baseball could not be considered interstate commerce" (Metzenbaum, 1996: 275).

> In 1922, Oliver Wendell Holmes, speaking for the majority, delivered the Supreme Court's opinion adjudicating Baltimore's case. The court considered the facts and then ignored them. Baseball, concluded the learned jurists, was not interstate commerce. Although baseball teams traveled from state to state, baseball games were merely "exhibitions" of talent and they were always played within the boundaries of a single state. This bizarre interpretation of the law was reaffirmed fifty years later in *Flood v. Kuhn*. In that decision, written by Harry A. Blackmun, the justices admitted that the predecessors had made a mistake, but they refused to correct the "established aberration" [Guttmann, 2004: 137].

The 1922 Supreme Court decision afforded Major League Baseball an exemption from antitrust legislation and the burden of fair competition dictated by the open, democratic market. The other major sport leagues never enjoyed the immunity given to MLB, but they too received a variety of protections by the courts and Congress that enabled owners to monopolize their industry and operate their sport leagues as cartels (Sage, 1996). "This has enabled owners to engage in collusion, price and wage fixing, and various restraints of trade (e.g., leaguewide negotiation of TV contracts), thus maximizing their profits. It has also protected each franchise within a league from competition because the number of franchises is controlled by the team owners; no franchise is allowed to locate in a given territory without approval of the owners" (Sage, 1996: 265).

Generally speaking, individual colleges and universities (as well as high school sport teams) are not viewed as cartels. However, the NCAA is. Economists generally view the NCAA as a cartel for a number of reasons, including that it:

1. Sets input prices that can be paid for student-athletes
2. Regulates the usage of those student-athletes in terms of duration and intensity
3. Regulates output in terms of the number and length of athletic contests
4. Occasionally pools and distributes the profits of the cartel earned from activities such as the television football package
5. Disseminates information concerning transactions, market conditions, and business accounting techniques
6. Polices the behavior of cartel members and levies penalties for infractions (Koch and Leonard, 1981: 253).

Despite the many similarities to illegal cartels, the NCAA and professional sports leagues are usually immune to antitrust policy in the United States. They are essentially business cartels that seem to enjoy an economic monopoly.

SPORT MONOPOLIES

Another term often associated with sport is monopoly. Monopolies and cartels are regularly intertwined. What is a monopoly? A monopoly is when one company controls a commodity or service in a particular market, or has such control over a commodity or service that it is capable of manipulating prices. Professional sports league act as unregulated monopolies wherein each league regulates itself almost exclusively without government interference. League officials can determine rules, schedules, promotions, expansion, media contracts, sanctions, and reward systems.

Of particular economic importance to sport league monopolies is their ability to negotiate their own television contracts. Economic growth in sport is due primarily to television revenue. And although it is true that some teams hold such high status that they can negotiate partial broadcast rights and keep their own revenue (e.g., Notre Dame home football games and the New York Yankee Network), revenue sharing dominates most American sport leagues (both collegiate and professional). Consider the money available for each franchise when the NFL agreed in 2004 to an $8 billion contract extension with FOX and CBS to televise games for six more years. FOX would pay $4.3 billion and CBS $3.7 billion to the NFL for the rights to broadcast games from 2006 to 2011 (*Post-Standard*, 2004). In 2002, the NBA signed a six-year contract with ABC, ESPN and TNT for $4.6 billion (Fendrich, 2002).

MLB also has a form of revenue sharing (total revenue was near $4.5 billion in 2005 — a large percentage comes from television) where each year a payroll threshold is established (in 2005 it was $128 million) and every team that exceeds that amount pays a "luxury tax" of 40 percent over the threshold. That revenue is shared with all the teams below the threshold level. The tax is designed to keep payrolls relatively competitive. The luxury tax has not led to payroll equity. In 2006, the New York Yankees paid more in luxury tax ($26 million) than the Florida Marlins' entire team payroll of $21 million (Blum, 2007).

Sports leagues resemble cartels but do not monopolize an entire business. Thus, sport leagues are more like cartels than monopolies. As Downward and Dawson (2000) explain, "The co-operation between teams required in cartels can echo monopoly behavior. However, it also implies less rigidity and conformity of behavior than implied in a monopoly *per se*, in which power must, by definition, reside with the league. In a cartel mutual behavior is by agreement only and these agreements need to be enforced. If they are not, or better opportunities for members of the cartel appear elsewhere, then they can break down. Paramount to the success of a cartel, thus, is the ability to reconcile potential conflicts of interest within the group. While aspects of a cartel's activities can resemble a monopoly ... the concept of a cartel is a better conceptual description of a sporting league" (p. 36). One of the critical elements of a cartel is to monopolize the market. The sport league attempts to limit the number of franchises and the placement of franchises in order to maximize the profits of all the teams in the league, as well as the league itself.

As a cartel, sports owners represent an oligarchy. An oligarchy occurs when power is in the hands of a few. And when power is in the hands of the few, the masses (fans) are generally at a major disadvantage. Owners often flaunt their power in the face of loyal fans. They charge outrageous prices for game tickets, parking, merchandise, and food concessions. Season ticket holders in particular carry the brunt of the economic burden. For example, NFL season ticket holders are required to purchase the meaningless preseason (exhibition) games. Adding insult to injury, the preseason tickets are stamped as "Game 1" and "Game 2"—as if they are real games. The season home opener game is stamped as "Game 3." Season ticket holders are not given a choice on whether they want to purchase the preseason games—they are automatically included in the season ticket package. (Delaney is a season ticket holder of an NFL franchise.)

However, being forced to pay for preseason tickets, overpriced tickets, and so forth pales in comparison to the worst atrocity committed by owners; namely, franchise relocation. If an owner decides to relocate a franchise fans have little recourse, legal or otherwise. No matter how loyal fans are to a team, franchise permanence is not guaranteed. The franchise remaining in the local community is critical to fans. Making profits is critical for owners. These two desires are not always congruent.

FRANCHISE RELOCATION

An all-too-common occurrence in professional sport is franchise relocation. Many owners claim that they are not making enough money or are actually losing money. Owners are tempted to leave one community (market) for a more lucrative one. Sometimes they are tempted by leaders in other communities who hope to entice them to relocate their sports franchise. Municipalities seek professional sport franchises for the perceived economic benefits which they bring to their community. To attract a franchise, a city (e.g., local government) without a presence in a major sports league may offer a variety of publicly-funded "sweetheart" benefits (subsidies). These benefits may come in the form of "guaranteed" sellouts, tax breaks, revenue generated from public parking fees, new stadiums, and a number of other "incentives."

The issue of franchise relocation is of great importance to the American and Canadian cities that host professional sports. (One of the primary reasons that some fans prefer college sports over professional sports is the reality that college sports teams will not relocate to a different market because they were offered financial deals.) Second to communities who hope to keep their teams are those communities that seek franchises. Many such communities must wait and hope for league expansion; others attempt to "steal" existing franchises away from existing host cities.

Before a franchise can abandon one community for another, each sports league requires the approval of a significant percentage of league owners. Because of the shared vested interest of the owners, approval is generally permitted, especially if a franchise can show that it is suffering economic hardship. Further, movement is seldom vigorously challenged by the other owners because each realizes that a potential move might be in their future as well. Economic hardship was a common reason for franchise relocation prior to the late 1950s. However, this all changed with the westward movement of the Brooklyn Dodgers and the New York Giants. Both the Dodgers and Giants were well supported by the hometown fans. However, the lure of the west coast and even bigger profits prompted these rival franchises to move regardless. "Civic inducement and factors other than a community's past support became the important variables in a franchise owner's location decision" (Johnson, 1983: 521). As Brooklyn Dodgers and New York Giants fans learned, even if a franchise has a long history of support from the community and every indication reveals that a profit is being made by the owner, there is still no guarantee of future stability of that franchise in the current community. Franchise relocations abound in the contemporary era; the most recent involves the NBA's Seattle Supersonics' move to Oklahoma City.

Sport Stadium Deals: Communities Held Hostage

Communities have to decide just how badly they want a professional sports franchise, and whether the taxpayers will incur the costs of building a stadium or pay renovation on existing stadiums. An owner of an existing sport franchise may threaten to relocate the franchise if a new stadium is not built, or renovations not made. A potential new franchise owner may hold competing communities at bay by waiting for the best stadium proposal from local community leaders. Support for seeking and securing a professional sport franchise at public expense usually comes from coalitions of urban elites: local politicians; businesses, especially restaurants and hotels; developers; construction firms; local mass media; and, of course, the pro-sport industry. Proponents argue that sports facilities eventually pay for themselves and usually require little beyond initial public backing for the bonds that finance them. Backers note the economic impact for nearby restaurants and other related businesses. Consequently, the public (taxpayers) often foot the bill for new stadiums and stadium renovations. Local governments offer public subsidies in order to keep existing sports franchises or to attract potential new franchises. The scarcity of professional sports teams and the tremendous fan interest in having a major sports franchise in their city fuels the desire for municipalities to offer deals attractive enough to entice a sports owner to relocate.

Nearly all stadiums are built with public subsidies, especially through revenue bonds. During the 1960s and 1970s a number of cities financed new stadiums for professional sports teams. The "cookie cutter" stadiums—the circular, fully enclosed, two-sport ballparks—made infamous in St. Louis, Atlanta, Cincinnati, Pittsburgh, and Philadelphia served their purpose and gave municipalities their money's worth, but were aesthetically unappealing. "The functional facilities opened to glowing reviews between 1966 and 1971. They were hailed as modernistic, space-age edifices with no poles obstructing views, symmetrical dimensions in the playing field and cutting-edge features such as huge scoreboards with computerized animation" (Dodd, 2005: 1C). These stadiums ranged in cost from Atlanta-Fulton County Stadium at $18 million (first game on April 12, 1966) to Philadelphia's Veterans Stadium at $52 million (first game played on April 10, 1971) (Dodd, 2005). By the end of 2005, the cookie cutter stadiums had all been demolished and replaced with newer stadiums—at great cost to taxpayers. The new stadiums have more aesthetic appeal and much higher price tags (for example, Atlanta's Turner Field, $242.5 million; St. Louis' Busch Stadium, $345 million; and Philadelphia's Veterans Stadium, $458 million). In addition to the "cookie cutter" stadiums that have been replaced by newer, flashier stadiums, the Houston Astrodome, formerly a symbol of progress and a source of pride for Houstonians—and once proclaimed as the "Eighth Wonder of the World"—was replaced as the home of Astros in 1999. The Astrodome opened in time for the 1965 Astros home opener at a cost of $35 million. A little more than three decades later, this "modern wonder" was deemed outdated by MLB. (It is still used today for other events.) In 2009, both the New York Yankees and the New York Mets moved into new stadiums.

Economic Benefits for Owners

Receiving financial assistance for new stadiums and renovations to old stadiums (e.g., adding "luxury" or "corporate" suites) is just one economic benefit enjoyed by sport franchise owners. The advantage held by sport owners is similar to that of other business cartels. The player "reserve clause" system utilized by professional sports through the early history of sports is a prime example of the economic benefits to owners. The reserve clause eliminated interclub competition for players' services, as once a player signed a contract with a professional sports team, he or she became the "property" of the team. The team holding the player contract had the sole right to unilaterally negotiate with players. The reserve clause, in essence, meant that players had no control over the team for which they played during their entire playing careers. This "forced loyalty" explains why players in the past stayed with just one team.

Today's professional players would be appalled by notions of a reserve clause and its restriction on individual activity. Contemporary athletes can thank Curt Flood, a baseball player for the St. Louis Cardinals. Flood first challenged the reserve clause in the early 1970s. (The Curt Flood case and the end of the reserve clause will be discussed later in this chapter.) Players have more rights and freedoms today than at any other time in sports history. However, the owners still enjoy a number of economic benefits, including tax breaks, gate receipts, and television revenue.

Tax breaks come in a variety of forms. In brief, the owner typically enjoys huge profits from the sale of a team, which is counted as capital gains—and therefore taxed at a lower rate than other sources of income such as salaries and wages. The Internal Revenue Service, for example, allows the owner to claim 60 percent of that cost for the franchise and 40 percent for player contracts. Players serve as tax write-offs because they are assumed to lose value with age; meaning, that their value can be depreciated. Thus, even when sports owners say they "lost" money and can show it on paper as a loss, they have most likely already made a huge profit. Further, owners may pay themselves exorbitant salaries which are counted as operating expenses (Zimbalist, 2000). Businesses that purchase sports-related commodities (e.g., game tickets, food and skyboxes) can write these costs off as business expenses.

Periodically, sports owners like to flex their muscles and demonstrate their power. This can be accomplished in such ways as "cutting" players who can no longer perform, suspending players for misbehavior, refusing to renegotiate contracts of players having a "break-out" season of peak performance, and so on. These displays of power are conducted on the micro level and generally affect one player at a time. Occasionally, team owners exert their power at a larger, macro level. They may engage in collusion (e.g., an informal agreement among owners to a "ceiling" salary, or "black-balling" a specific player) or in extreme cases, "lockouts." Collusion is a secret undertaking by two or more people engaged in for the purpose of fraud. In the mid–1980s, the owners of MLB were found guilty by arbitrators who ruled that they were colluding to suppress the pay of free agents. A lockout occurs when negotiations between players and owners have deteriorated to the point where owners simply close down operations and keep players from playing. Generally, lockouts follow failed negotiations where owners are claiming a loss and players are perceived to be demanding too much from them. The most recent lockout involving a major team sport in North America involved the National Hockey League. In 2004, the NHL instituted a lockout that lasted 301 days. An entire season was wiped out because of player and owner disputes centered on economic considerations. In July 2005, the owners of the NHL's 30 teams unanimously approved a new six-year collective bargaining agreement with the players. Among the most significant outcomes of the lockout was the introduction of a team salary cap of $39 million. The players were also forced to concede to a 24 percent across-the-board salary rollback, and an individual cap that keeps a player from earning more than 20 percent of his team's payroll (Farber, 2005). It could be argued that the players were the big losers in this dispute with ownership. The authors would argue that it was the fans— after all; they were, once again, powerless to do anything about the lockout.

The Role of Athletes

Throughout most of its history, professional baseball enjoyed a formal exemption from the Sherman Antitrust Act. Football, hockey and basketball generally benefited from lax enforcement of antitrust laws as well. Sports owners have typically argued that the reserve and draft systems promote competitive balance and are therefore necessary. The players, naturally, have a different perspective; they view the reserve clause as indentured servitude. The reserve system did, after all, make a drafted athlete the *property* of a team for his whole career. The signed (to a contract) athlete's skills and abilities were "reserved" for the original owner. The reserve clause guaranteed that a player could not join a rival team without the owner's permission. The marketplace for an athlete can be described in economic terms as a "monopsony." A monopsony refers to a situation where a seller (the player) is limited to only one buyer (the owner who the athlete is currently under contract or who has drafted him or her). The buyer controls the market because the seller is not allowed to sell his skills elsewhere in a free and open market.

A variation of the reserve clause, the option system, was used in football and basketball. Under the option system, a player was free to seek employment with another team one year after his contract had expired if the original owner did not re-sign him (at 90 percent of the previous year's salary) (Vogler and Schwartz, 1993). During much of the 1960s and 1970s, the NFL implemented the "Rozelle Rule"— named after then-NFL commissioner Pete Rozelle. The Rozelle Rule was a highly restrictive and secretive system designed to impede a player's attempt to sell his services to the highest bidder after playing out his option year of his contract. Any team that signed such a player was obligated to pay compensation (draft choices, money, or both) to the original team. No team was informed (prior to signing a player after his option year) as to what the compensation would be. Because of the Rozelle Rule, only four players who had played out their options were signed by other clubs between 1963 and 1976. The owners of professional sports had quasi-literally "owned" the athletic talents of their players.

Most athletes took offense to this. They believed that their skills should be marketed in the same manner as other people in other industries with the right to "sell" themselves to the team that made them the best offer. The majority of athletes realized that they were powerless in their struggle with ownership over the reserve clause and other restrictive practices that made them the property of sports owners. Eventually, a "sacrificial lamb" decided to challenge the reserve clause. This pioneer in the fight for economic rights for athletes was Curt Flood.

CURT FLOOD

Curt Flood was an outstanding centerfielder for the St. Louis Cardinals. He was a three-time All Star and seven-time winner of the Gold Glove for his defensive skills. Flood hit higher than .300 six times during his 15-year MLB career that began in 1956 and had a lifetime batting average of .293. Following the completion of the 1969 season, the Cardinals attempted to trade Flood (along with Tim McCarver, Byron Browne and Joe Hoerner) to the Philadelphia Phillies (for Dick Allen, Cookie Rojas, and Jerry Johnson). Flood refused to go. Among other things, Flood viewed Philadelphia as a racist city and the Phillies as a team with little hope of reaching the playoffs, plus he wanted to stay in St. Louis. He also felt insulted by the idea that he was being treated as a piece of property because of the reserve clause. The late 1960s were rebellious years with anti-war protests, civil rights movements, and a general questioning of

"The Establishment." Maintaining policies just because "that's the way we have always done it" no longer seemed valid to an increasingly large percentage of the American population.

Flood received the backing of the Players Association and former U.S. Supreme Court Justice Arthur Goldberg (who argued on Flood's behalf) and decided to forgo a relatively lucrative $100,000 contract to challenge the legality of the reserve clause. On January 16, 1970, Flood filed suit against MLB and its reserve clause in a case known as *Flood v. Kuhn* (407 U.S. 258) Kuhn was the MLB commissioner at the time. Flood sat out the entire 1970 season while he battled MLB. The Cardinals were forced to pay compensation (two minor leaguers) to the Phillies. Flood's *The Way It Is*, an autobiography which detailed his moral and legal objections to baseball's reserve clause, was published in 1970. In 1971, Flood joined the Washington Senators but his time away from baseball and his increasing age led him to quit the Senators after playing just 13 games. In June 1972, the Supreme Court ruled against Flood and upheld baseball's exemption from antitrust statutes. Justice Harry Blackmun's "majority opinion quoted from 'Casey at the Bat' and cited the fiction of Ring Lardner. Blackmun ... recited the names of Ty Cobb, Babe Ruth, and eighty-six other legendary players. Confronted with economic injustice and legal absurdity, the justices wallowed in nostalgia" (Guttmann, 2004: 137).

However, Flood's legal challenge of the reserve clause helped pave the way for Andy Messersmith and Dave McNally's 1975 successful challenge. In that year, baseball arbitrator Peter Seitz ruled that since Messersmith and McNally played for one season without a contract, they were "free agents" and allowed to place their athletic skills up for the highest bidder. After the Seitz decision, MLB commissioner Kuhn feared that baseball would be overrun by greedy ballplayers to the point that the game would not be able to survive (Wilson, 1994).

Flood died of throat cancer in 1997 at the age of 59. In honor of Flood's attempt to empower players' rights against the oligarchic power of owners, the "Curt Flood Act of 1998" was passed. This legislation makes it clear that major-league baseball players are covered under antitrust laws.

PLAYER BENEFITS AND INCREASED SALARIES

Curt Flood's challenge of baseball's reserve clause helped to change the face of sports forever. However, this change was relatively slow. Kuhn's proclamation that baseball was going to be driven to bankruptcy by greedy players did not come to immediate fruition. As Wilson (1994) explains, "Arbitration was undoubtedly a victory for the players, but Kuhn's picture is overdrawn. Between 1973 and 1989, fewer than one thousand cases were filed for arbitration out of a group of eight thousand eligible players; and of those cases, only 8 percent were actually arbitrated" (p. 112). However, the power of player unions would continue to increase after the Flood court case. Unions demanded better compensation, benefits and working conditions (e.g., better locker rooms, training facilities, travel provisions, and so on). The unions negotiated higher minimum salaries and better health and pension plans.

By the 1990s, it had become commonplace for players to come and go from one team to the next. Athletes were also able to sell themselves in the open market. And many athletes are enjoying a bloated sports market with some receiving astronomical salaries. Consider this sampling of player salaries:

- In 2007, the three highest paid MLB players were N.Y. Yankees: Alex Rodriguez ($27.7 million); Jason Giambi ($23.4 million); and Derek Jeter ($21.6 million). Manny Ramirez of the Boston Red Sox had the fourth highest salary in 2007 at $17 million.
- There were 425 MLB players making at least $1 million in 2007 and 66 players who earned more than $10 million. Fourteen MLB players have extended contracts totaling more than $100 million.
- Tiger Woods earned more than $22.9 million on the course in 2008. (As previously mentioned,

he has endorsement contracts totaling $100 million off the course.) It is estimated that Tiger Woods will reach the $1 billion plateau in total earnings by 2010.

- L.A. Lakers star Kobe Bryant's seven year contract pays him $136 million.
- Peyton Manning of the Indianapolis Colts (NFL) will earn $98 million over 7 years.
- In 2007, NASCAR's top earner was Jeff Gordon at $32 million (including $17 million from endorsements and royalties on merchandise). Dale Earnhardt, Jr., earned $31 million (but some of the money was split with his former race team, DEI).
- In 2007, David Beckman signed a five year, $250 million contract with the Los Angeles Galaxy (MLS) to play soccer with the L.A. franchise and to help promote soccer in the United States.

Players are earning more money today than ever before. Seemingly, there is no end to the escalation of player salaries. The typical person believes that athletes are overpaid. And yet, people continue to support athletic events and pay increasingly higher ticket prices. This pattern is consistent with many entertainers. Movie patrons pay outrageous ticket prices to watch feature films where elite actors are paid more than elite athletes. The point is, no matter how much people complain about the high prices of tickets, fans continue to financially support sport entertainers of all kinds. There are, however, some athletes in some sports who continue to struggle. American Olympians are a prime example. Nearly every nation, other than the United States, helps to fund its Olympic athletes. "Even Canada gives top amateurs a monthly stipend for expenses. Bonnie Blair, 41— the most decorated American in Winter Olympic history — tells us that it costs a speed-skater like her about $55,000 a year to compete. She had to pay her own way to Europe to practice and still is grateful for a $7,000 gift from a local police association" (Winik, 2005: 27). Elite Olympic athletes like Blair who do not participate in the "glamour" sports do not receive endorsement deals anywhere near those of other elite athletes, and there are no professional leagues where they can earn a high salary, or even a minimum salary of six figures. The rookie salary for Women's National Basketball Association players was $40,800 in 2004. The WNBA player salary cap was $87,000 in 2004.

In the elite sports, top athletes continue to command huge salaries. Many athletes are able to sell themselves on the open market to team owners with deep pockets. The owner-driven salary caps have helped lead to a high turnover of athletes from team to team in most major sports. It is often difficult to keep up with all the player movements in team sports. Today, a scorecard (or gameday program) is truly needed to have any idea who the players are on one's favorite team from year to year.

The Role of Sports Agents

Curt Flood's challenge of the reserve clause and subsequent successful legal battles by athletes against ownership coupled with the rise of power of player unions have greatly benefited professional athletes economically. However, many of today's elite athletes earn high salaries because they have entrusted their financial careers to sports agents. Some of these agents have become nearly as famous as their clients, due to their high-powered negotiating skills. Drew Rosenhaus, for instance, is one of the best known American Football sports agents and was reputedly the inspiration for the character "Bob Sugar" in the popular 1996 film *Jerry Maguire*. He has represented hundreds of players, including such stars as Edgerrin James, Willis McGahee, Santana Moss, Warren Sapp, Zach Thomas, and Terrell Owens.

While they can be extremely important in getting players the best deal possible, agents are constrained by many major league sports by collective bargaining agreements, which spell out in great detail the rights of owners and players. In addition, they can play a complicated role in their clients' lives, which can sometimes lead to misunderstandings and even lawsuits. As Tim Green (1996) points out:

To placate their clients, most agents will offer "full-service" representation, which means they will serve as financial advisor, marketing consultant, accountant, and glorified baby-sitter for their players. Thousands of players through the years have watched their money disappear because they've allowed their agents to manage it for them. The "full service" turns into self-service for the agent, who now has easy access to the player's money. The majority of agents are not qualified to provide anything but the most rudimentary advice regarding an investment portfolio. But it's easy for someone to palm himself off as an expert in this area to someone who has never held more than a few hundred dollars in his hand at one time. It is not unusual for the agent to purchase life insurance annuities, bond funds, and other investment products on behalf of a player and receive kickbacks or perks from the financial or insurance agent selling the product [pp. 195–196].

This chapter began by noting that some athletes may earn millions of dollars within 5 to 10 years, and can then live in comfort for the rest of their lives. But the reality is that often mismanagement of their funds by unscrupulous or incompetent managers and agents negates much of this, and they can find themselves scrambling to make a living. The great boxer Joe Louis, for instance, was cheated out of much of his wealth by his manager, and had to get by as a professional greeter in Las Vegas during his final years. Earning tremendous amounts of money in a short time is only half the battle — investing it wisely is quite often a task which professional athletes find more challenging than mastering the game that made them wealthy to begin with.

One final economic issue which confronts college athletes is the fact that they are not considered to be professionals. As such, they cannot draw a salary or be represented by agents. The NCAA has specified that individuals will be ineligible for participation in intercollegiate sports if they have agreed either orally or in writing to be represented by an agent. There have been challenges over the years to these restrictions, especially by those who claim that college athletics brings such large financial rewards to the host institutions that it is unfair not to pay the athletes for their work. Myles Brand, president of the NCAA, has taken a strong stand on this issue. In an interview with co-author Madigan (2003), Brand stated:

I am opposed to pay for play. The college game has integrity, and that integrity is directly tied to amateurism. To pay student-athletes for their play is just to turn the college game into the professional game, a third-rate professional game at that. Young athletes have opportunities to earn professional salaries, if they are capable of competing at the professional level. In basketball, hockey, soccer, boxing, ice skating, and other sports, college-age athletes become professionals. That is fine. Of course, these young men and women can and sometimes do attend college as they are working as professional athletes or after they complete their professional careers. Those athletes who choose to attend college are entitled to scholarship aid. I believe that they should also be entitled to at least some of the additional costs of attendance, and certainly too adequate health care and insurance. This is controversial, and not every institution is willing or able to assume these extra costs. The most important point is that student-athletes are entitled to the full opportunity for an excellent education. Every coach and athletics administration and every university president has a duty to take steps necessary to make that the case [Madigan, p. 12].

It is likely that the issue of paying student-athletes will continue to be hotly debated for years to come.

SUMMARY

Sports are part of the entertainment industry, and elite members of the sports world can earn huge amounts of money. Sports can provide upward mobility (directly or indirectly) for many athletes. Power is distributed unevenly in sports based on gender, race and ethnicity.

The socio-economic status of athletes can give them a standing in society which they would otherwise not have. Sports are an enigma. On the one hand, they are games, which are usually associated with play and fun. Yet they also comprise a multi-billion dollar industry. Much of the business of sport involves providing a product which is "marketable."

Because of the great number of potential sports consumers, the sports industry attempts to lure fans beyond the die-hard. The key is to provide a product that people will want to consume.

Because people have numerous choices in the products they consume, marketing can be the difference in financial success or failure. In an attempt to maximize financial potential, there are sports marketers who use sex to promote the sport and advertise their products. The right marketing campaign provides financial benefits for all involved. Corporate sponsorships are an effective way to handle costs. Such sponsorships are so prevalent that they have contributed dramatically to the over-commercialization found in sport today.

Athletes often endorse products for their corporate sponsors. Companies spend more than one billion dollars a year on athlete endorsements. There are expectations attached to such endorsement deals. It is important that athletes exercise a little common sense when they are offered deals to promote specific products.

Globalization of commercial sport is occurring on a growing scale. Large corporations have expanded their markets throughout the world and have spread their cultural influence into previously diverse cultures. Worldwide communications has allowed for the transmission of sports coverage in one nation to other parts of the world.

Owners play an important role in the economics of sport. The sports world is basically a self-regulating monopoly that acts as a cartel. Economic growth in sport is due primarily to television revenue. Sport league monopolies have an advantage in negotiating exclusive television broadcast rights.

A common occurrence in professional sport is franchise relocation. Communities can be adversely affected when they lose a sports franchise. They can also be held hostage when an owner threatens to relocate unless a new stadium is built at taxpayer expense. The advantage held by sports owners is similar to that of other business cartels. They receive a number of economic benefits, including tax breaks, gate receipts, and television revenue.

Players today have more rights and freedoms than at any other time in sports history, due to such pioneers in the fight for economic rights as Curt Flood. By the 1990s it was commonplace for players to change teams. Some athletes receive astronomical salaries, especially those in "elite" sports. Sports agents often negotiate choice deals, and manage their clients' investments as well, which can be a source of friction. The debate over whether college athletes should receive payment for their services is a major issue in the NCAA.

KEY TERMS

Achieved Status A social or economic standing achieved through high levels of education and/or successful personal and economic decisions.
Ascribed Status Social or economic standing inherited by those born in wealthy families, higher than those born in poorer families.
Collusion A secret undertaking by two or more people engaged in for the purpose of fraud.
Cultural Diffusion The spread of cultural aspects of one society to another.
Economic Dimension A stratification system involving two key variables: income and wealth.
Globalization A social process in which the constraints of geography on social and cultural arrangements recede and in which people become increasingly aware that they are receding.

Income The amount of money that a person, or family, receives over a period of time, generally a calendar year.

Lockout Occurs when negotiations between players and owners have deteriorated to the point where owners simply close down operations and keep players from playing.

Modernization Changes in society characterized by growth in technology (especially a reliance on the application of scientific knowledge); advances in agriculture (e.g., commercial production of corporate-run farms); the use of machinery (human and animal power being replaced by machines); and changing ecological arrangements (e.g., continued population shift from rural areas to urban ones).

Monopoly A single firm that supplies a market.

Monopsony A situation where a seller (the player) is limited to only one buyer (the owner who the athlete is currently under contract with or who has drafted him or her). The buyer controls the market because the seller is not allowed to sell his skills elsewhere in a free and open market.

Oligarchy A power structure in which control is in the hands of a few.

Option System An arrangement in which a player is free to seek employment with another team one year after his contract has expired if the original owner did not re-sign him.

Social Prestige A dimension of social stratification that is tied to what people think about others.

Social Stratification A ranking system of members of a social system into levels having different or unequal evaluations; it reveals patterns of social inequality.

Socio-economic Status A composite term that includes a person's income, wealth, occupational prestige, and educational attainment.

Sports Cartel An economic body formed by a small number of teams within the same league that make decisions on matters of common interest (e.g., rules, revenue-sharing, expansion, scheduling, and promotion) and exchange money as resources.

Wealth The total value of everything that a person or family owns, minus any debts owed.

Discussion Questions

- Do you think that college athletes should be paid? Why or why not?

- In what ways are sports a part of the entertainment business?

- Would you buy a product endorsed by an athlete? Is it important to you that the athlete actually uses the product he or she endorses? Think of some examples of current endorsements. Do you find these appropriate or inappropriate?

- Is it okay for marketers to use the sex appeal of athletes to promote their product? Why or why not?

- What is "collusion" and why have Major League Baseball owners been accused of engaging in it?

- What is your opinion of sports owners who move a franchise from one city to another without the consent of the original host city?

CHAPTER 13

Politics and Sport

Imagine amateur athletes training their entire lives for their one shot at Olympic glory only to have their aspirations crushed because their home nation is boycotting the Games. Imagine holding a "world" championship and not inviting one of the best countries in that sport to the event. How and why do things like this occur? The simple answer is politics. Politics, one of the subjects that everyone is warned not to discuss in public (or risk condemnation from someone with an opposing viewpoint), is very much a part of the world of sports. In Chapter 12, the introduction of the World Baseball Classic (WBC) in 2006 was discussed. Initially (in December, 2005), the United States government banned Cuba from the event. The Treasury Department cited the U.S. embargo on the communist nation as its reason to prohibit Cuba from the WBC. The International Baseball Federation (IBAF) announced that it would not sanction the WBC if Cuba was not allowed to participate (Chen, 2006). The U.S. government rescinded its prohibition on Cuba when Fidel Castro promised to donate all his country's WBC earnings to Hurricane Katrina victims. (All participating nations receive at least 1 percent of the tournament profits and the winner receives 10 percent.)

In this chapter, the role of government and politics in sports is explored at the national and international levels. A special emphasis is placed on the Olympics—the leading international multi-sports event.

The Role of Politics and Governments

Politics and governments have intruded into the domain of sports throughout the ages. (The terms politics and government are not used synonymously, but in juxtaposition with one another.) Politics refers to the methods or tactics of government, or governing, of a society, and the administration and control of its internal and external affairs. The political system operates on behalf of the government. The government is the governing body or organization that exercises authority via laws and customs.

The review of the history of sport provided in Chapter 3 revealed that politics and governments have traditionally played a major role in shaping sport participation and sport acceptability standards. In particular, the Olympics, dating back to its ancient origins, has routinely included political intrusion of one sort or another. Governments generally support sports for a variety of reasons. For example, the prevailing sport creed often includes values such as respect for authority, commitment to success, hard work and dedication, and perseverance that are cherished as "ideals" of acceptable behavior for citizens by governments around the world. The political domain is interested in athletes because they typically represent social organizations such as schools, communities, employers, regions, states, nations, and prevailing ideology. Politicians and governments are also interested in sports because they are so popular. This popularity represents potential power and ultimately, politics is about power, who has it, and how it is exercised.

However, as discussed in Chapter 12, when the government does not support the national sports team, as the Iraqi government barely acknowledged Iraq's first-ever Asian Cup championship in 2007, the importance of the sports accomplishment is minimized. The government was, more or less, forced to celebrate the event because of the importance placed on it by the people. However, in an attempt to maintain its power over the people, the victory celebration was held in the heavily fortified Green Zone, preventing the public from attending (Greenwell, 2007). Government and military dignitaries happily had their photos taken with the players in an attempt to boost their own images.

POLITICAL POWER AND AUTHORITY

A number of sociologists, economists, and political scientists have attempted to explain the concepts of power and authority, their role, and how they operate in society. Power and authority are exercised in nearly all social relationships, including small groups and large organizations and societies. George Homans, a social exchange theorist, focuses on micro-level relationships and views power and authority as similar concepts. According to Homans (1961) a person who has *influence* over other members of a group has authority. Possessing influence occurs when an individual has the ability to provide valuable rewards. Likewise, power is defined as the ability to provide rewards. Those with power and authority are small in number. Subordinates will accept the authority and power of leaders as long as they feel they are being treated equally (distributive justice).

Conflict theorists emphasize the role of power as a force that reveals social inequality throughout society. They claim that the dominant power group forces its values upon the rest of society, the subordinate groups. Karl Marx, whose works led to the formation of conflict theory, argued that power is attained strictly through economic means. He felt that those who control the means of production (the bourgeoisie) have power over the workers (the proletariat). In this regard, the owners of professional sport franchises hold a position of power over the players. The sports world is a multi-billion dollar industry. Therefore, from an economic standpoint, sport represents power. Our discussion of sport owners (see Chapter 12) highlighted the fact that only wealthy individuals and corporations can afford to own sport franchises.

THE ROLE OF GOVERNMENT IN SPORT

Governments around the world use sports as a tool for promoting the interests of politicians. The following represents a glimpse at the primary role of the government in sport in the United States.

1. *Rules and Safety.* Perhaps the most important role of the government is to assure the safety of its citizens. This includes providing safe sporting environments where safety rules are enacted, monitored, and enforced. "Without rules on civility and the resolution of conflicts, public life deteriorates into a jungle of passions" (Wiebe, 2003: 35). Rules regarding safety in sport include categorizing sports that are legal (e.g., football, basketball, baseball) or illegal (e.g., street luge, BASE jumping); setting age requirements for participation (usually expressed in terms of minimum age requirements); requiring safety personnel at ball games (e.g., trained rescue workers and ambulances at football games); restricting locations to those suitable for certain sports (e.g., BASE jumping may be allowed in "designated" areas); and, making laws that designed to stop discrimination (e.g., Title IX, which ensured that women had the right to play sports in school).

   There are other ways in which governments attempt to safeguard the public order, including protecting sports fans in public places via the placement of safety signs, caution cones, and barriers to control traffic flow, and mandating a large number of law enforcement officers and private security personnel. In addition, governments have to be concerned with the potential for fan violence, which can arise due to longstanding team rivalries, inebriation, provocation, and racial tensions. This is a particular problem in countries where sport hooligans or thugs are prevalent. Special care must be taken to monitor the potential for violent outbreaks, and police and medical personnel have to be available to contain the after-effects if violence does occur.

2. *Physical Fitness.* For thousands of years, warriors have prepared for the battlefield by training on the athletic fields. The original Olympics involved sports that accentuated the skills of soldiers. Medieval lords used such sports as jousting to train knights. The often cited quote that "The Battle of Waterloo [1815] was won on the playing fields of Eton" revealed the English belief that sports helped to prepare the English soldiers for battle. Baron Pierre de Coubertin, a French nobleman, pushed for the reintroduction of the Olympics after the pitiful performance of French soldiers in the 1870–71 Franco-Prussian War. Coubertin believed that France's military prowess could be re-established by means of a national fitness and sports program.

By the end of the nineteenth century, the Muscular Christianity movement had taken hold in the United States as an ideal of honorable sporting prowess. Muscular Christianity helped to generate the development of sports and fitness programs in the United States—primarily for boys—in the early twentieth century. The government's support of the playground movement was another sign of its role in encouraging health and fitness. During the 1950s, general fitness programs were the norm at schools.

Unfortunately, the U.S. government has done an inadequate job of maintaining health and fitness programs, especially in the schools. Obesity rates for children, as well as adults, have never been as high in the United States as they are now. Many schools have been forced to cut physical education and sports programs due to financial reasons. It is not a mere coincidence that as physical education programs have been increasingly disappearing or de-emphasized, the youth of today are increasingly overweight and out of shape. The U.S. government *must* reinvest in America's fitness programs. Daily physical education (for all able-bodied children) must become mandatory. After all, good healthy habits established in childhood are more likely to be maintained in adulthood. And with the increasing costs of health care, it is in everyone's (the government, as well as individuals) best interest to maintain good physical health.

3. *Promoting Prestige.* Sports provide opportunities for heroic performances, which in turn are prestigious. Athletes and teams that overcome huge odds to win a gold medal or world championship; a fallen athlete who finishes a race despite a great deal of pain; and host communities who make visitors feel welcomed are among the few ways of attaining honor, respect and prestige. Governments like to take advantage of opportunities that make them "look good," especially in front of the global community. It is this very quest for prestige that provides governments with the incentive to found sports programs and training centers. At the local level, community businesses and local governments support various sports teams (e.g., a Pop Warner football team, or high school sport teams) as a way of gaining a favorable presence in the community. Such an impression within the community is, of course, a sign of prestige.

The discussion on franchise relocation (see Chapter 12) revealed how prestigious owning a professional sports franchise is for local governments. A city is not a "major league" city until it owns a major sport franchise. A city that loses a sports franchise suffers a major loss of prestige. The reasoning goes, if a city cannot hold onto and support a major sports franchise, how are they going to conduct more mundane forms of business? Contrastly, a city that "wins" (or "steals") a sports franchise experiences an increased level of prestige. This reality helps to explain why local governments are so willing to give "sweetheart" deals to sports franchises. Such governments believe that the costs of owning a sports franchise are more than offset by the rewards of prestige.

Nations of the world find it important to win at international sporting events, as it gives them "bragging" rights in at least one social sphere. The governments of "power nations" want to beat other sporting elite nations because they believe it helps to justify their political ideology. The politicians in power can bask in the reflected glory of being identified with a winning team, especially one that has excelled on an international level.

Successfully hosting an international sporting event may also provide prestige. Consider China's hosting of the 2008 Summer Olympics. As the Chinese nation took political hit after

Construction costs of the new Yankee Stadium (MLB) will exceed $1.4 billion, much of which will be paid for by public funds (courtesy Tom Delaney).

political hit because of human rights issues, it became increasingly important for that society to "look good" within the international political world.

4. *National Identity.* Many nations possess an international identity because of their sporting prowess. For them, it becomes especially important to win the sports that they are "supposed" to win. The United States, for example, has taken an international sporting beating as a result of its failure to dominate basketball as it once did. On the other hand, when a nation beats a reigning power, the victory is all the sweeter. Furthermore, when a nation performs well when it was not expected to, they have positively contributed to their identity. Such is the case with the United States' recent success in soccer.

5. *Politicians Who Use Sports For Identity.* Sports reflect the culture of a society and provide a nation with a sense of prestige and national identity. As a result, politicians like to attach themselves to athletes; especially those who win championships. Politicians with varying rank from local community council members to the president of the country have taken advantage of the popularity of sports in an attempt to shape a positive identity with the citizens. A nation's top political leader shows respect for sports because of its cultural importance. In the United States, this tradition dates at least to President Theodore Roosevelt. Presidents routinely invite NCAA champions and professional sport champions to the White House for official photo-taking publicity shots and general "clowning" around. Nearly all presidents of the twentieth and twenty-first centuries have had a true love for sports; enhancing their identity via sport was "natural." President William Howard Taft, for example, had a brother who owned a professional baseball franchise and regularly attended professional baseball games. Taft started the annual custom of president's attending the opening day game. President John F. Kennedy's advisors used his love for touch football to "evoke images of youth and vigor" (Wilson, 1994: 271). President Gerald Ford, although perceived by the media as a bit of a klutz, played football at the University of Michigan. Ronald Reagan was a football announcer, aside from being an actor, before becoming president, and his most famous acting role was as Notre Dame football great George "the Gipper" Gipp in the 1940 film *Knute Rockne, All American.* President Bill Clinton possessed a great love for his home state University of Arkansas basketball team. And George W. Bush, a sports cheerleader at Yale, was the former owner of the Texas Rangers (MLB) and remains an avid fan of baseball. In addition, Presidents Jimmy Carter, Clinton and Bush all have their identities attached to being avid runners, and all have been identified with public advocacy of physical fitness—ironically enough, during a time when more and more Americans are becoming obese and out of shape.

At state and local levels, politicians from all ranks of government turn to sporting contests as a way of increasing a positive identity within the community. If a high school team from a small city or town wins a state championship it is understood among the townspeople that the mayor should be at the victory celebration. And generally speaking, politicians seldom skip out on publicity opportunities that place them in an environment where people are already celebrating and experiencing joy and happiness.

6. *Integration via Sport.* The U.S. government uses sports as a way to integrate different groups. Sport possesses integrative properties because it "has become one of culture's broadest common denominators.... Politicians and ministers use sports jargon to explain the world and morality" (Lapchick, 2003: 71). Recent immigrants to the U.S. can immediately feel a part of society through sports (as participants, fans, and spectators). Rich and poor, white and black, young and old, conservative and radical can all join together and become one collective when they cheer for the same team. Supporting local high school and college sports is an effective method of becoming a part of the community. Politicians are aware of the integrative power of sports. For example, "It is because sport is such a potent integrative symbol that congressmen combine romanticism and rationalism in their attitude toward it. They shift easily from seeing sport as the quintessence of private, voluntaristic behavior to seeing it as vital to the national purpose, a trust as sacred as the Constitution itself or a national monument" (Wilson, 1994: 273–273).

At a national level, the integrative properties of sport provide diverse members of a society an opportunity to form a national identity. Thus, recent immigrants to the United States will find assimilation easier when they cheer for American teams involved in international competition. Every nation of the world attempts to integrate its citizens in order to maintain stability. Sport is the common vehicle world-wide that is used to help citizens form a national identity.

Politics and American Sports

Despite the fact that many of the major American sports have foreign roots, the United States has succeeded in constructing its own sporting culture. With industrialization and the conclusion of the Civil War, the United States witnessed a rapid expansion of sport during the late 1800s and early 1900s. Commercial backing, the creation of governing bodies, and improvement in media technology (e.g., telegraph service, newspapers) coupled with an increasing number of Americans who enjoyed leisure time helped to create an American sporting culture that was unique from its colonial founders. The American sport culture was quite distinctive with its considerable emphasis on the team sports of baseball, American football, basketball and hockey (the "Big Four"). Bairner (2001) claims that "the emphasis on team sports as opposed to individual activities is itself a peculiarly American characteristic" (p. 95). This claim is not entirely accurate, as team sports such as hockey are a fabric of national identity in Canada and soccer is the very essence of such nations as Brazil, Argentina and England. What distinguishes American sporting culture from the rest of the world is a love for a wide variety of sports. Most people around the world are passionate about one sport. Although it is true that most American fans have a favorite sport, many are passionate for the sports played in each season. That is, any given fan will pay close attention to football during the fall, basketball and hockey during the winter and baseball in the spring and summer. Numerous other sports, including auto racing, tennis, golf and lacrosse will also grab the attention of Americans during the season of primary team sports.

Baseball played an important role in the development of the United States throughout the late nineteenth and twentieth centuries. Baseball was referred to as the "National Pastime." Playing baseball was encouraged by the U.S. government because the sport highlighted cultural ideals of fair play, individualism within the team framework, team spirit, respect for authority, and competitiveness. The integrative function of baseball was also viewed as a positive attribute of the sport. "One of the most dramatic developments in modern America was the migration of huge numbers of people from the rural communities to the rapidly growing cities. The game of baseball moved with them, not only physically but in some metaphysical sense as well. Indeed, for many young men, the game provided them with a sense of belonging otherwise absent from their new life experience" (Bairner, 2001: 98). The integration function was also deemed important as a means of "Americanizing" immigrants. Any boy, despite his national origins, that played baseball was in effect creating an identity as an American. This sporting identity was as imperfect as American society itself. For example, racism and sexism were found in both domains.

The Cold War sparked increased governmental involvement and political importance of Americans participating in international sporting events. The Soviet bloc nations were using sports as a way to promote their political ideology. The United States felt compelled to answer in kind. As Bairner (2001) states, "During the Cold War, sport clearly had a part to play in the promotion of American values. International events, such as the Olympic Games, acquired a new significance" (p. 112). The United States was working at a disadvantage. First, the U.S. was still using true amateur athletes in international sports competitions, whereas the Soviet bloc nations were using athletes trained by the government since early childhood. They were hardly ideal amateurs. Second, the Soviet bloc nations spent more money on their athletic training facilities than the U.S. Further, the primary sports in the U.S. were football and baseball, neither of which were Olympic sports. (Baseball has since been played in the Olympics and then, surprisingly, was removed.) Americans have always been more interested in their national sports than in international sports. The typical NFL and MLB fan would rather have their favorite team win the championship than an American national team win an international sports tournament.

U.S. government involvement in sport reached a new high in the 1970s. Legislation such as Title IX (See Chapter 10) had a dramatic impact on American sports. During the 1970s, the government also set its political attention toward the international sport scene by establishing the United States Olympic Committee (USOC). President Gerald Ford appointed a Commission on Olympic Sports in 1975 in an attempt to organize the governorship of U.S. amateur athletics. As a result of the presidential commission, the Amateur Sports Act of 1978 was passed. This act established the USOC as the chosen organization of the U.S. government to oversee, promote and support amateur athletic activities involving the United States in athletic competitions with foreign nations. Although the intentions of the Amateur Sports Act of 1978 were good, the legislation did not solve the problem of how amateur sports should be funded. The USOC had historically prided itself as the only national Olympics association that did not receive any government support — even though the government had given minimal support in the past. A decade later, the Olympic Coin Act of 1988 was passed and enabled the USOC to sell silver and gold commemorative coins printed by the U.S. Treasury.

The idea of international sporting events as a quasi-political field had played witness to a variety of political boycotts throughout the years in such competitions as the Olympics. President Jimmy Carter decided to have the U.S. boycott the 1980 Moscow Olympic Games, thus demonstrating the United States federal government's willingness to politicize international sporting events. A boycott is a form of collective action intended to pressure the target group to change its position or behavior. Soviet bloc nations returned in kind and boycotted the 1984 Los Angeles Olympic Games, still the most profitable (for the host country) of all the Games. In ancient times wars ended so that the Olympics could be played. The modern Olympics have been used as much as a political tool as an athletic event.

During the 1990s, the amateur ideal of Olympic competition was further compromised in the United States when the USOC allowed a number of professional athletes (e.g., NBA basketball players) to play in the Olympics. The quest for gold medals had replaced the ideals of amateurism. This trend has continued into the twenty-first century.

Former Athletes in Politics

Earlier in this chapter we discussed politicians who use sport for a sense of identity and opportunities to improve their own political standing with voters. In this section, athletes who turned to politics for a new identity and sense of power are discussed.

Former athletes have a number of potential advantages over non-athletes when running for political office. Their name recognition provided by the sports world is chief among them. The numerous political positions available and voter apathy are two other significant factors contributing to their success. In many nations around the world there would be fewer opportunities for an athlete to become a politician; however, the United States has more elections than any other democracy. "Voters not only fill positions that are typically appointive in other countries, such as judges, but they also select officials for many more layers of government, from the town or county to the federal level. Voters even select nominees for the ballot through primaries, instead of relying on party organizations to designate candidates" (Fowler, 1996: 430). In short, thousands of candidates compete for elected office each year. The large number of election opportunities clearly paves the way for nearly anyone to get elected to some level of political office including one of the authors. Ideally, candidates who will serve the needs of their constituents the best will be elected to office. Obviously, this is not always the case. In many instances unqualified persons who seek only to improve their own personal standings may be elected. Much of the blame resides with voters who choose candidates for reasons that have little or nothing to do with political qualifications. Voter apathy among the majority of citizens contributes to the problems of democracy as well. When thousands of election opportunities are combined with the voter apathy, unqualified candidates being elected to political office is often the result.

Ex-athletes who run for office may, or may not, be qualified for office. Each example would have to be evaluated a singular basis. To be fair, it should be pointed out that being qualified for a political office is not a characteristic of eligibility to run for office. For example, "By law, almost anyone can seek a seat in Congress; for the Constitutions sets only three criteria for members: age, citizenship, and residence in the state" (Fowler, 1996: 430). Athletes are certainly capable of meeting these three requirements. Further, most athletes possess the general characteristic of most politicians; they have a high socioeconomic status. They may also enjoy the benefit of name recognition with voters. It is often said by sports commentators that popular coaches, especially following a national championship, could run for office.

FORMER U.S. ATHLETES WHO TURNED TO POLITICS

As described earlier in this chapter, a number of U.S. presidents were involved in sports, or were sportsmen, before their political careers began. Abraham Lincoln was an equestrian, swimmer, wrestler, runner, and jumper; Theodore Roosevelt pursued baseball, lacrosse, polo, horseback riding, tennis, football, boxing, and rowing; Woodrow Wilson played and coached football; Franklin D. Roosevelt swam, rode horseback, and sailed; Harry Truman was an avid walker and umpired baseball games; Dwight D. Eisenhower played baseball and football in his youth, and in later life enjoyed golfing and fishing; John F. Kennedy swam, sailed, golfed, played tennis, and played touch football; Lyndon B. Johnson was a swimmer, equestrian, hunter, and fisherman; Richard M. Nixon played football at Whittier College; Gerald Ford played football at Michigan (earning the most valuable player award on the 1934 Michigan team and participating in two All-Star games) and later coached at Yale while pursuing his law studies (he also turned down professional offers from the Green Bay Packers and Detroit Lions); Jimmy Carter played basketball in high school; and Ronald Reagan played football at Eureka College (Leonard, 1992). George H. W. Bush was the captain of his baseball team. As these examples demonstrate, political leaders at the highest level participated in sports before they turned to politics. In the following pages, a number of other athletes who have successfully run for political office will be discussed. This is not, of course, an exhaustive list but instead provides ample evidence of the fact that the world of athletics and politics often intersect.

Among the more popular, or well-known, former U.S. athletes who have gone onto political careers are Jack Kemp, Bill Bradley, Steve Largent, and Jesse "The Body" Ventura. Jack Kemp was a star quarterback for 13 years with the AFL Buffalo Bills and San Diego Chargers. He led the Bills to back-to-back AFL championships in 1964 and 1965. Kemp co-founded the AFL Players Association and was elected president for five terms. His sports exploits and name recognition helped his initial election bid. Kemp, a Republican, served in the House of Representatives (representing the Buffalo area and western New York) from 1971 to 1989. He failed in a 1988 bid to earn the Republican Party presidential nomination but served as secretary of Housing and Urban Development for four years in George H.W. Bush's administration. Kemp was selected as Bob Dole's 1996 presidential running mate against Bill Clinton (and Al Gore). Clinton and Gore won in a landslide victory. (Ed Rutkowski, a teammate of Kemp's with the Bills, was also elected Erie County executive.)

Bill Bradley, a Rhodes Scholar after starring for Princeton's basketball team, where he was a three-time All-American (averaging 30.2 points per game throughout his three-year varsity career), played in the NBA for 10 years and won two NBA Championships with the New York Knicks (1970 and 1973). Bradley's excellence in professional basketball was honored by the Knicks when they retired his number 24 jersey. Bradley also served as captain of the 1964 gold-medal winning U.S. Olympic basketball team. Bradley turned his popularity in basketball into immediate success in the political arena. After retiring from basketball in 1977, Bradley ran for the U.S. Senate in New Jersey in 1978. He won and would serve 17 years in the Senate. Bradley ran unsuccessfully for the 2000 Democratic presidential nomination, losing out to Al Gore.

Steve Largent, never the fastest or the most gifted wide receiver, worked hard throughout his 14-year NFL career with the Seattle Seahawks and earned his induction into the Hall of Fame. The Oklahoma native was elected to the U.S. House of Representatives as a Republican in 1994. He was re-elected three times, always with a margin of over 60 percent of the vote. He identified himself with the Religious Right and led a revolt against House Speaker Newt Gingrich, whom he blamed for congressional losses in 1998. Largent relinquished his House seat to run for state governor in 2002. He lost his bid in a close election, being defeated by state senator Brad Henry by less than 7,000 votes. He is currently the CEO of a cellular phone lobbying organization.

Although professional wrestling in the United States is not considered to be a sport, we have decided to include Jesse "The Body" Ventura on the lists of athletes who have turned to politics. Ventura is a former Navy SEAL, professional wrestler, actor, mayor (St. Paul, Minnesota) and talk show host. A controversial man outside and inside the political arena, Ventura can credit his successful election as governor of Minnesota to his flamboyant personality. Ventura changed his wrestling nickname of "The Body"—a reference to his persona as bully with great physical prowess—to "The Mind"—to reflect a qualification deemed more desirable in the political world—during his foray into politics. Ventura, a member of the Reform party, served as governor from January 1999 to January 2003 but did not seek a second term.

There are other notable American athletes who have gone onto politics. For example, Ben Nighthorse Campbell (son of a Portuguese immigrant mother and Northern Cheyenne Indian father) is a former Republican senator from Colorado (he did not seek re-election in 2004). Elected to the U.S. Senate in 1992, Campbell was the first Native American to serve in the Senate in more than 60 years. He also served in the U.S. House of Representatives from 1987 to 1992. Campbell is a former three-time U.S. National judo champion (1961–63) and represented the United States at the 1964 Olympic Games in Tokyo. While serving in the Senate, Campbell was a member of the Senate's Committee on Indian Affairs. He remains as an outspoken critic of the use of Indian nicknames, mascots and logos in sports. Jim Bunning, MLB Hall of Fame pitcher, who had 1,000 strikeouts and 100 wins in both leagues, is a senator from Kentucky. Jim Ryun (R-Kansas), a three-time Olympic track star and former mile and 1,500-meter world-record holder, is a congressman. J.C. Watts, a two-time Orange Bowl MVP with the University of Oklahoma, played football in the Canadian League. Upon the completion of his CFL career, Watts was elected to the U.S. House of Representatives in 1994. Watts served four terms in Congress before leaving politics in 2003. Watts was one of the highest profile African Americans in the Republican Party.

INTERNATIONAL FORMER ATHLETES WHO TURNED TO POLITICS

The United States is not the only country with political leaders who were previously sports stars. Throughout the world former athletes have entered the realm of politics. Just as in the United States, some of these athletes have risen to the ranks of president. Russia's former president and current prime minister, Vladimir Putin, a one-time KGB agent, is a martial arts expert who still enjoys putting on displays. Other international star athletes have gone on to political careers.

Sebastian Coe, a British middle distance runner who dominated the 800 and 1500 meter races during the early 1980s, is the only man to win the Olympic gold medal in the 1500 twice (Moscow in 1980 and Los Angeles in 1984). He is one of the most decorated athletes in British history. Coe, a Conservative, was elected to the Parliament from 1992 to 1997, but lost his re-election bid. In 2000, Coe was elected to the House of Lords. He led London's successful bid to host the 2012 Summer Olympic Games and now serves as president of the organizing committee for those Games. Coe had to convince members of the International Olympic Committee that London's transport system could be overhauled and that there was public support for the Games.

A number of former Canadian NHL players have enjoyed success in the political arena after their playing careers were over. Howie Meeker's sporting and political professions overlapped, as he won the federal by election in the Ontario riding of Waterloo South in 1951 while he was still playing hockey for the Toronto Maple Leafs. The Conservative member of Parliament did not seek re-election in 1953. After retiring from hockey, Meeker became a Canadian hockey broadcasting icon who entertained viewers for 30 years with his trademark folksy phrases. Frank Mahovlich, who played professional hockey for 22 years (NHL and WHA), never ran for political office, but he was appointed to the Senate in 1998. He belongs to the Fisheries and Oceans and National Finance Senate committees. Ken Dryden, a former goaltender for the Montreal Canadians, successfully ran for office in the Parliament. He was named to the cabinet as minister of social development. There are rumors that Dryden ultimately plans on running for prime minister. It is reasonable to assume that if Wayne Gretzky stepped into Canada's political arena that he could successfully run for nearly any political office, including prime minister.

International Sports

Many nations around the world attempt to promote their socio-political ideology on the playing field. The sports environment provides a civil, universally accepted way for rival and friendly nations to compete. To assure the smooth functioning of international sports competition, each nation must abide by international rules that apply both on the field and off the field. Participating nations must realize that international rules may differ from those of their home nation. International basketball rules, for example, include a different three-point line than the one used in either the NBA or NCAA. Off the field issues usually come under the realm of foreign policy. As Nafziger (1995) states, "Foreign sports policy must comply with international law, including that governing nation groups such as the Commonwealth of Nations.... The Olympic Charter best evidences international custom pertaining to sports competition, Olympic or not. The Rules of the Charter are administered by a 'supreme authority,' the International Olympic Committee (IOC). The IOC is a corporate body having juridical status and perpetual succession.... Although the IOC is a nongovernmental organization that cannot in itself compel state obedience, its rules best evidence current international practice and therefore have legal significance" (p. 241). Thus, it is important for competing nations to understand international rules of the game and the legal authority of governing bodies. Developing coherent sports policy is an important and necessary function of government. Developing a suitable international sport policy assures that all participants, including the individual athletes as well as the governments of competing nations, fully understand the rules on and off the field.

Once an international sport policy is established, governments are ready for international sport participation, and there are a variety of political uses of international sport competitions.

POLITICAL USES OF INTERNATIONAL SPORTS COMPETITION

Ever since the reintroduction of the modern Olympic Games, the importance of international sport competition has increased tremendously. Nafziger and Strenk (1978) argue that there are six political uses of international sports competition: international cooperation, national ideology and propaganda, official prestige, diplomatic nonrecognition (and recognition), protest, and conflict. Of these categories of political uses of international sport competition, "only diplomatic nonrecognition and conflict are improper official uses of sports competition according to international law, although variations on the other uses may constitute unfriendly acts. Within this margin of discretion, it is necessary for governments to clarify their objects" (Nafziger, 1995: 239).

1. *International cooperation.* Ideally, sports foster cooperation and fair play between competitors. Nations that participate in international sporting competitions have, more or less, agreed to abide by international law. International sporting events provide a playing field where all participants play by the same rules that are, ideally, enforced fairly. The Goodwill Games were created by Ted Turner in response to the overly political Olympic Games. These Games were designed during the Cold War to promote friendly athletic competitions between nations that would be free from political problems that consume the Olympics. The first Goodwill Games were held in Seattle in 1990. According to the Goodwill Games home page (www.goodwill-games.com) the Games have discontinued after 16 years of existence, which included five Summer and one Winter Goodwill Games that included nearly 20,000 participants from over 100 countries. With the end of the Cold War, the need for such a competition has ceased to be, although the growing world tensions in other arenas might lead Turner to re-establish them in the future.

   Sporting venues also create opportunities for political diplomats to find a "common ground" that exists between them. For example, in 1999, following the World Cup championship match between the United States' and China's women's soccer teams, political diplomats from the two countries met in an attempt to ease tensions. As Sly (1999) stated, "Soccer diplomacy has scored its first victory, succeeding where regular diplomacy failed in easing friction between China and the United States. After a two-month freeze, China is signaling its willingness to soften its stance toward the United States, citing 'good sportsmanship' that the U.S. and Chinese teams displayed during their encounter in the women's World Cup final" (p. A-3). Tensions between China and the U.S. were very high in 1999, especially in light of the changing status of Taiwan, which was reluctant to relinquish independence status to China and received the support of the U.S. in its quest for independence. "But the soccer match had already helped break the ice, injecting a spirit of sporting competitiveness into a relationship that had seemed at times hovering dangerously on the brink of outright animosity" (Sly, 1999: A-3). Decades earlier, the United States and China used "ping pong" diplomacy as a means to open communications between the two polarized nations. Ping pong diplomacy is a phrase coined during the Nixon Administration to describe the use of sports as a means of bridging the political gap between the U.S. and the People's Republic of China. Americans and Chinese would later compete in other sports such as basketball, track and field, volleyball, and swimming, all the while increasing various cultural exchanges. Today, China and the U.S. are more active in trade than ever before.

In March 2006, President George W. Bush visited Pakistan. He met with Pakistan President Gen. Pervez Musharraf to praise the leader for his role in bringing democracy to Pakistan and serving as a valuable U.S. ally in the fight against terrorism. Fighting terrorism has been a hallmark of the Bush Administration. In a show of diplomacy, Bush participated in a game of cricket with Pakistani students on the lawn of the U.S. Embassy. Bush told reporters that he prefers baseball but diplomatically noted that he hasn't had time to master cricket skills. Simple gestures such as playing the national sport while touring a foreign nation can serve a positive function for a politician. It makes the politician appear concerned about the things that are popular within a culture.

2. *National Ideology and Propaganda*. Most nations attempt to use sports as a propaganda tool. Governments hope to showcase their athletes' triumphs as examples of national ideological superiority. Before the Soviet Union and East Germany attempted to demonstrate their perceived political ideological superiority via sport, Adolf Hitler had attempted to do the same thing during the 1936 Berlin Olympics. The IOC had awarded the Games to Berlin while the democratic Weimar Republic still existed. It was thought that this would be a way to demonstrate Germany's full integration back into the good graces of the world after the horrors of the First World War. Months later, however, Hitler's Nazi regime gained control of Germany. Hitler wanted Germany to host the Olympics so that he could showcase German athletes and glorify Nazism. Nazi political symbols entrenched the Games. For example, as the torchbearer brought the Olympic torch into the German stadium that served as host of the introductory ceremonies, Nazi banners were draped in a highly visible manner throughout the stadium. As described in Chapter 11, athletes such as American Jesse Owens crushed Hitler's delusional vision of German superior race.

Today, the world's elite nations, including the United States, continue to use international sporting events as an opportunity to showcase their athletic prowess as a sign of political ideological superiority. Tracking medal counts are important for nations that seek to showcase their political ideology as superior to others. The staggered stage set (gold medal winners are elevated above silver medal winners who are elevated over bronze medal winners) used to award medals to champions also reflects a power status. There are critics of this Olympic tradition of elevating gold winners over the others because they view such ceremony as elitist. These critics would prefer a technique used in the Special Olympics where all participants are treated equally. The idea of applying such an egalitarian format to international sporting events such as the Olympics and World Cup is, obviously, not at all popular with the masses, who believe winners should acknowledged for all their hard work.

3. *Official Prestige*. Concepts related to official prestige include a national identity and self-image. International sporting events provide a golden opportunity for nations of the world to earn prestige and a positive self-image. Victories gained on the playing field provide an affirmative national identity. Emerging nations are afforded an opportunity to create an image for themselves via international sporting events. Nations often use the sports world as a means of developing a national identity because it is easier to develop talents of athletes than it is to locate other precious commodities (e.g., oil, gold, diamonds, etc.). Nigeria and Kenya, for

example, have found it easier to develop prestige via their reputation as nations with great distance runners than by developing a strong international banking economy or space program. Each nation must learn to adapt to the level of natural resources and level of technology it possesses. In addition, by encouraging the talents of local athletes, nations can give a sense of hope to individuals who might otherwise despair of or even rebel against the government. And the identification certain countries, such as Brazil and Argentina, have with World Cup victories bolsters the esteem of their citizens.

4. *Diplomatic Recognition and Nonrecognition.* When a nation is allowed to compete in international sporting events, it becomes symbolic of political recognition. This often occurs during various Olympic Games. For example, Bosnia and Herzegovina (a former republic of Yugoslavia) was allowed to use its own national flag and anthem in the 1992 Barcelona Olympics. Bosnia and Herzegovina was among several small nations that emerged from the break-up of Yugoslavia, a heterogeneous country that was created after World War I by the victorious Western Allies. (Before Yugoslavia was ravaged by war during the 1990s, Sarajevo had played host to the 1984 Winter Olympic Games.) When a new nation sends its athletes to an international sporting event, it represents an innocent way to institute official contact. Thus, sports help to serve as a transitional step in the official diplomatic recognition of new governments. However, recognition can be denied a nation when other countries refuse to compete against it in sport. The former East Germany gained its official recognition via international sporting contests, thus separating itself from West Germany. The former South African government that employed a social system of apartheid (separation of races) felt the brunt of international nonrecognition in the sporting world, as most nations refused to compete with them on the playing fields. This former elite sporting nation suffered tremendously because of this nonrecognition. The racist South African government eventually collapsed.

5. *Protests.* The international sporting environment provides a major venue for protesting perceived social injustices. Social protests can occur at two levels: the individual or small group and the national or multi-national level. At any time, any number of athletes may attempt to stage a political protest during an international sporting event. If this individualistic act of protest is deemed unacceptable by the nation represented by the protestor(s), the athlete(s) risks great condemnation both nationally and internationally. On the other hand, the protesting athlete may actually gain sympathy through his or her public display of discontent. Perhaps the most famous protest conducted by American athletes during an international sporting event was exhibited by Tommie Smith and John Carlos, who gave black-power salutes during the medal ceremonies for the 200-meter race (Smith finished first and Carlos third) in the 1968 Mexico City Olympics. Smith and Carlos each raised one black-gloved hand during the playing of the national anthem. They were subsequently banned for life from all Olympic competition and ordered to leave Mexico. Of note, Harry Edwards, the sociologist who coined the term "sport sociology" (see Chapter 1), who was friends with the two athletes, had been the one who suggested the protest gesture to them. The protest perpetrated by Smith and Carlos was designed to send a global message about their feelings that the American society was racist. The majority of Americans were outraged by this public display meant to dishonor the United States. On the other hand, a number of people view the political gesture made by Smith and Carlos as a heroic stand against injustice.

Diego Maradona, a former Argentine soccer star, is involved in political protests in Argentina. In 2005, Maradona joined a huge protest rally in Mar Del Plata staged by demonstrators who were angry at President George W. Bush and his policies regarding free trade. Venezuelan President Hugo Chavez, a highly outspoken critic of Bush, was also at the protest with Maradona. Argentine President Nestor Kirchner, Maradona, Chavez and other Iberian political leaders were upset with the continuing U.S. government policy that they believe has led to numerous social problems, including poverty and misery throughout South America. Maradona used his weekly television show to combine his politics with sports analysis and remains hugely popular in Argentina.

A number of Cuban protestors took advantage of the international stage provided by Cuba's participation in the World Baseball Classic. There are millions of Cuban-Americans in the

United States. Many of these people were unsure whether to cheer for Cuba in the WBC. On the one hand, Cubans felt compelled to cheer for their ancestral home nation. However, as one Cuban American stated, "If Cuba wins, Fidel wins" (Wides-Munoz, 2006: D-1). A few highly publicized protests directed toward Castro were evident during Cuba's WBC games. During a March 13, 2006, game in San Juan, Puerto Rico, fans wore t-shirts that spelled out, "ABAJO FIDEL"—"Down with Fidel." An airplane with the same message flew over the stadium during the Cuba-Dominican Republic game, won by the Dominican Republic. This form of protesting was illegal, as the WBC organizers had banned signs with political messages to comply with an agreement made with Cuba. A number of counter-protestors chanted "Fuera!"—"take them out!"—as police intervened with the anti–Castro protestors.

Cuban officials were so upset with anti–Castro signs they refused to attend the news conference following the game for the second time in the tournament (protestors appeared in an earlier round game involving Cuba and the Netherlands). Cuban organizers had threatened to withdraw from the tournament after the March 9 game versus the Dutch, claiming there was a lack of security and respect for the Cubans. A Castro-led Cuban government will always generate protestors and counter protestors. An international sporting event provides both an opportunity to voice their grievances.

Individuals and groups may lead protests. However, protests at the national level also may occur. Protests at the national level generally involve a nation, or a number of nations, who engage in a boycott. The boycott is a type of sanction (punishment) directed toward the governmental policies of another nation(s). South Africa fell victim to an international sports boycott because of its repressive government. South Africa instituted its system of apartheid in 1948. The movement toward isolating (punishing) South Africa from the international sporting world began in 1964 when it was banned from the Tokyo Olympics. In 1970, the International Olympic Committee issued a permanent ban against South Africa, forbidding it from future Olympic competition until it ended its system of separation.

A number of significant boycotts have occurred throughout the history of the Modern Olympic Games; they will be discussed later in this chapter.

6. *Conflict.* The sports world mirrors the greater society, one that is filled with conflict and war. As explained in Chapter 9, conflict and violence are a part of sports; the international sporting arena is no different. Sport competition itself may lead to conflict and violence; for example, when athletes tangle in the "heat of the moment." This type of conflict and violence is generally short-lived and isolated. Conflict that started on the playing field sometimes spills over outside the sports arena. For example, in one rare case, a war broke out because of the events that took place on the playing field of an international sporting contest. In 1969, a best-of-three World Cup qualifier game between El Salvador and Honduras sparked an incident known as "The Soccer War." The intense rivalry between these two nations peaked when El Salvador won the best-of-three match, causing hostility. The borders between the two nations were closed. Six thousand people died and millions of dollars in damage occurred during the short war that followed. Clearly, these two rival nations had political conflicts (e.g., a long-standing dispute over the exact location of a border and the huge numbers of Salvadorans who had migrated into Honduras) prior to this short-lived war (four days), but the spectator violence that took place during the qualifying matches was enough to upset both nations to the point of war.

Conflict and violence directed at international sport participants may come from the outside and impose themselves upon the sports world. For example, in 1972, the Black September Movement (BSM) used the 1972 Munich Games to stage a violent conflict aimed at Israeli athletes. The BSM wanted to promote the recognition of Palestine and demonstrate its disdain toward Israel. The Palestinian terrorists broke into the Olympic Village and took Israeli athletes and coaches hostage. All hostages were eventually killed. The 2005 movie *Munich* recounts the tragic moments of this massacre and the subsequent hunting down of the terrorists by Israeli military personnel.

The Modern Olympics: The Ultimate International Sports Stage

The Modern Olympic Games, although often claiming a sense of idealism, have fallen far short of such lofty principles. When Baron Pierre de Coubertin, a French nobleman, attempted to establish the Modern Games, his intention was not solely to encourage the valued principles of sportsmanship and fair competitive games. Rather, it was the sad performance of French soldiers in the 1870–71 Franco-Prussian War that prompted de Coubertin's belief that France's military prowess could be re-established by means of a national fitness and sports program. Born in Paris on January 1, 1863, de Coubertin was just a child when France suffered its humiliating defeat at the hands of the Prussians at Sedan in 1870 (Guttmann, 1992).

De Coubertin believed that a national physical education program was the best means of "restoring the vigor of French youth and grandeur of France" (Senn, 1999: 2). He came to this conclusion because "he had been taken with the character-building claims of the game-playing curriculum of the upper-class-male British public schools.... He proposed that sport be extended to all in what he called a 'democracy of youth'" (Kidd, 1995: 233). De Coubertin faced far more obstacles getting his Olympic dream started than he did in establishing physical education programs for French youth. De Coubertin was confronted by political intrigues, antagonisms, and conflicts. Convincing athletes from different nations, such as Germany and France, to compete together under unified rules was another major challenge confronting the Baron. From the very first modern Olympic Games, held in Athens in 1896, de Coubertin realized that the Olympics would always be consumed by political interference. In 1908 he concluded, "The Games have become an affair of state" (Senn, 1999: 2). Senn (1999) states that early Games "had become a focal point of state policies and national ambitions. Ultimately, participation in the Games became a public affirmation of international recognition, and the possibility that some governments might even object to Games' practices arose, as the Russians did to the flying of the Finnish flag at the London Games of 1908.... The Olympic Games has seemed at times something like a disabled boat adrift in stormy international waters" (p. 2). Competing nations in the early Modern Games argued over what sports should be played, an argument that continues today. "The American sport czar James E. Sullivan, for example, argued that track and field constituted the most important sports and that most of those other types of competition should be excluded. Coubertin vigorously rejected this thought, insisting the Games should consist of many different types of competition" (Senn, 1999: 3).

Sullivan wanted track and field as the centerpiece of the Olympics because the United States dominated in those sports. American journalists documented every early success of American athletes, proclaiming such international victories as evidence of the superiority of the United States' social system (Riess, 1995). The 1904 St. Louis Games were completely dominated by American athletes; however, it should be pointed out that 432 of the 554 competitors were from the USA. The U.S. won seventy of 74 track and field medals, twenty-nine of 30 in rowing, and all the medals in boxing, cycling, wrestling, and women's archery (Riess, 1995). Nationalism was in full display by the 1908 Olympics. "Four years later at the 1908 London games, where national teams were employed, chauvinism became a dominant factor. By mistake, the host nation failed to display the American flag at the opening ceremonies. In response, several Americans carried their own U.S. flags in the opening parade and were the only athletes who did not dip their flags in respect when marching before King Edward VII. This gesture was seen as an affront to Great Britain, and British judges seemed to retaliate by cheating American athletes" (Riess, 1995: 28). Martin Sheridan, the American standard-bearer of the U.S. flag, responded to King Edward and Great Britain's perceived slight by stating the American flag dips to no earthly king.

The ceremonial opening parade of athletes remains a hallmark of the Olympics. Athletes march together by nation carrying their flags. This is a proud moment for the athletes and the nations they represent. It often brings chills to participants and viewers alike. There are a few detractors of this form of nationalism, but such critics should try explaining themselves to the athletes who relish this opportunity to represent their nation. For example, tell the Palestinian swimmers of the 2008 Olympics that athletes with national uniforms and flags marching during the opening ceremonies is not a good idea. There is no Olympic-sized pool in the territories the Palestinian athletes represent. Their training consisted of swimming in a 17-meter pool (Halpern, 2008). Furthermore, there was no budget to help support the Palestinian athletes. In short, there was little hope for these athletes to win medals in the 2008 Olympics—wearing their national uniforms and hoisting their flag during the opening ceremonies was their "gold medal." Would you take that opportunity away from them?

The great public exposure afforded by the Olympics all but guarantees political involvement (Hill, 1992). The modern Olympic Games have been plagued by political involvement and national self-interest. U.S. President Theodore Roosevelt and the city of St. Louis are credited with injecting politics into the modern games for the first time in 1904. Chicago was originally selected by the International Olympic Committee to host the games. St. Louis was already planning to host its Louisiana Purchase Exhibition World's Fair the same year and organizers managed to get the IOC to change its decision through pressure from Roosevelt (*Los Angeles Times*, 7/14/92). Politics have continued to play a negative role in the Olympics.

POLITICAL PROBLEMS WITH THE MODERN OLYMPICS

International sporting events are vulnerable to any number of political problems. Corruption, political boycotts, drug scandals and economic issues are among the primary politically-charged problems of the modern Olympic Games.

1. *Corruption.* The true level of corruption involved in the Olympics may never be known. Corruption may involve crooked judges who are paid to give high scores to specific athletes and low scores to his or her leading competitors and any number of other forms of illegal and unethical behavior. Among the more common known forms of Olympic corruption involves providing illegal payments and bribes to members of the International Olympic Committee from delegates of potential host cities who try to influence members of the IOC to vote favorably for their city. IOC President Juan Antonio Samaranch has admitted that it would be difficult for any city to secure the Games without some sort of "donation." The donation of $25 million to an Olympic museum, among many other contributions, led to a favorable vote in 1991 for Nagano's 1998 Winter Olympic Games (Theil, 1999). The Japanese government launched an investigation into the bidding activities that brought the Games to Nagano. In an official report generated by the Nagano Prefecture Investigation Group (2005), it was revealed that Japanese boosters lavished $24 million in cash gifts to members of the IOC in vying for favorable selection. The Investigation Group found that "during the period of activities promoting the bid for the Winter Olympics in Nagano, illegitimate and excessive levels of hospitality were offered" (*Nagano Prefecture Investigation Group*, 2005: 1). Many gifts to IOC members were "hidden" as souvenir-related expenses—a type of general fund that usually involves discretionary money. The large operating budgets of bidding cities provide a number of corruption opportunities.

   Thomas Welch, president of the Salt Lake City Olympic Bidding Committee for the 1998 Winter Games, learned of the "donation expectation" first-hand when, the night before the 1998 host city was announced, he was approached by IOC members who sought a cash payoff in exchange for votes. When Welch refused, the IOC voted 46–42 in favor of Nagano just a few hours later (Pound and Johnson, 1999). Welch learned his lesson; if Salt Lake City wanted to host the Games they were going to have to bribe some officials. Sure enough, Salt Lake City was selected to host the 2002 Winter Games and subsequently found itself in the center of an influence-buying and bribery scandal so serious that the very integrity of the Games is at question

(Allen, 1999). Many examples of corruption (e.g., several IOC members accepted inappropriately large gifts in exchange for voting to hold the Games in Salt Lake City) were revealed three years before the Games were held. Among the specific forms of corruption was a half-million dollar scholarship fund for relatives of six IOC members (*Buffalo News*, 12/13/98). In all, millions of dollars in gifts, scholarships, cash and gratuities for IOC members and their relatives were illegally provided as bribes to bring the Games to Salt Lake City. The fallout from the various investigations into the scandal includes the resignations of Frank Joklik, president of the Salt Lake City Organizing Committee, and Dave Johnson, vice president. Tom Welch had resigned before the scandal broke due to personal issues. Welch and Johnson were indicted in 2000 on 15 charges by a federal grand jury but in 2001 the charges were dropped (*Deseretnews.com*, 2001).

Allegations of corruption are common when representatives of bidding cities are willing to lavish "expected" gifts to unscrupulous IOC members. Money and other gifts exchanged hands during the bidding of the 2000 Sydney Summer Olympic Games that resulted in the resignation of at least one IOC member from Libya (*CNN.com*, 1999). In short, there is a great deal of corruption involved in the bidding for site locations.

2. *Boycotts*. A number of private groups have boycotted the Olympic Games. For example, European political leftists and socialist workers organizations protested the Olympics during the 1920s and 1930s. The NAACP, Jewish organizations, and half of the American public (according to a 1935 Gallop poll) protested American involvement in the 1936 Berlin Games (Wilson, 1994). However, when private groups and organizations attempt to disrupt the playing of the Games, they are unsuccessful. Significant and influential boycotts of Olympic Games are those perpetrated by a coalition of nations. For example, Israel was excluded from the 1948 Games because of an Arab-led threat of boycott. However, for the most part, before World War II, there was little interest among the nations of the world to boycott the Games. This would change in the 1950s. Olympic boycotts occurred in 1956 over the Soviet invasion of Hungary and the British invasion of Egypt. A number of nations also boycotted the 1976 Montreal Games because New Zealand was allowed to participate. (New Zealand was stigmatized at that time because of its refusal to boycott South African sports.)

Guttmann (1992) claims that the "era of the boycott" began in the 1970s. A number of nations sympathetic with the plight of Palestine boycotted the 1972 Games. As described earlier in this chapter, a political boycott was not sufficient for the Black September Movement (BSM). Twenty nations from Africa agreed to boycott the 1976 Montreal Games if New Zealand was allowed to participate. The African nations were upset with New Zealand because it allowed one of its rugby teams to play in South Africa, which was a violation of the international boycott imposed on all South African sports. China not only threatened to boycott the 1976 Games if Taiwan was allowed to participate in Montreal, the Chinese government threatened to renege on a trade agreement crucial to the Canadian economy. Taiwan enjoyed IOC recognition and host Olympic nations must welcome athletes from any country in good standing. The IOC was eager to have mainland China participate in the Olympics and as a result allowed them to participate. Nationalist China (Taiwan) was asked to participate under either a Taiwan or IOC flag. It refused, and boycotted the 1976 Games.

The 1980s witnessed the biggest and most significant political boycotts of the Olympics. A U.S.-led boycott of the 1980 Moscow Games was prompted by the 1979 Soviet invasion of Afghanistan. This boycott, in turn, resulted in a Soviet Union led 15 nation boycott of the 1984 Los Angeles Games. President Jimmy Carter initially had a hard time convincing foreign nations—let alone the United States Olympic Committee—to agree with his decision to boycott the Moscow Games. The U.S. had alienated the African nations by not joining them in their 1976 boycott and many European nations had questioned Carter's reasoning and justification for his political boycott of Moscow (Wilson, 1994).

> The Carter Administration's demand for a boycott by the USOC of the Moscow Games was based on what appeared to be unclear policy concerns. The Administration variously argued principles of diplomatic protection of its nationals, deterrence and retribution. The President first justified the boycott on the grounds of a presumed danger to American athletes and spectators, which was the

rationale parroted by the Soviet Union to justify its boycott of the 1984 Games. After having advanced this rationale for the compelled boycott, the White House later changed its mind by asserting that the real reason for the boycott was to deter future aggression and to send the Soviets 'a signal of world outrage.' [Nafziger, 1995: 239].

In the end, the largest Olympic boycott ever — 61 nations in all — responded to Carter's request that athletes stay home to protest the Soviet invasion of Afghanistan. Ironically, decades later, the U.S. would invade Afghanistan although for entirely different reasons.

Despite the Soviet led boycott of the 1984 Summer Games, Los Angeles earned a record $222 million-plus profit. (Peter Ueberroth, the organizer of the event, became famous for his managerial skills, and was shortly thereafter appointed the commissioner of Major League Baseball, serving from 1984 to 1989. He is presently the head of the United States Olympic Committee.) Of note, Nationalist China competed as Taiwan and the People's Republic of China competed as China. The 1988 Seoul Games enjoyed a near "normal" participation rate among the nations of the world. South Africa was still banned from the Games but only six invited countries (North Korea, Cuba, Ethiopia, Nicaragua, Albania, and the Seychelles) refused to participate (Figler and Whitaker, 1995). The "Era of the Boycott" appears to have concluded. The 1992 Barcelona Games represents the first Olympiad since 1972 that no country boycotted. A record 169 nations took part in the opening 1992 parade. Participation rates continue to soar into the Third Millennium. Many human rights groups called for a boycott — either by athletes or by world leaders attending the opening ceremonies— of the 2008 games in Beijing, in protest for China's occupation of Tibet and alleged human rights violations perpetrated on its inhabitants.

3. *Drug Use and Drug Testing.* Another problem facing the Olympics is one that exists at all levels of sports, drugs and the subsequent drug testing policy. Just as illegal drug use and drug testing is a major focus of governing bodies in American sports, so to is it a concern in the Olympics. Decades ago, sports fans marveled at the accomplishments of East German athletes; today, of course, we know the results are tainted because of illegal drug use. Athletes taking performance enhancing drugs such as anabolic steroids predates the East Germans. Hoberman (2005) explains that the doping of athletes "was evident long before the anabolic steroid epidemic began during the 1960s. As early as 1939, before doping was being recognized as a societal problem, a Danish exercise physiologist was reporting that the use of stimulants by athletes was fueling 'the record-breaking craze and the desire to satisfy an exacting public'" (p. 216).

The problem of illegal drug use in the Olympics has "reached epidemic proportions," according to Hoberman (2005). "The widespread and often undetected use of potentially dangerous synthetic hormones such as anabolic steroids, human growth hormone, and erythropoietin has provided a crisis of confidence in the integrity of such Olympic sports as track and field, swimming, cycling, and weightlifting. Hormone doping has made possible, or rendered suspect, numerous world records" (Hoberman, 2005: 239). The scandal of tainted drug records came to the forefront with Canadian sprinter Ben Johnson's positive drug test following his record-setting performance (100 meters in 9.79 seconds) in the 1988 Seoul Games (Coe, 1996). Although Johnson was caught, it is generally believed that that "for every one of those few track and field athletes who have been caught, we can only assume that there have been many dozens who have carefully, secretly and systematically relied on drugs in some form or another to help them towards a personal best, an international best, a place in the Olympic squad, an Olympic medal" (Coe, 1996: 112).

It is believed that many athletes get away with taking drugs because of ineffective drug testing policies in sport (Voy, 1991). As Hoberman (2005) explains:

> The failure of national and international sports federations to control doping is primarily a political, though it is conventionally misrepresented as being caused by the moral degeneracy of individual athletes. Media reports of doping scandals invariably stress the ethical failures of athletes and portray sports federations as beleaguered but honest regulators whose methods for detecting drugs cannot match the scientific ingenuity of the cheaters and those who aid and abet them. But the reality of doping is far more complicated.... The historical record shows that the minority of sports officials who have been openly dedicated to the eradication of doping have been unable to prevail

against less-dedicated colleagues bent on tolerating or covering up the doping practices of their athletes, coaches, and doctors [p. 240].

The culture that accepts athletes taking drugs must be changed if effective drug enforcement is to prevail. This culture includes the athletes, trainers, coaches, governments and fans of sport. They must all agree that taking performance enhancing drugs not only risks the health of the athletes but ultimately compromises their performance. During the 2002 Salt Lake City Games a number of athletes tested positive for drugs, including medal winners (e.g., Spain's Johann Muehlegg and Russia's Larissa Lazutina, who lost gold medals). Hoberman (2005) concludes that a "drug-free" sport is an illusion. "This is especially true at the elite levels, where athletes are subjected to constant physical and psychological stresses that are treated with drugs.... Doping has also spread to recreational sport and even sport for the handicapped, demonstrating once again how the modern fascination with performance extends far beyond the exclusive ranks of elite performers" (p. 275). The sobering outlook on drug use and the lack of quality drug testing described by Hoberman implies that doping will remain a problem in the Olympics.

4. *Economic Issues.* Host countries fight with each other intensely in order to have the Olympic Games held in one of their prominent cities. Partly this is done for prestige purposes, due to the great attention the country will receive from the mass media during the events. But the primary motivating factor seems to be the perceived economic benefits that will accrue from tourists, commercialization, and other revenue-enhancing areas connected with the events. Yet, with the noted exception of the 1984 Los Angeles Games, which were a great financial success, it is debatable just how positive the economic impact has been on the host cities. Most cities have claimed to have ended up losing money, although it is often said that the long-term benefits of adding new stadiums and other facilities more than makes up for any initial financial loss. Still, as Helen Jefferson Lenskyj (2000) points out, this too is debatable:

> Evidence from three decades of Olympic industry disasters has demonstrated what is arguably the most serious and sinister implication for citizens living in Olympic cities and states: the threat of disenfranchisement. The generally negative social, economic, and environmental impacts of hallmark events, as well as the documented concerns and experiences of anti–Olympic and Olympic watchdog groups on four continents, provide irrefutable evidence that Olympic bids and preparations exacerbate the problems of already disadvantaged populations. While some of the promised economic boosts may eventuate, there is little evidence that the people "at the bottom of the food chain" will reap any benefits. A beautified, gentrified city with state-of-the-art professional sports facilities has no value to men, women, and children whose basic human needs are not being met [pp. 192–193].

Idealistically, the Olympics are a symbol of cooperation among diverse nations. In reality, the Olympics are ripe with political problems and issues. Promoting one's ideology through international sport dominance remains as a characteristic of the elite nations of the world.

SUMMARY

The role of government and politics, at both the national and international levels, is an important aspect of sport. They have shaped sports participation and sport acceptability standards. Going back at least to the time of the ancient Olympic Games, political intrusions into the world of sport have occurred for a variety of reasons.

Governments around the world use sports as a tool for promoting the interests of politicians. Perhaps the most important role of the government is to assure the safety of its citizens, which includes providing safe sporting environments, and monitoring rules and safety regulations. Governments also have an interest in maintaining the physical fitness of their citizens, and sports participation is an excellent way to encourage this. In addition, sports promote national prestige and national identity.

Political leaders often identify themselves with athletes and sporting events. At state and local levels, politicians from all ranks of government turn to sporting contests as a way of increasing a positive identity within the community. On the national and international levels, they often try to connect athletic victories with their own governmental policies.

Sports provide mechanisms for integrating disparate groups within a society, by allowing them to form national identities. Even with the increasing role of globalization and the spread of international sport, nationalism remains an important issue.

Countries are often identified with specific sports: hockey in Canada, basketball and baseball in the United States, soccer in Brazil and Argentina. Such sports can highlight cultural ideals, as well as increase one's national identity. They are often supported, either directly or indirectly, by governmental subsidies.

Political issues can also intrude into the world of sports. Athletes can be co-opted into supporting political policies or identifying themselves with specific political leaders. In some instances, athletes themselves run for and obtain political offices.

Many nations attempt to promote their socio-political ideology on the playing field. The International Olympic Committee (IOC) is a nongovernmental organization which attempts to develop a coherent sport policy internationally. Ideally, sports foster cooperation and fair play between competitors. But national ideologies and propaganda techniques have sullied the sports world, including the Olympic Games themselves. The lofty principles of the modern Olympics often come into conflict with the political realities of the competing nations.

KEY TERMS

Apartheid Government-sanctioned separation of races.

Authority According to George Homans, a person who has *influence* over other members of a group. Authority is considered to be a type of legitimate power.

Boycott A form of collective action, in athletics involving withdrawal from participation, intended to pressure the target group to change its position or behavior.

Government The political unit that exercises authority via laws and customs.

Ping Pong Diplomacy A phrase coined during the Nixon Administration to describe the use of sports as a means of bridging the political gap between the U.S. and the People's Republic of China.

Politics Generally viewed as the guiding influence of governmental policy.

Power The ability to provide rewards.

DISCUSSION QUESTIONS

- Should the United States have stayed out of the 1980 Olympic Games? What arguments did President Jimmy Carter give to justify his order? Was this fair to the athletes who had prepared for four years or more to participate? Was the Soviet Union justified in keeping its teams out of the 1984 Games in retaliation?

- All nations must be interested in the physical well-being of their citizens. Should sports participation, particularly in the schools, be subsidized by government money? Why or why not?

- How do sports provide opportunities for promoting prestige among nations? Should citizens identify with their nations' sport teams during such international events as the Olympics or World Cup?

- Why might an athlete be a viable candidate for political office? What abilities, demonstrated on the playing field, might be applicable to holding a political position? What are some criticisms that could be given for supporting athletes who run for office?

- Are the ideals of the Olympics too lofty? Or do they still basically serve the goals of their initiators, who hoped to alleviate world tension and foster a sense of international cooperation?

CHAPTER 14

Religion and Sport

The game is on the line as the home team lines up for a last second, game-winning field goal attempt. The tension in the air is heightened when the visiting team calls a timeout in an attempt to "freeze" (add pressure to) the kicker. Tens of thousands of fans in the stadium and millions of fans watching on television hope for the best. Many of these fans, assuming that a higher power exists, offer up silent prayers to God for divine intervention. "Please, God, let the kicker make this field goal," pray the fans. Meanwhile, many of the opposing team's fans are praying to God that the kicker will miss the field goal. Whose prayers will God answer? Why do people think God cares whether the field goal is good and one team wins, or whether the field goal is missed and the other team wins? Why do people believe there is a God to pray to, for that matter? These are among the questions that prevail in an examination of sport and religion.

In this chapter, the role of religion (including prayer) in sport is examined. We will examine the social institution of religion, the relationship between sport and religion, the similarities and differences between sport and religion, and the secularization of sport (including a look at sport superstitions).

The Institution of Religion

Throughout humanity our species has struggled to survive among the bigger and much stronger species that inhabit the earth. Humans learned to rely on cunning ingenuity and eventually developed a superior intellect. This intellect allowed for the creation of tools that help the human species rise to the top of the food chain. Along with an evolving intellect came a thirst for answers to life's dilemmas that seemed overwhelmingly complicated to the average person. Lacking scientific knowledge, early humans developed crude, elementary forms of explanation. Humanity simply personified the forces of nature, thus creating a universe of spirits that were held accountable as explanations for natural phenomena (Prebish, 1993). Animism was the earliest form of religion. "Animism maintains that everything has two aspects, a physical manifestation and a spirit or soul. This duality enabled early humanity to explain the difference between life and death, as well as the images present in dreams. The presence in these spirits or *anima* suggested both a life after death and the existence of realms other than the human" (Prebish, 1993: 5). Over time, most religions shifted their belief systems from multiple gods to the concept of one true God.

How do people learn about religion? Much in the same manner that they learn about sport; that is, through the agents of socialization. Sport and religious participation are generally taught in early life through exposure to the ideals of each institution from significant others. Through participation individuals cultivate an increasingly more sophisticated level of understanding and knowledge of religion, as they do sport. Most people who are introduced to sport or religion early in life and had such ideals reinforced throughout childhood are likely to maintain their participation throughout their lifetimes. Prebish suggests, however, that people constantly seek more knowledge about sports than they do about religion. "Unlike religion, though, the sport cycle really does seem to be working. There are fewer and fewer adults who have not progressed beyond a child-like understanding of an ever-increasing variety of sports" (Prebish, 1993:xiv).

DEFINING RELIGION

Religion developed as a source of explanation for life's uncertainties. Religious explanations are not based on empirical science, but rather, a belief system. Science and religion are often at odds because of this fundamental difference. Whereas people of science rely on empirical data collection and analysis, religious adherents rely on faith and spiritual beliefs. A belief is a conviction of certainty about specific matters even without evidence of its truth. Every religion is structured on a system of beliefs. Religious beliefs are centered on an unquestioned conviction of ideals to which members of a particular religion adhere. Fans of Notre Dame University believe that "God made Notre Dame number one," but they have no empirical "proof" of this. Nonetheless, religious adherents form a sense of community based on their beliefs and spirituality. With this in mind, religion may be defined as a system of beliefs and ritualistic behaviors which unite a group of like-minded people together into a social group who adhere to ideals of spirituality.

FUNCTIONS OF RELIGION

Social institutions of Western society are organized pragmatically, rationally, and ideally, logically. Even so, religious ideals still dominate the private lives of most people. Religion exists because it serves so many functions in society. For this reason, sociologists examine religion on the basis of the functions it serves. (An understanding of the functions of religion will help the reader to better understand the similarities and differences between sport and religion to be discussed later in this chapter.) A function is viewed as behavior that is a contribution or service or serves a purpose to society. Functions of religion commonly cited among sociologists include the following:

1. *Religion provides order and meaning to life.* Religion helps to provide structure and order in the daily lives of adherents. It helps to explain and justify the role of individuals in the social world in order to move onto the next life. Religion offers simple and reassuring explanations about the meaning of life.
2. *Psychological support.* A chief function of religion is providing for the psychic needs of its followers, especially by providing emotional and spiritual support in times of crisis. With the death of a loved one, many people find comfort within the religious community because of the psychological support offered. Psychological support is also provided in happy times as well (e.g., marriages, confirmations, baptisms, and so on).
3. *Self Esteem and Identity.* Another function of religion that helps individuals is the affirmation of social status. Through religious membership, adherents enjoy a sense of belonging to a community of like-minded people, which in turn upholds the positive aspects of religious identity. A positive identity is acquired primarily through social interaction with others. This positive sense of identity, in turn, increases self-esteem.
4. *Social Solidarity and Integration.* As religion continues to alter the identities of individuals, a community of like-minded people forms. The integrative property of religion remains as one of the primary functions of religion; after all, the word "religion" comes from the Latin word "religare," meaning "to bind together." Religion shapes the group into a common way of thinking and adhering to common beliefs and values, where shared perspectives shape a "we" feeling (e.g., "we Baptists," "we Catholics," "we Hindus").
5. *Ceremonies of Status.* Ritualistic behavior among group members reaffirms the social solidarity

A religious mural on the side of the Library Building at the University of Notre Dame that overlooks the football field is affectionately nicknamed "Touchdown Jesus" because Jesus appears to be signaling "touchdown."

between them. Ceremonies of status are a form of ritualistic behavior that represents the passing from one level to the next. Baptisms, bar mitzvahs, confirmations, and other religious ceremonies characterize major steps in development for the younger members of the religious community. Such rituals indoctrinate the next generation into the mindset of the religious group; they also reinforce the collective sentiments held by those with full status.

6. *Social Control.* All religions have a set of rules that adherents are expected to abide by. Religious tenets (e.g., the Ten Commandments, the Golden Rule, the Koranic rules) are designed to keep believers in line with the norms, values, and beliefs of group. Most followers practice the beliefs taught to them by religious leaders in their daily lives. In some societies, the social control power of religion is as important as (or the same thing as) the government. In Western societies, such as the United States, there is generally a separation of church and state principle that allows civil law to supersede religious law in civil matters.

This concludes our brief review of the functions of religion. Next, we shall examine the overlap between the social institutions of religion and sport.

The Relationship Between Religion and Sport

Emile Durkheim argues that the relationship between sport and religion is sociological, rather than psychological or biological. From a Durkheimian perspective, the relationship between religion and sport represents the meeting of the sacred and the profane. Durkheim

(1912) described sacred items as those objects that we show reverence toward (e.g., a blessed rosary); they are set aside from the everyday items. In contrast, profane items are the ordinary, everyday objects (e.g., computers, cell phones, DVDs). Durkheim viewed religion as a social phenomenon, rather that a psychological one, because of its ritualistic behavior and use of symbols. As Birrell (1981) explains, "The conceptual definition of *ritual*, and the related concept *symbolic system*, on which this discussion of sport is based, are most familiar from Durkheim's *The Elementary Forms of Religious Life* where he presented his thesis concerning religion as a social rather than psychological experience" (p. 356).

Charles Prebish (1993) believes that the ritualistic behavior and use of symbolic language found in sport today qualifies it as religion. Furthermore, because followers of sport treat it as sacred, sport *is* religion. Harry Edwards (1973) claimed that if a universal popular religion exists in the United States, it is found within the institution of sport. This religious experience in sport is not confined to the actual participants (the players) but also extends to the fans. And, if sports fans believe, and players view, a sport as a type of religion, then it, in fact, becomes a religion.

Most sport sociologists argue that sport is not a religion in the same manner that Methodism, Presbyterianism, or Catholicism is a religion; rather, it is a secular or civil religion. Novak (1993) explains, "Sports are religious in the sense that they are organized institutions, disciplines, and liturgies; and also in the sense that they teach religious qualities of heart and soul. In particular, they recreate symbols of cosmic struggle, in which human survival and moral courage are not assured. To this extent, they are not mere games, diversions, pastimes. Their power to exhilarate or depress is far greater than that. To say: 'It was only a game' is the psyche's best defense against the cosmic symbolic meaning of sports events" (p. 153). To put it simply, sport can give *meaning* to a person's life, and for many it is the primary way they give importance to their own existence.

Similarities Between Sport and Religion

Harry Edwards (1973) argued that the universal "popular" religion of the United States is sports. To be considered a religion, sport must possess a number of characteristics common to religion. Edwards refers to thirteen essential features that sport shares with religion. Having researched the numerous similarities between sport and religion, as cited by Edwards and other sport sociologists, the authors have established a list of twenty similarities between these two powerful social institutions.

1. *Belief Systems.* Edwards (1973) argues that both sport and religion have a body of formally stated beliefs that are accepted on faith by a great number of adherents. Belief systems are centered on a creed that followers abide by in varying degrees. Fans are told to have "faith" in their team, especially in times of turmoil, much in the same manner that religious people are told to have faith in times where they doubt their religion or "God's plan." The philosopher William James coined the phrase "the will to believe" to express the view that sometimes believing that an event will occur can actually help make it happen. This can be applied to both athletes and fans, who feel that their strong dedication to winning might actually tip the scale and make victory occur.

2. *True Believers.* Neither sport nor religion can survive without followers, or true believers. Both social institutions rely on converting new members into their belief systems. This is accomplished through the socialization process (See Chapter 5). "True believers" are those who so strongly support the religious or sport ideals that they defend such social institutions passionately. They are unyielding in their support.

3. *Providing Testimony.* Religion and sport both have their pundits who promote their respective social institutions. Sports fans everywhere love to proclaim, "We're number one!" Religious adherents also believe that their religion is "number one" as well.

4. *Patriarchical Dominance.* Both institutions have been, historically, dominated by men. The passage of such legislation as Title IX and a greater acceptance of women in sport have lessened the male dominance once found in sport. Many of the world's major religions have failed to embraced gender equity. In the Catholic Church, for example, women are not allowed to join the ranks of priesthood. Muslim women are treated as a distant second-class citizen to the male Muslim. Hindu and Islamic nations seldom have women athletes or women's teams because women are not allowed to expose any parts of their bodies in public. Such a practice is clearly not conducive to gender equity. Both sport and religion have "ruling patriarchs"—males who carry the most influence within their respective institutions. The ruling patriarchs are often treated, and act, as saints or gods.

5. *The Worship of Saints and Gods.* As described above, the institutions of sport and religion have their saints and gods who personify the respective ideals of their institutions. Sports fans often idolize and "worship" athletes as if they are gods, much in the same manner religious adherents blindly revere and adore a variety of religious leaders. The various sports halls of fame are especially symbolic of the level of worship bestowed upon athletes by sports fans. Further, sport fans demonstrate their commitment to their earthly gods by regularly reading the sports pages for more information about their heroes and by collecting various sports memorabilia (e.g., autographed baseballs and other items and a wide variety of sport-related souvenirs) which are symbols of their faith in their gods. Religious adherents often have various religious items (e.g., crucifixes, holy books in their homes) that they also pay homage. Both institutions also have their "martyrs." With sport, Notre Dame football great George "the Gipper" Gipp, Yankee baseball legend Lou Gehrig, and Pat Tillman (see Chapter 4) might be considered in this category.

6. *High Councils.* Religion and sport are both consumed with rules and expectations of proper behavior. Rules are designed to maintain consistency within a group or society. Often, these rules contain moral and ethical undertones. As a result of rules and the need to enforce the rules, both social institutions have ruling councils that create, maintain, and interpret their respective rules. The Catholic Church, for example, requires that its priests remain celibate in order to preserve their purity and closeness with God. The hierarchy established in the Church will enforce such rules. In sport, such councils include the NCAA, USOC, and the various ruling professional sport league offices.

7. *Scribes.* Another commonality between sport and religion is the reliance on scribes to maintain the history of their social institutions and promote public awareness regarding the ongoing, daily events of the tradition.

8. *Seekers of the Kingdom.* Both sports and religion have hard-core, diehard followers who believe so strongly in the tenets they have been taught that they take the teachings literally and are willing to do anything to reach the "promised land." For the religious person, the "kingdom" may be Heaven or a higher reincarnated life form. In sport, the "kingdom" is the sporting event itself, especially when the game is played in a revered stadium or arena—and this scenario is true for both the athlete and the fan.

9. *Psychological Support.* As mentioned earlier in this chapter, one of the primary functions of religion is to provide psychological support to its adherents, especially in time of emotional crisis (as well as during happy occasions). Athletes and coaches are capable of providing psychological support to one another as well. Coaches (especially at the nonprofessional level) often console athletes after an individual failure or team loss. Teammates, also, generally support one another in time of crisis. In addition, coaches and teammates are there to celebrate victories with one another as well.

10. *Pilgrimages to a Shrine.* Diehard religious adherents and sports fans must have a destination, a promised land, to guide their paths through life. Depending on one's religion, hearing Mass at the Vatican, or saying prayers at Mecca, represent ideal destinations. In sport, the various halls of fame may be viewed as shrines honoring heroic figures accompanied by tales of greatness. Attending major sporting events and beloved stadiums are also viewed as shrines. The 1989 film *Field of Dreams,* with its mantra "If you build it, he will come," ably captures this mystical aspect.

11. *Buildings for Events.* Believers and followers of sport and religion generally have a place, sacred ground, where they meet to worship as a group. It is true that religious believers and sport followers can both practice their religion at home, but most will commune with others. Thus, both religion and sport provide physical locations which may qualify as "shrines" for people to worship collectively. All societies provide buildings (e.g., churches, synagogues, and mosques) for followers to worship and pay homage to their saints and gods. The parallel between sport and religion is obvious in this regard, as most towns and cities in the nation have a ballfield, high school stadium, and perhaps a university or major league stadium.

12. *Use of Symbols.* People communicate symbolically. Symbols are objects, ideas, and actions that possess meaning for those who adhere to such beliefs. Both religion and sport employ the use of symbols that possess a shared meaning for participants. Religion has such symbols as the Cross, the Star of David, the Rosary, and the Mezuzah, and sport has such symbols as championship trophies and rings, medallions, and ribbons. The Olympic torch as a symbol of pure, undying sportsmanship is another such example.

13. *Written Dramas.* In an effort to keep the attention of their followers, both religion and sport have created dramas to captivate adherents. Religion relies on prayer books as a means to keep followers interested in their teachings as well as provide guidelines for "proper" behavior. The sports world has playbooks and training manuals for athletes and media guides and programs for sport fans.

14. *Scheduled Events.* The primary reason for scheduled events is to keep followers in a routine of ritual. Religious people are expected to attend services on a regular basis; consequently, religious leaders designate specific days and times for adherence to such services. The sports world heavily promotes its schedule and has the assistance of the media.

15. *Special Days.* The routine can become boring, even to the strictest adherent to sports or religion. As a result, both the sport and religion create a number of "special" days to stimulate and excite followers. Religion promotes these special days (e.g., Easter, Passover, Christmas, and Hanukkah) as a time to re-commit to religious ideals and tenets. The sports world usually promotes special days at the conclusion of each season. Thus, the World Series (which follows the end of the regular and playoff season in MLB); the Super Bowl (which crowns the NFL champion); "March Madness" (the NCAA men's basketball championship single-game elimination series); and the World Cup are viewed as pinnacle days in sports.

16. *Collective Emotions.* Religious followers who share the same belief and come together in the form of a religious community often share collective emotions through ritualistic behaviors. The collective emotions shared by sports fans are especially obvious as they outwardly display their emotions: happiness and elation following a victory and sadness and despair following a loss. Both religion and sport allow men, in particular, the rare opportunity to cry in public and generally express their deepest emotions in an unabashed way.

17. *Ritualistic Behavior.* "Both sport and religion employ intricate rituals which attempt to place events in traditional and orderly view" (Slusher, 1993: 173). Religious services include a large number of ritualistic behaviors. Catholics, for example, make the sign of the cross after placing their index finger in a bowl of holy water upon entering the church. They kneel, sit, stand, and repeat. They shake hands with one another and receive communion. In religion, ceremonies and rituals are practiced to give order to man's existence (Slusher, 1993). The sports world is also filled with ritualistic behavior; although such behavior is often tied to superstitions. Chandler (1992) argues that "many rituals in sport are designed simply to assert superiority.... These rituals of superiority are worldwide.... These rituals of dominance simply underscore the sporting competitor's objective: to win." (p. 58). (We will discuss the role of ritualistic, superstitious behavior in sport later in this chapter.) Ritualistic behaviors are used to galvanize a community of adherents around a set of values (Hoffman, 1992).

18. *Competitive Nature.* Both sports and religion are in competition with challenges within their respective social institutions from competing elements. Each religion seeks to convert as many followers as possible in an attempt to outnumber its "enemies." Religions, by their very design, are unique and different, and each one believes it is "right" and therefore, by default, the others are "wrong." Consequently, each religion is in competition with the others. The

sports world is a "battlefield" of competition. Once again, by design, sports has as its primary goal for one athlete or team to demonstrate its superiority over competitors.

19. *Prayer.* Religious leaders and adherents, athletes, and sports fans utilize prayer as a means of attaining a favorable outcome. Although prayer in the religious world is generally thought of as within the sacred realm and prayer in the sports world as profane, there remains a common thread between the two. In all cases, those who rely on prayer are hoping for "divine" intervention. They have lost "faith" in human ability and have searched for unearthly assistance. The role of prayer in sport will be discussed later in this chapter.

20. *Sense of Identity.* Sport, as religion, helps to provide individuals with a sense of identity and self-esteem by creating a sense of belonging and providing meaning to life. Both sport and religion provide opportunities to reaffirm social solidarity through the creation of a bond among members, thus forming a sense of community. Bonding leads to feelings of identity, loyalty, commitment, and self-esteem.

Clearly, there are many similarities between sport and religion. In fact, it is difficult to argue with those who claim sport *is* religion; or at the very least, a quasi-religion. There are, however, a number of significant differences between sport and religion as well.

Differences Between Sport and Religion

The differences between sport and religion are highlighted by the fact that sport is centered on the profane, everyday, tangible world, whereas religion is centered on the sacred, spiritual world. The major distinctions between sport and religion are listed below.

1. *Sports are Real and Religion Is Spiritual.* Although sports fans express "faith" in their team, this is not the same thing as religious faith. Religious adherents pay homage to a "sacred" world that is not visible and that is promoted by people who cannot show empirical proof of their spiritual claims. Sports, on the other hand, are real, tangible, and visible. Sports fans and athletes need no other verification of the validity of sport than simply to observe the phenomena before their very eyes. Sports fans must have "faith" that their team or favorite athlete will prevail, but no such faith is necessary to verify its existence. Religious adherents are told to have faith in an entity unseen and unverifiable. Religious beliefs are based on a leap of faith. Sports fans keep tangible records and hope for victories in *this* world rather than the world to come.

2. *Sports Are a Part of the Here and Now.* Related to the first difference between sport and religion, sports are not only "real," they are a part of the here and now. The world of sport provides us with concrete time and space situations bound by the laws of nature. Time and space constraints also mean that sport is a human event that rests *within* humans (Slusher, 1993). The religious realm transcends time and space; it speaks of an afterlife, a world *outside* of human confines.

3. *Sports are Materialistically Driven.* Because sports are a part of the profane world, and economic success is a powerful force in Western culture, sports are materialistically driven. Athletes want big salaries. Sports owners want to make money. Sport sponsors want their athletes to win and promote their products. The media wants to sell commercial time in an attempt to make broadcasting profits. At every level, economics and materialism are a critical aspect of sport (See Chapter 12). Religion, because it is a part of the spiritual world, is for the most part nonmaterialistic. The primary goal of religion rests with providing adherents eternal salvation in the afterlife (or the next life). It should be pointed out, however, that because religion is a part of the everyday world, it relies on economics and materialistic goods for its survival. Most religions collect (and expect) money from its parishioners in order to "pay the bills." Some churches actually seek to make profits. The Catholic Church, for example, is said to own more real estate than any other entity in the world. And many prominent religious figures are noted for their extravagant lifestyle and opulent display of wealth. Still, the ideals for religious leaders and religions in general continue to be austerity, simplicity and concern with spiritual rather than material well-being.

4. *Rationalism.* Although both sports and religion have rules, sport is organized rationally and not supernaturally. The sports world is based on secular, civil rules that are equally applied to all. Religion is based on spiritual rules and faith and admits its dependence on the nonrational (Slusher, 1993). Religious athletes sometimes find conflict between their religious beliefs and commitments and the civil rules of sports. Attempts to embrace religious diversity combined with the American fundamental principle of the "separation of church and state" will assure that conflicts between these two institutions will steadily increase for as long as people cling to religious ideals in a civil and secular environment such as sports.

5. *Ritualistic Behavior Is Used Differently.* Religion and sports both utilize rituals; however, in sports, rituals are instrumental and goal-oriented; whereas, in religion, rituals are expressive and process-oriented. For sport fans, the ritualistic behavior of consuming a hot dog and peanuts at a baseball game is far different from the ritualistic behaviors associated with going to Mass for a religious person.

6. *Buildings for Events.* Although both religion and sport provide buildings for events, these structures take on different meanings. As Novak (1993) explains, a ballpark is not really a temple, but it is not a "fun house" either. Sport spectators are allowed, and expected, to yell and scream while they support their favorite player(s) and teams. Stadiums and arenas are viewed as secular meeting places where participants can relax and release a number of their inhibitions. Conversely, most religious services are conducted inside buildings where adherents are expected to abide by moral protocols (e.g., acting dignified and respectful). Of course, there are moments during sports events where solemnity is also expected, such as during the singing of the national anthem and "moments of silence" to honor the passing of socially significant persons.

7. *Attempts to Provide Answers to the Meaning of Life.* A major difference between sport and religion rests with religion's desire to explain the meaning of life, and an afterlife, while sport does not attempt such a grandiose ideal. Because religion is consumed with the spiritual realm, attempting to explain the meaning of life is among its primary goals. Sport, because it is immersed in the secular, everyday world, makes no proclamations regarding the meaning of life.

8. *Clear-cut Winners.* Although religion attempts to explain the meaning of life, it does so without scientific, empirical proof. Any answer to life's dilemmas provided by religion is suspect at best. Further, different religious perspectives may yield contrasting answers. Sport, however, provides clear-cut winners. Someone wins the game or race and the others do not. No religion has been able to correctly claim they are "right" or they are the "winner." While the spiritual realm remains unknown, the sports world is non-ambivalent.

Despite the differences between sport and religion, the two social institutions remain connected by the numerous similarities. For many people, sport is a religion, or is treated as importantly as religion. Others, of course, place a much greater value on religion than sport.

The Role of Prayer in Sport

It is fairly common for people to appeal to a higher authority in times of stress and hope. In the sports world, both sport fans and athletes have been known to pray for favorable outcomes. The role of prayer in sports, especially in school sports, is one of the more controversial topics in the discussion of the relationship between sport and religion.

TURNING TO PRAYER

Why do people turn to prayer? In the religious realm, prayer fosters the contemplative attitudes of listening and receptivity; it brings adherents closer to God. In the strictest sense, religious prayer is the preparation for contemplation and discussion with God. According to Keating (1994), prayer is supposed to reduce the obstacles caused by the hyperactivity of individuals' minds and lives so that adherents can concentrate on their "discussion" with God (or some other spirit). Religious people who believe in a Higher Power assume that God can do anything; after all, God is "all powerful." To move into the realm of prayer is to be open to infinite possibilities (Keating, 1995). Belief in religious prayer is equated to a belief in a God, or Holy Spirit, that is capable of anything. If God is capable of anything, then certainly influencing the outcome of a game is within the control of God. Prayer would seem, to some, as a "logical" path of communication between individuals and God when requesting a favorable outcome.

Although prayer, in the strictest sense, is a part of the religious realm, it has crossed over into the sports world as well. For sport participants, the team pregame prayer can help unify the players into one collectivity. Athletes may pray for safety and protection during competition, for a good individual or team performance, and especially for a victory. Many people, including athletes and sports fans, turn to prayer for a favorable outcome. They may make such promises as, "I promise to be a better person, just let my team win," as they bargain with God or some spiritual entity for divine intervention. Why would God answer such mundane prayers?

PRAYER IN SCHOOL

The United States, in theory, has a separation of church and state policy. However, religion intrudes in state affairs in a variety of ways, including the 1954 addition of the phrase "Under God" to the pledge of allegiance to the flag; the addition of "In God We Trust" on U.S. currency in 1956; the requirement to place one's right hand on the Bible in a court of law, and prayer in public school. The role of prayer in school is an especially hot topic. "For the greater part of this century, controversy has raged over the separation of church and state in the United States. Perhaps no issue has so fueled this controversy as religion in the public schools. Today, fifty years after *Everson v. Board of Education*, which brought Thomas Jefferson's famous phrase, 'a wall of separation between church and state' into modern Establishment Clause jurisprudence, the debate rages on. Despite the passage of more than thirty years since the *School District of Abington Township v. Schempp* and *Engel v. Vitale* decisions, which held that school-sponsored bible reading and prayer, respectively, are unconstitutional, public school religious exercises still breed controversy" (Ravitch, 1999: 3).

Many school districts simply ignore constitutional mandates forbidding bible reading and prayer in public schools. The growing power of conservative religious groups ("the Christian Right") in the United States has led to organized campaigns to influence school policy in favor of religious inclusion in public schools despite the rights of people who hold differing religious views or those who refrain from organized religion altogether. "United States history is replete with examples of religious exercise in public schools facilitating discrimination and intolerance against religious minorities and dissenters. In some cases, the discrimination has been an unintended byproduct of the exercises. At other times, it has been a significant purpose behind them. Regardless, a disturbing trend of discrimination results when public schools engage in religious exercises" (Ravitch, 1999: 4).

Interestingly, the first organized attempt to keep religion out of schools came from conservative Protestant groups who wanted to keep Catholicism out of the newly formed public schools in the mid–1800s (Greenawalt, 2005). In 1844 two riots, known as the Philadelphia Bible Riots of 1844, resulted as a reaction against Catholic immigration and participation in the public schools. The riots "were fueled by a fear of increasing religious and cultural pluralism as well as by anti-immigration zeal (Ravitch, 1999: 4). More than twenty people were killed during the riots (Delfattore, 2004). Until the mid–1800s, with few exceptions, religious pluralism was restricted to different the Protestant sects that existed at the time. Religious zealots, of any denomination, are not known for their tolerance for other people, they do not believe in what they preach: brotherhood to all. As Ravitch (1999) explains, "During the mid-nineteenth century,

Catholic children were sometimes whipped and beaten in public schools for refusing to engage in school-sanctioned religious exercises; a priest in Maine was tarred, feathered, and ridden on a rail as the result of a dispute over bible reading in the public schools; and other incidents occurred throughout the country" (p. 6). In 1878, the Supreme Court decided in the *Reynolds v. United States* case that George Reynolds, a resident of the Utah Territory and an active member of the Church of Jesus Christ of Latter-Day Saints (Mormon), could not practice his religious belief of polygamy (Smith, 1987). Examples of religious intolerance in the United States continued throughout the twentieth century and persist today.

Much of the current debate over prayer in public schools involves gray-area situations about where the lines should be drawn in respect to religious activity (Delfattore, 2004). Schools try to appease student-led, volunteer prayer groups, while staying within legal guidelines. As one form of compromise, many states and school districts have instituted moments of silence to replace oral prayer to begin the school day (Greenawalt, 2005). The state of Alabama, for example, passed a statute that required a period of silence at the beginning of the day (Fenwick, 1989). Moments of silence may be spent praying, contemplating the day's events, or daydreaming. The Supreme Court views the observing of a moment of silence as constitutional. (The Supreme Court rejected Alabama's law in 1985.) As Greenawalt (2005) explains, "A moment of silence impinges less on dissenters than does oral prayer. In this case, no students need participate in an offensive practice, or listen to words that offend their conscience, or risk peer disapproval by asking to be excused. Virtually all religious traditions accept silent prayer and mediation. Insofar as a moment of silence encourages prayer, it achieves nonpreference among religions more fully than can any oral prayer" (p. 58). By all indications, the debate over prayer and religious expression in school will continue for sometime. However, the focus of our attention rests with the role of religion in sport. Specifically, we are most interested in the demonstration of religious expression, including prayer, in sports in school and on the playing field.

The role of prayer in school, as discussed previously, is a fundamental issue in public schools that carries over into the domain of sports. In 1999, a Texas teenager decided not to lead her classmates in prayer before high school football games because she feared her role in a constitutional battle over prayer in school could get her expelled. "The 5th U.S. Circuit Court of Appeals ruled this year that student-led prayers were allowable at solemn events like graduations. But the court ruled out prayers before football games, saying they don't share the 'singularly serious nature' of graduation" (*Buffalo News*, 8/27/99:A8). In 2000, the Supreme Court passed a ruling (6–3) that forbids invocations at school activities, including pre-football game kickoffs, even when students organize them. "Ruling that pre-kickoff prayers violate the First Amendment's separation of church and state, the court provided an unusually direct condemnation of school-sanctioned prayer.... The Court's ruling generated particularly emotional reactions in the South, where pre-game prayers are as much a tradition as the coin toss" (Biskupic, 2000: 1A). Carelli (2000) adds, "As the latest word on a politically volatile issue that has bedeviled the nation's highest court for 40 years, the ruling offered a ringing reaffirmation of a landmark 1962 decision that outlawed organized, officially sponsored prayer in public schools" (p. A1).

In 2006, the authors conducted a survey on college students from a public state university and a private Catholic college. The respondents were asked a number of questions regarding prayer and religious expression in sport. Respondents were asked to identify their sex and whether or not they consider themselves to be religious. In each of the following tables, survey data were collected and analyzed and categorized in the following manner: by public university and private college, by sex (data from the state public university and private college were combined), and by non-religious and religious (data from the state public university and private college were combined). There were 127 respondents from the public state university (66 females and 61 males) and 105 respondents from the private college (72 females and 33 males).

Interestingly, there were an equal number of combined respondents who claimed to be religious (N=116) and nonreligious (N=116). There were 232 total respondents.

Survey respondents were asked, "Should prayer be allowed in sports in public schools?" (See Table 14.1.) Seventy-one percent of the religious respondents indicated that prayer should be allowed in public school sports compared to just 59 percent of the non-religious. Still, the fact that a clear majority of the non-religious respondents indicated that prayer is acceptable in public school sports indicates the growing tide of support of prayer, even in public schools. Predictably, a higher percentage of private college respondents than public university respondents favored prayer in public schools (the results were nearly identical to the non-religious and religious category). A higher percentage of males (70 percent) than females (63 percent) were in favor of public school prayer in sports.

TABLE 14.1. SHOULD PRAYER BE ALLOWED IN SPORTS IN PUBLIC SCHOOLS? (IN PERCENT)

	Non-Religious	*Religious*	*Public Univ.*	*Private College*	*Male*	*Female*
Yes	59	71	59	74	70	63
No	41	29	41	26	30	37

Although the survey was not an open-ended instrument, a number of respondents wrote that they were in favor of prayer in public school sports assuming it was voluntary and not forced onto the team. This is an important point to consider.

Respondents were asked whether or not prayer in sports in private schools should be allowed (see Table 14.2). This is an issue that seldom comes to the forefront of public concern for the simple fact that these schools are private and not publicly supported. (If a private school is publicly supported, it is a concern.) As suspected, an overwhelming percentage of respondents indicated that they were in favor of prayer in private school sports. Ninety percent of non-religious and religious respondents were in favor and a slightly higher percentage of males (94 percent) than females (92 percent) were in favor of prayer in sports in private schools. Nearly all private college respondents (97 percent) and the vast majority (86 percent) of public university respondents were in favor of prayer in private school sports.

TABLE 14.2. SHOULD PRAYER BE ALLOWED IN SPORTS IN PRIVATE SCHOOLS? (IN PERCENT)

	Non-Religious	*Religious*	*Public Univ.*	*Private College*	*Male*	*Female*
Yes	90	90	86	97	94	92
No	10	10	14	3	6	8

Over the past couple of decades an increasing number of athletes have incorporated religious gestures on the playing field or court. For example, Catholic athletes will often make the sign of the cross before attempting a free-throw. Christian athletes believe that God is personal and involved in their daily activities; consequently, paying religious homage on the playing field is deemed appropriate (Hoffman, 1992, and Czech, et al., 2004). "The extent of prayer and/or spiritual rituals before, during, and after sporting contests permeates today's prep, collegiate, club, and professional sports.... Prayer circles can be seen at almost every collegiate sporting event" (Czech, et al., 2004: 3). Respondents were asked if they think it is okay for athletes to make religious gestures (e.g., the sign of the cross) after some athletic achievement (see Table 14.3). An overwhelming percentage of respondents agree or strongly agree that athletes making a religious gesture on the playing field or court is appropriate behavior. The percentages are nearly equal despite the classification system: 92 percent of the non-religious agree or strongly agree and 93 percent of the religious agree or strongly agree; 81 percent of males and 85 percent of females agree or strongly agree; and 93 percent of public university respondents and 89 percent of private college respondents agree or strongly agree that it is okay for athletes to make a religious gesture on the playing field or court after some athletic achievement.

TABLE 14.3. AFTER SOME ATHLETIC ACHIEVEMENT ON THE PLAYING
FIELD/COURT IT IS OKAY FOR ATHLETES TO MAKE A RELIGIOUS GESTURE. (IN PERCENT)

	Non-Religious	Religious	Public Univ.	Private College	Male	Female
Agree	71	66	69	64	48	73
Strongly Agree	21	27	24	25	33	12
Disagree	7	6	5	9	6	6
Strongly Disagree	1	1	2	3	2	2

The bond shared among many religious athletes extends beyond the bond among teammates. One example involves professional and collegiate football players from opposing teams kneeling together in prayer on the field after the conclusion of the game. While other teammates go to their respective locker rooms a number of opposing players join together for a public display of prayer. With this idea in mind, respondents were asked whether it was okay for athletes from opposing teams to join together in prayer on the playing field (see Table 14.4). Consistent with previous responses found in the earlier tables, the vast majority of respondents agreed or strongly agreed that it is okay for athletes from opposing teams to join together in prayer on the playing field. The figures were nearly equal by all three categories: 76 percent of the non-religious and 79 percent of the religious agree or strongly agree; 77 percent of the public university respondents and 83 percent of the private college respondents agree or strongly agree; and 81 percent of males and 77 percent of females agree or disagree. It should be noted that some respondents wrote that they were in favor of athletes praying together when a player has been injured—a variable that the authors, admittedly, had not factored into the question.

TABLE 14.4. IT IS OKAY FOR ATHLETES FROM OPPOSING TEAMS
TO JOIN TOGETHER IN PRAYER ON THE PLAYING FIELD? (IN PERCENT)

	Non-Religious	Religious	Public Univ.	Private College	Male	Female
Agree	59	52	55	58	46	63
Strongly Agree	17	27	22	25	35	14
Disagree	16	19	20	13	14	21
Strongly Disagree	8	2	3	4	5	2

Anyone who has attended a sporting event has likely witnessed a spectator praying for a favorable outcome. Furthermore, most fans have found themselves praying for a favorable outcome on more than one occasion. Why? Why do people think praying has a correlation to winning? Fans may pray for a favorable outcome because they know they have no direct influence over the play of the game. Rather than rely on the skills of their favorite athletes to successfully prevail, fans turn to prayer. Do sports fans really think prayers help? Delaney (2001) conducted research on the Southern California Browns Backers (SCBBA) (an NFL booster group) during the 1990s. He asked members whether praying can influence the outcome of a Browns game. Only 19 percent agreed and 4 percent strongly agreed. During interviews conducted with members of the SCBBA, one respondent told Delaney (2001), "If all it took was prayers, the Browns would have won at least three Super Bowls by now" (p. 93). Millions of Browns fans have been praying for a Super Bowl victory (or appearance for that matter) for over forty years. Not only have their prayers not been answered, Cleveland temporarily lost their franchise shortly after this research was conducted. There are millions of other fans who have also never had the prayers answered when praying for a favorable outcome in a sporting event. And yet, many cling to their faith in prayer.

Athletes may also turn to prayer in hopes of a favorable outcome. This is quite disconcerting for most fans. After all, fans want to see confidence in their favorite players, not moments of doubt or signs of a reliance on variables outside of individual talent. Uncertainty and doubt are primary reasons athletes turn to prayer in sports. "Because sport competitions involve a high degree of uncertainty, it is not surprising that many athletes use religious prayer to make them feel as if they have some control over what happens to them on the playing field" (Czech, et al., 2004: 9). Thus, fans who rely on prayer do so because of the frustration and stress they experience due to the fact they have no direct influence on the game, while athletes turn to prayer because of their insecurities and doubts. Czech and associates (2004) believe that "many times, Christian athletes utilize their belief system as a performance enhancement technique. More specifically, prayer has been used as a coping mechanism for stress, to help with team cohesion, and to promote a morally sound life" (p. 4). In this matter, athletes who turn to prayer may do so because it adds to their self-confidence. This newly charged self-confidence, athletes believe, helps to motivate them to perform better.

In their 2006 study, Delaney and Madigan asked respondents whether or not praying can influence the outcome of the game (see Table 14.5). In Table 14.5 there are stark differences between respondents in all three categories. First, just 24 percent of the non-religious agree and zero percent strongly agree that praying can influence the outcome of the game, while 50 percent agree or strongly agree. Further, 37 percent of the non-religious, compared to 14 percent of the religious, strongly disagree that praying can influence the outcome of the game. The "religious" divide continues when comparing respondents from the public state university and the private Catholic college. Twenty percent of the public university respondents agree and 2 percent strongly agree that praying can influence the outcome of the game, compared to 48 percent of private college respondents who agree and 6 percent who strongly agree. Thirty-two percent of public university respondents strongly disagree, compared to 18 percent of private college students who disagree that praying can influence the outcome of the game. A significantly higher percentage of women (45 percent) than men (25 percent) agree or strongly agree that praying can influence the outcome of the game. More than twice as many males (38 percent) than females (16 percent) strongly disagree.

TABLE 14.5. PRAYING CAN INFLUENCE THE OUTCOME OF THE GAME. (IN PERCENT)

Non-Religious	*Religious*	*Univ.*	*Public College*	*Private Male*	*Female*	
Agree	24	44	20	48	22	41
Strongly Agree	0	6	2	6	3	4
Disagree	39	36	46	28	37	39
Strongly Disagree	37	14	32	18	38	16

This brief analysis on the role of prayer in sport indicates that a substantial number of college students believe that religion, including prayer, has a role in sport; including private and public schools. Only a small percentage of respondents, however, believe that prayer has any correlation to a positive sporting outcome. Fans and athletes alike have not relied solely on prayer for a positive intervention in their sporting endeavors. Many have turned to magic and superstition. Such behaviors reside in the secular world of sport.

Secularization and Sport

The social institutions of sport and religion are filled with ritualistic behavior. People turn to ritualistic behaviors for a variety of reasons. Malinowski (1927) suggests that ritual, or magical behavior, is associated with high risk activities. Risk is expressed in terms of physical danger to the participants or when the possibility of failure in an important endeavor is possible (Womack, 1992). Fortes (1936) argued that uncertainty plays a role in ritualistic behavior and that ritual is associated with behavior designed toward the safety of the group (rather than with individuals). Douglas (1966) believes that ritual is used to deal with elements of psychic danger, as well as with physical danger and threat of deprivation (Womack, 1992). Turner (1967) states that rituals are a way of demonstrating conformity to expected behavior while Geertz (1965) claims that rituals are an effective form of social control (Womack, 1992). Czech and associates (2004) state, "Throughout history, people have used rituals based on religion, magic and/or superstition to cope with uncertainties in their lives" (p. 9).

RITUALS IN SPORT

Ritualistic behavior possesses a number of qualities. According to Womack (1992), there are five key components of ritual:

1. *Repetitive.* It occurs again and again in a given context, or certain elements tend to be repeated throughout the behavioral sequence.
2. *Stylized.* It is formal, rather than spontaneous.
3. *Sequential.* There is an orderly procession from beginning to end. Transposition of elements within a ritual is thought to diminish its efficacy.
4. *Non-ordinary.* It is distinct from ordinary mundane activities and is not essential to technical performance.
5. *Potent.* It is believed to be either innately powerful, or powerful in controlling supernatural beings or forces (p. 192).

Ironically, ritualistic behavior is described as non-ordinary, and yet ritualistic behaviors become the ordinary when they become routinized.

Ritualistic behaviors are very common in sport, as many athletes, coaches, and fans engage in any number of rituals before, during or after the game. Fans of sport may wear specific clothing while viewing or attending a game, eat certain foods, take specific routes to the game or a friend's house to watch the game, engage in pre-game tailgating, and postgame festivities (e.g., meeting at certain "watering hole"). Highly identified fans may go through more ritualistic behaviors than athletes. They believe that their actions, somehow, contribute to the outcome of the game. Athletes may engage in a variety of rituals, including preparatory rites (pre-activity rituals that may include the shower routine and the refusal to shave on game day), day-of-game rituals (a specific meal or time of day to eat, putting clothes on in a specific order, or wearing "lucky" clothes under the uniform), pregame rituals (especially in terms of "warming up" for the athletic event, a field goal kicker who refuses to leave the field until he makes a practice field goal attempt), activity-specific rituals (behavior that psychs an athlete to play) (Womack, 1992).

Ritualistic behaviors help to relieve anxiety and stress and help athletes concentrate and face the competition with confidence. As Gmelch (1994) explains, "Rituals usually grow out of exceptionally good performances. When a player does well he seldom attributes his success to skill alone. Although his skill remains constant, he may go hitless in one game and in the next get three or four hits. Many players attribute the inconsistencies in their performances to an object, item of food, or form of behavior outside their play. Through ritual, players seek to gain control over their performance" (p. 355). Womack (1992) concludes that ritual is important in sport for the following reasons:

1. Ritual helps the player focus his attention on the task at hand. It can be used by the player to prevent anxiety or shut out excessive environmental stimuli — such as the chanting of fans — from interrupting his concentration.
2. Ritual can signal intent to the other team. Specifically, ritual can be used to "threaten" the other team.
3. Ritual provides a means of coping with a high-risk, high stress situation.
4. Ritual helps establish a rank order among team members and promotes intra-group communication.
5. Ritual helps in dealing with ambiguity in interpersonal relationships, with other team members, and with people on the periphery of the team, such as management and the public.
6. Ritual is a "harmless" means of self-expression. It can be used to reinforce a sense of individual worth under pressure for group conformity, without endangering the unity of the group.
7. Ritual directs individual motivations and needs toward achieving group goals (p. 200).

Regardless of the rituals employed, ultimately it is talent, skill, and ability that prevail. However, the element of luck inherent in any sporting event allows both fans and athletes to attribute outcomes to their specific ritualistic behaviors.

MAGIC

A number of ritualistic behaviors are grounded in the world of magic. Magic, like religion, assumes that supernatural powers exist; however, whereas religion is oriented to the otherworldly, magic is oriented toward the instant, sensible goals. Religion concerns itself with eternal salvation while magic is focused on the needs of the here and now. Religion preaches that adherents should behave in specific ways that are consistent with their teachings in order attain eternal salvation. People who turn to magic hope to manipulate events in such a way as to gain an advantage over their competitors. The world of religion deals with sacred items as emblems and symbols of faith (e.g., a blessed rosary or cross). In contrast, the world of magic relies on profane items as symbols of magical power (e.g., a lucky penny or a rabbit's foot).

Gmelch (1994), an anthropologist and former professional baseball player, classifies magic into three categories:

1. *Rituals.* Rituals emerge from exceptionally good performances. That is, the behaviors that preceded an outstanding performance are repeated because they are deemed to possess magical power.
2. *Taboos.* Taboos refer to behaviors that are avoided because they are deemed bad luck. "Taboos usually grow out of exceptionally poor performances, which players often attribute to a particular behavior or food. Certain uniform numbers may become taboo" (Gmelch, 1994: 355). Gmelch admits to his own "pancake taboo" — he refused to eat pancakes during the baseball season because he once ate pancakes before a game in which he struck out four times. Athletes today may refuse to stop on the foul lines on the baseball field as they run out to the field or back to the dugout.
3. *Fetishes or charms.* Material objects such as coins, old bats, or horsehide covers from old baseballs are credited with possessing special powers. "Ordinary objects acquire power by being connected to exceptionally hot batting or pitching streaks, especially ones in which players get

all the breaks. The object is often a new possession or something a player finds and holds responsible for his new good fortune" (Gmelch, 1994: 355).

Gmelch acknowledges that relying on magic would certainly seem to be illogical and yet, it serves a valuable function. He states, "Magic is a human attempt to impose order and certainty on a chaotic, uncertain situation. This attempt is irrational in that there is no causal connection between the instruments of magic and the desired consequences of the magical practice. But it is rational in that it creates in the practitioner a sense of confidence, competence, and control, which in turn is important to successfully executing a specific activity and achieving a desired result" (p. 352).

SUPERSTITIONS

Irrational beliefs in the power of magic are tied to superstitions as well. Superstitions are fragmentary remains of past rituals, systems of thoughts, and belief systems that have lost their original meaning to those who believe in them in the present. As Hole (1969) explains, "Superstitions are the living relics of ways of thought much older than our own, and of beliefs once strongly held but now abandoned and forgotten.... Absurd as some of them now seem in the light of knowledge, all were serious in their beginnings" (p. 7). Superstitious persons find causal relations between certain behaviors and outcomes where they do not really exist. Superstitions can be defined as beliefs or practices resulting from ignorance, fear of the unknown, or a belief in magic or chance. Superstitions can be found in all cultures. They can also be found in sports.

Generally speaking, superstitious behaviors in sports fall under the belief in magic or chance, rather than ignorance or fear of the unknown. As with other forms of ritualistic behaviors, athletes engage in superstitious behavior as a way to reduce their level of anxiety before and during the game. B.F. Skinner (1948) found that the acquisition of superstition as a conditioning process is the result of unrelated events that have been linked together. Thus, if an athlete wears blue socks (instead of the normal white socks that he or she typically wears) and breaks a personal losing streak, the athlete will attribute (link) the newfound favorable outcome to an unrelated procedure (wearing blue socks) if he or she is superstitious. If subsequent connections are made between the new ritual (e.g., wearing blue socks) and a favorable outcome the behavior becomes routinized as a superstition. When superstitious behaviors become a part of the regular pregame ritual the superstitious athlete will continue such behavior even when positive reinforcement (a favorable outcome) fails to occur. Sport superstitions can be defined as ritualized routines that are separate from athletic training and that are performed by athletes because they believe such behaviors are powerful enough to control external factors (e.g., the talents of opponents).

Superstitious behaviors are different from preperformance routines. Preperformance routines, such as relaxation techniques and focusing and coping strategies, are learned behavioral and cognitive strategies which are deliberately used by athletes to assist physical performance (Bleak and Frederick, 1998). Engaging in superstitious ritual, much like preperformance routines, provides the athlete with a feeling of control or sense of calm prior to athletic participation. Ritualistic superstitious behaviors are usually personalized by individual athletes; that is, many athletes have their own quirky behaviors separate from general taboos found in their sport.

Among the many general superstitious beliefs that have existed in sport for some time is the idea that athletes need to abstain from sex before participating in sports. Many male athletes have heard the superstitious warning, "Don't have sex the night before a game because it will make you weak in the knees." As previously mentioned, superstitions are tied to primitive beliefs of the past, and this is certainly the case in regard to the belief that a male athlete is weakened if he ejaculates before sport participation. In fact, this belief dates back to the ancient Greeks and continued through the nineteenth century. Primitive medical science equated the loss of semen to the loss of blood and brain power (Gordon, 1988). "It is easy to see how this concern with the dangers of sexual behavior became an issue for those involved in athletics. If all but the most circumscribed expenditure of semen could have serious effects on physical and mental well-being, it could certainly also take its toll on athletic performance. It would, therefore, be important to keep sex and sport as temporally separate as possible. Moreover, since the good athlete was supposed to be morally pure as well as physically fit, sexual indulgence had to be controlled" (Gordon, 1988: 257). Former heavyweight world champion boxer Muhammad Ali believed in sexual abstention before his boxing matches because he felt it kept him strong and angry (because he was sexually frustrated) (Fischer, 1997). Research in the area of athletic performance following sex has not shown any detrimental effects. In one specific study, there was no less strength in boxers' legs after sex (Fischer, 1997). Sexual abstinence in sport is not generally mandated today, but sexual modernism during the season has emerged as the prevailing ideology of the twentieth century (Gordon, 1988).

There are many superstitious behaviors among hockey players. For example, because of the importance of protective clothing and padding, players spend a great deal of time putting on equipment in a very precise, routinized manner. During on-ice warm-ups, hockey players employ a number of superstitious ritualistic behaviors. Team rituals may involve players skating towards the net in a particular order and with each player's movement a deliberate pattern. Usually the players skate by their goalie and give him a tap and offer words of encouragement. Every team has a player that *has* to be the last one off the ice or a player who has to be the last one to shoot a puck in the goal (Keating and Hogg, 1995). Research conducted on Division I and Division III hockey players reveals that the frequency of superstitious behaviors engaged in by the two levels of athletes is quite similar (Todd and Brown, 2003). Thus, the level of competition does not determine the use or frequency of superstitious behavior.

The belief in superstitions reflects the idea that elements other than personal ability affect behavioral outcome. Athletes that rely on superstition do so in an attempt to gain some sense of control over an event. Gaining any type of "edge" in athletic performance is the goal of all athletes. In their research on NCAA track and field athletes, Todd and Brown (2003) found a positive relationship between athletic identity and superstitious behavior, suggesting that student athletes high in athletic identity use more superstition in sport competitions. Although logic dictates that superstitious behaviors have no direct bearing on the outcome of the game, if athletes believe in superstitions it may provide them with a psychological edge. This edge may lead to victory. In this manner, superstitious behavior is more likely to lead to a favorable sporting outcome than prayer.

SUMMARY

Individuals learn about religion much in the same manner that they learn about sport: through the agents of socialization. Sport and religious participation are generally taught in early life through exposure to the ideals of each institution from significant others.

Religion arose from the need to explain and understand life's mysteries. Religion provides a meaning or interpretation of life, reinforces the morals and norms held by the collectivity, and provides authority figures that supervise behavior. These are traits that are also associated with sport.

Primitive games developed out of the human need to compete and dominate. Emile Durkheim argued that the relationship between religion and sport represents the meeting of the sacred and the profane. Sport sociologists generally argue that sport is not a religion in the same manner that Methodism, Presbyterianism or Catholicism is a religion; rather, it is a secular or civil religion. Sport and religion do have a relationship, which can be traced from ancient times to the present. There are many similarities between the two. In fact, it is difficult to argue with those who claim sport *is* a religion, or at the very least, a quasi-religion. There are, however, a number of significant differences between the two, highlighted by the fact that sport centers on the profane, everyday, tangible world, whereas religion is centered on the sacred, spiritual world.

It is fairly common for people to appeal to a higher authority in times of stress and hope. This is especially true in the sports world. One aspect of this is team prayer as an example of the bonding experience in action. Although there appears to be a growing number of athletes who have incorporated religion into the sports world, not all athletes are eager participants in such ritualistic behavior.

The role of prayer in public schools is a fundamental issue that carries over into the domain of sports. The social institutions of sport and religion are filled with ritualistic behaviors, which help to relieve anxiety and stress and help athletes concentrate and face the competition with confidence. A number of such ritualistic behaviors are grounded in the world of magic and superstition. Many athletes are superstitious and engage in a wide variety of ritualistic behaviors.

KEY TERMS

Animism The earliest form of religion, it maintains that everything has two aspects, a physical manifestation and a spirit or soul.

Beliefs Things that people presume to be true; whereas, they may, or may not be true.

Function A contribution, service, or behavior purposive to society.

Preperformance Routines Learned behavioral and cognitive strategies which are deliberately used by athletes in order to assist physical performance.

Profane Items The ordinary, mundane, commonplace items of society.

Religion A system of beliefs and rituals that serves to bind people together into a social group while attempting to answer the dilemmas and questions of human existence by making the world more meaningful to its adherents.

Religious Beliefs Ideals to which members of a particular religion adhere.

Sacred Items Objects and behaviors that are deemed part of the spiritual realm and are set apart from the ordinary; they are worshipped.

Sport superstitions Ritualized routines that are separate from athletic training and that are performed by athletes because they believe such behaviors are powerful enough to control external factors (e.g., the talents of opponents).

Superstitions Beliefs or practices resulting from ignorance or fear of the unknown, or a belief in magic or chance.

DISCUSSION QUESTIONS

• Why do fans pray at sporting events? Do you think they seriously believe that God will be influenced by their prayers?

- What is the difference between sacred and profane items, and how does this relate to the sporting world?
- What do you think is the purpose of a sports hall of fame? Do these museums have a religious connotation? Why or why not?
- One definition of "religion" is that it is an institution that binds people together. Why do some people say that sport is their "religion"? Do you think they are merely speaking figuratively or might there be more to it?
- Do you think that prayer should be allowed in sports in public school? Why or why not?
- What are some athletic superstitions that you are familiar with? Do you have any yourself? Why do you think such rituals continue, and how might they serve a purpose?

CHAPTER 15

The Media in Sport

There is an old philosophical question, "If a tree falls in the woods and no one is there to hear it, does it make a sound?" With the growing influence of the mass media over sport, we might amend this question to, "If they hold a sports event and the media is not there, is it really a sports event?" Today, nearly all sporting events are covered by some aspect of the mass media. Whether it is television, radio, or newspaper coverage, the media are there to report sports— and sports at all levels including youth, high school, college and professional. The role of the media in sports has not always been as inclusive as it is today, but the mass media and mass interest in sport grew together and now enjoy a symbiotic relationship. The results of this convergence between the media and sports will be discussed throughout this chapter, but it is worth noting here that the media have such a pervasive influence on sport that entertainment is now more important than sport competition.

ESPN, a 24-hour sports network, is the leading representative of emphasizing entertainment over sport. This is most clearly exemplified by the fact that the "E" (for "entertainment") comes before the "S" (for "sports") in ESPN (the "P" and "N" stand for "programming" and "network" respectively). Some viewers would find it hard to imagine ESPN without the "E" aspect of its coverage. Other viewers would prefer that the "E" was eliminated and the coverage restricted to the "S"—sports coverage without all the frills and sidebars. However, all indicators point to a continuing emphasis on the entertainment value of sports as we move through the twenty-first century.

The Institution of the Media

The media, or more specifically, the press, has enjoyed much power throughout history. The creators of the U.S. Constitution were so passionate about the rights of the press that the First Amendment guarantees the freedom of speech and freedom of the press. Dating back to the era of the penny press (one-page newspapers sold for a penny so that the masses could afford to read the news), the media have attempted to inform the masses of important news events. Providing news, information, and entertainment are the trademarks of the contemporary mass media. The term "media" has been used since the 1920s. According to Real (1996), "The term *media* refers to all communication relays and technologies" (p. 9). The word "mass" refers to large size of the media's audience (Ryan and Wentworth, 1999). Put together, the mass media become the medium by which large numbers of people are informed about important happenings in society. The mass media grew from their humble printing press beginnings to their current omnipresent existence due to the incorporation of the ever-expanding level of technology.

Typically, the media are divided into two major categories: the print media, which include newspapers, magazines, and books; and the electronic media, which include television, radio, motion pictures, sound recordings and the Internet. Traditionally, the mass media have been viewed as forms of communication that permit a one-way flow of information from a source to an audience (Ryan and Wentworth, 1999). However, as Delaney and Wilcox (2002) indicate, with the increased use and development of interactive television, the ability to text message such things as votes for the next "American Idol," call-in radio programs, and the Internet, the idea of the media as merely a one-way form of communication is outdated.

The Relationship Between the Media and Sport

Throughout the nineteenth century, sports became increasingly important in American society. The print media were there since the beginning. As Rader (1984) states, "Even early in the nineteenth century, print media — whether in the form of weeklies, newspapers, fiction, biography, or autobiography — enhanced public interest in sports" (p. 18). The print media quickly took notice of the rise of a leisure class and the growing popularity of sports on college campuses. "To increase circulation, newspapers frequently became promoters of sports. As early as 1873, James Gordon Bennett, Jr., the eccentric owner of the New York *Herald*, began awarding cups and medals to intercollegiate track and field champions" (Rader, 1984: 19).

The sports page was taking shape in many newspapers in the 1880s and 1890s. By the 1920s, the sports page was a fixture in all major daily newspapers. Readers of the sports pages in the early twentieth century enjoyed sports columns for the same reasons people enjoy them today; that is, the sports pages provide information consisting of clear-cut winners and losers and provide continuity and orderliness to a segment of life. The sports pages became so popular by the early twentieth century that writers began to specialize in sports. Today, a number of people are employed as sports journalists. The development of such new media technology as radio, motion pictures and television was also applied to the world of sports in an attempt to reach the largest possible audience.

LINKING THE MASS MEDIA TO SPORTS

As previously stated, newspapers began to cover sports in the late 1800s. William Randolph Hearst, publisher of the *New York Journal*, is often credited as the first person to develop the "sports section" of a newspaper (McChesney, 1989). By 1900, the sports section represented about 15 percent of all general news covered in leading newspapers (Eitzen and Sage, 1989). Throughout the early half of the twentieth century newspapers contributed to the popularity of sports. Along with sponsoring sporting events, newspapers provided sports information to growing leisure class that featured millions of sports fans who thirsted for information about their favorite athletes and sports teams. The print media became the conduit between the masses and their desire for sports information. Sports information and sensational story-telling on the part of sports journalists helped to establish athletes as stars worthy of adulation.

Rader (1984) claims that newspaper sportswriting in the pre-television era fell into three large, sometimes overlapping categories: the tall tale, verse, and the true story. The tall tale, the oldest form of story telling, is the result of oral accounts of great feats. The verse refers to poetic-style writing of sportswriters. Grantland Rice's depiction of Notre Dame's famous "Four Horsemen" and their 1924 victory over powerful Army is the classic example of the verse style of sportswriting: "Outlined against a blue-grey October sky, the Four Horsemen rode again. In dramatic lore they are known as Famine, Pestilence, Destruction, and Death. These are only aliases. Their real names are Stuhldreher, Miller, Crowley, and Layden" (Rader, 1984: 21). The true story approach to sportswriting revealed the frailties and failures of athletes.

Newspaper stories were enhanced by accompanying photographs. This proved to be especially significant. As Whannel (2002) explains, "The emergence of sports sections, and the growing use of photography helped to establish the beginnings of an individualization of sport in which star individuals began to inhabit the public imagination" (p. 31). The introduction of cigarette cards that featured photos of athletes further aided the creation of the star status among the elite ball players. Cigarette cards, which are believed to have originated in France around the 1840s, were cardboard stiffeners used as promotion (Whannel, 2002). (Cigarettes were sold loosely or in paper packs that required a stiffener in the late 1800s and early 1900s.) These cards usually featured "glamour" shots of women (as most smokers were men), but a series of sport cards were introduced in the United States toward the end of the nineteenth century. Tobacco companies assumed that male smokers cared the most about three things: sport, women and the military (Whannel, 2002).

Other forms of print media include magazines and books. Before the sport section appeared in newspapers, a number of magazines and books were written, and continued to be written, about athletes and sports. Magazines on horse racing, hunting, and fishing were popular since the 1830s. During the twentieth century every sport developed its own specialized magazines, and many popular magazines such as *Sports Illustrated*, *Sport*, *Inside Sport*, and *The Sporting News* enjoy a huge circulation. Books have existed for centuries. The mass readership of books coincided with mandatory education laws (which transformed a nearly completely illiterate mass into a literate one) and industrialization (which allowed for the production of dime novels around the time of the U.S. Civil War). There were a variety of books written on the topic of sport dating back to the late nineteenth century. During the twentieth century it became popular to have books written on sports teams and individual athletes from a wide range of sports. Athletes, with the assistance of ghost writers, often write books about their sporting exploits. At times, these books include the "tell all" variety where the athletes expose the "secret" world of sport. Baseball player Jim Bouton's *Ball Four* (1970) remains a classic must-read. "Tell all" books remain in vogue today, as evidenced by Jose Canesco's *Juiced* (2005), an exposé about the alleged rampant abuse of steroids in professional baseball.

Beginning in the early twentieth century, motion pictures brought to life many sporting stories and events that fans had only heard about. Cinema newsreel was very popular in England and the United States by the 1920s and 1930s. "By 1919, 50 percent of the British population went to the cinema once or twice a week. During the 1920s and 1930s there was a substantial increase in investment in cinemas, with around one thousand being built between 1924–31. The introduction of sound at the end of the twenties provided a boost to industry and encouraged investment in new cinemas.... By 1940 the average weekly audience was 21 million" (Whannel, 2002: 32–33). In the United States, an estimated eighty-five million Americans saw one movie per week (Eitzen and Sage, 1989). While movies such as *Knute Rockne, All American* (1940), *The Pride of the Yankees* (about Lou Gehrig, 1942) and *Somebody Up There Likes Me* (about Rocky Graziano, 1956) were popular films, oddly, sports movies were a rarity until the 1970s. Today, a number of sports movies have enjoyed great success. (Sports movies were previously discussed in Chapter 1 regarding the pervasiveness of sports in society).

A major breakthrough in sports coverage occurred with the introduction of the radio. Sport stories retold in motion pictures and books are dated by the time they reach their audience. Magazine sport stories are relatively recent and newspaper coverage is at least a day removed from the sports event. But radio provided immediate coverage — and to a large audience. As Whannel (2002) explains, "If cinema brought action and movement, radio provided immediacy and it brought sport into the domestic sphere for the first time. In both Britain and the USA early radio broadcast experiments were underway by the start of the 1920s.... The percentage of households with radio rose rapidly in the inter-war period, from 10 percent in 1924 to 71 percent in 1938. In the USA, too, radio rose to prominence and sport broadcasts played a significant role in its popularity. By 1929 one-third of American households had radio" (p. 33).

Fans across the U.S. listened to the radio for the play-by-play accounts of sporting events, especially baseball, boxing, horse racing, and football. Unlike the newspaper, which informed sport enthusiasts about sporting events *after* they occurred, radio provided sounds and descriptions of sporting events *while* they occurred. In spite of the overwhelming presence of television in sports, radio broadcasts remain popular today. In certain markets local games of interest may not be televised but are offered on the radio. Many fans listen to sporting events on the radio while they are at work or riding in their cars. Some fans become so attached to the voice and personality of their favorite radio announcers that they listen to the radio while watching televised broadcasts (with the television volume muted).

The next major break-through of media technology to the sports world was television. Television fundamentally changed sport. It not only provides immediacy, as radio, but it also provides all the action and movement of motion pictures. "Like the radio, this medium allows live reporting, but because it transmits not only sound but also live images, the feeling of 'being there' is even stronger for television spectators than for radio listeners. So, with television, major sporting contests are no longer available just to spectators witnessing the event in person, but also to many millions more who can view the spectacle in their own homes, thanks to their television sets. The added value stemming from this medium is evident: close-ups, replays, slow motion, the different angles from different cameras, and cameras that follow the action. It can be more exciting to be spectator in front of the television screen than to be a spectator in the stadium, far away from the playing field or arena floor" (Beck and Bosshart, 2003: 10).

According to Duncan and Brummett (1987) there are four dimensions of televised sports in the contemporary era: narrative, intimacy, commodification, and rigid time segmentation.

1. *Narrative.* Televised sports programs are presented in a predictable fashion using predictable plots and familiar characters. Then again, as Hilliard (1996) explains, "The athletic contest itself provides a basis for narrative." In other words, a sporting event is a story that unfolds before the viewer and the job of the commentator is to simply describe the events.
2. *Intimacy.* Televised sports programs provide viewers an opportunity to become closer to the sport participants. Intimacy "refers both to the visual closeness of the television viewer to the subject matter and to the development of an emotional attachment between actor and viewer.... The development of audience identification with characters is a principal means by which viewers' attention to the narrative is maintained" (Hilliard, 1996: 116).
3. *Commodification.* In an attempt to keep viewers tuned to televised commercials, television executives look for advertisers whose products fit the needs and interests of the viewing audience. Today, a great number of televised commercials are elaborate and entertaining and more than keep the interests of viewers. In the case of the Super Bowl, millions of viewers tune in to the game *primarily* to watch the commercials! Furthermore, there is as much discussion in the media the Monday after the Super Bowl about the commercials as there is about the game itself.
4. *Rigid Time Segmentation.* It has often been said that soccer will never be a marketable success in the United States because it does not possess built-in stoppages of play that allow for the airing of commercials. In an attempt to remedy this, many televised soccer matches superimpose commercial brand logos on-screen. Most other sports events are organized into short, rigid blocks of time that allow for commercials during timeouts or stoppages of play. An obvious example of this is the "television timeout" after the first dead ball every four minutes (16:00, 12:00, 8:00, and 4:00 minute mark in each half) in college basketball. The "TV timeout" allows for a regular presentation of commercials. (More recently, the "TV timeout" has been described as a "media timeout." But let's be honest, do radio stations or sports journalists have the power to stop the game for a commercial break?) It also stops the flow of the game and allows coaches to save timeouts for more critical times. And it provides TV commentators time to discuss the plays and compare them with past performances and other arcane bits of information.

Television is critical for the economic success that all those in sports enjoy. The revenue generated by television all but guarantees that NFL franchises operate at a profit (because all the teams in the NFL share the television revenue equally). And despite the long, drawn out pregame hype that coincides with such sporting events as the Super Bowl, without television, these games would hardly be *events*. The very fact that the media, especially television, are responsible for creating events ties to the question in the introduction of this chapter: Without the media, is it *really* a sporting event?

Today, with the advent of cable and satellite television and streaming Internet broadcasts, nearly any game is accessible to sports fans. Television is responsible for creating billions of sports consumers around the world. (Technological advancements in the mass media since the development of cable television will be discussed later in this chapter.)

VIDEO GAMES

Many people play video games. The sports industry is aware of this fact. As a result, there are a number of sports-related video games available for gamers. A gamer is a person who plays video games. In general, there are two types of sports gamers, those who want a realistic game experience and those who want extreme forms of gaming. An example of a realistic sports video game would be the annual Madden NFL games. The Madden NFL series is among the top sellers, regardless of genre, for all video games. Most major sports leagues are represented in the lucrative gaming market. There are also video games for a wide variety of sports beyond the "big four," including rugby, lacrosse, archery, and auto racing. Among the more provocative extreme sports video games is "Blitz: The League." "Blitz" (made by Midway Amusement Games, known for their "Mortal Combat" video game) is not like Madden's NFL version of video football. In this fictitious football league, there is an emphasis on the off-the-field behavior of players, including gambling, barroom fights, use of profanity, taking steroids, and sex with prostitutes.

FUNCTIONS OF THE SPORTS MEDIA

As with the media in general, the sports media serve a number of functions, including the following:

1. *Information.* The sports media provide scores, statistics, highlights, and general information on a variety of sporting events, athletes, and teams. Information on sports may also come in the form of interviews and live coverage.
2. *Interpretations.* Coverage of sporting events and the provision of information are accompanied by media interpretation, and possible biases. ESPN's Mel Kiper, Jr., makes a living providing his "NFL Draft Analysis"; which, of course, is based on his interpretation of potential draftees. Sport media "experts" offer opinions on teams they think will make the playoffs (e.g., what teams are "on the bubble" and which ones will be selected as "at large" bids for the NCAA tournament?) or whether or not a particular athlete will break a record, or who will win a boxing match, auto race, and so on.
3. *Entertainment.* The sports media are all about entertainment. As mentioned earlier, the "E" comes before the "S" in ESPN, signifying the importance placed on entertainment. The wide variety of sporting events available all but guarantees that the sports media will find any number of sporting events worthy of coverage and description.
4. *Excitement.* People love sports because they find them exciting. The game or event itself is enough to draw fans' interest to sports. Stimulating arousal and excitement in fans helps the media serve an affective function.
5. *Escape and Diversion.* Sports provide people with an opportunity to "lose themselves" for a period of time while they immerse themselves in a sporting event. Ideally, sports allow people to temporarily escape from frustrations and life problems. Unfortunately, the highly identified

fan may actually incur greater affective costs if the sporting event does not turn out favorably. Thus, if a person watches sport for an "escape" from problems and then his or her favorite athlete or team loses, it is like adding salt to an open wound.

6. *Economics.* The mass media have completely changed the design and financial makeup of the sports world. The economic aspect of the media in sport will be discussed later in this chapter both in terms of their positive and negative role.

7. *Integration.* Sports provide people with a chance to bond with fellow fans. This is true for the spectators in the stands who cheer for the same team as well as friends bonding together at home or at a bar while watching sports. Friends who watch historic sporting events together are linked together forever and think of each other whenever the game or key play is replayed. At the macro level, members of a nation can unite together while cheering for their national teams during international sporting events.

8. *National Identity.* International media sports coverage places a bright spotlight on the host city and nation. This is especially true for World Cup games, the Olympics and the Super Bowl. The fact that the whole world is watching is a source of pride and national identity (Beck and Bosshart, 2003).

The link between the mass media and sport is firmly entrenched. In fact, they enjoy a symbiotic relationship where each social institution attempts to create the most marketable product possible. The sports media, especially television (and in particular specialty networks like ESPN that are dependent on sports for their 24-hour entertainment broadcasts) need sports in order to provide an endless supply of entertainment programming. As a result, these networks pay huge sums of money for the broadcast rights of various sports events. At the same time, the sports industry needs the mass media in order to keep functioning as an elite social institution, and one that handsomely rewards those involved with great finances. The mass media and sport institutions cooperate with one another but they are not dependent on each other. The media can survive without sports because people will always find something to watch on television, listen to on the radio, or read in the print media. Furthermore, sports have existed throughout recorded history, and there are enough athletes to play sports and fans who will follow sports whether the media covers them or not. The ancient Greeks managed to stage the Olympics and other Panhellenic games long before the existence of the mass media; surely modern sports can survive without the media. Still, never before in the history of humanity has sport received such a mass popularity, due primarily to the symbiotic relationship between sports and the media.

Presently, sports and the mass media are loyal partners. The merger between these two social institutions has created a number of both positive and negative outcomes.

The Media's Positive Impact on Sport

Although sports survived for millennia without media coverage, the structure of contemporary sport has benefited tremendously because of its relationship with the media. Perhaps the most significant aspect of the media's role in sport centers on economics.

ECONOMICS

A great deal of the economic success that commercialized sports enjoy is the result of the media and its commitment to sports entertainment programming. As discussed in Chapter 12, television pays huge sums of money for the broadcasting rights of various commercial sports. For example, ESPN pays the NFL more than $1 billion a year (2006–2011) for the rights to broadcast *Monday Night Football* and NBC pays the NFL $650 million a year (2006–2011) to broadcast on Sunday nights. Commercial sports operate as they do because of television money. (Sporting events also generate money through such means as gate receipts, merchandising, fundraisers, and sponsorship support.) Sport leagues and conferences as a whole benefit from the economic infusion by the media.

Individual athletes and sport celebrities have also benefited tremendously from the economic involvement of the media. Prior to the late 1970s, a successful athlete could enjoy relatively modest upward mobility via the financial aspect of professional sport participation. The economic riches afforded successful athletes today have inspired a large number of young, especially lower socio-economic youths, to pursue sports as a means of upward mobility. Successful athletes today earn multiple millions of dollars to play sports. For example, in 2000, MLB's Texas Rangers signed Alex Rodriguez to a record ten-year, $252 million contract, beginning with the 2001 season. Rodriguez's quest for financial success first and team loyalty second remains a primary reason why so many baseball fans continue to view him as an anti-hero. The contract offered to Rodriguez was $2 million more than owner Tom Hicks, a media millionaire, paid George W. Bush and Rusty Rose for the franchise three years earlier (Antonen, 2000). (Rodriguez later left the Rangers to play for the New York Yankees and has had his contract renegotiated so that he can earn more money.)

The minuscule number of youth who will ever directly benefit financially from sport is a distortion of reality that is ignored by most individuals who seek economic riches via sport.

In sum, the media contribute greatly to the financial success of commercialized sport both at the macro level (sport leagues, conferences, and teams) and the micro level (individual sport athletes and celebrities). Television and other media outlets make stars out of athletes and sport celebrities (e.g., high profile announcers like Dick Vitale or John Madden) which in turn, affords greater economic success to those in sports.

SOCIAL EVENTS AND SPECTACLES

The media have the power to transform a ball game into a social event or spectacle. When the media become involved in a sporting event a number of elements arise. "First, the media will hype the game in order to draw more attention and awareness to the event. Increased awareness leads to a greater number of viewers, which equals more advertising revenue and results in more profits. Second, by the very fact that the media have chosen to broadcast a particular game reveals the importance of it. Third, many people attend the game not only to support their team, but in hopes of being 'seen' on television. In other words, the game has now become a social event" (Delaney and Wilcox, 2002: 206). People will do almost anything to be on television. ESPN's Game Day crew attends sporting events and broadcasts hours before the start of that game, drawing huge crowds. In nearly all cases, those who show up want to be seen on television as much as they want to attend a media-staged pep rally hours before the start of the game. During a game, fans cheer wildly when the camera is turned in their direction. The game and the crowd combined are social events and spectacles when television coverage is involved.

During the early years of television, the coverage of sport was limited primarily to the "Big Four" professional sport leagues (NFL, MLB, NBA, and NHL), big-time college sports, and to a lesser degree, the more marketable individual sports (professional tennis, auto racing, and golf). With the advent of cable and satellite television and the introduction of ESPN came the realization among television sports executives that sports coverage would have to extend to a variety of sports in order to fill in "blank" (times when few or no major sporting events occur) airing spots. During its infancy (and before it attained the rights to major sporting events) ESPN broadcast a wide variety of sports—including world championship frisbee, badminton, table-tennis, and calf wrestling—from around the globe. Among the more popular nontraditional sports covered by ESPN during its early history was Australian Rules Football. ESPN created cult followings during the late 1980s and early 1990s with its Aussie football coverage. Despite its overwhelming focus on commercial sports, ESPN continues to broadcast a variety of nontraditional sporting and recreational activities, including dog shows, fishing, and poker. ESPN created the "X-Games," which features a large number of nontraditional sports including extreme sports such as snowboarding and motocross racing.

The exposure to a wide variety of sports is viewed as a positive function of the media because millions of people, especially youth, may be disenchanted with commercialized sport and yet still enjoy sports, leisure and recreation in general. Exposing the public to viable alternatives to commercialized sports may help stimulate youth, and adults, into participating in healthy sporting endeavors.

PUBLIC FORUM

The success of sports broadcasting is dependent upon two critical issues, the actual broadcasting of the sporting event and access to the athletes for insightful and exclusive comments. The mass media creates a public forum where athletes can discuss aspects of the game. For their part, sport leagues, including the NCAA, have rules that make it mandatory that athletes make themselves available to the media for post-game interviews. This intrusion into the athlete's inner world extends to the locker rooms where athletes shower and dress. "Potentially, all parties involved with sports benefit from this relationship. The media are given a product to sell; the sports fans are given 'inside' information about the events of the game; and the athletes are given an opportunity to present and review events from their perspective" (Delaney and Wilcox, 2002: 207).

Successful and high profile athletes are celebrities and are sometimes viewed as heroes and role models. The broadcast media relies on sound bites to sell viewer interest in their broadcasts and, therefore, turns to athletes for comments and opinions (mostly about sports but other interests as well). The media will especially target fan favorites and "controversial" athletes because they hold the greatest interest to sports consumers. Stories and sound bites from fan favorites such as Tiger Woods, Brett Favre, Peyton Manning, Dale Earnhardt, Jr., Allen Iverson and Kobe Bryant all but guarantee viewership interest. The media will even allow athletes to "plug" various causes and charities or provide opportunities for them to air their views on certain matters. Some athletes have their own media shows (e.g., radio call-in shows, websites, and television shows or segments) where they can present their views in a public forum.

The media will usually provide an athlete with an opportunity to "correct" him- or herself following an "inappropriate" comment. The media also provides opportunities for athletes to apologize for any past indiscretions. Controversial athletes such as Terrell Owens and Chad Johnson are media favorites because they seem to be lightning rods for trouble or controversy — which always provides for analysis and interpretation among sport broadcasters and personalities.

ENTERTAINMENT

One of the primary functions of the sports media is to provide entertainment. Sports are commercialized, but most fans realize that commercials are a price worth paying when sports coverage is the return. Providing information, entertainment, and a temporary escape from the everyday life activity is perhaps the most enjoyable feature of the sports media. Despite any warranted criticisms of ESPN, sports fans are glad it exists. Originally funded by the Getty Oil Company through the use of 625 television cable systems and a satellite for transmission, ESPN initially reached just 20 percent of the nation's television viewers. Today, ESPN (along with its sister networks that include ESPN2, ESPN News, ESPN U, ESPN 360, ESPN Deportes, and so on) is available to most everyone in North America. ESPN inspired other networks to increase the quality of their sports broadcasting. The growth of cable and satellite television has assisted the sports industry in their attempt to entertain us, the sport viewers. Many people start their days with ESPN's SportsCenter so that they are up to date with all the latest sports news and entertainment.

The Media's Negative Impact on Sport

Undoubtedly, the media have quite an influence on sports. The distinction between the media's positive role and negative role in sport is often a matter of perspective. For example, the Chicago Cubs used to play only day games at Wrigley Field. Major League Baseball and the Chicago Cubs organization realized that greater broadcast revenue could be generated with televised night games. In order to do this, lights were added to the ballpark. This modernization of one of professional baseball's oldest stadiums was not initially popular with most Cubs fans, who preferred the tradition of day games. Ultimately, the fans' voices were ignored and lights were added in an attempt to attract increased revenue via night time broadcasts of Cubs games (there are more people available to watch games at night than during the day when people work and children go to school). Was television's influence that led to lights being installed at Wrigley Field positive or negative? The answer lies with one's perspective. On the one hand, a long-standing tradition was destroyed; on the other hand, more people had access to Cubs games both live and on television.

Some examples of the media's negative role in sport are detailed in the following pages, bearing in mind that there is room for disagreement on these outcome evaluations.

ECONOMICS

As stated earlier in this chapter, the media — primarily television — have positively impacted the economic fortune of athletes and team owners. The large sums of money provided by television to the sports industry led to, among other things, dramatically higher salaries for athletes in all commercial sports. Although the yearly salaries of most athletes in commercial sports are usually higher than the lifetime income of average Americans, contemporary athletes continue to demand more money and greater "perks." The revenue sports teams earn as a result of media contracts is generally insufficient in covering the operating expenses (which includes player salaries) of a ball club. In order to cover their expenses, sports owners and promoters have continued to raise ticket prices. It has become increasingly difficult for families to afford the price of attending a ballgame, auto race, international sporting event, and so on.

Based on research provided by the *Team Marketing Report* (a trade publication that surveys ticket and concession prices for all major sports), of the four major team sports in North America, the NFL had the highest average ticket price, at nearly $60 per ticket in 2007 (*The Buffalo News*, 5/21/08). The New England Patriots have the highest average ticket price ($90.89), while the Buffalo Bills had the lowest ($46.26). It is not surprising that the NFL has the highest ticket price considering that each franchise has only eight regular season home games. In contrast, Major League Baseball franchises have 81 regular season home games and predictably have the lowest average ticket price ($25.40) of the four major team sports in 2008. The 2008 average MLB ticket price was, however, up nearly 11 percent from 2007.

Small market teams find it difficult to compete with larger market teams because of the differences in fan-base size. It is easier to diffuse the high ticket costs in large markets because of the greater number of people who can afford to attend games compared to small markets and the lower total numbers of people. Thus, small market teams can raise their prices only so high.

INFLUENCE OVER SCHEDULING AND RULE CHANGES

Television has great influence over the sports industry when it comes to scheduling games or start times. The actual date of a game may be moved to accommodate television. This is especially true for high profile games and events and especially the playoffs (and tournaments). "The start time of games are nearly always scheduled in an attempt to maximize viewership. This is most evident during playoffs, where networks worry about broadcasting a night game during the week. If the game starts too late in the Eastern time zone, viewers may turn off the game before the end because it is so late. But, if the game starts too early in the Pacific time zone, potential viewers are still at work, or driving home from work" (Delaney and Wilcox, 2002: 209). Scheduling start times to accommodate television broadcasts is often upsetting to coaches and players as well as viewers and spectators.

Television has also played a role in a variety of rule changes in sports. The television time-out in televised sports events (especially in basketball and football) is especially frustrating to spectators and viewers, and sometimes to the athletes and coaches as well (e.g., when the television timeout stops a team's momentum). The television timeout is designed to provided structured stoppages in play in order to broadcast commercials—which is the source of revenue for television. A number of rule changes in sports have been influenced by television in an effort to provide more action. Television executives realize that American viewers want to watch sporting events with action that leads to scoring. Over the past few decades a number of rules changes have been enacted to increase offense (action). Three examples from baseball include lowering the pitcher's mound, which takes away a certain amount of the "edge" that the pitcher has (the higher the hill, the greater the edge the pitcher has), moving the outfield fences closer to home plate, and decreasing the foul ball territory (and replacing it with high-priced luxury seats). The enactment of the 3-point shot rule dramatically changed the game of basketball. Teams that find success from "behind the line" can reduce a deficiency or build a big lead quickly. The 3-point shot was first introduced in college basketball in the 1980–81 season. It was introduced in the NBA on a trial basis a season earlier. The American Basketball Association already had the 3-point shot, which spearheaded the NBA's interest in this exciting rules change. The spot for kickoffs in football, once at the 40 yard line, has been moved back to the 30 yard line in the NFL and the 35 yard line in college.

CONTROLLED PRODUCTION

The media provide information to listeners and viewers. This information is filtered through a restricted presentation of descriptions of events. The presentation of televised sports involves a highly structured and controlled production. Because of the complexity involved with producing a sports event, it is important to control as many variables as possible. The production staff generally includes a "hierarchical division of labor, typically between the producer, the director, commentators, camera operatives, vision and sound mixers, and technicians. Each individual has clearly defined responsibilities, which they are expected to fulfill despite any deficiencies in equipment.... Each is employed in a particular role according to skills and previous experience, although flexibility is also a desired quality. The pressures involved are not just of time but also of uncertainty, in that producers have to react to unpredictable occurrences both within the event and external to it" (Brookes, 2002: 22). Thus, the game itself may be unscripted, but the production of the sporting event is as organized as possible. Ideally, the production of the televised sporting event meets the expectations of the viewers.

In most cases, the viewers are relatively happy with the production of televised sporting events. Viewers want and expect accurate information and descriptions of events. There are times when television (and radio) announcers flat-out miss calls (e.g., use the wrong name of an athlete, fail to see a penalty that was clear to viewers), announcers think and act as if *they* are as important as the sporting event, television breaks away to commercials too quickly (action is missed) or return from commercials too late (action is missed). Any die-hard fan can attest to the numerous mistakes of media personnel during the production of any given game. This is because many viewers are actually more knowledgeable about sports (or a particular sport or game) than those announcing it.

The media provides much of what fans expect and desire. However, they do so in a very controlled context. This is especially true in sports highlights shows (e.g., ESPN's *SportsCenter*). The mass sports media discuss the topics what *they* want to discuss. The recaps and reviews provided in newspapers, magazines, and televised news reports may be quite different from the perspective of spectator who actually attended the game. Highlight shows and news articles may be presented in such a way that one team or player is highlighted at the expense of the competitor even though the competitor ultimately wins. "Production staff, on-air announcers, and editors, often reveal their own biases as to what they think is important for the viewer to watch. This is potentially very negative as the media are capable of manipulating the audience into thinking that the game was one thing, when it actually could be something quite different" (Delaney and Wilcox, 2002: 210–211). ESPN's *SportsCenter*, a sports highlight show that is watched regularly by avid sports fans, is both enlightening (a great deal of information is provided) and frustrating. *SportsCenter* is often difficult to watch because of its "helter skelter" approach to broadcasting. In a typical one-hour broadcast, highlights of one sport (e.g., college basketball) are shown, followed by an abrupt move to another topic (e.g., golf), and without a transition on to another topic (e.g., the NFL draft). Commercial breaks follow. The next set of highlights may go back to a previously discussed sport (e.g., college basketball), a new topic (e.g., MLB's spring training), and back to another previously discussed topic (e.g., golf). In this regard, the "controlled" production is not fan-friendly and the seemingly unorganized approach utilized by *SportsCenter* is a common complaint among sports fans.

Another problem associated with the media's controlled production aspect involves the media's insistence on overwhelming sports consumers with stories and information they have little or no desire to hear about. For example, in August 2005, ESPN ran an online poll question asking, "How do you feel about Terrell Owens?"—the answers to choose from were: "I'm sick of hearing about him"; "I only care what he does on the field"; and "I can't wait to see what he does next." When one of the authors (Delaney) voted on this question a total of 77,617 votes had been cast at that time. Eighty-one percent voted for "I'm sick of hearing about him"; 13 percent voted for "I only care what he does on the field"; while just 6 percent voted for "I can't wait to see what he does next." ESPN went on to discuss Terrell Owens ad nauseam for the rest of that week and inevitably for the entire 2005 NFL season. The mass media need to realize that most fans do not care about the every move of Terrell Owens, Barry Bonds, Chad Johnson, and other athletes that they (the media) deem need to be followed.

In sum, the sports media provides information on sports to a mass audience. The controlled aspect of the production allows media outlets an opportunity to shape people's perception of events. As the leader in sports entertainment broadcasting, ESPN has great influence sport consumers. Its attempt to dominate the sports market includes the controlled production of an award show known as *The ESPYs* (Excellence in Sports Performance Yearly Awards). *The ESPYs* is an awards show created and produced by ESPN wherein media stars (mostly movie and television entertainers) present various awards to athletes. Fans are allowed to vote for specific plays (chosen by ESPN) in each category and the winners are announced at the annual ESPYs show. This light-hearted production is a clear example of the marriage between the mass media and athletics.

LOSS OF HEROES

Heroes have most likely existed throughout history. One becomes aware of heroic deeds through two primary means: first-hand observation of heroic deeds and through some form of communication. Before written languages were created, stories of heroes were passed down from one generation to the next (and undoubtedly they were embellished every step of the way). With written language, tales of heroic deeds were expressed in poems and short stories. Over time, technology improved and expanded upon these early versions of communication, leading to the creation of a mass media that included newspapers and eventually, radio, motion pictures, television, satellite, and the Internet. All of these media outlets have helped to establish hero status for certain individuals. However, as quick as the media often is to bestow hero status to some athletes, the media is just as quick to reveal stories of an athlete who has fallen short of heroic behavior, thus knocking him or her off the hero pedestal.

Throughout most of the history between sports and the media, journalists and others involved in the media kept the private lives of athletes out of their commentary, which in turn kept the hero myth alive for many athletes who did not lead ideal lives. For example, most people did not know that during Mickey Mantle's entire baseball career he had a drinking problem. This was not revealed until years after his career ended and Mantle admitted that he could have been an even greater player if he had taken better care of his body. Today, the private lives of many athletes have become overly public. As a result, fans know too much about their sports heroes (and athletes in general). In short, the media are capable of placing someone on a hero pedestal and equally capable of knocking someone off it. To their credit, however, the media generally provide an athlete an opportunity (public forum) to tell his or her side of the story or a chance to publicly apologize, and therefore provide the avenue for "fallen" athletes to regain their positive image. The fact remains, though, that the media are partly responsible for the decreasing number of sports heroes found in contemporary society.

THE MEDIA'S PORTRAYAL OF GENDER

A basic adage of advertising involves a simple concept: "Sex sells." Everyone knows and understands this to be true. Images of sex appeal are commonly used to sell a wide variety of products. Commercialized sports are products to be consumed by a mass audience. The sports mass media often utilize the "sex sells" mentality in their approach to promoting and selling sports. As a result, a great deal of objectification of athletes occurs in sports. For example, Olympic beach volleyball was chastised by feminists as a sport that did little more than display scantily clad women for the delight of television viewers and spectators in the stands. Duncan (1993) states that patriarchal social practices in the media are responsible for the objectification of women in sport. Burstyn (1999) uses the term "hypermasculinity" to describe this patriarchal approach to sport coverage by the media. Burstyn (1999) argues that hypermasculinity is a cultural force that inhibits gender equity in society in general and sport specifically.

The objectification of women in sports leads to distorted body images for girls. Young girls and women are being told by the media to be thin and sexy. Bissell (2004) states, "Thin-ideal media content is said to be one of the factors responsible for promoting distorted body image perceptions in young girls and college women" (p. 108). Promoting fitness is certainly a positive attribute of the media, as obesity continues to be a growing problem in society. Being too thin, of course, is not only unhealthy, it is not attractive.

At present, gender objectification not only still exists, it seems to be extending to men as well. Society, including the media, has increasingly stepped up its pressure on men to look aesthetically pleasing. Many men have cosmetic surgery and male television announcers wouldn't think about going on the air without makeup. However, women still face far greater scrutiny about their image than men do. For example, women athletes have long faced the "stigma" that all female athletes are lesbians. To circumvent this "problem" the sports media often employ a feminine apologetic approach to their coverage of women's sports in which they heterosexual-ize female athletes through emphasizing their relationships with men (Knight and Giuliano, 2003). Rarely do the media find the need to point out that male athletes are involved with women. The media explicitly refer to a female athlete's attractiveness and attempt to show them as feminine. There is a reason why the sports media hype such female athletes as Michele Wie and Danica Patrick; they are athletically successful, but also young, feminine, heterosexual, and aesthetically pleasing women.

Sport Journalism and Broadcasting

Many sports fans rely on sports coverage provided by journalists and broadcasters. As a primary social institution, sport commands the attention of millions. Sports journalists and broadcasters are relatively influential people in shaping public opinion on a variety of topics.

Sports Journalism

Journalists provide information to an audience. Sports journalists, of course, focus on ele-ments related to the institution of sport. Today, it is common for sports coverage to account for nearly 20 to 25 percent of the content of major newspapers in most cities. As a result, sports journalists experience a certain level of prestige within the newspaper business, as sports cov-erage represents the largest specialization within most newspapers. The sports department of a typical daily newspaper will often consist of a separate editor, desk, sub-editors, and reporters.

There are many similarities between news and sports journalists. For example, just as news journalists, sports journalists generally have a degree in journalism. As news journalists, sports journalists provide information; specifically, on sporting events and stories of relevance to either athletes, sports teams, or the institution of sport in general. As with other news reporters, sports journalists are trained to be and expected to be objective and neutral in their reporting. Although sports provide ample opportunities for sensational story-writing, most stories written by sports journalists are routine. As Brookes (2002) explains, "Most journalism concerning sport is much more routine and everyday. There is a danger that in focusing on the most spectacular news related to sport we ignore what sports journalism does day in, day out" (pp. 32–33). Thus, sports journalists, as do news journalists, generally deal with the routine story but occasionally get involved with sensational stories. Those sport journalists who concentrate on spectacular stories are looking for high profile topics and scandals that cross over to "newsworthiness," such as the steroid scandal in baseball. A sports journalist who can provide evidence that Barry Bonds is on the "juice" will have successfully crossed over to newsworthiness. Ever since Major League Baseball was taken to task by the U.S. Congress in the mid–2000s, stories on steroid use in sports have taken on a higher priority in sports journalism because they have cross-over appeal to the news world. Sports journalists who write serious, newsworthy stories are utilizing the "hard" news approach to journalism. The hard news style is more factual and objective in con-tent. It reflects the serious nature of sports journalism. In hard news articles, journalists often seek out "experts" in the field to provide quotes for their articles. This helps to bring legitimacy to their reports. It also makes it "hard" news.

In contrast, there are journalists, both in sports and out of sports, who prefer to cover "soft" news. Soft news journalists discuss gossip and scandals. Scandals of any kind are often covered by journalists. Sports scandals follow this pattern. As Brookes (2002) explains, the sports scan-dal story "predominates in mass circulation and elite publications. The newsworthiness of the story depends on the combination of elements of sex, violence, crime, drugs and greed" (p.

34). Gossip may include rumors about athletes to be traded and behind the scenes reports of the activities and behaviors of athletes and sports personnel. The soft news approach also involves journalistic coverage of local sporting events, such as high school ball games. These sport journalists are dealing with the profane, everyday world of sports where the coverage is expected to be "light" and noncontroversial. These sport journalists generally enjoy a regular audience, but such an audience is localized. The sport journalist who covers the everyday sporting events serves an important function for smaller newspapers that rely on hometown coverage of sporting events, perhaps including a slant in storytelling that favors the home team.

Whether sports journalism centers on "hard" news or "soft" news, it has the potential to shape gender and racial images of sport participants. Throughout the past few decades, most sport journalists who cover women's sports have presented it in a positive manner. This positive image has helped to shape the greater society to the point where most people completely accept women in sports. However, even as coverage of women's sports has generally been positive, it is not equal to that of men's. The unequal coverage of women's and men's sporting events perpetuates the idea that sports remain primarily a male institution. In addition, stereotypical images of men and women are enhanced through sports journalism. Female athletes are often described in terms that highlight their femininity and how they "look" (aesthetically speaking), while male athletes are described in masculine terms (e.g., strength and toughness). In this manner, sport journalists often reinforce stereotypical gender roles for males and females.

Typecasting males to a masculine ideal is known as hegemonic masculinity. Trujillo (2000) describes former MLB pitcher Nolan Ryan as a perfect example of the hegemonic masculine athlete because sports journalists describe Ryan as "the ageless wonder," a "living legend," and a "great family man." Based on these descriptions, males are expected to remain as primary breadwinners for their families in order to be valued. Further, media commentary promotes masculinity in a purely heterosexual manner (Trujillo, 2000). The portrayal of sports as a male domain also makes it difficult for women who attempt to become sports journalists. Despite gender obstacles, the number of women in sport journalism and broadcasting continues to increase. This is also true for minorities in journalism.

As described in Chapters 11 and 12, sports are viewed, and sometimes used, as a means of upward mobility for persons from lower socio-economic groups. Athletes from disadvantaged groups tend to dominate sports, as minority members are more likely to view sports as the best option for getting ahead. Many sports journalists have bought into the false notion of a superior athlete based on skin color. This misconception reinforces the belief among many lower socio-economic group members that sports are indeed the best way to find success in a society that often discriminates against them. On the other hand, sport remains as one of the primary cultural institutions where minorities, especially blacks, are viewed as equals (Hardin, Dodd, Chance, and Walsdorf, 2004).

The majority of sports journalists are from middle-class backgrounds, college-educated, and generally white. As they interview athletes, who are often from lower socio-economic groups and less educated, but substantially higher paid, it is common for journalists to exploit athletes in an attempt to level the playing field. As a result, friction often develops between sport journalists and professional athletes. Athletes may respond violently or by refusing to talk with certain journalists. Both journalists and athletes need to realize they need each other, at least in part, in order to reach the highest level of success in their respective fields. After all, journalists must be able to interview athletes in order to gain inside information that the readers want to know, and athletes need to present themselves in a positive light with the public if they are to take advantage of all the opportunities that may be afforded them (e.g., endorsements).

Sports Broadcasting

The mass audience of sports fans and consumers affords opportunities for some sport journalists and broadcasters to become stars in their own right. In this regard, sports journalists and broadcasters may attain celebrity status by virtue of their occupation. ESPN sports anchors in particular reach the homes of millions of viewers. The celebrity status enjoyed by the top sports journalists and broadcasters is often both exciting and filled with "perks."

Sports broadcasters often serve as icons for fans. The "voice" of a particular team is heard repeatedly by fans. Many fans listen to that same "voice" for years, even decades. Among the "old-school" broadcasters who enjoyed iconic status were Red Barber, Mel Allen, Curt Gowdy, and "Chick" Hearn. Vin Scully, Dick Vitale, Al Michaels, and John Madden enjoy such iconic status today. John Madden is so popular that his name is used to sell the official annual NFL video game that is a hit with youth today.

Sports broadcasters and journalists are such a big part of sport that they are eligible for various sports halls of fame. For many fans, broadcasters and journalists bring to life sporting events they have not seen and recreate images of games and events they have seen. There is no doubt that the media will continue to have a strong role in sports. The thirst for sports knowledge among millions of fans will continue to stimulate further technological growth in the sports media industry.

Technology and the Future of Media in Sport

As described throughout this chapter, the primary role of the media is to provide information. Sports fans do want information. Sports fans do not always want to know about the personal lives of athletes, but they do want all the latest statistics and up-to-date scores. In the past three decades, the media has met this demand and fueled an ever-increasing desire for instantaneous gratification.

Sports Media Conglomerates

On September 7, 1979, ESPN aired its first broadcast. Sports fans at this time could only imagine the dramatic effect ESPN would have on sports broadcasting. Students today should take note of the fact that most viewers in 1979 had just three broadcast networks and possibly an independent station to choose from. Further, except for major events, sports were televised only on weekends. Today, the combined ESPN networks air about 600 hours of sports programming a week. "With ESPN — now in 82% of the USA's 108 million homes — viewers will get 2,293 live or taped events in 2004, occurring on every day of the week" (Martzke and Cherner, 2004: 2C).

Although it is a media conglomerate today, ESPN began modestly enough with one satellite and crude studios in 1979. In 1984, ABC acquired ESPN and began combining and sharing their operations and on-air personnel. On January 1, 1992, ESPN Radio premiered. In October, 1993, ESPN2 began telecasting. In May 1994, ESPN Regional Television was formed. This network allowed for regional coverage of sports events, especially college football and basketball. Today, ESPN Regional is the nation's largest syndicator of college sports programming (Martzke and Cherner, 2004). On April 1, 1995, ESPN's Web site was launched. ESPNews began broadcasting on November 1, 1996. ESPN continued its growth by purchasing Classic Sports Network — known today as ESPN Classic. In an attempt to make a mark in the print media, ESPN debuted *ESPN the Magazine* in March 1998. Capitalizing on its name appeal, the first ESPN Zone restaurant opened in Baltimore in July 1998. On April 1, 2001, ESPN *Deportes*, a Spanish-speaking network, debuted. It is available in most Spanish-speaking nations in North America and South America. In 2003 ESPN began broadcasting in HD (high definition television), further enhancing the quality of viewing. Also in 2003, ESPN introduced its first video game with "ESPN NFL Football." Digital production of ESPN broadcasts began in 2004 (Rose, 2005). In April 2006 ESPN began airing one day a week in Japan. ESPN has created the *X-Games*, the *Great Outdoors Games*, original programming (e.g., the *Playmakers*), and continues to add new networks (e.g., ESPN U) to its growing conglomerate.

ESPN is much more than a 24-hour sports channel, it is a sports media conglomerate. Emphasizing the entertainment aspects of its broadcasts, ESPN is a personality-driven medium. "ESPN's product is its attitude, exemplified by the personalities created and its distinctly irreverent style" (Martzke and Cherner, 2004). ESPN is clearly the dominant force in the provision of sports entertainment. It is also intent on remaining the leader in sports broadcasting in North America.

ESPN does have some competition. Cable news network giant CNN attempted to compete with ESPN with its own sports network, CNN/SI. Unavailable in most homes, CNN/SI never mounted a legitimate challenge to ESPN. The FOX network established FOX Sports Net (FSN) in an attempt to challenge ESPN's dominance in sports broadcasting. FSN failed in its attempt to challenge ESPN's *SportsCenter* with its *National Sports Report*. FSN's *The Best Damn Sports Show Period*, a two hour show resembling a talk show with a variety of a panelists, represents the network's most unique feature. A number of smaller sports networks also exist. Cable stations include the Golf Channel and Speed TV. A few MLB franchises also have their own sports network (e.g., the YES network for Yankee baseball and NESN for Red Sox baseball). None of these networks represent a challenge to ESPN's dominance in North American sport broadcasting.

As yet another example of the "marriage" between the media and sports, many media conglomerates own sports franchises. This relationship was especially evident in the 1990s. For example, the Walt Disney Co. owned the Mighty Ducks of Anaheim (NHL) and the Anaheim Angels (MLB) (it also owned ESPN and ABC); Time Warner (owners of CNN, CNN/SI, TBS, TNT, and *Sports Illustrated*) owned the Atlanta Hawks (NBA), Atlanta Braves (MLB), and the Atlanta Thrashers (NHL); News Corp. (owners of FOX, FX, Fox Sports Net, and the *New York Post*) owned the Los Angeles Dodgers (MLB), New York Knicks (NBA) and the New York Rangers (NHL); and John Rigas (founder of Adelphia Communications Corp.) owned the Buffalo Sabres (Strauss, 1998).

As with many marriages, the partnership between the media and sports has experienced some difficulties and "divorces." The trend established in the mid–1990s of media conglomerates owning sports teams had reversed itself in the mid–2000s. A private business person, Frank McCourt, became the majority owner of the Los Angeles Dodgers after he purchased the team from News Corp. Other wealthy private business owners have also purchased sports teams from media conglomerates, including Arturo Moreno, who purchased the Anaheim Angels (and renamed the team the Los Angeles Angels of Anaheim) from the Walt Disney Company (a rival of News Corp.) and B. Thomas Golisano— a billionaire from Rochester, New York, and founder of Paychex, Inc.— who purchased the Buffalo Sabres from John Rigas (Adelphia Communications). Time Warner has sold its sports franchises as well. In short, a clear trend was established in the mid–2000s away from the joint ownership of media and sports (Bellamy and Walker, 2005). Although the joint ownership of media and sports is disappearing, the symbiotic relationship between sports and the media remains strong and shows no signs of dissipating.

TECHNOLOGY AND THE FUTURE

Technology exerts a great deal of influence in nearly all spheres of life. Technological advancements in the mass media and communications have had a tremendous influence in the sports world. Sports fans who want inside information about athletes do not have to turn to sports highlight shows—which should focus on highlights instead of insipid stories of athletes—as many athletes have their own personal Web sites or blogs. Personal Web sites provide athletes with a forum where they can control the production and presentation of their lives. These Web sites generally provide bulletin boards or e-mail addresses where fans can leave messages for the athlete. Sports fans may also set up Web sites or blogs on their favorite (or most despised) athletes and teams. Blogs are similar to personal journals or diaries but they are posted online for others to read. All major sport teams have official Web sites where fans can visit and learn about the team, specific athletes, the organization, upcoming events, news stories, and so on.

So-called "reality shows" became popular in the late 1990s and continue to air in the 2000s. The sports world was a little slow to enter this domain, perhaps expecting the interest in such broadcasts would have subsided long ago. However, there are a growing number of sports-based reality shows. Bobby Knight, when head basketball coach of Texas Tech, had a reality show called *Knight School* that followed his team throughout the 2005–06 season. In 2006, the short-lived *Bonds on Bonds* debuted on ESPN2. This quasi-infomercial provided Barry Bonds with an opportunity to answer the questions he would have preferred the media ask him, before the steroid scandal raging about him caused the show to be cancelled. Another reality series airing in 2006, on the Lifetime network, was *Cheerleader Nation*, a 10-week reality series on a championship team from Lexington, Kentucky. Prominent athletes such as Emmitt Smith and Jason Taylor have appeared on ABC-TV's *Dancing with the Stars*. Smith won the pairs competition in 2006 (with partner Cheryl Burke), and Taylor (and his partner Edyta Sliwinska) finished second in 2008. The marriage between sport and entertainment combined with the current interest in reality television programming all but guarantees additional sports reality shows and athletes on reality shows in the future.

The primary concern of sports fans is receiving information on games and sporting events. To this end, technology of the early 21st century has revolutionized sports coverage much as television had decades ago. Sports fans not only enjoy the opportunity to view numerous sporting events every day of week thanks to cable television, satellite coverage has expanded sport viewership opportunities to a nearly inconceivable level. "Thanks to the development of satellite technology and cable television, and the growing popularity and marketability of sports, televised sports coverage has proliferated" (Rada and Wulfemeyer, 2005: 65). If there is a game broadcast anywhere in the world, a satellite can beam the broadcast in an instant around the globe. One merely needs to possess the proper technology to receive such broadcasts. Satellite television is popular in many parts of the world, including Europe. As Whannel (2002) explains, "The deregulation of rights negotiation allowed television channels to acquire the rights to the European games of specific clubs and competition between the five terrestrial channels and Sky meant that there was more live football on television than ever before" (p. 38). Not only has the quantity of sporting events available to consumers increased, thanks to digital technology the quality of the broadcasts has also improved tremendously.

Cable and satellite TV coverage of sport represents the mere beginning of the technological advancements that have led to the proliferation of sports programming and consumer availability. The Internet is another vehicle used by many sports fans in their search of sports broadcasts and information. Advances in computer technology have led to dramatic memory increases and high-speed data transfer rates. This technology combined with satellite technology makes it inevitable that unlimited sports broadcast programming will be available online. Right now, fans can visit official Web sites of major sports leagues and gain access to a wide variety of sports information, statistics, and play by play of accounts of games in progress. Some sites have audio links as well. Most official Web sites are relatively sophisticated. At MLB.com, for example, a baseball diamond is presented graphically. It shows the location of any base runners

Phone technology allows sports fans to get up-to-the-minute scores online via such outlets as ESPN.

and "locates" the defensive players on field. Statistics are provided for the batter's history against the pitcher, as well as the pitcher's history against the batter, and so on. In short, there is no shortage of sports information available online. International travelers are especially happy with the information available online because they can find sports information and ball game results wherever they are.

In 2006, CBS offered, for the first time, free video streaming of the first 56 NCAA tournament games. Streaming allows sports fans to watch the "game on the go" or while they are at work online. A "boss" button option is available on most programs. When the viewer presses the "boss" button, a spreadsheet instantly pops on the screen — so that you won't get caught watching the game. The ease with which technology allows people to watch sporting events, especially major events, at work is of concern to employers.

Advancements in cell phone technology over the past two decades are nearly astronomical. Cell phones have been available for twenty years, but the phones used today are dramatically different from the first, almost primitive variations. Today's cell phones not only take pictures and videos and permit text messaging, they allow for streaming video with the newest models.

Undoubtedly, technology will continue to advance at a rapid pace. Wireless outlets will be everywhere and will most likely be free to consumers. Computers and mobile phone storage will increase radically. In the future live video and audio broadcasts of sporting events will be available on the Internet and cell phones. The overall quality of broadcasts will continue to increase as advancements in digital technology progress. Consumers will be able to record events online and on mobile phones in the future similar to the use of TiVo or DVRs today. Satellite and cable subscribers will be able to watch whatever game they want on a pay-per-view basis.

The broadcast media will continue to find new ways to entertain sports viewers. There will be more cameras used in sports broadcasts than viewers can possibly imagine. That is hard to imagine! There are cameras everywhere, including helmet cam, goalie cam, cameras in the floors at NBA games, overhead cameras at football games, cameras inside race cars, and so on. What remains? Television will find the answer. Television introduced the public to instant replay. The NFL incorporated instant replay into a rule change that allows coaches to issue "challenges" wherein certain plays are allowed to be reviewed for accuracy. Although many fans are happy when an incorrect call is overruled, the time spent making this decision almost mocks technology. Better implementation of technology will eventually speed up reviews of controversial plays.

Technology will be infused in sport in a variety of ways. For example, the authors predict that inevitably, tiny transmitters will be incorporated inside hockey pucks and digital lines will be installed over the goal line in an attempt to reach undisputable evidence of whether a goal was scored. The NFL could also utilize this technology by installing a transmitter inside a football and digital devices used at yard makers in order to determine such things as first downs and whether or not the ball crosses the end zone.

At this pace, technology will continue to play a significant role in presenting and shaping sporting events. From this perspective, the media's future role in sport is secure.

SUMMARY

Today, nearly all sporting events are covered by some aspect of the mass media. The role of the media in sports has not always been as inclusive, but both the mass media and mass interest in sport grew together and now enjoy a symbiotic relationship.

The media play a huge role in most cultures, and this is especially true in societies of the West, including the United States and Canada. Most people watch television, go to the movie theater, listen to the radio, read a newspaper, or log on to the Internet on a regular basis. Such media provide information, interpretations of events, and entertainment. They also promote social integration and social change.

As sports became increasingly important in American society, the print media were there since the beginning. By the 1920s, the sports page was a fixture in all major daily newspapers. The sportswriter helped to establish athletes as stars worthy of adulation. Newspaper stories were enhanced by accompanying photographs. Beginning in the early twentieth century, motion pictures brought to life many sporting stories and events. A major breakthrough in sports coverage occurred with the introduction of the radio. But the greatest application (to date) of media technology to the sports world is television.

Television is critical to the economic success that all those in sports enjoy. In the early 1960s there were only three networks and a few independent television stations, so the amount of sports coverage was limited. Today, with the advent of cable and satellite television, nearly any game that is broadcast is accessible to sports fans.

The link between the mass media and sport is firmly entrenched. They enjoy a symbiotic relationship where each social institution attempts to create the most marketable product possible. Presently, sports and the mass media are loyal partners. The merger between these two social institutions has created a number of both positive and negative outcomes.

The success of sports broadcasting is dependent upon two critical issues, the actual broadcasting of the sporting event and access to the athletes for insightful and exclusive comments. Among the primary functions of the sports media is to provide entertainment. ESPN is one of the most important venues today; it provides almost constant sports entertainment. However, the media's insistence on overwhelming sports consumers with stories and information they have little or no desire to hear about can be disturbing.

Sports journalists provide information on sporting events and stories of relevance to either athletes, sports teams, or the institution of sports in general. Sports broadcasters often serve as icons for fans. The thirst for sports knowledge among millions of fans will continue to stimulate further technological growth in the sports media industry.

KEY TERMS

Cigarette Cards Believed to have originated in France around the 1840s, these were cardboard stiffeners used as promotion.
Electronic Media Includes television, radio, motion pictures, and the Internet.
Gamer A person who plays video games.
Hegemonic Masculinity Typecasting males to a masculine ideal.
Mass Media The medium by which large numbers of people are informed about important happenings in society.
Medium A means of communicating information.
Print Media Includes newspapers, magazines, and books.
Streaming A technological advancement in sport broadcasting that allows sports fans to watch the game "on the go" or while they are at work online.
Tall Tale The oldest form of story telling is the result of oral accounts of great feats of accomplishments, usually exaggerated.
True Story An approach to sportswriting which reveals the frailties and failures of athletes.
Verse Refers to the poetic-style writing of sportswriters.

DISCUSSION QUESTIONS

- Why does ESPN place the word "entertainment" before the word "sports" in its title? Do you think this is significant?
- Do you think there is too much sports coverage on television today? Why or why not?
- Why is the connection between sports and the mass media called a "symbiotic" one? What are some of the positive and some of the negative aspects of this connection, in your view?
- Do you feel that individual athletes receive too much attention today? Does the fact that we often know a great deal about an athlete's personal life detract from the need for sports heroes?

CHAPTER 16

The Benefits of Sport Participation

As demonstrated throughout the text, the role of sport in society is multi-faceted. Sport is inter-connected with every major social institution found in society. As with every social institution, sport has its positive and negative features. Furthermore, sport has been a feature of societies around the world throughout history. It gives meaning and excitement to the lives of most human beings; it is a force for social cohesion as well as for social inequities.

In this final chapter, we take a slightly different approach. The authors believe that it is important to demonstrate how sport participation can benefit people with special needs and help reduce obesity by emphasizing physical education in the schools as well as in adulthood. Furthermore, the authors believe that the sportsmanship aspect of sport needs to be underscored. After all, sport participation and competition should involve learning the fundamentals of a game, while instilling a desire to compete to win, but it should also be about having respect for the game, the other participants, and oneself. Playing sports, especially nonprofessional sports, should be about having fun while exercising and building a bond with others. The age-old desire to connect sport and character remains a viable one. Sport can be the means to make people feel more involved with those around them and more in control of their own lives as well. This can be particularly so when addressing the growing concerns for those with disabilities in our society.

Sport and Autism

Over the past few years, a number of articles have been written and stories told about the benefits of sport participation for children with autism. In 2006, for example, ESPN broadcast a story involving Jason McElwain (J-Mac), an autistic high school student at Greece Athena High School in Rochester, New York. McElwain, a student-manager on the boys' high school basketball team, was sent into a game at the end of the season by his coach. The student body cheered wildly for him. Not only that, but Jason sank one basket after another, causing a tidal wave of emotion to spill onto the court at the conclusion of the game. Later that year (and after Jason met President Bush and appeared on *Oprah*), ESPN awarded McElwain an EPSY in the "Best Moment" category, beating out his personal idol Kobe Bryant, who was nominated for his 81-point game with the Lakers earlier in the season. Bryant was one of the first to congratulate J-Mac, who was accompanied to the stage by his older brother Josh, whom he credited for getting him interested in sports. It was another magic moment for Jason, his family and friends, and for countless fans and supporters.

Proponents of mainstreaming autistic children viewed Jason's accomplishments as inspirational. Others, however, cautioned that Jason is labeled as a "highly functional" autistic person and that his experience with sport, especially being touched and lifted off the court by his teammates, may not be a common outcome for autistic youth who are not as "highly functional." So, what is autism, and can sport benefit these special needs youth?

Explaining Autism

Autism is a behavioral type of spectrum disorder that is usually detected in early childhood. Autism does not discriminate based on race, ethnicity, or social class and is known worldwide. Autism awareness is on the rise. Thirty years ago, there were just 4 or 5 reported cases per 10,000 people. "Today, its prevalence is estimated at one in every 500 people" (Bruey, 2004: 4). The cause of autism is still unknown, although most researchers agree that the central nervous system does not develop normally in an autistic child. The brain of an autistic person does not respond in the typical fashion of a non-autistic person. The autistic person is overly sensitive to some stimuli and under sensitive to others. Among the primary characteristics of an autistic person are impairments in social interactions; delays or impairments in both verbal and nonverbal communication; repetitive patterns of behavior (e.g., flapping of hands, twisting, and obsession with specific objects); and withdrawal into one's own private world. Other common symptoms of autism include tantrums, lack of eye contact, and basic lack of emotional contact with others.

Generally speaking, people are either born with autism or it develops early on in a child's life. Many autistic children are overly-sensitive to smells, and even as an infant, the autistic child may throw a tantrum or retreat into their own world as a result of certain smells. The earliest symptoms in an autistic child include a failure to maintain and develop relationships with others, a lack of interest in typically "exciting" events, and little or no desire to interact with others. As recently as the 1980s, most doctors advised parents of autistic children to institutionalize their child with schizophrenics and people with far more serious disorders. Today, many people are learning to deal with autistic spectrum disorder (ASD) in a more positive manner. As Greenspan and Wieder explain:

> Perhaps the most influential myth relates to the ability of children with ASD to love and form loving relationships.... Whereas initially children with ASD were thought to have a fundamental autistic aloneness, currently the ability to form intimate relationships is viewed as a continuum.... Evidence from our work with children with autism indicates that they feel a personal sense of love, specifically with their mother, father, or other primary caregiver, because other adults often won't produce in the child that same degree of intimacy, or of comfort in a moment of fear or need. In fact, after treatment, the children not only show no sense of aloneness but may become more loving than their typically developing peers [2006: 12–13].

Knowledge about autism and other related syndromes is increasing, due in no small part to the work of members of the athletic community. Many people in the sports world are responsible for encouraging awareness and finding the cause of autism. For example, when Detroit Tigers broadcaster Jim Price and his wife, Lisa, learned that their son Jackson was autistic, they turned for help and found little available. As a result, they established the "Jack's Place for Autism" community center designed to meet the needs of children with autistic spectrum disorder as they grow into adulthood. Jackson is one of an estimated 1.5 million American children and adults with autism. Other organizations, such as the "Doug Flutie, Jr. Foundation for Autism" are responsible for autism awareness, research, and education. The Doug Flutie Foundation was established by Doug and Laurie Flutie in 1998 after their son, Doug, Jr., was discovered to be autistic. The foundation provides financial aid to families with an autistic child who need help, raises money for education and research, and serves as a clearinghouse and communications center for new programs and services designed for individuals with autism (Doug Flutie Jr. Foundation for Autism Web site). Since 1998, the Fluties have raised over $10 million for autism through corporate and individual donations, fundraisers, endorsement promotions featuring Doug and Doug, Jr., as well as sales of Flutie Flakes (breakfast cereal) and other related items.

Among the characteristics of autism are severe social isolation and a lack of communication between the autistic person and others (e.g., family members and teachers). Autistic children often look forward to participating in recreational activities and sports but it is difficult for them because of possible lack of coordination and difficulty understanding what sport entails (e.g., the rules and close contact with others). Playing sports in a structured format such as J-Mac's participation in high school scholastic sports presents a difficult challenge for most autistic children. Successful experiences with organized sport participation have a great deal to do with where a child falls on the autism spectrum, high or low functioning.

As previously mentioned, J-Mac is a highly functional autistic person, which makes organized sport participation easier for him than for autistic persons low on the spectrum. Nonetheless, recreational activities are important for autistic children. Autistic children can develop motor skills through sport participation. Playing catch within a group setting encourages sharing and communication. Long distance running is beneficial for some autistic people because it is a solitary, repetitive activity that requires determination and stamina, traits that most autistic people have. Anthony Crudale, an autistic adult, wrote about his experiences as a long distance runner in a *Sports Illustrated* article. Crudale, the first autistic person to graduate from the University of Nevada at Las Vegas, is a highly functional autistic person who has enjoyed long distance running for most of his life. Crudale (2001) credits his sport participation for his good physical health and the close friends he has made by running in marathons.

All kinds of sports can potentially help autistic children overcome social barriers. This includes surfing. One might think that autistic kids are afraid of the ocean, but this is not necessarily the case. According to an ESPN report on *SportsCenter* (aired on March 27, 2006), Danielle and Izzy Paskowitz gave birth to an autistic child they named Isaiah. Izzy, a care-free professional surf champion, had a particularly tough time dealing with a son who was autistic. Danielle explains that having an autistic child can be hard on some couples. Initially, it was easier for Izzy to find excuses not to hang out with his often agitated autistic son. Eventually, Izzy tried surfing with his son. Isaiah loved it. Izzy and Danielle Paskowitz decided provide a day of surfing for other autistic children. By 2000, Surfers Healing, a non-profit group, was established to give autistic children a free day of surf lessons and fun in the sun and ocean.

Most autistic kids panic upon their initial indoctrination to surfing. A stranger is touching them, they are paddled out into the ocean facing seemingly insurmountable waves and they feel helpless. The autistic children often claw at the surf instructors. And then, a major transformation usually occurs. They ride a wave. An instantaneous and unstoppable gigantic grin and smile overwhelms the same children that often don't even speak. The day of surfing is day of bliss for both the autistic children and their parents or guardians. Surfing is not a cure for autism, but it has proven to be highly effective in bringing smiles of acceptance to over 3,000 children with autism. Every year, dozens of Surfers Healing events are held on both the east and west coasts.

Autistic children, as do children with other special needs, enjoy participating in sport and recreational activities. The Special Olympics were designed to help provide a sporting experience for the physically challenged where participation and good sportsmanship prevail.

Sport for the Physically Challenged

Sports and recreational activities are enjoyed by billions of people around the world. Physically challenged people are among those who enjoy playing sports. Sports activities are available for people with developmental disabilities, cerebral palsy, dwarfism, visual impairments and other conditions. These sporting opportunities provide disabled athletes and non-disabled athletes an opportunity to come together in a positive manner. Disabled athletes participate in sport and recreation for the same reasons as nondisabled athletes do. They enjoy interacting with others, they enjoy friendly competition, and they have fun doing it. Participating in sports assists with the physical health of the disabled, who might otherwise lead sedentary lives. In turn, the physical act of playing sports improves the mental health of disabled athletes. In short, sports help the disabled find happiness through participation.

The history of promoting sports for the disabled is rooted in a hospital in England. World War II veterans with injuries were seeking a physical form of rehabilitation. In 1948, Stoke Mandeville Hospital created competitive games for veterans. Before long, sporting events for the disabled sprang up throughout England. In 1967, the National Handicapped Sports (NHS) organization was established by a group of Vietnam veterans to provide physical rehabilitation and sports programs for vets (Jones and Paciorek, 1994). Over the years, the NHS has opened chapters throughout the United States and Canada and is open to all people with physical disabilities. The NHS offers such activities as water skiing, other water sports, fitness programs, and a large number of special sporting events. The participants may include persons with visual impairments, amputations, spinal cord injuries, cerebral palsy, head injuries, and other disabilities.

Today, an increasing number of disabled persons are playing sports because of technological advancements. For example, biotics are being used to improve the quality of artificial legs and arms. Wheelchairs are specially made for speed, control and stability. There are numerous organizations that provide sporting activities for the physically challenged. They include:

- The Children's Hospital Handicapped Sports Program (TCHHSP) (formerly known as The Handicapped Ski Program), which provides resources and programs for children with physical disabilities.
- The National Disability Sports Alliance (NDSA), dedicated to providing sporting opportunities for all people with any type of disability.
- The National Handicapped Sports (NHS) program.
- The National Sports Alliance (NSA) program.
- The American with Disabilities Act, designed to help all people with disabilities to work together to solve problems they face.
- The U.S. Association for Blind Athletes (USABA) and the U.S. Cerebral Palsy Athletic Association (USCPAA), which offer chances for all those seeking sporting opportunities.
- The Dwarf Athletic Association of America (DAAA), which is designed to help provide sporting opportunities and competitions for dwarf athletes.
- Kids Enjoy Exercise Now (KEEN), an organization that encourages one on one participation in recreational activities among individuals with disabilities.

The best-known sporting organization for disabled persons is the Special Olympics. The Special Olympics is an international nonprofit organization that is devoted to providing individuals with disabilities (including autism) an opportunity to participate and compete in sports in a "safe" environment. More than 200 programs serve over 2.25 million persons with intellectual disabilities. There are Summer and Winter Special Olympics, similar to the regular Olympics, with many of the same events. The Special Olympics help to unite families and facilitate positive self-esteem in participants. The games were initiated in 1968 by Eunice Kennedy Shriver, sister of the late President John F. Kennedy, in part to honor their sister, Rosemary Kennedy, who was mentally retarded. According to Ana Bueno (1994): "On July 19, in 1968, one thousand athletes from 26 states and Canada traveled to Chicago. On July 20th, after breakfast, the athletes got on chartered school buses and were driven to Soldier Field for the Chicago Special Olympics. It was the beginning of a history-making day. Just a couple of years earlier, the idea of people with mental retardation getting together to compete in athletic events seemed incredible. Even in 1968, parents were still being counseled to place their developmentally disabled children into institutions and forget them" (p. 27).

Since that time, the Special Olympics, which now features athletes from all 50 states and several countries, has helped to de-stigmatize mental retardation and provides an opportunity for millions of children to excel. Its motto remains: "Let me win. But if I cannot win, let me be brave in the attempt."

Promoting Sport and Physical Education

The authors argue that sports and physical education are not emphasized enough in society. Although it is not necessary for every person to play sports, everyone should attempt to maintain physical fitness. Clearly, this is not the case, as there is a growing social problem in society: obesity.

OBESITY

Take a walk in any public place (e.g., a grocery store, mall, or ball game) and observe the people in the immediate area. Statistically speaking, two out of ten will be obese. Further, six out of 10 adults (aged 20 years and older) will be overweight. According to Centers for Disease Control and Prevention, the prevalence of obese persons (both adults and children) has increased from 15 percent in the late 1970s to nearly 33 percent in 2004 (CDC, 2007). The American Heart Association claims that the obesity rate among American men nearly tripled to 28 percent between 1960 and 2002, and more than doubled to 34 percent for women (McCutcheon).

How are the categories of "overweight" and "obesity" determined? The formula used by the Centers for Disease Control and Prevention (CDCP) in determining obesity is based on a body mass index (BMI). BMI is calculated by converting the weight of person into kilograms, divided by an individual's height in meters squared. A BMI over 30 is considered obese. This formula has (at least) one major flaw, in that it is not a good indicator for someone who is muscular and works out a lot. Mississippi, Alabama, West Virginia, Louisiana, and Tennessee, all southern states, have the highest percentage of obese people. In the entire nation only Oregon isn't getting any fatter (according to statistics gathered by the CDCP the previous year).

Adults are not the only Americans getting fatter. There are more than 9 million children and adolescents (16 percent of the U.S. population) who are overweight or obese. This figure is nearly four times higher than 40 years ago (Clinton, 2005). Some small children are so obese they cannot fit into car seats, thus risking their immediate safety. The additional weight that young people carry around with them may cause numerous physical health problems in adulthood, including high cholesterol, high blood pressure, type 2 diabetes, heart disease, stroke, and premature death. "If childhood obesity continues to increase, it could cut two to five years from the average lifespan. That could result in our current generation of children becoming the first in American history to live shorter lives than their parents" (Clinton, 2005: 5). The primary culprit in the fattening of America's youth is a lack of physical exercise and unhealthy eating habits. Many schools no longer allow vending machine junk foods or soda. This represents a good start in the fight against obesity. All parents need to encourage their children to exercise regularly and eat properly. The fact that so many adults are overweight indicates that they should lead by example. Negative habits such as a lack of exercise and poor eating routines learned in childhood generally set the stage for poor health in the future. Conversely, proper exercise routines and eating habits learned in childhood will likely be continued in adulthood. As a result, it is critical for parents to talk to their children about weight.

Dr. Stephen Daniels, chairman of the American Heart Association's Council on Cardiovascular Disease in the Young, stresses the importance of parents discussing health with their children and yet being aware of how sensitive most young people are about their appearance. Daniels (2005: 6) offers these tips to parents when communicating the importance of good health and exercise to their children: always give love and support, be positive, avoid criticism, work together as a family, be honest about yourself, make if fun, and teach self-monitoring.

Dr. Isadore Rosenfeld (2005) points out that healthy eating habits and regular exercise will help keep the heart strong. Poor habits will likely lead to the hardening of the arteries in the heart, brain, kidneys, eyes, and legs. Healthy habits established in childhood decrease the likelihood of these problems occurring. Overweight children, those who regularly eat high-calorie foods, and children who are not physically active run the greatest risk of heart disease and related problems. Rosenfeld (2005) recommends that by age 10, every child should have the following tests: a cholesterol-level screening, a blood sugar test, and a blood-pressure check.

Obesity is a real problem in the United States. The Centers for Disease Control report that 112,000 deaths occur each year as a result of obesity. This figure is nearly three times the number of deaths from all drugs and alcohol. The economic costs are just as staggering. Direct health-care costs of obesity have soared from $52 billion in 1995 to $75 billion in 2003. As high as obesity health-related costs are, the direct health care costs for smoking are twice that of obesity (Jackson, 2005). Clearly, a person who smokes and does not exercise regularly or eat properly is running a substantial health risk and is all but guaranteed to have their life span decreased.

The obesity problem is not limited to the United States. There are overweight people around the globe. In fact, the high number of children worldwide who are obese represents a great threat to public health care and the economies of many nations. Kirka (2006) states, "Nearly half of the children in North and South America will be overweight by 2010, up from what recent studies say is about one-third, according to a report published by the International Journal of Pediatric Obesity. In the European Union, about 38 percent of all children will be overweight if present trends continue — up from about 25 percent in recent surveys" (p. A-5). It is estimated that one in five children in China will be overweight by 2010 (Kirka, 2006).

In short, obesity is reaching near global epidemic proportions. An increasing number of adults and children are growing fat. It is especially important to curtail unhealthy eating habits of children. Children must be taught not to (and not be allowed to) eat junk food on a regular basis (an occasional bag of potato chips will not cause obesity); this includes a ban on soda pop. Proper eating habits are the first step toward eliminating obesity. A regular regimen of physical activity is a second way to combat obesity.

LACK OF PHYSICAL ACTIVITY

Physical fitness is one of the best and easiest ways to protect one's health and reduce the risk of nearly every major health problem, including heart disease, cancer, diabetes, and Alzheimer's disease. Unfortunately, there are many people who do not exercise regularly (3 to 5 times a week for a minimum of 30 to 60 minutes). As a result, there are many people "out of shape" and physically "unfit." Treadmill tests on a representative sample of more than 5,300 Americans 12 to 49 years old found poor cardiovascular fitness in 20 percent of participants. There were far more teenagers physically unfit (33 percent) than adults (14 percent) who were out of shape. Based on these results, there are an estimated 7.5 million adolescents and 8.5 million adults out of condition (Stein, 2005). Teens and adults with poor fitness were two to four times more likely to be overweight or obese than those considered moderately or highly fit (Tanner, 2005).

The lack of physical activity leaves many people in a sedentary lifestyle. Based on statistics from the U.S. Census Bureau, Statistical Abstract of 2006, Americans were playing fewer sports in 2005 than in 2004, but they were watching more sports events in person and on television (Ohlemacher, 2005). "Participation in almost every recreational sport, from golf and tennis to bowling and snow skiing, was down ... while attendance at professional sporting events was up" (Ohlemacher, 2005: 32). Adult Americans are not only spending less time participating in sports, their favorite leisure activities (e.g., dining out, entertaining friends and family at home, reading books) are increasingly moving indoors. When "baby boomers" were growing up, they wanted to be outdoors playing with friends, bicycling, swimming, fishing, playing ball, and so on.

Today's youth enjoy indoor activities such as playing video games, watching television, and surfing the Internet. "The average child spends nearly six hours a day sitting in front of a television, computer, or video game" (Cauchon, 2005:A2). This sedentary lifestyle is not conducive to a healthy existence. According to statistics compiled by the *USA Today* (2005), traditional childhood outdoor activities were less popular in 2004 than just a decade earlier. For example, in 1995, 68 percent of 7 to 11 year olds participated in bicycling, compared to just 47 percent in 2004. Sport participation in other activities for this age group also declined: swimming, 60 percent in 1995, 42 percent in 2004; baseball, 29 percent in 1995, 22 percent in 2004; fishing, 25 percent in 1995, and 11 percent in 2004; and touch football, 16 percent in 1995, 10 percent in 2004 (Cauchon, 2005).

Mandatory Physical Education at School and Home

The trends of an alarming, growing rate of obesity; an increasing percentage of juveniles and adults who are physically unfit; a general lack of physical activity among youth and adults; and sedentary life habits are alarming and further justify the promotion of sports and physical education in school. Despite warnings for years about the obesity problem in the United States, there have been disturbing societal trends that discourage exercise among children (e.g., the elimination of mandatory physical education classes in many schools and sedentary habits of playing video games, surfing the Internet, and watching television). According to O'Shea (2005B), "Illinois is now the only state in the nation that makes physical education classes a requirement for grades K-12. As for recess, as many as 40% of our elementary schools no longer set aside time for play. The end result has been a sharp increase in obesity among youngsters" (p. 8). It is a tragic shame that physical education is not mandatory in all schools for all grades. This must be corrected or the obesity epidemic will continue to expand. The related health care costs will become a burden to all, including physically fit persons. Parents must demand that their schools utilize a physical education program. Because of economic budget concerns this may mean that some parents will have to volunteer their time and serve as physical educators (assuming they have the background). Ideally, it should be mandatory that all schools hire at least one full-time physical education instructor.

Participating in physical activities is not limited to the school environment. Parents can organize walking, running, or biking groups with their children (as well as with children whose parents are busy working). Adults can also organize physical activities with other adults. It is not necessarily to join a gym or health club to work out, one merely needs to step outside and start walking. Treadmills are responsibly priced and allow people to work out year round despite potential inclement weather outside. Those who can afford to join a health club should take advantage of the facilities and personal trainers available. Dr. Gail Saltz (2005) recommends these five practical tips to help motivate parents and their children to exercise more:

1. *Lead by example.* Children are more likely to be motivated to exercise if there is a positive role model to pattern behavior after.
2. *Take a non-negotiable position.* Just as parents will not put up with children who refuse to brush their teeth or swim without supervision, the same logic applies to keeping children from being sedentary.

3. *Promote the concept of personal best.* Physical exercise is not the same thing as competitive sports. Children can participate in physical activity (e.g., bike riding, dancing, yoga, and aerobics) without the worry of being compared to others. To keep themselves motivated they can attempt to meet and beat their own personal best performances. Parents should give positive feedback to their children who surpass previous performances.
4. *Limit sedentary activities.* Parents must limit the amount of time their children spend in front of the television, computer, and video screen. One hour of physical activity should be the goal for every child and teenager.
5. *Make it "cool."* If the fitness program is viewed as relatively entertaining (e.g. combing music with a workout, promoting diverse activities such as martial arts) it is more likely to be looked upon in favorable terms.

In sum, children and adults should engage in physical activities on a regular basis. Physical exercise along with a proper diet will increase the likelihood of a healthy, long life. Most people who exercise regularly actually find it difficult to miss a workout routine. This is why some people exercise while on vacation while others simply overeat and pursue sedentary activities.

Sportsmanship

Promoting healthy eating habits and sport participation or physical exercise should be accompanied by lessons in sportsmanship. Although sportsmanship (sportspersonship) has been discussed throughout this book, it is important to revisit this critical element of sport in our concluding remarks regarding sports' role in society.

Former NBA player and current NBA broadcaster Bill Walton believes that too many people involved in sports place an excessive emphasis on winning instead of sportsmanship, character development, and plain old fun. Walton (2005) claims it is especially important to emphasize sportsmanship, teamwork, attitude and respect, and playing sports for the fun of participation at the youth level. Walton believes that children have enough peer pressure and competition to contend with in their daily lives without having a win-at-all-cost mentality thrust upon them in the sports domain. As an active member of a Junior NBA/Junior WNBA program that conveys on a global scale the values of fair play and sportsmanship, Walton argues that it is important young people be taught the fundamentals of the game, safety tips, and the importance of qualities such as confidence, hustle, and dedication. "They also need to learn how to win and lose with class and dignity, plus how to compete like true sportsmen at every level of competition" (Walton, 2005: 13A). Walton was deeply upset with the NBA Indiana-Detroit brawl involving players and spectators (see Chapter 9) because of the potential significant influence that negative behavior can have on young people's behaviors and perceptions. The authors agree with Bill Walton's take on youth sport; specifically, that the prime emphasis at this level of sport competition should be learning fundamentals of the game, teaching sportsmanship and respect for the game and other participants, providing playing time for all athletes, and finding a way to make participation fun.

Around the time youth reach high school the prominent aspects of sports begin to shift toward winning. Some parents, coaches, and young athletes begin to lose sight of notions of fair play and a respect for the rules and ideals of the game. As Reeds (2004) points out, "The games we play and the rules we play them by have been established as meaningful boundaries defining fair play and should not be recognized as a set of trivial pursuits merely getting in the way of victory.... Social learning theory tells us that we learn through reinforcements for behaviors that bring us success. Winning as the desired outcome is a learned behavior and may require a subset of undesired behaviors. Rule violations have been institutionalized into our way of thinking. Sports are played and followed by folks who expect and accept the systematic breaking of rules" (p. 88).

Personal achievement is another aspect that gains prominence at the high school level of sport participation. At this point in personal development a number of young athletes' sporting talents have begun to clearly outshine others. Participants begin to realize their potential and their limitations. While it is important to encourage the continued play of those less talented, the winning priority dictates that their playing time will be reduced. Star athletes are encouraged to develop their talents so that they might play at the next level (e.g., college or professional sports, Olympic training). When athletes put forth extraordinary performances, especially against relatively equal opposition, they are praised. However, questions centered on sportsmanship and fair play come to the forefront when a star athlete puts forth a dominating effort against a clearly out-matched opposition. In some sports, such as girls' high school basketball, there is great disparity between the quality of play from team to team (Feinberg, 2006). As a result, final scores often reflect this disparity of talent. There are times when the losing team may accuse the opposition of "running up" the score—a violation of fair play and sportsmanship. The ethical debate over whether a team, or individual player, should play to its full potential, even if it means running up the score, or show "mercy" against an out-matched opponent is centered on the premise of sportsmanship and fair play.

A great example of this ethical dilemma took place on February 1, 2006, when Epiphanny Prince, a member of the Murry Bergtraum High School girls' basketball team, scored 113 points in a game against Brandeis High School. Prince's 113 points broke the national girls' record of 105 set in 1982 by Hall of Famer Cheryl Miller. Murry Bergtraum H.S. was ranked 2nd in the nation by the *USA Today* when they played Brandeis H.S., a team that had won only four league games and lost to Murry Bergtraum by 93 points earlier in the season. The demoralized Brandeis team, which trailed at halftime 74–11, reportedly gave up playing defense in the second half of the game (Feinberg, 2006). Prince had 58 points at the half and her coach, Ed Grezinsky, reasoned she had a good chance to break Miller's record and decided to keep her in the game—despite the lopsided score—so that she could go after the record. Prince made an incredible 54 of 60 shots and had only one free throw (reflecting that her opponents had given up playing defense). The ethical issue centers on whether or not Prince should have been kept in the game and given the opportunity to break the record against an obviously out-matched team. Brandeis Head Coach Vera Springer did not think so and interpreted the record-breaking performance as an example of poor sportsmanship on the part of Head Coach Ed Grezinsky. Cheryl Miller recalled that her coach, Floyd Evans, at Riverside Poly was questioned about keeping her in the game long enough to score 105 points.

It should be noted that running up the score against an over-matched opponent is generally viewed as poor sportsmanship at the youth and high school levels of sport competition. It becomes less clear at the professional level. For example, when L.A. Lakers star Kobe Bryant scored 81 points on January 22, 2006, against the Toronto Raptors, no one accused Lakers coach Phil Jackson of running up the score or keeping Kobe in the game in an attempt to beat Wilt Chamberlain's record of 100 points in a single game in 1962. This is primarily due to the fact that their opponent was another NBA team, the score was close (final score was 122–104), and this was professional sports. However, New England Patriots Coach Bill Belichick was criticized by many for running up the score against several opponents during the 2007 NFL season, in addition to illegally videotaping defensive signals of some of the teams (the so-called "Spygate" scandal).

Sport competition at the collegiate level represents a peculiar attempt to blend the ideals of sportsmanship and need (economically and otherwise) to win mentality. As demonstrated in Chapter 7, many colleges treat sport as a money-making industry and have their image so closely attached to sporting prowess that winning becomes important to the point that a number of unsportsmanlike behaviors are tolerated. Many people enjoy Division III sports because the pressures of "Big-Time" sports seldom invade their playing domain. Division III athletes (nonscholarship athletes) play for the love of their sport. They realize that a professional career as an athlete is highly unlikely, and yet they continue to play sports. Ideals of sportsmanship are emphasized more directly in Division III sports than in Division I. For example, the State University of New York Athletic Conference makes this announcement before all men's and women's basketball games:

> The student-athletes of the State University of New York Athletic Conference ask our fans to support our goal of promoting positive sportsmanship and developing an enjoyable sporting atmosphere. Just as we compete with respect for our opponents, we expect our fans, both local and visiting, to be courteous to our student athletes, our referees, our coaches, our administrators, and one another. For a positive student experience, profanity, racial or sexist comments, taunting, and other intimidating actions cross the line into poor sportsmanship and are grounds for removal from the site of competition. Let's cheer for our teams, have fun, and support the goals of Division III athletics [Source: Copy of the statement used at SUNY Oswego basketball games].

The importance placed on sportsmanship at the Division III level applies to athletes, coaches, referees, administrators, and fans. This practice should be applied to all levels of collegiate and professional athletics. As Reeds (2004) explains, "Winning fair and square, without seeking an unfair advantage through the breach of rules or through intimidation has a smell all of its own. It smells clean like a load of fresh air-dried laundry. Victories secured through rules violations or perverse posturing or taunting also have a smell all of their own, they stink. They smell like a decaying cesspool. When you hang up your championship banner may it exude the sweet smell of an honest effort and not the exhumed odor of a tainted death" (pp. 89–90).

As stated throughout this book, sport mirrors society; it is not bigger than life or separate from life, it is a part of life. There are positive aspects and there are negative aspects of both. The behaviors tolerated on the playing field or court are tolerated in society and we should not be surprised that they do not vary drastically. Promoting good sportsmanship will take away many of the negative aspects of sports (e.g., deviance, violence and inequality). Sport, as society, is filled with people who do not treat others fairly and who do not always demonstrate the ideals of good sportsmanship. It is important to continue to work toward a more equitable and fair society and sports institution. Many people are fighting this good fight.

In an attempt to recognize the humanitarian efforts of athletes, the World Sports Humanitarian Hall of Fame was established in 1994 and is located on the campus of Boise State University. This meaningful Hall of Fame annually inducts individuals who are world-class in athletic ability, serve as positive role models and have a strong record of humanitarian efforts. According to its Web site, the mission statement of the World Sports Humanitarian Hall of Fame is "to promote and recognize athletes who are role models and humanitarians for the purpose of inspiring individuals of all ages to reach their full potential" (Humanitarian Hall of Fame, 2006). The first three inductees were Chi Chi Rodriguez, Arthur Ashe, and Rafer Johnson. Other past inductees include Roberto Clemente, Bonnie Blair, Pele, Jackie Joyner-Kersee, Mary Lou Retton, the Harlem Globetrotters, Jackie Robinson, Jesse Owens, and Kathy Kusner. When people begin to visit and pay attention to this Hall of Fame as much as the ones located in Cooperstown (MLB), Canton (NFL), Springfield (NBA), or Toronto (NHL), we will notice that sportsmanship has become the dominant aspect of sport; not winning.

Summary

The sociology of sport serves an important function, by keeping an eye out on the ways in which sports operate in society, as well as by offering prescriptions for dealing with deviant behaviors, racism, sexism and other detrimental aspects of the sporting world. We hope that we have shown throughout this book the central role which sport plays in the lives of billions of individuals. At times, it can cause dissension, lead to violence, and mirror the overall disparities of the social systems in which it operates. At other times, it can provide meaning to people's lives, give a cathartic outlet for aggressive behavior, and bring out the best aspects of the social systems in which it operates, particularly in the realm of sportsmanship. And on some occasions, such as the J-Mac phenomenon, it can, for a brief shining moment, unite millions of people by bringing them the experience of pure joy.

People love sports for a variety of reasons. There are often euphoric moments in sports that allow for temporary escapes from the everyday, mundane world. One positive aspect is the way in which people with disabilities can benefit from sports participation. Many professional athletes devote a good amount of their time to promoting awareness of this topic.

Sports and physical education need to be emphasized more as a way of dealing with the contemporary problem of chronic obesity. This is a worldwide issue, but is especially a problem in the United States. More and more people are leading a sedentary lifestyle.

Sportsmanship remains a vital part of sports sociology. Sports competition should involve learning fundamentals of a game, learning sportsmanship and respect for the game and other participants, playing time for all athletes, and finding a way to make participation fun.

Sports mirrors society; it is not bigger than life or separate from life, it is a part of life.

KEY TERMS

Autism A developmental disability that begins in early childhood, characterized by marked deficits in communication and social interaction.

Body Mass Index Calculated by converting the weight of person into kilograms, divided by an individual's height in meters squared.

Personal Achievement Realizing one's potential and limitations.

Sedentary Lifestyle A lack of physical activity leading to one becoming out of shape or physically unfit.

DISCUSSION QUESTIONS

• Do you agree or disagree with the claim that participating in sports is basically a positive experience?

• What are some reasons why Americans are leading sedentary lifestyles, and what might be done to counter this trend?

• Do you think that physical education should be mandatory in school and at home? Why or why not? How might such a policy be implemented?

• What is "sportsmanship" and how can it be promoted?

Glossary

Academic Admissions Requirements Certain minimum standards that must be met for admission to a college or university.

Achieved Status A social or economic standing achieved through high levels of education or successful personal and economic decisions.

Acute Injuries Sports injuries which occur quickly as a result of a traumatic event and are followed immediately by a pattern of signs and symptoms such as pain, swelling, and loss of function.

Agents of Socialization The people, groups or institutions that teach us what we need to know in order to function properly in society.

Aggression Behavior which leads to personal injury, or the intent to harm others.

Aggression in Sport Verbal and physical behavior grounded in the intent to successfully accomplish a task even if it means to dominate, control, or harm, physically or psychologically, an opponent.

Amenorrhea The complete loss of menstruation. It can be termed as three or fewer menstrual cycles in a year or no cycle for six consecutive months.

Animism The earliest form of religion, it maintains that everything has two aspects, a physical manifestation and a spirit or soul.

Anomie Theory Developed by Robert Merton, the premise that society encourages all persons to attain culturally desirable goals, but the opportunity to reach these goals is not equal for all members of society.

Anorexia An eating disorder characterized by a purposeful weight loss far beyond the normal range.

Apartheid Government-sanctioned separation of races.

Ascribed Status Social or economic standing inherited by those born in wealthy families, higher than those born in poorer families.

Athlete A person who trains to compete in athletics.

Athletic Director A person who has full control over all aspects of college athletics, including the department's employees (staff, coaches, and student-athletes).

Athletic Scholarships Either full or partial, these provide financial assistance, usually in the form of room and board (paying for admissions, textbooks and school supplies) as well as per diem (meal allowance).

Athletic Stress Forces that cause bodily or mental strain.

Athletic Trainers Professionals who specialize in proper health care for athletes and in prevention, evaluation, management and rehabilitation of injuries.

Athletics Exercises and games that require physical skill, strength and endurance.

Attention Deficit Hyperactivity Disorder (ADHD) A behavior disorder identified by three characteristics: inattentiveness, impulsiveness, and hyperactivity.

Authoritarian Coach An overbearing coach obsessed with winning who may ruin the sport experience of participants.

Authority According to George Homans, a person who has *influence* over the thoughts and behaviors of other members of a group. Authority is considered to be a type of legitimate power.

Autism A development disability that begins in early childhood, characterized by marked deficits in communication and social interaction.

Babe Ruth Baseball/Softball Program Using regulation competitive baseball and softball rules, this program teaches skills, mental and physical development, a respect for the rules of the game, and basic ideals of sportsmanship and fair play.

BASE Jumping Parachuting from stationary objects (e.g., buildings, bridges, steep mountains). BASE is an acronym for building, antenna, span and earth.

Beliefs Things that people presume to be true, whereas they may or may not be true.

BIRG ("Basking in Reflected Glory") Individuals find meaning in their lives through their identification with successful people and teams.

Blood-doping Introducing a surplus of an athlete's own blood into his or her body in the hopes of improving performance.

Blue Laws So-called because they were once printed on blue paper, these are laws restricting activities or sales of goods on Sundays or holy days.

Bodily Strain Physical impairment caused by excessive demands on the body.

Body Mass Index Calculated by converting the weight of person into kilograms, divided by an individual's height in meters squared.

Bookies People who take illegal bets.

Boosterism Efforts to engender pride in one's hometown. Having a major league sports franchise can be a means to show pride in one's hometown.

Boycott A form of collective action, in athletics involving withdrawal from participation, intended to pressure the target group to change its position or behavior.

Bulimia An eating disorder characterized by repetitive cycles of dieting, then overeating — binging — followed by behaviors that get rid of, or purge, the food eaten.

Cal Ripken Baseball Division Part of the Babe Ruth Baseball/Softball Program, this division is for kids 12 and under.

Catastrophic Injury A sports injury which involves damage to the brain or spinal cord, or both, and is potentially life threatening or permanent.

Character Individual personality and behavioral traits, both good and bad, which define who a person is.

Character Development Gaining qualities that will make a person better able to deal with life's problems; many believe sports enhance character development.

Cheating In school sports it can take multiple forms (e.g., violating rules of sportsmanship, taking performance-enhancing drugs), all of which undermine the idealism of sport as an institution of character building.

Cheerleader A person who leads, calls for, and directs organized cheering at sporting events from the sidelines of the field or court.

Chivalry The qualities idealized by knighthood in the Middle Ages, such as bravery, courtesy, honor, and gallantry toward women.

Chronic Injuries Sports injuries which linger and develop over an extended period of time and are not tied to a single traumatic event.

Cigarette Cards Believed to have originated in France around the 1840s, these were cardboard stiffeners used as promotion.

Coaches Individuals who guide athletes on the rules of the game, methods of training, and ideally, help to develop the athletes' skills.

College Conferences Collective units which serve for instilling standards in college sports.

Collusion A secret undertaking by two or more people engaged in for the purpose of fraud.

Commitment Involves an emotional attachment to the object of loyalty.

Competitive Cheer Squads Groups which compete against other cheer squads in front of judges rather than cheering for a sports team.

Conflict Theories Theories which examine the role of and imbalances in power, especially in light of economic and social inequalities found in all societies.

Conspicuous Consumption A term coined by Thorstein Veblen; it refers to spending money, time and effort quite uselessly in the pleasurable business of inflating the ego.

Conspicuous Leisure A term coined by Thorstein Veblen; it refers to living a lifestyle where the pursuit of leisure and the appearance of privilege are used instrumental in one's behavior. In other words, it involves participating in nonproductive activities.

Consumer Culture Using consumer goods to express cultural categories and principles, cultivate ideals, create and sustain lifestyles, construct notions of the self, and create (and survive) social change.

Contest An organized competition. It may be between two individuals, between two teams, between an individual and a group, between an individual or team and inanimate nature, between a person or group and animate nature, or between an individual or team and an ideal standard.

CORF ("Cutting off Reflective Failure") Individuals distance themselves from unsuccessful people and teams.

Cultural Diffusion The spread of cultural aspects of one society to another.

Culture The shared knowledge, values, language, norms, and behavioral patterns of a given society that are handed down from one generation to the next and form a way of life for its members.

Development of Self The result of a number of interactions with others over a period of time in a variety of social and cultural contexts.

Deviance Any act or behavior that is likely to be defined, by some members of society, or specific subcultural groups, as an unacceptable violation of a social norm and elicits negative reactions from others.

Deviants Those who stray from the norm by committing acts of deviance.

Differential Association Theory The view that it takes continued association and reinforcement in order for a behavior to be indoctrinated.

Direct Upward Mobility A rise in socio-economic status that is accomplished when an athlete signs a lucrative professional contract.

Discrimination Behavior that treats people unequally on the basis of an ascribed status, such as race or gender.

Disrupting Play Generally takes place in the form of a spectator(s) running onto the field or court.

Diversity of Culture The result of each society's adaptation to their specific natural environments (e.g., climate and geography) and a number of traditional customs, habits, values and norms that develop over time to form a way of life for people.

Economic Dimension A stratification system involving two key variables: income and wealth.

E-gambling Gambling on the Internet.

Electronic Media Includes television, radio, motion pictures, and the Internet.

Elite Athlete Someone who has reached a level of competition at or near a national standard. He or she is considered the best in their sport; they are often shown special favor by coaches and schools.

Elite Deference Refers to the special privileges that are afforded athletes.

Ethnic Group A category of people who are recognized as a distinct group based on social or cultural factors.

Ethnocentrism The tendency for members of a society to use their culture's norms and values as standards for judging other cultures.

External Social Control (sometimes called **direct social control**) Regulation of behavior comes from "outside" social control agents, such as coaches, trainers, administrators and referees and umpires.

Extreme Sports A collective idiom used to describe a number of relatively newer sporting activities that involve risky, adrenaline-inducing action. Features of extreme sports may include speed, height, danger, peril, stunts, and illegality.

False Consciousness A term used by Marxists to signify the inability to clearly see where one's own best interests lie.

Folk Games Popular and traditional games, primarily played in rural areas and passed along from one generation to another.

Fraternal Bond A process whereby members of a group foster and reinforce team camaraderie and a commitment to group goals.

Function A contribution, service, or behavior purposive to society.

Functional Imperatives A term coined by Talcott Parsons, who argued that there are four basic "system needs" (adaptation, goal attainment, integration, and latency; or AGIL) necessary in order for any society (club, organization, team, etc.) to run smoothly.

Functional Theory The idea that there is a general consensus in values and norms of society and that the social institutions found within a society are integrated into a functioning whole.

Gamer A person who plays video games.

Gender This refers to socially determined expectations placed on individuals because of their sexual category. Males are expected to act masculine, while females are expected to act feminine.

Gender Roles A social by-product of cultural expectations. Gender role expectations extend to all realms of the social life, including mannerisms, behaviors, attitudes, styles of dress, and activities, including sports, that are deemed appropriate for men and women.

Generalized Other A person's conscious awareness of the society that he or she is a part of; the community or communities one belongs to.

Genocide The intentional attempt to exterminate a race of people by a more dominant population.

Genomics The use of genetic engineering to enhance athletic performance.

Globalization A social process in which the constraints of geography on social and cultural arrangements recede and in which people become increasingly aware that they are receding.

Government The political unit that exercises authority via laws and customs.

Harm Principle Philosopher John Stuart Mill's view that the only justification for interference with personal behavior is to prevent harm to others.

Hazing An all-encompassing term that covers silly, potentially risky, or degrading tasks required for acceptance by a group of full-fledged members.

Hegemonic Masculinity Typecasting males to a masculine ideal.

Hero Someone who is admired for his or her achievement, courage, skill, dedication, or integrity.

Heterogeneous Societies Consist of people who are dissimilar in regard to social characteristics such as religion, race, ethnicity, politics, and economic backgrounds.

Homogeneous Societies Consist of people who share a common culture and are generally from similar social, religious, political and economic backgrounds.

Homophobia Fear and dislike of homosexuals, often leading to persecution and discrimination against them.

Hypermasculinity The belief that ideal manhood lies in the exercise of force to dominate others.

Identity Involves those aspects of one's life that are deemed as essential to the character and maintenance of self.

Ideological Sexism The belief that one sex is inferior to another; it stresses gender-appropriateness based on gender roles.

Illegal Recruiting Tactics These may include rival recruiters spreading misinformation, lies or innuendoes to prized athletes in such ways as suggesting the other school is about to be placed on probation, they are going to raise admissions requirements, or that the head coach is about to quit or be fired.

Income The amount of money that a person, or family, receives over a period of time; generally a calendar year.

Indirect Upward Mobility A rise in socio-economic status that occurs when an athlete earns a college degree and finds gainful employment because of his or her educational credentials.

Industrialization The process of transforming an agricultural (farming) economy into an industrial one, through an increase in large factories, rapid population growth, and urbanization.

Informal Sports Those which are player-controlled, free from governing bodies and adult supervision, and allow the participant an opportunity to have fun in a self-expressing format.

Institutional Sexism Systematic practices and patterns within social institutions that lead to inequality between men and women.

Instrumental Aggression Behavior that is non-emotional and task oriented and driven by the quest for achieving some nonaggressive goal.

Instrumental Relationships Those relationships based on pragmatic principles that assist individuals in their pursuit of goals.

Intimidation Behavior that involves words, gestures and actions that sometimes may threaten violence or aggression in an attempt to pressure and put fear in the opponent.

Jousting Competition between two knights in full armor who ride at high speed directly toward one another with the object to unhorse one's opponent with a long tilting spear.

Labeling Theory The theory which examines the effects of a "label" being placed on a person and his or her subsequent behavior.

Language A set of symbols that can be strung together in an infinite number of ways that expresses ideas and abstract thoughts and enables people to think and communicate with one another.

Leisure Unobligated time that is free of work or maintenance responsibilities.

Leisure Class A term used by Thorstein Veblen to describe people who engaged in non-productive economic behavior.

Letter of Intent Treated as a legal contract, this states that the athlete promises to attend a particular school for four years.

Licensing Profits from merchandise sales.

Little League Baseball A program for youth, geared to provide a safe and healthy environment where they can learn the fundamentals of baseball while becoming good and decent citizens.

Little Leaguism A term used to describe youth sports that have become bureaucratic, standardized, efficiency-driven, rationalized, calculated, and predictable.

Lockout Occurs when negotiations between players and owners have deteriorated to the point where owners simply close down operations and keep players from playing.

Marquis of Queensbury Rules Set of rules agreed upon in the 1860s which became the standard of modern boxing, including requiring boxers to wear padded gloves and limiting rounds to three minutes.

Mass Media The medium by which large numbers of people are informed about important happenings in society.

Material Culture The physical, tangible creations of a society, such as clothing, merchandise, football stadiums, sporting equipment, automobiles, and art.

Medium A means of communicating information.

Mental Strain Distress caused by internal pressure that the youth places on self-performance.

Middle Ages A transitional period between a time when a large, unified nation or civilization (the Roman Empire) had disappeared and a later time when nations regained strength and stability (the Renaissance).

Mob Mentality Collective thinking and action that develops when a group reacts nearly simultaneously to a stimulus.

Modernization Changes in society characterized by growth in technology (especially a reliance on the application of scientific knowledge); advances in agriculture (e.g., commercial production of corporate-run farms); the use of machinery (human and animal power being replaced by machines); and changing ecological arrangements (e.g., continued population shift from rural areas to urban ones).

Monopoly A single firm that supplies a market.

Monopsony A situation where a seller (the player) is limited to only one buyer (the owner who the athlete is currently under contract with or who has drafted him or her). The buyer controls the market because the seller is not allowed to sell his skills elsewhere in a free and open market.

Muscular Christianity A term used to describe the religious philosophy of teaching morals and values through sport.

National Collegiate Athletic Association The NCAA supervises the organization of college sports, the conduct of athletes, coaches and others involved with college sports, and the academic qualification to which athletes must adhere. It attempts to act in the best interests of college athletics.

Natural Sciences Disciplines such as astronomy, biology, chemistry, geology, and physics, which focus their studies on the physical features of nature and the manner in which they interact and change.

Negro Baseball A collective term used to describe the various teams and leagues that existed from the early 1900s until the 1950s.

Nonmaterial Culture The more abstract creations of society, such as beliefs, values, ideology, and norms.

Oligarchy A power structure in which control is in the hands of a few.

Option System An arrangement in which a player is free to seek employment with another team one year after his contract has expired if the original owner did not re-sign him.

Organized Play Activities which are bound by rules, in which there are designated time limits and boundaries and nearly always a clear winner and loser.

Osteoporosis A condition of decreased bone mass that can lead to bone fractures.

Other-regarding Acts Behaviors which may cause harm to others and, therefore, fall outside the dominion of acceptable forms of violence.

Pankration A Greek word that means "complete strength" or "complete victory."

Patriarchy A male-dominated society or ideology.

Personal Achievement Realizing one's potential and limitations.

Phenomenological Approach A type of symbolic interactionism which examines sport through the senses and emotions of the player.

Ping Pong Diplomacy A phrase coined during the Nixon Administration to describe the use of sports as a means of bridging the political gap between the U.S. and the People's Republic of China.

Play An activity that is performed voluntarily during leisure.

Politics Generally viewed as the guiding influence of governmental policy.

Pop Warner Football The most recognized formal and organized youth football program.

Positivism A way of understanding the world based on science. Positivists believe that the social world can be studied in the same manner as the natural sciences and believe that "laws" exist that apply to the human species; they merely have to be discovered by social scientists.

Power The ability to provide rewards.

Practice Any meeting, activity or instruction involving sports-related information and having an athletics purpose, held for one or more student-athletes at the direction of, or supervised by, any member or members of an institution's coaching staff.

Prejudice Negative beliefs and overgeneralizations concerning a group of people which involves a judgment against someone based on a rigid and fixed mental image of some group of people that is applied to all individuals of that group.

Preperformance Routines Learned behavioral and cognitive strategies which are deliberately used by athletes in order to assist physical performance.

Primary Group An intimate association where members share a sense of "we-ness"—a sort of sympathy and mutual identification for which "we" is a natural expression. The primary group is relatively small, often informal, involves close personal relationships, and has an important role in shaping an individual's sense of self.

Print Media Includes newspapers, magazines, and books.

Profane Items The ordinary, mundane, commonplace items of society.

Proportionality In Title IX, the total number of varsity male and female athletes must be proportional to the gender division of the general student body.

Race A group of people who share some socially recognized physical characteristic (such as skin color or facial features) that distinguishes them from other groups of people and are recognized by themselves and others as a distinct group.

Racism Any attitude, belief, behavior, or social arrangement that has the intent, or the ultimate effect, of favoring one group over another.

Reactive Aggression Actions with the primary goal of inflicting bodily injury or physical harm to an opponent.

Recreation A leisure activity designed to refresh the mind and/or body.

Recreational Gambling Gambling among friends and co-workers.

Recruitment A college's act of seeking out an athlete, rather than the reverse.

Religion A system of beliefs and rituals that serves to bind people together into a social group while attempting to answer the dilemmas and questions of human existence by making the world more meaningful to its adherents.

Religious Beliefs Ideals to which members of a particular religion adhere.

Role Exit A process of leaving a role through being socialized into a new role.

Sacred Items Objects and behaviors that are deemed part of the spiritual realm and are set apart from the ordinary; they are worshipped.

Scientific Method The pursuit of knowledge involving the stating of a problem, the collection of facts through observation and experiment, and the testing of ideas to determine whether they are right or wrong.

Secondary Group A collectivity whose members interact with one another formally and impersonally.

Secularism The process of moving from a religious orientation toward one that is focused on the world.

Sedentary Lifestyle A lack of physical activity leading to one becoming out of shape or physically unfit.

Self-fulfilling Prophecy Occurs when people take to heart the labels bestowed upon them, come to see themselves in regard to those labels, and then act correspondingly to those labels.

Self-regarding Acts Behaviors that may cause harm only to the individual performing them and, therefore, fall within the realm of acceptable violence.

Sex This refers to one's biological classification. Males and females differ biologically in regards to their internal and external reproductive organs and genitalia, types and levels of hormones and chromosomal structure (females have an XX and males an XY design).

Sexism Behavior that discriminates against a member(s) of one sex due to preferential treatment aimed to assist a member(s) of the other sex.

Sexual Harassment Deliberate or repeated unsolicited verbal comments, gestures, or physical contact of a sexual nature that are unwelcome by the recipient and create an intimidating or hostile work environment.

"Significant Others" Those specific individuals with whom a child interacts with on a regular basis, generally the child's immediate family members and friends (a term used by George Herbert Mead). Those persons play a major role in shaping a person's self.

Soccer Mom Someone who drives her children to soccer games and watches them compete.

Social Institutions A set of organized beliefs and rules that establishes how a society will attempt to meet its basic social needs.

Social Learning Theories An individual learns behavior through interaction with others; whether directly (being taught) or indirectly (through observation).

Social Norms The rules that govern behavior.

Social Prestige A dimension of social stratification that is tied to what people think about others.

Social Sciences Disciplines such as sociology, anthropology, economics, history, psychology, and political science, which concentrate their study on the various aspects of human society.

Social Stratification A ranking system of members of a social system into levels having different or unequal evaluations; it reveals patterns of social inequality.

Social Structure The organization of society — its social positions and the ongoing relationships among these social positions, the different resources allocated to these social positions, and the social groups that make up the society.

Social Theory Focuses on interactions, patterns and events found in the social environment and attempts to explain such observed phenomena.

Social Worlds Group members who share a subcultural perspective and are held together through interaction and communication.

Socialization A process of social development and learning that occurs as individuals interact with one another and learn about society's expectations of acceptable behavior.

Socialization into Sport A process whereby an individual is encouraged by the agents of socialization to partake in sport either as a participant or as a spectator or consumer.

Socialization out of Sport A desocialization process where an individual leaves sport and experiences a modification of sense of self. For professional athletes, exiting sport can be very difficult.

Socialization Process The ways in which individuals learn cultural norms, values, beliefs and expectations.

Socialization via Sport The social processes and significant others that influence an individual's decision to remain in sport.

Society The largest collection of a group of people who interact with one another as members of a collectivity within a defined boundary. A society also consists of a number of highly structured systems of human organization and this organized system helps to form the social structure of society.

Socio-economic Status A composite term that includes a person's income, wealth, occupational prestige, and educational attainment.

Sociological Imagination A term coined by C. Wright Mills. Sociological imagination stresses the importance of the historical social context in which an individual is found, and the ways in which our private lives are influenced by our social environment and existing social forces.

Sociology The systematic study of human society and social interaction. Note the difference from page 4, where sociology is defined as the systematic study of groups, organizations, social institutions, societies, and the social interaction among people.

Sociology of Sport The systematic study of the processes, patterns, issues, values and behaviors found in the institution of sport.

Spontaneous Play A type of play which is voluntary, flexible, and uncertain with latitude for innovation.

Sport An institutionalized, structured, and sanctioned competitive activity beyond the realm of play that involves physical exertion and the use of relatively complex athletic skills.

Sport Books Legally placed bets on a wide variety of sporting events, allowed in some casinos.

Sport Specialization Concentrating on just one sport, year-around, instead of enjoying participating in multiple sports.

Sport Superstitions Ritualized routines that are separate from athletic training and that are performed by athletes because they believe such behaviors are powerful enough to control external factors (e.g., the talents of opponents).

Sport Violence Intentional aggressive physical behavior that causes harm, occurs outside the rules of the game, is unrelated to ideals of sportsmanship, or which destroys the property of another sportsperson.

Sports Cartel An economic body formed by a small number of teams within the same league that make decisions on matters of common interest (e.g., rules, revenue-sharing, expansion, scheduling, and promotion) and exchange money as resources.

Streaming A technological advancement in sport broadcasting that allows sports fans to watch the game "on the go" or while they are at work online.

Subculture A distinctive group of people within a greater culture who possess distinctive cultural values, behavioral patterns, ethnicity, or some other trait that distinguishes it from dominant groups in the greater society.

Superstitions Beliefs or practices resulting from ignorance or fear of the unknown, or a belief in magic or chance.

Symbolic Interactionism The view that that human behavior involves choices and that choices are made based on *meanings,* or *definitions of the situation.*

Symbols Items that represent something else by association, resemblance, or convention to a people in a society.

Tall Tale The oldest form of story telling is the result of oral accounts of great feats of accomplishments, usually exaggerated.

T-ball A game designed to indoctrinate young children (starting around age 5) into the game of baseball.

Terrorism The unlawful use of — or threatened use of — force or violence against individuals or property to coerce or intimidate governments or societies, often to achieve political, religious, or ideological objectives.

Theory A statement that proposes to explain or relate observed phenomena or a set of concepts through a logically-based system of general propositions. It involves a set of inter-related arguments that seek to describe and explain cause-effect relationships.

Totemism As described by Emile Durkheim, a primitive form of a religious system in which certain things, particularly animals and plants, come to be regarded as *sacred* emblems.

Tournaments Public contests held in the Middle Ages between armed horsemen in simulation of real battle; these were restricted to the upper classes.

True Story An approach to sportswriting which reveals the frailties and failures of athletes.

Urbanization The process by which a country's population changes from primarily rural to urban. It is caused by the migration of people from the countryside to the city in search of better jobs and living conditions.

Vandalism The willful or malicious destruction or defacing of public or private property.

Verbal Assaults The use of obscenities, vulgarities, and threatening words directed by sports spectators at the targets of their scorn.

Verse Refers to the poetic-style writing of sportswriters.

Violence Entails great physical force used intentionally by one person(s) to cause another person(s) harm or aggressive behavior which destroys the property of another.

Walk-on A nonscholarship athlete who tries out for a sport.

Wealth The total value of everything that a person or family owns, minus any debts owed.

Bibliography

ABC News. 2005. "How to Handle 'Sideline Rage.'" Available: http://abcnewsgo.com/gma/print?id=1034449.

Abend, Gabrel. 2008. "The Meaning of 'Theory'" *Sociological Theory*, 26(2): 173–199.

AOL Sport News. 2005. "Richardson Against NBA's New Dress Code." October 20. Available: http://aolsvc.news.aol.com/sports/article.adp.

_____. 2005. "DeBerry Reprimanded for Comments About Black Athletes." October 26. Available: http://aolsvx.news.aol.com/sports/article.adp.

Aboulafia, Mitchell. 1986. *The Mediating Self: Mead, Sartre and Self-Determination*. New Haven: Yale University Press.

Adelman, Melvin. 1997. "The Early Years of Baseball, 1845–60," pp. 58–87 in *The New American Sport History*, edited by S.W. Pope. Chicago: University of Illinois Press.

Adorno, Theodor W. 1981. *Prisms*, translated by Samuel and Shierry Weber. Cambridge, MA: MIT Press.

Albanese, Jeanne. 1997A. "Youth Coach Accused of Assaulting Boy." *The Post-Standard*. January 28: D-1.

_____. 1997B. "Dad Barred From Games." *The Post-Standard*. January 28: D1.

Alexander, Elton. 2005. "When it Comes to Shoes, Athletes Know Best." *The Cleveland Plain Dealer*. October 23: C2.

Allardt, E. 1970. "Basic Approaches in Comparative Sociological Research and the Study of Sport," pp. 14–30 in *Cross-Cultural Analysis of Sport and Games*, edited by Günther Luschen. Champaign, IL: Stipes.

Allen, Karen. 1999. "Controversy Has Marked Modern Olympics." *USA Today*. January 7: 5E.

American Sociological Association. 2005. "Reflecting on ASA's Centennial Year, 2005." May/June: 1.

Anshel, Mark. 1994. *Sport Psychology*, 2nd edition. Scottsdale, AZ: Gorsuch Scarisbrick.

Antonen, Mel. 2000. "A-Rod Gets $252 Million and a New Address in Texas." *USA Today*. December 12: 1C.

Aran, K., and M. Sangiacomo. 1993. "Sockalexis Kin Say He Likes Team Name." *Cleveland Plain Dealer*. June 12: 2B.

Arens, Elizabeth. 1999. "Title IX is Unfair to Men's Sports," pp. 127–135 in *Sports and Athletes: Opposing Viewpoints*, edited by Laura Egendorf. San Diego: Greenhaven.

Arnold, Brandon. 2006. "History of Snowboarding." Available: http://snowboarding.about.com/65/basics1/a/history.html.

Arnold, Serena. 1980. "The Dilemma of Meaning," pp. 5–18 in *Recreation and Leisure: Issues in an Era of Change*, edited by Thomas Goodale and Peter Witt. State College, PA: Venture.

Atlanta Braves History. 2000. "All Dressed up in History." Available: www.atlantabraves.com.

Auer, Holly. 2003. "Betting Against All Odds." *Buffalo News*. April 21: A-1.

Babe Ruth League. 2005. Home website. Available: http://www.baberuthleague.org.

Bagnall, Janet. 2005. "Hazing Rituals Should Not Be Tolerated." *The Gazette*. September 23: A27.

Bailey, Darlene. 2000. "Women in Sports: Seeking Balance," pp. 102–114 in *Sports in School*, edited by John R. Gerdy. New York: Teachers College Press.

_____. 2006. "J-Mac: The Story Behind The Kid in the Highlights." *The Post-Standard* (originally printed in the *Daily Messenger* of Canandaigua, New York). February 24: A-1, A-6.

Baird, Woody. 2007. "Pregnant Athlete Loses Her Funding." May 13: A-16.

Bairner, Alan. 2001. *Sport, Nationalism, and Globalization*. Albany, NY: State University of New York Press.

Baker, W. J. 1982. *Sports in the Western World*. Totowa, NJ: Rowan & Littlefield.

Bartollas, Clemens. 1985. *Correctional Treatment Theory and Practice*. Englewood Cliffs, NJ: Prentice Hall.

Baumeister, R. F. 1991. *Meanings of Life*. New York: Guilford Press.

Bazzano, Carmelo. 1994. "The Italian-American Sporting Experience," pp. 103–116 in *Ethnicity and Sport in North American History and Culture*, edited by George Eisen and David K. Wiggins. Westport, CT: Greenwood Press.

BBC News. 2000. "Jumbo Race a 'Big Success.'" July 16. Available: http://news.bbc.co.uk.

Beaton, Rod. 2002. "Age May be Off for Hundreds in Baseball." *USA Today*. February 26: C1.

Bechtel, Mark. 2005. "The Right Way to Cheat: Pulling a Fast One is Sometimes Part of the Game." August 24. Available: http://sportsillustrated.cnn.com.

Beck, Daniel, and Louis Bosshart. 2003 (Winter). "Sports, Media, Politics, and National Identity." *Communication Research Trends*. 22(4): 10–15.

Beezley, William H. and Joseph P. Hobbs. 1989. "Nice Girls Don't Sweat: Women in American Sport," pp. 337–349 in *Sport in Contemporary Society*, 3rd

319

edition, edited by D. Stanley Eitzen. New York: St. Martin's.

Bell, J. Bowyer. 1987. *To Play the Game*. New Brunswick, NJ: Transaction Books.

Bell, Jarrett. 2005. "Progress Would Have Pleased Pollard, Grandson Says." *USA Today*. August 8: 8C.

Bellamy, Robert V. Jr., and James R. Walker. 2005. "Whatever Happened to Synergy? *Nine*, 13(2): 19–31.

Bender, Thomas. 1991. *Community and Social Change in America*. Baltimore: Johns Hopkins University Press.

Berg, Francis M. 1997. *Afraid to Eat: Children and Teens in Weight Crisis*. Hettinger, ND: Healthy Weight Publishing Network.

Berger, Peter. 1963. *Invitation to Sociology: A Humanistic Perspective*. New York: Doubleday (Anchor edition).

Best, Joel, and David F. Luckenbill. 1994. *Organizing Deviance*. Englewood Cliffs, NJ: Prentice Hall.

Bigelow, Bob. 2000. "Is Your Child Too Young for Youth Sports or is Your Adult Too Old?" pp. 7–17 in *Sports in School*, edited by John R. Gerdy. New York: Teachers College Press.

Birrell, Susan. 1981. "Sport as Ritual: Interpretations from Durkheim to Goffman." *Social Forces*, 62(2): 354–376.

Biskupic, Joan. 2000. "School Prayer Rejected: High Court Bars Student-Led Acts." *USA Today*. June 20: 1A.

Bissell, Kimberly L. 2004. "What Do These Messages Really Mean? Sports Media Exposure, Sports Participation, and the Body Image Distortion in Women Between the Ages of 18 and 75." *Journalism and Mass Communication Quarterly*. 81(1): 108–123.

Bjarkman, Peter C. 1996. *Baseball with a Latin Beat*. Jefferson, NC: McFarland.

Bleak, Jared L., and Christina M. Frederick. 1998. "Superstitious Behavior in Sport: Levels of Effectiveness and Determinants of Use in Three Collegiate Sports." *Journal of Sport Behavior*. Vol. 21 (March), No. 1: 1–15.

Blum, Matt. 2007. "Big-League Wallets Bursting With Cash." *The Post-Standard*. April 3: D-4.

Blum, Ronald. 2006. "Life of Luxury Costly for Yanks." *The Post-Standard*. December 23: D-2.

Blumer, Herbert. 1969. *Symbolic Interaction*. Englewood Cliffs, NJ: Prentice Hall.

Borges, Ron. 2005. "Frivolity Didn't Wash." *The Boston Globe*. August 21: C12.

Borte, Jason. 2000. "George Freeth." Available: http://www.surfing.com/surfa2/freeth_george.cfm.

Bowen, William G., and Sarah A. Levin. 2003. *Reclaiming the Game: College Sports and Educational Values*. Princeton, NJ: Princeton University Press.

Bowman, John, and Joel Zoss. 1989. *Diamonds in the Rough: The Untold Story of Baseball*. New York: Macmillan.

Brady, Erik. 2002. "Cheerleading in the USA: A Sport and an Industry." *USA Today*. April 26–28: 1A.

_____. 2002. "Title IX Hits Middle America." *USA Today*. June 13: 1A, 2A.

Brayshaw, R.D. 1974. "Leisure Counseling for People in Correctional Institutions." *Leisurability*, Vol. 1: 10–14.

_____. 1978. "Reducing Recidivism: A Community Responsibility." *Leisurability*, Vol. 5: 30–32.

_____. 1981. "The Future of Correctional Recreation." *Journal of Physical Education, Recreation and Dance*, Vol. 52: 53.

Brohm, Jean-Marie. 1976. *Sport — A Prison of Measured Time*, translated by Ian Fraser. London: Ink Links.

Brookes, Rod. 2002. *Representing Sport*. New York: Oxford University Press.

Bruey, Carolyn Thorworth. 2004. *Demystifying Autism Spectrum Disorders: A Guide To Diagnosis for Parents and Professionals*. Bethesda, MD: Woodbine House.

Bueno, Ana. 1994. *Special Olympics: The First 25 Years*. San Francisco, California: Foghorn Press.

Buffalo News. 1998. "Site Selection Bribery Charges Rock IOC." December 13: D3.

_____. 1999. "Fears Stop Teen From Saying Prayer at Football Games." August 27: A8.

_____. 2000. "Parents in Brawl After Youth Football Game." September 25: A3.

_____. 2008. "Chart: The Buffalo Bills Average Ticket Prices in 2007 Were the Lowest in the NFL." May 21. Available: http://www.buffalonews.com/sports/bills nfl/story/34986.html.

Burstyn, Varda. 1999. *The Rites of Men: Manhood, Politics, and The Culture of Sport*. Toronto: University of Toronto Press.

Cahn, Susan K. 2003. *Coming on Strong: Gender and Sexuality in Twentieth Century Women's Sports*. Cambridge, MA: Harvard University Press.

Calhoun, Donald W. 1987. *Sport, Culture and Personality*. Champaign, IL: Human Kinetics.

Caponi-Tabery, Gena. 2002. "Jump for Joy: Jump Blues, Dance, and Basketball in 1930s African America," pp. 39–74 in *Sports Matters: Race, Recreation and Culture*, edited by John Bloom and Michael Nevin Willard. New York: New York University Press.

Carelli, Richard. 2000. "Ruling Bars Prayers Led by Students at Games." *Buffalo News*. June 19: A1.

Carroll, John. 1999. *Red Grange and the Rise of Modern Football*. Chicago: University of Illinois Press.

Cauchon, Dennis. 2005. "Childhood Pastimes are Increasingly Moving Indoors." *USA Today*. July 12: A1, A2.

Center for Disease Control. 2002. "Injury Fact Book: 2001–2002." Available: http://www.cdc.gov/fact-book.

_____. 2007. "Obesity and Overweight: Introduction." Available: http://www.cdc.gov.

Chalip, Laurence and B. Christine Green. 1998. "Establishing and Maintaining a Modified Youth Sport Program: Lessons from Hotelling's Location Game." *Sociology of Sport Journal*. 15: 326–342.

Chandler, Joan M. 1992. "Sport Is Not a Religion," pp. 55–61 in *Sport and Religion*, edited by Shirl J. Hoffman. Champaign, IL: Human Kinetics.

Chanen, David, and David Shaffer. 2005. "Culpepper, 3 Others Charged in Boat Party." *Minneapolis Star Tribune* (as appeared in *The Post-Standard*). December 16: C-1.

Chavira, R. 1977. "Three to Cheer." *Nuestro*, 1 (August): 34–35.

Chen, Albert. 2006. "Scoreboard: World Serious." *Sports Illustrated*. January 16: 16–17.

Chronicle of Higher Education. 1988. "Sidelines." Vol. 34 (May 11): A32.

Cialdini, Robert, Richard Borden, Arril Thorne, Marcus Walker, Stephen Freeman, and Lloyd Sloan. 1976.

"Basking in Reflected Glory: Three (Football) Field Studies." *Journal of Personality and Social Psychology*, 34: 366–375.

The Citizen. 2005. "Report: Three Panthers Filled Steroid Prescriptions with S.C. Doctor." March 30: B3.

_____. 2006. "Autistic Hoops Sensation Meets President Bush." March 15: B1.

Clark, Michael A. 2000. "Who's Coaching The Coaches?" pp. 55–65 in *Sports in School: The Future of an Institution*, edited by John R. Gerdy. New York: Teacher's College, Columbia University.

Clark, N., M. Nelson, and W. Evans. 1998. "Nutrition Education for Elite Female Runners." *The Physician and Sports Medicine*. 16 (Feb.): 124–134.

Clinton, Bill. 2005. "We Must Act Now." *Parade*. September 25: 4–5.

CNN.COM. 1999. "Money Offered Night Before Sydney Won Olympics." January 22. Available: http://www.cnn.com/world/europe/9901/122/olympics.031.

_____. 2003. "High School's Sports Participation at Record Level." Available: http://cnnfyi.printthis.clickability.com.

_____. 2005. "Then & Now: Bethany Hamilton — June 22, 2005." Available at: http://cnn.worldnews.printthis.clickability.com.

Coakley, Jay. 1981. "The Sociological Perspective: Alternate Causations of Violence in Sport." *Arena Review*, 5 (Feb.): 44–56.

_____. 2006. *Sports in Society*, 9th edition. Boston: McGraw-Hill.

Cockerham, William. 1995. *The Global Society*. New York: McGraw-Hill.

Coe, Sebastian, with Nicholas Mason. 1996. *The Olympians: A Century of Gold*. London: Pavilion.

Connors, Greg. 2002. "Action Figures." *Buffalo News*. July 14: B1.

Cooley, Charles. 1909. *Social Organization*. New York: Scribners.

Craig, Steve. 2002. *Sports and Games of the Ancients*. Westport, CT: Greenwood Press.

Crepeau, Richard. 1985. "Where Have You Gone, Frank Merriwell? The Decline of the American Sports Hero," pp. 76–82 in *American Sport Culture*, edited by Wiley Lee Umphlett. Lewisburg: Bucknell University Press.

Crow, R. Brian, and Scott R. Rosner. 2004. "Hazing and Sport and the Law," pp. 200–223 in *The Hazing Reader*, edited by Hank Nuwer. Bloomington, IN: Indiana University Press.

Crudale, Anthony. 2001. "Livin' It: For the 24-Year-Old Author, the Best Therapy for Autism is Running." *Sports Illustrated*. June 18: 28.

Curry, Tim. 1991. "Fraternal Bonding in the Locker Room: A Pro Feminist Analysis of Talk About Competition and Women." *Sociology of Sport Journal*. 8: 119–135.

Curry, Timothy J., and Robert M. Jiobu. 1984. *Sports: A Social Perspective*. Englewood Cliffs, NJ: Prentice Hall.

Curtis, James, William McTeer, and Philip White. 2003. "Do High School Athletes Earn More Pay? Youth Sport Participation and Earnings as an Adult." *Sociology of Sport Journal*. 20: 60–76.

Czech, Daniel R., Craig A. Wrisberg, Leslee A. Fisher, Charles L. Thompson, and Gene Hayes. 2004. "The Experience of Christian Prayer in Sport: An Existential Phenomenological Investigation." *Journal of Psychology and Christianity*. 25(1): 3–11.

Daniels, Stephen. 2005. "How to Talk to Your Kids About Weight." *Parade*. September 25: 6.

Daymont, Thomas N. 1981. "The Effects of Monopsonistic Procedures on Equality of Competition in Professional Sport Leagues," pp. 241–250 in *Sport, Culture, and Society*, 2nd edition, edited by John W. Loy, Jr., Gerald S. Kenyon and Barry D. McPherson. Philadelphia: Lea & Febiger.

Delaney, Tim. 2001. *Community, Sport and Leisure*. Auburn, NY: Legend Books.

_____. 2002. "Sport Violence," pp. 1560–1563 in the *Encyclopedia of Crime and Punishment*, Vol. 4, edited by David Levinson. Thousand Oaks, CA: Sage.

_____. 2004. *Classical Social Theory: Investigation and Application*. Upper Saddle River, NJ: Prentice Hall.

_____. 2005. *Contemporary Social Theory: Investigation and Application*. Upper Saddle River, NJ: Prentice Hall.

_____. 2006A. *Seinology: The Sociology of Seinfeld*. Amherst, NY: Prometheus Books.

_____. 2006B. *American Street Gangs*. Upper Saddle River, NJ: Prentice Hall.

_____. 2007. "Basic Concepts of Sports Gambling: An Exploratory Review." *New York Sociologist*, 2: 93–102.

Delaney, Tim, and Allene Wilcox. 2002. "Sports and the Role of the Media," pp. 199–215 in *Values, Society & Evolution*, edited by Harry Birx and Tim Delaney. Auburn, NY: Legend Books.

Delfattore, Joan. 2004. *The Fourth R*. New Haven, CT: Yale University Press.

Denzin, Norman. 1969. "Symbolic Interaction and Ethnomethodology: A Proposed Synthesis." *American Sociological Review*, 34(6): 922–934.

Deseretnews.com. 2001. "S.L. Bid Scandal Leads to Olympic Reforms." Available: http://deseretnews.com.

Devereaux, E. 1976. "Backyard Versus Little League Baseball: The Impoverishment of Children's Games," pp. 37–50 in *Social Problems in Athletics*, edited by D. Landers. Urbana, IL: University of Illinois Press.

Dobie, Michael. 2004. "Frequently Asked Questions." *Newsday.com*. July 11. Available: http://www.newsday.com/sports/ny-pris/-side4,0,3111 317.

Dodd, Mike. 2005. "Last Cookie Cutter Crumbles." *USA Today*. September 21: 1C–2C.

Dorfman, H.A. 2003. *Coaching the Mental Game*. New York: Taylor.

Dorinson, Joseph. 1997. "Black Heroes in Sport: From Jack Johnson to Muhammad Ali." *Journal of Popular Culture*, 31 (Winter): 115–135.

The Doug Flutie, Jr., Foundation for Autism. 2006. "Homesite." Available: www.dougflutiejrfoundation.org.

Douglas, Mary. 1966. *Purity and Danger*. London: Routledge & Kegan Paul.

Downward, Paul and Alistair Dawson. 2000. *The Economics of Professional Team Sports*. New York: Routledge.

Drahota, Jo Anne Tremaine, and D. Stanley Eitzen. 1998. "The Role Exit of Professional Athletes." *Sociology of Sport Journal*. 15: 263–278.

Dubbert, J.L. 1979. *A Man's Place*. Englewood Cliffs, NJ: Prentice Hall.

Duderstadt, James J. 2003. *Intercollegiate Athletics and the American University: A President's Perspective*. Ann Arbor: University of Michigan Press.

Duncan, Margret Carlisle. 1993. "Beyond Analyses of Sport Media Texts: An Argument For Formal Analyses of Institutional Structures." *Sociology of Sport Journal*. 10: 353–372.

Duncan, Margaret Carlisle, and B. Brummett. 1987. "The Mediation of Spectator Sport." *Research Quarterly*, 38: 168–177.

Dunning, Eric. 1999. *Sport Matters: Sociological Study of Sport, Deviance, Violence and Civilization*. New York: Routledge.

Durkheim, Emile. 1963 [1912]. *The Elementary Forms of Religious Life*. New York: Free Press.

Easterbrook, Gregg. 1999. "College Athletes Should Receive Scholarship Extensions," pp. 78–81 in *Sports and Athletes*, edited by Laura Egendorf. San Diego, CA: Greenhaven.

Edwards, Harry. 1969. *The Revolt of the Black Athlete*. New York: Free Press.

_____. 1973. *Sociology of Sport*. Homewood, IL: Dorsey.

Eitzen, D. Stanley, and George H. Sage. 1989. *Sociology of North American Sport*, 4th edition. Dubuque, IA: Wm. C. Brown.

Eltman, Frank. 2003. "High School Ballplayers Allegedly Visited Strip Club." *The Buffalo News*. May 9: A-8.

Entine, Jon. 2000. *Taboo: Why Black Athletes Dominate Sports and Why We're Afraid To Talk About It*. New York: Public Affairs/Perseus.

Erie County Interscholastic Conference. 2001. "Appendix A: Academic Eligibility." New York State Public High School Athletic Association and the Erie County Interscholastic Conference (E.D.I.C.).

ESPN. 2005. "Many Ginobili — Special Report." Original airdate: June 11.

_____. 2005. "50 States in 50 Days: Idaho." Original airdate: July 24.

_____. 2007. "Outside the Lines." Original airdate: June 2.

ESPN Page 2. 2005. "Page 2's Top 20 Sports Movies of All-Time." July 30. Available: http://espn.go.com/page2/movies/s/top20/fulllist.html.

Euchner, C.C. 1993. *Playing the Field: Why Sports Teams Move and Cities Fight to Keep Them*. Baltimore: Johns Hopkins University Press.

Falkener, Edward. 1961. *Games, Ancient and Oriental and How to Play Them*. New York: Dover.

Farber, Michael. 2005. "Scorecard: Cold Warriors." *Sports Illustrated*. July 4: 16–17.

Feinberg, Doug. 2006. "Poor Sportsmanship or Good Shooting: Should Epiphanny Prince Have Stayed in to Score 113 Points Against a Helpless Team?" *The Post-Standard*. February 3: C-9

Feldman, Jay. 1993. "Roberto Clemente Went to Bat for Latino Ballplayers." *Smithsonian*, Vol. 24: 128.

Fendrich, Howard. 2002. "NBA Inks New Six-Year, $4.6 Billion Deals with ESPN, ABC, TNT." *The Buffalo News*. January 24: C-5.

Fenwick, Lynda Beck. 1989. *Should The Children Pray?* Waco, TX: Markham Press.

Figler, Stephen and Gail Whitaker. 1991. *Sport and Play In American Life*, 2nd edition. Dubuque, IA: Wm. C. Brown.

_____. 1995. *Sport and Play in American Life*, 3rd edition. Chicago: Brown and Benchmark.

Fink, Dale Borman. 2000. *Making a Place for Kids with Disabilities*. Westport, CT: Praeger.

Fischer, Claude E., and C. Ann Stueve. 1977. "Authentic Community: The Role of Place in Modern Life," pp. 163–186 in *Networks and Places*, edited by Claude S. Fischer. New York: Free Press.

Fischer, Gloria. 1997. "Abstention from Sex and Other Pre-Game Rituals Used by College Male Varsity Athletes." *Journal of Sport Behavior*. 20(2): 176–185.

Fisher, Donald M. 2001. "Chief Bill Orange and the Saltine Warrior: A Cultural History of Indian Symbols and Imagery at Syracuse University," pp. 25–45 in *Team Spirits: The Native American Mascots Controversy*. Lincoln, NE: University of Nebraska Press.

Fitzgerald, Jim. 2001. "Iona-Mississippi 'Rivalry' has a History." *Buffalo News*. March 15: B11.

Fleisher Arthur A., III, Brian L. Goff, and Robert D. Tollison. 1992. *The National Collegiate Athletic Association: A Study in Cartel Behavior*. Chicago: University of Chicago Press.

Forbes. 2006. "What is Your Team Worth?" (As appearing in *The Post-Standard*.) September 5: D-8.

Fortes, Meyer. 1936. "Ritual Festivals and Social Cohesion in the Hinterland of the Gold Coast." *American Anthropologist*, 38: 602.

Fowler, Linda L. 1996. "Who Runs for Congress?" *PS: Political Science and Politics*. Vol. 29, No. 3 (Sept.): 430–434.

Francis, Leslie. 2001. "Title IX: Equality for Women's Sports?" pp. 247–266 in *Ethics in Sport*, edited by William J. Morgan, Klaus V. Meier, and Angela J. Schneider. Champaign, IL: Human Kinetics.

Freeman, William. 1997. *Physical Education and Sport in a Changing Society*. Boston: Allyn and Bacon.

Frey, James H. 1978. "The Organization of Amateur Sport: Efficiency to Entropy." *American Behavioral Scientist*. 21: 361–378.

Frey, James H., and Tim Delaney. 1996. "The Role of Leisure Participation in Prison: A Report From Consumers." *Journal of Offender Rehabilitation*, Vol. 23 (1/2):79–89.

Frey, James H., and David R. Dickens. 1990. "Leisure as a Primary Institution." *Sociological Inquiry*. 60 (3): 264–273.

Frey, James H., and D. Stanley Eitzen. 1991. "Sport and Society." *Annual Review of Sociology*, 17: 503– 522.

Fridman, Sherman M. 2004. "The Adult Face of Youth Sport Violence." Available: http://community.healthgate.com.

Frith, David. 2001. *Silence of the Heart: Cricket Suicides*. Edinburgh: Mainstream Publishing.

Fryer, Jenna. 2005. "Four Networks Flag NASCAR." *The Post-Standard*. December 8: D-2.

Gardiner, E. Norman. 1930. *Athletes of the Ancient World*. Oxford: Clarendon Press.

Garfinkel, Harold. 1956. "Conditions of Successful Degradation Ceremonies." *American Journal of Sociology*. 61: 420–424.

Geertz, Clifford. 1965. "Religion as a Cultural System," in *Anthropological Approaches to the Study of Religion*, edited by Michael Banton. London: Tavistock.

Gerdy, John R. 1997. *The Successful College Athlete Program: The New Standard.* Phoenix, AZ: Oryx.

_____, ed. 2000. *Sports in School: The Future of an Institution.* New York: Teachers College, Columbia University.

Giesen, Bernhard. 2005. "Performing Transcendence in Politics: Sovereignty, Deviance and the Void of Meaning." *Sociological Theory,* 23(3): 275–285.

Gifford, Aaron. 2004. "Many Ex-Players Find Life After Pros Difficult." *The Post-Standard.* October 2: A-5.

Gilligan, Carol. 1993. *In a Different Voice.* Cambridge, MA: Harvard University Press.

Gmelch, George. 1994. "Ritual and Magic in American Baseball," pp. 351–361 in *Conformity & Conflict: Readings in Cultural Anthropology,* 8th edition, edited by James P. Spradley and David W. McCurdy. New York: HarperCollins.

Goldstein, Richard, 1993. *Ivy League Autumns: An Illustrated History of College Football's Grand Old Rivalries.* New York: St. Martin's Press.

_____. 2005. "Norman Mager, 78, Player Tarnished by Gambling Scandal." *New York Times.* March 23: C15.

Gordon, Michael. 1988. "College Coaches' Attitudes Toward Pregame Sex." *The Journal of Sex Research.* Vol. 24: 256–262.

Green, Tim. 1996. *The Dark Side of the Game: My Life in the NFL.* New York: Warner Books.

_____. 1997. "Cheating to Win is Rule of Thumb for Teams' Survival." *USA Today.* November 6: 4C.

Greenawalt, Kent. 2005. *Does God Belong in Public Schools?* Princeton, NJ: Princeton University Press.

Greenberg, Jon. 2008. "Team Marketing Reports 2008 MLB Fan Cost Index." Available: http://www. teammarketing.com.

Greenspan, Stanley I., and Serena Wieder. 2006. *Engaging Autism.* New York: Da Capo Press.

Greenwell, Megan. 2008. "Muted Return for Champs." *The Post-Standard.* August 4: A-12.

Griffin, Pat. 1998. *Strong Women, Deep Closets: Lesbians and Homophobia in Sport.* Champaign, IL: Human Kinetics.

Griffin, Robert S. 1998. *Sports in the Lives of Children and Adolescents: Success on the Field and in Life.* Westport, CT: Praeger.

Gruneau, R. S. 1975. "Sport, Social Differentiation, and Social Inequality," pp. 117–184 in *Sport and Social Order,* edited by D. Ball and J. Loy. Reading, MA: Addison-Wesley.

Gurko, Miriam. 1974. *The Ladies of Seneca Falls.* New York: Schocken Books.

Guttmann, Allen. 1978. *From Ritual to Record: The Nature of Modern Sports.* New York: Columbia University Press.

_____. 1988. *A Whole New Ball Game.* Chapel Hill, NC: University of North Carolina Press.

_____. 2002. *The Olympics: A History of the Modern Games,* 2nd Edition. Urbana, IL: University of Illinois Press.

_____. 2004. *Sports: The First Five Millennia.* Amherst and Boston: University of Massachusetts Press.

Hadden, Richard. 1997. *Sociological Theory.* Orchard Park, NY: Broadview.

Halpern, Orly. 2008. "For Palestinian Swimmers, It's a Chance to Swim." *The Globe and Mail* (Vancouver, BC). July 7: A3.

Hamilton, Brian. 2005. "How to Operate a 'Whizzinator'—and Its History." *The Mercury News.* May 11. Available: http://www.mercurynews.com/mld/ mercurymnews/sports/11623290.htm.

Hardin, Marie, Julie Dodd, Jean Chance, and Kristie Walsdorf. 2004. "Sporting Image in Black and White: Race and Newspaper Coverage of the 2000 Olympic Games." *The Howard Journal of Communications,* 15: 211–227.

Harrison, Lisa, and Amanda Lynch. 2005. "Social Role Theory and the Perceived Gender Role Orientation of Athletes." *Sex Roles: A Journal of Research.* Vol. 52 (3–4): 227–236.

Hartmann, Susan. 1998. "Feminism and Women's Movement," pp. 41–45 in *Reading Women's Lives,* edited by Mary Margaret Fonow. Needham Heights, MA: Simon and Schuster.

Hellendoorn, Joop, Rimmert van der Kooij, and Brian Sutton-Smith. 1994. *Play and Intervention.* Albany, NY: State University of New York Press.

Hellison, D. 1995. *Teaching Responsibility Through Physical Activity.* Champaign, IL: Human Kinetics.

Heywood, Leslie. 1998. *Pretty Good for a Girl.* New York: Free Press.

Heywood, Leslie, and Shari L. Dworkin. 2003. *Built to Win: The Female Athlete as Cultural Icon.* Minneapolis, MN: University of Minnesota Press.

Hill, Christopher. 1992. *Olympic Politics.* New York: Manchester University Press.

Hilliard, Dan C. 1996. "Televised Sport and the (Anti) Sociological Imagination," pp. 115–125 in *Sport in Contemporary Society: An Anthology,* 5th edition, edited by D. Stanley Eitzen. New York: St. Martin's Press.

Hoberman, John. 2001. "Listening to Steroids," pp. 107–118 in *Ethics in Sport,* edited by William Morgan, Klaus Meier, and Angela Schneider. Champaign, IL: Human Kinetics.

_____. 2005. *Testosterone Dreams: Rejuvenation, Aphrodisia, Doping.* Berkeley, CA: University of California Press.

Hoch, Paul. 1972. *Rip Off the Big Game: The Exploitation of Sports by the Power Elite.* Garden City, NY: Anchor.

Hoffer, Richard. 2006. "Scorecard: Goodbye, Mr. Chips." *Sports Illustrated.* May 15: 18–19.

Hoffman, Roy. 1996. "It's a Bird, It's a Plane, It's a Flying Anvil." *The Post Standard.* November 7: A-18.

Hoffman, Shirl, editor. 1992. *Sport and Religion.* Champaign, IL: Human Kinetics.

Hole, Christina. 1969. *Encyclopedia of Superstitions.* Chester Springs, PA: Dufour.

Homans, George. 1961. *Social Behavior: Its Elementary Forms.* New York: Harcourt, Brace and World.

Honolulu Star-Bulletin. 2000. "Rainbow Comments Upset Gay Activists." July 28. Available http://starbulletin.com/2000/o7/28/sports/story1 /html.

Hook, Sidney. 1943. *The Hero in History.* Boston: Beacon Press.

Horn, J.C. 1977. "Parent Egos Take the Fun out of Little League." *Psychology Today,* 11(9): 18, 22.

Hornak, Joan N., and James E. Hornak. Winter 1997. "The Role of the Coach with Eating Disordered Ath-

letes: Recognition, Referral, and Recommendation."
Physical Educator. Vol. 54 (1): 35–40.

Houlihan, Barrie. 1999. *Dying to Win.* Strasbourg, Germany: Council of Europe Publishing.

Howell, R. 1982. "Generalizations on Women and Sport, Games and Play in the United States from Settlement to 1860," pp. 87–95 in *Her Story in Sport: A Historical Anthropology of Women in Sports,* edited by R. Howell. West Point, NY: Leisure Press.

Humanitarian Hall of Fame. 2006. "Mission Statement." Available: http://www/sportshumanitarian. com/quick_facts/quick_facts.html.

Hutslar, J. 1985. *Beyond Xs and Os.* Welcome, NC: Wooten.

Jamieson, Katherine M. 1998. "Reading Nancy Lopez: Decoding Representations of Race, Class, and Sexuality." *Sociology of Sport Journal.* 15: 343–358.

Jay, Kathryn. 2004. *More Than Just a Game.* New York: Columbia University Press.

Johnson, Arthur T. 1983. "Municipal Administration and the Sports Franchise Relocation Issue." *Public Administration Review.* Nov/Dec: 519–527.

Johnson, L.A. 2002. "Girls Who Play Sports Grow up to be Leaders." *The Post-Standard* (originally appeared in *Pittsburgh Post-Gazette*). May 20: E-1.

Johnson, Patricia Altenbernd. 2000. *On Wollstonecraft.* New York: Wadsworth.

Jones, Jeffery A., and Michael J. Paciorek. 1994. *Sports and Recreation for the Disabled.* Indianapolis, IN: Master Press.

Kammerer, R. Craig. 2001. "What is Doping and How Is it Detected?" pp. 3–28 in *Doping In Elite Sport,* edited by Wayne Wilson and Edward Derse. Champaign, IL: Human Kinetics.

Kane, Mary Jo, and Lisa Disch. 1993. "Sexual Violence and the Reproduction of Male Power in the Locker Room: The 'Lisa Olson Incident.'" *Sociology of Sport Journal.* 10: 331–352.

Katz, B. 1994. "Seize Every Team!" *The Nation.* September 26: 259, 297.

Keating, Thomas. 1994. *Intimacy with God.* New York: Crossroad.

_____. 1995. *Open Mind, Open Heart.* New York: Continuum.

Kenyon, Gerald S., and John W. Loy. 1965. "Toward Sociology of Sport." *Journal of Health, Physical Education, and Recreation,* 36(5): 24–25, 68–69.

Kenyon, Gerald S., and Barry D. McPherson. 1981. "Becoming Involved in Physical Activity and Sport: A Process of Socialization," pp. 217–234 in *Sport, Culture and Society,* edited by John W. Loy, Gerald Kenyon and Barry McPherson. Philadelphia: Lea & Febiger.

Kerr, John H. 2005. *Rethinking Aggression and Violence in Sport.* New York, NY: Routledge.

Kidd, Bruce. 1995. "Inequality in Sport, the Corporation and the State: An Arena for Social Scientists." *Journal of Sport and Social Issues.* Vol. 19 (Aug.), No. 3: 232–248.

King, C. Richard, and Charles Fruehling Springwood. 2001. *Team Spirits: The Native American Mascots Controversy.* Lincoln, NE: University of Nebraska Press.

Kinoy, Barbara P., Adele M. Holman, and Ray Lemberg. 1999. "The Eating Disorder: An Introduction," pp. 2–6 in *Eating Disorders: A Reference Sourcebook,* edited by Raymond Lemberg with Leigh Cohn. Phoenix, AZ: Oryx.

Kirka, Danica. 2006. "Threat of Worldwide Childhood Obesity Looms, New Study Warns." *The Post-Standard.* March 6: A-5.

Kirst, Sean. 2004. "Violence in Sports Included a Riot in Syracuse." *The Post-Standard.* November 29: B-1.

Knight, Jennifer L., and Traci A. Giuliano. 2003. "Blood, Sweat, and Jeers: The Impact of the Media's Heterosexist Portrayals on Perceptions of Male and Female Athletes." *The Journal of Sport Behavior.* Volume 26: 230.

Koch, James V., and Wilbert M. Leonard. 1981. "The NCAA: A Socio-economic Analysis: The Development of the College Sports Cartel from Social Movement to Formal Organization," pp. 251–258 in *Sport, Culture and Society: A Reader on the Sociology of Sport,* edited by John W. Loy, Gerald S. Kenyon and Barry D. McPherson. Philadelphia: Lea & Febiger.

Kuehn, Don. 2005. "Wanna Bet?" *On Campus.* Vol. 25 (Nov.), No.3: 15.

Kuhn, Cynthia, Scott Swartzwelder, and Wilkie Wilson. 2000. *Pumped: Straight Facts for Athletes about Drugs, Supplements, and Training.* New York: Norton.

Labinger, Lynette. 1999. "Title IX is Necessary for Women and Is Not Unfair to Men's Sports," pp. 136–139 in *Sports and Athletes: Opposing Viewpoints,* edited by Laura Egendorf. San Diego: Greenhaven.

Ladouceur, Robert, Jean-Marie Boisvert, Michel Pepin, Michael Lorranger, and Caroline Sylvain. 1994. "Social Cost of Pathological Gambling." *Journal of Gambling Studies.* 10(4): 399–409.

LaFeber, Walter. 1999. *Michael Jordan and the New Global Capitalism.* New York: Norton.

Lapchick, Richard. 2003. "Sports and Public Behavior," pp. 71–79 in *Public Discourse in America,* edited by Judith Rodin and Stephen P. Steinberg. Philadelphia: University of Pennsylvania Press.

Le Bon, Gustave. 1952. *The Crowd.* London: Benn.

Lee, Yueh Ting. 1993. "In Group Preference and Homogeneity Among African American and Chinese American Students." *Journal of Social Psychology.* 133: 225–235.

Leitch, Will. 2005. "On the Financial Gridiron." *PRIMEDIA,* February 1: 1.

Lemyre, L., and P.M. Smith. 1985. "Inter-group Discrimination and Self-Esteem in the Minimal Group Paradigm." *Journal of Personality and Social Psychology.* 49: 660–670.

Lenskyj, Helen Jefferson. 2000. *Inside the Olympic Industry.* Albany, NY: State University of New York Press.

Leonard, Wilbert M., III. 1988. *A Sociological Perspective of Sport.* New York: Macmillan.

Lesieur, Henry. 1998. "Costs and Treatment of Pathological Gambling," pp. 153–171 in *The Annals,* edited by James H. Frey. Thousand Oaks, CA: Sage.

Levin, Susanna. 1996. "The Spoils of Victory: Who Gets Big Money from Sponsors, and Why," pp. 367–372 in *Sport in Contemporary Society: An Anthology.* New York: St. Martin's Press.

Levin, William. 1991. *Sociological Ideas,* 3rd edition. Belmont, CA: Wadsworth.

Lipsyte, Robert. 1985. "Varsity Syndrome: The Unkindest Cut," pp. 111–121 in *American Sport Culture*, edited by Wiley Lee Umphlett. Lewisburg: Bucknell University Press.

Little League Baseball 2008. Home webpage. Available: http://www.littleleague.org.

Lomax, Michael. 2004. "Major League Baseball's Separate-and-Unequal Doctrine," pp. 59–94 in *Race and Sport: The Struggle for Inequality On and Off the Field*, edited by Charles K. Ross. Jackson, MS: University Press of Mississippi.

Los Angeles Times. 1993. "There Always Is One Person on Your Side." September 9: C2.

_____. 1992. "Politics and the Olympics." July 14: C8.

Loy, John, and Alan Ingham. 1981. "Play, Games, and Sport in the Psychological Development of Children and Youth," pp. 189–216 in *Sport, Culture and Society*, edited by John Loy, Gerald Kenyon and Barry McPherson. Philadelphia: Lea & Febiger.

Lumpkin, Angela. 1994. *Physical Education and Sport*, 3rd edition. St. Louis: Mosby.

Lupica, Mike. 1996. "5 Ways to Better Sports." *USA Weekend.* October 25–27: 4–5.

Luschen, Günther. 1967. "The Sociology of Sport: A Trend Report and Bibliography." *Current Sociology*, 15(3): 5–140.

_____. 1970A. *The Cross-Cultural Analysis of Sports and Games*. Champaign, IL: Stipes.

_____. 1970B. "Cooperation, Association and Contest." *Journal of Conflict Resolution.* 14(1): 21–34.

_____. 1981. "The Interdependence of Sport and Culture," pp. 287–295 in *Sport, Culture and Society*, edited by John W. Loy, Gerald Kenyon and Barry McPherson. Philadelphia: Lea & Febiger.

Madigan, Tim. 2003. "An Interview with Myles Brand." *Philosophy Now*, May/June (41): 12.

Magoun, Francis Peabody. 1966 [1938]. *History of Football*. New York: Johnson. Mahon, M.J., and C.C. Bullock. 1991. "Recreation and Corrections: A Review of the Literature Over the Past Two Years." *Correctional Recreation Today*, Vol. 5: 7–15.

Malinowski, Bronislaw. 1927. *Coral Gardens and Their Magic*. London: Routledge & Kegan Paul.

Mandell, Richard. 1984. *Sport: A Cultural History*. New York: Columbia University Press.

Mann, L. 1979. "Sports Crowds Viewed From the Perspective of Collective Behavior," pp. 337–368 in *Sports, Games and Play*, edited by J.H. Goldstein. Hillsdale, NJ: Erlbaum.

Marger, Martin. 2006. *Race and Ethnic Relations: American and Global Perspectives*, 7th edition. Belmont, CA: Wadsworth.

Margolis, Jeffrey A. 1999. *Violence in Sports*. Berkeley Heights, NJ: Enslow.

Martens, Rainer. 1988. "Helping Children Become Independent, Responsible Adults Through Sports," pp. 297–307 in *Competitive Sports for Children and Youth: An Overview of Research and Issues*, edited by E.W. Brown & C.F. Branta. Champaign, IL: Human Kinetics.

Martens, Rainer, and Vern Seefeldt, editors. 1979. *Guidelines for Children's Sports*. Washington, D.C.: National Association for Sport & Physical Education.

Martzke, Rudy, and Reid Cherner. 2004. "Channeling How to View Sports: ESPN's 25th Anniversary Seen in Changing TV Sports Patterns." *USA Today*. August 17: C1, C2.

McChesney, Robert W. 1989. "Media Made Sport: A History of Sports Coverage in the USA," in *Media Sports and Society*, edited by L. Wenner. London: Sage.

McCutcheon, Chuck. 2006. "Feeling the Strain." *The Post-Standard.* September 18: D-2.

McIntosh, Peter. 1993. "The Sociology of Sport in the Ancient World," pp. 19–38 in *The Sports Process*, edited by Eric Dunning, Joseph Maguire, and Robert Pearton. Champaign, IL: Human Kinetics.

McKibben, Dave. 2006. "Tennis, Anyone? Anyone??" *The Los Angeles Times*. January 6: A21.

McLellan, David. 1987. *Marxism and Religion*. New York: Harper and Row.

McPherson, Barry D. 1981. "Past, Present and Future Perspectives for Research in Sport Sociology," pp. 10–20 in *Sport, Culture and Society*, 2nd edition, edited by John W. Loy, Gerald S. Kenyon, and Barry D. McPherson. Philadelphia: Leatfebiger. Reprinted from *International Review of Sport Sociology*, 10(1): 55–72, 1975.

Mead, George Herbert. 1934. *Mind, Self & Society*, edited by Charles W. Morris. Chicago: University of Chicago Press.

Meadows, Karin. 2000. "Down, Dad! A Tough Lesson in Sportsmanship." *Buffalo News*. February 16: A1.

Melnick, Merrill, and Donald Sabo. 1994. "Sport and Social Mobility among African American and Hispanic Athletes," pp, 221–241 in *Ethnicity and Sport in North American History and Culture*, edited by George Eisen and David K. Wiggins. Westport, CT: Greenwood Press.

Merrill, Christopher. 1993. *The Grass of Another Country: A Journey Through the World of Soccer*. New York: Henry Holt.

Merton, Robert. 1938. "Social Structure and Anomie," *American Sociological Review*, 3: 672–682.

_____. 1968 [1949]. *Social Theory and Social Structure*. New York: Free Press.

Messner, Michael. 2002. "Sports and Male Domination: The Female as Contested Ideological Terrain," pp. 267–284 in *Ethics in Sport*, edited by William J. Morgan, Klaus Meier, and Angela J. Schneider. Champaign, IL: Human Kinetics.

Messner, Michael, and Donald Sabo. 1990. "Toward a Critical Feminist Reappraisal of Sport, Men, and the Gender Order," pp. 1–15 in *Sport, Men, and the Gender Order*, edited by Michael Messner and Donald Sabo. Champaign, IL: Human Kinetics.

Metzenbaum, Howard. 1996. "Baseball's Antitrust Immunity Should Be Repealed," pp. 275–277 in *Sport in Contemporary Society: An Anthology*, 5th edition, edited by D. Stanly Eitzen. New York: St. Martin's Press.

Michael, Matt. 2007. "Study: Fewest Blacks in Baseball Since '80s." *The Post-Standard*. April 3: D-3.

Micheli, Lyle J., with Mark D. Jenkins. 1990. *Sportswise an Essential Guide for Young Athletes, Parents and Coaches*. Boston: Houghton Mifflin.

Mihoces, Gary. 2005. "Wrestling's New World Rises from Sand." *USA Today*. July 12: 3C.

Mill, John Stuart. 1996 [1859]. *On Liberty*, edited by Currin V. Shields. Upper Saddle River, NJ: Prentice Hall.

Miller, David. 1973. *George Herbert Mead: Self, Language, and the World*. Austin: University of Texas Press.

Miller, Walter B. 1958. "Lower Class Culture as a Generating Milieu of Gang Delinquency." *Journal of Social Issues*, 14(3):5–19.

Mills, C. Wright. 1959. *The Sociological Imagination*. New York: Oxford University Press.

Mitchell, Wesley C., editor. 1964. *What Veblen Taught: Selected Writings of Thorstein Veblen*. New York: Kelley.

Miyazaki, Anthony D., and Angela G. Morgan. 2001 (Jan). "Assessing Market Value of Event Sponsoring: Corporate Olympic Sponsorships." *Journal of Advertising Research*. Vol. 41: 11–20.

Moffatt, Gregory K. 2002. *Violent Heart: Understanding Aggressive Individuals*. Westport, CT: Praeger.

Moffi, Larry, and Jonathan Kronstadt. 1994. *Crossing the Line: Black Major Leaguers, 1947–1959*. Jefferson, NC: McFarland.

Morgan, William, Klaus Meier, and Angela Schneider. 2002. *Ethics in Sport*. Champaign IL: Human Kinetics.

Morrison, L. Leotus. 1993. "The AIAW: Governance by Women for Women," pp. 59–66 in *Women in Sport: Issues and Controversies*, edited by Greta L. Cohen. Newbury Park, CA: Sage.

Moses, Sarah. 2006. "Native Athletes to Compete in Denver." *The Post-Standard*. April 7: B-3.

Murphy, Melissa. 2007. "Anti-Gay Remarks Bench Hardaway." *The Post-Standard*. February 16: C-8.

Museum of Appalachia. 2005. "July 4th Celebration and Anvil Shoot." Available: www.museumofappalachia. com.

Nafziger, James A., and Andrew Strenk. 1978. "The Political Uses and Abuses of Sports." *Connecticut Law Review*. 10: 280–89.

Nagano Prefecture Investigation Group Report. 2005. "A Focused on the Promotional Activities Aimed at Bringing the 1998 Winter Olympics to Nagano City." November 22. Available: www.pref.nagano.jpkeisi/ seisakj/tyosai/05/125/hokokueng.pdf.

National Center for Sports Safety. 2008. "Sports Injuries Facts." Available: http://www.sportsafety. org/sports-injury-facts/

NBA.com. 2005. "NBA Player Dress Code." Available: http://aol.nba.com/news/player_dress_code_051017. html.

NCAA Manual. 2004. "2004–05 NCAA Manual." Indianapolis, IN: The National Collegiate Athletic Association.

NCAA News. 2001. "2001 NCAA Drug Use Survey." October 13: 1, 17. Available: www.ncaa.org.

Nerz, Ryan. 2006. *Eat This Book*. New York: St. Martin's Press.

Nesmith, Jeff. 2007. "Frontier of Sports Cheating: Genomics." *The Post-Standard*. October 23: D-7.

Nixon, Howard L., II 1984. *Sport and the American Dream*. New York: Leisure Press.

Nixon, Howard L., II, and James H. Frey. 1996. *A Sociology of Sport*. Belmont, CA: Wadsworth.

Novak, Michael. 1993. "The Joy of Sport," pp. 151–172 in *Religion and Sport*, edited by Charles S. Prebish. Westport, CT: Greenwood Press.

Nuwer, Hank. 1999. *Wrongs of Passage*. Bloomington, IN: Indiana University Press.

_____, editor. 2004. *The Hazing Reader*. Bloomington, IN: Indiana University Press.

Oakes, P. J., and J. C. Turner. 1980. "Social Categorization and Inter-Group Behavior: Does Minimal Inter-Group Discrimination Make Social Identity More Positive?" *European Journal of Social Psychology*, 10: 295–301.

Oakley, J. Ronald. 1994. *Baseball's Last Golden Age, 1946–1960: The National Pastime in a Time of Glory and Change*. Jefferson, NC: McFarland.

Ohlemacher, Stephen. 2005. "Fewer Got Game: More Watching, Less Playing." *New York Post*. December 22: 32.

Orr, Scott. 2005. "Teen Steroid Use on the Rise: Web Feeds Demand for Drugs." *The Post-Standard*. April 3: A-17.

O'Shea, Michael. 2005. "Better Fitness." *Parade*. August 28: 8.

_____. 2005B. "Better Fitness." *Parade*. November 27: 8.

Otis, Carol L., and Roger Goldingay. 2000. *The Athletic Woman's Survival Guide: How to Win the Battle Against Eating Disorders, Amenorrhea, Osteoporosis*. Champaign, IL: Human Kinetics.

O'Toole, Catie. 2005. "Meet Oswego's New Team: The Admirals Junior Hockey Team Starts Its First Season." *The Post-Standard*. September 8: B-1.

O'Toole, Thomas. 2002. "Crisis on Campus: Fan Disturbances After Sports Events More Common, Destructive." *USA Today*. April 9: 1C.

Pampel, Fred. 2000. *Sociological Lines and Ideas*. New York: Worth.

Parsons, Talcott. 1951. *The Social System*. Glencoe, IL: Free Press.

Passer, Michael. 1986. "When Should Children Begin Competing? A Psychological Perspective," pp. 55–58 in *Sport for Children and Youths*, edited by Maureen Weiss and Daniel Gould. Champaign, IL: Human Kinetics.

Pate, Russell, Stewart G. Trost, Sarah Levin, and Marsha Dowda. "Sports Participation and Health-Related Behaviors Among U.S. Youth." *Archives of Pediatric Adolescent Medicine*. Vol. 154, September 2002: 904–911.

Patrick, Dick. 2005. "Graham Can't Outrun Questions." *USA Today*. August 8: 6C.

Peterson, Robert. 1984. *Only the Ball Was White: A History of Legendary Black Players and All-Black Professional Teams*. New York: McGraw-Hill.

Petrie, J., and Trent Anderson. 1996. "Gender Differences in the Perception of College Student-Athletes' Academic Performance." *College of Student Affairs Journal*, 61(1): 62–69.

Pfeiffer, Ronald P., and Brent C. Mangus. 2002. *Concepts of Athletic Training*, 3rd edition. Boston: Jones and Bartlett.

Pfuetze, Paul. 1954. *Self, Society and Existence: Human Nature and Dialogue in the Thoughts of George Herbert Mead and Martin Buber*. New York: Harper Torch Books.

Phillips, John. 1993. *Sociology of Sport*. Boston: Allyn & Bacon.

The Plain Dealer. 2000. "Massillon Fans Arrested." November 5: 19C.

Poliakoff, Michael. 1987. *Combat Sports in the Ancient World*. New Haven, CT: Yale University Press.

Poliquin, Bud. 2005. "Sex Appeal, True Talent an Exciting Combination." *The Post-Standard.* June 16: D-1.

_____. 2005. "Mantle: Flawed Hero." *The Post-Standard.* July 18: C-2.

Poltilove, Josh. 2005. "NFL Cheerleader, Woman Held After Nightclub Fracas." TBO.com Sports. Available: http://bucs.tbo.com/bucs.

Porto, Brian. 2003. *A New Season: Using Title IX to Reform College Sports.* Westport, CT: Praeger.

The Post-Standard. 1997. "Youth Teams Brawl." February 26: D7.

_____. 2000. "15-Year-Old Boy Banned for Life for Attack on Ref." August 19: D-9.

_____. 2004. "1791 Ban on Baseball Rewrites History." May 12: A-2.

_____. 2004. "Gambling Becomes a National Addiction." May 26: A-12.

_____. 2004. "And We Quote." June 30: D-1.

_____. 2004. "NFL Signs $8 Billion TV Deals." November 9: D2.

_____. 2005. "Vikings' 'Whiz' Kid Tries to Put One Past Airport Security." May 12: D-1.

_____. 2005. "Montgomery Admits his Drug Use to Grand Jury." June 25: D-1.

_____. 2005. "A Ban on Cursing in English Soccer? No Bloody Way." August 11: A4.

_____. 2006. "Yet Another Newborn has been Named After ESPN." October 7: D-1.

_____. "Orioles Scout Indicated in Sports Gambling Probe." July 12: C-5.

Potrikus, Alaina. 2006. "Tribe's Living Heritage." *The Post-Standard.* March 23: B-3.

Potter, Dena. 2008. "Study: Winning in Sports Really Does Bring Universities More Students." *The Post-Standard.* March 8: B-5.

Pound, Edward T., and Kevin Johnson. 1999. "Salt Lake Took Lessons to Heart." *USA Today.* February 17: 3C.

Powell, Robert Andrew. 2003. *We Own This Game.* New York: Atlantic Monthly Press.

Prebish, Charles. 1984. "Heavenly Father, DivinecGoalie: Sport and Religion." *The Antioch Review*, 42 (Summer): 306–318.

Putnam, Douglas T. 1999. *Controversies of the Sports World.* Westport, CT: Greenwood Press.

Quintanilla, Michael. 1998. "Surf's Up, Big Kahuna." *Los Angeles Times.* June 3: D1.

Rada, A., and K. Tim Wulfemeyer. 2005 (March). "Color Coded: Racial Descriptions in Television Coverage of Intercollegiate Sports." *Journal of Broadcasting & Electronic Media.* 49(1): 65–86.

Rader, Benjamin. 1984. *In Its Own Image: How Television Has Transformed Sports.* New York: Free Press.

_____. 2004. *American Sports*, 5th edition. Upper Saddle River, NJ: Prentice Hall.

Rank, Otto. 2004 [1909]. *The Myth of the Birth of the Hero: A Psychological Exploration of Myth.* Baltimore, MD: Johns Hopkins University Press.

Ravitch, Frank S. 1999. *School Prayer and Discrimination: The Civil Rights of Religious Minorities and Dissenters.* Boston: Northeastern University Press.

Real, Michael R. 1996. *Exploring Media Culture: A Guide.* Thousand Oaks, CA: Sage.

Redondo Beach Chamber. 2005. "George Freeth Memorial." Available at: http://www.redondo chamber.com/visitors/freeth_memorial.htm.

Reeds, Greg. 2004. "Winning and Losing: A Case Study for Fair Play," pp. 87–90 in *Social Diseases: Mafia, Terrorism, Totalitarianism*, edited by Tim Delaney, Valeri Kuvakin, and Tim Madigan. Moscow, Russia: Russian Humanist Society.

Rees, C. Roger. 1998. "Globalization of Sport Activities and Sport Perceptions Among Adolescents from Berlin and Suburban New York." *Sociology of Sport Journal.* 15: 216–230.

Reeser, J. C. 2005. "Gender Identity and Sport: Is the Playing Field Level?" *British Journal of Sports Medicine.* Vol. 39: 695–699.

Relin, David Oliver. 2005. "Who's Killing Kids' Sports?" *Parade Magazine.* August 7: 4.

Reynolds, Larry. 1993. *Interactionism: Exposition and Critique*, 3rd edition. Dix Hills, NY: General Hall.

Riess, Steven. 1989. *City Games.* Chicago: University of Illinois Press.

_____. 1995. *Sport in Industrial America 1850–1920.* Wheeling, IL: Harlan Davidson.

Ritzer, George. 2000. *Classical Social Theory*, 3rd edition. Boston: McGraw-Hill.

Robinson, Jackie. 1995. *The Autobiography of Jackie Robinson*, with an introduction by Hank Aaron and foreword by Cornel West. Hopewater, NJ: Ecco Press.

Rojek, Chris. 1985. *Capitalism and Leisure Theory.* New York: Tavistock.

Rosemond, John. 2000. "A Rough Time with Sports." *Buffalo News.* April 17: C3.

Rosen, L., D.B. McKeon, and D.O. Hough. 1986. "Pathogenic Weight-Control Behavior in Female Athletes." *The Physician and Sports Medicine.* 16 (Jan.): 79–86.

Rosenfeld, Isadore. 2005. "Heart Health Should Start Early." *Parade.* September 25: 6–7.

Rosson, Philip. 2001. "Football Shirt Sponsorships: SEGA Europe and Arsenal FC." *International Journal of Sports Marketing & Sponsorship* (June-July), 3(2): 157–183.

Ruibal, Sal. 1999. "Pirates Provide a Ray of Light." *USA Today.* September 29: 13C.

_____. 2004. "Gene Alteration Sets off Alarm in Doping Fight." *USA Today.* April 15: 3C.

Rushin, Steve. 2005. "A Double Whammy." *Sports Illustrated.* October 17: 18.

Ryan, Joan. 2000. *Little Girls in Pretty Boxes: The Making and Breaking of Elite Gymnasts and Figure Skaters.* New York: Warner.

Ryan, John, and William M. Wentworth. 1999. *Media and Society.* Boston: Allyn and Bacon.

Ryckman, Richard, and Jane Hamel. 1992. "Female Adolescents' Motives Related to Involvement in Organized Team Sports." *International Journal of Sport Psychology.* 23: 147–160.

Sabo, Don. 1985. "Sport, Patriarchy and Male Identity: New Questions about Men and Sport." *Arena Review*, 9: 2.

Sack, Allen L., and Ellen J. Staurowsky. 1998. *College Athletes for Hire: The Evolution and Legacy of the NCAA's Amateur Myth.* Westport, CT: Praeger.

Sage, George H., editor. 1970. *Sport and American Society: Selected Readings.* Reading, MA: Addison-Wesley.

_____. 1979. "Sport and the Social Sciences." *The Annals of the American Academy of Political and Social Sciences*, 445: 1–14.

Saltz, Gail. 2005. "5 Ways to Get Your Child Moving." *Parade*. September 25: 8.

Sansone, David. 1998. *Greek Athletics and the Genesis of Sport*. Berkeley: University of California Press.

Saxon, Lisa Nehus. 1999. "College Athletes Should Be Encouraged to Make Education a Priority," pp. 82–85 in *Sports and Athletes: Opposing Viewpoints*, edited by Laura K. Egendorf. San Diego, CA: Greenhaven Press.

Schaaf, Phil. 1995. *Sports Marketing: It's Not Just a Game Anymore*. Amherst, NY: Prometheus.

_____. 2005. *Sports, Inc.: 100 Years of Sports Business*. Amherst, NY: Prometheus.

Schreiber, Lee. 1990. *The Parent's Guide to Kids' Sports*. Boston: Little, Brown.

Seattle Post-Intelligencer. 2005. "Elma School Officials Ban Short Cheerleader Skirts." September 9. Available: http://seattlepi.nwsource.com.

Sefton, Dru. 2004. "Cup Stacking: The Next Pro Sport?" *The Post-Standard*. September 19: A-16.

_____. 2005. "Poker Site Lures Gamblers with College Tuition Jackpot." *The Post-Standard*. May 21: A-1.

Semyonov, M., and M. Farbstein. 1989. "Ecology of Sports Violence: The Case of Israeli Soccer." *Sociology of Sport Journal*, Vol. 6: 50–59.

Senn, Alfred Erich. 1999. *Power, Politics, and the Olympic Games*. Champaign, IL: Human Kinetics.

7online.com. 2005. "The Football Game That Nobody Saw." Tristate News from WABC-TV. Available: http://abclocal.go.com./wabc/story.

Shafer, Howard J. 2003. "A Critical View of Pathological Gambling and Addiction," pp. 175–190 in *Gambling Who Wins? Who Loses?*, edited by Gerda Reith. Amherst, NY: Prometheus.

Shahzad, Asif. 2006. "Kite-Flying Banned After Strings Kill 7." *The Post-Standard*. March 12: A-6.

Sheridan, Chris. 2004. "Artest Suspended for Season." *Buffalo News*. November 22: D7.

Shropshire, Kenneth L. 1996. *In Black and White: Race and Sports in America*. New York: New York University Press.

Shulman, James L., and William G. Bowen. 2001. *The Game of Life*. Princeton, NJ: Princeton University Press.

Silby, Caroline, with Shelley Smith. 2000. *Games Girls Play: Understanding and Guiding Young Female Athletes*. New York: St. Martin's Press.

Simon, Robert L. 1985. *Sports and Social Values*. Englewood Cliffs, NJ: Prentice Hall.

_____. 1991. *Fair Play*. Boulder, CO: Westview.

Sirak, Ron. 2008. "The Rich Get Richer." *Golf Digest*. February: 96–100.

Skinner, B.F. 1948. "Superstition in the Pigeon." *Journal of Experimental Psychology*, 38: 168–172.

Slusher, Howard. 1993. "Sport and the Religious," pp. 173–196 in *Religion and Sport*, edited by Charles S. Prebish. Westport, CT: Greenwood Press.

Small, Eric, with Linda Spear. 2002. *Kids & Sports*. New York: New Market Press.

Smelser, Neil. 1966. *Social Structure and Mobility in Economic Development*. Chicago: Aldine.

Smith, Claire. 1999. "Pee Wee Reese: A Down-to-Earth, Generous Hero in Life and Baseball." *Philadelphia Inquirer*. August 16: T11.

Smith, Michael D. 1974. "Significant Others' Influence on Assaultive Behavior of Young Hockey Players." *International Review of Sport Sociology*, 3–4: 45–56.

_____. 1983. *Violence and Sport*. Toronto: Butterworths.

_____. 1996. "A Typology of Sports Violence," pp. 161–172 in *Sport in Contemporary Society*, 5th edition, edited by D. Stanley Eitzen. New York: St. Martin's Press.

Smith, Rodney K. 1987. *Public Prayer and the Constitution: A Case Study in Constitutional Interpretation*. Wilmington, Delaware: Scholarly Resources.

Smith, Ronald E. 1986. "A Component Analysis of Athletic Stress," pp. 107–111 in *Sport for Children and Youths*, edited by Maureen R. Weiss and Daniel Gould. Champaign, IL: Human Kinetics.

_____. 1988. *Sports and Freedom: The Rise of Big-Time College Athletics*. New York: Oxford University Press.

Snyder, C. R., M.A. Lassagard and C.E. Ford. 1986. "Distancing After Group Success and Failure: Basking in Reflected Glory and Cutting off Reflected Failure." *Journal of Personality and Social Psychology*, 51: 382–388.

Snyder, Eldon E., and Elmer Spreitzer. 1978. *Social Aspects of Sport*. Englewood Cliffs, NJ: Prentice Hall.

Snyder, John. 2001. *Soccer's Most Wanted: The Top 10 Book of Clumsy Keepers, Clever Crosses, and Outlandish Oddities*. Washington, DC: Brassey.

The Special Olympics. 2008. Homepage. Available: http://www.specialolympics.org.

Special Olympics 37th Anniversary. 2005. "Special Olympics Celebrates 37 Years of Achievement, Empowerment and Growth." Available: http://www.specialolympics.org/special+olympics.

Sperber, Murray. 1990. *College Sports Inc*. New York: Henry Holt.

Sports Illustrated. 2003. "Moral Merger: Vanderbilt Eliminates Athletic Department, Keeps Sports Team. September 9. Available: http://si.printthisclickability.com.

_____. 2005. "Sued." April 11: 25.

_____. 2005. "Get on the Stick." April 25: 56–67.

_____. 2005. "Picture This." August 1: 28.

_____. 2005. "Banned." August 15: 22.

_____. 2005. "Shame on Vacation." August 29: 25.

_____. 2005. "Charged." October 10: 22.

_____. 2005. "Stinging Endorsements." November 14: 22.

_____. 2005. "Clarified." November 28: 26.

_____. 2005. "For the Record: Challenged." November 28: 24.

_____. 2006. "Queen of the Mat." February 13: 30.

_____. 2006. "Sign of the Apocalypse." September 11: 28.

_____. 2008. "For the Record: Owed." May 26: 18.

_____. 2008. "Getting Belichicky." June 23: 28.

_____. 2008. "For the Record: Confessed." July 14–21: 22.

SportsIllustrated.com. 2005. "Going for the Jugular?" October 31. Available: http://sportsillustrated.cnn.com/2005/football/ncaa.

Stacy, Mitch. 2001. "Youth Referee Jailed in Knifing of Coach." *Buffalo News*. February 15: A4.

Stanley, Gregory Kent. 1996. *The Rise and Fall of the*

Sportswoman: Women's Health, Fitness, and Athletics 1860–1940. New York: Peter Lang.

Stauble, Vernon B. 1994. "The Significance of Sports Marketing and the Case of the Olympic Games," pp. 14–21 in *Sport Business*, edited by Peter Graham. Madison, WI: Brown & Benchmark.

Staurowsky, Ellen. 1998. "An Act of Honor or Exploitation? The Cleveland Indians: Use of the Louis Francis Sockalexis Story." *Sociology of Sport Journal.* 15: 299–316.

Stein, Rob. 2005. "Physical Fitness Study Confirms Fears on Health of Many Americans." *Buffalo News* (originally published in the *Washington Post*). December 21: A1, A6.

Stevenson, C. L., and J. E. Nixon. 1972. "A Conceptual Scheme of the Social Functions of Sports." *Sportwissenschaft*, 2: 119–132.

Stewart, Larry. 2002. "'Chickisms' Include Mustard and Everything Else in the Refrigerator." *Los Angeles Times.* August 6: D3.

Stinchfield, Randy, and Ken C. Winters. 1988. "Gambling and Problem Gambling Among Youths," pp. 172–185 in *The Annals*, edited by James H. Frey. Thousand Oaks, CA: Sage.

Stoll, Sharon and Jennifer Beller. 2000. "Do Sports Build Character?" pp. 18–30 in *Sports in School: The Future of an Institution*, edited by John Gerdy. New York: Teachers College Press.

Strauss, Lawrence. 1998. "Does Money Tilt the Playing Field?: When Covering Becomes Marketing." *Columbia Journalism Review.* Vol. 37 (Sept./Oct.), Issue 3: 16–17.

Suggs, Welch. 2005. *A Place on the Team: The Triumph and Tragedy of Title IX.* Princeton, New Jersey: Princeton University Press.

Sutherland, Edwin, and Donald R. Cressey. 1978. *Criminology*, 10th edition. Philadelphia: Lippincott.

Swaddling, Judith. 1980. *The Ancient Olympic Games.* Austin: University of Texas Press.

Swartz, Jon. 2004. "Behind Fun Façade, Professional Wrestling Sees 65 Deaths in 7 Years." *USA Today.* March 12: 1A.

Szymanski, Stefan, and Andrew Zimbalist. 2005. *National Pastime.* Washington, D.C.: Brookings Institution Press.

Tanner, Lindsey. 2005. "Teens' Physical Fitness Found Lacking by Study." *The Post-Standard.* December 21: A-18.

Telander, Rick. 1988. "Sports Behind the Walls." *Sports Illustrated*, October 17: 82–88.

Theberge, N. 1981. "A Critique of Critiques: Radical and Feminist Writings on Sport." *Social Forces*, 60(2): 341–353.

Theil, Art. 1999. "Scandal Virus Deeply Rooted." *The Post Standard.* January 27: C2.

Thelin, John R. 1994. *Games Colleges Play: Scandal and Reform in Intercollegiate Athletics.* Baltimore, MD: Johns Hopkins University Press.

Todd, Melissa, and Chris Brown. 2003. "Characteristics Associated with Superstitious Behavior in Track and Field Athletes: Are There NCAA Divisional Level Differences?" *Journal of Sport Behavior.* 26(2): 168–179.

Todhunter, Andrew. 2000. *Dangerous Games.* New York: Doubleday.

Tuley, Dave. 2005. "Old Friend or Two-Faced Acquaintance?" July 21. Available: http://www.lexisnexis.com/unworse/document.

Turner, Jonathan. 1975. "A Strategy for Reformulating the Dialectical and Functional Theories of Conflict." *Social Forces*, 53 (3): 433–444.

_____. 2006. *Handbook of Sociological Theory.* New York: Springer.

Turner, Victor. 1967. *The Forest of Symbols.* Ithaca, NY: Cornell University Press.

Underwood, John. 1989. "What's Wrong with Organized Youth Sports and What We Should Do About It," pp. 120–132 in *Sport in Contemporary Society*, 3rd edition. New York: St. Martin's Press.

U.S. Census Bureau. 1999. "Current Business Reports BS/98, Service Annual Survey: 1998. Washington, D.C.: USGPO.

_____. 2004. "Official Statistics." Available: www.uscensus.gov.

_____. 2004. "Historical Income Tables." October 3. Available: www.uscensus.gov.

U.S. Embassy. 2008. "Sports in America—Soccer." Available: Http://usembassy.de/sports-soccer. htm.

USA Today. 1999. "New Deal." June 7: C1.

_____. 1999. "Women's Marathon Times." December 30: 1C.

_____. 2000. "Coach-Parent Brawl Ends 8–9 Soccer Match." September 11: 1C.

_____. 2000. "Marinovich Back at Work Today." April 27: 17C.

_____. 2004. "Nike Ad Causes Stir in Singapore." November 26: 4C.

Vandy Sports. 2005. "Monday Morning Coffee." October 3. Available: http://vanderbilt.rivals. com/content.asp?sid+1087&cid+247065.

Van Keuren, K. 1992. "Title IX 20 Years Later: Has Sport Actually Changed?" *CSSS Digest.* Summer: 9.

Veblen, Thorstein. 1934 [1899]. *The Theory of the Leisure Class: An Economic Study of Institution.* New York: Random House.

Veroff, J. 1969. "Social Comparison and the Development of Achievement Motivation," pp. 46–101 in *Achievement-Related Motives in Children*, edited by C.P. Smith. New York: Russell Sage Foundation.

Vertinsky, Patricia A. *The Eternally Wounded Woman.* Urbana and Chicago: University of Illinois Press.

Vogler, Conrad and Stephen Schwartz. 1993. *The Sociology of Sport: An Introduction.* Englewood Cliffs, NJ: Prentice Hall.

Volberg, Rachel. 1994. "The Prevalence and Demographics of Pathological Gamblers: Implications for Public Health." *American Journal of Gambling Studies.* 10(4): 399–409.

Voy, Robert. 1991. *Drugs, Sport and Politics.* Champaign, IL: Leisure Press.

Wade, Stephen. 2005. "More Than Tires Divide F-1 Series." *The Post-Standard.* June 21: D-9.

Wahl, Grant. 2005. "Yes, Hard Feelings." *Sports Illustrated.* March 28: 54–57.

Walton, Bill. 2005. "Good Sportsmanship is Losing out to Winning." *USA Today.* December 21: 13A.

Wann, Daniel, and Nyla Branscombe. "Die-Hard and Fair-Weather Fans: Effects of Identification on BIRGing and CORFing Tendencies." *Journal of Sport and Social Issues.* 14(2): 103–117.

_____. 1993. "Sports Fans: Measuring Degree of Identification with Their Team." *International Journal of Sport Psychology*, 24: 1–17.

Wann, Daniel L., Merrill J. Melnick, Gordon W. Russell, and Dale G. Pease. 2001. *Sport Fans*. New York: Routledge.

Warren, William E. 1997. *Coaching & Control*. Paramus, NJ: Prentice Hall.

Waters, Malcolm. 1995. *Globalization*. London: Routledge.

Webb, Donnie. 2007. "The Money Game." December 5. Available: www.syracuse.com.

Wedgwood, Nikki. 2004. "Kicking Like a Boy: School Girl Australian Rules Football and Bi-Gendered Female Embodiment." *Sociology of Sport Journal*. 21: 140–162.

Weiner, Richard. 1999. "Marinovich Attempts Carve out Comeback," *USA Today*. May 12: 8C.

Weir, Tom. 2004. "Online Sports Betting Spins out of Control." *USA Today*. August 22: A-1.

Werner, Erica. 2005. "Indian Casinos See Rapid Growth." *The Post-Standard*. February 16: A-6.

Wertheim, L. Jon. 2002. *Venus Envy*. New York: Perennial.

Whannel, Garry. 2002. *Media Sport Stars*. New York; Routledge.

White, G. Edward. 1996. *Creating the National Pastime: Baseball Transforms Itself 1903–1953*. Princeton, NJ: Princeton University Press.

Whitmire, Tim. 1999. "Reese was the Man of Boys of Summer." *Buffalo News*. August 19: F1.

Wides-Munoz, Laura. 2006. "Who Should We Root For?" *The Post-Standard*. March 21: D-1.

Wiebe, Robert H. 2003. "Primary Tensions in American Public Life," pp. 35–49 in *Public Discourse in America*, edited by Judith Rodin and Stephen P. Steinberg. Philadelphia: University of Pennsylvania Press.

Wilcox, Ralph C. 1994. "The Shamrock and the Eagle: Irish Americans and Sport in the Nineteenth Century," pp. 55–74 in *Ethnicity and Sport in North American History And Culture*, edited by George Eisen and David K. Wiggins. Westport, CT: Greenwood Press.

Will, George. 2000. "Sports Gambling Bill a Bad Bet." *Buffalo News*. March 13: B3.

Williams, Henry. 1895. "The Educational and Health Giving Value of Athletics." *Harper's Weekly*. February 16: 166.

Williams, Larry R. 1981 (Apr.). "Women's Correctional Recreation Services." *Journal of Physical Education, Recreation and Dance*, Vol. 52 (4): 56.

Wilson, John. 1994. *Playing by the Rules*. Detroit: Wayne State University Press.

Winik, Lyric Wallwork. 2005. "U.S. Olympians Need YOU!" *Parade*. November 20: 27.

Winter, Bud. 1981. *Relax & Win*. San Diego: A. S. Barnes.

Wohl, A. 1970. "Competitive Sport and Its Social Function." *International Review of Sport*, 5: 117– 125.

Womack, Mari. 1992. "Why Athletes Need Ritual: A Study of Magic Among Professional Athletes," pp. 191–202 in *Sport and Religion*, edited by Shirl J. Hoffman. Champaign, IL: Human Kinetics.

Women's Sports Foundation. 2004. "27 Year Study Shows Progression of Women in College Athletics." Available: http://www.womenssportsfoundation.org.

_____. 2005. "Gender Equity in High School and College Athletics: Most Recent Participation & Budget Statistics." Available: http://www.womenssports foundation.org.

The World Sport Stacking Association. 2008. "WSSA Mission Statement." WSSA homepage: Available: http://www.worldsportsstackingassociation.org/abo ut.htm.

Yesalis, Charles, and Virginia Cowart. 1998. *The Steroids Game*. Champaign, IL: Human Kinetics.

Yiannakis, Andrew, Thomas McIntyre, Merrill Melnick, and Dale Hart. 1978. *Sport Sociology: Contemporary Themes*. Dubuque, IA: Kendall Hunt.

Young, Perry Deane. 1995. *Lesbians and Gays and Sports*. New York: Chelsea House.

Zillmann, Dolf, Bryant Jennings, and Barry Sapolsky. 1979. "The Enjoyment of Watching Sport Contests," pp. 297–335 in *Sport, Games and Play*, edited by Jeffrey H. Goldstein. Hillsdale, NJ: Laurence Earlbaum.

Zimbalist, Andrew. 1999. *Unpaid Professionals*. Princeton, NJ: Princeton University Press.

Zirin, David. 2005. "When the Arm Breaks: John Chaney and the Rules of Violence." *PoliticalAffairs. net*. Available: http://www.politicalaffairs. net/arti cle/view/729/1/80/.

Zwerman, G. 1995. *Martina Navratilova: Lives of Notable Gay Men and Lesbians*. New York: Chelsea House.

Index

agents of socialization 79–80, 82–84
aggression 158; instrumental 158; reactive 158
Amateur Athletic Union (AAU) 181
amenorrhea 188
ancient sports 39–41
animism 259
Anomie/Strain theory 137
anorexia 186
anvil shooting 10
archery 45, 47
Armstrong, Lance 71
Association for Intercollegiate Athletics for Women (AIWA) 182–183, 193
athlete, defined 15; elite 81–82
athletic director 125
athletic scholarships 124–125
athletics, defined 15
authority 240
autism 299; and sport 298–300
auto racing 165, 220

Babe Ruth Baseball 102–103
BASE jumping 54–55
baseball 49–50, 53, 164–165, 200, 243–244
basketball 48, 162–163, 201
Basking in Reflected Glory (BIRG) 34
"Battle of the Sexes" 184
bicycling 180
billiards 52
BIRG and CORF theories 34–36
blood doping 145–146
blood sports 47
Blumer, Herbert 29
bocce ball 207
boxing 161, 206
bowling 46
Brand, Myles 118
broadcasting, sports 292
bulimia 187–188
buzkashi 13–14

Cal Ripken Baseball Division 102–103
Campbell, Ben Nighthorse 246–247
cartels, sport 228–229
Cartwright, Alexander 49
character 97; good 97–98
Chief Illiniwek 214

Chief Osceola 213
chivalry 44
cholitas 56
Clemente, Roberto 70, 209–210
coaching 127–130; authoritarian 117
college sports 121; scholarships, recruitment, eligibility and academic requirements 122–124; student-athlete 121–122
Comte, Auguste 4
conflict theory 26–29, 139
conspicuous consumption 7, 16
conspicuous leisure 7
consumerism 219–220
contests 17–18
Cooperstown, Major League Baseball Hall of Fame 49, 69
culture, defined 59
cup stacking 11
Cutting Off Reflective Failure (CORF) 34

de Coubertin, Baron 50–51, 252
development of self 80–81
deviance 136; and coaching 140; and referees and officials 141; off-the-field 142–145; on-the-field 139–140; spectator 142; sports entertainment and media 141–142
discrimination 199
diversity of culture 62
Donaghy, Tim 141
Doubleday, Abner 49
Durkheim, Emile 261–262
dysfunctional acts 24

Edwards, Harry 6, 9
e-gambling 152
elephant racing 11
endorsements 223–225
ESPN 53, 292–293, 298, 300
ex-athlete 92
extreme sports 53–55

false consciousness 27
female sport participation 178–182; early history 179–180; early 1900s 181–182; myths 178–179; post–World War II 182; Victorian Era 180–181
feminist theory 32–34
Flood, Curt 232–235
folk games 44

football 53, 103, 122, 159–161
former athletes in politics 245–247
franchise relocation 230–231
Freeth, George 59
functional imperatives 26
functionalism 23–26

gambling 150–154; in sports 153–154; see also e-gambling
game stage 22–23
generalized other 23
genetics and sports 203–204
gladiator games 43–44
globalization 226
golf 52
government in sport 240–243
Greek festivals 42

Harm principle 171
hazing 130–133
Hera 42
heroes 67; as representatives of culture 67–68; categories of 70–72; demise of 74–75, 289; functions of 68–70
high school sports 117; academic requirements 117–118; athletic training 119–120; economics 120–121; negative effects 121; participation and administration 118–119
Hoch, Paul 27
hockey 161–162, 215
hooligans, soccer 169
horse racing 48–49
Human Growth Hormone (HGH) 148–149
hypermasculinity 169–170

identity, sports 81–82
imitation stage 22
income 219
Indian imagery 212
industrialization 47
informal youth sports 106–107
International Olympic Committee (IOC) 51
international sports 247–248; political uses 248–251
intimidation 157

journalism, sports 290–291
jousting 44–45

kickboxing 55
kite fighting 14

Labeling theory 138–139
lacrosse 14, 61–62, 214–215
lawn jockey 199
leisure 15–16
leisure groups 65–67
letter of intent 123–124
Little League Baseball 102–103
Lopez, Nancy 210
Lupica, Mike 65

magic 273–274
manifest functions 25
Marinovich, family 96, 108, 204
Marquis of Queensbury 48
Marx, Karl 26–27
material culture 60
Mead, George Herbert 22, 81
media 278; functions of 282–283;
    negative aspects on sports
    286–290; positive impact on
    sports 283–286; sport conglomer-
    ates 292–293; technology and the
    future 293–296
Merton, Robert 24
Middle Ages 44
Mill, John Stuart 171
Mills, C. Wright 4–5
mob mentality 168, 170
modern sports, characteristics of
    51–52
modernization 226
monopolies, sport 229–230
Morgan, William G. 48
Muscular Christianity 100, 207

Naismith, James 48
National Collegiate Athletic Associ-
    ation (NCAA) 126; purpose and
    development 126–127, 193
Native American nicknames, logos,
    and mascots 211–214
Negro Baseball 200
nonmaterial culture 60

obesity 302–303
Olympics, ancient 42–43, 239
Olympics, modern 50–51, 252–253;
    political problems 253–256
O'Neal, Shaquille 31
option clause 233
Owens, Jesse 200–201
owners 227–228; economic benefits
    232–233

pankration 40
Parsons, Talcott 24
patriarchy 177
Pepe, Maria 183
performance-enhancing drugs
    146–150

personal achievement 306
play 16–17
play stage 22
player endorsements 223–225
Pop Warner Football 103
politics 239, 243–245
positivism 4
power elites 28
prayer and sport 266–272
preindustrial sport 46–47
prejudice 199
primary group 79
print media 279–280
pula 40–41

race 198
racinos 150
racism 198–203; in sports in the
    past 199–201; in sports in the
    present 201
radio and sports 280–281
Redskins 213
Relaxation theory 31
religion 260; differences between
    sport and religion 265–266; func-
    tions of 260–261; relationship to
    sport 261–262; similarities with
    sport and religion 262–265
reserve clause 233–234
resocialization 91–92
Rickey, Branch 208
Robinson, Jackie 208–209
Roman spectacles 43
Roman sport 43–44
rounders 46
rowing 206

sacred emblems 211
secondary groups 79
secularization of sport 44, 51,
    272–275
sex, defined 177
sex sells 186, 224
skateboarding 53–54
snowboarding 53–54
soccer 104, 164
social system 24
social learning and differential the-
    ory 138
social theory 21
social worlds 88
socialization into sport 85–87
socialization process 77
socialization out of sport 89–91
socialization via sport 87–89
socioeconomic status (SES) 219
sociological imagination 4–5
sociology, defined 4
Southern California Browns Backers
    Association (SCBBA) 34–36,
    66
Special Olympics 104, 301–302
specific performance clause 64

sport 3, 10, 18; consumers 82;
    defined 12–13; in prison 172–174;
    as a social institution 8, 60; soci-
    ological perspective 3
sports agents 235–236
sports entertainment 220
sports marketing 220–221
sports sponsorship 221–223
sportsmanship 88, 110–111, 305–307
steroid use 109
stick fighting 40
stool ball 46
Subcultural/Cultural Deviance The-
    ory 137–138
subcultures 62–63
superstitions 274–275
Symbolic Interactionism 29–32;
    phenomenological approach 31
symbols 60

tennis 52, 103–104, 180–181
terrorism 167
theory, defined 21–22
Title IX 183, 192–195; compliance
    192; reactions 193–194; unfair to
    men's sports 194
totemism 211

Ultimate fighting 55
upward mobility 204–205, 219

vandalism 166
Veblen, Thorstein 6–7, 16
video games 282
video streaming 295
violence 157–159; player 159–165;
    spectator 165–171; sport violence
    and the law 171–172
volleyball 48

Walton, Bill 305
wealth 219
women's sports: aesthetic fitness
    186–188; homosexuality and
    homophobia 190–192; lack of
    women in power positions 185;
    male resistance 186; obstacles to
    continued growth 185; quest for
    equality in the male preserve
    189–190; sexism 188–189; sexual
    harassment 189
Woods, Tiger 53–53

X-games 53

youth sport: criticisms of 105; dis-
    turbing trends 107–110; evalua-
    tions 111–113; objectives 101;
    participation 97–100

Zeus 42